D0023369

# Tin Pan Alley

*OTHER BOOKS BY THE AUTHOR*

*By DAVID A. JASEN*
*Recorded Ragtime 1897–1958*
*A Century of American Popular Music*

*By DAVID A. JASEN and GENE JONES*
*Spreadin' Rhythm Around*
*That American Rag!*
*Black Bottom Stomp*

*By DAVID A. JASEN and TREBOR J. TICHENOR*
*Rags and Ragtime*

# Tin Pan Alley

## AN ENCYCLOPEDIA OF THE GOLDEN AGE OF AMERICAN SONG

David A. Jasen

Routledge
New York and London

Published in 2003 by

Routledge
29 West 35th Street
New York, NY 10001
www.routledge-ny.com

Published in Great Britain by
Routledge
11 New Fetter Lane
London EC4P 4EE
www.routledge.uk.co



All illustrations are from the collection of David A. Jasen.

Routledge is an imprint of Taylor and Francis Books, Inc.

Printed in the United States of America on acid-free paper.



10 9 8 7 6 5 4 3 2 1

**Cataloging-in-Publication Data**

**Library of Congress Cataloging-in-Publication Data**

Jasen, David A.
Tin Pan Alley : an encyclopedia of the golden age of American song / David A. Jasen.
p. cm.
Includes bibliographical references.
ISBN 0-415-93877-5 (hardback : acid-free paper)
1. Popular music—United States—Encyclopedia. I. Title.
ML102.P66J37 2003
782.42164′0973—dc21

2003002699

*To*
*Richard Carlin*
*A Most Creative and Dedicated Editor*

*You write in the morning, you write at night. You write in a taxi, in the bathtub, or in an elevator. And, after the song is all finished it may turn out to be very bad, but you sharpen your pencil and try again. A professional songwriter has his mind on his job all the time.*
*—Irving Berlin*

# Contents

The Tin Pan Alley home of Jerome H. Remick Publishers, 45 W. 28th Street, c. 1905.

# Introduction

The history of Tin Pan Alley is the history of the United States as seen by its tunesmiths. Songs seem to have mirrored every aspect of American life from the 1890s to the digital technology of the 2000s. We can chronicle the changing musical tastes of Americans, along with our social, economic, and political concerns, by the kinds of popular music we bought, played, and listened to: from the tearjerker to the latest rock song.

Just what is Tin Pan Alley, and where is it located? In the era before Elvis Presley made a song's performance more important than its publication, when a song's popularity was determined not by the number of records it sold but by the number of copies of sheet music it sold, Tin Pan Alley was the name given to the branch of the music publishing business that hired composers and lyricists on a permanent basis to create popular songs. Publishers marketed songs in sheet music form by means of extensive promotional campaigns. Originally, Tin Pan Alley was a nickname given to West Twenty-eighth Street between Broadway and Sixth Avenue in Manhattan, where many of the fledgling popular music publishers had offices. In time, it became the generic term for all publishers of popular American sheet music, regardless of their geographic location.

## How Tin Pan Alley Got Its Name

According to legend, the naming of Tin Pan Alley came at the turn of the twentieth century, when Monroe Rosenfeld, a prolific composer-lyricist, wrote a series of articles for the *New York Herald* on the new and energetic popular-music publishing business. For research, he visited the office of Harry Von Tilzer, located at 42 West Twenty-eighth Street, between Broadway and Sixth Avenue. Many other fledgling publishers were located on this street of reconstructed brownstone flats. Their "offices" usually consisted of a broken-down, out-of-tune piano, a secondhand desk and chair, file cabinets, and wooden racks holding the stock of sheet music. Rosenfeld heard a din of competing pianists as he left Von Tilzer's office, and he recorded that this street, with dozens of demonstrators working at the same time, sounded like a bunch of tin pans clanging. He characterized the street where all of this activity was taking place as "Tin Pan Alley."

## The Heydey of the Alley: 1880–1950

Pop music today means music videos, cassettes, compact discs, and flat disc recordings. Popular music itself is called rock, and it is produced by high-powered electronic machines that create a multitude of layered sounds. But today's approach to pop music is a far cry from its beginnings. Throughout the Alley's seventy years, popular music emerged in a variety of forms—love ballads, syncopated tunes, Latin American music, nonsense songs, show tunes—all marketed for adults. The music was presented and promoted in sheet music for voice and piano. The public was induced to purchase the music sheets when they saw and heard their favorite performers incorporate the songs in their acts, first in the theater and in vaudeville, then through recordings (first on cylinders, then on flat discs that turned at 78 revolutions per minute), and later on radio, then in films, and finally on television.

Through most of the years of Tin Pan Alley, sheet music publishers dominated the music business. What was this "popular" American business, and how did it differ from the development and selling of martial music, children's music, folk music, religious music, and classical music? Surely, each of these kinds of music has representative pieces, vocal and instrumental, that were and are truly popular.

Before the 1890s, the occupations of composers, lyricists, and even publishers of popular music did not exist. This is not to say that popular songs were not written and published, but that nobody was hired expressly to compose and write them on demand. That demand came later, after the Alley was firmly established. Stars wanted songs suited to their personalities, and publishers demanded songs of a type that a rival publisher had and that the public was currently buying.

Pre-1890s music publishers were either classical publishers, music store owners, or local printers who, along with such commodities as stationery, books, broadsides, magazines, advertisements, and posters, printed sheet music. Music from these printing houses and stationers was sold in their own stores, with larger firms getting salesmen of other goods to handle this product as a sideline. Because these early printers could not afford their own full-time sales forces, they hired salesmen of clothing, notions, and supplies to carry sample cases of music with them when they made the rounds of their territories. (Meredith Willson's Professor Harold Hill in *The Music Man* was a humorous caricature of these early music salesmen.) These multi-product peddlers got commissions on orders sent in by local music store owners.

Before long, these salesmen not only knew the likely customers for music among these local store owners, but they also knew which songs were selling best in which areas. Some of them began to think that they could write better songs than those they were selling on commission. For less than a $1,000 worth of credit, a salesman could write, publish, and go on the road to sell his own songs. From such roots, Tin Pan Alley was born. The first of these "salesman-composer-publisher" firms were Charles K. Harris in Milwaukee, Will Rossiter and Victor Kremer in Chicago, Jerome Remick in Detroit, John Stark in St. Louis, Vandersloot in Williamsport, Pennsylvania, Walter Jacobs in Boston, and the Witmarks, Joseph Stern, Maurice Shapiro, F. A. Mills, Harry Von Tilzer, T. B. Harms, Leo Feist, and Howley, Haviland and Company in New York City.

Many famous publishing names got into the business as an afterthought. Full-line music stores like Sherman, Clay and Company of San Francisco, Lyon and Healy of Chicago, Oliver Ditson of Boston, Grinnell Bros. of Detroit, and Carl Hoffman and J. W. Jenkins' Sons of Kansas City began their own publishing imprints, although music publishing was always incidental to their main store operations. Men like Edward P. Little and Elmer Grant Ege, who founded and ran Sherman, Clay and J. W. Jenkins' Sons' publishing departments, respectively, deserve the billing of publishers as much as Jerome H. Remick, Leo Feist, and Edward B. Marks do, because they initiated and developed their businesses with the same care as did those who had their names on the doors. However, it took Little and Ege a long time to be made directors of their firms.

These young, dynamic publishers had a common goal: to get enough potential sheet-music customers to hear the music and then buy it. The new wrinkle for this new business was song promotion. Anywhere and everywhere people congregated was fair game: vaudeville, bars, lobster palaces, beer gardens, theaters, brothels, nickelodeons. In the beginning, the publisher himself made the rounds of the entertainment centers, some publishers visiting as many as sixty places a week. These publishers also printed what they called "professional copies"—cheap newsprint song editions without fancy illustrated covers—to give to orchestra leaders and singers to induce them to perform their numbers, often sealing the deal with free drinks. These energetic publisher-salesmen also offered star performers gifts and, later, money to feature their songs in their acts.

## Vaudeville

Among the important factors in the rise of Tin Pan Alley was the rapid growth of vaudeville. In the 1890s and early 1900s, theaters were constructed across the country in great numbers. Names like Strand, Lyceum, Proctor's, Pantages, Keith, and Orpheum sprouted in towns and villages everywhere. All, including the independently owned theaters, were supplied talent by booking agencies such as William Morris, Keith-Albee, and Klaw and Erlanger.

Each year, before they set out to tour the country, vaudeville performers would stop at publishing houses for songs to freshen up their acts. They went to each publisher's professional department, where they were taken to a small room with an upright piano. At the piano sat an accompanist, and sometimes a lyricist was in a nearby chair. The vaudevillians would listen to new songs, often demonstrated by their composers, and when a singer liked a number, the accompanist would immediately teach it to him or her. On the spot, a song could be tailored to the range and style of the singer, and all possible problems of key or tempo eliminated. For a star, these staff composers and lyricists (with a weekly draw of $25.00 against future royalties) would create special material for exclusive use. The professional manager not only supervised these piano rooms and demonstrators, but also chose the material for the star performers and directed the plugging activity of the firm.

## Music Publishing in New York

The entertainment industry in New York City in the 1880s was centered around Union Square, on East Fourteenth Street. Tony Pastor (1837–1908) operated the leading music hall of the day (1875–1906), on East Fourteenth Street near Third Avenue, where the most famous singers entertained. The singers always included old favorites in their acts, as well as new songs that were sung exclusively by them—many were created specifically for them. Fourteenth Street between Broadway and Third Avenue was the mecca of musical show business. The premier popular song publisher of the 1880s was Willis Woodward, who had his office in the Star Theatre Building, on Thirteenth Street at Broadway. Woodward issued such hits as "White Wings," "The Song That Reached My Heart," and "Always Take Mother's Advice." He was king of the tearjerkers. T. B. Harms and Co. published most of the musical stage songs of the day, and William A. Pond and Company published the Harrigan and Hart songs and the authorized versions of Gilbert and Sullivan music.

Early in the 1890s, a new, young breed of popular music publishers came into being. These publishers were, essentially, salesmen who didn't sit in their offices waiting for performers to come to them, but went out to the entertainment palaces and badgered singers, orchestra leaders, dancers, acrobats, and comedians to use their numbers. They hustled themselves, as well as their hired singers and whistlers, into the finest theaters and the lowest dives. As the decade progressed, vaudeville houses began to move uptown, along with the leading restaurants. It is no wonder, then, that the new popular music publishers moved and expanded their businesses, as did theatrical agents and the show business trade journals.

As the new publishers who actively plugged their songs flourished at the turn of the twentieth century, they needed more physical space. Their plugging methods became more sophisticated, and there was a need to create departments to fulfill various kinds of promotions. Since it was no longer considered fashionable or productive to see performers after their shows, publishers began to invite performers to their offices to demonstrate new songs. They needed a fancy suite of demonstration rooms, sometimes even a small auditorium, where performers could try out the tunes under conditions similar to those they faced in theaters.

Publishers also needed space for band and orchestra departments, which were responsible for arranging the tunes from lead sheets to orchestral parts. Each band and orchestra department became an industry in itself, arranging for different musical combinations and issuing the parts in enticing forms. Orchestral parts didn't have colorful covers, as did the piano-vocal sheets; rather, they were sold much the way book clubs operate today: by establishing a "club" so that performing organizations could "subscribe" to the publisher's works for a year at a time. "Member" bands and orchestras performed the songs publicly (which constituted plugs), so they were sent all of the firm's numbers during the year, fully orchestrated.

The Remick, Feist, Stern, Witmark, and Shapiro organizations either took over an entire floor of a building or leased an entire building for their vast departments. Their businesses had outgrown the one-room offices of the 1890s and now required large spaces for fast-growing operations.

For instance, in January 1903, when Feist moved into its own brownstone at 134 West Thirty-seventh Street, the basement housed the acquired catalog of Century Music, which contained twelve hundred songs. The main floor consisted of the general offices, managed by Edgar Bitner, and the reception room. The second floor housed the illustrators department, the professional parlor, and the band and orchestra department, under Abe Holzmann, who also managed the piano rooms. The third floor included the ladies' reception rooms, stock circular department, more piano rooms, and the teachers' department, under the supervision of Robert A. Keiser. The fourth floor housed the advertising department, addressing department, stock room, folio department, and the private office of Leo Feist.

When Remick leased its building at 219–221 West Forty-sixth Street in October 1912, its setup was slightly different: the basement held the stock room and shipping department; the ground floor had the band and orchestra department (run by Abe Holzmann), the sales department (of which F. J. Burt was in charge), the publicity department (headed by Sam

Speck), and a two hundred-seat auditorium used as a demonstration and rehearsal hall. The second floor was given over to the professional department, under Mose Gumble's direction. Gumble's assistant, Tom Penfold, took charge of the fifteen piano rooms. Also on the second floor were the slide department and a room devoted to the storage of stationery and advertising campaigns. The third floor contained the executive offices of Fred E. Belcher, Jerome Keit, Belcher's private secretary, and Jerome H. Remick, when he was in town. The arranging department, with a dozen arrangers headed by J. Bodewalt Lampe, was also located on this floor.

Conventional wisdom has it that the publishers of popular music in New York kept changing their business locations to follow the center of the theater district in its thirty-year progression uptown. The old-line publishers of the 1870s and 1880s clustered around the Bowery, in lower Manhattan, and later around Union Square (Fourteenth Street and Broadway). In the 1890s, West Twenty-eighth Street attracted the new, plugging publishers. Between 1903 and 1908, Tin Pan Alley moved uptown again, heading toward West Forty-second Street. By the 1920s, many song publishers were entrenched in Upper Longacre Square (West Forty-second to Fifty-sixth streets), where the Great White Way is still to be found.

Although half of the ten major publishers never set foot on West Twenty-eighth Street (the Tin Pan Alley of legend), five of them did, however briefly. At the turn of the twentieth century and during its first decade, many minor publishers did have offices there. From 1911 to 1919, most of the majors and minors settled in the West Forties, with the Exchange Building, located at 145 West Forty-fifth Street, the focal point of the small-to-medium-sized publishers. This thirteen-story building seems to have housed nothing but publishers during the 1910s. It presaged the coming of the Brill Building.

## Hollywood Buys into the Alley

With the advent of talking pictures, Hollywood changed Tin Pan Alley by buying up most of the larger publishers. Warner Brothers made the first move to acquire song catalogs when it bought out Witmark and Harms (from Max Dreyfus) in 1929, and Jerome H. Remick Company from Jerome Keit later that year. MGM bought Leo Feist, Inc., in 1934, and Robbins Music Corp. in the following year. After adding Miller Music, Inc., MGM formed the combine Robbins-Feist-Miller, known as The Big Three. Paramount Pictures created Famous Music Corporation in 1928, and soon bought out Spier and Coslow to add to the Famous catalog.

These Hollywood-based firms created new ways to plug songs, using the media to advantage. Radio became the most important way to present a song, and bandleaders and singers were constantly badgered by pluggers. Harry Von Tilzer, still at it in the 1920s, sang his own songs over the radio and even made a talking picture plugging his then latest number, demonstrating at the piano how he wrote "Just Around the Corner May Be Sunshine for You."

The 1920s saw the biggest outpouring of songs of all the decades in Tin Pan Alley's history. The good times were reflected in the popularity of jazz bands and in the number of dance bands that were being recorded around the country. The entertainment industry was going full-blast, with the sale of player pianos and piano rolls peaking in 1926. Vaudeville attendance was at an all-time high, and so was the number of musical comedy productions on Broadway (the 1927–1928 season produced fifty-three musicals, according to *Variety*). Everything came to a halt by the end of 1929, when, in *Variety*'s famous headline, "Wall Street Lays an Egg."

By the start of the 1930s, radio had become a most important force in the popular music industry, reaching vast numbers of people and heralding the age of the disc jockey. Talking pictures created another outlet for music publishers, since movie musicals were starting to appear in great numbers. Films became a most important source of income for the songwriters and publishers of Tin Pan Alley, because film producers had to buy songs. Film companies found it more convenient to purchase established publishing firms with catalogs of favorite songs for their constantly growing roster of films. The Depression saw the cost of sheet music drop from thirty to twenty-five cents. Ironically, during the early 1930s, dance bands were increasing in size from twelve to fifteen players, and they came to be known as big bands. Pluggers went after performers with radio shows and sought bandleaders with permanent ballroom jobs.

In the 1930s, the movies, a favorite entertainment medium, at long last began to talk. More important, they began to sing and dance, using thousands of songs—both old and new. The major film studios created their own publishing units and bought up several of the largest Tin Pan Alley publishers. The most important composers and lyricists got fat contracts to work in Hollywood, either picture by picture or on a long-term basis. The Big Band era began with Benny Goodman being crowned "King of Swing." Guy Lombardo made it equally big and was named "King of Sweet." Broadway musicals were enriched with works by Richard Rodgers and Lorenz Hart, Cole Porter, and Harold Arlen. Bing Crosby became the most popular male vocalist of the decade, and all of Tin Pan Alley helped people forget the Depression.

## Death of Tin Pan Alley

At first, Alley operations at the beginning of the 1950s seemed like a continuation of the 1940s, with songs plugged on radio, in movies, on records, and on the new electronic novelty, television—all done with the time-honored aim of selling sheet music. And as the Alley was coming to its untimely end, there appeared on the top charts a greater variety of song types than ever before. Not only were ballads, the staples of the Alley, popular ("My Heart Cries for You"), there was also success for Latin American songs ("Vaya con Dios"), syncopated rag ("Music! Music! Music!"), hillbilly ("Your Cheatin' Heart"), homespun ("Dearie"), ethnic ("Come on-a My House"), folk ("Goodnight, Irene"), novelty ("Molasses, Molasses"), and polka ("Hopscotch Polka").

In the major publishing firms, the general professional manager bought the songs, directed the pluggers, and decided which songs deserved money for advertising. The pluggers, or "contact men," as they were now called, went after bandleaders who had radio programs, solo singers who made recordings and worked the nightclubs, artist and repertoire (called "A and R") heads of record companies, and (since the end of the war) announcers of popular music record shows, called disc jockeys (or "deejays").

The most famous of the deejays was Martin Block of radio station WNEW in New York City, who had started his career by playing records during pauses in the station's live coverage of the Bruno Hauptmann trial in 1935. He created the *Make Believe Ballroom* show, which quickly caught on. Block came to know publishers, songwriters, A and R men, singers, and pluggers, all of whom he interviewed on his program. He was even invited to recording sessions, and his knowledgeable commentary on songs and performers was entertaining as well as informative. He drew a large following. When Block plugged recordings, they became hits.

Al Jarvis, on KLAC in Los Angeles (the first all-deejay station), Eddie Hubbard on WIND (Chicago), Kurt Webster on WBT (Charlotte, North Carolina), Al "Jazzbo" Collins (a hip, jazz-oriented deejay who worked for several stations in different locations), Bob Horn on WFIL (Philadelphia), Bob Clayton on WHDH (Boston), Eddie Gallagher on WTOP (Washington, D.C.), Ed McKenzie as "Jack the Bellboy" on WJBK (Detroit), and Bill Randle on WERE (Cleveland, Ohio) were among the popular deejays who individually made recordings into hits in their areas and led to nationwide airings of their selections. Some, like Bill Randle, discovered singers (Johnnie Ray and Tony Bennett) and pushed their discoveries' recordings onto the charts. The deejay became the most important factor in the success of popular recordings. The pluggers, who used to give "professional copies" to bandleaders and singers, now gave sample records to deejays.

As plugging methods changed, recordings at the beginning of the 1950s started to sound different. New electronic gimmickry included overdubbing, echo effects, and multitrack recordings, which resulted in such distinctive approaches as Patti Page's singing a duet with herself in "Tennessee Waltz," Les Paul and Mary Ford creating the sound of many guitars and singers from one guitar and one voice in "How High the Moon," and Ross Bagdasarian's (under the pseudonym of David Seville) "The Chipmunk Song," with his own voice becoming those of the three individualized chipmunks—Alvin, Theodore, and Simon—on a record engineered by him. "Chipmunk" sold two and a half million discs in two weeks.

With these new sounds came new audiences. During the early 1950s, nobody in the Alley realized that a shift was taking place in the demographics of popular music. As Western movies became more popular, country and western songs (formerly known as hillbilly music) became more popular, starting with the Gene Autry and Roy Rogers oaters of the early 1940s. Using Alley techniques, the Aberbach brothers, Jean and Julian, pushed country and western songs through their companies: Hill and Range Songs, Alamo Music, and, finally, Elvis Presley Music.

A new black sound arose after World War II, becoming known as rhythm and blues. It was vocal music to be danced to, but the words weren't as important as the beat. Charts in the trade papers noted some top-selling records in these new categories during the late 1940s, although they hadn't yet had much influence on the pop charts. But, around 1952–1953, songs on these black and country charts started being "covered" by major white pop singers for a growing audience of teenagers, who would soon dominate the popular music scene as the purchasers of pop singles. Thus, at the beginning of the 1950s pop songs didn't reflect this emerging audience, as publishers ignored the rhythm and blues and country songs that were captivating the youngsters. Instead, published songs continued to reflect the taste of the young and middle-aged adults who had always bought sheet music. This stagnation would prove fatal to the Alley.

Symbolically, Tin Pan Alley died on April 12, 1954, when Bill Haley (1925–1981) and his Comets recorded Max Freedman and Jimmy De Knight's (pseudonym of publisher James Myers, 1920–2001) "Rock Around the Clock." It had been published a year earlier and did not create a sensation, but Haley's recording (Decca 29214) would ultimately sell twenty-five million copies worldwide. It became the first international rock and roll best-seller. *The Blackboard Jungle* (1955) sound track gave the song and Haley's performance an additional context, and rebellious teenagers took it as their anthem. The song was such a powerful influence that two movies were built around the song and its performance: *Rock Around the Clock* (1956) and *Don't Knock the Rock* (1957). The recording surfaced again in the films *American Graffiti* (1973) and *Superman* (1978). It was also featured in the television series *Happy Days* (1974–1984). Bill Haley and his Comets had one more million seller, "See You Later, Alligator" (1956), which they introduced in the film *Rock Around the Clock* (Decca 29791).

Before rock and roll, songs and their publication had been the main thrust of the creation and promotion of popular music. With rock and roll, recorded performance became more important than written music and words. Publishers were no longer in charge of a song's promotion, and sheet music sales became insignificant to the pop music business. From 1956 on, rock and roll songs dominated the Hit Parade and Top 40 lists. The Alley publishers, who had done so much to develop and promote hit songs for seventy years, could no longer hold their power.

New groups and soloists wrote their own songs, controlled their publishing rights, recorded their own numbers, and generally wrote their own tickets. And while the theater was still producing musical shows, and film companies still used established songs and newly created ones, the music business changed so much that the Alley and its products became obsolete.

Nonetheless, the legacy of Tin Pan Alley continues to have an impact on American popular song. Long after the Alley's demise, on a building at the comer of Twenty-eighth Street and Broadway, Tin Pan Alley was officially recognized for its part in our musical history when a plaque was installed on July 26, 1976, as part of the Bicentennial celebration. It read:

> A Landmark of American Music
> Tin Pan Alley
> 28th Street Between Broadway and Sixth Avenues Was the Legendary
> Tin Pan Alley Where the Business of the American Popular Song
> Flourished During the First Decades of the 20th Century.

Tin Pan Alley's legacy is part of our heritage, and the sheet music and recordings it gave us remain a valuable part of our lives.

# Maurice Abrahams

Composer, music publisher (b. Russia, March 18, 1883; d. New York City, April 13, 1931). Abrahams was a pop song composer of the 1910s and 1920s who is best remembered for the 1912 novelty hit "Ragtime Cowboy Joe," written with LEWIS MUIR and lyricist Grant Clarke (1891–1931). Abrahams was composing pop songs by the early 1910s. After his hit with "Ragtime Cowboy Joe," Abrahams collaborated again with Clarke (along with EDGAR LESLIE as colyricist) on the 1913 hit "He'd Have to Get Out and Get Under," celebrating the difficulties of owning the newfangled automobile. Maurice published it through his own firm. In 1914, Clarke and Abrahams celebrated another new technology, record players, in "They Start the Victrola (and Dance Around the Floor)." That same year, Abrahams was among the charter members of ASCAP. Other hits from the 1910s include 1912's "Hitchy Koo" (music composed with Muir, lyrics by L. WOLFE GILBERT); "Pullman Porters on Parade," a hit for AL JOLSON in 1913 (Columbia A1374), and 1914's "Ruff Johnson's Harmony Band" (with lyrics by Shelton Brooks). For Jolson's wife, Broadway star Belle Baker (1893–1957), Abrahams composed "High, High, High Up in the Hills" in 1926, with words by SAM LEWIS and JOE YOUNG.

# Stanley Adams

Lyricist (b. New York City, August 14, 1907; d. Great Neck, New York, December 27, 1994). Adams worked with several major composers, including HOAGY CARMICHAEL, VICTOR HERBERT, FATS WALLER, and Max Steiner. His best-known song was 1934's "What a Diff'rence a Day Made," a popular Spanish song composed by Maria Grever; Adams provided the English lyrics. Though originally recorded by the Dorsey Brothers, it was Dinah Washington's 1959 recording (Mercury 71435) that made it into a pop standard. Also in 1934, Adams provided lyrics to XAVIER CUGAT's theme "My Shawl," a major hit for the bandleader. With Carmichael, Adams wrote "Little Old Lady" (1936) for the revue *The Show Is On*. Adams also scored several films, including *Duel in the Sun* (1946). He served as president of ASCAP from 1953 to 1956 and again from 1959 to 1980.

# Harold Adamson

Lyricist (b. Greenville, New Jersey, December 10, 1906; d. Beverly Hills, California, August 17, 1980). Adamson was a prolific and successful lyricist for Broadway and the movies, working from the late 1920s through the 1950s. He attended the University of Kansas, where he began writing songs for shows, and then Harvard, where he provided material for the famed Hasty Pudding shows. His first Broadway success came with "Time on My Hands," with colyricist Mack Gordon and music by VINCENT YOUMANS. In the early 1930s, Adamson moved to Hollywood, where he provided lyrics for musical films. In the mid-1930s, Adamson worked on several films with composer WALTER DONALDSON, scoring hits with 1935's "Tender Is the Night" for *Here Comes the Band*, and "Did I Remember?" (1936) for Jean Harlow's *Suzy*. Also in 1936, the Adamson/Donaldson team wrote "It's Been So Long" and "You" for *The Great Ziegfeld*. Adamson often worked with composer JIMMY MCHUGH; among their Hollywood hits were "Blame It on the Rumba," from the film *Top of the Town* (1937), and "It's a Most Unusual Day," from *A Date with Judy* (1948). During the 1940s, the duo collaborated on the Broadway shows *Banjo Eyes* and *As the Girls Go*, and they scored big with the wartime hit, "Comin' in on a Wing and a Prayer" (1943). Adamson also collaborated with DUKE ELLINGTON, VERNON DUKE, BURTON LANE, and many others. During the 1950s, he contributed lyrics for the title songs for several nonmusical films, including *An Affair to Remember* (1957, with HARRY WARREN and Leo McCarey), and *Around the World in 80 Days* (1956, with VICTOR YOUNG). He retired in the early 1960s.

# Richard Adler

Composer, lyricist, Broadway producer (b. New York City, August 3, 1921). Adler is best remembered for two 1950s musicals, *The Pajama Game* and *Damn Yankees*, written with his partner, lyricist Jerry Ross (b. Jerold Rosenberg, The Bronx, New York, March 9, 1926; d. New York City, November 11, 1955). The two began working together in the early 1950s to compose pop songs. They scored big with 1953's "Rags to Riches," a two-million-selling #1 hit for Tony Bennett (Columbia 40048). Its success led to the opportunity to write for Broadway, first for *John Murray Anderson's Almanac*, a revue, and then *The Pajama Game* (1954), which produced hits for Rosemary Clooney with "Hey There" (Columbia 40266), along with classics like "Hernando's Hideaway" and "Small Talk." This was followed a year later by *Damn Yankees*, which produced pop hits for Eddie Fisher ("Heart," RCA 6097) and for DINAH SHORE (RCA 6077) and Sarah Vaughan (Mercury 70595) ("Whatever Lola Wants"). Ross died of leukemia in November 1955, and Adler has never been able to equal his initial success on his own.

# Milton Ager

Composer (b. Chicago, Illinois, October 6, 1893; d. Los Angeles, California, April 6, 1979). Ager is best remembered for several hits of the 1920s, written with lyricist JACK YELLEN, including "Hard-Hearted Hannah" and "Crazy Words, Crazy Tune." He began his career plugging and demonstrating music at the Chicago branch of Waterson, Berlin and Snyder in 1910. From there, he became the vaudeville accompanist to Gene Greene, who was at that time singing "Melancholy Baby." (Earlier, Greene had sung Ager and Charley Straight's "King of the Bungaloos," a wonderful ragtime song.) When Ager came to New York in 1914, he learned what made a song popular by scoring for the staff writers at Waterson, Berlin and Snyder. He met PETE WENDLING there, and the two composed a few undistinguished fox-trots. When he returned from his military service at Fort Greenleaf, Georgia (1917–1918), Ager got a job with LEO FEIST and collaborated with GEORGE MEYER and lyricist Grant Clarke on two "experience-based" songs: 1918's "Everything Is Peaches Down in Georgia," followed in 1919 by "Anything Is Nice if It Comes from Dixieland." These were both peppy numbers, not far removed from the instrumental fox-trots Ager had turned out several years before.

Around 1920, Ager met his permanent lyricist, Jack Yellen, and the two of them formed Ager, Yellen and Bornstein, with professional manager Ben Bornstein, in August 1922. Their first published number was "Lovin' Sam (The Sheik of Alabam')," a song SOPHIE TUCKER turned into a hit. It started Yellen's association with Tucker. He would write special material for her over the next twenty years. "Louisville Lou" and "Mamma Goes Where Papa Goes," 1923 hits by the partners, were both introduced by Sophie Tucker. The comedy team of Greenlee and Drayton helped promote the first; Jane Green with the Virginians recorded the second (Victor 19215), and Belle Baker helped it along in vaudeville.

"I Wonder What's Become of Sally," their big number of 1924, was introduced by VAN AND SCHENCK, who made it a million-seller. The Ager-Yellen team wrote three more numbers that year. The first was "Big Boy," a super tune that the Wolverines recorded (Gennett 5565), featuring Bix Beiderbecke on cornet and also briefly on piano. Sophie Tucker wasn't the only singer who liked the Ager-Yellen songs. Margaret Young did, too, and she recorded many of them on Brunswick. "Hard-Hearted Hannah" was introduced on Broadway by Frances Williams in *Innocent Eyes*. PAUL WHITEMAN covered it (Victor 19447), as did Herb Wiedoeft's Orchestra (Brunswick 2751) on disc. The team's comedy number that year was "Big Bad Bill Is Sweet William Now," which enjoyed great popularity on Margaret Young's record accompanied by RUBE BLOOM (Brunswick 2736), and with Healy and Cross in vaudeville.

"Could I? I Certainly Could," one of Ager and Yellen's two 1926 novelty entries, was introduced by Sophie Tucker. The recording by Bob Haring's orchestra (Cameo 926) almost matched Sid Sydney's (Victor 20029) for cleverness in arrangement. This was a fine, spirited comic song that would be heard over the next year. The other novelty was "Hard-to-Get Gertie," given a peppy treatment by Irving Aaronson and his Commanders (Victor 20100).

The big year for Ager and Yellen was 1927, with five huge successes. "Ain't That a Grand and Glorious Feeling" was the first, followed by a big comic number, "Crazy Words, Crazy Tune (Vo Do De O)," which Irving Aaronson's orchestra (Victor 20473) made into a hit (revived in the mid-1950s by Jerry Lewis). "Is She My Girlfriend?" was given a huge send-off by the COON-SANDERS NIGHTHAWKS (Victor 21148). The Ager-Yellen ballad "Forgive Me" was sung by Lillian Roth, and Nat Shilkret made a beautiful arrangement (Victor 20514). Their CHARLESTON number, "Ain't She Sweet?," was their biggest hit. Frank Banta recorded it as a marvelous piano solo (Victor 20610).

"Hungry Women" (1928) was interpolated by EDDIE CANTOR into *Whoopee*, and it brought the house down. The team wrote most of the score of *Rain or Shine* (February 9,

1928), but only the title song made a stir. "My Pet" (1928) was given a boost by the recording of Ernie Golden's orchestra (Domino 4146).

The Ager-Yellen team went to Hollywood, where in 1929, they wrote the score for Sophie Tucker's first film, *Honky Tonk*, which gave her "I'm the Last of the Red Hot Mamas." They also wrote the theme song for Dolores Costello's *Glad Rag Doll*. For the MGM musical *Chasing Rainbows*, they wrote what became the theme song of the New Deal, the song Democrats have used as their party's song ever since, "Happy Days Are Here Again." It was revived by Barbra Streisand in 1963.

Ager and Yellen broke up in 1930, when Yellen was bought out of their publishing company. Ager spent the next fourteen years with many different lyricists, but created no real hits. He left the business in 1944 when Warner Bros. bought his catalog and combined it with Advanced Music.

# Fred E. Ahlert

Composer (b. New York City, September 19, 1892; d. New York City, October 20, 1953). Ahlert's biggest hits came in the 1920s and 1930s, when he was working with lyricist Roy Turk (1892–1934). He was a staff arranger for Waterson, Berlin and Snyder and had his first number, "Beets and Turnips," published by them in 1915. It was a syncopated fox-trot, composed with Cliff Hess (1894–1959). Vic Meyers and his orchestra made a fine recording of it in 1924 (Brunswick 2664), as did the Varsity Eight (Cameo 640) for a revival. "I'd Love to Fall Asleep and Wake Up in My Mammy's Arms" (1920) was Ahlert's first big hit, with lyrics by Sam Lewis and Joe Young. It was helped along by the Benson Orchestra's recording (Victor 18697). "Maybe She'll Write Me (Maybe She'll Phone Me)" (1924) was a cute novelty composed with music publisher Ted Snyder, with lyrics by Roy Turk. Paul Whiteman and his orchestra gave it a nice treatment (Victor 19284).

"There's a Cradle in Caroline" (1927) was written with Sam Lewis and Joe Young. Frankie Trumbauer and his orchestra, with Bix Beiderbecke, made a lovely recording of it with a vocal by Seger Ellis (1904–1995) (Okeh 40879). "I'll Get By" (1928), written with Roy Turk, was Ahlert's biggest seller. Ruth Etting sang it to hit status originally (Columbia 1733-D), and the Irving Aaronson Orchestra recording (Victor 21786) gave it a boost. It was revived in the film *A Guy Named Joe* (1944), sung by Irene Dunne. The King Sisters made a best-selling record the following year (Bluebird 0821), and Dan Dailey sang it in the film *You Were Meant for Me* (1948). It was used later as a theme song for a film of the same name in 1950.

"Mean to Me" (1929) was another big success for Ahlert and Turk. Again, Ruth Etting recorded it (Columbia 1762-D), as did Helen Morgan (Victor 21930). When Ruth Etting's life got the Hollywood treatment in *Love Me or Leave Me* (1955), Doris Day, who portrayed Etting, sang it in that film. "Walkin' My Baby Back Home" (1930) continued the Ahlert-Turk team's streak, featured by singer Harry Richman. It was revived in 1952 by Johnnie Ray (Columbia 39750), and was sung by Donald O'Connor in the 1953 film of the same name.

"I Don't Know Why (I Just Do)" (1931), by the Ahlert-Turk combination, gave Kate Smith one of her early hits (Columbia 2539-D). It was revived during the 1940s and 1950s by the Andrews Sisters, Tommy Dorsey's orchestra, the King Cole Trio, Frank Sinatra, and Bobby Sherwood and his orchestra. That same year, Ahlert and Turk wrote "Where the Blue of the Night (Meets the Gold of the Day)" (1931) with some assistance from Bing Crosby, who sang it to success and made it his radio theme song (Brunswick 6226). Crosby was so closely identified with the song that he was asked to include it in *The Big Broadcast* (1932). "I'll Follow You" and "Love, You Funny Thing!" (1932) were the last two hits written by the Ahlert-Turk team. The first was a Kate Smith favorite, and the second was made famous by Bing Crosby.

"I'm Gonna Sit Right Down and Write Myself a Letter" (1935), Ahlert's last big hit, was written with Joe Young. Fats Waller introduced it, and his recording became a best-seller (Victor 25044). It was revived in 1956 by Billy Williams (Coral 61830) and sold over two million copies. Ahlert's hit-making days were over, although he kept writing until World War II. He was president of ASCAP from 1948 to 1950.

# Harry Akst

Composer (b. New York City, August 15, 1894; d. Hollywood, California, March 31, 1963). Akst is best remembered for writing several pop and jazz standards, including "Dinah" and "Am I Blue?" He took classical piano lessons at the age of five but learned ragtime so that he could become a demonstrator for Leo Feist. For a brief time, he accompanied Nora Bayes in her vaudeville appearances. He was drafted during World War I and was sent to Camp Upton, where he met Private Walter Donaldson and Sergeant Irving Berlin. At war's end, Akst joined Berlin in his new publishing company as a staff pianist and his amanuensis. He and Berlin wrote "Home Again Blues" in 1921 and scored with their effort. Aileen Stanley made the best recording of it (Victor 18760). "A Smile Will Go a Long, Long Way" (1923) was a collaboration between Akst and lyricist Benny Davis. Henry Santrey's plug began its sale of a million copies, and it later became the theme song of Sam Lanin and his orchestra.

"Dinah" (1925) was Akst's first collaboration with the old pros Sam Lewis and Joe Young. It was introduced in *The New Plantation Club Revue* by Ethel Waters, who also made the first recording of it (Columbia 487-D). It was a late interpolation by Eddie Cantor into *Kid Boots* (December 31, 1923), and it has been performed throughout the years in various films, notably *Show Business* (1944). Dinah Shore used it as her theme on radio and television. "Steppin' in Society" (1925) was a syncopated fox-trot made popular by Ben Selvin (Vocalion 15038).

"Everything's Gonna Be All Right" (1926) had a Benny Davis lyric and was featured on record by Jane Gray, accompanied by Rube Bloom (Harmony 128), and by the Coon-Sanders Nighthawks (Victor 20003). Akst and Davis's huge success of 1926 was "Baby Face," which Eddie Cantor made famous. The first recording was made by Jan Garber's orchestra, with Benny Davis as vocalist (Victor 20105). Al Jolson sang it on the sound track of *Jolson Sings Again* (1949). Art Mooney's orchestra had revived it in 1948 for a million-seller (MGM 10156).

The last major song by Akst was written with Grant Clarke for Ethel Waters's first film, *On with the Show* (1929). She brought the house down with her poignant rendition of "Am I Blue?" Her recording (Columbia 1837-D), accompanied by the Dorsey brothers and Frank Signorelli, was enormously popular. Akst spent the rest of his professional life touring with Al Jolson, serving as his accompanist until Jolson's death in 1950.

# Lou Alter

Composer (b. Louis Alter, New York City, June 18, 1902; d. New York City, November 5, 1980). Alter is remembered primarily for "Do You Know What It Means to Miss New Orleans?" a pop and jazz standard. Alter began his career composing for Broadway revues. His first hit came in 1926 with "Hugs and Kisses," with lyrics by Raymond Klages (1888–1947), written for the fifth edition of *Earl Carroll's Vanities*. Art Landry and his orchestra (Victor 20285) had the most successful recording, but it was also covered by Jack Albin's orchestra (Edison Diamond Disc 51829-L). "Blue Shadows" was another popular number from the show. Alter also wrote with Lew Brown, producing minor hits with "I've Loved the Same Girl for Fifty Years" and "If Love Makes You Give Up Steak and Potatoes, Then I Don't Want Love" in 1934. In the later 1930s, Alter moved to Hollywood. His first big success came in 1941 with the song "Dolores" for the film *Las Vegas Nights*, with lyrics by Frank Loesser; it was an Oscar nominee for best song. Tommy Dorsey, with vocalist Frank Sinatra, had the hit recording. But it was 1946's "Do You Know What It Means to Miss New Orleans?" with lyrics by Eddie De Lange (1904–1949), that is Alter's best-loved song. It was introduced by Louis Armstrong and Billie Holiday in the film *New Orleans*, and became a standard in Armstrong's repertoire.

# Amateur Composers

Tin Pan Alley consisted of professional, full-time composers and lyricists, men and women who made their living writing songs to be issued by publishers who made their living by issuing them, plugging them nationally, seeing that they were performed in vaudeville, on radio, in nightclubs, and on discs. But nearly everyone, it seemed, thought that they could write a song hit. Several publishers issued monthly magazines plugging their songs. Music publisher Walter Jacobs's magazine ran a column devoted to critiquing amateurs' songs sent in hopes of being published. It was often searing in the comments on these submissions:

> Your poem "There's a Song in My Heart That My Tongue Can't Express" would never get by in this world as a song lyric. Neither would "I Will Work for My Board for a Season or Two." Same applies to "You're Only Flirting with a Roast," "I Have Corns," and "Poor Butterfly Is Working in a Dairy Now." If you spend a few minutes a day looking over songs that have been published in the last few years, they might give you some idea what to write about and what not to write about. I haven't the remotest idea where you get such strange titles and plots for your lyrical endeavors. Please use pen and ink; pencil copy is very hard to read.

To another would-be songwriter, Jacobs's columnist wrote:

> "Influenza Fox Trot" has three quite catchy strains, but the first two are too short. Your first strain is only eight measures long and should be sixteen. This applies also to your second strain. The trio will pass as it is as far as length is concerned, but there should be less repeating on the melody. As it stands, it is rather monotonous . . . whatever you do with, or do to, this composition, dress it with a new title, as "Influenza" has already been used. "Ringworm Waltz" is as flat and ridiculous as its titles. . . . The melodies to this waltz are vague and get nowhere. Tear it up.

Very few amateur songwriters went on to enjoy professional careers. Those amateurs who achieved a few hits quickly turned professional; the rest continued to dream of a career as a songwriter, without ever achieving fame beyond their own piano stool. Big publishers were wary of amateur songwriters, fearing lawsuits and bad songs. Until the end of the Alley, songwriting was for professionals only.

# Leroy Anderson

Composer and conductor who created unusual instrumentals featuring sound effects (b. Cambridge, Massachusetts, June 29, 1908; d. Woodbury, Connecticut, May 18, 1975). Anderson's conceptions, which exhibited a genial sense of humor, were sometimes enhanced after their composition with lyrics by MITCHELL PARISH, including "The Syncopated Clock," "Serenata," "Sleigh Ride," "Blue Tango," and the beautiful "Forgotten Dreams." Parish, the house lyricist for MILLS MUSIC—not so coincidentally Anderson's publisher—specialized in taking instrumentals and making hit songs from them. Not a songwriter in the Alley sense, Anderson described his work as concert music with a pop quality. His early career was as permanent orchestrator for the Boston Pops under Arthur Fiedler. There, he arranged many pop songs for symphony orchestra. His recording of his instrumental "Blue Tango" (Decca 27875) in late 1951 sold over two million copies. During the early days of television, *The Late Show*, featuring movies in the early morning hours, used Anderson's recording of "The Syncopated Clock" as its theme song; unsurprisingly, it sold over a million copies (Decca 16005). Almost as famous were "Trumpeter's Lullaby" (1952) and "The Typewriter" (1953). In 1958, *Goldilocks*, his only Broadway score, was produced. It was a charming show about the silent movie days. Anderson's later career was as a conductor of major symphony orchestras.

# Andrews Sisters

Singers LaVerne, Maxine, and Patty were all born in Minneapolis, Minnesota (LaVerne, b. July 6, 1915; d. Brentwood, California, May 8, 1967; Maxine, b. January 3, 1918; d. Hyannis, Massachusetts, October 23, 1995; Patty, b. February 16, 1920). The sisters began their popularity with a string of hits for Decca Records, starting in 1938 with "Bei Mir Bist Du Schoen" (Decca 1562), and followed in 1939 with "Hold Tight—Hold Tight" (Decca 2214) and "Beer Barrel Polka" (Decca 2462). They revived a 1920 hit, "Down by the O-HI-O," twenty years later (Decca 3065), and another 1920 hit "(I'll Be with You) in Apple Blossom Time" (Decca 3622), in the 1941 Abbott and Costello film, *Buck Privates*, which also featured their blockbuster "Boogie Woogie Bugle Boy" (Decca 3598), revived in 1973 by Bette Midler (Atlantic 2964). Their appearance in a 1942 film, *Give Out, Sisters,* led to another big hit, "Pennsylvania Polka" (Decca 18398). That same year saw their "Strip Polka" become a hit (Decca 18470), followed the next year by "Shoo-Shoo Baby" (Decca 18572). Their biggest hit during the war years came in 1945, when a calypso tune, "Rum and Coca-Cola," gave them a million-selling record (Decca 18636). In a move to get more mileage from its top-selling stars, Decca paired the sisters with GUY LOMBARDO's orchestra for the Christmas perennial "Winter Wonderland"—backed by "Christmas Island" (Decca 23722)—and scored another million-seller in 1946. Decca also paired the sisters with its #1 best-selling artist, BING CROSBY, to produce two million-selling hits, "Pistol Packin' Mama" (Decca 23277) and "Don't Fence Me In" (Decca 23364). Their Christmas coupling of "Jingle Bells" and "Santa Claus Is Comin' to Town" (Decca 23281) in 1947 gave them yet another double-barreled hit. The sisters' last million-seller came in 1949 with "I Can Dream, Can't I?" (Decca 24705), and their last #1 charted hit came in 1950 with "I Wanna Be Loved" (Decca 27007). Their many films (especially the Abbott and Costello features) solidified their status as the most important female trio of the 1940s and early 1950s. They had their own radio show and were featured on a host of others. They retired in the late 1950s when rock and roll took over the pop charts. They made guest appearances in the late 1960s, and Maxine and Patty starred in a Broadway musical, *Over Here*, in 1974.

# Animal Dances

Animal dances were popular during the second decade of the twentieth century. Many of these dances originated among African-Americans, who performed them informally at house parties and small gatherings. Of all of them (grizzly bear, bunny hug, turkey trot), the easiest to do, and the longest lasting, was the fox-trot. Because of their great popularity, the animal dances inspired music by the Alley's top composers. "The Grizzly Bear Rag" was composed by George Botsford in 1910; "The Turkey Trot" (1912), by J. Bodewalt Lampe under the pseudonym of Ribe Danmark; and "The Bunny Hug" (1912), by HARRY VON TILZER. Some of the Alley's fox-trot dances were "Rabbit's Foot" by GEORGE L. COBB (1915), "The Weeping Willow" by PERCY WENRICH (1914), "Some Chocolate Drops" by Fred Irvin and Will Vodery (1914), "Doctor Brown" by Fred Irvin (1914), "Sugar Lump" by Fred Bryan (1914), "Supper Club" by HARRY CARROLL (1917), "Pozzo" by Vincent Rose (1916), "The Kangaroo Hop" by Melville Morris (1915), and "Cruel Papa" by WILL MARION COOK (1914). The extraordinarily popular songs "Ballin' the Jack," by CHRIS SMITH, and "Walkin' the Dog," by SHELTON BROOKS, were turned into instrumentals for fox-trotting.

# Harry Archer

Composer and bandleader (b. Harry Auracher, Creston, Iowa, February 21, 1888; d. New York City, April 23, 1960). Archer was a successful dance band leader of the 1920s and 1930s who scored several Broadway shows. After attending Michigan Military School, where he played trombone, he studied at Knox College and then Princeton University. Archer settled in Chicago, forming his first dance band. His first Broadway score came in 1912 for *Pearl Maiden*; he continued to compose for shows and revues through the mid-1920s. His greatest success came with the score for 1923's *Little Jesse James*, which produced the hit "I Love You." It was introduced in the show by John Boles and Margaret Wilson. PAUL WHITEMAN's orchestra (Victor 19151) and Carl Fenton's orchestra, featuring the duo pianists Arden and Ohman (Brunswick 2487), had the hit recordings. Archer married actress Ruth Gillette, and retired after World War II.

# Harold Arlen

Composer best remembered for his classic "Stormy Weather" (b. Hyman Arluck, Buffalo, New York, February 15, 1905; d. New York City, April 23, 1986). Arlen was given piano lessons as a child, and he loved to sing. His main interest was jazz. He once said, "I even

Harold Arlen as a young pianist, c. mid-1920s.

ran away from home once to hear the ORIGINAL MEMPHIS FIVE, a Dixieland group. They were my heroes." When he began to compose pop songs, it was in jazz bands that he found his inspiration. When he was sixteen, he formed the Snappy Trio to play in Buffalo cafés. The group expanded to become the kind of five-piece jazz band he loved to listen to. Arlen then joined the Buffalodians, an eleven-piece dance band, as pianist, arranger, and singer. This group came to New York City in 1925 and played the Palace Theatre, where bandleader Arnold Johnson heard Arlen and hired him as arranger, pianist, and vocalist for his band. The Arnold Johnson Orchestra played for *George White's Scandals of 1928*, and Arlen sang a medley of songs in the pit during intermission.

In the fall of 1929, VINCENT YOUMANS hired Arlen to sing a song in his upcoming show, *Great Day*, but the number was cut during rehearsal. When the rehearsal pianist took ill, Arlen replaced him. While rehearsing the chorus in a number, Arlen started fooling around with the introductory vamp, playing it over and over. Each time, he would improvise a bit of melody, then change the harmony, until WILL MARION COOK, the director of the chorus, told him that he ought to polish up the tune and write it down before someone stole it. Arlen took it to his friend HARRY WARREN, then on the staff at JEROME H. REMICK AND COMPANY, who introduced him to lyricist TED KOEHLER. Koehler gave the song its lyric and title, "Get Happy." It was put into the *Nine-Fifteen Revue* (February 11, 1930) and sung by RUTH ETTING. Although the revue lasted only seven performances, Remick published the song. The song's success allowed Arlen to give up performing and concentrate on songwriting.

Ted Koehler became his full-time lyricist, and together they got the assignment to write the Cotton Club shows, replacing the team of JIMMY MCHUGH and DOROTHY FIELDS. Harlem's Cotton Club featured black performers, but catered to an exclusively white clientele. The first revue there for Arlen and Koehler was *Rhythmania* (1931), and for BILL "BOJANGLES" ROBINSON they wrote "Between the Devil and the Deep Blue Sea." Also in the score were a production number, "I Love a Parade," and a Minnie-the-Moocher song for CAB CALLOWAY, "Kickin' the Gong Around."

*Earl Carroll Vanities—Tenth Edition* (September 27, 1932) included two Arlen-Koehler songs, "Rockin' in Rhythm" and the classic "I Gotta Right to Sing the Blues." The latter was jazz singer-trombonist Jack Teagarden's theme from 1939 to 1947. *Americana* (October 5, 1932) was a Shubert revue with only one Arlen song, "Satan's Lil Lamb," which marked the first time he worked with lyricists E. Y. "YIP" HARBURG and JOHNNY MERCER. Arlen would work with each separately, and most rewardingly, later.

*Cotton Club Parade—Twenty-first Edition* (October 23, 1932) boasted a smash hit in "I've Got the World on a String," sung by Aida Ward. "Minnie the Moocher's Wedding Day" was tailor-made for Cab Calloway and his orchestra, who featured it in the show. *Cotton Club Parade—Twenty-second Edition* (April 6, 1933) was, by all accounts, the most successful of the series, thanks in great measure to Arlen's score, which included "Happy as the Day Is Long," "Raisin' the Rent," and the classic "Stormy Weather," introduced in the show by ETHEL WATERS. This was her first time performing before a white audience, and it gave her career a tremendous boost. She made the song hers (Brunswick 6564), until Lena Horne sang it in the 1943 film of the same name. It was Waters's superb rendition that prompted IRVING BERLIN to cast her in his Broadway revue, *As Thousands Cheer*, later in 1933. GEORGE GERSHWIN remarked on the originality of the structure of the song, pointing out that there is no repetition of any phrase from the opening through "keeps rainin' all the time." "Stormy

Weather" broke with the conventions of popular song. Leo Reisman and his orchestra had Arlen as the vocalist on the hit recording (Victor 24262). Next, Arlen produced one of his few songs not from a show or film score. "Shame on You" had lyrics by EDWARD HEYMAN.

*Crazy Quilt of 1933*, for its post-Broadway tour, interpolated "It's Only a Paper Moon," with lyrics by E. Y. Harburg and BILLY ROSE, into its score. The song was then placed in the film version of *Take a Chance* (1933), sung by June Knight and Buddy Rogers. It first appeared, however, as "If You Believed in Me," in the flop play *The Great Magoo* (December 2, 1932).

"Let's Fall in Love" (1933) was Arlen's first movie assignment, written for the film of the same name (1934), in which singer Art Jarrett and actress Ann Sothern introduced the number. It promptly became a success.

*Cotton Club Parade—Twenty-fourth Edition* (March 23, 1934) included "Ill Wind," which Aida Ward introduced, and "As Long as I Live," introduced by sixteen-year-old Lena Horne and twenty-four-year-old Avon Long. BENNY GOODMAN and his orchestra recorded "As Long as I Live" with a swinging vocal by Jack Teagarden (Columbia 2923-D). It was the last of Arlen's major collaborations with Koehler.

*Life Begins at 8:40* (August 24, 1934), a title takeoff on a popular book of the day (*Life Begins at Forty*), was a revue with lyrics by "Yip" Harburg and IRA GERSHWIN. The score had two hits, "Let's Take a Walk Around the Block" and "You're a Builder Upper," which was introduced by Ray Bolger and Dixie Dunbar.

"Last Night When We Were Young" (1935) was another pop song Arlen wrote without a show or film connection. Lyrics were by Harburg. They wrote it in appreciation of Lawrence Tibbett, whose Hollywood house they rented for their first stay. Tibbett recorded the song and it became a standard (Victor 11877).

*Hooray for What!* (December 1, 1937) had an Arlen-Harburg score and a cast headed by Ed Wynn. It included "Buds Won't Bud," which was to be sung by Hannah Williams (later Mrs. Jack Dempsey), but both she and the song were dropped before the show opened on Broadway. It was later sung by JUDY GARLAND in *Andy Hardy Meets a Debutante* (1940). "Down with Love" was introduced in *Hooray* by Jack Whiting, June Clyde, and Vivian Vance. "In the Shade of the New Apple Tree" had a fine vocal arrangement by Hugh Martin, who sang it in the show. Martin would become prominent in the 1940s as a composer for films. "Moanin' in the Mornin' " was a feature for Vivian Vance and the "Singing Spies."

*The Wizard of Oz* (1939) is one of the great musical films of all time. The score by Arlen and Harburg is a masterpiece, with six knockout songs. The most famous, and the only Academy Award–winning song for Arlen, is "Over the Rainbow." Judy Garland wrote to Arlen's biographer, Edward Jablonski: "I have sung it dozens of times and it's still the song that is closest to my heart. It is very gratifying to have a song that is more or less known as my song, or my theme song, and to have had it written by the fantastic Harold Arlen." The other songs—"Ding-Dong! The Witch Is Dead," "If I Only Had a Brain," "The Jitter-bug," "The Merry Old Land of Oz," and "We're Off to See the Wizard"—fit perfectly with the film. An incredible blending of talents created a magnificent whole.

*At the Circus* (1939) starred the Marx Brothers, and Arlen and Harburg wrote "Lydia, the Tattooed Lady" for Groucho. This movie song became one of Groucho's most requested numbers. "When the Sun Comes Out" (1941) briefly reunited Ted Koehler with Arlen. It was a hit, but it was soon overshadowed by Arlen's next film score.

*Blues in the Night* (1941) had a score with lyrics by Johnny Mercer. Its four songs are varied, yet all are of high quality. "Hang onto Your Lids, Kids" is a snappy, jive-laden song that perfectly fit the swing era. "Says Who, Says You, Says I!" and "This Time the Dream's on Me" were sung by Priscilla Lane. The title song became a hit almost as soon as the movie was released. DINAH SHORE had her first million-selling disc with it (Bluebird 11436), and it also became identified with Jack Teagarden. It has remained a classic.

*Star Spangled Rhythm* (1942) was Paramount's wartime tribute in revue. The most memorable song was "That Old Black Magic," sung by Johnny Johnston, then danced by ballerina Vera Zorina. It later became identified with singer Billy Daniels. "Hit the Road to Dreamland" was sung in the film by Mary Martin and Dick Powell, to the counterpoint melody of the Golden Gate Quartet.

*Cabin in the Sky* (1943) was a film based on VERNON DUKE's Broadway show. For this treatment, MGM called Arlen and Harburg to add three songs. "Life's Full of Consequence," a duet for Eddie "Rochester" Anderson and Lena Horne, and "Happiness Is a Thing Called Joe," an inspiring, warm-glow number for Ethel Waters, were the two most significant.

*Bloomer Girl* (October 5, 1944) was the first Broadway show Arlen had written since he joined the Hollywood colony. It was a nostalgic look at the Civil War era. The best songs were "Evelina," "The Eagle and Me," and "Right as the Rain."

*Here Come the Waves* (1945) brought Arlen back to Hollywood. It also gave BING CROSBY the chance to make two Arlen-Mercer song hits: "Let's Take the Long Way Home" and "Accent-tchu-ate the Positive." Crosby also reprised "That Old Black Magic," spoofing his rival, FRANK SINATRA, singing it. *Out of This World* (1945) contains another Sinatra spoof, this time involving an absent Crosby. Star Eddie Bracken "sings" the title song, with Crosby's voice on the sound track. "June Comes Around Every Year" is a DOUBLE SONG, the only one Arlen wrote, and it stands up to those written by Irving Berlin.

*St. Louis Woman* (March 30, 1946) is thought by aficionados to be the best Arlen score, some maintaining that it is the best Broadway score ever. Two of the Arlen-Mercer songs became standards: "Any Place I Hang My Hat Is Home" and "Come Rain or Come Shine." The other songs include "I Had Myself a True Love," "Legalize My Name," "Cakewalk Your Lady," "I Wonder What Became of Me?," "Ridin' on the Moon," and "A Woman's Prerogative," all of which have entered the nightclub repertoire. *Casbah* (1948) contained two fine songs by Arlen and LEO ROBIN, both sung by the film's star, TONY MARTIN: "For Every Man There's a Woman" and "Hooray for Love." *The Petty Girl* (1950), a film score with lyrics by Mercer, sported "Fancy Free."

*A Star Is Born* (1954) starred Judy Garland and featured songs by Arlen and Ira Gershwin. Of the charming score, "Gotta Have Me Go with You," "It's a New World," and "The Man That Got Away" are the most important. This last song became almost as important to Garland's career as "Over the Rainbow," and was one of her most requested numbers in later years.

*House of Flowers* (December 30, 1954) starred Pearl Bailey and Diahann Carroll singing the Arlen songs, with lyrics by Arlen and Truman Capote. The Broadway show's gems include "A Sleepin' Bee," "House of Flowers," "I Never Has Seen Snow," and "Two Ladies in de Shade of de Banana Tree." *Jamaica* (October 31, 1957) reunited Arlen with Harburg and gave Lena Horne two more stage hits, "Cocoanut Sweet" and "Napoleon." *Saratoga* (December 7, 1959) brought Mercer and Arlen back to the stage and offered the fine "Goose Never Be a Peacock." *Gay Purr-ee* (1962) is an animated cartoon feature, with the voice of Judy Garland singing "Little Drops of Rain," an Arlen-Harburg gem. "That's a Fine Kind o' Freedom," with lyrics by Martin Charnin (1965), was Arlen's last song.

As publisher Edwin H. Morris told Edward Jablonski, "Anybody can walk in off the street and give you a hit. That doesn't make him a great songwriter. Harold has always been a long-pull composer who expresses himself honestly. His songs last and are ultimately more valuable, even financially, than the off-the-street hit."

# Louis Armstrong

Trumpeter and singer who was arguably the most creative and inspiring musician in jazz history (b. New Orleans, Louisiana, August 4, 1901 [not July 4, 1900, as he sometimes claimed]; d. New York City, July 6, 1971). Trumpeters (and other jazzmen, such as pianist Earl Hines) took inspiration from his phrasing and either directly copied him or tried to make his ideas their own.

Armstrong began recording with his Hot Five in November 1925, for Okeh Records. The personnel included Louis Armstrong, cornet; Kid Ory, trombone; Johnny Dodds, clarinet; Lil Armstrong, piano; and Johnny St. Cyr, banjo. Along with the Original Dixieland Jazz Band, Jelly Roll Morton's Red Hot Peppers, and King Oliver's recordings, Armstrong's Hot Five and Hot Seven discs provide the basic jazz repertoire. Kid Ory's classic "Muskrat Ramble" was initially recorded by the Hot Five (Okeh 8300), as was the flip side, Boyd Atkins's "Heebie Jeebies" (1926). "Heebie Jeebies" is the only song sheet with a photo of the Hot Five on the cover. Armstrong composed such tunes for his band as "My Heart," "Cornet Chop Suey," "Potato Head Blues," "Wild Man Blues," "Struttin' with Some Barbecue," and the later "Someday You'll Be Sorry."

Throughout his working life, Louis Armstrong brought out the best in jazzmen and songwriters. Beginning in 1929, he recorded pop songs, featuring both his trumpet playing and his singing. His discs helped to make the songs standards, and encouraged jazzmen to use pop songs in their repertoires. In 1932, his career in the movies got a boost when Fleisher Studios made a cartoon short of Louis playing and singing "I'll Be Glad When You're Dead, You Rascal You" (Okeh 41504). 1932 saw several pop hits for Armstrong, including vocal versions of "All of Me" and "Chinatown, My Chinatown." Armstrong's vocal phrasing—derived from his trumpet playing—influenced every jazz vocalist (and many pop singers) who followed, notably Billie Holiday. His wordless scat singing also was widely admired and copied.

In 1935, Armstrong signed with new label Decca, continuing his move into the field of pop recording. His next hits came in the mid-1940s, including a Top 10 R and B hit in

Louis Armstrong (right) and Bing Crosby in a still from the film *High Society* (1956).

1945 with "I Wonder" and two hit duets with Ella Fitzgerald, "You Won't Be Satisfied (Until You Break My Heart)" (which hit 10 on the pop charts in 1945) and "The Frim Fram Sauce" (a 1946 Top 10 R and B hit). Also, Armstrong began establishing himself as a screen persona, enlivening such musical films as *New Orleans* (1947) and *The Benny Goodman Story* (1955). His performance of "A Kiss to Build a Dream On" in the 1951 film *The Strip* (composed by HARRY RUBY with lyricists OSCAR HAMMERSTEIN II and Bert Kalmar) was a Top 10 pop hit in early 1952; the recording was featured prominently in the sound track for the film *Sleepless in Seattle* (1993). In COLE PORTER's hit *High Society* (1956), Armstrong gave one of his most memorable performances, singing "The Calypso" and a duet with BING CROSBY, "Now You Has Jazz."

Armstrong continued to be an influential pop singer through his entire career. In 1956, he had a Top 20 pop hit with his version of "Mack the Knife" (Columbia 40587), recorded with his small All-Stars group. In 1964, his recording of "Hello, Dolly!" (Decca 30091) displaced the Beatles from their accustomed rank at the top of the charts. Armstrong also won a Grammy for Best Vocal Performance, Male, for this recording. His 1967 performance of "What a Wonderful World" was used in the sound track of the 1987 movie *Good Morning, Vietnam*, returning it to the pop charts.

# Gus Arnheim

Bandleader, songwriter (b. Philadelphia, Pennsylvania, September 11, 1897; d. Los Angeles, California, January 19, 1955). Arnheim was a West Coast–based popular bandleader of the 1920s and 1930s who enjoyed a few hits. He began his career working with ABE LYMAN's popular dance bands, and the pair wrote the popular "I Cried for You" in 1923; it was revived in 1939 by JUDY GARLAND in the film *Babes in Arms*. In 1927, Arnheim struck out on his own, and two years later, he undertook a very successful tour of the United States and Europe. The band helped launch the career of two major pop vocalists of the 1930s. RUSS COLUMBO was originally a member of Arnheim's string section who quickly achieved success on his own as a singer. A young BING CROSBY also worked with the band; Arnheim provided Crosby with an early hit, 1930's "It Must Be True," and Crosby's recordings of "I Surrender, Dear" and "Wrap Your Troubles in Dreams" with Arnheim's band led to his solo stardom. From 1936 to 1938, Arnheim tried to remake his dance band into a swing ensemble, briefly employing Stan Kenton as a pianist. He retired from musicmaking in the early 1940s but attempted a comeback on television shortly before his death.

# ASCAP

The American Society of Composers, Authors, and Publishers is the oldest collection agency for songwriters and their publishers. The need arose for such an agency when it was realized that although Tin Pan Alley songwriters depended on royalties from the sale of sheet music for their income, many places of business were using music but not paying the songwriters. The Copyright Act of 1909 was supposed to protect songwriters so that no one could use their creations without permission. This aspect of the copyright law was being ignored by restaurants, hotels, amusement parks, recording companies, piano roll manufacturers, and others who engaged soloists and orchestras to entertain the public. The lawyer Nathan Burkan noted that Europeans had an organization to collect a fee for each time a musical composition was performed. It was called SACEM (Société des Auteurs, Compositeurs, et Editeurs de Musique), and it had been collecting royalties for its members since 1871. On February 13, 1914, at a meeting attended by 22 publishers and 107 composers and authors, ASCAP came into being. Burkan was its attorney, and George Maxwell became president; VICTOR HERBERT, vice president; the lyricist Glen MacDonough, secretary; and the lyricist-theatrical producer John Golden, treasurer. It wasn't until the end of the 1920s that ASCAP became a force, when radio stations and motion picture houses contributed the lion's share of the annual fees paid to the membership.

ASCAP evolved a complicated and highly arbitrary system for distributing the monies it collected. A songwriter could become a member if he had a minimum of five songs published in sheet music. He would then be placed in a category, depending upon the number of performance hours his works earned. As long as his work was being performed, he or his estate would be paid, even if he had stopped writing or had died.

In 1940, ASCAP's greed nearly ruined the organization. Its contract with over six hundred radio stations was expiring, and the new contract called for doubling the yearly fees for the following five years. Radio executives were stunned, and refused to discuss the issue. They pulled all ASCAP music from the airwaves, using only music in the public domain, hillbilly music, rhythm and blues, Latin American music, folk songs, and songs written by young composers and lyricists who didn't have the credits to join ASCAP. They also created their own collection agency, called BMI (Broadcast Music Incorporated), which didn't set onerous restrictions on joining and allowed any member to start collecting full fees at once, with performance ranks determining the amount distributed each year. While ASCAP distributed its royalties based on longevity within its ranks, BMI paid off immediately. It also accepted nontraditional popular songwriters, while ASCAP limited its members to creators of the popular songs of the day, Broadway show tunes, and songs from films. BMI grew quickly, taking advantage of the new youth market at the end of World War II and accepting rock and roll composers and lyricists, giving airplay to this new sound, and building radio programming devoted exclusively to contemporary popular music.

Changes in ASCAP and BMI permitted membership in both organizations (the use of pseudonyms for composers and authors, creation of other music firms for publishers), for the further benefit of their members.

# Fred Astaire

Dancer and singer (b. Frederick Austerlitz, Omaha, Nebraska, May 10, 1899; d. Beverly Hills, California, June 22, 1987). Astaire is considered one of the most talented dancers on stage and in films. He devised and performed elegant, innovative, and intricate dance routines. Of all his films, the best-remembered are the ten he made with GINGER ROGERS. Astaire introduced many standard songs in a light and sophisticated manner. His charm, combined with his easy articulation of lyrics, made him a favorite performer among songwriters. In 1936, he became one himself when he and JOHNNY MERCER wrote "I'm Building Up to an Awful Letdown" (Brunswick 7610). He made famous songs by GEORGE and IRA GERSHWIN, IRVING BERLIN, COLE PORTER, and JEROME KERN. Among the songs associated with him are "Oh, Lady Be Good"; "Fascinating Rhythm"; "'S Wonderful"; "Night and Day" (Victor 24193); "Cheek to Cheek" (Brunswick 7486); "Top Hat, White Tie and Tails" (Brunswick 7487); "Let's Face the Music and Dance" (Brunswick 7806); "The Way You Look Tonight" (Brunswick 7717); "A Fine Romance" (Brunswick 7716); "They Can't Take That Away from Me" (Brunswick 7855); "A Foggy Day" (Brunswick 7982); and "Steppin' Out with My Baby" in the 1948 film *Easter Parade*. In 1953 he recorded a four-LP set, *The Fred Astaire Story* (Mercury 1001–1004), which featured many songs he made famous and revived interest in them for a new generation. He continued to make films throughout the 1960s.

# Gene Austin

Composer and singer (b. Gainesville, Texas, June 24, 1900; d. Palm Springs, California, January 24, 1972). Popular singer Austin composed two hit songs in 1924, "How Come You Do Me Like You Do?" and "When My Sugar Walks Down the Street." Other hits were

"The Lonesome Road" (1929) and "Ridin' Around in the Rain" (1934). His soft voice and easygoing style made him a favorite on records and on radio, where he was billed as "The Voice of the Southland." His duet with Aileen Stanley on "When My Sugar Walks Down the Street" was a hit in 1925 (Victor 19585). With ukulele accompaniment by Billy Carpenter, his "Yes Sir! That's My Baby" (Victor 19656) also topped the charts that year. In 1926, he had two more hits, "Five Foot Two" (Victor 19899) and "Bye, Bye, Blackbird" (Victor 20044). 1927 was his banner year, with "Tonight You Belong to Me" (Victor 20371), "Forgive Me" (Victor 20561), and his biggest hit and the all-time nonholiday hit before the rock era, a five-million seller, "My Blue Heaven" (Victor 20964). 1928 saw two more hits, "Ramona" (Victor 21334) and "Jeannine" (Victor 21564), both written for silent films. 1929 brought "Carolina Moon" (Victor 21833), "Wedding Bells Are Breaking Up That Old Gang of Mine" (Victor 21893), "Ain't Misbehavin' " (Victor 22068), and "My Fate Is in Your Hands," with FATS WALLER at the piano (Victor 22223). 1931 gave him "Please Don't Talk About Me When I'm Gone" (Victor 22635) and "Lies" (Perfect 15542). He made a few films in the early 1930s, but in the mid-1930s, his recording sales dropped off. He continued working in nightclubs and on radio. He bowed out of show business during World War II.

# Gene Autry

Singer (b. Tioga Springs, Texas, September 29, 1907; d. Los Angeles, California, October 2, 1998). Autry was the first singing cowboy star of the movies, and he actually worked as a cowboy during the early 1920s. He began singing on local Oklahoma radio in the late 1920s, and appeared on Chicago's popular *National Barn Dance* program during the early 1930s. Autry went to Hollywood in 1934, and made over one hundred films by the mid-1950s. He had his own radio show, *Melody Ranch*, from 1940 through the mid-1950s. He made over one hundred half-hour television shows. His recording career spanned twenty years, starting in 1933. His first million-seller came in 1935 with his own tune, "That Silver-Haired Daddy of Mine" (Vocalion 2991). He had another million-selling disc in 1947 with "Here Comes Santa Claus," which he cowrote (Columbia 37942). In the 1949 Christmas season, his recording of Johnny Marks's "Rudolph, the Red-Nosed Reindeer" (Columbia 38610) began its climb to selling over eight million copies during the next four years. His version of "Frosty the Snowman" (Columbia 38907) sold over a million copies in 1950. Beginning in the mid-1950s, Autry concentrated on his non–show business empire, his radio and television stations, and his baseball club, the California Angels.

# B

## Mildred Bailey

Singer (b. Tekoa, Washington, February 27, 1907; d. Poughkeepsie, New York, December 12, 1951). A warm, jazz-tinged vocalist, Bailey had a big career throughout the 1930s. Her family moved to Spokane, Washington, where, in 1923, she played piano in movie houses. She later was a sheet music demonstrator in a shop, where she was discovered by a nightclub owner. In 1929, she became PAUL WHITEMAN's first female vocalist. Bailey had her first record success with the band in 1931 on "When It's Sleepy Time Down South" (Victor 22828), quickly followed in early 1932 by "All of Me" (Victor 22879). That same year she was accompanied by Matt Malneck's orchestra on "Georgia on My Mind" (Victor 22891). Back with Whiteman she recorded "I'll Never Be the Same" (Victor 24088). In 1933, she introduced "Lazy Bones" (Brunswick 6587), backed by the Dorsey Brothers Orchestra, featuring Bunny Berigan in a GLENN MILLER arrangement. Her 1937 recording of "Rockin' Chair" (Vocalion 3553), based on an Eddie Sauter arrangement, gave her the nickname "The Rockin' Chair Lady." Bailey next joined her husband, bandleader Red Norvo, for a series of discs that earned them the nickname "Mr. and Mrs. Swing." "I've Got My Love to Keep Me Warm" (Brunswick 7813) and "Love Is Here to Stay" (Brunswick 8068) showed Bailey's great skill at jazz singing. 1938 was her peak year, with "Don't Be That Way" (Vocalion 4016); "I Let a Song Go Out of My Heart" (Vocalion 4083), and "My Reverie" (Vocalion 4408). Illness restricted her to intermittent work during the last decade of her life.

# Ernest R. Ball

Successful composer of the first two decades of the twentieth century (b. Cleveland, Ohio, July 22, 1878; d. Santa Ana, California, May 3, 1927). Ball specialized in Irish songs and sentimental ballads, and became the mainstay of M. WITMARK AND SONS, who gave him a twenty-year contract that was renewed for another ten years, the longest association any composer had with one publisher.

Ball scored his first big hit with "Will You Love Me in December as You Do in May?" (1905), and in the following year he established his reputation when he wrote the million-selling "Love Me and the World Is Mine." Henry Burr (1882–1941), the most famous ballad singer on records from 1890–1930, had the hit recording (Columbia 3499). With Irish tenor Chauncey Olcott and lyricist Rida Johnson Young, Ball wrote "Mother Machree" for Olcott when he starred in the 1910 Broadway show *Harry of Ballymore*. John McCormack (1884–1945), the most famous Irish tenor of all time, made the best-selling recording (Victor 64181). Ball's next big hit for Olcott came in 1912 with "When Irish Eyes Are Smiling." It was put into *The Isle of Dreams* the following year, and Olcott had the #1 disc (Columbia A-1310). Baritone George MacFarlane made Ball's next hit when he sang "A Little Bit of Heaven (Shure They Call It Ireland)" in the 1914 Broadway show *Heart of Paddy Whack*. Ball's last big ballad came in 1919 when Elizabeth Spencer and Charles Hart made a hit of "Let the Rest of the World Go By" (Victor 18638). Ball kept writing and performing until his death. Hollywood made a biopic, *Irish Eyes Are Smiling* (1944), starring Dick Haymes.

# Ballroom Dances of the Ragtime Era (1900s–1910s)

In dance, the first decades of the twentieth century were the calm before the storm. The waltz maintained its lead as the universal favorite. The two-step gave the younger generation a kick while the older generation clucked its disapproval. No one could foresee what popular dance would be like in the 1920s.

The most popular of the ballroom dances during this period was the two-step. Like the CAKEWALK, the music for it was lightly syncopated, and therefore easily danced to. At first, dance tunes were in 6/8 time, but when publishers added the designation "characteristic march and two-step," the public understood it to mean a syncopated number, usually in 2/4 time. An alternative to piano RAGTIME, two-steps were easier for the amateur pianist to learn, yet they hinted at the exhilaration that ragtime could provide. Two-steps were published through the 1900s and into the 1910s, to be succeeded by the ANIMAL DANCES and the one-step just before World War I.

Some of the most successful two-steps include CHARLES L. JOHNSON's "All the Money" (1908), S. R. Henry's "The Colored Major" (1900) and "Peter Piper" (1905), ALBERT VON TILZER's "Cotton" (1907), HARRY VON TILZER's "The Cubanola Glide" (1909), Duane Crabb's "Fluffy Ruffles" (1907), Malvin M. Franklin's "The Lobster Glide" (1909), William H. Tyers's "Panama" (1911), and Henry Frantzen's "Kentucky Kut Up" (1907).

During this decade the waltz was holding its own, as evidenced by the great popularity of Harry Von Tilzer's "Down Where the Wurzburger Flows"(1902), "Under the Anheuser Bush"(1903), and "On a Sunday Afternoon" (1902); George Evans's "In the Good Old Summertime" (1902); EGBERT VAN ALSTYNE's "In the Shade of the Old Apple Tree" (1905); Kerry Mills's "Meet Me in St. Louis, Louis" (1904); GUS EDWARDS's "In My Merry Oldsmobile" (1905) and "School Days" (1907); and Leo Friedman's "Meet Me Tonight in Dreamland" (1909).

# Roy Bargy

Pianist and bandleader (b. Newaygo, Michigan, July 30, 1894; d. Vista, California, January 16, 1974). Bargy began his career as piano roll artist for Imperial Roll Company in Chicago in August 1919. He created some of the most diabolical and difficult-to-play novelty rags: "Omeomy" (Imperial 513980), "A Blue Streak" (Imperial 513600), "Sweet and Tender" (Imperial 512980), and "Slipova" (Imperial 513070) in 1920. He made piano solo recordings in 1922 and 1924: "Knice and Knifty" (Victor 18969), "Pianoflage" (Victor 18969), "Jim Jams!" (Victor 19537), and "Sunshine Capers" (Victor 19320). Bargy led the Benson Orchestra of Chicago from 1920 to 1924. He was with the ISHAM JONES Orchestra from 1924 to 1928, and then became pianist and chief arranger for the PAUL WHITEMAN Orchestra from 1928 to 1938. Finally, he served as comedian JIMMY DURANTE's musical director until Durante retired in 1961.

# Harry Barris

Composer (b. New York City, November 24, 1905; d. Burbank, California, December 13, 1962). Barris started as a professional pianist at age fourteen and became one of PAUL WHITEMAN's Rhythm Boys in late 1926, singing with Al Rinker and BING CROSBY. "Mississippi Mud" (1927), his first song hit, was written while he was a member of the Rhythm Boys trio. Paul Whiteman and his orchestra recorded it, with Bix Beiderbecke on cornet and the Rhythm Boys as vocalists (Victor 21274). "From Monday On" (1928), another great feature for the Rhythm Boys, was issued on the flip side of "Mississippi Mud."

"It Must Be True" (1930) was written with bandleader GUS ARNHEIM and lyricist Gordon Clifford (1902–1968) for Bing Crosby and the Rhythm Boys (Victor 22561); bandleader Ted Weems also featured this hit. "I Surrender, Dear" (1931), with lyrics by Clifford, was featured by Bing Crosby (Victor 22618). KATE SMITH as well as GUY LOMBARDO's band also plugged it successfully. "Lies" (1931), with lyrics by George Springer, was introduced by popular crooner RUSS COLUMBO. Guy Lombardo's orchestra also helped to turn it into a standard. This song has the shortest note span in all of pop music; only four full tones are used in verse and chorus.

"Wrap Your Troubles in Dreams" (1931), with lyrics by TED KOEHLER and Billy Moll, was a big hit for Bing Crosby (Victor 22701). "It Was So Beautiful" (1932) was written with film producer/lyricist Arthur Freed for Connee Boswell. It was sung by Kate Smith in the film *The Big Broadcast* (1932). "I'm Satisfied" (1934), with lyrics by Ralph Freed (1907–1973), was introduced by Horatio Zito. "Little Dutch Mill" (1934) also has words by Ralph Freed, and was a hit for Bing Crosby (Brunswick 6794). It was the last hit for Barris, who retired from show business before he was forty.

# Phil Baxter

Bandleader, pianist, and songwriter (b. Navarro County, Texas, September 5, 1896; d. Dallas, Texas, November 1972). Baxter, a popular bandleader active from the mid-1920s through the mid-1930s, composed a number of hits in both the mainstream pop and the cowboy styles. His band was active throughout the Midwest, and made at least two recordings, the first in St. Louis in 1925 and the second in Dallas, Texas, in 1929. In 1921, Baxter heard singer Carl "Deacon" Moore (1905–1985) leading a small band in rural Arkansas; Moore soon joined Baxter's more established band, and the two worked together through the late 1920s; they also composed the novelty hit "Ding Dong Daddy from Dumas." Moore subsequently had a long career as a cowboy singer and country comedian. In June 1927, Baxter's band, known as The Texas Tommies, became the house band at a new St. Louis ballroom, the El Torreon, which would later be the legendary home for famed St. Louis groups including Bennie Moten's band (which featured a young pianist named Count Basie). Baxter remained there through 1933, and composed a theme song for the club that opened and closed each evening's performance; the band also broadcast from the club each evening over St. Louis radio. Baxter's best-known hit was 1929's "Piccolo Pete," with a typical Western flavor, which was a major hit for popular bandleader Ted Weems. By the mid-1930s, Baxter had to retire from performing due to severe arthritis, and subsequently left the music business.

# Nora Bayes

Vocalist (b. Dora Goldberg, Joliet, Illinois, 1880; d. Brooklyn, New York, March 19, 1928). Bayes was known as "The Wurzburger Girl." In 1902, on her opening night at the Orpheum Theatre in Brooklyn, she forgot the words to "Down Where the Wurzburger Flows." The composer, HARRY VON TILZER, stood up in the audience and sang the song for her. She picked it up on the second chorus and got a great hand. The management hired Von Tilzer to repeat the stunt for the rest of the week, generating tremendous interest in the song. That song made her a star.

Bayes and her husband, Jack Norworth, wrote "Shine On, Harvest Moon" and featured it in Ziegfeld's *Follies of 1908*. It was their biggest song success. Later that year, Norworth wrote the lyrics for ALBERT VON TILZER's "Take Me Out to the Ball-Game," and Bayes sang it in her act for the next two years. From that time on, she was a top act in vaudeville, headlining every bill she was on.

In the custom of the time, Bayes interpolated several numbers into the score of *The Jolly Bachelors*, which opened on January 6, 1910. She and her husband provided a new title and lyrics for an English song, "Come Along, My Mandy," which Bayes sang. The biggest hit in the show, however, was another English song with Americanized lyrics, "Has Anybody Here Seen Kelly?" It brought the house down nightly. For *Little Miss Fix-it* (April 3, 1911), the team interpolated their sequel to "Shine On, Harvest Moon," "Mr. Moon Man, Turn Off Your Light." Their recording of it demonstrates their star quality (Victor 70038).

Singing star Nora Bayes featured on the sheet music cover of her own "Fox-Trot."

George M. Cohan's "Over There," published by the William Jerome Publishing Company, carried a photograph of Nora Bayes on the first edition. This 1917 effort was the biggest seller of more than one thousand songs written about World War I, due in great measure to its plugging by Bayes.

Bayes starred in the Broadway musical *Ladies First* (October 24, 1918) and sang two interpolated numbers by George Gershwin. The first was "Some Wonderful Sort of Someone," published only with the pre-Broadway show title, *Look Who's Here*. The second, "The Real American Folk Song Is a Rag," not published until 1959, was the first song written by George and Ira Gershwin. It was filled with the syncopations that George would use throughout the 1920s. Ira's lyrics suited the melody perfectly, and it was Ira who gave the song to Ella Fitzgerald in 1959, when she asked to make the first recording of it. Her performance featured the expert backing of ragtime pianist Lou Busch on the LP, *Ella Fitzgerald Sings the George and Ira Gershwin Song Book*, Volume Two (Verve MGV-4025).

Although Bayes remained a headliner in vaudeville through the mid-1920s, her last two big song hits came in 1920. For composer Albert Von Tilzer, she sang "I'll Be with You in Apple Blossom Time," and for the new team of Richard Whiting and Raymond Egan, she made "The Japanese Sandman" a two-million seller (Columbia A-2997).

# Bennie Benjamin

Composer and lyricist (b. St. Croix, Virgin Islands, November 4, 1907; d. New York City, May 2, 1989). Popular song composer of the 1940s and 1950s, Benjamin is best remembered for his first hit, "I Don't Want to Set the World on Fire." He came to New York City in the 1920s, working as a dance band guitarist and for various music publishers. His big hit came in 1941 with "I Don't Want to Set the World on Fire," which he composed with jazz trombonist Eddie Durham (b. San Marcos, Texas, August 19, 1906; d. New York City, March 6, 1987); lyrics were by Eddie Seiler (1911–1952) and Sol Marcus (1912–1976). The Ink Spots (Decca 3987) had a major hit with it. Marcus and Seiler continued to write with Benjamin through the mid-1940s, and then Benjamin partnered with George Weiss (b. New York City, April 9, 1921) through the mid-1950s. The duo wrote dozens of songs, most notably the major hit "Wheel of Fortune," a #1 hit for Kay Starr in 1952 (Capitol 1964). After breaking with Weiss, Benjamin teamed again with Marcus, achieving his last major hit with "Don't Let Me Be Misunderstood" (written with Gloria Caldwell), originally recorded by Nina Simone, and revived by the British Invasion group The Animals in 1965 (MGM 13311) for a Top 20 pop hit.

# Irving Berlin

Composer, lyricist, plugger, performer, and publisher who personifies Tin Pan Alley in all its glory (b. Israel Baline, Temun, Russia, May 11, 1888; d. New York City, September 22, 1989). Berlin, who began as a boy singer and in a few years became the most famous Alley songwriter, came with his family to the United States when he was four years old. Young Izzy Baline found a job plugging the songs of HARRY VON TILZER, singing them from the balcony at Tony Pastor's on Fourteenth Street. When he was eighteen, Izzy became a singing waiter at Pelham's Café in Chinatown. He served customers and cleaned up the café when it closed for the night, but his main function was to entertain the customers with popular songs of the day. Around the corner from Pelham's was Callahan's, whose proprietor boasted that one of his waiters, George Ronklyn, had written the lyrics for the newly published "My Mariuccia Take a Steamboat." Pelham owner Mike Salter, convinced that his waiter could write a better song, encouraged his pianist, Mike Nicholson, to compose a tune for which Izzy would write the lyrics. In frank imitation of their rivals at Callahan's, they called their effort "Marie from Sunny Italy." It was published on May 8, 1907, by JOSEPH W. STERN AND COMPANY. On that day, Izzy Baline became I. Berlin, the name by which he was credited on the cover and on the title page. To avoid tempting fate, "I." became "Irving," and the name "Berlin" stuck. His total royalty on this, his first published song, was thirty-seven cents.

It is well known that the man who wrote more hits than anyone else in all three song categories—pop songs, show tunes, and movie songs—could not read a note of music, could not write music, could hardly play the piano, and played in only one key—F sharp. He got his start in the Alley when he wrote a lyric about the Italian marathon runner Dorando, who was disqualified in the 1908 Olympics. Berlin took the lyric to the young TED SNYDER COMPANY, where co-owner Henry Waterson said he would buy it for $25.00 if Berlin would write a melody. Berlin dictated one to an arranger on the spot. Several weeks later, singer Amy Butler took Ted Snyder to Jimmy Kelly's, on Union Square, to hear Berlin (still a singing waiter) perform his parodies of current songs. Berlin was hired as staff lyricist for a $25.00 a week draw against future royalties, and immediately turned out a song, with music by Snyder. "She Was a Dear Little Girl," was interpolated into a show, *The Boys and Betty* (November 2, 1908), by Marie Cahill (1870–1933). Though the song didn't set the world—or the show—on fire, its historic value is obvious. With lyricist EDGAR LESLIE making his publishing debut, Berlin wrote the music in 1909 for "Sadie Salome, Go Home," which FANNY BRICE used to audition for her first *Ziegfeld Follies* (the 1910 edition). That same year, Berlin wrote two rag songs of modest success, "That Mesmerizing Mendelssohn Tune," which was plugged by vaudevillian-turned-songwriter CON CONRAD, and "Yiddle on Your Fiddle Play Some Ragtime." Also in 1909, Berlin wrote lyrics for Ted Snyder's hugely successful piano rag, "Wild Cherries." Just as SCOTT JOPLIN deserved the title "King of Ragtime Writers," so Berlin would soon be "King of Ragtime Songs." During the next few years, he would write "That Beautiful Rag," "That Opera Rag," "Stop That Rag," "Dat Draggy Rag," "Dance of the Grizzly Bear," "Everybody's Doin' It Now," "Dying Rag," "Ragtime Violin," "That Mysterious Rag," "Whistling Rag," "Ragtime Jockey Man," "Ragtime Soldier Man," "That Society Bear," "They've Got Me Doin' It Now," "That International Rag," "Ragtime Opera Medley," "When the Band Played an American Rag," "Everything in America Is Ragtime," "Ragtime Razor Brigade," and "That Revolutionary Rag." His "Alexander's Ragtime Band" (1911) became the most popular and most profitable "ragtime" song ever written, although, of course, it isn't ragtime at all. It is a song *about* ragtime, not a song *in* ragtime. Its marchlike melody is taken from a bugle call and a phrase from Stephen Foster's "Swanee River."

Early in 1911, Berlin became a member of the Friars Club and was asked to perform in its annual *Frolic*. This was a special occasion for him, so he wanted to write a special song. The year before, he had written lyrics for a melody by Ted Snyder titled "Alexander and His Clarionet." He rewrote them to fit his new idea and his own melody. Old-time coon shouter EMMA CARUS put "Alexander's" into her vaudeville act in Chicago, where it brought the house down. When Berlin sang it as his contribution to the *Frolic*, he received high praise from his audience and from newspaper critics covering the event. The song was copyrighted on March 18, 1911, and was first published with Emma Carus's photograph on the cover. The song became so popular that sixty-five performers—a record number—eventually had their photos individually printed on sixty-five editions, as "successfully sung by." On September 9, the Victor Military Band made its famous version for the Victor Talking Machine Company (Victor 17006). Snyder issued the song later that month as a two-step instrumental.

Berlin's next big hit was an exuberant song about the South, "When the Midnight Choo-Choo Leaves for Alabam' " (1912), which became a favorite in vaudeville. Shortly after this song was published, he was made a publishing partner and the firm's name was changed to Waterson, Berlin and Snyder.

Berlin married Dorothy Goetz, sister of songwriter E. RAY GOETZ, after a whirlwind courtship of only a few weeks, on February 3, 1912. They honeymooned in Cuba, where she contracted typhoid fever. When she died five months after their wedding, Berlin was inconsolable. His brother-in-law suggested that he assuage his grief by writing a ballad. Later in the year he wrote his first heartrending ballad, "When I Lost You," which sold two million copies. He would write many other hit ballads, fortunately without such tragedy to inspire them. However, he had a rocky time when it came to courting Ellin Mackay, the woman who became his second wife on January 4, 1926. For her, he wrote "All Alone," "What'll I Do?," "Remember," and, shortly before their wedding, "Always."

The story goes that Berlin and his current pianist were sitting at a table in a Florida restaurant with the pianist's girlfriend. The talk at the table revolved around the Alley and how much hit songs made, and the girl finally gathered up enough nerve to ask, "Mr. Berlin, would you write a song about me sometime?" Berlin, in an expansive mood, said, "Why sometime? Why not right now?" He asked her name, and she replied, "Mona." With that, Berlin leaned back in his chair and hummed a simple melody, adding words to it. The pianist copied the tune and words on a napkin, and when he got back to New York, transcribed it onto music paper and put it in the file. A few years later, Berlin had a huge hit in "Remember," and his firm wanted to follow it up with another waltz. Someone went through the file and found "Mona." They played it and said it was a natural. But no one in the office knew who Mona was. When Berlin came in, he said he didn't know either, and further, didn't remember

Irving Berlin in the 1920s.

writing the song! Asked to change the lyric, he decided to make the opening line "I'll be loving you, always." He said, "That will take care of everybody."

Late in 1914, Berlin created his first complete score for a musical. He had stated in an interview that he wanted to write a ragtime opera. What he meant was that he wanted to include syncopated songs in a musical show, providing toe-tapping music for ballroom dancing. Dancing schools were opening everywhere to teach the new "animal dances," the tango, and others steps popularized by VERNON AND IRENE CASTLE. The team had, seemingly overnight, captivated the public with their dancing. It was the idea of producer Charles Dillingham to put Irving Berlin together with the Castles to provide Broadway with *Watch Your Step* (December 8, 1914). The songs from this score were the first that Berlin published. (For his nonshow songs, he remained with Waterson, Berlin and Snyder.) He was proud of his first score, and issued twenty of its numbers in advance of the show's opening on Broadway. It was unusual for so many songs to be published from one show. Most publishers would test the waters with three or four songs from the out-of-town tryouts, then, after the Broadway opening, issue a few others that received audience and reviewers' approval. Of the many numbers published from the show, only two stood out. "The Syncopated Walk" was featured in the overture, as the first act's major production number, as the finale to the first act, as an entr'acte, and as the grand finale. It is curious, given the show's hype as "A Syncopated Musical," that there is very little syncopation in the melody. The verse is practically in even time. The real gem of the show was called "Simple Melody," later known as "Play a Simple Melody." It was the first of four numbers Berlin wrote that contain double tunes—two different melodies and lyrics for the same chorus, each sung separately and then combined (requiring two people to sing). One of the melodies to "Simple Melody" is very raggy, justifying the subtitle of the show. Berlin was to write three more of these tricky "double songs": "You're Just in Love," for *Call Me Madam* (1950); "Empty Pockets Filled with Love" for his last Broadway musical, *Mr. President* (1962); and "An Old-Fashioned Wedding," written for the revival of *Annie Get Your Gun* (1966).

A new Berlin show followed a year later, with Gaby Deslys and Harry Fox starring in *Stop! Look! Listen!* (December 25, 1915). It contained fifteen published numbers, three of them noteworthy. With "Everything in America Is Ragtime," Berlin maintained his rag song crown. "The Girl on the Magazine" made a wonderful production number, re-created in the film *Easter Parade* (1948). The song that became a standard, and Berlin's avowed favorite, was "I Love a Piano."

The big noise (literally) from the Alley in 1917 was a new music called jazz. Jazz was both a style of playing popular songs as well as a body of instrumental syncopated melodies written for small (five-to-seven-piece) bands. The jazz style featured ensemble playing and individual improvisations. It required a tremendous amount of energy to play, to listen to, and especially to dance to. Jazz differed from traditional dance band music. In addition to reading arrangements from printed scores, jazz players would syncopate the melody and ad-lib solos in a faster rhythm, and in ensemble they sounded "hotter" than the smooth dance orchestras. Because it was featured by bands and was played in nightclubs for dancing, jazz supplanted piano ragtime in popularity. The syncopation involved in jazz was, of necessity, less than in piano ragtime, and in time jazz became more melodious for dancing. New dance steps were created for this fast, wild-sounding music, and the fox-trot and the one-step became the most suitable styles of dancing to it. The new music gave a shot in the leg to all those under thirty and, thanks to the pioneer recordings of the ORIGINAL DIXIELAND JAZZ BAND (ODJB), became a cause célèbre among ministers and most older folk. Just under thirty at this time, Berlin, as always, sided with youth and wrote "Mr. Jazz Himself."

When America entered World War I, Irving Berlin was drafted. He was assigned to Camp Upton at Fort Yaphank on eastern Long Island, where he had to get up at five in the morning every day. (He had been accustomed to working until two or three in the morning, so he had previously arisen around noon.) Something had to be done, so his creativity came to the rescue. He discovered many actors, musicians, and other show business characters also stationed in the camp. He went to his commanding officer and pointed out that if they could use their talents in putting together a show for other soldiers, it would help in recruitment and boost the morale of everyone. The officer gave his permission, and while working on the show, Berlin could get up whenever he wanted to. This incident gave rise to his most famous war song, "Oh! How I Hate to Get Up in the Morning." He sang it in the show, which was called *Yip, Yip, Yaphank* (August 19, 1918). There were ten songs published from this show, including a farewell to ragtime, "Ragtime Razor Brigade," and a hello to jazz, "Send a Lot of Jazz Bands Over There." His soon-to-be-famous "Mandy" was originally written for this show, but in the following year was rewritten, to be placed in the *Ziegfeld Follies of 1919* (June 16, 1919).

At the beginning of 1919, Berlin, a civilian once again, dissolved his partnership and severed his connection with Waterson, Berlin and Snyder. On June 1, he and his new partner, Max Winslow, also his professional manager, opened Irving Berlin, Inc., taking the third floor of 1587 Broadway (at Forty-eighth Street), with Saul Bornstein as general manager. The firm's first published song was "The New Moon," a theme for the Norma Talmadge silent film of the same name. Berlin had written it as a favor to a childhood friend, movie producer Joseph M. Schenck, Talmadge's husband. Berlin next wrote "Eyes of Youth" for the "photo-play" of the same name, starring Clara Kimball Young. His first million-selling success for his own firm was "Nobody Knows and Nobody Seems to Care," which his company plugged for over seventy weeks!

When Sam Harris broke up his producing partnership with GEORGE M. COHAN, Berlin teamed with Harris to build a new theater on Broadway. They named it The Music Box, and it opened on September 22, 1921, to general approbation for its architecture and furnishings. The first *Music Box Revue* (with, of course, a Berlin score) also opened that night to critical acclaim. The hit of the opulent show was "Say It with Music." "The Schoolhouse Blues" was his first nod to this new form of music. (He was late in coming to it.) His next year's *Revue* (October 23, 1922) contained three future standards: "Crinoline Days," "Lady of the Evening," and "Pack Up Your Sins and Go to the Devil." The third annual *Revue* (September 22, 1923) featured "Learn to Do the Strut" and "An Orange Grove in California." After its opening, Berlin added "What'll I Do?"

*The Cocoanuts* (December 8, 1925), starring the Marx Brothers and Margaret Dumont, should have yielded at least one Berlin hit, but didn't. When the film was made in 1930, Berlin wrote a new song for it that became popular: "When My Dreams Come True."

At star Belle Baker's insistence that he supply her with a song for the Rodgers and Hart show *Betsy* (December 28, 1926), Berlin wrote "Blue Skies." While revues always featured interpolated numbers, it was rare for a book show in the late 1920s to include one. This was especially true of the Rodgers and Hart shows, which by contract prohibited anyone from interpolating songs into their scores. Berlin would not have contributed his number if Baker had not requested it. Much to Rodgers and Hart's annoyance, Berlin's song was the only hit to come from that show. It was also the only time they allowed a song to be interpolated into one of their scores.

An often overlooked aspect of sheet music publishing is the simplified arrangement made for the amateur pianist. This arrangement not only must be easy to play but also must highlight the melody. The finest arranger of such music was HELMY KRESA, who had worked for the Irving Berlin corporation since 1926. When he first came to New York, Kresa was given a job as arranger by Berlin's professional manager, Ben Bloom. It was to be only temporary—to last one week while another arranger was on vacation. However, Kresa's good work came to Berlin's attention. (His first job was arranging HARRY WOODS's "When the Red, Red Robin Comes Bob, Bob, Bobbin' Along.") After Berlin dictated "Blue Skies" to Kresa, he made Kresa's stay permanent. As Berlin's personal arranger from that time forward, Kresa was employed by Irving Berlin, Inc. for sixty-five years.

Though he wouldn't become fully committed to the movies until 1935, Berlin was asked by Joe Schenck to write more theme songs, and he did. In 1928, Berlin wrote three: for *Coquette*, starring Mary Pickford; "Marie," the theme song of *The Awakening*, which starred Vilma Banky (a song TOMMY DORSEY was to record with spectacular success nine years later); and "Where Is the Song of Songs for Me" for *Lady of the Pavements* (or, as it was first titled, *Masquerade*), starring Lupe Velez. For the all-black cast of King Vidor's "talking-singing" *Hallelujah* (1929), Berlin wrote "Swanee Shuffle" and "Waiting at the End of the Road." For his friend AL JOLSON's *Mammy* (1929), Berlin wrote three songs. The best, and most characteristic of the Jolson personality, was "Let Me Sing and I'm Happy." He also wrote three songs for HARRY RICHMAN's *Puttin' on the Ritz* (1929), but only the title song became a hit. For the Douglas Fairbanks–Bebe Daniels film *Reaching for the Moon* (1931), Berlin obliged once more with a title song.

His first complete film score was for *Top Hat* (1935), starring FRED ASTAIRE and GINGER ROGERS. Because he was allowed to attend story conferences, his songs grew from the plot. (The film song that makes the strongest impression is the one which is firmly rooted to a situation. Such a song stands a good chance to have popularity apart from the film, while the more generic song, which would seem to have the edge, really doesn't.) This is probably why the five songs from *Top Hat* have remained standards and the film is generally regarded as the best of the Astaire-Rogers series. "Top Hat, White Tie and Tails" is immediately identified with Fred Astaire. It matched his persona, as "Let Me Sing and I'm Happy" had matched Jolson's. The others in the score are "Cheek to Cheek," "Isn't This a Lovely Day," "No Strings," and "The Piccolino."

*Follow the Fleet* (1936) followed *Top Hat* and boasted an original Berlin score of seven songs. Though it featured the same stars and production team, the songs didn't seem to be integral parts of the film, so only two have had longevity: "I'm Putting All My Eggs in One Basket" and "Let's Face the Music and Dance." *On the Avenue* (1937) had a score of six published numbers for this Dick Powell–Alice Faye–Madeleine Carroll starrer, with two outstanding hits, "I've Got My Love to Keep Me Warm" and "Slumming on Park Avenue."

*Alexander's Ragtime Band* (1938) took the title of Berlin's first monumental hit, and this movie again proved the song's power by its place as the biggest-grossing musical film of the 1930s. For once, Twentieth Century-Fox's hype was on the mark when it proclaimed it the "Greatest of All Motion Pictures." Starring Tyrone Power, Alice Faye, Don Ameche, ETHEL MERMAN, and Jack Haley, the film consisted mainly of Berlin hits of bygone years. It also holds the record for having more songs published from a single film—32—than any other movie musical.

*Carefree* (1938) starred Fred Astaire and Ginger Rogers; of the four new Berlin songs published from it, only "Change Partners" became successful. Berlin's next assignment, *Second Fiddle* (1939), had an even less distinguished score. But Berlin outdid himself with his next score, for *Holiday Inn* (1942), a tuneful film starring BING CROSBY, Fred Astaire, Marjorie Reynolds, and Virginia Dale. He wrote ten new songs and interpolated "Easter Parade" from his 1933 Broadway revue *As Thousands Cheer*, since the plot dealt with celebrating holidays. The blockbuster was "White Christmas," and it won Berlin his only Academy Award for Best Song. Bing Crosby's recording of it (Decca 18429) has sold over twenty-five million copies, and in total record sales the song is the all-time biggest. It further holds the distinction of having been heard more often on *Your Hit Parade* than any other song in that program's history. It was on thirty-three times, ten in the #1 position. It has sold more than five million copies of sheet music, and over a million copies of vocal and band arrangements. It has been recorded in over thirty languages for total record sales in excess of 140 million. In short, as *Variety* has pointed out, it is the most valuable copyright in the world.

*This Is the Army* (1943) was a movie made from Berlin's Broadway show of the previous year. The composer set up a special company, This Is the Army, Inc., to deal with its profits, which he turned over to the Army Relief Fund. Both the Broadway and the film version were based on his *Yip, Yip, Yaphank* of twenty-five years earlier. This all-soldier revue contained all new material for World War II, except for the inclusion of "Oh! How I Hate to Get Up in the Morning," which again (on stage and film) featured the composer singing it in his thin voice. (When Berlin was recording the song for the sound track, a crew member remarked to a colleague, "If the guy who wrote this song could hear the way this guy is singing it, he'd turn over in his grave!")

The movie cast included two actors who would later become interested in politics, George Murphy and Ronald Reagan. KATE SMITH sang "God Bless America," which she had introduced on radio on November 10, 1938. Her record became a multimillion seller, and it was used for years at ball games, political rallies, movie theaters, and presidential birthday balls (Victor 26198). In time, it became the best-known patriotic song in the United States. It has been considered our unofficial national anthem, ranking only slightly behind "The Star-Spangled Banner" in performances of a patriotic nature. Berlin assigned all earnings from this song to be shared equally by the Boy Scouts and Girl Scouts of America. *This Is the Army* also included such hits as "This Is the Army, Mr. Jones," "I'm Getting Tired So I Can Sleep," "With My Head in the Clouds," "How About a Cheer for the Navy," and "I Left My Heart at the Stage Door Canteen."

*Blue Skies* (1946) again teamed Bing Crosby and Fred Astaire. Its seventeen songs mixed the old with the new. Naturally, the title song was a standout, along with the 1921 favorite "All by Myself," "A Pretty Girl Is like a Melody," "I'll See You in C-U-B-A," "Always," and a new hit written for the film, "You Keep Coming Back Like a Song."

*Easter Parade* (1948) couldn't help but become a classic film musical, because it starred Fred Astaire and JUDY GARLAND. Set in 1910, it became the perfect vehicle for such golden oldies as "When the Midnight Choo-Choo Leaves for Alabam', " "Snooky Ookums," "I Want to Go Back to Michigan," "Everybody's Doin' It," and the title song. Berlin's new songs were equally good, and the public put its seal of approval on "It Only Happens When I Dance with You," "We're a Couple of Swells," and "Stepping Out with My Baby."

*White Christmas* (1954) deserved and got a delightful cast, with Bing Crosby, Danny Kaye, Rosemary Clooney, and Vera-Ellen starring in this charming film, another mixture of old Berlin songs and new ones. The new ones included "Sisters" and "Count Your Blessings Instead of Sheep." The latter, as recorded by Eddie Fisher, (Victor 47-5871), appeared on the *Hit Parade* for sixteen weeks.

*There's No Business like Show Business* (1954) was the last of the Berlin mix-and-match movies. This extravaganza starred Ethel Merman, Donald O'Connor, Marilyn Monroe, Dan Dailey, and Mitzi Gaynor. It contained thirteen numbers, only two of them new. Marilyn Monroe cemented her reputation as a sexpot with "Heat Wave," an old song, and "After You Get What You Want, You Don't Want It," an older one. The title song has become the unofficial anthem of the entertainment industry, which this film celebrates. It is fitting that Berlin's last movie assignment was to write a theme for *Sayonara* (1957), starring Marlon Brando. He finished his movie career as it had begun, writing theme songs.

After his late-1920s film themes, and with the Great Depression in full force, Berlin reactivated his career on Broadway. He made his comeback in a revue, *Face the Music* (February 17, 1932), which sported the ballad "Soft Lights and Sweet Music," the marvelous comic song "I Say It's Spinach (and I Say the Hell with It)," and what became a theme song for hard times, "Let's Have Another Cup of Coffee." That same year Berlin came out with two of his most haunting ballads, "How Deep Is the Ocean?" and RUDY VALLEE's smash hit, "Say It Isn't So" (Columbia 2714-D).

*As Thousands Cheer* (September 30, 1933) was a midway high point in Berlin's theatrical career. This show was the last to star Marilyn Miller, the famous *Follies* personality and

Ziegfeld favorite. It also featured Clifton Webb, Helen Broderick, and singer-dancer ETHEL WATERS in her first white show. The score's eight numbers were highly contrasted, from the tragic "Supper Time" to the joyous "Easter Parade," which was rewritten from his 1917 "Smile and Show Your Dimple." "Not for All the Rice in China" and "Heat Wave" were other hits in this show.

*Louisiana Purchase* (May 28, 1940) starred William Gaxton, Vera Zorina, Victor Moore, and Irene Bordoni. The show's score provided no hits, but the optimistic "It's a Lovely Day Tomorrow" was one of Berlin's happiest numbers. It was used as a closing theme for *The Garry Moore Show* on television in the 1950s.

*Annie Get Your Gun* (May 16, 1946) was Berlin's greatest score and, with 1,147 performances, his longest-running show. It is a masterful blending of script and music. The Annie Oakley story was originally slated to have a JEROME KERN score, but Kern's death gave Berlin the opportunity to create one of the most nearly perfect scores in Broadway history. Two of the songs, "Doin' What Comes Natur'lly" and "They Say It's Wonderful," made the *Hit Parade*; and "The Girl That I Marry," "I've Got the Sun in the Morning," "I'm an Indian Too," "Anything You Can Do," "You Can't Get a Man with a Gun," and "There's No Business Like Show Business" have become standards. Ethel Merman got her part of a lifetime, and was so thoroughly identified with "Annie" that when the show was revived twenty years later, she again played the role.

*Miss Liberty* (July 15, 1949) was only a modest success, and thus a disappointment after the incredible *Annie*. However, the show boasted two memorable songs: "Give Me Your Tired, Your Poor," based on the poem by Emma Lazarus, and "Let's Take an Old-Fashioned Walk," in Berlin's happiest waltz vein.

*Call Me Madam* (October 12, 1950) starred Ethel Merman in another role that suited her down to the ground. She portrayed a fabulous party giver (based on the real-life hostess Perle Mesta) in Washington, D.C., and gave spark to "The Hostess with the Mostes' on the Ball." "You're Just in Love" has been mentioned as one of the "double songs" Berlin had a patent on. "They Like Ike" was so successful that when the show was done on television in 1968, it was retitled "We Still Like Ike." The most-remembered song, however, was "It's a Lovely Day Today."

*Mr. President* (October 20, 1962) also gave Berlin a political subject. His last Broadway musical contained many fresh numbers, including "The Washington Twist," reminiscent of the novelty dance number in *Call Me Madam*, the "Washington Square Dance." "Don't Be Afraid of Romance" and the "double song" "Empty Pockets Filled with Love" provided the ballads for the show.

When *Annie Get Your Gun* was revived at the New York State Theatre in 1966, Berlin wrote his final published show song for it. It was his last double song, "An Old Fashioned Wedding," and it stopped the show nightly.

There is simply no parallel to Irving Berlin's career in Tin Pan Alley. For over seventy years, he was America's most widely performed songwriter, in spite of the ever-changing styles of popular music. He created more standards than anyone else. Of his professional skill, Virgil Thomson once wrote, "I don't know of five American 'art composers' who can be compared as songwriters, for either technical skills or artistic responsibility, with Irving Berlin." And Jerome Kern once said, "Irving Berlin has no place in American music. He *is* American music."

## American Published Individual Songs of Irving Berlin

"Abie Sings an Irish Song" (1913)
"Abraham" (1942), *Holiday Inn* (film)
"After the Honeymoon" (1911)
"After You Get What You Want, You Don't Want It" (1920)
"Alexander and His Clarionet" (1910)
"Alexander's Bag-Pipe Band" (1912), *Hokey-Pokey* (show)
"Alexander's Ragtime Band" (1911)
"Alice in Wonderland" (1916), *Century Girl* (show)
"Alice in Wonderland" (1924), *Music Box Revue* (show)
"All Alone" (1924), *Music Box Revue* (show)
"All by Myself" (1921)
"All of My Life" (1944)
"Along Came Ruth" (1914), *Along Came Ruth* (show)
"Always" (1925)
"Always Treat Her like a Baby" (1914)
"American Eagles" (1942), *This Is the Army* (show)
"And Father Wanted Me to Learn a Trade" (1915), *Stop! Look! Listen!* (show)
"Angelo" (1911), *Jumping Jupiter* (show)
"Angels of Mercy" (1941)
"Anna Lize's Wedding Day" (1913)
"Antonio, You'd Better Come Home" (1912)
"Any Bonds Today?" (1941)
"Anything You Can Do" (1946), *Annie Get Your Gun* (show)
"Apple Tree and the Bumble Bee" (1913)
"Araby" (1915)
"Arms for the Love of America" (1942)
"Army's Made a Man out of Me" (1942), *This Is the Army* (show)
"At Peace with the World" (1926)
"At the Court Around the Corner" (1921), *Music Box Revue* (show)
"At the Devil's Ball" (1913)
"At the Picture Show" (1912), *Sun Dodgers* (show)
"Back to Back" (1939), *Second Fiddle* (film)
"Be Careful, It's My Heart" (1942), *Holiday Inn* (film)
"Beautiful Faces" (1920), *Broadway Brevities of 1920* (show)
"Because I Love You" (1926)
"Becky's Got a Job in a Musical Show" (1912)
"Before I Go and Marry" (1910)
"Begging for Love" (1931)
"Behind the Fan" (1921), *Music Box Revue* (show)
"Belle of the Barbers' Ball" (1912)
"Bells" (1920), *Ziegfeld Follies of 1920* (show)
"Best of Friends Must Part" (1908)
"Best Thing for You" (1950), *Call Me Madam* (show)
"Best Things Happen While You're Dancing" (1954), *White Christmas* (film)
"Better Luck Next Time" (1948), *Easter Parade* (film)
"Bevo" (1918), *Yip, Yip, Yaphank* (show)
"Bird of Paradise" (1915)
"Blow Your Horn" (1915), *Stop! Look! Listen!* (show)
"Blue Devils of France" (1918), *Ziegfeld Follies of 1918* (show)
"Blue Skies" (1926), *Betsy* (show)
"Bring Back My Lena to Me" (1910), *He Came from Milwaukee* (show)
"Bring Back My Lovin' Man" (1911)
"Bring Me a Ring in the Spring" (1911)
"Bring on the Pepper" (1922), *Music Box Revue* (show)
"Business Is Business, Rosey Cohen" (1911)
"But (She's a Little Bit Crazy About Her Husband, That's All)" (1920)
"But Where Are You?" (1936), *Follow the Fleet* (film)
"Butterfingers" (1934)
"Call Again" (1912)
"Call Me Up Some Rainy Afternoon" (1910)
"Call of the South" (1924), *Music Box Revue* (show)
"Can You Use Any Money Today?" (1950), *Call Me Madam* (film)
"Change Partners" (1938), *Carefree* (film)
"Cheek to Cheek" (1935), *Top Hat* (film)
"Chicken Walk" (1916), *Century Girl* (show)
"Chinese Firecrackers" (1920), *Ziegfeld Follies of 1920* (show)
"Choreography" (1954), *White Christmas* (film)
"Christmas Time Seems Years and Years Away" (1909)
"Circus Is Coming to Town" (1918), *Everything* (show)
"Climbing Up the Scale" (1923), *Music Box Revue* (show)
"Cohen Owes Me Ninety-seven Dollars" (1915)
"Colonel Buffalo Bill" (1946), *Annie Get Your Gun* (show)
"Colored Romeo" (1910)
"Come Along Sextette" (1920), *Ziegfeld Follies of 1920* (show)
"Come Along to Toy Town" (1918), *Everything* (show)
"Come Back to Me" (1912)
"Come to the Land of the Argentine" (1914), *Watch Your Step* (show)
"Coquette" (1928), *Coquette* (film)
"Count Your Blessings Instead of Sheep" (1954), *White Christmas* (film)

"Couple of Swells" (1948), *Easter Parade* (film)
"Crinoline Days" (1922), *Music Box Revue* (show)
"Cuddle Up" (1911), *A Real Girl* (show)
"Daddy, Come Home" (1913)
"Dance and Grow Thin" (1917), *Dance and Grow Thin* (show)
"Dance of the Grizzly Bear" (1910), *Ziegfeld Follies of 1910* (show)
"Dance to the Music of the Ocarina" (1950), *Call Me Madam* (show)
"Dance with Me" (1940), *Louisiana Purchase* (show)
"Dancing Honeymoon" (1922), *Music Box Revue* (show)
"Dat Draggy Rag" (1910)
"Dat's-a My Gal" (1911)
"Dear Mayme, I Love You" (1910)
"Devil Has Bought Up All the Coal" (1918)
"Diamond Horseshoe" (1922), *Music Box Revue* (show)
"Ding Dong" (1918), *Yip, Yip, Yaphank* (show)
"Do It Again" (1912)
"Do Your Duty, Doctor" (1909)
"Doggone That Chilly Man" (1911), *Ziegfeld Follies of 1911* (show)
"Doin' What Comes Natur'lly" (1946), *Annie Get Your Gun* (show)
"Don't Be Afraid of Romance" (1962), *Mr. President* (show)
"Don't Leave Your Wife Alone" (1912)
"Don't Put Out the Light" (1911)
"Don't Send Me Back to Petrograd" (1924), *Music Box Revue* (show)
"Don't Take Your Beau to the Seashore" (1911), *Fascinating Widow* (show)
"Don't Wait Too Long" (1924), *Music Box Revue* (show)
"Dorando" (1909)
"Down in Chattanooga" (1913)
"Down in My Heart" (1911), *Little Millionaire* (show)
"Down to the Folies Bergere" (1911), *Gaby* (show)
"Down Where the Jack o' Lanterns Grow" (1917), *Cohan Revue of 1918* (show)
"Dream On, Little Soldier Boy" (1918), *Yip, Yip, Yaphank* (show)
"Dreams, Just Dreams" (1910)
"Drowsy Head" (1921)
"Drum Crazy" (1948), *Easter Parade* (film)
"Dying Rag" (1911)
"Easter Parade" (1933), *As Thousands Cheer* (show)
"Elevator Man" (1912)
"Empty Pockets Filled with Love" (1962), *Mr. President* (show)
"Ephraham Played upon the Piano" (1911), *Ziegfeld Follies of 1911* (show)
"Everybody Knew but Me" (1945)
"Everybody Step" (1921), *Music Box Revue* (show)
"Everybody's Doing It Now" (1911)
"Everything in America Is Ragtime" (1915), *Stop! Look! Listen!* (show)
"Everything Is Rosy Now for Rosy" (1919)
"Extra! Extra!" (1949), *Miss Liberty* (show)
"Eyes of Youth" (1919), *Eyes of Youth* (film)
"Eyes of Youth See the Truth" (1917), *Cohan Revue of 1918* (show)
"Falling Out of Love Can Be Fun" (1949), *Miss Liberty* (show)
"Father's Beard" (1912)
"Fella with an Umbrella" (1947), *Easter Parade* (film)
"Fiddle-Dee-Dee" (1912)
"First Lady" (1962), *Mr. President* (show)
"Five o'Clock Tea" (1925), *The Cocoanuts* (show)
"Florida by the Sea" (1925), *The Cocoanuts* (show)
"Follow Me Around" (1912), *My Best Girl* (show)
"Follow the Crowd" (1914), *Queen of the Movies* (show)
"Fools Fall in Love" (1940), *Louisiana Purchase* (show)
"For the Very First Time" (1952)
"For Your Country and My Country" (1917)
"Free" (1950), *Call Me Madam* (show)
"Freedom Train" (1947)
"Friars' Parade" (1916), *Friars' Frolic of 1916* (show)
"From Here to Shanghai" (1917)
"Funnies" (1933), *As Thousands Cheer* (show)
"Furnishing a Home for Two" (1914), *Society Buds* (show)
"Gee, I Wish I Was Back in the Army" (1954), *White Christmas* (film)
"Get Thee Behind Me, Satan" (1936), *Follow the Fleet* (film)
"Getting Nowhere" (1946), *Blue Skies* (film)
"Girl of My Dreams" (1920), *Ziegfeld Follies of 1920* (show)
"Girl on the Magazine" (1915), *Stop! Look! Listen!* (show)
"Girl on the Police Gazette" (1937), *On the Avenue* (film)
"Girl That I Marry" (1946), *Annie Get Your Gun* (show)
"Give Me Your Tired, Your Poor" (1949), *Miss Liberty* (show)
"Glad to Be Home" (1962), *Mr. President* (show)
"God Bless America" (1939)
"God Gave You to Me" (1914)
"Good Times with Hoover, Better Times with Al" (1928)
"Goodbye, France" (1918)
"Goodbye, Girlie, and Remember Me" (1909)

"Goody, Goody, Goody, Goody, Good" (1912)
"Hand That Rocked My Cradle Rules My Heart" (1919)
"Happy Easter" (1948), *Easter Parade* (film)
"Happy Holiday" (1942), *Holiday Inn* (film)
"Happy Little Country Girl" (1913)
"Harem Life" (1919), *Ziegfeld Follies of 1919* (show)
"Harlem on My Mind" (1933), *As Thousands Cheer* (show)
"Haunted House" (1914)
"He Ain't Got Rhythm" (1937), *On the Avenue* (film)
"He Promised Me" (1911)
"He Sympathized with Me" (1910), *Getting a Polish* (show)
"Heat Wave" (1933), *As Thousands Cheer* (show)
"Heaven Watch the Philippines" (1945)
"Help Me to Help My Neighbor" (1947)
"Herman, Let's Dance That Beautiful Waltz" (1910), *Two Men and a Girl* (show)
"He's a Devil in His Own Home Town" (1914)
"He's a Rag Picker" (1914)
"He's Getting Too Darn Big for a One-Horse Town" (1916)
"He's So Good to Me" (1913)
"Hiram's Band" (1912), *Sun Dodgers* (show)
"Home Again Blues" (1921)
"Homesick" (1922)
"Homeward Bound" (1914), *Watch Your Step* (show)
"Homework" (1949), *Miss Liberty* (show)
"Hon'rable Profession of the Fourth Estate" (1949), *Miss Liberty* (show)
"Hostess with the Mostes' on the Ball" (1950), *Call Me Madam* (show)
"How About a Cheer for the Navy?" (1942), *This Is the Army* (show)
"How About Me?" (1928)
"How Can I Forget?" (1917)
"How Deep Is the Ocean?" (1932)
"How Do You Do It, Mabel, on Twenty Dollars a Week?" (1911)
"How Many Times?" (1926)
"How's Chances?" (1933), *As Thousands Cheer* (show)
"Hurry Back to My Bamboo Shack" (1916)
"I Beg Your Pardon, Dear Old Broadway" (1911), *Gaby* (show)
"I Can Always Find a Little Sunshine in the YMCA" (1918), *Yip, Yip, Yaphank* (show)
"I Can Make You Laugh" (1954), *There's No Business Like Show Business* (film)
"I Can't Do Without You" (1928)
"I Can't Remember" (1933)
"I Didn't Go Home at All" (1909)
"I Got Lost in His Arms" (1946), *Annie Get Your Gun* (show)
"I Got the Sun in the Morning" (1946), *Annie Get Your Gun* (show)
"I Hate You" (1914), *Watch Your Step* (show)
"I Have Just One Heart for Just One Boy" (1918), *The Canary* (show)
"I Just Came Back to Say Goodbye" (1909)
"I Keep Running Away from You" (1957)
"I Left My Door Open and My Daddy Walked Out" (1919)
"I Left My Heart at the Stage Door Canteen" (1942), *This Is the Army* (show)
"I Like Ike" (1952)
"I Like It" (1921)
"I Lost My Heart in Dixieland" (1919)
"I Love a Piano" (1915), *Stop! Look! Listen!* (show)
"I Love to Dance" (1915), *Stop! Look! Listen!* (show)
"I Love to Have the Boys Around Me" (1914), *Watch Your Step* (show)
"I Love to Quarrel with You" (1914)
"I Love to Stay at Home" (1915)
"I Love You More Each Day" (1910)
"I Never Had a Chance" (1934)
"I Never Knew" (1919)
"I Paid My Income Tax Today" (1942)
"I Poured My Heart into a Song" (1939), *Second Fiddle* (film)
"I Say It's Spinach" (1932), *Face the Music* (show)
"I Threw a Kiss in the Ocean" (1942)
"I Used to Be Color Blind" (1938), *Carefree* (film)
"I Want to Be in Dixie" (1912)
"I Want to Go Back to Michigan" (1914)
"I Want You for Myself" (1931)
"I Was Aviating Around" (1913)
"I Wonder" (1920)
"I Wouldn't Give That for the Man Who Couldn't Dance" (1918), *The Canary* (show)
"I'd Like My Picture Took" (1949), *Miss Liberty* (show)
"I'd Rather Lead a Band" (1936), *Follow the Fleet* (film)
"I'd Rather See a Minstrel Show" (1919), *Ziegfeld Follies of 1919* (show)
"If All the Girls I Knew Were Like You" (1912)
"If I Had You" (1914)
"If I Thought You Wouldn't Tell" (1909)
"If That's Your Idea of a Wonderful Time" (1914)
"If the Managers Only Thought the Same as Mother" (1910), *Jolly Bachelors* (show)
"If You Believe" (1954), *There's No Business Like Show Business* (film)
"If You Don't Want Me" (1913)
"If You Don't Want My Peaches, You Better Stop Shaking My Tree" (1914)
"Ike for Four More Years" (1956)
"I'll Capture Your Heart Singing" (1942), *Holiday Inn* (film)

"I'll Dance Rings Around You" (1945)
"I'll Miss You in the Evening" (1932)
"I'll See You in C-U-B-A" (1919)
"I'll Share It All with You" (1946), *Annie Get Your Gun* (show)
"I'll Take You Back to Italy" (1917), *Jack o'Lantern* (show)
"I'm a Bad, Bad Man" (1946), *Annie Get Your Gun* (show)
"I'm a Happy Married Man" (1910)
"I'm Afraid, Pretty Maid, I'm Afraid" (1912)
"I'm an Indian Too" (1946), *Annie Get Your Gun* (show)
"I'm Beginning to Miss You" (1949)
"I'm Down in Honolulu Looking Them Over" (1916)
"I'm Getting Tired So I Can Sleep" (1942), *This Is the Army* (show)
"I'm Going Back to Dixie" (1912), *She Knows Better Now* (show)
"I'm Going Back to the Farm" (1915)
"I'm Going on a Long Vacation" (1910), *Are You a Mason?* (show)
"I'm Gonna Get Him" (1962), *Mr. President* (show)
"I'm Gonna Pin a Medal on the Girl I Left Behind" (1918), *Ziegfeld Follies of 1918* (show)
"I'm Looking for a Daddy Long Legs" (1922), *Music Box Revue* (show)
"I'm Not Afraid" (1954)
"I'm Not Prepared" (1916)
"I'm on My Way Home" (1926)
"I'm Playing with Fire" (1932)
"I'm Putting All My Eggs in One Basket" (1936), *Follow the Fleet* (film)
"I'm Sorry for Myself" (1939), *Second Fiddle* (film)
"I'm the Guy Who Guards the Harem" (1919), *Ziegfeld Follies of 1919* (show)
"In a Cozy Kitchenette Apartment" (1921), *Music Box Revue* (show)
"In Acapulco" (1948)
"In Florida Among the Palms" (1916), *Step This Way* (show)
"In My Harem" (1913)
"In Our Hideaway" (1962), *Mr. President* (show)
"In the Morning" (1929)
"In the Shade of a Sheltering Tree (1924), *Music Box Revue* (show)
"Innocent Bessie Brown" (1910)
"Is He the Only Man in the World?" (1962), *Mr. President* (show)
"Is There Anything Else I Can Do for You?" (1910)
"Isn't This a Lovely Day?" (1935), *Top Hat* (film)
"It All Belongs to Me" (1927), *Ziegfeld Follies of 1927* (show)
"It Can't Be Did!" (1912), *Jumping Jupiter* (show)
"It Gets Lonely in the White House" (1962), *Mr. President* (show)
"It Isn't What He Said" (1914)
"It Only Happens When I Dance with You" (1947), *Easter Parade* (film)
"It Takes an Irishman to Make Love" (1916), *Century Girl* (show)
"It'll Come to You" (1940), *Louisiana Purchase* (show)
"It's a Lovely Day Today" (1950), *Call Me Madam* (show)
"It's a Lovely Day Tomorrow" (1940), *Louisiana Purchase* (show)
"It's a Walk-in with Walker" (1925)
"It's the Little Bit of Irish" (1918), *The Canary* (show)
"It's up to the Band" (1927), *Ziegfeld Follies of 1927* (show)
"I've Got-a-Go Back to Texas" (1914), *Watch Your Step* (show)
"I've Got a Sweet Tooth Bothering Me" (1916), *Step This Way* (show)
"I've Got My Captain Working for Me Now" (1919)
"I've Got My Love to Keep Me Warm" (1937), *On the Avenue* (film)
"I've Got to Be Around" (1962), *Mr. President* (show)
"I've Got to Have Some Lovin' Now" (1912)
"Jake! Jake! The Yiddisher Ball-Player" (1913)
"Jimmy" (1927), *Ziegfeld Follies of 1927* (show)
"Just a Blue Serge Suit" (1945)
"Just a Little Longer" (1926)
"Just a Little While" (1930)
"Just Like the Rose" (1909)
"Just One Way to Say I Love You" (1949), *Miss Liberty* (show)
"Kate" (1947)
"Keep a Taxi Waiting, Dear" (1911), *Gaby* (show)
"Keep Away from the Fellow Who Owns an Automobile" (1912)
"Keep On Walking" (1913)
"Ki-i-yodeling Dog" (1913)
"Kiss Me, My Honey, Kiss Me" (1911)
"Kiss Your Sailor Boy Goodbye" (1913)
"Kitchen Police" (1918), *Yip, Yip, Yaphank* (show)
"Knights of the Road" (1930), *Mammy* (film)
"Ladies of the Chorus" (1918), *Yip, Yip, Yaphank* (show)
"Lady of the Evening" (1922), *Music Box Revue* (show)
"Latins Know How" (1940), *Louisiana Purchase* (show)
"Laugh It Up" (1962), *Mr. President* (show)
"Law Must Be Obeyed" (1915), *Stop! Look! Listen!* (show)
"Lazy" (1924)

"Lead Me to Love" (1914), *Watch Your Step* (show)
"Lead Me to That Beautiful Band" (1912), *Cohan and Harris Minstrels* (show)
"Learn to Do the Strut" (1923), *Music Box Revue* (show)
"Learn to Sing a Love Song" (1927), *Ziegfeld Follies of 1927* (show)
"Leg of Nations" (1920), *Ziegfeld Follies of 1920* (show)
"Legend of the Pearls" (1921), *Music Box Revue* (show)
"Let Me Sing and I'm Happy" (1929), *Mammy* (film)
"Let Yourself Go" (1936), *Follow the Fleet* (film)
"Let's All Be Americans Now" (1917)
"Let's Face the Music and Dance" (1936), *Follow the Fleet* (film)
"Let's Go Back to the Waltz" (1962), *Mr. President* (show)
"Let's Go 'Round the Town" (1914), *Watch Your Step* (show)
"Let's Have Another Cup of Coffee" (1932), *Face the Music* (show)
"Let's Start the New Year Right" (1942), *Holiday Inn* (film)
"Let's Take an Old-Fashioned Walk" (1948), *Miss Liberty* (show)
"Lindy" (1920)
"Listening" (1924), *Music Box Revue* (show)
"Little Bit of Everything" (1912), *Ziegfeld Follies of 1912* (show)
"Little Bungalow" (1925), *The Cocoanuts* (show)
"Little Butterfly" (1923), *Music Box Revue* (show)
"Little Fish in a Big Pond" (1949), *Miss Liberty* (show)
"Little Old Church in England" (1941)
"Little Red Lacquer Cage" (1922), *Music Box Revue* (show)
"Little Things in Life" (1930)
"Lock Me in Your Harem and Throw Away the Key" (1914), *Watch Your Step* (show)
"Lonely Heart" (1933), *As Thousands Cheer* (show)
"Look Out for the Bolsheviki Man" (1919), *Ziegfeld Follies of 1919* (show)
"Looking at You (Across the Breakfast Table)" (1930), *Mammy* (film)
"Lord Done Fixed Up My Soul" (1940), *Louisiana Purchase* (show)
"Louisiana Purchase" (1940), *Louisiana Purchase* (show)
"Love and the Weather" (1941)
"Love, You Didn't Do Right by Me" (1954), *White Christmas* (film)
"Lucky Boy" (1925), *The Cocoanuts* (show)
"Maid of Mesh" (1923), *Music Box Revue* (show)
"Man Chases a Girl (Until She Catches Him)" (1948) *There's No Business Like Show Business* (Film)
"Mandy" (1918), *Yip, Yip, Yaphank* (show)
"Mandy" (1919), *Ziegfeld Follies of 1919* (show)
"Manhattan Madness" (1932), *Face the Music* (show)
"Marie" (1928), *The Awakening* (film)
"Marie from Sunny Italy" (1907)
"Marrying for Love" (1950), *Call Me Madam* (show)
"Maybe I Love You Too Much" (1933)
"Me" (1931)
"Me an' My Bundle" (1949), *Miss Liberty* (show)
"Me and My Melinda" (1942)
"Meat and Potatoes" (1962), *Mr. President* (show)
"Meet Me Tonight" (1911)
"Million Dollar Ball" (1912), *Hanky Panky* (show)
"Minstrel Parade" (1914), *Watch Your Step* (show)
"Miss Liberty" (1949), *Miss Liberty* (show)
"Mr. Jazz Himself" (1917)
"Mr. Monotony" (1947), *Miss Liberty* (show)
"Molly O! Oh, Molly!" (1911)
"Monkey Doodle Doo" (1913), *All Aboard* (show)
"Monkey Doodle-Doo!" (1925), *The Cocoanuts* (show)
"Mont Martre" (1922), *Music Box Revue* (show)
"Moonshine Lullaby" (1946), *Annie Get Your Gun* (show)
"Morning Exercises" (1914)
"Most Expensive Statue in the World" (1949), *Miss Liberty* (show)
"Move Over" (1914), *Watch Your Step* (show)
"My Bird of Paradise" (1915)
"My British Buddy" (1943), *This Is the Army* (touring show)
"My Defenses Are Down" (1946), *Annie Get Your Gun* (show)
"My Little Book of Poetry" (1921), *Music Box Revue* (show)
"My Melody Dream" (1911)
"My New York" (1927), *Ziegfeld Follies of 1927* (show)
"My Sergeant and I Are Buddies" (1942), *This Is the Army* (show)
"My Sweet Italian Man" (1913)
"My Sweetie" (1917)
"My Tambourine Girl" (1919), *Ziegfeld Follies of 1919* (show)
"My Walking Stick" (1938), *Alexander's Ragtime Band* (film)
"My Wife Bridget" (1910), *Getting a Polish* (show)
"My Wife's Gone to the Country (Hurrah! Hurrah!)" (1909)
"New Moon" (1919), *The New Moon* (film)
"Next to Your Mother, Who Do You Love?" (1909)
"Night Is Filled with Music" (1938), *Carefree* (film)

"No One Could Do It like My Father" (1909)
"No Strings" (1935), *Top Hat* (film)
"Nobody Knows (And Nobody Seems to Care)" (1919)
"Not for All the Rice in China" (1933), *As Thousands Cheer* (show)
"Now It Can Be Told" (1938), *Alexander's Ragtime Band* (film)
"Ocarina" (1950), *Call Me Madam* (show)
"Oh, How I Hate to Get Up in the Morning" (1918), *Yip, Yip, Yaphank* (show)
"Oh, How That German Could Love" (1910), *The Girl and the Wizard* (show)
"Oh, What I Know About You" (1909)
"Oh, Where Is My Wife Tonight?" (1909)
"Old-Fashioned Tune Is Always New" (1939), *Second Fiddle* (film)
"Old-Fashioned Wedding" (1966), *Annie Get Your Gun* (show)
"Old Maid's Ball" (1913)
"Old Man" (1952), *White Christmas* (film)
"On a Roof in Manhattan" (1932), *Face the Music* (show)
"Once Ev'ry Four Years" (1962), *Mr. President* (show)
"Once upon a Time Today" (1950), *Call Me Madam* (show)
"One Girl" (1923), *Music Box Revue* (show)
"One o'Clock in the Morning I Get Lonesome" (1911)
"Only for Americans" (1949), *Miss Liberty* (show)
"Ooh, Maybe It's You" (1927), *Ziegfeld Follies of 1927* (show)
"Opera Burlesque on the Sextette from Lucia" (1912), *Hanky Panky* (show)
"Orange Grove in California" (1923), *Music Box Revue* (show)
"Out of This World into My Arms" (1955)
"Over the Sea, Boys" (1918)
"Pack Up Your Sins and Go to the Devil" (1922), *Music Box Revue* (show)
"Pair of Ordinary Coons" (1915), *Stop! Look! Listen!* (show)
"Paris Wakes Up and Smiles" (1949), *Miss Liberty* (show)
"Passion Flower" (1920), *Passion Flower* (show)
"Piano Man" (1910)
"Piccolino" (1935), *Top Hat* (film)
"Pick, Pick, Pick, Pick on the Mandolin, Antonio" (1912)
"Pickaninny Mose" (1921)
"Pigtails and Freckles" (1962), *Mr. President* (show)
"Plenty to Be Thankful For" (1942), *Holiday Inn* (film)
"Policemen's Ball" (1949), *Miss Liberty* (show)
"Polly, Pretty Polly" (1917), *Cohan Revue of 1918* (show)
"Poor Joe" (1962), *Mr. President* (show)
"Poor Little Rich Girl's Dog (1917), *Rambler Rose* (show)
"Porcelain Maid" (1922), *Music Box Revue* (show)
"President's Birthday Ball" (1942)
"Pretty Girl Is like a Melody" (1919), *Ziegfeld Follies of 1919* (show)
"Pullman Porters on Parade" (1913)
"Puttin' on the Ritz" (1929), *Puttin' on the Ritz* (film)
"Queenie (My Own)" (1908)
"Race Horse and the Flea" (1945)
"Ragtime Jockey Man" (1912), *Passing Show of 1912* (show)
"Ragtime Mocking Bird" (1912), *She Knows Better Now* (show)
"Ragtime Opera Medley" (1914), *Watch Your Step* (show)
"Ragtime Razor Brigade" (1918), *Yip, Yip, Yaphank* (show)
"Ragtime Soldier Man" (1912)
"Ragtime Violin" (1911)
"Rainbow of Girls" (1927), *Ziegfeld Follies of 1927* (show)
"Reaching for the Moon" (1930), *Reaching for the Moon* (film)
"Relatives" (1920)
"Remember" (1925)
"Road That Leads to Love" (1917)
"Rockabye Baby" (1924), *Music Box Revue* (show)
"Roses of Yesterday" (1928)
"Rum Tum Tiddle" (1913)
"Run Home and Tell Your Mother" (1911)
"Russian Lullaby" (1927)
"Sadie Salome (Go Home)" (1909)
"Sailor Song" (1915), *Stop! Look! Listen!* (show)
"Sailor's Not a Sailor" (1954), *There's No Business like Show Business* (film)
"Sam, Sam (The Man What Am)" (1961)
"San Francisco Bound" (1913)
"Say It Isn't So" (1932)
"Say It with Music" (1921), *Music Box Revue* (show)
"Sayonara" (1957), *Sayonara* (film)
"Schoolhouse Blues" (1921), *Music Box Revue* (show)
"Secret Service" (1962), *Mr. President* (show)
"Send a Lot of Jazz Bands Over There" (1918), *Yip, Yip, Yaphank* (show)
"Serenade to an Old-Fashioned Girl" (1946), *Blue Skies* (film)
"Settle Down in a One-Horse Town" (1914), *Watch Your Step* (show)
"Shaking the Blues Away" (1927), *Ziegfeld Follies of 1927* (show)
"She Was a Dear Little Girl" (1909), *The Boys and Betty* (show)
"Show Us How to Do the Fox Trot" (1914), *Watch Your Step* (show)

"Si's Been Drinking Cider" (1915)
"Simple Melody" (1914), *Watch Your Step* (show)
"Sing and Dance" (1943), *Holiday Inn* (film)
"Sisters" (1954), *White Christmas* (film)
"Sittin' in the Sun" (1953)
"Slumming on Park Avenue" (1937), *On the Avenue* (film)
"Smile and Show Your Dimple" (1917)
"Snooky Ookums" (1913)
"Snow" (1953), *White Christmas* (film)
"So Help Me" (1934)
"Soft Lights and Sweet Music" (1932), *Face the Music* (show)
"Sombrero Land" (1911)
"Some Little Something About You" (1909)
"Some Sunny Day" (1922)
"Somebody's Coming to My House" (1913)
"Someone Else May Be There While I'm Gone" (1917)
"Someone Just Like You, Dear" (1910)
"Something to Dance About" (1950), *Call Me Madam* (show)
"Song for Belly Dancer" (1962), *Mr. President* (show)
"Song for the U.N." (1971)
"Song Is Ended (But the Melody Lingers On)" (1927)
"Song of Freedom" (1942), *Holiday Inn* (film)
"Song of the Metronome" (1939), *Second Fiddle* (film)
"Spanish" (1917), *Cohan Revue of 1918* (show)
"Spanish Love" (1911), *Gaby* (show)
"Spring and Fall" (1912)
"Stay Down Here Where You Belong" (1914)
"Steppin' Out with My Baby" (1947), *Easter Parade* (film)
"Sterling Silver Moon" (1918), *Yip, Yip, Yaphank* (show)
"Stop! Look! Listen!" (1915), *Stop! Look! Listen!* (show)
"Stop, Stop, Stop" (1910)
"Stop That Rag" (1909), *Jolly Bachelors* (show)
"Sunshine" (1928)
"Supper Time" (1933), *As Thousands Cheer* (show)
"Swanee Shuffle" (1929), *Hallelujah* (film)
"Sweet Italian Love" (1910), *Up and Down Broadway* (show)
"Sweet Marie Make-a-Rag-a-Time Dance wid Me" (1910), *Jolly Bachelors* (show)
"Sweeter Than Sugar" (1919)
"Syncopated Cocktail" (1919), *Ziegfeld Follies of 1919* (show)
"Syncopated Vamp" (1920), *Ziegfeld Follies of 1920* (show)
"Syncopated Walk" (1914), *Watch Your Step* (show)
"Take a Little Tip from Father" (1912)
"Take a Little Wife" (1922), *Music Box Revue* (show)
"Take Me Back" (1913), *All Aboard!* (show)
"Take Off a Little Bit" (1915), *Stop! Look! Listen!* (show)
"Tango Melody" (1925), *The Cocoanuts* (show)
"Teach Me How to Love" (1915), *Stop! Look! Listen!* (show)
"Tell All the Folks in Kentucky" (1923)
"Tell Her in the Springtime" (1924), *Music Box Revue* (show)
"Tell Me a Bedtime Story" (1923), *Music Box Revue* (show)
"Tell Me, Little Gypsy" (1920), *Ziegfeld Follies of 1920* (show)
"Telling Lies" (1910)
"Thank You, Kind Sir! Said She" (1911), *Jumping Jupiter* (show)
"That Beautiful Rag" (1910), *Jolly Bachelors* (show)
"That Hula Hula" (1915), *Stop! Look! Listen!* (show)
"That International Rag" (1913)
"That Kazzatsky Dance" (1910)
"That Mesmerizing Mendelssohn Tune" (1909)
"That Monkey Tune" (1911)
"That Mysterious Rag" (1911), *A Real Girl* (show)
"That Opera Rag" (1910), *Mrs. Jim* (show)
"That Revolutionary Rag" (1919), *The Royal Vagabond* (show)
"That Russian Winter" (1942), *This Is the Army* (show)
"That Society Bear" (1912), *Whirl of Society* (show)
"That's a Good Girl" (1926)
"That's How I Love You" (1912)
"That's My Idea of Paradise" (1914), *Society Buds* (show)
"That's What the Well-Dressed Man in Harlem Will Wear" (1942), *This is the Army* (show)
"There Are No Wings on a Foxhole" (1944), *This Is the Army* (touring show)
"There Are Two Eyes in Dixie" (1917)
"There's a Corner Up in Heaven" (1921)
"There's a Girl in Arizona" (1913)
"There's a Girl in Havana" (1911), *The Never Homes* (show)
"There's No Business like Show Business" (1946), *Annie Get Your Gun* (show)
"There's Something Nice About the South" (1917), *Dance and Grow Thin* (show)
"They Always Follow Me Around" (1914), *Watch Your Step* (show)
"They Call It Dancing" (1921), *Music Box Revue* (show)
"They Like Ike" (1950), *Call Me Madam* (show)
"They Love Me" (1962), *Mr. President* (show)

"They Say It's Wonderful" (1946), *Annie Get Your Gun* (show)
"They Were All Out of Step but Jim" (1918)
"They're Blaming the Charleston" (1925)
"They're on Their Way to Mexico" (1914)
"They've Got Me Doin' It Now" (1913)
"This Is a Great Country" (1962), *Mr. President* (show)
"This Is the Army, Mr. Jones" (1942), *This Is the Army* (show)
"This Is the Life" (1914)
"This Time" (1942)
"This Year's Kisses" (1937), *On the Avenue* (film)
"Ting-a-Ling, the Bells'll Ring" (1926), *The Cocoanuts* (show)
"To Be Forgotten" (1928)
"To My Mammy" (1930), *Mammy* (film)
"Together We Two" (1927)
"Tokio Blues" (1924), *Music Box Revue* (show)
"Tonight at the Mardi Gras" (1940), *Louisiana Purchase* (show)
"Top Hat, White Tie and Tails" (1935), *Top Hat* (film)
"Tra-La-La-La" (1913)
"True Born Soldier Man" (1912)
"Try It on Your Piano" (1910)
"Unlucky in Love" (1921), *Music Box Revue* (show)
"Until I Fell in Love with You" (1915), *Stop! Look! Listen!* (show)
"Venetian Isles" (1925)
"Virginia Low" (1911)
"Voice of Belgium" (1915)
"Wait Until Your Daddy Comes Home" (1912)
"Waiting at the End of the Road" (1929), *Hallelujah* (film)
"Waltz of Long Ago" (1923), *Music Box Revue* (show)
"Was There Ever a Pal like You?" (1919)
"Washington Square Dance" (1950), *Call Me Madam* (show)
"Washington Twist" (1962), *Mr. President* (show)
"Wasn't It Yesterday?" (1917)
"Watch Your Step" (1914), *Watch Your Step* (show)
"We Have Much to Be Thankful For" (1913)
"We Saw the Sea" (1936), *Follow the Fleet* (film)
"We Should Care (Let the Lazy Sun Refuse to Care)" (1925), *The Cocoanuts* (show)
"We Should Care (Let the Sky Start to Cry)" (1925), *The Cocoanuts* (show)
"Welcome Home" (1913)
"We'll Never Know" (1926, 1938)
"We'll Wait, Wait, Wait" (1909)
"We're on Our Way to France" (1918), *Yip, Yip, Yaphank* (show)
"What Are We Going to Do with All the Jeeps?" (1944), *This Is the Army* (touring show)
"What Can You Do with a General?" (1948), *White Christmas* (film)
"What Chance Have I with Love?" (1940), *Louisiana Purchase* (show)
"What Do I Have to Do to Get My Picture in the Paper?" (1949), *Miss Liberty* (show)
"What Does He Look Like?" (1943), *This Is the Army* (film)
"What Does It Matter?" (1927)
"What Is Love?" (1914), *Watch Your Step* (show)
"What'll I Do?" (1924)
"When I Discovered You" (1914), *Watch Your Step* (show)
"When I Get Back to the U.S.A." (1915), *Stop! Look! Listen!* (show)
"When I Hear You Play That Piano, Bill" (1910)
"When I Leave the World Behind" (1915)
"When I Lost You" (1912)
"When I'm Alone, I'm Lonesome" (1911)
"When I'm Out with You" (1915), *Stop! Look! Listen!* (show)
"When I'm Thinking of You" (1912)
"When It Rains, Sweetheart, When It Rains" (1911)
"When It's Night Time Down in Dixie Land" (1914), *Watch Your Step* (show)
"When Johnson's Quartette Harmonize" (1912)
"When My Baby Smiles" (1919)
"When My Dreams Come True" (1929), *The Cocoanuts* (film)
"When That Man Is Dead and Gone" (1941)
"When That Midnight Choo-Choo Leaves for Alabam' " (1912)
"When the Black Sheep Returns to the Fold" (1916)
"When the Boys Come Home" (1944)
"When the Curtain Falls" (1917), *Going Up* (show)
"When the Folks High-Up Do the Mean Low-Down!" (1931), *Reaching for the Moon* (film)
"When This Crazy World Is Sane Again" (1941)
"When Winter Comes" (1939), *Second Fiddle* (film)
"When You Kiss an Italian Girl" (1911)
"When You Walked Out, Someone Else Walked Right In" (1923)
"When You're Down in Louisville, Call on Me" (1915)
"When You're in Town" (1911)
"Where Is My Little Old New York?" (1924), *Music Box Revue* (show)
"Where Is the Song of Songs for Me?" (1928), *Lady of the Pavements* (film)
"While the Band Played an American Rag" (1915)
"Whistling Rag" (1911)
"White Christmas" (1942), *Holiday Inn* (film)
"Who?" (1924), *Music Box Revue* (show)

"Who Do You Love, I Hope?" (1946), *Annie Get Your Gun* (show)
"Whose Little Heart Are You Breaking Now?" (1917)
"Why Do You Want to Know Why?" (1926), *The Cocoanuts* (show)
"Wild About You" (1940), *Louisiana Purchase* (show)
"Wild Cherries" (1909)
"Wilhelmina" (1945)
"Will She Come from the East?" (1922), *Music Box Revue* (show)
"Wishing" (1910), *The Girl and the Drummer* (show)
"With My Head in the Clouds" (1942), *This is the Army* (show)
"With You" (1929), *Puttin' on the Ritz* (film)
"Woodman, Woodman, Spare That Tree" (1911), *Ziegfeld Follies of 1911* (show)
"Yam" (1938), *Carefree* (film)
"Yankee Love" (1911)
"Yascha Michaeloffsky's Melody" (1928)
"Yiddisha Eyes" (1910)
"Yiddisha Nightingale" (1911)
"Yiddisha Professor" (1912)
"Yiddle, on Your Fiddle, Play Some Ragtime" (1909)
"Y.M.C.A." (1918), *Yip, Yip, Yaphank* (show)
"You Can Have Him" (1949), *Miss Liberty* (show)
"You Cannot Make Your Shimmy Shake on Tea" (1919), *Ziegfeld Follies of 1919* (show)
"You Can't Brush Me Off" (1940), *Louisiana Purchase* (show)
"You Can't Get a Man with a Gun" (1946), *Annie Get Your Gun* (show)
"You Can't Lose the Blues with Colors" (1957)
"You Keep Coming Back like a Song" (1945), *Blue Skies* (film)
"You Picked a Bad Day Out to Say Goodbye" (1913)
"You'd Be Surprised" (1919), *Ziegfeld Follies of 1919* (show)
"You're Easy to Dance With" (1942), *Holiday Inn* (film)
"You're Just in Love" (1950), *Call Me Madam* (show)
"You're Laughing at Me" (1937), *On the Avenue* (film)
"You're Lonely and I'm Lonely" (1940), *Louisiana Purchase* (show)
"You're So Beautiful" (1918), *The Canary* (show)
"You've Built a Fire Down in My Heart" (1911), *Ziegfeld Follies of 1911* (show)
"You've Got Me Hypnotized" (1911)
"You've Got Your Mother's Big Blue Eyes!" (1913)

# Leonard Bernstein

The most charismatic American-born conductor of classical music during the last half of the twentieth century, and noted classical and popular composer (b. Lawrence, Massachusetts, August 25, 1918; d. New York City, October 14, 1990). Bernstein's impact on Tin Pan Alley comes from the scores he wrote for Broadway. In 1943, Bernstein scored Jerome Robbins's ballet *Fancy Free*, which was so successful it inspired a Broadway musical, *On the Town*. Lyrics were provided by the team of BETTY COMDEN and ADOLPH GREEN, and the show produced hits with "New York, New York," "Lonely Town," "I Get Carried Away," and "Lucky to Be Me." In 1949 it was made into a film starring Gene Kelly and FRANK SINATRA, which further popularized these songs. Comden and Green and Bernstein reunited for 1953's *Wonderful Town*. 1956 saw Bernstein's *Candide* premiere on Broadway; although unsuccessful at the time, it has become a classic in revivals. Bernstein's greatest success on the musical stage came in 1957 with *West Side Story*, with choreography by Robbins and lyrics by a Broadway newcomer, Stephen Sondheim. The show produced numerous hits, including "To-night," "A-mer-ica," and "I Feel Pretty," all of which have become standards. Bernstein also wrote the film score for the 1954 movie *On the Waterfront*. Bernstein attempted to return to Broadway with the ill-fated *1600 Pennsylvania Avenue* (with lyrics by ALAN JAY LERNER) in the mid-1970s, but the balance of his career was spent as a classical music composer and conductor.

# Big Three

Trade name for the music publishing combine formed by MGM when it purchased three independent music publishers and combined their operations: LEO FEIST (purchased in 1934), ROBBINS MUSIC CORPORATION, and Miller Music (purchased a year later).

# Edgar F. Bitner

Music publishing executive whose cost-cutting decisions changed the entire industry (places and dates of birth and death unknown). When LEO FEIST and Joe Frankenthaler started their concern in August 1897, their first employee was Edgar F. Bitner, who was hired as book-keeper, porter, and errand boy. Within ten years, Bitner had become general manager of the firm, in charge of the New York office and of all five branches, which employed a total of 250 people. He eventually became vice president of the corporation. With the cost of paper rising, and in order to keep the publisher's cost down, he introduced in March 1916 a new kind of music sheet, without an insert page. The music was printed complete on the inside

The staff of Leo Feist publishers, 1902, l to r: Abe Holzmann (plugger and composer), Edgar F. Bitner (general manager), Robert Keiser (major composer), and Leo Feist (owner and former corset salesman).

of the front and back covers. Not only did this save paper, it also reduced shipping charges. He saved paper again when, in August 1918, he issued a smaller (10 ¼ inches × 7 inches) wartime version of the song sheet, also without an insert page.

# Eubie Blake

African-American composer and pianist (b. Baltimore, Maryland, February 7, 1883; d. Brooklyn, New York, February 12, 1983). His first published compositions were "The Chevy Chase," a rag with an especially fine trio section, and "Fizz Water," both issued in 1914 by Joseph W. Stern and Company. He met his lifelong friend and lyricist, Noble Sissle (b. Indianapolis, Indiana, July 10, 1889; d. Tampa, Florida, December 17, 1975), in 1915, and they soon wrote their first song, "It's All Your Fault," which Sophie Tucker introduced in her vaudeville act. It didn't do much commercially, but it paved the way for their own sensational act, which they called the "Dixie Duo." As headliners in vaudeville, they featured their own songs, with Blake at the piano. They made many recordings of their works. Sissle

Eubie Blake tickling the ivories in the mid-1970s.

and Blake were the most successful black act of their time, and wrote the first all-black musical to play Broadway since *His Honor the Barber* (1911). Their *Shuffle Along* (May 23, 1921) ran for a record-breaking 484 performances. Among its hits were "Bandanna Days," "Gypsy Blues," "Good Night, Angeline," "I'm Craving for That Kind of Love," "I'm Just Simply Full of Jazz," "If You've Never Been Vamped by a Brownskin (You've Never Been Vamped at All)," "In Honeysuckle Time," "Love Will Find a Way," "Low Down Blues," and their biggest and most durable song, "I'm Just Wild About Harry." This last was composed by Blake as a waltz, but when his star, Lottie Gee, complained, he turned it into a snappy fox-trot. Sissle's lyrics were virtually the same as those for their 1916 song "My Loving Baby."

In 1923, the team made a sound-on-film short for broadcast pioneer Lee De Forest, *Sissle and Blake's Snappy Songs*, which included their "Affectionate Dan" and "All God's Chillun Got Shoes." This short, probably the first film musical ever made, has survived and has been shown on several television documentaries. For *Andre Charlot's Revue of 1924*, the team wrote "You Were Meant for Me" (not to be confused with the song of the same title written by NACIO HERB BROWN and ARTHUR FREED in 1929). This was the first song that NOEL COWARD and Gertrude Lawrence sang together in a show.

*The Chocolate Dandies* (September 1, 1924) was the team's next Broadway show. Though it was a slick and lavish production, the only song to emerge was the beautiful "You Ought to Know." (The haunting "Jassamine Lane" and Blake's own favorite of his songs, "Dixie Moon," were also in this score.) The team recorded "You Ought to Know" in March 1926 (Edison Bell Winner 4417). "I Wonder Where My Sweetie Can Be" (1925) appeared under the Jack Mills imprint and was recorded by the writers (Edison Bell Winner 4371), with an especially fetching ragtime solo chorus by Blake.

For *Blackbirds of 1930* (October 22, 1930), Blake wrote "You're Lucky to Me," "That Lindy Hop," and his lovely "Memories of You," all with lyricist ANDY RAZAF. Even though Will Morrissey's *Hot Rhythm* (August 21, 1930) was a flop, Blake's "Loving You the Way I Do" was definitely a hit.

Blake continued to compose songs for revues through the 1930s and 1940s, and then, thanks to the ragtime revival, began playing and composing ragtime pieces in the early 1950s and continued through his death. In 1969 Columbia issued a two-LP set, *The 86 Years of Eubie Blake*, featuring both his ragtime and his show music (along with a reunion with Noble Sissle), which helped renew interest in his career. During the last decades of his life, Blake had his own record label, Eubie Blake Music. Eubie's music returned to Broadway in an anthology revue of his works titled *Eubie!* (September 23, 1978), which enjoyed a run of 439 performances. The show's namesake attended several times and performed a few songs on opening night.

# Rube Bloom

Composer, pianist, and arranger (b. New York City, April 24, 1902; d. New York City, March 30, 1976). Although Bloom could not read or write down music, he became a sought-after accompanist for singers, pianist for jazz bands, and arranger of pop songs for major publishers. He composed the novelty rag piano solos "Spring Fever" (1927), "Soliloquy" (1927), and "Jumping Jack" (1929). His famous pop songs include "Fools Rush In" (1940), "Stay on the Right Side, Sister" (1933), "Song of the Bayou" (1929), "Don't Worry 'Bout Me" (1939), "Truckin' " (1935), "Big Man from the South" (1930), "Day In—Day Out" (1939), and "Give Me the Simple Life" (1945).

# Blues

Based on a traditional African-American folk form, commercial blues were first published in Memphis in 1912, when W. C. HANDY began to write and issue his compositions. He was by far the most successful blues writer, and his 1914 "St. Louis Blues" became the most famous blues written and the most recorded blues tune ever.

The word "blues" became a fad (1919–1924) and was used in the titles of many compositions, whether they were true blues or not. Many of these were syncopated fox-trots ("Jazz

Me Blues," "Chasing the Blues"). Others were ordinary pop songs ("Wang Wang Blues," "Wabash Blues"). Some were even real blues ("Decatur Street Blues," "Laughin' Cryin' Blues"). For years, writers on jazz and blues who are not musicians have stuck to a formula which dictates that a blues is a twelve-measure song of three four-measure lines, with the first two lines being practically identical and the last being the punch line, wrapping up a story. Since this formula describes fewer than half of the songs published as blues, it isn't a trustworthy guide to the genre. To further confound nonmusical writers, the term "blues" refers not only to specific songs and instrumentals, but also to a manner in which pop songs can be sung. A good example is the J. RUSSEL ROBINSON-Roy Turk song "Aggravatin' Papa" (1922). As performed by the Virginians (on Victor 19021), it is a snappy fox-trot, but as performed by Bessie Smith (on Columbia A–3877), it becomes a blues.

# BMI

Broadcast Music Incorporated was formed by radio station owners in 1940 to compete with ASCAP and to provide music to air over their stations. Its founding was inspired by ASCAP's 1939 showdown with the radio industry, in which ASCAP enforced a ban on the performance of its members' music in an attempt to collect higher fees for radio play. For a period of time, only public domain music was performed over the air. Determined not to be held hostage by ASCAP again, the radio station owners formed their own agency.

As a collection agency, BMI provided more equitable payment to its members. It also had fewer membership restrictions than ASCAP. Instead of requiring five published songs, BMI admitted to membership those who had one published song or one recording of a song. It especially welcomed country music and rhythm and blues songwriters, who traditionally were not welcomed by ASCAP. During the 1950s, BMI also embraced the early rock and roll writers and bested ASCAP in annual earnings.

# Boswell Sisters

Connie, Martha, and Vet were the most popular female vocal trio before the ANDREWS SISTERS (Constance [Connie], b. Kansas City, Missouri, December 3, 1907; d. New York City, October 11, 1976; Martha, b. Kansas City, Missouri, 1905; d. Peekskill, New York, July 2,

1958; Helvetia [Vet], b. Birmingham Alabama, 1909; d. Peekskill, New York, November 12, 1988). Connie, who had a successful solo career after the trio broke up, played the cello in addition to being the lead singer and chief arranger; Martha played piano; and Vet, the violin. They were often backed by famous jazzmen of the period. In 1931, they had three hits: "When I Take My Sugar to Tea" (Brunswick 6083), "Roll On, Mississippi, Roll On" (Brunswick 6109), and "I Found a Million-Dollar Baby" (Brunswick 6128). "Was That the Human Thing to Do?" (Brunswick 6257) was their only hit of 1932. 1935 was their banner year, starting with their biggest #1 song, "The Object of My Affection" (Brunswick 7348), followed by "Dinah" and its flip side, "Alexander's Ragtime Band" (Brunswick 7412), and "Cheek to Cheek" (Decca 574). Their last solid hit came early in 1936, with "I'm Gonna Sit Right Down and Write Myself a Letter" (Decca 671). Connie had made solo recordings during this period, and went on as a solo artist after the group broke up, now spelling her first name "Connee."

# Perry Bradford

African-American publisher, composer, vaudevillian, artists' manager, and record producer (b. Montgomery, Alabama, February 14, 1893; d. New York City, April 22, 1970). He was the fourth black publisher to make a mark in Tin Pan Alley (after GOTHAM-ATTUCKS, PACE AND HANDY, and CLARENCE WILLIAMS). In 1916, while Bradford was playing the Standard Theatre in Philadelphia with his partner Jeanette Taylor, he published his "Lonesome Blues." Apparently this edition was a well-kept secret, for he sold the piece to a New York publisher two years later. Moving to New York, Bradford became involved with record companies, managing to talk Fred Hager (formerly of the publishing firm of Helf and Hager, 1905–1909) of Okeh Records into letting black singer Mamie Smith record two of Bradford's blues compositions. Because of Bradford's tenacity, in 1920, Mamie Smith, became the first black singer to record with a black jazz band, The Jazz Hounds (Okeh 4169). She was also the first singer to record a blues. Because of her success at selling records—as well as the impressive sales of Bessie Smith, Clara Smith, Trixie Smith, and Ida Cox, among others—the field of blues singing was dominated by women until the late 1930s.

Bradford started in Tin Pan Alley by opening the Perry Bradford Music Company in the Gaiety Building at 1547 Broadway, and by publishing his first million-selling hit, "Crazy Blues." Bradford also owned Blues Music Company and Acme Music Publishing Company. His first firm had an important catalog of blues, mostly his own compositions, such as the famous "It's Right Here for You"; "That Thing Called Love," which SOPHIE TUCKER helped make popular; "You Can't Keep a Good Man Down"; and Lemuel Fowler's "He May Be Your Man, But He Comes to See Me Sometimes." Perry Bradford Music Company went out of business in 1928.

# Fanny Brice

Comedienne and singer (b. New York City, October 29, 1891; d. Los Angeles, California, May 29, 1951). She started out in burlesque and vaudeville, then starred on Broadway, appeared as Baby Snooks on radio (1939–1945), and made a number of fine recordings. Her first hit came in the *Ziegfeld Follies of 1910*, when she introduced Joe Jordan's "Lovie Joe." She had her first double-sided hit in 1922, with "My Man" and "Second Hand Rose" (Victor 45263), and followed it up with "I'm an Indian" (Victor 45303). In 1928 she was asked to rerecord "My Man" with the new electrical process (Victor 21168). She introduced "I'd Rather Be Blue" in the film *My Man* (1929) and had a hit recording (Victor 21815). Brice made sporadic appearances in films through 1945, and continued to be an attraction on stage and on radio. Her second husband was showman/songwriter BILLY ROSE. Brice's life and career were immortalized in the Broadway show *Funny Girl* (1964) by JULE STYNE and BOB MERRILL, starring Barbra Streisand.

# Brill Building

It wasn't until 1931, when the Brill Building was built at 1619 Broadway (at Forty-ninth Street), that the popular music publishing industry established a stable location. Named for Morris Brill, who had a clothing store on the ground floor, this building was the last hub of the music business. Among its early tenants were MILLS MUSIC, FAMOUS MUSIC, FRED FISHER Music, and IRVING CAESAR Music. As Hal David, lyricist and former president of

The Brill Building, 1619 Broadway, a major home of Tin Pan Alley publishers, in the mid-1930s.

ASCAP, recalled, "The preponderance of songwriters were in the Brill Building, the energy was in the Brill Building, the publishers were there, and if you had to be someplace else, you always wound up back at the Brill Building sometime during the day." During the late 1950s and early 1960s, the building became famous for the songwriting factories that churned out the teen-pop hits of the day, particularly Aldon Music, which nurtured the talents of songwriters like Carole King and Gerry Goffin.

# Broadway Show and Revue Songs

*The Black Crook* was the first musical to have songs published from its score (1866). It wasn't until 1891 that *A Trip to Chinatown* provided the first Broadway song hit ("The Bowery"). The biggest-selling show song of all time in sheet music was "Swanee," by George Gershwin and IRVING CAESAR (1919), interpolated by AL JOLSON into his show *Sinbad.* His recording sold over one million copies (Columbia A-2884). What do two shows, from 1921 and 1962, respectively, have in common? If they are the EUBIE BLAKE/Noble Sissle *Shuffle Along* and IRVING BERLIN's *Mr. President,* the answer is that they tie for having the most songs published separately (twenty-one songs each).

In the days before talking pictures, Broadway was the major launching spot for hit songs. As the center of entertainment for the entire country, if a song was successfully sung there, sheet music sales would follow. Publishers did their best to place songs in shows; unlike today, when a musical show's score is usually written specifically for the show, extra songs (called "interpolations") were often added to a popular show as a means of promoting them.

The most significant publisher of show tunes during the first sixty years of the Alley was T. B. HARMS COMPANY. During the 1920s, the English firm of Chappell combined with Harms, and together they published over 90 percent of all Broadway show songs. They set up smaller firms within their large company for special composers: New World for the Gershwins, Buxton Hill for COLE PORTER, and Williamson for RICHARD RODGERS and OSCAR HAMMERSTEIN. JEROME KERN bought a quarter partnership in Harms early in his career.

First editions are important to show tune collectors, but there are no easy ways to determine whether a song is a first edition. One way is to locate the printed price on the cover (especially for shows done after 1950). Another way is to count the number of songs published separately when they are listed on the front or back cover. Many shows issued just a few songs from the score until the show was firmly established on Broadway. Then, when it looked like a hit, more songs were printed. Revivals of shows usually have different stars, and often different producers—all listed on the covers.

Sometimes you'll notice that songs from the same show have different covers. That's because they were issued by different publishers when interpolated into existing shows. Chances are that the composers and lyricists are not those who did the main songs from the score. Many pop songs are also interpolated into shows, and have different artwork on the covers (usually a pop star's photo).

# Shelton Brooks

Composer (b. Amesburg, Ontario Canada, May 4, 1886; d. Los Angeles, California, September 6, 1975). He grew up in Detroit and started out as a pianist playing ragtime. He then created a comic vaudeville act by doing an imitation of Bert Williams. When Williams saw Brooks's performance, he said, "If I'm as funny as he is, I got nothin' to worry about."

There is a story about Brooks walking around for days with a tune in his head, but unable to find the proper lyrics to fit it. One afternoon he overheard a couple quarreling.

"Better not walk out on me, man!" said the angry woman. "Some of these days, you're gonna miss me, honey." The words fell into place. He spent $35.00 to get the song printed by the William Foster Music Company in Chicago, then showed it to SOPHIE TUCKER, whose maid, a friend of his, introduced them. Tucker liked it so much that she put it into her act the next day. "Some of These Days" (1910) was well received, and the star got WILL ROSSITER to take over the copyright and give it a big promotion. Tucker continued to use it as her theme song, and took its title for her autobiography. The sheet music sold well over two million copies. Brooks's next song, "All Night Long" (1912), also a Rossiter publication, had a middling sale. It wasn't until 1916, when he wrote a fine fox-trot, "Walkin' the Dog," that Brooks got his next hit.

In 1917, just as ragtime was starting to be edged out by blues and jazz, Brooks came up with his syncopated smash, "The Darktown Strutters' Ball." It was introduced in vaudeville by the team of Benny Fields, Jack Salisbury, and (soon-to-be songwriter) BENNY DAVIS. It was one of the two selections given to the ORIGINAL DIXIELAND JAZZ BAND to record at their first session for Columbia on January 30, 1917. The disc became such an incredible hit that LEO FEIST bought the publishing rights from Rossiter and plugged the song sheet to over three million sales. It is still the favorite of dixieland jazz bands. Two years later, Brooks composed "Jean," which became a modest hit when recorded by the Chicago songwriter-bandleader ISHAM JONES and his orchestra (Brunswick 5012).

From the early 1920s through World War II, Brooks continued to appear in vaudeville and films, and on radio. He made a tour of Europe in the 1920s as part of Lew Leslie's Blackbirds, and appeared on Broadway in the *Plantation Revue* (1922) and *Dixie to Broadway* (1924).

# Lew Brown

Lyricist, and publisher (b. Odessa, Russia, December 10, 1893; d. New York City, February 5, 1958). He came to the United States when he was five, and as a teenager was writing parodies and song lyrics. His first success was with ALBERT VON TILZER, "I'm the Lonesomest Gal in Town" (1912). He worked with composers RAY HENDERSON, CON CONRAD, HARRY WARREN, HARRY AKST, CLIFF FRIEND, LOU ALTER, SAM STEPT, Jay Gorney, SAMMY FAIN, and HAROLD ARLEN before and after joining BUDDY DESYLVA and Ray Henderson in 1925 as a songwriting team and music publishers. With Albert Von Tilzer, Brown wrote "Oh, by Jingo" for the 1919 show *Linger Longer, Letty*. Frank Crumit made the hit disc (Columbia A-2935), and SPIKE JONES revived it in his 1942 recording (Bluebird 0812). Crumit made it a point to record several of Brown's early 1920s songs, starting with "Chili Bean" (1920) and "Dapper Dan" (1921). In 1924, Brown helped CECIL MACK rewrite the lyrics to Ford Dabaney's 1910 song "Shine." The California Ramblers secured its inclusion as a dixieland standard (Columbia 127-D). It was revived by BING CROSBY and the MILLS BROTHERS in 1932 (Brunswick 6276), and again in 1948 by Frankie Laine (Mercury 5091). 1925 saw Brown collaborating with BILLY ROSE and Ray Henderson on "Don't Bring Lulu," and with Sidney Clare and Cliff Friend on "I Wanna Go Where You Go . . . Then I'll Be Happy." For the *George White Scandals'* eleventh edition in 1931, Brown and Henderson wrote "Life Is Just a Bowl of Cherries," which RUDY VALLEE turned into a hit (Victor 22783). Shep Fields and his Rippling Rhythm had the number-one recording of "That Old Feeling" (Bluebird 7066), from the film *Vogues of 1938*. In 1939, Brown took an old Czechoslovakian song and turned it into "Beer Barrel Polka." Accordionist-bandleader Will Glahe turned it into a million-seller (Victor V-710). Brown's last standard "Don't Sit under the Apple Tree" came from the 1942 film *Private Buckaroo*. GLENN MILLER's version with vocals by Marion Hutton, Tex Beneke, and the Modernaires made it a favorite with World War II soldiers (Bluebird 11474). Brown retired from songwriting shortly thereafter.

# Nacio Herb Brown

Composer (b. Deming, New Mexico, February 22, 1896; d. San Francisco, California, September 28, 1964). He is best remembered for the title song of one of the greatest movie musicals of all time, *Singin' in the Rain* (1952), sung by the film's three stars, Donald O'Connor, Debbie Reynolds, and Gene Kelly. Brown started his career as piano accompanist to vaudeville singer Alice Doll, and toured with her for a year on the Orpheum circuit. Wanting to be part of the Hollywood scene, he opened a custom tailor shop, attracting such clients as Charlie Chaplin, Rudolph Valentino, and Wallace Reid. Brown then went into Beverly Hills real estate and became extremely successful. He started composing songs in his spare time. His first number, with lyrics by King Zany, was "Coral Sea," which Sherman, Clay and Company published in 1920. PAUL WHITEMAN and his Alexandria Hotel Orchestra started plugging it in Los Angeles. When Whiteman recorded it later that year, it became a modest hit.

Brown's first real smash, a novelty piano rag called "Doll Dance" (1927), was interpolated into the *Hollywood Music Box Revue*, featuring Doris Eaton. It was almost as big as ZEZ CONFREY's "Kitten on the Keys" had been six years earlier. Sheet music sales boomed for this marvelous, technically difficult composition, written in the seldom-used key of D major (despite the tricky fingering required, D is the easiest key in which to play it). Frank Banta, using the pseudonym "Jimmy Andrews," made a spectacular recording of it (Banner 6116). At the urging of his publisher, Brown followed it up with "Rag Doll" (1928), not quite as overwhelming but selling over half a million copies. San Francisco vaudeville pianist Edna Fischer had the hit recording (Victor 21384).

Brown was asked by MGM production chief Irving Thalberg to compose the score for MGM's first all-sound musical, *The Broadway Melody* (1929), with lyricist ARTHUR FREED, who was soon to become an MGM producer of musical films. "You Were Meant for Me," "Broadway Melody," and "Wedding of the Painted Doll" became enduring hits. "Singin' in the Rain," by the new team of Brown and Freed, was put into MGM's next musical, *Hollywood Revue* (1929). It was introduced by CLIFF EDWARDS. It was later given to JUDY GARLAND in *Little Nellie Kelly* (1940). Finally, it became the title song of the classic 1952 musical film. Gene Kelly sang and danced to it in an elaborate sequence. The majority of the score reprised earlier hits by Brown and Freed, and this film remains the fans' favorite.

*The Pagan* (1929) introduced "Pagan Love Song," sung by star Ramon Novarro. "Should I?" came from *Lord Byron of Broadway* (1929). "Paradise" (1931) was the waltz theme of Pola Negri's *A Woman Cammands*, and it has been used in several nonmusical films through the years.

"Temptation" (1933) was the huge success of *Going Hollywood*, dramatically sung by BING CROSBY, who later made a hit recording (Brunswick 6695). Perry Como revived it with a best-selling disc in 1945 (Victor 20-1658). Red Ingle and Jo Stafford sold a million copies of their takeoff, "Tim-Tayshun," in 1948 (Capitol 412).

"All I Do Is Dream of You" (1934) was the Brown-Freed hit from *Sadie McKee*, introduced by Gene Raymond. It was revived by Debbie Reynolds in *Singin' in the Rain*. "You Are My Lucky Star" (1935) was featured in *The Broadway Melody of 1936* (1935) by Eleanor Powell. In the same year's Marx Brothers movie, *A Night at the Opera*, "Alone," was sung by Kitty Carlisle and Allan Jones. "Would You?" (1936) was sung by JEANETTE MACDONALD in *San Francisco*.

"Good Morning" (1939) was introduced by Judy Garland and Mickey Rooney in the film version of *Babes in Arms*. It was revived by Debbie Reynolds, Donald O'Connor, and Gene Kelly in *Singin' in the Rain*. "Love Is Where You Find It" (1948) was written with Edward Heyman and Earl Brent for Kathryn Grayson in *The Kissing Bandit*. Her recording of it helped put over this last gem by Brown (MGM 30133). Brown retired after World War II.

# Joe Burke

Composer (b. Philadelphia, Pennsylvania, March 18, 1884; d. Upper Darby, Pennsylvania, June 9, 1950). Burke was a very successful composer who had major hits in the 1920s ("Tip Toe Through the Tulips") and 1930s ("Moon over Miami"). Burke studied piano as a child, then played in his school orchestra and at the University of Pennsylvania. After college, he worked in his home town for local music publishers, and then moved to New York City in the mid-1910s. He began publishing songs immediately, but didn't have a big hit until the mid-1920s. In 1924, Burke teamed with lyricist BENNY DAVIS and bandleader MARK FISHER to write the million-selling hit "Oh, How I Miss You Tonight," recorded by the Oriole Orchestra (Brunswick 2874), with a vocal by Fisher, the Oriole leader and banjoist. "Yearning (Just for You)" (1925), with lyrics by Benny Davis, made the best-seller list with recordings by Ben Bernie and his Hotel Roosevelt Orchestra (Vocalion 15002) and ROGER WOLFE

Kahn and his Hotel Biltmore Orchestra (Victor 19616). "She Was Just a Sailor's Sweetheart" (1925), composed and written by Burke, was featured by the Six Jumping Jacks (Brunswick 3094). It was revived in the early 1950s by the Frank Petty Trio (MGM 11186).

"Just the Same" (1927), with lyrics by Walter Donaldson, was given a splendid treatment by Roger Wolfe Kahn and his orchestra, featuring Joe Venuti on violin and Eddie Lang on guitar (Victor 20634). "Carolina Moon" (1928), with lyrics by Benny Davis, was first plugged and recorded by Gene Austin (Victor 21833). Later, it was used by singer Morton Downey as his theme on radio.

*Gold Diggers of Broadway* (1929) brought Burke together with lyricist Al Dubin for two memorable songs, "Painting the Clouds with Sunshine" and "Tip Toe Through the Tulips with Me," both sung in the film by Nick Lucas. The second song was revived in 1968 on a best-selling record by Tiny Tim (Reprise 0679).

"Dancing with Tears in My Eyes" (1930) was written with Al Dubin for the film *Dancing Sweeties*, but was not used. Burke was so angry that he left Hollywood and returned to the Alley. He proved the movie moguls wrong when he got Rudy Vallee to introduce the song on his radio program, and it became a smash. The team then wrote "For You," which was successfully recorded by Glen Gray and the Casa Loma Orchestra with vocalist Kenny Sargent (Brunswick 6606). Ricky Nelson revived it with a best-selling recording in 1964 (Decca 31574). *Dancing Sweeties* used one Burke-Dubin song, "The Kiss Waltz," which was sung by Sue Carol. It, too, sold many copies.

When he resettled in the Alley in the mid-1930s, Burke teamed with Edgar Leslie, and they knocked out seven of the biggest hits of the decade. In 1935 alone, they had four huge successes: "On Treasure Island," "A Little Bit Independent," "In a Little Gypsy Tea Room," and "Moon over Miami," the last introduced by Ted Fio Rito and his orchestra. Eddy Duchin also helped plug it (Victor 25212). The new team of Burke and Leslie scored twice in 1936, with "Midnight Blue," an interpolation into *The New Ziegfeld Follies of 1936*, and "Robins and Roses," which Bing Crosby made famous (Decca 791). "It Looks Like Rain in Cherry Blossom Lane" (1937), one of Burke's loveliest melodies, took him twenty minutes to compose. Leslie's lyrics fit perfectly, and Guy Lombardo's recording helped to make it another hit (Victor 25572). Poppa John Gordy revived it in the 1950s (RCA Victor LPM 1060).

Burke was less active in the 1940s, but managed to produce one last big hit in 1948, "Rambling Rose," with words by Joseph McCarthy Jr. It was popularized on disc by Perry Como and Gordon MacRae, among others.

# Johnny Burke

Lyricist and publisher (b. Antioch, California, October 3, 1908; d. New York City, February 25, 1964). Burke was raised in Chicago, where he studied piano and drama. He came to New York in the mid-1920s, and began as a piano salesman. He had his first hit song in

1933 with "Annie Doesn't Live Here Anymore" (with colyricist JOE YOUNG and music by Harold Spina), which was recorded by GUY LOMBARDO. More collaborations with Spina yielded few hits, although FATS WALLER successfully recorded their "My Very Good Friend the Milkman" (1935).

In 1936, Burke moved to Hollywood. His biggest hit came that year with "Pennies from Heaven," from the movie of the same name; the music was by ARTHUR JOHNSTON. Working with composer JIMMY MONACO, Burke produced the 1938 hit "I've Got a Pocketful of Dreams" for the film *Sing, You Sinners.* "Too Romantic" (1940) was another hit for Monaco and Burke, written for the *Road to Singapore*, the first Bing Crosby-Bob Hope picture in the successful *Road* series. Also in 1940, Burke partnered with JIMMY VAN HEUSEN for his longest-lasting collaboration. The duo supplied songs for sixteen Crosby films through 1950, including the Academy Award–winning "Swinging on a Star" (for the film *Going My Way*). Burke returned to New York during the 1950s and continued to write pop songs, most notably supplying lyrics for the Erroll Garner jazz classic "Misty" (1954).

# Henry Busse

Trumpeter and composer (b. Magdeburg, Germany, May 19, 1894; d. Memphis, Tennessee, April 23, 1955). Busse was a novelty trumpet player best remembered for his instrumental hits "Wang Wang Blues" and "Hot Lips." After immigrating to the United State in 1916, he played in movie house bands and led his own small ensembles until hooking up with popular West Coast bandleader ABE LYMAN around 1918. When PAUL WHITEMAN's band toured the West Coast in 1919, he heard the band perform, including their popular number "Wang Wang Blues," which was written by Lyman band members Busse, trombonist Albert "Buster" Johnson, and clarinetist Gus Mueller. Whiteman enlisted Busse for his band, and used "Wang Wang" as his audition number for Victor Records. The group recorded it at its first session for the label on August 9, 1920 (Victor 18694), and it was subsequently a major hit for the young band. (Other 1920s popular recordings of the tune were made by BLUES shouter Lucille Hegamin and DUKE ELLINGTON's band.) "Wang Wang" was followed by the million-selling "Hot Lips" (Victor 18920), composed by another band member, Henry Lange (1895–1985), Busse, and Lou Davis (1881–1961). It became a popular feature for Busse, and he continued to perform it while leading his own ensembles through the rest of his career. Busse left Whiteman in 1928 and subsequently led his own bands for a number of decades, and also appeared in a number of Hollywood features in the 1940s, including the GEORGE GERSHWIN biopic, *Rhapsody in Blue* (1945). Ten years later, he died of a heart attack before a scheduled performance in a Memphis, Tennessee, hotel.

# C

## Irving Caesar

Lyricist and publisher (b. New York City, July 4, 1895; d. New York City, December 17, 1996). One of the leading lyricists of the 1920s and 1930s, Caesar collaborated with GEORGE GERSHWIN (cowriting Gershwin's hit "Swanee"), VINCENT YOUMANS, VICTOR HERBERT, SIGMUND ROMBERG, RUDOLF FRIML, RAY HENDERSON, CLIFF FRIEND, ROGER WOLFE KAHN, and GERALD MARKS. Following his first major hit, "Swanee" (1919), he and Gershwin came up with "I Was So Young (You Were So Beautiful)." "Yankee Doodle Blues" came from a show, *Spice of 1922*, but it really scored on disc with Jazzbo's Carolina Serenaders (Cameo 258) and Ladd's Black Aces (Gennett 4995). "What Do You Do Sunday, Mary?" came from the 1923 show *Poppy*, starring W. C. Fields; the Ambassadors had the hit recording (Vocalion 14681).

From the 1924 Broadway show *No, No, Nanette* came the standards "I Want to Be Happy," which made Jan Garber's orchestra happy (Victor 19404), and "Tea for Two," for which the Benson Orchestra of Chicago had the hit recording (Victor 19438). It was revived in 1938 by Bob Crosby's orchestra, with Bob Zurke at the piano (Decca 1850). From the 1927 show *Hit the Deck* came the stupendous hit "Sometimes I'm Happy," first recorded by the Roger Wolfe Kahn orchestra (Victor 20599). Kahn also had the hit recording of Caesar's

1928 standard "Crazy Rhythm" (Victor 21368). Ted Lewis and his orchestra had the #1 hit recording of the 1930 winner "Just a Gigolo" (Columbia 2378-D). Shirley Temple introduced "Animal Crackers in My Soup" in her 1935 film *Curly Top*. Al Jolson asked Caesar for another Dixie song, and in 1936, Caesar and Gerald Marks gave Jolson "Is It True What They Say About Dixie?" Bob Eberly with the Jimmy Dorsey orchestra had the #1 recording (Decca 768). Caesar issued a collection of songs (music by Gerald Marks) in a 1937 folio, called *Sing a Song of Safety*, that included "Let the Ball Roll" and "Remember Your Name and Address." His last hit, "Umbriago," was written with Jimmy Durante, who recorded it in 1944 (Decca 23351); it became one of the comic singer's signature tunes.

# Sammy Cahn

Lyricist (b. Samuel Cohen, New York City, June 18, 1913; d. Beverly Hills, California, January 15, 1993). Cahn produced many hit songs from the mid-1930s through the late 1950s. His major collaborators were Saul Chaplin, Jule Styne, and Jimmy Van Heusen. Cahn was an extremely quick writer whose quality belied his huge output.

Cahn was raised on New York's Lower East Side, the son of Jewish immigrants from Poland. He learned to play the violin from his mother, and began playing in local bands and at burlesque houses. As a teenager, he wrote his first lyric. He met future composer Saul Chaplin in one of the bands, and convinced him to be his songwriting partner. Their first hit came in 1935, with "Rhythm Is Our Business" when the Jimmie Lunceford orchestra had the #1 disc (Decca 369). Andy Kirk and his Twelve Clouds of Joy had the hit recording of "Until the Real Thing Comes Along" (1936), and it became their theme song (Decca 809). In the same year, Cahn and Chaplin scored with "Shoeshine Boy," which came from the revue *Connie's Hot Chocolates of 1936*. "Bei Mir Bist Du Schon," Cahn and Chaplin's adaptation of a traditional Yiddish song, started the Andrews Sisters' career in 1937 with a #1 hit (Decca 1562). The duo were contracted by Warner Bros. to supply film songs, and worked together through 1942.

In 1942, Cahn formed a partnership with composer Jule Styne. From the 1942 film *Youth on Parade*, Harry James introduced their "I've Heard That Song Before," and had a #1 million-seller that charted for twenty-five weeks (Columbia 36668). In the 1944 film *Follow the Boys*, Dinah Shore came up with the #1 hit "I'll Walk Alone" (Victor 20–1586). Frank Sinatra had the hit 1944 record of "I Should Care," from the film *Thrill of a*

*Romance* (Columbia 36791). He also scored with Cahn's 1946 entry "Day by Day" (Columbia 36905).

Cahn's first Broadway show was *High Button Shoes* (1947), which yielded a hit for Doris Day, "Papa, Won't You Dance With Me?" (Columbia 37931). The following year Day had a million-seller from the film *Romance on the High Seas*, when she introduced "It's Magic" (Columbia 38188). Mario Lanza starred in the 1950 film *The Toast of New Orleans* and sang "Be My Love," which gave him a two-million-selling record (RCA Victor 20-1561). Cahn wrote this number with his new collaborator, Nicholas Brodszky. Lanza scored again in his 1952 film *Because You're Mine*, with the title song, which sold over a million copies on disc (RCA Victor 20-3914). Frank Sinatra sang the title song of the 1954 film *Three Coins in the Fountain* (Capitol 2816), which reunited Cahn with Styne and became Cahn's first Academy Award winner. "Love and Marriage" was the first song hit to come from an original television musical (*Our Town*, in 1955), and also marked the beginning of Cahn's collaboration with Jimmy van Heusen. Frank Sinatra introduced it in the show and had the hit recording (Capitol 3260). This recording was later used as the theme song for TV's *Married with Children*. Also in 1955 Sinatra starred in *The Tender Trap* and had the hit recording of the title song (Capitol 3290). Sinatra scored again in 1957 with "All the Way," from the film *The Joker Is Wild*, for which Cahn won his second Academy Award (Capitol 3793). "High Hopes," from the 1959 film *A Hole in the Head*, again starred Sinatra, who gave Cahn his third Academy Award winner (Capitol 4214). In 1963 Cahn won his fourth Academy Award for "Call Me Irresponsible" from the film *Papa's Delicate Condition*.

Cahn was less active after the mid-1960s, although he did stage a revue of his own material, called *Words and Music*, on Broadway in 1972, the year he was inducted into the

Sammy Cahn in the mid-1980s.

Songwriters Hall of Fame. He took the show to England two years later, and revived it in 1987. He died at his California home in 1993.

# Cakewalk

This dance sensation, along with the jaunty music written for it, first appeared in music halls and theaters in the mid-1890s. Its popularity was based on tuneful, lightly syncopated music written for high-strutting, prancing dance steps. It was composer-publisher KERRY (FREDERICK ALLEN) MILLS who started the rage for this dance music with his first publication, "Rastus on Parade," in 1895. The tune had the distinction of establishing what soon became a harmonic cliché of cakewalks by beginning in a minor key and moving to the relative major, a construction that later writers followed with a subdominant trio section. It was another Mills cakewalk, however, "At a Georgia Camp Meeting" (1897), that became the standard against which all other cakewalks were measured. Although a highly singable and danceable number, it was rejected by all major publishers of the day. Their costly mistake firmly set up the house of F. A. Mills for the next twenty years. His 1899 hit "Whistling Rufus" successfully competed with E. T. McGrath's "A Breeze from Blackville," Bernard Franklin's "Blackville Society," Arthur Pryor's "A Coon Band Contest," Jean Schwartz's "Dusky Dudes," George Rosey's "A Rag-Time Skedaddle," and Abe Holzmann's "Smokey Mokes"—all winners in the glorious "year of the cakewalk." The following year, J. Bodewalt Lampe published his "Creole Belles" in his hometown of Buffalo, New York. Not until Whitney-Warner purchased it the following year did it became a million-seller. Although Kerry Mills went on to compose several lovely Tin Pan Alley songs, some of which ("Meet Me in St. Louis, Louis" and "Red Wing") became standards, he occasionally harked back to his cakewalk roots: "Kerry Mills Ragtime Dance" (1909) and "Kerry Mills' Cake Walk" (1915).

In their Tin Pan Alley form, cakewalks were 2/4 instrumentals, with occasional vocal trios, founded on a simple march framework and using simple syncopation in a single rhythm pattern. Compositionally, they were unpianistic pieces involving single-note, easily remembered melody lines that one could sketch out on a piano with one finger without disturbing their harmony. Though cakewalks were often arranged for piano (as were marches), their sheet music covers typically displayed other instruments, usually trombones and banjos, and they were often performed by marching or circus bands, as well as by string bands consisting of violin, banjo, and string bass. The earliest cakewalk hits were popularized by the premier concert band of John Philip Sousa, who was responsible for the cakewalk's European popularity. Sousa detested the cakewalk but clearly perceived its commercial possibilities. He had his solo trombonist, Arthur Pryor, make the arrangements and conduct the Sousa band when it recorded cakewalks.

# Anne Caldwell

Lyricist, playwright, and singer (b. Anne Payson Caldwell, Boston, Massachusetts, August 30, 1876; d. Beverly Hills, California, October 22, 1936). Caldwell originally aspired to be a singer and dancer, but began writing lyrics after a mishap on stage laid her up with a broken leg. Arriving in New York City at the end of the first decade of the twentieth century, she met lyricist James O'Dea, whom she soon wed. The two first collaborated on "Top o' the World" in 1910, but Caldwell initially gained fame as a playwright with the nonmusical play *The Nest Egg* that same year. Her first big hit was 1914's *Chin-Chin*, which featured her own book and lyrics, although its success was tempered by the death of her husband after a long bout of pneumonia. She collaborated with many leading New York composers, including JEROME KERN, with whom she worked on a number of shows. Their first collaboration was in 1919, and their first big success came a year later with *The Night Boat*, which produced the hits "Left All Alone Again Blues" (originally recorded by singer Marion Harris [Columbia A2939]) and the sprightly "Whose Baby Are You?" A year later, the duo offered *Good Morning, Dearie*, featuring "Ka-lu-a," which was popularized at the time by singer Elsie Baker and revived in the 1946 JUDY GARLAND feature *Till the Clouds Roll By*. In 1929, Caldwell moved to Hollywood, where she worked on scripts for *Dixiana* (and also supplied lyrics for some of the songs, although she went uncredited) and *Flying Down to Rio*. She died in Hollywood at the age of sixty.

# Cab Calloway

Bandleader, composer, lyricist, singer, and actor (b. Rochester, New York, December 25, 1907; d. New York City, November 19, 1994). As a performer, he featured jive talk and personified the hep-cat from the early 1930s through World War II. He was famous for his "Hi-De-Ho" scat singing and his flamboyant manner of conducting his orchestra, which included some of the finest jazzmen of the time. As a composer, he contributed "Minnie the Moocher" (his 1931 theme song, based on the 1927 "Willie the Weeper"), "The Scat Song" (1932), "Boog-It" (1940), "Are You All Reet?" (1941), and "Let's Go, Joe" (1942). His hit recordings started in 1931 with "Minnie the Moocher" (Brunswick 6074); "St. James' Infirmary," which was banned from the airwaves (Brunswick 6105); and "Kickin' the Gong Around" (Brunswick 6209). 1932 continued his jive numbers with "Minnie the Moocher's Wedding Day" (Brunswick 6321) and "Reefer Man" (Brunswick 6340). His million-seller came in 1939 with his own tune, "(Hep-Hep!) The Jumpin' Jive" (Vocalion 5005). His 1942 hit "Blues in the Night" featured Dizzy Gillespie on trumpet (Okeh 6422). During the 1950s and 1960s, Calloway appeared as Sportin' Life in a touring company of *Porgy and Bess* and on Broadway in *Hello Dolly!* He made a memorable late-career appearance in the comedy film *The Blues Brothers* (1980).

# Hughie Cannon

Composer and pianist (b. Detroit, Michigan, 1877; d. Toledo, Ohio, 1912). Cannon is best remembered as the composer of the jazz standard "Bill Bailey, Won't You Please Come Home?" (1902). Cannon worked as a pianist for a number of vaudeville singers, and apparently also sang himself. He first worked as a composer in collaboration with lyricist John Queen, producing "Just Because She Made Dem Goo-Goo Eyes" in 1900, followed by "I Hates to Get Up Early in the Morning" a year later. "Bill Bailey," with his own lyrics and tune, was an immediate hit as introduced by Queen on the vaudeville circuit and on record initially by Arthur Collins, who made several recordings for different labels in 1902. There are many conflicting stories about who the real "Bill Bailey" was, but everyone seems to agree that there was an actual Bill Bailey who, after being kicked out of his house by his wife, was let back in. This is one of the greatest syncopated rag songs, but because of its caricature cover, it was considered a COON SONG. It was so popular that it inspired a host of other songs about Bill Bailey, including "I Wonder Why Bill Bailey Don't Come Home," "Since Bill Bailey Came Back Home," "Bill Bailey's Left His Happy Home Again," and "Bill Bailey's Application." Cannon produced his own follow-up, "He Done Me Wrong," telling the story of Bailey's death; it borrowed its title from the refrain of the famous folk ballad "Frankie and Johnnie." "Bill Bailey" was long a standard in jazzman Louis Armstrong's repertoire, whose version was much imitated; teen popster Bobby Darin had a million-selling hit with his version released in 1959 (Atco 6167).

# Eddie Cantor

Very popular comedian and singer (b. Edward Israel Iskowitz, New York City, January 31, 1892; d. Hollywood, California, October 10, 1964). Orphaned at a young age, Cantor was raised by his grandmother, and as a young teen sang on street corners for pocket change. Around 1910, he joined the Gus Edwards troupe in vaudeville, along with his friend George Jessel. He next formed an act with Lila Lee and went on to play the Palace Theatre. He became famous singing "That's the Kind of a Baby for Me" (Victor 18342) in the *Ziegfeld Follies of 1917*. He played in the *Follies of 1918* and *1919*, *Broadway Brevities of 1920*, *Midnight Rounders of 1921*, *Make It Snappy* (1922), and *Ziegfeld Follies of 1923*, and starred in *Kid Boots* (1924) and *Whoopee* (1928). His last Broadway show was *Banjo Eyes* (1942). He began his movie career in 1930, eventually making fourteen films. In 1953, the biopic *The Eddie Cantor Story* starred Keefe Brasselle in the title role, for which Cantor dubbed the songs.

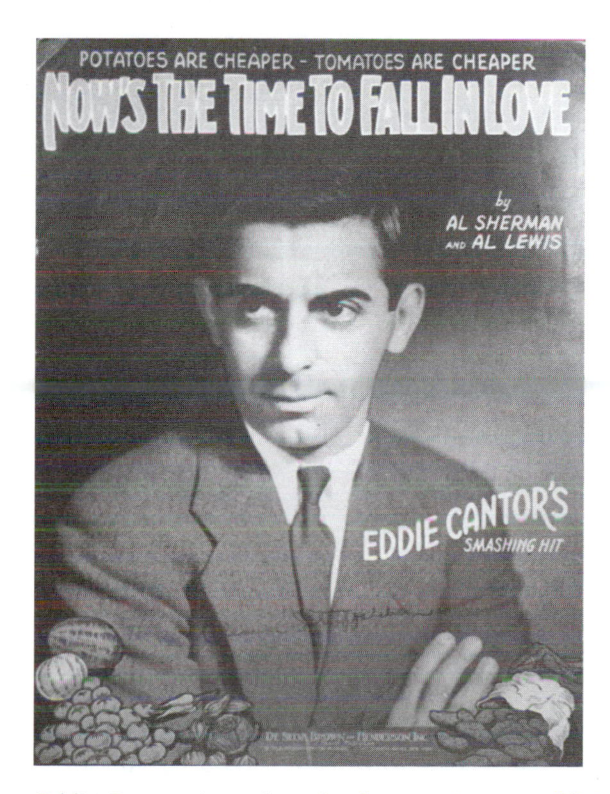


Eddie Cantor pictured on the sheet music cover of "Now's the Time to Fall in Love," by Al Sherman and Al Lewis, published by De Sylva, Brown, and Henderson, Inc.

Cantor's recording career began in 1917 and continued into the era of the LP. He was a star of radio in the 1920s and had a top-rated program throughout the 1930s and 1940s, using "One Hour with You" as his closing theme. He helped singers Deanna Durbin and Bobby Breen achieve stardom in the 1930s, and helped DINAH SHORE in the 1940s. Eddie Fisher was the recipient of his good offices during the early 1950s. His *Colgate Comedy Hour* television show was a consistent favorite.

Throughout his career, Cantor was known for "You'd Be Surprised" (Emerson 10102), "Margie" (Emerson 10301), "Oh! Gee, Oh! Gosh, Oh! Golly I'm in Love" (Columbia A-3934), "If You Knew Susie" (Columbia 364D), "Ida" (Decca 23987), "Makin' Whoopee!" (Victor 21831), and "Now's the Time to Fall in Love" (Decca 23985). He wrote two autobiographies, *My Life Is in Your Hands* and *Take My Life*.

# Hoagy Carmichael

Composer (b. Bloomington, Indiana, November 22, 1899; d. Palm Springs, California, December 27, 1981). He learned to play piano by listening to his mother, who accompanied silent movies, and from a local black pianist, Reggie Duval. While attending Indiana University's law school, he became friendly with Bix Beiderbecke and invited Beiderbecke's Wolverines to play at parties his fraternity gave. As a result of that friendship, his first composition, "Riverboat Shuffle," was recorded by the Wolverines (Gennett 5454) in May 1924. Jack Mills published it in 1925, giving cocomposer credit to Wolverine pianist Dick Voynow and to publisher Irving Mills. MITCHELL PARISH added lyrics in 1939. "Washboard Blues" (1928) was Carmichael's next tune, with lyrics by Fred B. Callahan. PAUL WHITEMAN and his orchestra recorded it in November 1927, with Beiderbecke on cornet and Carmichael as pianist, also performing his first vocal on record (Victor 35877).

In 1927 Carmichael composed the melody of "Star Dust" one evening when he went to the Book Nook at the University to play the broken-down upright piano there. His school friend Stuart Gorrell named the tune that resulted because "it sounded like dust from stars drifting down through the summer sky." Carmichael first recorded the tune as a "stomp" with Emil Seidel's band, under the name of Hoagy Carmichael and His Pals (Gennett 6311). Carmichael played the piano on this recording of October 31, 1927. MILLS MUSIC published it as an instrumental number in January 1929. In May of that year, Mitchell Parish added lyrics. The song didn't begin to be popular until ISHAM JONES and his orchestra recorded it as a dreamy ballad in an arrangement by Jones's pianist-arranger, VICTOR YOUNG (Brunswick 4886), in May 1930. RCA-Victor Records broke with tradition in 1936 when it issued a single record containing two completely different versions of the song. BENNY GOODMAN, using a FLETCHER HENDERSON arrangement, recorded it with his orchestra on April 23. TOMMY DORSEY, with vocalist Edythe Wright, had recorded the song eight days earlier. Both versions were issued back to back on Victor 25320. The two biggest swing bandleaders of the day proved their popularity by making this disc a best-seller. ARTIE SHAW and his orchestra made their recording in 1940, and it sold over two million copies (Victor 27230). The song has since been recorded over a thousand times in the United States alone. Carmichael recorded it several times during his long career, and his best is the 1942 version, accompanied by Artie Bernstein on string bass and SPIKE JONES on drums (Decca 18395).

"Rockin' Chair" (1930) was Carmichael's next important song. He recorded it with LOUIS ARMSTRONG and his orchestra (Okeh 8756) in December 1929, with vocals by the two of them. Carmichael also sang it with what now looks like an all-star band in May 1930: Bix Beiderbecke and Bubber Miley (from Duke Ellington's band), cornet; Tommy Dorsey, trombone; Benny Goodman, clarinet; Bud Freeman, tenor sax; Joe Venuti, violin; Irving Brodsky, piano and vocal; Eddie Lang, guitar; Harry Goodman, tuba; and Gene Krupa, drums. Carmichael joined in on Brodsky's vocal (Victor 38139).

"Georgia on My Mind" (1930) had lyrics by Carmichael's school chum Stuart Gorrell. Carmichael first recorded it with his own hand-picked group in September 1930 (Victor 23013). FATS WALLER recorded it (Victor 27765) in 1941, and Ray Charles revived it in 1960 for a best-selling disc (ABC Paramount 10135). Charles performed it in Georgia's state legislative chamber on the day it was named the state song.

"Lazy River" (1931) was written with Sidney Arodin. Carmichael sang it on a record with another all-star band that he brought together (Victor 23034). The MILLS BROTHERS also had a best-selling disc (Decca 28458). It was revived in 1961 by Bobby Darin (Atco 6188) and also by Si Zentner, whose orchestral performance won him a Grammy (Liberty 3216). "Come Easy, Go Easy, Love" (1931), with lyrics by Sunny Clapp (1899–1962), was recorded by Clapp's band with Carmichael as vocalist. Sidney Arodin is the clarinetist in the band, and Clapp plays alto saxophone (Victor 22776).

Hoagy Carmichael (left) and Duke Ellington in the mid-1930s.

"Lazybones" (1933) has lyrics by JOHNNY MERCER. If ever there was a natural collaboration between similar musical personalities, this was it. Carmichael recorded it (Victor 24402), as did Mercer (Varsity 8031). It was also popularized by MILDRED BAILEY, Ben Bernie, and RUDY VALLEE. "Skylark" (1942), another collaboration with Mercer, gave DINAH SHORE a #5 hit that year (Bluebird 11473). In 1944, they again joined forces to produce "How Little We Know" for the film *To Have and Have Not.*

"Little Old Lady" (1936) has lyrics by STANLEY ADAMS. It was written for a revue, *The Show Is On.* During rehearsals, the producer wanted to remove it because he felt it didn't have a proper setting. E. Y. HARBURG, who was working on the show, liked the song so much that he created a special situation for Mitzi Mayfair and Charles Walters, who sang and danced to it. "The Nearness of You," with lyrics by NED WASHINGTON, was written for Gladys Swarthout to sing in the film *Romance in the Dark* (1938). It wasn't published until 1940—as a pop song, with no mention of its film connection. "Heart and Soul," with lyrics by FRANK LOESSER, was written for a Paramount short, *A Song Is Born* (1938), which featured bandleader Larry Clinton and his orchestra. The Loesser-Carmichael team also wrote "Two Sleepy People" for Bob Hope and Shirley Ross in the film *Thanks for the Memory* (1938).

"Hong Kong Blues" (1939) was an independent number that didn't take off until the composer himself sang it in the film *To Have and Have Not* (1944). From this time on, Carmichael would include film acting in his varied career. "Doctor, Lawyer, Indian Chief" (1945), with lyrics by Paul Francis Webster, was written for the Betty Hutton film *The Stork Club.* Her recording made it a hit (Capitol 15230). "Ole Buttermilk Sky" (1946) was written with Jack Brooks for Carmichael to sing in a nonmusical film, *Canyon Passage.*

Carmichael continued to be active through the mid-1950s. One of his biggest late career hits was "In the Cool, Cool, Cool of the Evening" (1951), with lyrics by Johnny Mercer, which was written for BING CROSBY and Jane Wyman in *Here Comes the Groom.* It received the Academy Award for Best Song, Mercer's second of four Oscars. Carmichael wrote nine songs for the 1953 Marilyn Monroe-Jane Russell film *Gentlemen Prefer Blondes,* working with lyricist HAROLD ADAMSON, but all but two were cut from the final version. He did a few more films, with his last assignment, 1962's *Hatari,* producing a top-ten sound track album. Meanwhile, his venerable standards, including "Star Dust" and "Georgia on My Mind," were constantly revived, keeping Carmichael's name and music present to the public.

# Harry Carroll

Composer and pianist (b. Atlantic City, New Jersey, November 28, 1892; d. Mount Carmel, Pennsylvania, December 26, 1962). A self-taught pianist, Carroll was playing in local movie houses by his early teens, and then moved to New York City. He worked as an arranger on Tin Pan Alley during the day, and as a café pianist at night. The Schuberts hired him to write songs for *The Whirl of Society* (1912), which led to his first hit, "On the Mississippi," written with Arthur Fields and lyricist Ballard MacDonald. With MacDonald, Carroll scored additional hits a year later, including "The Trail of the Lonesome Pine," which became a major hit for cowboy singers over the decades. The title was taken from a popular novel of the day by John Fox Jr., the husband of singer Fritzi Scheff. The novel referred to the Cumberland Mountains of Kentucky, but MacDonald, who obviously hadn't read the book, wrote a lyric about "the Blue Ridge Mountains of Virginia." This was the song Laurel and Hardy sang in their 1937 film *Way Out West.* (It was also the favorite of Gertrude Stein.)

In 1914, Carroll wrote the popular "By the Beautiful Sea," this time in collaboration with lyricist Harold Atteridge. It has become a classic summertime anthem often associated with Carroll's hometown of Atlantic City. From 1914 to 1917, Carroll was a director of ASCAP. In 1918, he produced his own Broadway show, *Oh, Look*, which featured the million-selling hit "I'm Always Chasing Rainbows," its melody borrowed from Chopin's Fantasie Impromptu in C# Minor; the lyric was by JOSEPH McCARTHY. The vaudevillian Dolly Sisters made it a big hit, and it was featured in the 1946 biopic of the singers, starring Betty Grable and June Haver. A year later, Perry Como had a major hit with his recording. About 1918, Carroll wed vaudevillian Anna Wheaton, and the two toured for many years, first on the vaudeville circuit and eventually in smaller clubs.

# Cartoon Characters

Newspaper owners discovered that comic strips added substantially to their daily sales, and popular sheet music publishers found that using characters from popular comic strips increased music sales as well. The first modern newspaper cartoonist was Richard Outcault, and through the years, he created several characters. His first was the Yellow Kid, and although the Kid appears on about a dozen song sheets, it seems that not one was drawn or signed by Outcault himself. However, he signed the illustrations for his Buster Brown and Li'l Mose songs.

Animated cartoon characters started to appear on sheets with Max Fleisher's Ko Ko the Clown on the 1923 song sheet "Out of the Bottle." The most popular song embodying a newspaper cartoon was the 1923 song by CON CONRAD and BILLY ROSE, "Barney Google." Ernest Hare and Billy Jones had the #2 hit recording (Columbia A-3876), but also recorded it for Okeh, Emerson, Brunswick, Edison, and Vocalion. Pat Sullivan's creation Felix the Cat was turned into a song by that name in 1928 by PETE WENDLING, Max Kortlander, and Alfred Bryan. The Fleisher Studios scored in 1932 when JOHNNY GREEN and EDWARD HEYMAN wrote the theme song for the Betty Boop series, and again in 1934 when Sammy Lerner wrote "I'm Popeye the Sailor Man" for their Popeye series by Segar.

*See also* DISNEY CARTOON SONGS *for the use of music in Walt Disney's animated features.*

# Emma Carus

Performer (b. Berlin, Germany, March 18, 1879; d. New York City, November 19, 1927). Drama critic Amy Leslie wrote, "Emma Carus is about the only one of the big-time singers who has a cultivated and genuine voice. It is a sweet contralto voice with excellent mezzo register and she uses it well." Carus was discovered by songwriter MONROE H. ROSENFELD, and her first song success was his "Take Back Your Gold" (1897).

Appearing on the vaudeville stage, Carus was known for her comic re-creations of various ethnic types. "I'm the human dialect cocktail," she quipped. "A little Scotch, considerable Irish, a dash of Dutch, and a great deal of Negro, together with a bit of British." The somewhat hefty Carus opened her act by saying, "I'm not pretty, but I'm good to my folks," which became her well-known tag line. She belted out her songs and was billed as a coon shouter. Carus introduced IRVING BERLIN's first big hit, 1911's "Alexander's Ragtime Band," while performing in Chicago; by the end of a week, the song was an enormous hit. She was so effective as a plugger of this song that her name remained on the song sheet in all of its sixty-five editions—above the title. In 1914, Jack Glogau (1886–1953) wrote a snappy fox-trot, "The Carus Breeze," in her honor.

# Vernon and Irene Castle

Dancers (b.Vernon Blythe, Norwich, England, May 2, 1887; d. Fort Worth, Texas, February 15, 1918, and Irene Foote, New Rochelle, New York, April 17, 1893; d. Eureka Springs, Arkansas January 25, 1969). The duo met in the early 1910s in Paris, where both were scraping by as dance performers; asked to demonstrate the latest American dance fads, they quickly wrote home and got information about the turkey trot and other new dances. Creating a sensation in Paris, the couple realized they had hit on a unique formula for success. The Castles inspired a national craze for ballroom dancing when they returned to the United States in 1912. They appeared on Broadway in *The Lady of the Slipper* (October 28, 1912). *The Sunshine Girl* (February 3, 1913), which starred Julia Sanderson, featured Julia and Vernon doing the tango, as the song sheet cover of "The Argentine" illustrates. From the same show, the cover of Dan Caslar's one-and-two-step, "Tres Chic," pictures Irene and Vernon in a pose from their routine. In the same year, Arthur N. Green composed three numbers that featured the Castles on their covers: "Tango Argentine," "Innovation Tango,"

Vernon and Irene do the "Castle Lame Duck Waltz" on the cover of the sheet music by James Reese Europe and Ford T. Dabney, published by Joseph W. Stern.

and "Maxixe Brasilienne." His "Royal Arab" one-step and fox-trot of 1915 also features the duo on its cover. They starred in Irving Berlin's first complete musical show, *Watch Your Step* (1914).

The publishing house of JOSEPH STERN, which had been an early booster of ragtime, black songwriters, and new fads, showed its intuition by signing the Castles to pose for the covers of a series of dance tunes written by black bandleaders JAMES REESE EUROPE and Ford T. Dabney (1883–1958). Dabney had accompanied the Castles with Europe's Society Orchestra. The Stern series of dance songs consisted of "The Castle Combination" (waltz-trot), "Castle Innovation Waltz," "Castle Lame Duck Waltz," "Castles' Half and Half," "Castle Innovation Tango," "Castle Maxixe," "Castle Perfect Trot," "Castle Valse Classique," "The Castle Walk," "Castles in Europe," and "Castle House Rag."

Vernon was also a fine comedian and drummer. A picture of him at the drums is on the cover of Carey Morgan's "Trilby Rag" (1915). Irene, slim, tall, and graceful, was the first stage star to wear her hair bobbed. Unlike Vernon's previous dancing partners, who were too short, she was the right height for her husband. In fact, she was the first tall, slim stage personality in an era whose female stars, notably SOPHIE TUCKER and EMMA CARUS, were considerably more substantial. They were featured nightly at Castles-in-the-Air, their dance pavilion in New York City. During the summers they appeared at Castles-by-the-Sea in Long Beach, Long Island.

At the height of their popularity in 1917, Vernon enlisted in a British flying unit in France to do aerial photography at the front. He was soon transferred to the United States as a flying instructor at the Fort Worth Flying School, where he died in a plane crash. Irene immediately retired from show business.

Before she did, and while Vernon was away, she appeared as a solo dancer in the revue *Miss 1917* (November 5, 1917). She also made a silent movie called *Patria* (1917) for International Studios, and she composed the music for its theme. She appears on the song's cover wrapped in an American flag.

The Castles' major rivals were Maurice and Florence Walton, who were featured on several song sheet covers, the best being the instrumental composed for them by Paul Biese and F. Henri Klickmann, appropriately entitled "The Maurice Walk" (1913). The following year, silent film star Mae Murray, who had danced in vaudeville, was featured on the cover of "The Murray Walk," also composed by Biese and Klickmann. The Castles were the subject of the 1939 biopic *The Story of Vernon and Irene Castle*, the last feature pairing FRED ASTAIRE and GINGER ROGERS, who re-created the Castles' famous dances.

# Saul Chaplin

Composer and arranger (b. Saul Kaplan, Brooklyn, New York, February 19, 1912; d. Hollywood, California, November 15, 1997). Chaplin was a popular songwriter of the 1930s, best known for his collaborations with SAMMY CAHN. Their hits included "Until the Real Thing

Comes Along" (1936, written with Mann Holiner, Alberta Nichols, and L. E. Freeman; recorded by FATS WALLER and Connee BOSWELL, among others, and revived in the 1950s by the vocal group The Ravens) and "Please Be Kind" (1938). Lou Levy approached the duo to write English lyrics for the Yiddish song "Bei Mir Bist Du Schoen"; the result was a top 1938 hit for the ANDREWS SISTERS (Decca 1562). With AL JOLSON, Chaplin collaborated on the hit "The Anniversary Song," which was written for the biopic *The Jolson Story* (1946). In the early 1940s, Chaplin and Cahn went to Hollywood to work for Columbia Pictures, and during the 1950s Chaplin was a Hollywood arranger, most notably for *An American in Paris* (1951), and then turned to producing films in the 1960s.

# Chappell and Company

British music publishing company dating back to the early nineteenth century. In 1920, with a floundering New York office, Chappell approached MAX and Louis DREYFUS of T. B. HARMS, proposing a partnership. Max was already part-owner of Harms, and entered into a separate partnership with Chappell. In 1929, Max sold his holdings in Harms to Warner Brothers. His brother Louis went to England to run Chappell, now fully owned by the Dreyfuses; Max remained in the United States. The firm took offices in the RKO Building in 1934. Chappell quickly became a power in the Alley by specializing in publishing songs from Broadway shows. In 1943, Chappell purchased Williamson Music (the Rodgers and Hammerstein catalog) for its list, developing the largest catalog of show music. When Louis Dreyfus died in 1980, the Rodgers and Hammerstein estate, along with music publisher Freddy Bienstock (of Carlin Music), purchased the firm. They in turn sold Chappell to Warner Brothers in 1987, and the new firm was named WARNER/CHAPPELL MUSIC.

# Charleston

The dance that defined the defiant spirit of the 1920s is the Charleston, which first appeared in the Broadway show *Runnin' Wild* (October 29, 1923). Elisabeth Welch introduced the song in this score, composed by JAMES P. JOHNSON with lyrics by CECIL MACK. (They also wrote the standard "Old Fashioned Love" for this production.) Johnson claimed he was inspired by his neighbors in New York's Hell's Kitchen, many of whom had originally come from South Carolina. They would hold house parties at which they did this unusual dance, for which Johnson developed a unique rhythmic accompaniment. Johnson and Mack's "Charleston" influenced other songs with its rhythm, and it inspired a host of numbers that used the word in their titles: "Charleston Baby of Mine," "Charleston Ball," "Charleston Cabin," "Charleston Capers," and "Charleston Charlie." ZEZ CONFREY wrote "Charleston Chuckles," and FATS WALLER wrote "Charleston Hound." Others included "The Charleston Didn't Come from Charleston," "Charleston Rhythm," "Charleston Stampede," "Charleston Your Blues Away," and, in 1926, William Holmes's "Everybody's Charleston Crazy." Johnson and Mack followed their original hit with "Everybody's Doin' the Charleston Now."

Two other dances, novelties and variations of the Charleston, didn't last very long. However, their songs have become standards. One was the DE SYLVA, BROWN AND HENDERSON "Black Bottom," which first appeared in *George White's Scandals* (June 14, 1926). It was introduced by little Ann Pennington, who had performed in the *Ziegfeld Follies* since 1913. The same trio wrote "The Varsity Drag" (1927) for their show *Good News*.

# Charts

In 1913, *Billboard* started charting sheet music sales, using figures compiled from the leading five-and-ten chains (Woolworth's, McCrory's) and major music stores around the country. It wasn't until 1934 that the trade papers *Billboard* and *Variety* began to run Top 10 charts on a weekly basis. From 1935 to 1958, *Your Hit Parade* featured the top ten songs of the week, performed by the talent on the show rather than by artists who made the songs famous. The weekly survey was undertaken by the sponsor's advertising agency and was based on sheet music and record sales and radio performances. Radio exposure of songs was monitored by the *Accurate Report* and the *Peatman Report*, two daily services provided to the music and advertising industries, which listed every plug on radio in the New York metropolitan area, and graded the kinds of plugs: whether played on a local station or on a network, in a medley or alone. After World War II, recordings replaced the live performances of singers and big bands on radio, as the disc jockey playing records took over. Since the 1940s, *Billboard* has had different charts, such as Best-Sellers in Stores, Most Played by Jockeys, Most Played in Juke Boxes, Top 100, Hot 100, Hot 100 Singles Sales, and Hot 100 Airplay. The last three charts are still in use today. Also after World War II, *Billboard* began separate charts for country and western and rhythm and blues, marking the beginning of the division of the pop music industry into many subcategories, which continues today.

# Frank E. Churchill

Composer (b. Rumford, Maine, October 20, 1901; d. Hollywood, California, May 14, 1942). Best known for his assocation with Walt Disney, Churchill joined the Disney firm in 1932, replacing Carl Stallings (who went to work for Warner Bros., composing music for the Looney Tunes series). Churchill's first hit was "Who's Afraid of the Big Bad Wolf?," written for a 1933 Three Little Pigs short. Working with lyricist Larry Morey, Churchill memorably scored *Snow White and the Seven Dwarfs* (1937), which produced the standards "Someday My Prince Will Come" and "Whistle While You Work." The duo reunited for *Dumbo* (1941) and for Churchill's last feature, *Bambi* (1942), released after his death at the age of forty-one. Eleven years after his death, Disney released *Peter Pan*, a cartoon that had first been planned in 1939. Churchill's "Never Smile at a Crocodile," with lyrics by Jack Lawrence, had been written for the proposed film and was eventually used in the finished product, becoming a children's song classic.

# Classical Music Appropriated

Taking melodies from the classics has a long tradition in the Alley. "Iola" (1906) was taken from Johann Strauss Sr., and "I'm Always Chasing Rainbows" (1918) from Chopin, who also contributed the melody for "Till the End of Time" (1945). "Song of Love" (1921) came from Schubert, and Ferde Grofe made a fabulous arrangement for PAUL WHITEMAN's orchestra of "Song of India," originally by Rimsky-Korsakov (1922). The period from the late 1930s through World War II saw a plethora of great classical-pop songs: "My Reverie" (1938) by Debussy, "The Lamp Is Low" (1939) by Ravel, "Tonight We Love" (1941) by Tchaikovsky; and "Full Moon and Empty Arms" (1946) by Rachmaninoff. "Stranger in Paradise" (1953) had a melody taken from Borodin. When pop composer FRED FISHER went to Hollywood in 1929, producer Irving Thalberg asked him if he could write a symphony. He replied, "When you buy me, you're buying Chopin, Liszt, and Mozart. You're getting the very best!"

# Maggie Cline

Performer (b. Haverhill, Massachusetts, January 1, 1857; d. Fair Haven, New Jersey, June 11, 1934). Cline worked in a shoe factory from the age of twelve, and was determined to escape to a life of performing. She began her career in 1879 as the first female comic Irish singer. Her biggest hit was her 1890 "Throw Him Down, McCloskey." She had met the composer, John W. Kelley, known as vaudeville's "Rolling Mill Man," and asked him if he had any loose songs on him. He told her he had one that no one wanted, and she could have it for $2.00. She bought it from him on the spot, and for twenty-three years she used it. Her performance was spectacular. At the words "Throw him down, McCloskey!," everybody backstage took whatever they could grab and threw it on the floor with as much force as they could muster. Those who could not find pieces of furniture or iron weights grabbed steam whistles, thunder sheets, and other noisy devices. Since Cline got encore after encore, she and her crew would be exhausted by the time they finished the performance. Cline once said that she performed the song over 75,000 times. She retired in 1917.

# George L. Cobb

Composer (b. Mexico, New York, August 31, 1886; d. Brookline, Massachusetts, December 25, 1942). Trained in music at Syracuse University, Cobb won a composition contest in Buffalo, where he lived after college. He started out writing rags, then came to the Alley and wrote a few hit songs. He went to work for Boston publisher Walter Jacobs, writing more rags and anything else the publisher needed. When Jacobs began a monthly magazine, *The Tuneful Yankee*, early in 1917 (the name was changed the following year to *Melody*), Cobb wrote a column to answer the questions of would-be songwriters. He also reviewed current pop songs, and the magazine printed several in each issue, often including one from the pen of George Cobb. His first rag, "Rubber Plant Rag," was published by Jacobs in 1909 and became fairly well known. His fine "Canned Corn Rag" was issued by the Bell Music Company of Buffalo in 1910. His "Bunny Hug Rag" of 1913 created a stir, because it was aimed at the new craze for ANIMAL DANCES. The same year, he and fellow Buffalonian, lyricist JACK YELLEN, wrote a syncopated hit, "All Aboard for Dixie Land." Elizabeth Murray sang it as an interpolation in RUDOLF FRIML's operetta *High Jinks* (December 10, 1913), and turned it into a hit. Two years later, she introduced another of their songs, "Listen to That Dixie Band," and also scored with it. She could do no wrong for the boys, so later that year they gave her "Alabama Jubilee," which sold nearly a million copies. It was revived in the early 1950s. The team from North Buffalo, where the winters are below freezing, remained enamored of the South, and their last hit was "Are You from Dixie?" (1915).

Then, Cobb came up with a rag for dancer Maizie King called "The Midnight Trot." It was published by WILL ROSSITER in 1916, and its harmonic changes in the trio are adventurous for its time. Cobb gave Rossiter his 1918 adaptation of Rachmaninoff's "Prelude in C Sharp Minor," and the publisher called it "Russian Rag." It sold over a million copies and was the vaudeville virtuosos' favorite for years. Joe "Fingers" Carr made the definitive recording of it in the early 1950s (Capitol 1311). The song was in such demand that in 1923 Rossiter asked Cobb to write another rag, using more of the same Prelude. Cobb called it "The New Russian Rag." Amateur pianists have been cursing him for these tricky masterpieces ever since. But pianists with technique love him, and so do audiences when they hear Cobb's syncopated gems played well.

# George M. Cohan

Well-loved Broadway star, playwright, and songwriter (b. Providence, Rhode Island, July 3, 1878 [despite his claim to have been "born on the 4th of July"]; d. New York City, November 5, 1942). He could be described, without exaggeration, as having been "born in a trunk," since his parents were touring vaudevillians, and he joined their act as a human prop while still a baby. His first speaking role came at the age of nine. His education consisted mainly of lessons learned on the vaudeville circuit. By eleven, he was contributing sketches to his parents' act and serving as their business manager. After his marriage in 1894 to Ethel Levey, who joined the act as a singer-actress, Cohan began to write for the musical theater and to expand his vaudeville sketches for the legitimate stage.

His first song was published by the WITMARKS, who had Walter Ford rewrite the lyrics, turning "Why Did Nellie Leave Home?" from a comic number into a tearjerker. Cohan met May Irwin and, in 1896, collaborated with her on a COON SONG, "Hot Tamale Alley," which she sang in vaudeville. Two years later, writing his own words and music, Cohan came out with "I Guess I'll Have to Telegraph My Baby," his first real hit song.

The precocious youngster set about changing musical comedy in America by giving it an American feeling, *his* feeling—full of brashness, brightness, and patriotic fervor. Before

Cohan, musical comedy consisted of vaudeville stars doing their turns in exotic costumes in front of colorful scenery, using scripts that had little or no plot. The more exotic, the more popular, it seemed. American stages were crowded with stories that unfolded in such foreign locales as "Ruritania." Then came Cohan to write about American characters in American places. He made it acceptable for things American to be written about, and even glorified, on the stage and in song.

In time, Cohan became famous not only as a song-and-dance man, but also as a playwright, director, composer, lyricist, publisher, dramatic actor, and producer—the first complete man of the American theater. His theatrical talents encompassed the scope of the business, and we can barely imagine now how one man could dominate the medium of the stage doing everything himself—not just once, but time and again for over fifteen years!

Cohan's list of Broadway productions, starting with *The Governor's Son* (February 25, 1901), included twenty-two musicals and thirteen straight plays. His most impressive years as producer-performer-playwright were 1904–1920, when he partnered with Broadway producer Sam Harris (1872–1941). Late in his life, Cohan scored a triumph as a dramatic actor in Eugene O'Neill's *Ah, Wilderness!* and in Kaufman and Hart's *I'd Rather Be Right.*

Cohan's first two Broadway shows were merely expansions of his family's vaudeville sketches. It is not surprising that they failed with spectacle-dazed Broadway audiences. However, audiences around the country liked them, and *The Governor's Son* and *Running for Office* (April 27, 1903) made money in their out-of-town runs. The first had an interesting song, "I Love Everyone in the Wide, Wide World," and twelve songs from the score were published by F. A. MILLS. The second show also issued twelve songs, a good one being "Sweet Popularity," published by the short-lived Cohan, Nobel and Cohan firm.

The best Cohan musicals are the eight in which he starred. They featured his most famous songs during the first decade of the twentieth century. *Little Johnny Jones* (November 7, 1904) had a score that contained three genuine hits: "The Yankee Doodle Boy," "Give My Regards to Broadway," and "Life's a Funny Proposition After All." The next important Cohan show, *Forty-five Minutes from Broadway* (January 1, 1906), was the first to star someone other than himself. Three of its six published songs were hits: the title song, "Mary's a Grand Old Name," and "So Long, Mary." One song, a comic number titled "Stand Up and Fight like Hell," shocked Broadway, since words like "hell" and "damn" had been forbidden on stage in the nineteenth century. Cohan's audiences were titillated by his use of them in what was thought to be family entertainment. (It may be remembered that it took many years for such language to be considered acceptable on television.)

Unable to stay out of his own shows, Cohan wrote, produced, and starred in *George Washington, Jr.* (February 12, 1906), from which came the patriotic "The Wedding of the Blue and Gray" and everyone's Cohan favorite, "You're a Grand Old Flag." But not everyone was happy with the song when he first published it. The song's original title came from a conversation Cohan had with a Civil War veteran who had been a color-bearer during Pickett's charge at Gettysburg. The old man alluded proudly to his standard, saying, "She's a grand old rag." After opening night and a first publication bearing that title and phrase in the lyric, patriotic societies complained that referring to our country's flag as a "rag" was an insult. Cohan recalled the initial sheet music and substituted "flag" for "rag."

Cohan's musical for 1907, a rehash of *Running for Office*, was called *The Honeymooners* (June 3, 1907), and featured an unusual (for him) syncopated tune called "Popularity." The show also included the comic "If I'm Going to Die, I'm Going to Have Some Fun." Cohan's next musical, *The Talk of NewYork* (December 3, 1907), starred Victor Moore, who had made a splash in his debut in *Forty-five Minutes from Broadway.* He made the character "Kid Burns" so famous that Cohan wrote a play which featured him. The show included "I Want the World to Know I Love You," "I Have a Longing for Longacre Square," "When We Are M-A double R-I-E-D," and "When a Fellow's on the Level with a Girl That's on the Square."

Cohan's third show of the 1907–1908 season was *Fifty Miles from Boston* (February 3, 1908), and he energized its score with "Harrigan." *The Yankee Prince* (April 20, 1908) contained "Come On Downtown." With this show, the producers started their own publishing firm, Cohan and Harris, with Jerome H. Remick and Company as their exclusive selling agent. *Cohan and Harris' Minstrels* (August 3, 1908) starred George "Honey Boy" Evans and interpolated William Jerome and Jean Schwartz's "Meet Me in Rose Time, Rosie." *The American Idea* (October 5, 1908) featured "The American Ragtime."

*The Man Who Owns Broadway* (October 11, 1909) starred Raymond Hitchcock and featured a song with a show business inside joke, "I'm All O.K. with K. and E." "K. and E." was the theatrical producing colossus Klaw and Erlanger, which controlled most of the Broadway theaters through World War I. The last of Cohan's book shows, *The Little Millionaire* (September 25, 1911), starred the author-composer and included Cohan's "Come with Me to the Bungalow."

In his last three productions before the end of the war, Cohan explored the revue format. The first, *Hello, Broadway* (December 25, 1914), was subtitled "A Musical Crazy Quilt Patched and Threaded Together with Words and Music by George M. Cohan." It co-starred Cohan and William Collier, and featured "Down by the Erie Canal." *The Cohan Revue of 1916* (February 9, 1916) included the cute "The Frisco Melody." His last Broadway effort of the decade, *The Cohan Revue of 1918* (December 31, 1917), had a score by Cohan and

George Cohan in his later years as a dramatic actor, c. the mid-1930s.

Irving Berlin. When Cohan managed to fast-talk Berlin into working with him for this revue, it became the first and, so far, only instance of two famous individual composer-lyricists working together on a single Broadway production. "Polly, Pretty Polly" had music by Berlin and words by Cohan.

It is ironic that Cohan's biggest song hit, "Over There," did not come from one of his shows. "Over There" was written expressly for and about World War I. It was first published by the William Jerome Publishing Corporation, which Cohan had backed financially. Nora Bayes introduced it and, by her thrilling performances, turned it into such a hit that Leo Feist bought it for his firm for the then unprecedented amount of $25,000. Feist's pluggers turned it into a more than two-million-seller. Cohan donated his share of the profits to war charities. President Woodrow Wilson said the song was a "genuine inspiration to all American manhood." It was so inspiring, in fact, that Congress in 1940, upon the urging of President Franklin D. Roosevelt, issued a special Medal of Honor to Cohan for writing it. Upon Cohan's death, President Roosevelt wrote, "A beloved figure is lost to our national life."

Cohan's career slowed after he sided with the producers over his fellow actors during the famous actors' strike of 1919. During the 1920s, he performed in a few more musical shows, but was viewed as somewhat of a relic. He then turned to dramatic roles for most of the balance of his career. In 1937, he returned to musical theater, portraying President Franklin Roosevelt in the Rodgers and Hart musical *I'd Rather Be Right*. Cohan made his last Broadway appearance in 1940, in a straight dramatic part in *Return of the Vagabond*. His songs were revived in the 1942 Hollywood biopic, *Yankee Doodle Dandy*, featuring a toe-tapping performance by James Cagney as Cohan, and again in the 1968 musical, *George M.*, in which Joel Grey portrayed the composer. Today, Cohan's upbeat, patriotic songs are considered American classics.

# Cole and Johnson Brothers

Bob Cole was a black composer and lyricist (b. Athens, Georgia, July 1, 1868; d. Catskills, New York, August 2, 1911). His first big break occurred in 1890, when he was hired as a comedian in Sam T. Jack's *Creole Show* and also served as its stage manager. In the cast was soubrette Stella Wiley, who would soon marry Cole. Next, he got a job as a playwright and stage manager for Worth's Museum All-Star Stock Company, which James Weldon Johnson described in his book *Black Manhattan* as "the first place where a group of coloured performers were able to gain anything approaching dramatic training and experience on the strictly professional stage." Cole's next experience was writing songs and performing the songs of others with *Black Patti's Troubadours*, a touring concert-vaudeville show produced by whites.

After a dispute over salary, Cole left to form his own production company and write his own show. He formed a partnership with Billy Johnson (1858–1916), a fellow actor-dancer who wrote lyrics and costarred with Cole in *A Trip to Coontown*. This landmark production opened in New York City at the very out-of-the-way Third Avenue Theatre on April 4, 1898. It was the first musical written, performed, and produced entirely by blacks. It was in this show that Bob Cole portrayed a tramp called "Willie Wayside" to great acclaim. Some of the songs in the show were the title song (with words by the new partners and music by Bert Williams), "I Hope These Few Lines Will Find You Well," "The Wedding of the Chinee and the Coon," and "In Dahomey," all with music by Bob Cole and lyrics by Billy Johnson. The show toured the country for two years. After the tour came to an end, so did this Cole-Johnson partnership. The next partnership that Cole would form with the Johnson Brothers would last until his death by drowning.

John Rosamond Johnson (b. Jacksonville, Florida, August 11, 1873; d. New York City, November 11, 1954) was a noted composer; his brother, James Weldon Johnson (b. Jacksonville, Florida, June 17, 1871; d. Wiscasset, Maine, June 26, 1938), was a lyricist. The brothers joined forces with Bob Cole in 1900. Their first number was "If That's Society, Excuse Me." The team wrote two hits during the next two years that were independent of shows: "My Castle on the Nile" (1901) and "Oh! Didn't He Ramble" (1902), the latter written under the pseudonym "Will Handy."

Their first show assignment was for a white production, *The Belle of Bridgeport* (October 29, 1900), which starred May Irwin, who sang their "Why Don't the Band Play" and "I've Got Troubles of My Own." These two numbers were published by JOSEPH W. STERN and Company, which would publish most of the team's work during this decade. (HOWLEY, HAVILAND AND COMPANY had been the publisher of the first Cole and Johnson team.)

*The Sleeping Beauty and the Beast* (November 4, 1901) contained a few of their numbers, "Come Out, Dinah, on the Green" being the best of them. Another show of that year, *The Little Duchess* (October 14, 1901), starred Anna Held, who interpolated their famous "The Maiden with the Dreamy Eyes." Marie Cahill starred in *Sally in Our Alley* (August 29, 1902) and interpolated Bob Cole's "Under the Bamboo Tree," which became so identified with her that she took the song into her next show, *Nancy Brown* (February 16, 1903). Cahill also sang their "The Katydid, the Cricket and the Frog" and the Johnson Brothers' "Congo Love Song." For the University of Pennsylvania's Mask and Wig Club's eighteenth production, the team supplied four numbers, of which "Won't Your Mamma Let You Come Out and Play" (1906) was the most successful.

Bob Cole and the Johnson Brothers wrote two complete scores for Broadway musicals with white casts. The first was *Humpty Dumpty* (November 14, 1904), an American adaptation of an English show, which included "Mexico" and "Sambo and Dinah." The second was *In Newport* (December 26, 1904), which starred Fay Templeton and Peter Dailey, formerly of the WEBER AND FIELDS MUSIC HALL gang, with Templeton singing "Lindy."

The team wrote two Broadway musicals for all-black casts. Their first was *The Shoo-Fly Regiment* (August 6, 1907), in which Cole and John Rosamond Johnson costarred. Their two big numbers were "On the Gay Luneta" and "Who Do You Love?" The team's other black show was *The Red Moon* (May 3, 1909). While this one didn't have any hits, the score was praised by *The Dramatic Mirror*, whose critic tended to be tough on black shows. He wrote, "The score is often quite ambitious and always pleasing to hear." Some of the more "pleasing" songs were "As Long As the World Goes Round," "The Big Red Shawl," and "On

Sheet music cover for Cole and Johnson's "Picaninny Days," from the musical *The Red Moon*, published by Jerome H. Remick & Co.

the Road to Monterey." *Red Moon* toured for the rest of the season, at the end of which the team announced their retirement from producing and writing Broadway musicals. The start of the 1910 season saw the team reenter vaudeville with an act consisting of Bob Cole singing and John Rosamond Johnson at the piano. They toured throughout the United States.

# Russ Columbo

Leading pop singer of the 1920s and early 1930s (b. Eugenio Ruggerio de Rudolpho Columbo, Camden, New Jersey, January 14, 1908; d. Hollywood, California, September 2, 1934). Columbo, along with RUDY VALLEE and BING CROSBY, was one of the first pop crooners. His parents were both musicians, and the family moved several times during Columbo's early years, first to Philadelphia when he was five years old; then to California, settling in San Francisco; and then, when Columbo was a teenager, to Los Angeles. Columbo played violin and accordion in theater orchestras from a young age. In 1927, he joined GUS ARNHEIM's popular dance band as a violinist, and his vocal skills were soon discovered. He formed his own band in 1931. In addition to making major hits of other songwriters' material, Columbo wrote a few numbers himself, notably "You Call It Madness, But I Call It Love" and "Prisoner of Love," both in 1931, with CON CONRAD, who was Columbo's manager. By this time, Columbo was a star on equal footing with Crosby and Vallee, as immortalized in the Tin Pan Alley ditty "Crosby, Columbo, and Vallee" by JOE BURKE and AL DUBIN. A major radio star in the early 1930s, dubbed "The Romeo of the Radio," Columbo also starred in a few musical films before dying in a tragic accident when he and a friend staged a mock duel with antique pistols. One pistol accidentally fired, and Columbo was killed.

# Comden and Green

Broadway and film librettists and lyricists (Betty Comden, b. New York City, May 3, 1915; Adolph Green, b. New York, December 2, 1915; d. New York City, October 23, 2002). Comden and Green began their career as part of the Revuers, a New York-based act featuring a young, soon-to-be-star singer/actress, Judy Holliday. They got their big break in 1944 when they provided lyrics for the musical *On the Town*, with a score by LEONARD BERNSTEIN. The show produced several hits, including "New York, New York" and "Lonely Town." Comden and Green continued to work on Broadway and in Hollywood through the 1950s, scoring major hit shows that included several collaborations with composer JULE STYNE, notably *Peter Pan* (1952) and *Bells Are Ringing* (1956), with its hit title song and "The Party's Over," a hit for Nat King Cole in 1957 and now a cabaret standard. Comden and Green continued to write for Broadway, with hit shows *Applause* (1970), *On the Twentieth Century* (1978), and *The Will Rogers Follies* (1991).

# Composing a Pop Song

Tin Pan Alley songsmiths wrote songs primarily for two purposes: stand-alone compositions that they hoped would become hits, and songs for specific Broadway shows or revues. This distinction developed over a number of decades, because at first many songs were "interpolated" (or added to) a Broadway show or revue as a means of promoting them. Vaudeville stars also were paid to sing a specific number, "plugging" it either on stage, radio, or record. Even when songs were written for a specific show, they might not necessarily complement the show's (often admittedly loose) story line. It was only with the success of more modern, so-called integrated or book musicals, that songs began to serve the show's plotline—and thus could not be replaced at will.

The most frequently asked question of songwriters is, "Which comes first, the words or the music?" (Lyricist IRVING CAESAR used to say, "What comes first is the contract!") More often than not, the music came first. The Alley composer, once he had thought up a tune, wrote it down or, in some cases, played it for a copyist to take down. The lead sheet was then given to the lyricist, who usually knew enough about notation to make out the general rhythm and the important accents. The sheet served as his lead or guide, hence the name. Theater composer JEROME KERN always wrote the music first. RICHARD RODGERS wrote the music first when collaborating with LORENZ HART; however, when writing with OSCAR HAMMERSTEIN II, Rodgers wrote his music to Hammerstein's lyrics. IRVING BERLIN, who wrote both words and music, did it both ways, although the words usually came first. In his book *Great Men of American Popular Song*, David Ewen quotes Berlin as stating: "I usually get a phrase first—words. I keep repeating it over and over, and the first thing I know, I begin to get a sort of rhythm, and then a tune. I don't say all my songs are written that way. Sometimes I hear a tune first, and then I start trying to fit words to it."

Even the roles of "lyricist" and "composer" were often blurred. Sometimes the song would be a true collaborative effort, with two or three people working together at the same time. Sometimes, after the heat of fashioning a song, no one remembered who did what. Teams such as De Sylva, Brown, and Henderson worked collaboratively, bouncing lyric and musical ideas off each other, so that characterizing one person as "lyricist" and the other as "composer" is really beside the point.

Creating an independent song required just a kernel of an idea, either verbal or musical. In the world of Tin Pan Alley, sometimes the title would be the first to come. Of course, topical songs taken from newspaper headlines have always been in vogue, starting with the beginning of Tin Pan Alley when Isadore Witmark composed "President Grover Cleveland's Wedding March" (1886), when it was revealed that he would be getting married in the White House, the first president to do so. Songs were also written to order to respond to specific fads: a hit written on the subject of a new invention (such as the automobile) would inspire dozens more on the same subject. Specific genres of songs—such as coon songs, dialect songs, or dance songs—developed over time and could inspire many new creations.

Writing a song for a theatrical production presents special problems for its creators, since most character- or plot-specific songs are not potential "hits." Beginning with Rodgers and Hammerstein's 1943 hit, *Oklahoma!*, the notion of fitting the songs to complement the musical's story became all-important, rather than simply dropping songs into a show almost as an afterthought. The first thing the theater composer and lyricist do is to plan how many songs they will need and the purpose each will serve in the context of the show. Will a song be used to create a mood, or can this mood be better expressed in dialogue? Would this song be sung by this character at this point in the show?

However, as Tin Pan Alley composers became more focused on providing songs for Broadway shows, it became more difficult for them to produce stand-alone hits. Changing musical tastes—such as the development of country, R and B, and rock and roll—also contributed to a changing pop-music landscape that the Alley composers did not recognize quickly. Some publishers spotted the new markets and responded by producing songs geared toward them; others remained committed to the earlier styles. Few composers, however, could adapt their styles to the new world; Irving Berlin retired decades before his death when he realized that he could no longer create songs to fit contemporary popular tastes.

# Zez Confrey

Composer (b. Edward Elzear Confrey, Peru, Illinois, April 3, 1895; d. Lakewood, New Jersey, November 22, 1971). Confrey composed more than ninety piano pieces, influencing the playing of his contemporaries and creating the vogue for novelty rags in the 1920s. He studied at Florenz Ziegfeld Sr.'s, Chicago Musical College, where he was exposed to the French impressionist composers, who had a profound influence on his own composition. In 1915, he obtained a job demonstrating music for the Chicago branch of the HARRY VON TILZER MUSIC Publishing Company. At the start of World War I, he enlisted in the Navy and was featured in a skit with a touring show, *Leave It to the Sailors.* Part of the routine paired Confrey with a violinist from Waukegan who would become known as Jack Benny. When the show broke up and he left the Navy, Confrey auditioned for the QRS piano roll company, where he was hired as an arranger and pianist. During his stay at QRS, he arranged and played 123 rolls. His arrangements were tasteful and filled with rollicking inspiration. His proficiency at making rolls and composing hit tunes led him into recording (piano solos for Brunswick, Edison, and Emerson, playing with an orchestra for Victor) and appearing in vaudeville. His first novelty rag was the revolutionary "My Pet," closely followed by "Greenwich Witch," "Poor Buttermilk," "You Tell 'Em Ivories," "Coaxing the Piano," and, in 1921, his landmark "Kitten on the Keys." To ensure the proper effect in "Kitten on the Keys" third section, Confrey advised, "Be sure to scramble up the octaves in the part which is supposed to sound like a cat bouncing down the keyboard. In other words, make a fist when simulating the cat running up and down, otherwise it won't sound real." The sheet music sold over one million copies, as did his recording of it (Victor 18900). It was like "Maple Leaf Rag" all over again: another difficult piano rag defined a genre and became a hit at the same time. Though "Kitten" was the most technically advanced rag yet published, it sold quickly and enormously.

In 1922, Zez Confrey had three hits: "Dumbbell," "Tricks," and, the perennial favorite, "Stumbling," the first pop song to use a 3/4 rhythm inside a 4/4 time signature. Its opening figure is built on the five-tone scale, later used by IRVING BERLIN in "Always"; by RICHARD

A smiling Zez Confrey at the height of his fame in the 1920s.

Whiting in "Louise" and "Breezin' Along with the Breeze"; by Vincent Rose in "Linger Awhile"; by Hoagy Carmichael in "Ole Buttermilk Sky"; by George Gershwin in "Looking for a Boy" and "They All Laughed"; by Livingston and Evans in "Buttons and Bows"; and by Paul Denniker in "S'posin."

The following year, Confrey came out with another smash novelty piano rag, "Dizzy Fingers," as well as the clever "Nickel in the Slot." He was such an outstanding talent that he was asked to participate in a historic concert at Aeolian Hall in New York City. Held on February 12, 1924, the concert was billed as "Paul Whiteman and his Palais Royal Orchestra will offer an Experiment in Modern Music, assisted by Zez Confrey and George Gershwin." Later that year, he contracted to make piano rolls exclusively for Ampico. In 1933, he and Byron Gay wrote the hit "Sittin' on a Log (Pettin' My Dog)."

# Con Conrad

Composer (b. Conrad K. Dober, New York City, June 18, 1891; d. Van Nuys, California, September 28, 1938). His debut in show business was as a pianist at the Vanity Fair Theatre on 125th Street in New York City. He soon met Jay Whidden (1886–1968), a boilermaker who wanted to be a violinist. They teamed up to play on the Keith circuit, had their first song published as "Down in Dear Old New Orleans" (1912), and were signed for a London revue. Conrad came back home from World War I and wrote the hit "Oh! Frenchy" (1918).

Early in the 1920s, teamed with pianist-composer J. Russel Robinson, Conrad turned out three hits in a row. The first was "Margie" (1920), with words by Benny Davis; the second was "Singing the Blues," with words by Sam Lewis and Joe Young; and the third was "Palesteena," which they wrote by themselves. The Original Dixieland Jazz Band (ODJB) recorded a double-sided best-seller (Victor 18717) that produced *three* hits; the "Margie" side included a chorus of "Singing the Blues" (as noted on the record label) and "Palesteena" was on the other side of the disc. The pianist for this recording, not very coincidentally, was Robinson. The record sold over two million copies. In one form or another, these recorded performances were in print from the time of the record's release in September 1920 to late 1975, when the ODJB LP was finally deleted from the Victor catalog. No other record has been in print continuously for so long a time.

"Ma! (He's Making Eyes at Me)" was Conrad's 1921 entry in the hit parade. With words by Sidney Clare (1892–1972), it gave Eddie Cantor another in the series of songs permanently identified with him. Cantor featured it in his revue *The Midnight Rounders*. And Eubie Blake made an outstanding piano recording that year (Emerson 10450). Another song of 1921, for which Conrad wrote both words and music, was "Moonlight." It was a beautiful ballad that received its major boost from Paul Whiteman's recording (Victor 18756).

Starting in 1923, Conrad teamed with BILLY ROSE, and they wrote three songs that are still played by jazz bands. The first was "Barney Google," based on Billy De Beck's comic strip. Olson and Johnson first featured it in their vaudeville act by having an actor in a horse costume ridden in the aisles by another actor dressed like Barney Google while the team sang the song. It caught on, with Eddie Cantor plugging it and with Georgie Price's recording (Victor 19066). The writers capitalized on the song with a follow-up, "Come On, Spark Plug!" The covers of both songs had drawings by De Beck to help sell them. The last of their 1923 hits became a jazz standard, "You've Got to See Mamma Ev'ry Night (Or You Can't See Mamma at All)," initially made famous by "the Last of the Red-Hot Mamas," SOPHIE TUCKER (Okeh 4817). "Lonesome and Sorry" (1926), with Benny Davis as lyricist, was featured by Davis in vaudeville. It was also featured by a young comedian, Milton Berle. JEAN GOLDKETTE and his orchestra recorded it (Victor 20031).

Conrad went to California to write for the movies. His first assignment was for William Fox in 1929, to write the score for the Fox *Movietone Follies*. "Walking with Susie" was the best of the lot. In 1931, Conrad discovered RUSS COLUMBO and became his manager, writing "Prisoner of Love" and "You Call It Madness but I Call It Love," for him to do vocal battle with his rival, BING CROSBY. Conrad teamed with Herb Magidson (1906–1986) to write for films in 1934. That year, they won the first Oscar for Best Song with "The Continental," from RKO's *The Gay Divorcee*, starring FRED ASTAIRE and GINGER ROGERS. Although Conrad continued to compose for films until his death, he never again achieved a major hit from films.

# Will Marion Cook

Composer (b. William Mercer Cook, Washington, D.C., January 27, 1869; d. New York City, July 19, 1944). Cook was one of the first great African-American theatrical composers and a major influence on DUKE ELLINGTON. Both of his parents attended Oberlin College, and his father was a lawyer in Washington, D.C. Cook also was educated at Oberlin, and then studied composition in Germany from 1888 to 1890, thanks to family friend Frederick Douglass. When he returned to Washington, Cook formed his own orchestra, again thanks to Douglass's patronage, and took the stage name "Will Marion Cook." Douglass arranged for Cook to provide music for "Colored Folks' Day" at the 1893 Chicago World's Fair. In 1894, Cook arrived in New York and began studying with composer Antonin Dvorak, and briefly worked for theater producer Bob Cole's All-Star Stock Company, his introduction to the world of popular music. Around the beginning of 1897, Cook met the famed vaudevillians WILLIAMS AND WALKER, and pitched to them an idea for a musical play about the development of the CAKEWALK. With lyricist (and famed poet) Paul Laurence Dunbar, he wrote *Clorindy, or the Origin of the Cakewalk*, which premiered on July 5, 1898, with Cook conducting. Its syncopated numbers—notably the COON SONG "Who Dat Say Chicken in Dis Crowd?"—were an immediate sensation, introducing ragtime rhythms to Broadway.

Cook continued to write shows, scoring his next big hit again with Williams and Walker in the show *In Dahomey* (1903), this time with lyrics by Ernest Hogan. Cook and Hogan collaborated next on another show, *The Southerners*, and then formed a "singing orchestra," known as The Memphis Students, to perform Cook's songs. When Hogan split from Cook, Cook took the renamed Tennessee Students on a successful European tour in 1905. Cook scored two other Williams and Walker shows, most notably 1908's *Bandanna Land*, which featured the song "Bon Bon Buddy" (with lyrics by Alex Rogers), which Walker made into Cook's biggest popular hit. In 1912, Cook's music was featured in a landmark Carnegie Hall concert staged by JAMES REESE EUROPE; it featured his choral works "Rain Song" and "Swing Along," which became his best-known compositions thanks to their publication for vocal choir by G. Schirmer that year. Cook would never again enjoy such popular success, although he continued to work as a composer and bandleader until his death from cancer in 1944.

# Coon-Sanders Nighthawks

The Coon-Sanders Original Nighthawk Orchestra was a unique band. Its popularity transcended its own time, and it is honored today by a fan club that meets annually, with a festival devoted entirely to it and its tunes. The original band, its arrangements, and particular members had a sound and spirit unlike any of the hundreds of other bands in the 1920s.

Carleton A. Coon (1894–1932) and Joe L. Sanders (1896–1965) met in a Kansas City, Missouri, music store. As a result of that chance meeting, they formed a jazz-oriented dance band. Coon was the drummer and shared vocal duties with Sanders, the pianist and arranger. The distinctive arrangements made by Sanders featured the spreading of the voicings in the saxophone section, letting each instrument be heard clearly, whether in solo or ensemble playing. The Sanders arrangements included modern harmonies and sophisticated modulations, sometimes within a measure of an ancient ragtime break. Their careful blend of old and new sounds made this band distinctive. Sanders composed instrumentals and pop songs that became audience favorites.

This band was one of the first to appear on radio, with a nightly show on station WDAF in the Muehlebach Hotel in Kansas City. They broadcast from eleven at night till two in the morning, forming the "Knights and Ladies of the Bath" and giving themselves the name Nighthawks. Western Union installed a ticker tape in the ballroom so that the leaders could play requests and acknowledge their fans while on the air. During those pioneering radio days, the band, broadcasting late at night, could be heard halfway around the country. Their announcer—or, as they called him, "The Merry Old Chief"—was Leo Fitzgerald. Sanders was a grand showman and air personality, full of warmth and good cheer. Coon and Sanders were featured on practically every number, either separately or in duet, their voices blending perfectly.

In 1924, the Nighthawks went to Chicago, where they played at the Congress Hotel. They started making their more than eighty sides for the Victor Talking Machine Company in April of that year. Their first recording was of their theme song, "Night Hawk Blues" (1924), with words and music by Sanders (Victor 19396). The band became so popular that when Chicago's Blackhawk Restaurant opened in 1926, it booked the Coon-Sanders Orchestra. It also began broadcasting nightly over station WGN, solidifying its nationwide popularity. Its tours, college dances, and one-night stands were always sold out.

The Sanders instrumentals included "High Fever" (1926, Victor 20461), "Brainstorm" (1926, Victor 20390), "Roodles" (1927, Victor 20785), and "Blazin' " (1928, Victor 21680). Sanders's pop songs included "Sluefoot" (1927, Victor 21305), "What a Girl! What a Night!" (1928, Victor 21803), "Little Orphan Annie" (1928, Victor 21895), with lyrics by GUS KAHN, and "Tennessee Lazy" (1929, Victor 21939), with lyrics by Carleton Coon.

During the twelve years it was together (1920–1932), the band's personnel remained amazingly constant. The men's personalities were reflected in their lively, happy music. For the last seven years, the personnel didn't change at all. The band consisted of Bob Pope and Joe Richolson, trumpets; Rex Downing, trombone; Harold Thiell, John Thiell, and Floyd Estep, on clarinet, alto sax, and tenor sax, respectively; Joe Sanders, piano and vocal; Russ Stout, banjo; Elmer Krebs, tuba; and Carleton Coon, drums and vocal. The band's big request number was "Here Comes My Ball and Chain" (1929), a marvelous comic song written by J. FRED COOTS and Lou Davis (Victor 21812). They also scored heavily with "Darktown Strutters' Ball" (Victor 22342), "Some of These Days" (Victor 19600), and "On Revival Day" (Victor 22979).

The Coon-Sanders Orchestra was truly a 1920s musical highlight.

# Coon Songs

It is an American characteristic to ridicule, caricature, parody, lampoon, and generally make fun of ethnic groups. During the waves of immigration and dating back as far as slavery, ethnic songs abounded. So-called "coon songs" emerged as a specific genre in the 1890s and enjoyed great popularity over the next two decades, and many songwriters produced hits.

The first black face on a sheet music cover was the drawing on "Coal Black Rose," issued around 1829. The rise of blackface minstrelsy in the 1840s popularized two stereotyped black images: "Zip Coon," an up-to-date dandy, and "Jim Crow," a slow-witted, rural dweller. These stereotypes were given prominence through early song hits such as Dan Rice's "Jump Jim Crow" and the dance tune "Old Zip Coon," now better-known as "Turkey in the Straw." Stephen Foster is perhaps the most famous composer of minstrel-style songs (although he also wrote songs in other styles).

Coon songs were descendants of these earlier minstrel hits. Their major innovation was the introduction of syncopation. Thanks to the rise of Tin Pan Alley publishers, the songs were also national hits (whereas earlier minstrel numbers were published and performed regionally). Despite their somewhat prejudiced lyrics and themes, coon songs were written by both black and white composers seeking hits; "serious" African-American composer WILL MARION COOK, and pop songwriters Ernest Hogan (writing the still shocking "All Coons Look Alike to Me") and COLE AND JOHNSON all produced coon melodies, and well-known poet Paul Laurence Dunbar wrote coon lyrics.

Although there were dozens of hit coon songs published from the mid-1890s through the mid-1910s, most have been forgotten today. Some of the more lasting coon songs were HUGHIE CANNON's "Bill Bailey, Won't You Please Come Home" (1902); George Fairman's "The Preacher and the Bear" (1904); Barney Fagan's "My Gal Is a High Born Lady" (1896); and Theodore Metz's "Hot Time in the Old Town" (1896).

# J. Fred Coots

Composer (b. Brooklyn, New York, May 2, 1897; d. New York City, April 8, 1985). He started in the Alley as a stock clerk and piano demonstrator in the New York branch of Chicago's McKinley Music. His first big hit, "Doin' the Raccoon" (1928), with lyrics by Ray Klages, was made by the George Olsen band's recording (Victor 21701). The same year, Coots and Lou Davis wrote "A Precious Little Thing Called Love," which was introduced by Nancy Carroll in the film *The Shopworn Angel* (1929). It sold over two million copies of sheet music.

"I Still Get a Thrill Thinking of You" (1930), with words by BENNY DAVIS, was popularized by Hal Kemp and his orchestra. It was revived in 1950 by DINAH SHORE. "Love Letters in the Sand" (1931) was written with Charles and Nick Kenny. It was introduced by Dolly Dawn and became the theme song of George Hall and his orchestra. RUSS COLUMBO made a hit recording of it. It was revived with a best-selling record by Pat Boone in 1957 (Dot 15570). Boone also sang it in the film *Bernadine*. "Two Tickets to Georgia" (1933), with lyrics by Joe Young and Charles Tobias, was introduced by Ted Lewis and popularized by the Pickens Sisters.

"For All We Know" (1934), with lyrics by Sam M. Lewis, is one of the most beautiful ballads ever composed. Introduced by Morton Downey, it was featured by Isham Jones (Victor 24681). In a revival, The Voices of Walter Schumann made a magnificent recording (Capitol 1505). "Santa Claus Is Coming to Town" (1934), with lyrics by Haven Gillespie (1888–1975), is Coots's Christmas standard. It was introduced by Eddie Cantor on his radio program and became an instant hit, selling over four million copies. Hit recordings were made by Bing Crosby with the Andrews Sisters (Decca 23281), the Pied Pipers with Paul Weston's orchestra (Capitol 15004), Ozzie Nelson and his orchestra (Columbia 35786), and Tommy Dorsey and his orchestra (Victor 25145).

"A Beautiful Lady in Blue" (1935) has lyrics by Sam M. Lewis. Jan Garber and his orchestra had the hit recording (Deccca 651). "You Go to My Head" (1938), with lyrics by Haven Gillespie, became the theme song of Mitchell Ayres and his orchestra. Its first recording was by Larry Clinton and his orchestra, with a vocal by Bea Wain (Victor 25849). This classic was later recorded by Glen Gray and the Casa Loma Orchestra, Frank Sinatra, Doris Day, and Billy Eckstine.

# Sam Coslow

Lyricist and vocalist (b. New York City, December 27, 1902; d. New York City, April 2, 1982). Coslow was one of the key lyricists of pop songs of the 1920s and 1930s, often working with composer Arthur Johnston (b. New York City, January 10, 1898; d. Corona del Mar, California, May 5, 1954). Coslow began writing songs in school, and had a hit in 1920 with "Grieving for You." He struggled for success on Broadway, but meanwhile formed a publishing company, Spier and Coslow, and also recorded as a popular vocalist. Coslow moved to Hollywood in 1929 at the birth of the sound film. Working primarily with Johnston, he provided lyrics for dozens of films through the 1930s, producing hits with songs including "Learn to Croon" from 1933's *College Humor*, starring Bing Crosby who also had the hit on record "My Old Flame," introduced by Mae West *in Belle of the Nineties* (1934) and recorded by her with Duke Ellington's orchestra, and later a favorite of 1950s jazz musicians; and "Cocktails for Two," featured in the 1934 film *Murder at the Vanities*, and a # 1 hit for Ellington (Victor 24617). In 1939, the duo wrote "I'm in Love with an Honorable Mr. So-and-So" for the dramatic film *Society Lawyer*, sung in a nightclub sequence by Virginia

Bruce. In the early 1940s, Coslow and Franklin Roosevelt's son James founded the Soundies Company, which forecast the music video craze by four decades. The idea was to have coin-operated machines installed in bars (like jukeboxes) that would play short musical films instead of records. After World War II, Coslow founded a business publishing newsletters outside of the music industry before his retirement.

# Noel Coward

Composer, lyricist, playwright, actor, and singer (b. Noel Pierce Coward, Teddington, England, December 16, 1899; d. Port Maria, Jamaica, March 26, 1973). A well-known, witty British lyricist, Coward produced songs that have been cabaret favorites, although most were not originally charting hits.

Coward's father was a piano salesman, and Coward began playing piano by ear as a young child. He also appeared in a London Christmas pantomime in his early teens. He wrote his first song at age sixteen, and placed a song in the London show *Tails Up* in June 1918. His songs were first heard in America in *Andre Charlot's Revue of 1924*, which included Coward's "Parisian Pierrot." Two years later, Coward's songs were the main feature of the *Charlot Revue of 1926*, including the hit "Poor Little Rich Girl," which was recorded by British songstress Gertrude Lawrence.

As an actor, Coward starred in his own plays, recorded his own songs, and costarred with Gertrude Lawrence in *Tonight at 8:30*. He recorded many of his songs, including two he wrote for the 1929 musical *Bitter Sweet*: "I'll See You Again" (Victor 27228; also a hit for Leo Reisman and his orchestra) and "Zigeuner" (Victor 24772). In 1930, he interpolated "Someday I'll Find You" into his play *Private Lives*. "Mad Dogs and Englishmen" came from the 1931 musical revue *The Third Little Show* (Victor 24332); it was sung on stage by Beatrice Lillie. "Half Caste Boy" was sung the same year by HELEN MORGAN in that year's *Ziegfeld Follies*. "Mad About the Boy" was a 1932 entry, not written for a show; it was revived by RAY NOBLE and his orchestra in autumn 1935 for a record hit. "I'll Follow My Secret Heart" (1934) came from his play *Conversation Piece*, and also was popularized on disc by Noble. "Mrs. Worthington" found great success as a party piece and was published in 1935.

Coward was active through the 1940s and 1950s on stage and as a performer. His live album, *Noel Coward at Las Vegas*, charted in January 1956, and he also was featured in a TV special that year with Broadway singer Mary Martin. The 1960s saw two Coward musicals on Broadway, *Sail Away* (1961) and *The Girl Who Came to Supper* (1963). His lyrics, which sparkled with wit and elegance, matched his gorgeous melodies, and in the 1972–1973 season many found their way into a Broadway revue, *Oh, Coward!*

# Francis Craig

Bandleader and songwriter (b. Dickson, Tennessee, September 10, 1900; d. Sewanee, Tennessee, November 19, 1966). Following service in World War I, Craig attended Vanderbilt University and in 1920 founded his first dance band. Upon graduation in 1922, he went professional, leading a popular dance band at Nashville's Hermitage Hotel from 1924 through 1946; the band gained national exposure through a radio hookup via Nashville's powerful WSM (home of *The Grand Ole Opry*). Vocalists who got a start with the band included DINAH SHORE, Anita Kerr (later a leader of the famous Anita Kerr Singers), and Kenny Sargent. Craig decided to give up the band in 1946, and made one final recording as his swan song. It was the song "Near You" with lyrics by Kermit Goell, which was released by the fledgling Nashville-based Bullet label in 1947, featuring vocalist Bob Lamm accompanied by Craig and his band; it became a major hit, and was subsequently given a long afterlife when Milton Berle adopted it as his sign-off tune for his popular television program. In 1948, he wrote "Beg Your Pardon" with Beasley Smith, which reached #3 on the pop charts. Craig also composed "Red Rose," which he used as his band's theme song. He subsequently returned to radio work in Nashville and died in 1966.

# Henry Creamer

See *Turner Layton*

# Bing Crosby

Composer, singer, and film actor (b. Harry Lillis Crosby, Tacoma, Washington, May 2, 1903; d. Madrid, Spain, October 14, 1977). Crosby was the outstanding popularizer of songs in his time, thanks to hosting a network radio show for fifteen years, prolific recordings, and introducing songs in film. As a composer, he co-wrote his theme song "Where the Blue of the Night," "From Monday On," "At Your Command," "I Don't Stand a Ghost of a Chance With You," and "Love Me Tonight."

Crosby was nicknamed "Bing" as a child after a cartoon character whose exploits he followed in a local newspaper. By his teens, he was playing drums in a local band, and during the early 1920s, while attending college, partnered with another local would-be entertainer, Al Rinker, whose sister, singer MILDRED BAILEY, was already successfully performing in Los Angeles. In 1925, Crosby dropped out of college after Bailey arranged for him and Rinker to tour the West Coast as a vaudeville duo. They made their recording debut in autumn 1926, and that December they were hired by PAUL WHITEMAN to join Harry Barris and become The Rhythm Boys. Whiteman toured the vocal trio separately from his band from August 1927 for about a year, following the hit release "Muddy Water" (lyrics by Jo Trent, with music by Peter DeRose and HARRY RICHMAN) that featured Crosby's lead vocals which was released that June. After making the movie *King of Jazz* (1930), they left Whiteman to join GUS ARNHEIM's orchestra at the Cocoanut Grove in Los Angeles.

Crosby began his solo career in 1931 with a nightly radio show. His theme song was "Where the Blue of the Night," which he kept throughout his career. He began to record extensively and to appear in feature films, the first of which was *The Big Broadcast* (1932). His first starring role came in his next film, *College Humor* (1933). He traded his heavily romantic crooning for a lighter, more airy style, helped in great part by John Scott Trotter's arrangements (he was Crosby's musical director on radio and on records). His most successful recordings, starting in 1931, include "Out of Nowhere" (Brunswick 6090), "Just One More Chance" (Brunswick 6120), and "At Your Command" (Brunswick 6145). In 1932 he had "Dinah" (Brunswick 6240), "Where the Blue of the Night" (Brunswick 6226), "Please" (Brunswick 6394), and "Brother, Can You Spare a Dime?" (Brunswick 6414). From the 1933 film *Forty-second Street* came "You're Getting to Be a Habit with Me" (Brunswick 6472) and "Shadow Waltz" from the film *Gold Diggers of 1933* (Brunswick 6599). 1934 saw three more #1 hits: "Little Dutch Mill" (Brunswick 6794); "Love in Bloom," which became Jack Benny's theme song (Brunswick 6936); and "June in January" (Decca 310). 1935 brought "Soon" from his film *Mississippi* (Decca 392), "It's Easy to Remember" (Decca 391), "Red Sails in the Sunset" (Decca 616), and "Silent Night, Holy Night," which over the years proved one of the biggest discs of all time, selling an estimated ten million copies. "Pennies from Heaven" came from the 1936 film of the same name (Decca 947).

Bing Crosby (right) chats with composer Irving Berlin, c. the mid-1930s.

1937 saw five Crosby songs in the #1 position on the pop charts. The first was the million-seller and Academy Award winner "Sweet Leilani" (Decca 1175), followed by "Too Marvelous for Words" (Decca 1185), "The Moon Got in My Eyes" (Decca 1375), "Remember Me?" (Decca 1451), and "Bob White (Whatcha Gonna Swing Tonight?)" (Decca 1483). 1938 gave him three #1 hits: "I've Got a Pocketful of Dreams" (Decca 1933), "Alexander's Ragtime Band" with Connee Boswell (Decca 1887), and "You Must Have Been a Beautiful Baby" (Decca 2147). 1940 also saw three #1 hits: "Sierra Sue" (Decca 3133), "Trade Winds" (Decca 3299), and "Only Forever" (Decca 3300). 1942 brought Crosby's biggest-selling record and best-selling disc of all time, "White Christmas," which has sold more than thirty million copies (Decca 18429). From his film *The Road to Morocco* came another #1 hit, "Moonlight Becomes You" (Decca 18513). 1943's #1 hits were "Sunday, Monday, or Always" (Decca 18561), which sold over a million copies, as did "I'll Be Home for Christmas" (Decca 18570). 1944 had four #1 Crosby hits—with two million-sellers: "San Fernando Valley" (Decca 18586) and "I Love You" from the show *Mexican Hayride* (Decca 18597). Also in 1944 came "I'll Be Seeing You" (Decca 18595); "Swinging on a Star," which won the Academy Award for Best Song (Decca 18597); and "Too-Ra-Loo-Ra-Loo-Ral" (Decca 18621). 1945 brought two more #1 hits: "It's Been a Long, Long Time" (Decca 18708) and "I Can't Begin to Tell You" (Decca 23457), which sold over a million copies. "McNamara's Band" sold a million copies in 1946, not bad for a song published in 1917 (Decca 23405). "Alexander's Ragtime Band" proved lucky once more, as Crosby's 1947 duet with AL JOLSON sold over a million copies (Decca 40038). Another million-seller of 1947 was "The Whiffenpoof Song," originally published in 1909 (Decca 23990). 1948 brought yet another million-seller with "Now Is the Hour" (Decca 24279). In 1949, "Galway Bay," charting at only #3 still sold over a million copies (Decca 24295), as did Bing's #2 hit, "Dear Hearts and Gentle People" (Decca 24798). His next million-seller came in 1950 when he and son Gary recorded IRVING BERLIN's 1914 double song "Play a Simple Melody" (Decca 27112). Decca Records teamed Crosby with the ANDREWS SISTERS occasionally from 1939 to 1951, and they came up with two million-selling successes: "Pistol Packin' Mama" (Decca 23277) in 1943 and "Don't Fence Me In" (Decca 23364) in 1944. Crosby ended his hit-making career on discs with his 1956 million-selling recording with Grace Kelly of "True Love" (Capitol 3507).

Crosby was one of the greatest entertainers of the twentieth century, recording more than two thousand songs, selling a total of over five hundred million copies, with "White Christmas" alone accounting for more than thirty million discs. He was a movie star for over twenty years, appearing in over sixty films, and winning an Academy Award for *Going My Way* in 1944. He was in the Top 10 box office stars for five consecutive years in the 1940s and was listed among the Top 10 radio personalities for over twenty years.

Crosby's brother, Bob Crosby (b. Spokane, Washington, August 25, 1913; d. La Jolla, California, March 9, 1993), was a noted bandleader and helped promote many songs through recordings and radio appearances.

# Xavier Cugat

Popular Latin-styled bandleader (b. Gerona, Spain, January 1, 1900; d. Barcelona, Spain, October 21, 1990). Cugat was a favorite on television during the early 1950s, when the cha-cha became popular, and he was an important vehicle for the new Latin sounds invading the Alley. He organized a band specializing in Latin music, and opened at the Cocoanut Grove in Los Angeles. Besides being the most famous bandleader in this style, Cugat was also a noted caricaturist. His artwork often appeared on sheet music covers. He composed a beautiful theme, "My Shawl" (1934), with lyrics by STANLEY ADAMS (Victor 24508). His other compositions include "Rain in Spain" (1934, Victor 24387), "Night Must Fall" (1939, Victor 26074), and "Nightingale" (1942, Columbia 36559).

From the 1930s through the 1950s, Cugat made many successful appearances at the Waldorf-Astoria Hotel in New York City. The Cugat band was one of three featured on the now-historic *Let's Dance* program (which brought fame to BENNY GOODMAN and his orchestra). During the 1940s, Cugat had several radio programs and often appeared as a guest on the shows of others. He was a regular on the Garry Moore–JIMMY DURANTE show.

Cugat and his orchestra appeared in more films than any other dance band: *Go West, Young Man* (1936), *You Were Never Lovelier* (1942), *The Heat's On* (1943), *Stage Door Canteen* (1943), *Bathing Beauty* (1944), *Two Girls and a Sailor* (1944), *Weekend at the Waldorf* (1945),

Xavier Cugat pulls the bow on the cover of his "It's Easy When You Know How," published by Pemora Music Co.

*Holiday in Mexico* (1946), *No Leave, No Love* (1946), *This Time for Keeps* (1947), *A Date with Judy* (1948), *Luxury Liner* (1948), *On an Island with You* (1948), *Neptune's Daughter* (1949), *Chicago Syndicate* (1955), and *The Phynx* (1969).

A typical roster of Cugat personnel included Phil Hart and Joseph Piana, trumpets; Ruben Moss and Max Nadel, clarinet, alto sax, and tenor sax; Xavier Cugat and Max Warnowsky, violins; Nilo Menendez, piano; Billy Hobbs, piano-accordion; Pedro Berrios, guitar; Florence Wightman, harp; Charles Gonzales, string bass; Albert Calderon and Catalino Rolon, drums, maracas, claves; Antonio Lopez, bongos. His vocalists included Carmen Castillo, Lina Romay, and Miguelito Valdes. And Charo!

Among Cugat's many record hits were "Isle of Capri" (Victor 24813), "The Lady in Red (Victor 25012), "Begin the Beguine" (Victor 25133), "Say 'Si Si' " (Victor 25407), "Perfidia" (Victor 26334), "The Breeze and I" (Victor 26641), "La Cucaracha" (Columbia 36091), and "Thrill Me" (Columbia 38558).

# Cut-In

Someone other than the composer and lyricist getting credit for writing a song. Usually, the person being cut in on the royalty is either a big-name performer or a publisher. The purpose of the cut-in was to get the performer to promote a song; by giving him or her a cut of the royalty, a publisher gave the performer a financial incentive to make a song into a hit. AL JOLSON and Milton Berle were notorious for getting their names on songs they promoted but didn't write. Irving Mills and CLARENCE WILLIAMS were publishers who attached their names to songs they published but didn't write; in effect, they were double-dipping, taking a cut of the writer's royalty when they were already profiting from publishing the song itself. During the 1950s, when deejays became powerful in promoting songs, they were often cut in as a song's "composer," again as an incentive to promote the song by giving it additional airplay.

# D

## Charles N. Daniels

Composer (b. Leavenworth, Kansas, April 12, 1878; d. Los Angeles, California, January 21, 1943). He grew up in Kansas City, Kansas. In high school, he studied music theory, piano, and music calligraphy. Upon graduation, he joined the Carl Hoffman Music Company as a song demonstrator during the day, and he accompanied singers for the Kronberg Concert Company at night. In 1898, the Hoffman firm offered a prize of $25.00 for the best two-step by a local composer. Daniels, after much prodding by friends, competed for the prize, winning it with his song "Margery." At that time John Philip Sousa was playing at the Coats Opera House there. Sousa heard of the contest, offered to perform the winning work, and, much to everyone's amazement, made it an instant success. This led to a lasting friendship with Sousa, which came in handy for Daniels throughout his career. Though "Margery" sold 275,000 copies, the Hoffman firm owned the copyright, so Daniels had to be content with his prize money and some favorable publicity. But the tune's success led to his promotion as manager for Hoffman.

In December 1898, Daniels, acting for the firm, purchased SCOTT JOPLIN's "Original Rags," thus beginning his involvement with ragtime. In time, he became the most significant ragtime entrepreneur after JOHN STARK. He purchased Charles L. Johnson's "Dill Pickles" for Jerome Remick and made it into a million-selling sensation, thereby contributing greatly to the boom years of ragtime. He encouraged the composing of rags by his firm's staff, accepted unsolicited manuscripts, and purchased small-town publishers' rags. He nurtured ragtime until it was a flourishing and significant part of the popular sheet music industry. Curiously, for all his promotion of rags, he composed only a few of them, notably "Classic Rag" in 1909, under his famous pseudonym "Neil Moret," and the rag "Cotton Time" in 1910.

The same year that he purchased Joplin's "Original Rags," Daniels composed a song, "You Tell Me Your Dream, I'll Tell You Mine," which became a big hit, and also founded the publishing firm of Daniels, Russel and Boone. The next year, he left Kansas City for St. Louis, where he managed the sheet music department of the Barr Dry Goods Company. In 1901, Daniels published his Indian song, "Hiawatha," which became a success after Daniels prevailed upon Sousa to perform and record it (Victor 2443). The following year, when Jerome Remick purchased Whitney Warner of Detroit, he paid Daniels $10,000 for his firm so that Remick could have "Hiawatha." It was the highest sum yet paid for a song. With it went an offer to head up the Whitney Warner company as manager, so Daniels moved to Detroit in 1902. The following year, James O'Dea added words to "Hiawatha," and sales zoomed again when it became a song. Thus started the trend of Indian songs, which were extremely popular during the first decade of the twentieth century.

When he moved to San Francisco in 1912, Daniels formed another company, this time in partnership with Weston Wilson. Most notably, in 1918 they published Daniels's title song commissioned by Mack Sennett for *Mickey*, his silent film starring Mabel Normand. This was the first motion picture title song. It is remarkable that promoting a silent movie with a song took as long as it did. (The first silent film, "The Sneeze," an extremely short subject starring Fred Ott, was made in 1893.) But once producers caught on to this marketing gimmick, they didn't stop, and we find that most of the songs written for films today are title songs.

From 1924 to 1931, Daniels was president of Villa Moret, Inc., in San Francisco. Sensing that movies, with their new "sound tracks," and commercial radio were cutting into sheet music sales, Daniels decided to withdraw from active management in the music business. During the years he owned his own firms, Daniels composed hit songs that sold into the millions: "Moonlight and Roses," "Mello Cello," "Song of the Wanderer," "Chloe," "She's Funny That Way," "In Monterey," and "Sweet and Lovely."

# Benny Davis

Vocalist and lyricist (b. New York City, August 21, 1895; d. Miami, Florida December 20, 1979). Davis worked as a singer on the vaudeville circuit, and began composing songs in the late 1910s with various collaborators. His first major hit was 1920's "Margie," written with

Con Conrad and J. Russel Robinson, which became a major hit for Eddie Cantor (Emerson 10301). Davis continued to be successful, working with several leading composers of the 1920s and 1930s, scoring hits with 1924's "Oh, How I Miss You Tonight," written with Joe Burke and Mark Fisher, and recorded by Ben Selvin and his orchestra; "Yearning (Just for You)" (1925) and "Carolina Moon," a big hit for crooner Gene Austin (Victor 21833) and revived in 1958 by Connie Francis, both written with Burke; and 1925's "Baby Face," composed with Harry Akst, which Eddie Cantor made famous. The first recording was made by Jan Garber's orchestra, with Davis as vocalist (Victor 20105). Davis would continue to be active through the 1960s, achieving latter-day pop hits with Connie Francis, who scored a #1 hit in 1962 with Davis and composer Carl Fischer's "Don't Break the Heart That Loves You" (MGM 13059). Davis also owned several music-publishing businesses.

# Gussie L. Davis

African-American songwriter (b. Gussie Lord Davis, Dayton, Ohio, December 3, 1863; d. Whitestone, New York, October 18, 1899). Davis was a Gay Nineties songwriter most famous for the sentimental hit "In the Baggage Coach Ahead."

Davis moved to Cincinnati in his middle teens to attend Nelson Musical College. Because he was black, his application was rejected, so he made a deal with the administration to trade janitorial services for private lessons. His first song, "We Sat Beneath the Maple on the Hill," was published by Helling and Company, a local printer, in 1880. Whenever he saw the song in a shop window, Davis would point and say, "That's me. I done it." Davis partnered with a local music publisher and lyricist, George Propheter, in the early 1880s to compose songs; in 1886, Propheter moved his business to New York City, inviting Davis to accompany him as his musical director.

It took seven years, but Davis finally scored a hit with the tear-jerking ballad "The Fatal Wedding," with lyrics by black singer William H. Windom. Its success led to Davis's being made secretary of the black entertainers guild, the Colored Professionals Club. In 1894, he was asked to join Bob Cole's All-Star Stock Company as a resident composer (Will Marion Cook was the other composer for the company). And in 1895, Davis entered a contest sponsored by the *New York World* to find the ten best songwriters in the United States. He came in second with his tearjerker "Send Back the Picture and the Ring."

However, Davis's biggest hit—and best-remembered song—would come in 1896. Before he came to New York and became a full-time songwriter, Davis worked as a Pullman porter. On one train trip, he came upon a little girl crying bitterly. When he asked about her trouble, the child informed him that her mother was in the baggage coach ahead, in a coffin. Several years later he remembered that incident, wrote "In the Baggage Coach Ahead," and sold it outright to Howley, Haviland and Company. The publisher turned it into one of the hits of 1896, in part due to the plugging by the "Queen of Song," Imogene Comer. Davis's versatility was shown in that turning-point year of 1896, when he gave T. B. Harms and Company his coon song takeoff on Little Egypt's dance at the World's Fair, "When I Do the Hoochy-Coochy in de Sky."

In 1899, Davis scored his only show, *A Hot Time in Dixie*, which began a tour of Midwest theaters that August. He died in October, while the show was still touring.

# Joseph M. Davis

See *Triangle Music Publishing Company*

# Doris Day

Singer and film actress (b. Doris Mary Anne von Kappelhoff, Cincinnati, Ohio, April 3, 1922). Day was already performing as a dancer around her hometown as a young teenager, partnering with local dancer Jerry Dougherty. However, an automobile accident in 1937 sidelined her dance career, and she decided to take up singing. She first sang with Barney Rapp and His New Englanders; it was Rapp who gave her the surname "Day," inspired by the 1938 hit "Day After Day." She then moved to Bob Crosby's orchestra, and in August 1940, she began her career as a vocalist with Les Brown's band. She had several hits as lead vocalist with Brown's band, starting in 1944 with the #1 hit "Sentimental Journey" (lyrics by Bud Green; music by Les Brown and Ben Homer). She remained with Brown's band through 1947, scoring five more Top 10 hits.

In 1948, singing with vocalist Buddy Clark, Day had a million-selling #1 hit with "Love Somebody," written by Joan Whitney and Alex Kramer (Columbia 38174); that same year she entered the films. Many of her song hits came from her films, including the #2 hit that sold over a million copies, "It's Magic," from the film *Romance on the High Seas* (Columbia 38188), also in 1948. In 1952, she had another million-seller in "A Guy Is a Guy" (Columbia 39673). In 1953, she introduced "Secret Love" in the film *Calamity Jane*, which won the Academy Award for Best Song (Columbia 40108) and sold over a million copies. Her 1956 #2 hit, "Que Sera, Sera (Whatever Will Be, Will Be)," which won the Academy Award for Best Song and sold over a million copies, came from her film *The Man Who Knew Too Much* (Columbia 40704).

In the later 1950s, Day had several Top 10 hit albums, beginning with *Day by Day*, released in August 1957. Her final Top 10 single hit was "Everybody Loves a Lover" (lyrics by Richard Adler, music by Robert Allen) in 1958; that same year, her *Greatest Hits* album went gold. Day's film career, mostly focusing on nonsinging roles, continued through 1968, and she spent the balance of her career as a television personality. Her son, Terry Melcher, was a noted pop music producer and songwriter in the 1960s and 1970s.

# Sylvia Dee

See *Sid Lippman*

# Eddie De Lange

Vocalist, lyricist, and bandleader (b. Edgar De Lange, Long Island City, New York, January 15, 1904; d. Los Angeles, California, July 15, 1949). De Lange was a popular bandleader of the 1930s and 1940s who provided lyrics for a number of hit songs. After working as a singer with various bands, he began to write lyrics around 1934, scoring his first hit with "I Wish I Were Twins," on which he partnered with Frank Loesser; Joseph Meyer composed the tune. Also in 1934, he wrote his first major hit, "Moonglow," with a melody by Will Hudson.

The duo led a light swing band together from 1936 to 1938, and then De Lange struck out on his own. Other hits include "Solitude," which was successfully recorded by Duke Ellington in 1935. During the later 1930s, he worked with composer Jimmy Van Heusen, notably on the Broadway musical *Swingin' the Dream* (November 29, 1939). A later career hit was "Do You Know What It Means to Miss New Orleans?" with music by Lou Alter, from 1946. De Lange died in 1949, at the age of forty-five.

# Demonstrator

From the beginning of the Alley, pianists were hired to perform their publishers' numbers in music stores and at music counters in department stores. Department stores also hired pianists to play whatever songs their customers brought to them. This was before recordings

A female song demonstrator (sitting at the piano, far right) working at Hillman's, a sheet music store, 1906.

made an inroad into the sheet music business. Demonstrators lasted until the end of World War II. Many famous composers began their careers working as demonstrators. GEORGE GERSHWIN and VINCENT YOUMANS were hired as demonstrators by MOSE GUMBLE, who worked for JEROME H. REMICK; in this way, Gumble nurtured their careers, because it was not unusual for a demonstrator to pitch his own material for publication. MILDRED BAILEY got her start as a demonstrator singing pop songs in a local music store, another way that young talent was given a chance to be "discovered." When records became increasingly available and popular, music stores that sold discs installed "listening booths" as a means for customers to preview a record before purchasing it. In this way, live demonstrators were more or less put out of business.

# B. G. De Sylva

Lyricist, publisher, and film producer (b. George Gard De Sylva, but known as "Bud" or "Buddy," New York City, January 27, 1895; d. Los Angeles, California, July 11, 1950). De Sylva is most famous for his partnership with LEW BROWN and RAY HENDERSON.

De Sylva's father was a vaudevillian who performed as Hal De Forrest, but gave up his career for marriage and the more secure occupation of lawyer. Buddy appeared on stage as early as age four, and also began studying the violin as a youngster; by college age, he was writing songs. He got his big break when singer AL JOLSON, passing through California, heard his song "'N' Everything" and recorded it in 1917 (the composition was credited to Jolson, De Sylva, and GUS KAHN). De Sylva moved to New York City, and took a job as a staff composer for JEROME REMICK. There, he met young GEORGE GERSWHIN, who was working as a demonstrator, and the two collaborated on the shows *La, La, Lucille* (additional lyrics by Arthur Jackson) and *Gest's Midnight Whirl* (with lyricist John Henry Mears), both in 1919. Meanwhile, Jolson asked De Sylva to create a song based on his tag line "You ain't heard nothin' yet." Working again with Kahn, Jolson and De Sylva came up with a song of that title, a 1920 hit.

In the early 1920s, Al Jolson introduced and made famous a few of De Sylva's songs, including "Look for the Silver Lining" (1920), written with JEROME KERN for the show *Sally* (1920). Jolson also scored with "April Showers" from the 1921 show *Bombo* (music by Louis Silvers; Columbia A-3500), and "California, Here I Come" with ukulele backing by De Sylva (Brunswick 2569) in 1924. PAUL WHITEMAN's orchestra had the #1 hit in 1922, "I'll Build a Stairway to Paradise" (colyricist IRA GERSHWIN; music by George Gershwin; Victor 18949), and the #1 hit in 1924, "Somebody Loves Me" (music by George Gershwin; Victor 19414). Although Jolson introduced "Alabamy Bound" in 1925, Blossom Seeley had the #2 hit (colyricist Bud Green; composed by Ray Henderson; Columbia 304-D). The same year, Eddie Cantor had the #1 hit "If You Knew Susie" (music by Joseph Meyer; Columbia 364-D). From the Broadway musical *Take a Chance*, Paul Whiteman had two De Sylva hits, "Rise 'n' Shine" (Victor 24197) and "You're an Old Smoothie" (Victor 24202).

De Sylva joined Lew Brown and Ray Henderson in 1925 as a songwriting team and music publishers. In 1931, the trio broke up, and De Sylva remained in Hollywood, becoming a producer; by 1941 he was head of production at Paramount. After World War II, with songwriter Johnny Mercer and music store owner Glenn Wallichs, De Sylva founded Capitol Records, which became a major outlet for pop songs. He died in 1950, following a heart attack.

# De Sylva, Brown, and Henderson

The songwriting team of De Sylva, Brown, and Henderson was unique in the Alley. Although Buddy De Sylva and Lew Brown nominally wrote the words and Ray Henderson the music, these three functioned as one creator, sharing the same thought, feeling, purpose, and style. Each contributed both words and music. Before their teaming, each had written hits with others: De Sylva's, "Look for the Silver Lining" with Jerome Kern, "Somebody Loves Me" with George Gershwin, and "A Kiss in the Dark" with Victor Herbert; Lew Brown's, "I'm the Lonesomest Gal in Town," "Oh, by Jingo," and "Dapper Dan (The Sheik of Alabam')" with Albert Von Tilzer, "I Wanna Go Where You Go" with Cliff Friend, and "Collegiate" with Moe Jaffe; and Henderson's, "That Old Gang of Mine," with Mort Dixon and Billy Rose, "Five Foot Two, Eyes of Blue," and "I'm Sitting on Top of the World," with Sam Lewis and Joe Young. As a trio, they would come up with an unusual number of hits, mostly in the theater, some in the movies, and, occasionally, as pop tunes.

The trio formed when George White needed songs for his 1925 *Scandals*, after George Gershwin, who had composed the music for the last five editions, decided to concentrate on book musicals. White hired Ray Henderson to write the music for his revue and independently hired De Sylva and Brown to write the lyrics. The score the team produced (June 22, 1925) was published by T. B. Harms. It was not distinguished, but they created their first hit soon after they began their own publishing company. "It All Depends on You" (1926) was sung by Al Jolson (in whiteface, for a change) in his show *Big Boy*. "South Wind" (1926) was given a snappy interpretation by The Dixie Jazz Band (Oriole 896).

The next year, for *George White's Scandals of 1926* (June 14, 1926), the team turned out hit after hit, including "(This Is My) Lucky Day," "The Girl Is You and the Boy Is Me," and "The Birth of the Blues," all of which were introduced by Harry Richman in the show, and "Black Bottom," a challenge to the "CHARLESTON," which was sung and danced by Ann Pennington, the McCarthy Sisters, Frances Williams, and Tom Patricola. It was George White himself who created the spectacularly frenetic dance with which Ann Pennington stopped the show nightly and which helped make this edition the best of all his *Scandals*. Ohman and Arden with their orchestra (Brunswick 3242) and Howard Lanin's orchestra (Columbia 689-D) gave audiences something to remember the show by on discs.

The songwriting trio went from this revue to a Broadway book musical for their next offering. They chose college life, as Guy Bolton-P. G. WODEHOUSE-Jerome Kern had done ten years earlier, to showcase the fads of the day. The show was awash with raccoon coats, porkpie hats, ukuleles, and sorority emblems embroidered on tight-fitting sweaters. It featured George Olsen and his band, who ran down the aisle, yelling college cheers, before jumping into the pit, where they struck up the overture. Even the ushers wore college jerseys. The show, *Good News* (September 26, 1927), ran for 551 performances and made a star of the high-kicking Zelma O'Neal, who introduced "Good News" and "The Varsity Drag." The bright, fresh show abounded with other hits, such as "Lucky in Love," "Just Imagine," and "The Best Things in Life Are Free."

In addition to clicking their first time out with a book show, the team wrote three solid pop songs in this creative year of 1927, and another one under a pseudonym. The pseudonymous song was "The Church Bells Are Ringing for Mary" (1927), credited to "Elmer Colby." Belle Baker made "(Here Am I) Broken Hearted" famous, and their "Just a Memory" was used in *Manhattan Mary*. Lou Gold's orchestra helped make "Magnolia" famous.

Their *George White Scandals of 1928* can be summed up nicely by a song title from the show, "Not As Good As Last Year." So the team plunged ahead with their next book show, *Hold Everything* (October 10, 1928), a show about boxing, that starred Ona Munson, Betty Compton, Jack Whiting, Bert Lahr, and Victor Moore. Their resounding song in that show was "You're the Cream in My Coffee." Ted Weems's orchestra recorded it and helped establish its place on the all-time hit parade (Victor 21767).

While Al Jolson was making *The Singing Fool* (1928) for Warner Bros., the team was on the road in Atlantic City, New Jersey, trying out *Hold Everything*. One night they received a phone call from Jolson, asking De Sylva to write a song immediately. It had to be about a child, Jolson's son in the movie, and he wanted it to make the audience cry. As soon as De Sylva hung up, the team went to work, as related by David Ewen in *Great Men of American Popular Song*,

> not on a beautiful ballad, but on the corniest creation they could dream up—just one more practical joke. In no time at all, they called Jolson back, all three singing into the receiver. Jolson loved it. 'It'll be the biggest ballad I've ever sung,' he told the songwriters excitedly. The three could hardly keep from laughing, but they solemnly assured Jolson that they would send him the words and music immediately. When he finally hung up, they started to laugh—and never stopped. What they had written as a joke was the hit of the picture, 'Sonny Boy.' It sold a million and a half copies of sheet music and became a best-seller in Jolson's recording (Brunswick 4033).

"Together" was the team's pop hit of 1928. PAUL WHITEMAN, with vocalist Jack Fulton, made the first recording (Victor 35883). DINAH SHORE's record in 1944 made it a hit again (Victor 20-1594), and in 1961 Connie Francis made yet another best-selling recording of the song (MGM 13019). The big song in *Follow Thru* (January 9, 1929), the trio's show about golf, was "Button Up Your Overcoat," which was sung by Zelma O'Neal and Jack Haley. After a vocal chorus, Eleanor Powell tap-danced to it. Helping to make it big on records were Fred Waring's Pennsylvanians (Victor 21861). It was revived in the mid-1950s on disc by the Glenn Brown Trio (Cornet 550).

The teams' only original film score was for *Sunny Side Up* (1929), which featured Janet Gaynor and Charles Farrell singing "If I Had a Talking Picture of You." The title song was sung by Janet Gaynor, as was as "I'm a Dreamer, Aren't We All?" The team's last Broadway show, *Flying High* (March 3, 1930), exploited the aviation craze in the headlines about Charles Lindbergh, Amelia Earhart, and Admiral Byrd. The score boasted one enduring song "Thank Your Father," which was sung by Grace Brinkley and Oscar Shaw. The team broke up at this time, with De Sylva going it alone, while Brown and Henderson continued to work together.

Hollywood used the cream of their catalog in a "biography" of the team starring Dan Dailey, Gordon MacRae, and Ernest Borgnine. It was called *The Best Things in Life Are Free* (1956).

# De Sylva, Brown, and Henderson, Inc.

The successful writing team of De Sylva, Brown, and Henderson formed their own publishing company at the end of 1926, with Robert Crawford as president and general manager. He had been with Irving Berlin, Inc., as sales manager since that company's inception. The founding trio maintained the company until 1934, at 745 Seventh Avenue. The current owner of the catalog is Warner/Chappell Music.

# Howard Dietz

Lyricist (b. New York City, September 8, 1896; d. New York City, July 30, 1983). Dietz partnered Arthur Schwartz in many Broadway shows, but also wrote with Jerome Kern, Vernon Duke, Jimmy McHugh, and Ralph Rainger.

Dietz was the son of a Russian immigrant jeweler. While he was a junior at Columbia, he won an advertising slogan contest, which led to a job as an ad writer for a New York firm that represented, among other accounts, MGM. Dietz is credited with creating the MGM logo (Leo the Lion) and the slogan "Ars Gratia Artis." After serving in World War I, he joined MGM in 1924 as advertising and publicity director, and held the job until he retired. Although he had been writing lyrics since 1922, his first big hits did not come until 1929, from the Broadway revue *The Little Show.* RUDY VALLEE had a #2 hit with "I Guess I'll Have to Change My Plan" in 1932 (Columbia 2700-D), while Libby Holman made a hit of "Moanin' Low" (Brunswick 4445). The next year Holman did it again with "Something to Remember You By," from the show *Three's a Crowd* (Brunswick 4910). BING CROSBY had the first hit recording of "Dancing in the Dark," which came from the musical *The Band Wagon* in 1931 and became Dietz's most famous song (Brunswick 6159). In 1932, he followed up with "A Shine on Your Shoes" from the musical *Flying Colors*, recorded by ROGER WOLFE KAHN and his orchestra, featuring ARTIE SHAW on clarinet (Columbia 2722-D). 1934 saw "You and the Night and the Music" from the musical *Revenge with Music*, with the hit record belonging once more to Libby Holman (Victor 24839). "I See Your Face Before Me" came from the 1937 musical *Between the Devil*, with GUY LOMBARDO having the hit recording (Victor 25684). The team's last hit, "That's Entertainment," was written in 1953 for the film *The Band Wagon*, and it has become a show business standard. After a long hiatus, Dietz and Schwartz wrote two more scores for Broadway, *The Gay Life* in 1961 and *Jenny* in 1963. Dietz wrote his autobiography, *Dancing in the Dark*, in 1974.

# Disney Cartoon Songs

Walt Disney created many animated cartoons, and in all of them, songs were central to his ideas. As soon as sound came in, he used songs in most, if not all, of his films, whether one- or two-reelers or full-length productions. Given the popularity of his cartoons, it was only natural that the songs composed for his films should also be successful. Seven of the songs won Oscars. Since the films are periodically revived, the songs remain part of our popular music heritage.

"Minnie's Yoo Hoo" (1930) was the Mickey Mouse cartoons' theme song and the first Disney song to become popular. It had words and music by Carl Stalling. "Who's Afraid of the Big Bad Wolf?" (1933) was composed by FRANK CHURCHILL, a staff composer for Disney, with words by Ann Ronell. It was featured in the "Silly Symphony" *The Three Little Pigs.* "The World Owes Me a Living" (1934) was composed by LEIGH HARLINE, with lyrics by Larry Morey (1905–1971), for the "Silly Symphony" *The Grasshopper and the Ants.*

*Snow White and the Seven Dwarfs* (1937) was Disney's first full-length cartoon feature. It had a brilliant score by Churchill and Morey, including "Heigh-Ho," "Whistle While You Work," "Some Day My Prince Will Come," "I'm Wishing," and "With a Smile and a Song." *Pinocchio* (1940) had a glorious score by Leigh Harline and Ned Washington. The top songs were "Give a Little Whistle," "Hi-Diddle-Dee-Dee," "Jiminy Cricket," and the first of the two Academy Award Disney songs, "When You Wish upon a Star," which was used as the theme song for the Disney television show of the 1950s.

"Der Fuehrer's Face" (1942), with words and music by Oliver Wallace (1887–1963), was written for a short, *Donald Duck in Nutzi Land*. The song proved so popular during World War II that the short was retitled to bear the name of the song. Spike Jones started his career as a musical satirist with this number, the only song to become popular by making fun of Hitler. The recording by Jones and his City Slickers sold over a million and a half discs (Bluebird 11586).

"Brazil" (1939) was composed by Ary Barroso, with an English lyric by S. K. Russell. It was included in the score of the film *Saludos Amigos* (1943). "Tico-Tico" (1943), composed by Brazilian Zequinha Abreu, with an English lyric by Ervin Drake, was a big feature for Xavier Cugat and his orchestra. It was also heard in the film.

*Song of the South* (1946) was a full-length feature combining live actors with cartoon characters. The score included "Uncle Remus Said," by Johnny Lange, Hy Heath, and Eliot Daniel. "Everybody Has a Laughing Place" and "Zip-A-Dee-Doo-Dah" were composed by Allie Wrubel, with lyrics by Ray Gilbert (1912–1976). It was sung in the film by James Baskett, and it had its hit recording by Johnny Mercer with the Pied Pipers (Capitol 323). It won an Oscar for best song.

*So Dear to My Heart* (1949) included the gem "Lavender Blue (Dilly Dilly)," composed by Eliot Daniel, who took the melody from a seventeenth-century English folk song, with lyrics by Larry Morey. It was sung twice in the film, first by Dinah Shore and later by Burl Ives, and was a hit record in 1959 for Sammy Turner (Big Top 3016).

*Cinderella* (1950) was composed by Jerry Livingston, with lyrics by Mack David and Al Hoffman. The score included "Bibbidi, Bobbidi, Boo," "The Work Song," and "A Dream Is a Wish Your Heart Makes." The last was sung on the sound track by Ilene Woods.

*Alice In Wonderland* (1951) contained "I'm Late," composed by Sammy Fain, with lyrics by Bob Hilliard. "Dear Hearts and Gentle People" (1949) has lyrics by Hilliard. It was an enormously popular song, thanks to Dinah Shore (Columbia 38605) and Bing Crosby (Decca 24798).

*Peter Pan* (1953) had a score that featured songs by Frank Churchill and Jack Lawrence, including the hit "Never Smile at a Crocodile." Churchill had worked on the film in 1939 when Disney first proposed it, but died in 1942. The film itself was not completed until eleven years later, and featured a score by several songwriters.

*Adventures in Music* (1953) featured "A Toot and a Whistle and a Plunk and a Boom," composed by Sonny Burke, with lyrics by Jack Elliott. Spike Jones and his City Slickers made the hit recording (Victor Y-472). "Mickey Mouse March" (1955), words and music by Jimmy Dodd, was the theme song of television's *Mickey Mouse Club*. Dodd was the leader of the Mouseketeers.

After many years without producing new animated musicals, Disney returned big time to the genre from the late 1980s through the 1990s. *The Little Mermaid* (1989), with music by Alan Mencken (b. New Rochelle New York, July 22, 1949) and lyrics by Howard Ashman

(b. Baltimore, Maryland, May 3, 1950; d. Los Angeles, California, March 14, 1991), won the Academy Award for Best Song, "Under the Sea," the first since 1946. *Beauty and the Beast* (1991), also by Mencken and Ashman, won the Oscar for Best Song with the title song. Celine Dion and Peabo Bryson had a hit recording that sold over one million copies (Epic 74090). It was later transported by Disney to Broadway for a long run. Ashman and Mencken's last collaboration, *Aladdin* (1992), won another Academy Award for Best Song; "A Whole New World," which was sung by Peabo Bryson and Regina Belle, became a #1 hit, selling more than half a million copies (Columbia 74751). *The Lion King* (1994), with music by Elton John and lyrics by Tim Rice, garnered another Academy Award for best song with "Can You Feel the Love Tonight," composed and sung by Elton John for a #4 hit that sold more than half a million copies (Hollywood 645431). He also scored with "Circle of Life" from the same film (Hollywood 64516). A clever Broadway adaptation staged by Julie Taymor, involving large puppets, opened on Broadway in 1997 and has been Disney's most successful live production in New York. *Pocahontas* (1995) was the last Academy Award winner for Best Song by the Disney group, for "Colors of the Wind," which was sung by Vanessa Williams and reached the #4 position selling over half a million copies (Hollywood 64001). *Tarzan* (1999) featured Phil Collins singing his song, "You'll Be in My Heart" (Walt Disney 60025).

# Mort Dixon

Lyricist (b. New York City, March 20, 1892; d. Bronxville, New York, March 23, 1956). Dixon began his career as a vaudevillian prior to serving in World War I, and then began writing lyrics in the early 1920s. His first hit came in 1923 in collaboration with Billy Rose on "That Old Gang of Mine," with music by Ray Henderson, a hit on record for Billy Murray and Ed Smalle, among others. He continued to produce major hits through the 1920s, including "Bye, Bye, Blackbird" (with Rose, and music by Henderson), a defining song of the decade that was a recorded hit for Nick Lucas (Brunswick E18878) and Gene Austin (Victor 20044B); "I'm Looking over a Four Leaf Clover" (composed by Harry Woods; the Jean Goldkette recording, featuring Bix Beiderbecke, helped make the sheet music a million-seller [Victor 20466]); and "Nagasaki" (with music by Harry Warren and a favorite of stride pianist Willie "The Lion" Smith). The early 1930s saw another collaboration with Billy Rose on the show *Crazy Quilt*, with music by Harry Warren, producing the hit "I Found a Million Dollar Baby (in a Five and Ten Cent Store)," revived in later decades by Nat "King" Cole and Barbara Streisand in the film *Funny Lady* (1975). 1931 also saw other hits, including "You're My Everything," with lyrics by Dixon and Joe Young and music by Harry Warren, and "River, Stay 'Way from My Door," a major hit for Kate Smith (Columbia 2578-D). Dixon spent much of the 1930s in Hollywood, working with composer

Allie Wrubel for Warner Bros.; the duo scored a number of films through the end of the decade, when Dixon decided to retire.

# Walter J. Donaldson

Composer and publisher (b. Brooklyn, New York, February 15, 1891; d. Santa Monica, California, July 15, 1947). Although he wrote "Just Try to Picture Me Back Home in Tennessee" (with lyrics by William Jerome) in 1915, it was many years after he published the tune that he finally saw the state which was so closely identified with him. Donaldson loved writing songs so much that he was fired from his first job in the Alley for doing so during business hours, when he was supposed to be plugging the firm's tunes for performers. His first published song was "Just Try to Picture Me," issued in 1915 by Waterson, Berlin and Snyder. States and cities proved to be lucky for him, and his next published song that year was the hit "We'll Have a Jubilee in My Old Kentucky Home." He followed this one with "On the Gin, Gin, Ginny Shore," "Carolina in the Morning," "Kansas City Kitty," and "Lazy Louisiana Moon." His first post-World War I number to become a million-selling success was "How Ya Gonna Keep 'Em Down on the Farm" (1919). During the war, when he was stationed at Camp Upton as an entertainer, he wrote "The Daughter of Rosie O'Grady." It was at this camp where he met his future employer, Irving Berlin, who was also serving his country in khaki.

In Donaldson's first year as a civilian working for Waterson, Berlin and Snyder (1919), he teamed with the lyric duo of Sam M. Lewis and Joe Young for four hits: the aforementioned "How Ya Gonna Keep 'Em Down on the Farm," "Don't Cry Frenchy, Don't Cry," "I'll Be Happy When the Preacher Makes You Mine," and "You're a Million Miles from Nowhere."

At the beginning of the 1920s, Donaldson began roaring with a Hawaiian number, "My Little Bimbo Down on the Bamboo Isle," with lyricist Grant Clarke. In 1921 he wrote, with Lewis and Young providing the words, "My Mammy," which Al Jolson made "his" song, performing it on bended knee with white-gloved hands outstretched. This song became Jolson's trademark, and from that time forward, any interpreter of mother songs was known as a "mammy singer." Donaldson next wrote "Georgia" (1922), with lyrics by Howard Johnson (1887–1941), a lovely melody made famous by Paul Whiteman and his orchestra (Victor 18899).

Donaldson's next collaboration was with the celebrated lyricist Gus Kahn, a Chicagoan who refused to live in New York, remaining in the Windy City before he went to Hollywood. Their first number, "My Buddy" (1922), was a hit. They followed it with "Carolina in the Morning" the same year. The next year, they scored with "Beside a Babbling Brook." In 1925, the team of Donaldson and Kahn had four multimillion-selling songs: "My Sweetie Turned Me Down," which the Dixie Stars (singer Al Bernard and pianist-composer J. Russel Robinson) made famous (Columbia 389-D); "That Certain Party," popularized by Eddie

Walter Donaldson at the keyboard in the 1920s.

CANTOR; and two great CHARLESTON numbers, "I Wonder Where My Baby Is Tonight" and "Yes Sir, That's My Baby." This last was written for Eddie Cantor, at Cantor's house. One of the comedian's five daughters had a mechanical toy pig, which attracted Gus Kahn's attention. As the pig jiggled across the floor, Kahn recited the lines, "Yes sir, that's my baby, no sir, don't mean maybe" to the movements, and another of their hits was born. GENE AUSTIN made a best-selling record (Victor 19656).

The following year Donaldson produced "What Can I Say After I Say I'm Sorry?" with bandleader ABE LYMAN. It was sung with great success by two singers, torcher RUTH ETTING and jazzbaby Bee Palmer. With Gus Kahn, Donaldson produced two more hits in 1926, "There Ain't No Maybe in My Baby's Eyes" and "Let's Talk about My Sweetie."

If 1925 was big for Donaldson, 1927 was even bigger. He again had four hits, but their sales figures were much greater. With Gus Kahn, he wrote "He's the Last Word." Donaldson then started writing both words and music, and came up with "At Sundown," introduced at the Palace Theatre by CLIFF EDWARDS; "Changes," featured by Paul Whiteman's orchestra (and given a spectacular piano roll arrangement by Vee Lawnhurst on Welte 75333), and "Sam, the Old Accordion Man," made famous by Ruth Etting. In his only collaboration with GEORGE WHITING, Donaldson came up with "My Blue Heaven." Gene Austin recorded it (Victor 20964), selling over five million copies, and Eddie Cantor plugged it in vaudeville and in the *Ziegfeld Follies of 1927*. It was the biggest song in the history of LEO FEIST, Inc., according to Feist's son, Leonard. It sold over five million copies of sheet music.

On June 1, 1928, Donaldson formed a publishing house with Walter Douglas and the ace of pluggers, MOSE GUMBLE. Their first issues were from the score of Donaldson's only Broadway show, *Whoopee!* (December 4, 1928). Gus Kahn wrote the lyrics, and Eddie Cantor starred with Ruth Etting and Tamara Geva. Two songs were hits and became standards:

"Making Whoopee" and "Love Me or Leave Me." When the show was made into a movie two years later, Donaldson and Kahn added "My Baby Just Cares for Me," which Eddie Cantor turned into a hit.

By himself, Donaldson wrote "Because My Baby Don't Mean Maybe Now" in the first year of his publishing company. It was recorded by Paul Whiteman and his orchestra (Columbia 1441-D), Ruth Etting (Columbia 1920-D), and George Olsen and His Music (Victor 21452). It has been a favorite of jazz bands and singers ever since. In the following year, Donaldson wrote the wonderfully comic " 'Tain't No Sin to Dance Around in Your Bones" with EDGAR LESLIE.

Before he went to Hollywood in 1930, Donaldson wrote "Little White Lies" for newcomer ETHEL MERMAN, and one of his biggest hits, "You're Driving Me Crazy," initially made famous by RUDY VALLEE and later by GUY LOMBARDO and his orchestra, which seems to be revived every twenty-five years or so.

Donaldson went to Hollywood, but his output diminished there. He contributed a score to Eddie Cantor's *Kid Millions* (1934), which included "Okay, Toots." For *Here Comes the Band* (1935), he and HAROLD ADAMSON wrote "Tender Is the Night." The following year, again with Adamson, he wrote "Did I Remember?" for Jean Harlow's *Suzy* and "It's Been So Long" and "You" for *The Great Ziegfeld.* This last song later became the theme song of *Art Linkletter's House Party* on television. Donaldson and Kermit Goell (1915–1997) wrote "Tonight" for the all-star Universal movie *Follow the Boys* (1944). Soon after this, Donaldson was forced to retire due to ill health.

# Dorothy Donnelly

See *Sigmund Romberg*

# Jimmy Dorsey

Alto saxophone, clarinet, and trumpet player, older brother of trombonist TOMMY DORSEY, (b. James Francis Dorsey, Shenandoah, Pennsylvania, February 29, 1904; d. New York City, June 12, 1957). Both Jimmy and his brother Tommy were trained in music by their father,

Thomas Francis Dorsey, who led a marching band. Jimmy began playing cornet at age seven, but by the time he was eleven, he had switched to reed instruments. He formed some small combos with his brother, and then worked for a variety of leaders and was a prolific sideman in recording studios in the 1920s. In 1928, Jimmy formed Dorsey Brothers Band with Tommy for recording, and then as a performing band in 1934, but by June 1935, Jimmy took over the band, while Tommy took over Joe Haymes's band. In 1936, Jimmy's band became the house band for BING CROSBY's radio show, *Kraft Music Hall*. Jimmy's first #1 chart hit came in 1936 with "Is It True What They Say About Dixie?," with vocal by Bob Eberly (Decca 768). His next came in 1938 with "Change Partners," again with vocal by Eberly (Decca 2002). In 1940 he again scored with a #1 hit, "The Breeze and I" (Decca 3150). The next year he had six #1 hits, two of them million-sellers. The first was "I Hear a Rhapsody" (Decca 3570), followed by "Amapola," which sold over a million copies (Decca 3629) and had vocals by Bob Eberly and Helen O'Connell. "My Sister and I" had a vocal by Eberly (Decca 3710); "Green Eyes" had a vocal by Eberly and O'Connell (Decca 3698) and sold over a million copies. The flip side, "Maria Elena," with vocal by Eberly, also charted #1. "Blue Champagne" was the last #1 hit in 1941, with Bob Eberly taking the vocal once more (Decca 3775). The 1942 #1 hit was "Tangerine," from the film *The Fleet's In*, with Eberly and O'Connell singing (Decca 4123). In 1944, "Besame Mucho," a Mexican song with vocal by Eberly and Kitty Kallen, was the million-selling #1 hit (Decca 18574). After World War II, with the decline of the big bands, Jimmy rejoined Tommy in 1953, and the twosome hosted a television variety show from 1954 to 1956; in 1955, young singer Elvis Presley made his TV debut on it. Tommy died in November 1956, and Jimmy took over the band, although he was suffering from throat cancer and had to give up leading it in early 1957. Just before he died, in 1957, Jimmy Dorsey scored his last million-seller with a revival of the 1937 hit "So Rare" (Fraternity 755).

# Tommy Dorsey

Bandleader best remembered as the greatest trombonist of all time at playing popular ballads (b. Shenandoah, Pennsylvania, November 19, 1905; d. Greenwich, Connecticut, November 26, 1956). He and his older brother, JIMMY DORSEY (another top bandleader, and master of the clarinet and alto saxophone), grew up in Shenandoah, Pennsylvania, playing in their father's parade and concert band. They came to New York City in 1925 and, as freelancers, quickly became established as recording studio sidemen and as hot soloists. They organized the Dorsey Brothers' Orchestra in 1928, mostly for recording purposes, and started their dance band in 1934. They broke up in September 1935. Jimmy stayed with their band, and Tommy took over the nucleus of the Joe Haymes band.

Tommy recorded extensively for RCA-Victor for the next fifteen years. His theme song was "I'm Gettin' Sentimental over You" (Victor 25236), composed by George Bassman (1914–1997) and written by NED WASHINGTON. He had his own radio shows, as well as feature spots on other programs, but he finally hit it big on January 29, 1937, when he recorded his arrangement of "Song of India," backed by IRVING BERLIN's "Marie," with the band singing riffs behind Jack Leonard's straight vocal (Victor 25523). The "Marie" arrangement was originally created for Doc Wheeler's Sunset Royal Serenaders, but Tommy traded Wheeler eight Dorsey arrangements for that one. It was a profitable trade, since over the next few years, the Tommy Dorsey Orchestra would record other hits in that style: "Who?" (Victor 25693), "Yearning" (Victor 25815), "Blue Moon" (Victor 26185), and "East of the Sun" (Bluebird 10726). This last number had a lead vocal by FRANK SINATRA, whom he had hired away from GLENN MILLER in 1940. Tommy Dorsey's band would change personnel considerably over the years, but the band that gave him his 1937 double-sided hit consisted of Bunny Berigan, Steve Lipkins, Joe Bauer, and Bob Cusumano, trumpets; Tommy Dorsey, Les Jenkins, and Artie Foster, trombones; Joe Dixon, clarinet and alto sax; Fred Stulce and Clyde Rounds, alto saxes; Bud Freeman, tenor sax; Dick Jones, piano; Carmen Mastren, guitar; Gene Traxler, string bass; Dave Tough, drums; Jack Leonard, vocals.

Tommy Dorsey's biggest recordings included "Once in a While" (Victor 25686), "Music, Maestro, Please" (Victor 25866), "I'll Be Seeing You" (Victor 26539) (the flip side of which had Frank Sinatra's first hit with the band, "Polka Dots and Moonbeams"), "I'll Never Smile Again" (Victor 26628), and "This Love of Mine" (Victor 27508). Tommy formed a "band within the band," his Clambake Seven, a modern dixieland combo that also made some hit recordings.

The Tommy Dorsey band appeared in the following movies: *Las Vegas Nights* (1941), *Ship Ahoy* (1942), *DuBarry Was a Lady* (1943), *Girl Crazy* (1943), *Presenting Lily Mars* (1943), *Broadway Rhythm* (1944), and *Thrill of a Romance* (1945). In 1947, both Dorseys starred in their biographical movie, *The Fabulous Dorseys*. The two brothers got back together in 1953 after Jimmy folded his band, and began hosting their own variety show on TV a year later. In November 1956, Tommy died in his sleep; Jimmy died shortly afterward in 1957, from throat cancer.

# Double Song

The trickiest kind of song to compose, consisting of two different melodies and lyrics for the same chorus, each sung separately and then combined (requiring two people to sing). IRVING BERLIN wrote four of them across his career ("Simple Melody" in 1914, "You're Just in Love" in 1950, "Empty Pockets Filled with Love" in 1962, and "An Old Fasioned Wedding" in 1966). HAROLD ARLEN wrote one in 1945 ("June Comes Around Every Year").

# Paul Dresser

Songwriter (b. Paul Dreiser, Terre Haute, Indiana, April 21, 1857; d. New York City, January 30, 1906). He was the older brother of novelist Theodore Dreiser. His father, a deeply religious man, wanted Paul to become a priest. Since the boy's interest lay in music, he ran away from home at sixteen and joined a medicine show, changing his last name at this time. Dresser joined several minstrel troupes and wrote songs relentlessly. It was in 1885, when he was with the Billy Rice Minstrels, that he wrote his first hit, "The Letter That Never Came." He followed it two years later with "The Convict and the Bird," published by WILLIS WOODWARD, and with his 1891 hit, "The Pardon Came Too Late." By this time, Dresser had made a solid reputation as the foremost writer of sentimental ballads. When HOWLEY AND HAVILAND started their firm, they hired Dresser to write for them. He continued to write his ballads and to plug them in touring shows. He was in great demand as an actor and singer. In 1897 he created his immortal "On the Banks of the Wabash, Far Away." His brother later took the credit for writing some of the lyrics, but according to the arranger, Max Hoffman, this isn't true. Hoffman wrote of witnessing the creation of this famous song, quoted in Isidore Witmark's autobiography, *From Ragtime to Swingtime*:

> I went to his room at the Auditorium Hotel in Chicago where, instead of a piano, there was a small folding camp organ, which Paul always carried with him. It was summer; all the windows were open and Paul was mulling over a melody that was practically in finished form. But he did not have the words. So he had me play the full chorus over and over again for at least two or three hours, while he was writing down words, changing a line here and a phrase there until at last the lyric suited him. He had a sort of dummy refrain, which he was studying; but by the time he finished what he was writing down to my playing, it was an altogether different lyric.
>
> When Paul came to the line, "Through the sycamores the candle lights are gleaming," I was tremendously impressed. It struck me at once as one of the most poetic inspirations I had ever heard.
>
> I have always felt that Paul got the idea from glancing out of the window now and again as he wrote, and seeing the lights glimmering out on Lake Michigan. We spent many hours together that evening, and when Paul finished, he asked me to make a piano part for publication at the earliest moment. I happened to have some music paper with me, and I wrote one right out, on the spot. This I mailed to Pat Howley, one of Dresser's partners, sending it to the New York Office at Thirty-second Street and Broadway. At Paul's request, I also enclosed my bill.
>
> This piano part contained the lyric as Paul (and no one else) wrote it that night in my presence. The song was published precisely as I arranged it.

In August 1900, the publishing firm became Howley, Haviland and Dresser. Paul kept pouring out his ballads. On December 7, 1903, Haviland left the firm, and by June 1904, Howley, Dresser and Company was bankrupt. Dresser wrote what was to be his greatest hit, "My Gal Sal," late in 1905. He didn't have the money to plug it properly, although he did manage to publish it. It was not until his protégé, Louise Dresser (who adopted his last name), sang it and JOSEPH W. STERN and Company took over its publication that it became a hit.

# Dave Dreyer

Composer and pianist (b. Brooklyn, New York, September 22, 1894; d. New York City, March 1967). Dreyer first worked as a song plugger and staff pianist on Tin Pan Alley. He then became an accompanist on the vaudeville circuit, working at various times for Al Jolson, Frank Fay, and Sophie Tucker. His most famous song collaborations were 1927's "Me and My Shadow," with lyricist Billy Rose, which was plugged heavily by Jolson on stage and radio, though "Whispering" Jack Smith (Victor 20626) had the hit recording; 1928's "Back in Your Own Backyard," also with lyrics by Rose, for which Jolson took a "cocomposer" credit, and "There's a Rainbow 'Round My Shoulder," featured by Jolson in the film *The Singing Fool* and widely recorded, including instrumental versions by The Original Wolverines and McKinney's Cotton Pickers; and 1931's "Wabash Moon,"with lyrics by Morton Downey, and recorded by crooner Nick Lucas (Brunswick E36425). The hits ceased for Dreyer after the early 1930s.

# Max Dreyfus

Major music publisher and early employer of George Gershwin (b. 1874; d. 1964, full dates unknown). One of the first employees of Howley, Haviland and Company, who not only arranged the songs of the firm's top composers, including Paul Dresser, but also had great skill as an "inside" plugger, teaching performers the firm's songs on the premises. When he went to M. Witmark and Sons in 1895 to interest them in his own compositions, they did not want his songs but did want him. Witmark's (a larger firm than Howley, Haviland) hired him to arrange and plug its numbers. Dreyfus joined the old-line firm of T. B. Harms and Company in 1898 as their chief arranger and occasional composer. He purchased a 25 percent interest in the firm in 1901. Though brothers Thomas B. and Alex T. Harms had the idea of specializing in theater music, they also had outside interests and were not aggressive businessmen. They did not plug their music very effectively, possibly because Tom was more interested in Wall Street. Thus their business dwindled, and the newer houses of Stern and

Max Dreyfus (seated) with brother Louis, c. the late 1940s.

Witmark went after their theater music writers and customers. Dreyfus finally bought out the Harms brothers in 1904, retaining the firm's name and eventually turning it into the most prestigious popular music publisher in Tin Pan Alley. Dreyfus discovered and promoted the most distinguished theater composers of the century: Jerome Kern, George Gershwin, Vincent Youmans, Richard Rodgers, and Cole Porter, among many others. In time, he published about 90 percent of all Broadway scores and show tunes.

In 1908, the British firm Francis, Day and Hunter entered into partnership with T. B. Harms, with Max and his brother Louis owning two-thirds of the business, and Fred Day owning the remaining third. Twelve years later, William Boosey and Chappell and Company of London approached Dreyfus about the possibility of taking over their New York business. Day sold out and returned to London, Louis Dreyfus took over Chappell New York, and Max became the manager of the newly named Harms, Inc. In 1917, songwriter Jerome Kern bought a quarter share in the firm. In 1927, Dreyfus made an arrangement with George and Ira Gershwin to form a subsidiary, New World Music Corporation, to hold their copyrights, with Harms owning a large stake in the new corporation. In 1929, the Dreyfus brothers sold Harms to Warner Bros. Pictures, which combined the firm with its other music holdings to form Music Publishing Holding Corporation.

The brothers continued to work in the music business, now running Chappell. They built a considerable catalog by focusing on Broadway shows, and also through acquiring other lists, including Rodgers and Hammerstein's music publishing operation. They remained active in music publishing until their deaths, Max establishing himself as an important player on the Broadway scene thanks to Chappell's interest in musical theater publishing.

# Al Dubin

Lyricist best known for his work on the classic film *42nd Street* (b. Alexander Dubin, Zurich, Switzerland, June 10, 1891; d. Hollywood, California, February 11, 1945). The Dubin family immigrated to the United States when Al was very young, and settled in Philadelphia. He began writing lyrics as a schoolchild, but his parents hoped he'd become a doctor. These plans were dashed when he was expelled in 1911, and he then went to New York in search of work. Dubin had only moderate success before World War I, and even after service, he was still struggling to get a toehold in the industry. Traveling to Hollywood in the late 1920s, he teamed with JOE BURKE, finally achieving success with "Tip Toe Through the Tulips," introduced in the film *Gold Diggers of Broadway* (1929) by NICK LUCAS, and revived in 1968 on a best-selling record by Tiny Tim (Reprise 0679). His greatest success came in partnership with composer HARRY WARREN, beginning with *42nd Street*, including the classic title song along with "We're in the Money," "Shuffle off to Buffalo," and "You're Getting to Be a Habit with Me." The duo worked together through the end of the decade, producing dozens of standards, including "The Boulevard of Broken Dreams," written for the 1934 film *Moulin Rouge* and sung in the film by Constance Bennett; "I Only Have Eyes for You," a 1934 hit for Ben Selvin and his orchestra; and 1935's "Lulu's Back in Town," a major hit for FATS WALLER (Victor 25063) and later revived by Mel Torme. Dubin also collaborated with other composers, including JOHNNY MERCER, SAMMY FAIN, JIMMY MCHUGH, VICTOR HERBERT, and DUKE ELLINGTON. A prodigious drinker, eater, and womanizer, Dubin succumbed to a drug overdose in 1945.

# Vernon Duke

Composer (b. Vladmiri Dukelsky, Parafianovka, Russia, October 10, 1903; d. Santa Monica, California, January 17, 1969). After completing his education at Kiev Conservatory, Duke left Russia and spent time in Europe. He came to the United States permanently in 1929, composed his first Broadway score in 1932, and became a citizen in 1938.

*Walk a Little Faster* (December 7, 1932) contained Duke's most famous song, "April in Paris." The lyrics were written by E. Y. HARBURG. It was introduced by Evelyn Hoey but didn't attract much attention. Featured in nightclubs, it became a café society perennial thanks to chanteuse Marian Chase. Freddy Martin's orchestra had the hit (Brunswick 6717). When a film of the same name was made in 1952, DORIS DAY sang it.

*Thumbs Up* (December 27, 1934) another revue, contained only one song by Duke, who wrote its words and music. A follow-up to his previous hit, it was called "Autumn in New York." It was introduced in the show by J. Harold Murray and, like "April in Paris," which it resembled in no other way, it had to wait a number of years before it became a recognized classic. FRANK SINATRA made the hit recording of it in 1949 (Columbia 38316). It is a brilliantly original conception, melodically and harmonically superior to most Alley songs. It truly deserves its permanent fame.

*Ziegfeld Follies of 1936* (January 30, 1936) had the hit "I Can't Get Started," with lyrics by IRA GERSHWIN. It was introduced by Bob Hope and Eve Arden. Two Hollywood writers were working on the *Big Broadcast of 1936* for Paramount when they saw Hope do the number. They hired him for their film, and his long movie career began. The song also established the career of swing trumpeter Bunny Berigan, who made the best-selling recording, both singing and playing it, in 1938 (Victor 25728). It remained identified with Berigan throughout his career. A WNEW-AM listener poll in 1985 named the Berigan record the "best pop recording ever made!"

*Cabin in the Sky* (October 25, 1940) gave Duke his last Broadway hit. "Taking a Chance on Love" had lyrics by John Latouche and Ted Fetter. It was introduced by ETHEL WATERS in her greatest musical role. She stopped the show regularly, giving half a dozen encores nightly. She also sang it in the film version (1943). When Duke first played the song for Waters, she stopped him after the first eight bars and said, "Mister, our troubles are over." In 1941, he wrote the songs for EDDIE CANTOR's comeback show, *Banjo Eyes*. He continued to write shows through the war, and also led an Army band.

Duke was less successful in the 1950s, although he still managed to work on occasion. His title song for the 1952 Doris Day film *April in Paris* was a hit for Count Basie on the R and B charts four years later. His last Broadway show was 1957's *Time Remembered*, which featured only two songs along with his incidental music. Further attempts to launch shows over the next decade failed to come to fruition, and Duke succumbed to cancer in 1969.

# Jimmy Durante

Singer and comedian (b. James Frances Durante, New York City, February 10, 1893; d. Santa Monica, California, January 29, 1980). Durante began his career as a pianist at Coney Island in Brooklyn, where he was known as "Ragtime Jimmy." He also organized a five-piece jazz band there. While he is best known as a comedian, first with the team of Clayton, Jackson, and Durante in the mid-1920s and later as a single in radio, movies, and television, he composed his own specialty numbers ("Inka, Dinka, Doo," "I'm Jimmy the Well-Dressed Man," and "Umbriago"). He also turned out a batch of songs in the early 1920s, which created quite a stir.

His big year as a composer was 1921, first with the smash hit "I've Got My Habits On," which he composed to the lyrics of Chris Smith and Bob Schafer (1897–1943). Bennie Krueger, the original alto saxophonist with the ORIGINAL DIXIELAND JAZZ BAND, had his own dance orchestra and created a big plug with his recording (Brunswick 2181). This reception of a Durante tune led Joe Davis to sign him to a contract as a staff composer with his TRIANGLE MUSIC firm. With the same team, Durante wrote "Daddy, Your Mama Is Lonesome for You." Then, with Schafer and Dave Ringle (1893–1965), he wrote "Sweetness." With SAM COSLOW, he wrote the harmonically interesting "I Didn't Start in to Love You" (a tricky piece that, when well played, is a mighty fine blues number); "I'm on My Way to New Orleans" and "One of Your Smiles" were written with Bartley Costello (1871–1941).

"I Ain't Never Had Nobody Crazy over Me" (1923), a fine, jazzy blues number, written with two drummers, Johnny Stein and Jack Roth. "Papa String Bean" (1923) had lyrics by Al Bernard, the performing partner of J. RUSSEL ROBINSON. Durante spent the rest of a long career working in nightclubs, radio, films, and television.

# E

## Nelson Eddy

Singer (b. Providence, Rhode Island, June 29, 1901; d. Hollywood, California, March 6, 1967). Eddy was a self-trained baritone who honed his skills by listening to opera recordings. His family moved to Philadelphia when he was in his teens, and he took a number of day jobs while pursuing his passion for singing. He studied in Europe in 1923, and then returned to New York, where he did some concert and radio work. Eddy caught the eye of MGM head Louis B. Mayer and was signed to a contract in 1933. However, it wasn't until two years later, when he teamed with JEANETTE MACDONALD, that he achieved stardom (1935–1942). Eddy was a favorite on radio, hosting his own shows as well as doing spots on *The Voice of Firestone* and *The Chase and Sanborn Hour* from the mid-1930s to the early 1950s. His important recordings include two from 1935, from the film version of *Naughty Marietta*: "Ah! Sweet Mystery of Life" (Victor 4281) and "I'm Falling in Love with Someone" (Victor 4280). "When I Grow Too Old to Dream" came from the 1935 film *The Night Is Young* (Victor 4285). "Indian Love Call," from the film *Rose Marie*, sold over a million copies with Eddy and MacDonald's vocal (Victor 4323).

After breaking with MacDonald, Eddy made a few more films, and then returned to performing on radio and in stock productions and nightclubs. He died shortly before a scheduled appearance at a Miami Beach hotel.

# Cliff Edwards

Singer and comedian (b. Hannibal, Missouri, June 14, 1895; d. Hollywood, California, July 17, 1971). Known as Ukulele Ike, he was a favorite in vaudeville, Broadway musicals in the 1920s, and films and radio through the 1930s and 1940s. His soft and friendly voice was heard on many recordings, starting in 1924 with "It Had to Be You" (Pathe 032047), followed by "All Alone" (Pathe 032090). He appeared on Broadway in *Lady, Be Good* (1924) and made hit records of "Fascinating Rhythm" (Pathe 025126) and "Oh, Lady Be Good" (Pathe 025130). He interpolated "Who Takes Care of the Caretaker's Daughter?" into the show and turned that into a hit (Pathe 025128) as well. The same year he made "Paddlin' Madeline Home" (Pathe 025149). His recording of "I Can't Give You Anything but Love," from the Broadway musical *Blackbirds of 1928*, became a #1 hit (Columbia 1471-D), and the following year he introduced "Singin' in the Rain" in the film *Hollywood Revue of 1929*. His recording made the #1 position (Columbia 1869-D). He was the voice of Jiminy Cricket in Disney's *Pinocchio* (1940), and he had a double-sided hit with "When You Wish Upon a Star" (which won the Academy Award in 1940 for Best Song) and "Give a Little Whistle" (Victor 26477). He followed this role a year later with a part in Disney's animated feature *Dumbo*, with less success. Through the early 1960s, Edwards continued to work for Disney, primarily recording children's records.

# Gus Edwards

Composer (b. Hohensalza, Germany, August 18, 1879; d. Hollywood, California, November 7, 1945). He came to America when he was eight years old, and his family settled in the Williamsburg section of Brooklyn. He soon discovered Manhattan's Union Square, and began to hang around the vaudeville houses there. In 1893, singing star LOTTIE GILSON discovered his sweet singing voice and hired him to act as a stooge for her. He made his debut in the balcony of Hurtig and Seamon's, where he would sing along with Gilson on the chorus of such songs as "The Little Lost Child." Gilson was the first to use this particular routine, and Edwards was the first teenage boy to be used to plug a song in that manner. He became such a favorite that he was soon in demand to sing with MAGGIE CLINE, Helene Mora, and Imogene Comer. One day a vaudeville booking agent discovered him and created an act called the Newsboy Quintet, in which he and four other boys dressed in ragged clothes sang hits of the day. PAUL DRESSER gave pointers to Edwards and allowed him to use a piano at the offices of HOWLEY, HAVILAND AND COMPANY. It was Howley who, in 1898, published Edwards's first tune, a COON SONG called "All I Wants Is My Black Baby Back." It was featured not only by the Newsboy Quintet, but also by Bob Alden, The Ragtime Man. Edwards met Will D. Cobb (1876–1930), and they joined forces to produce "I Couldn't Stand to See My Baby Lose," introduced by the famous coon shouter May Irwin. In 1905, Edwards collaborated with Vincent Bryan for the Indian spoof "Tammany." The song was a takeoff on political hijinks, written for an affair sponsored by the National Democratic Club of New York and well received by this special audience. When Jefferson DeAngelis sang it in vaudeville, it became a hit. The same year, the same team struck it rich for the Witmarks with a great automobile song, "In My Merry Oldsmobile." The impetus to write the song came from newspaper stories about two Oldsmobiles being driven from Detroit to Portland, Oregon, in forty-four days, the first cross-country trip. It is the most successful automobile song and the most memorable. However, try as he might, Edwards could never get the Oldsmobile company to give him one of their cars.

Bankrolled by two hits published by WITMARK, Edwards decided to open his own publishing company toward the end of 1905, and his firm lasted until 1908, when he sold it to the Witmarks. His first numbers were both hits, "Sunbonnet Sue" (which sold over a million copies) and "I Just Can't Make My Eyes Behave" (which Anna Held introduced in the show *A Parisian Model* and used as her theme song ever after). Both of these had lyrics by his old friend Will D. Cobb. They did it again with their biggest seller, the 1907, three-million-copy success "School Days," which they wrote for Edwards's vaudeville act called "School Boys and Girls." Edwards wrote the act, directed it, and starred in it, and introduced, over the years, many young performers who would become famous in show business. He played the part of a schoolmaster, and some of his "students" included EDDIE CANTOR, George Jessel, Walter Winchell, Earl Carroll, Lilyan Tashman, Lila Lee, Georgie Price, Groucho Marx, Ray Bolger, Herman Timberg, Charles King, Mae Murray, Louise Groody, Bert Wheeler, Jack Pearl, Eleanor Powell, Sally Rand, Eddie Buzzell, Mitzi Mayfair, Ona Munson, Ann Dvorak, Larry Adler, and the Duncan Sisters. Georgie Price introduced the Edwards-Edward Madden favorite "By the Light of the Silvery Moon" in 1909. That same year, the song entered the *Ziegfeld Follies*, where Lillian Lorraine sang it and boosted its sale to well over two million copies.

Edwards composed the fine "Merry-Go-Round Rag" and published it at the end of 1908. It was one of the last tunes issued by the Gus Edwards Music Publishing Company. Edwards spent most of the balance of his career in vaudeville with his school act, and later worked in Hollywood.

# Ray Egan

See *Richard A. Whiting*

# Duke Ellington

Famed jazz composer and pianist (b. Edward Kennedy Ellington, Washington, D.C., April 29, 1899; d. New York City, May 24, 1974). Ellington led an outstanding band for more than fifty years. They started recording in 1924 as The Washingtonians, but from 1927 on, under the Ellington name. His sidemen over the years comprised a Who's Who of Jazz. Several who were with him from the beginning until their deaths were Otto Hardwick (alto sax), Fred Guy (banjo, guitar), Arthur Whetsol (trumpet), and Freddy Jenkins (trumpet). In December 1927, Ellington first headlined at the Cotton Club, and he remained there until 1931. Ellington formed an early important partnership with MILLS MUSIC's Jack and Irving Mills. Irving managed the band and often took composer's credit on early Ellington numbers; he also arranged for Ellington's major recording dates. Ellington's band toured the U.S. until the late 1950s, and toured Europe first in 1933 and sporadically thereafter. Ellington kept his band until the end—touring, playing jazz festivals and concerts, and recording. He wrote his autobiography, *Music Is My Mistress*, in 1973.

Although he wrote many extended works for orchestra, it is Ellington's pop songs that are important here. His first hit recording came in 1930. "Three Little Words," with vocal by the Rhythm Boys (BING CROSBY, Al Rinker, and HARRY BARRIS), was one of two in the Ellington canon not composed by the leader (Victor 22528). The other was the SAM COSLOW-Arthur Johnston "Cocktails for Two," which came from a 1934 film, *Murder at the Vanities* (Victor 24617). His first major pop composition was the 1931 "Mood Indigo," recorded with his Cotton Club Orchestra (Victor 22587). His 1932 "It Don't Mean a Thing (If It Ain't Got That Swing)" had a vocal by Ivie Anderson and solos by Johnny Hodges and Joe Nanton (Brunswick 6265). "Sophisticated Lady," a 1933 instrumental, became his most famous composition (Brunswick 6600). Billy Eckstine revived it in a 1946 recording that wasn't released until 1948 (National 9049). "Solitude" received an instrumental treatment in 1934, with a hit recording (Brunswick 6987) featuring the baritone sax of Harry Carney. "Caravan" was a hit in 1937, with cocomposer Juan Tizol featured on valve trombone (Master 131). "I Let a Song Go Out of My Heart" was a #1 hit in 1938, which featured alto saxophonist Johnny Hodges, Barney Bigard on clarinet, Harry Carney on baritone sax, and Lawrence Brown on trombone (Brunswick 8108). "I Got It Bad (And That Ain't Good)" came from Ellington's revue *Jump for Joy* in 1941 (Victor 27531), with vocalist Ivie Anderson, and solos by Ellington and Hodges. Recorded in 1940 as "Never No Lament," it was rereleased in 1943 as "Don't Get Around Much Anymore" (Victor 26610).

Ellington's alter ego and arranger Billy Strayhorn (b. Dayton, Ohio, November 29, 1915; d. New York City, May 31, 1967) composed Duke Ellington's 1940s theme song, "Take the "A" Train." Strayhorn also wrote "Lush Life" and "Satin Doll," first recorded by Ellington in 1953 (Capitol 2458), although it was not copyrighted until five years later. Strayhorn's role in Ellington's band was very important, but he did not produce many pop hits.

# Ethnic Songs

Vaudeville and turn-of-the-century entertainment were rife with ethnic characterizations. Jewish performers, such as WEBER AND FIELDS, portrayed "Dutch" comedians; AL JOLSON and EDDIE CANTOR appeared in blackface; MAGGIE CLINE portrayed a comic Irish character. Waves of new immigrants led to heightened interest in Italian, German, Jewish, and Irish characters, in both comic and sentimental portrayals. Many of the ethnic communities supported these characterizations, which were not entirely viewed as negative.

It is not surprising that Tin Pan Alley catered to this interest, both by providing songs for ethnic character performers and by creating subgenres of ethnic songs. COON SONGS were tremendously popular from the 1880s through the 1920s in various guises. The influx of black performers into Northern urban centers, along with the transformation of the minstrel show into vaudeville, made black characterizations—including comedy, dance, and music—a major part of any stage entertainment. IRVING BERLIN had his first hit writing a pseudo-Italian song, "Marie, from Sunny Italy," at the request of bar owner Mike Salter (who employed him as a singing waiter). It seems that Salter's major competitor, a bar around the corner, had scored big with *its* pseudo-Italian ballad, so Salter thought he ought to have one, too. Berlin would go on to write songs in many different "ethnic" styles.

Sentimental and comic songs written in an "Irish" style also were tremendously popular, and were embraced warmly by the Irish. Songs like "Danny Boy" eventually transcended ethnic characterization and became major pop hits as generic ballads. Touring Hawaiian musicians and dancers inspired a spate of Hawaiian-flavored numbers, often merging stereotypes, such as the Irish-Hawaii comic novelty, "O'Brien Is Tryin' to Learn to Talk Hawaiian (To His Honolulu Lu"). Such genre mixes helped extend popular song forms.

# Ruth Etting

Popular singer of the 1920s, (b. David City, Nebraska, November 23, 1903; d. Colorado Springs, Colorado, September 24, 1978). Etting was a singing star in Chicago in the early 1920s on radio and in nightclubs. She came to New York to appear on Broadway in the

*Ziegfeld Follies of 1927* and became the toast of the town. In the *Follies of 1931,* she revived the Nora Bayes-Jack Norworth song "Shine On, Harvest Moon," which tore the house down at each performance (Columbia 3085-D). Her hit recordings started in 1926 with "Lonesome and Sorry" (Columbia 644-D). It was followed in 1927 with "Thinking of You" (Columbia 827-D), "Sam, the Old Accordion Man" (Columbia 908-D), and "Shaking the Blues Away" (Columbia 1113-D), which she introduced in the 1927 *Follies*. 1929 brought several top hits, including "Love Me or Leave Me," which became her theme song (Columbia l680-D) and the title of her biopic, starring DORIS DAY, in 1955; "I'll Get By" (Columbia 1733-D); and "Mean to Me" (Columbia 1762-D). Etting introduced "Ten Cents a Dance" in the musical *Simple Simon* and had the hit recording in 1930 (Columbia 2l46-D). "Reaching for the Moon" (Columbia 2377-D) and "Guilty" (Columbia 2529-D) were her hits in 1931. "Can't We Talk It Over" made its debut on disc that same year (Banner 32398).

During the 1930s, Etting made three films, and also starred in a London revue, *Transatlantic Rhythm*, in 1936. Her last U.S. pop hit came in 1935, with a #1 winner, "Life Is a Song" (Columbia 3031-D). Less active after World War II, she had a brief return to popularity as a nightclub singer in the late 1940s and then retired from performing.

# James Reese Europe

African-American bandleader and composer (b. Mobile, Alabama, February 22, 1881; d. New York City, May 9, 1919). Europe was one of the first successful black bandleaders; his orchestra played syncopated dance music that forecast the coming jazz band style. He founded Harlem's Clef Club, an organization of black musicians and composers, and helped promote black songwriters and their work. He was hired by VERNON AND IRENE CASTLE, the popular white dance pair, to provide music for their dance programs during the 1910s, helping to introduce the fox-trot and other dance forms. Europe also composed a number of custom instrumentals for the Castles to showcase their dancing. In 1914, Europe helped lyricist Chris Smith turn his hit song, "Ballin' the Jack," into an instrumental number to accompany the newly created dance. During World War I, Europe was drafted and led the 396th Regiment Band, known as the Hellfighters; when this all-black regiment returned from its triumphant tour of duty, a parade was held in Harlem that became a source of considerable pride. Europe's performances in Europe helped introduce ragtime rhythms there, and paved the way for the subsequent enormous success enjoyed by black musicians abroad. Singer/lyricist Noble Sissle and pianist/composer EUBIE BLAKE were given early career boosts by Europe, who left Sissle in charge of his New York band when he was leading the Hellfighters. Europe's career was tragically ended when a jealous band member stabbed him to death in May 1919, in an argument over a woman.

# Sammy Fain

Composer (b. Samuel Feinberg, New York City, June 17, 1902; d. Los Angeles, California, December 6, 1989). Fain had a long career, scoring pop hits from the 1920s through the 1960s.

Fain's father was a cantor, and Fain taught himself to play piano. After graduating from high school, he got a job as staff pianist at the MILLS MUSIC firm. His first big hit was his first published song, "Nobody Knows What a Red Head Mamma Can Do" (1924). The lyrics were by AL DUBIN and Irving Mills, and the best-selling recordings were those of Margaret Young (Brunswick 2806) and Ray Miller and his orchestra (Brunswick 2778). "Let a Smile Be Your Umbrella" (1927) has lyrics by Irving Kahal (1903–1942) and Francis Wheeler. ROGER WOLFE KAHN and his orchestra made a splendid recording (Victor 21233). Milton Berle, "The Wayward Youth," plugged it in vaudeville, and it was revived in the film *Give My Regards to Broadway* (1948).

"Wedding Bells Are Breaking Up That Old Gang of Mine" (1929) has lyrics by Kahal and Willie Raskin (1896–1942). Johnny Perkins introduced the song, and it was revived in 1954 by The Four Aces (Decca 29123). "You Brought a New Kind of Love to Me" (1930) was composed with Pierre Norman Connor (1895–1952), with lyrics by Irving Kahal. It was introduced by Maurice Chevalier in *The Big Pond* (Victor 22405). When the Marx Brothers wanted to kid Chevalier, they used this song in *Monkey Business* (1931). It was revived in 1963, as the theme for the film *A New Kind of Love*. "Was That the Human Thing to Do?"

(1931) has lyrics by Joe Young and was introduced and made famous by Guy Lombardo and the Royal Canadians.

"By a Waterfall" (1933), with lyrics by Irving Kahal, was introduced by Dick Powell and Ruby Keeler in *Footlight Parade*. It was given an incredibly elaborate twelve-minute sequence in the film, a splashy interlude featuring Busby Berkeley's exotic choreography. "That Old Feeling" (1937) was written with Lew Brown for Virginia Verrill to sing in the film *Vogues of 1938*. Count Basie and his orchestra (Columbia 36795) helped it to success, and later it was revived by Peggy Lee (Capitol 10012). Jane Froman sang it on the sound track of *With a Song in My Heart* (1952). "I Can Dream, Can't I?" was written with Kahal for Tamara to sing in the show *Right This Way* (1937). It was revived on a best-selling record by the Andrews Sisters in 1949 (Decca 24705). "Are You Having Any Fun?" (1939) was written with Jack Yellen for Ella Logan to sing in *George White's Scandals of 1939*. She also made the hit record (Columbia 35251).

"I'll Be Seeing You" (1938), again with lyrics by Kahal, was placed in the *Royal Palm Revue*, a Los Angeles showcase, which starred Harry Richman, Tony Martin, Abe Lyman, Rudy Vallee, and the DeMarcos. It was next used in the film of the same name (1944), where it scored solidly. Hit recordings were made by Hildegarde (Decca 23291) and by Frank Sinatra with Tommy Dorsey's orchestra (Victor 26539). "Dear Hearts and Gentle People" (1949) has lyrics by Bob Hilliard. It was an enormously popular song, thanks to Dinah Shore (Columbia 38605) and Bing Crosby (Decca 24798).

"Secret Love" (1953), with lyrics by Paul Francis Webster (1907–1984), was written for Doris Day to sing in the film *Calamity Jane* (1953). It earned the first of Fain's two Oscars for Best Song. Day's record sold over a million copies (Columbia 40108). "Love Is a Many-Splendored Thing" (1955), again with lyrics by Webster, was written for the film of the same name and won the second Oscar for Fain. The recording by The Four Aces sold over a million copies (Decca 29625). "A Certain Smile" (1958) was written with Webster as a film's title song. Johnny Mathis made the million-selling record (Columbia 41193). "A Very Precious Love" (1958), with Webster's lyrics, appeared in the film *Marjorie Morningstar*, introduced by Gene Kelly. "April Love" (1957), with lyrics by Webster, came from the movie of the same name. Pat Boone's recording sold over a million copies (Dot 15660). "Tender Is the Night" (1961), with lyrics by Webster, was an important part of the plot of a nonmusical film of the same name, based on the Scott Fitzgerald novel.

# Famous Music (1928–Today)

Founded as the music-publishing arm of Famous-Lasky Corporation (the predecessor of Paramount Pictures), Famous was originally built solely from new songs by Paramount's staff composers. (Warner Bros. and MGM chose to purchase the back catalogs of other firms in order to start their music-publishing businesses.) Famous holds over 100,000 copyrights of popular songs and movie music. It is now part of the media conglomerate Viacom, which purchased Paramount and its assets in the mid-1990s.

# Leo Feist

Music publisher (b. Leopold Feist, 1869; d. 1930, full dates unknown). A sales manager for a corset company, Feist liked to write songs, and he convinced EDWARD B. MARKS to publish a couple of them. When sales did not live up to expectations, Feist decided to give up songwriting, but he liked the business so much that he joined with Joe Frankenthaler to publish other, more successful, songwriters. Among the first songs Feist and Frankenthaler issued were two in 1897 by the prolific HARRY VON TILZER. A year later, Feist issued Abe Holzmann's "Smoky Mokes," a big hit that firmly established their business. Feist was an

Leo Feist at the height of his publishing career, 1907.

expert salesman, and he often approached orchestra leaders himself and personally sold copies at various stores. His biggest coup was getting John Philip Sousa to program "Smoky Mokes" in his band concerts. He also had an excellent staff, including EDGAR F. BITNER, who helped build the firm into a powerhouse. It was Bitner's 1917 innovation to eliminate the loose, middle sheet from the firm's publications, thus saving money on paper.

Hits for Feist from the 1910s include Fred Fisher's "Peg o' My Heart" (1913) and the World War I classic "Over There" and "Everybody Loves a 'Jazz' Band," popularized by big-lunged singer EMMA CARUS (both 1917). A year later, Feist had the major hit "K-K-K-Katy," one of several wartime favorites. Feist published such 1920s classics as "Five Foot Two, Eyes of Blue" and "Toot-Toot-Tootsie! (Goo'bye)." "My Blue Heaven," a major hit for crooner GENE AUSTIN, was said to be the firm's best-seller ever, selling over five million sheets.

The Feist firm was purchased by MGM in 1934 and combined with ROBBINS MUSIC CORPORATION and Miller Music, a year later under the name Robbins-Feist-Miller, but more widely known as The BIG THREE.

LEO FEIST, INC. (1897–1934)

| | |
|---|---|
| 1897–1899 | 1227 Broadway/42 West 30 Street (as Feist and Frankenthaler) |
| 1900–1901 | 36 West 28th Street |
| 1902– | 36 West 28th Street (as Leo Feist, Inc.) |
| 1903–1912 | Feist Building, 134 West 37th Street |
| 1913–1916 | Feist Building, 231–235 West 40th Street |
| 1917– | Feist Building, 240 West 40th Street |
| 1918–1930 | Feist Building, 235 West 40th Street |
| 1930–1934 | 56 Cooper Square |

# Dorothy Fields

One of the few successful female lyricists of the Alley (b. Allenhurst, New Jersey, July 15, 1905; d. New York City, March 28, 1974). Daughter of comedian Lew Fields, Dorothy collaborated mainly with JIMMY MCHUGH, JEROME KERN, and Cy Coleman, writing extensively for Broadway and Hollywood in a career that spanned 1928–1973. Her siblings included Joseph, who established himself as a playwright, and Herbert (b. July 26, 1898; d. March 24, 1958), who was also a noted lyricist and often partnered with his sister.

Dorothy began her career as an actress in an early RICHARD RODGERS–LORENZ HART show, *You'd Be Surprised*, which played for one night in 1920 at the Plaza Hotel. She initially wrote lyrics for composer J. FRED COOTS, but soon after, met her first main collaborator, Jimmy McHugh, when both were employed by MILLS MUSIC. With McHugh, Dorothy wrote the lyrics for *Blackbirds of 1928*, from which came "I Can't Give You Anything but

Love," "Diga Diga Doo," and "Doin' the New Low Down." From the 1930 musical *International Revue* came "On the Sunny Side of the Street" and "Exactly Like You."

In 1930, the McHugh-Fields team moved to Hollywood, as did many other Tin Pan Alley songwriting teams. A 1931 film title song, "Cuban Love Song," enjoyed success on a RUTH ETTING recording (Columbia 2580-D). In 1935, Fields formed a partnership with composer Jerome Kern. They wrote "I Won't Dance" for the film *Roberta. Every Night at Eight* was the first film to have a complete score by McHugh and Fields. "I'm in the Mood for Love" was the big hit. In the 1936 film *Swing Time*, she had "The Way You Look Tonight" and "A Fine Romance," both introduced by FRED ASTAIRE.

By the end of the 1930s, Fields had returned to working on Broadway. In the early-to-mid-1940s, she collaborated with her brother Herbert on the librettos for three COLE PORTER Musicals: *Let's Face It*, *Something for the Boys*, and *Mexican Hayride*. In 1945, the duo wrote the book (with Dorothy supplying lyrics, and music by Sigmund Romberg) for the successful *Up in Central Park*, followed a year later by the classic book for *Annie Get Your Gun* (with music and lyrics by IRVING BERLIN). Fields produced a series of less successful shows in the 1950s with various collaborators. Her last hits came from the 1965 musical *Sweet Charity*: "If My Friends Could See Me Now" and "Big Spender," with music by Cy Coleman. Her last show was 1973's *Seesaw*, also written with Coleman. Fields died in early 1974.

# Film Music

## Silent Films

During the years 1918–1928 Tin Pan Alley cemented its association with the movies. Even though the screen couldn't talk, music played an important part in the viewing environment as accompaniment to the action, usually provided by a pianist in the theater.

CHARLES N. DANIELS, using his pseudonym "Neil Moret," and lyricist Harry Williams wrote the first commissioned title song for a motion picture. The song was "Mickey" (1918), and it was published by Daniels and Wilson of San Francisco to coincide with the release of the film. It starred Mabel Normand, whose photograph adorns the sheet music cover. The song was acquired later that year by Waterson, Berlin and Snyder, which published it in two different small-sized editions. The Mack Sennett star and song got plenty of exposure. This started the vogue for title songs, which is still going strong.

The most famous stars of the silent screen—Charlie Chaplin, Mary Pickford, and Pearl White (star of the *Perils of Pauline* serials)—appeared on sheet music covers as early as 1914 (the two women) and 1915 (Chaplin). "March of the Movies" by M. A. Althouse (1915) features a drawing of an audience in a nickelodeon, watching Chaplin in his tramp costume, with a pianist in the pit. "Those Keystone Comedy Cops," by Charles McCarron (1915), has a typical photograph of Sennett's Keystone Kops on its cover, with Ford Sterling on the telephone and Fatty Arbuckle trying to overhear the conversation. Over the next two decades, the movies would provide big plugs for songs, and major studios would purchase some of the Alley's largest firms to take care of their musical needs.

Composer ERNO RAPEE did much to popularize the use of "themes"—stock melodies that could be used to accompany typical silent-film scenes—through two popular collections that he published in the mid-1920s. Many orchestra leaders in smaller towns and cities used these books as guides for providing music for films. Rapee also composed many original scores, most notably 1926's *What Price Glory*; its theme song was given lyrics by LEW POLLACK and became a major hit, "Charmaine."

## Talkies

With the advent of "talking pictures," the importance of music to film became even greater. Broadway musicals were naturals for importation into the new medium, and film studios realized that they would need to hire composers and lyricists to provide both background music and songs for their pictures. Hit songs could also be ideal promotional vehicles to bring audiences into the theaters, and film studios began purchasing music publishers in order to be able to profit from their output. Warner Bros., MGM, and Paramount all became involved in music publishing in a big way.

The Great Depression had a huge impact on the Broadway stage, and many writers who previously could count on contributing to the many revues and shows on Broadway now looked to Hollywood for employment. Although many were unhappy when their songs were treated as mere product that could be added (or dropped) into almost any film, some did find films a creative medium. Over the coming years, unique musical films, such as the classic *Over the Rainbow*, were created and showcased songs that were every bit as good as the Broadway hits of the past.

## Movie Songs

Sheets relating to films began to be published in 1914 with "Nat-u-ritch," the song from a film called *Squaw Man*. From then until now, movie title songs have been a staple of sheet music publishing. Songs from films reached their peak with the deluge of musicals in the 1930s. When television began in the 1950s, production of movie musicals fell off, and by the 1960s, the main use of music was for theme songs, usually played under the title and credits. Many a pop song was interpolated into a film score and appeared with a film cover. The biggest-selling film songs are "White Christmas," "Ramona," and "As Time Goes By." The largest score published from a film was *Alexander's Ragtime Band*, with twenty-nine individual songs with the same standard cover. By far, the oddest publications from a film were the *Oklahoma!* songs. Their cover doesn't give any indication that they are from a film; there is no studio name or logo, nor a listing of any star credits. Bourne, Inc. published the reprints of the Disney songs that Irving Berlin, Inc. originally published. Some songs from American films were issued only in foreign editions.

## Biopics

One easy way to incorporate music into films was by filming the "true life story" of a major musician or composer. This had the added value of enabling movie studies to draw on their back catalogs of songs, pulling out "golden oldies" to sprinkle liberally through a score. *Variety*, the show business newspaper, coined the term "biopic" for these mostly fictional accounts of the lives of composers and lyricists. Many of these feature laughable plot lines and improbable scenes in which Hollywood actors mime playing musical instruments. Nonetheless, these biopics did much to repopularize older songs and introduce new ones.

## Best-Known Biopics

| Year | Composer/Performer Profiled | Title | Lead Actor |
|---|---|---|---|
| 1936 | Florenz Ziegfeld | *The Great Ziegfeld* | William Powell |
| 1939 | Victor Herbert | *The Great Victor Herbert* | Walter Connolly |
| 1940 | Stephen Foster | *Swanee River* | Don Ameche |
| 1940 | Lillian Russell | *Lillian Russell* | Alice Faye |
| 1942 | George M. Cohan | *Yankee Doodle Dandy* | James Cagney |
| 1942 | Paul Dresser | *My Gal Sal* | Victor Mature |
| 1943 | Dan Emmett | *Dixie* | Bing Crosby |
| 1944 | Ernest R. Ball | *Irish Eyes Are Smiling* | Dick Haymes |
| 1944 | Nora Bayes | *Shine On, Harvest Moon* | Ann Sheridan |
| 1945 | Texas Guinan | *Incendiary Blonde* | Betty Hutton |
| 1945 | George Gershwin | *Rhapsody in Blue* | Robert Alda |
| 1946 | Dolly Sisters | *The Dolly Sisters* | Betty Grable and June Haver |
| 1946 | Al Jolson | *The Jolson Story* | Larry Parks |
| 1946 | Cole Porter | *Night and Day* | Cary Grant |
| 1946 | Jerome Kern | *Till the Clouds Roll By* | Robert Walker |
| 1948 | Rodgers and Hart | *Words and Music* | Tom Drake and Mickey Rooney |
| 1949 | Al Jolson | *Jolson Sings Again* | Larry Parks |
| 1950 | Kalmar and Ruby | *Three Little Words* | Fred Astaire and Red Skelton |
| 1951 | Gus Kahn | *I'll See You in My Dreams* | Danny Thomas |
| 1953 | Eva Tanguay | *The I Don't Care Girl* | Mitzi Gaynor |
| 1953 | Eddie Cantor | *The Eddie Cantor Story* | Keefe Brasselle |
| 1954 | Sigmund Romberg | *Deep in My Heart* | Jose Ferrer |
| 1955 | Ruth Etting | *Love Me or Leave Me* | Doris Day |
| 1956 | De Sylva-Brown-Henderson | *The Best Things in Life Are Free* | Dan Dailey, Gordon MacRae, Ernest Borgnine |
| 1958 | W. C. Handy | *St. Louis Blues* | Nat "King" Cole |

# Ted Fio Rito

Composer (b. Newark, New Jersey, December 20, 1900; d. Scottsdale, Arizona, July 22, 1971). Fio Rito began his musical career as a demonstrator, playing piano for composer-publisher Al Piantadosi. Next, he formed a band to open the Oriole Terrace in Detroit, with Dan Russo as coleader. NICK LUCAS, later known as "The Singing Troubadour" in vaudeville, was their vocalist.

Fio Rito's most successful time as a songwriter was the 1920s, although his heyday as a bandleader came in the 1930s. His Oriole Terrace Orchestra was in such demand that he took it to Chicago for a record-breaking, four-year engagement at the Edgewater Beach Hotel. It was during this stay in Chicago that Fio Rito wrote with master lyricist GUS KAHN.

Their first hit, "Toot, Toot, Tootsie, Goodbye!" (1922), was written with Ernie Erdman (1879–1946) and Dan Russo (1885–1956). The song was used in *Bombo* (October 6, 1921), enthusiastically sung by AL JOLSON. Jolson would eventually sing it in four films, spanning his entire movie career. The Oriole Terrace Orchestra's recording of it was definitive (Brunswick 2337). The next big Fio Rito-Kahn song was "No, No, Nora" (1923), thanks to RUTH ETTING's plugging it and the Benson Orchestra's making a record of it (Victor 19121). Max Kortlander made a wonderful arrangement for piano roll (QRS 2398).

The new team scored again with "Charley My Boy" (1924). Charley Straight made one of his knockout arrangements for QRS, and Bennie Krueger's orchestra helped make it a success (Brunswick 2667). A few years later, it became popular all over again when Lindbergh made his historic flight. Their other 1924 number, "I Need Some Pettin'," with Robert A. King (1862–1932) as cocomposer, became the jazz lovers' favorite because of the recording made by the Wolverine Orchestra (Gennett 20062) in June. The group consisted of Bix Beiderbecke, cornet; Jimmy Hartwell, clarinet and alto sax; George Johnson, tenor sax; Dick Voynow, piano; Bob Gillette, banjo; Min Leibrook, tuba; and Vic Moore, drums.

"Alone at Last" (1925) was another Fio Rito hit with Gus Kahn, this time because of a COON-SANDERS recording (Victor 19728). The band featured the beautiful ballad nightly at the Congress Restaurant. "I Never Knew" (1925) was the team's last hit together, and ROGER WOLFE KAHN's recording helped it along (Victor 19845).

"King for a Day" and "Laugh, Clown, Laugh" (both 1928) were written with lyricists SAM LEWIS and JOE YOUNG, the latter as the theme for Lon Chaney's film of the same name. Again writing with Lewis and Young, Fio Rito had his last hit with "Then You've Never Been Blue" (1929).

His band took up much of Fio Rito's attention during the 1930s, when, at different times, he had young Betty Grable and June Haver as vocalists before they became movie stars. Fio Rito and his orchestra appeared in films with Dick Powell and did many radio shows. He continued to lead an orchestra on the West Coast until the 1960s.

# Fred Fisher

Composer active in the first three decades of the twentieth century (b. Cologne, Germany, September 30, 1875; d. New York City, January 14, 1942). Fisher came to the United States in 1900 and settled in Chicago, where a black saloon pianist gave him lessons. His first hit, for which he wrote both words and music, was "If the Man in the Moon Were a Coon" (1905), published by WILL ROSSITER, who had just reentered the music business after a five-year absence. It eventually sold over three million copies and gave Fisher the start of his career. The next year he wrote "I've Said My Last Farewell," with lyrics by Ed Rose.

In 1910 Fisher wrote two million-selling songs. "Any Little Girl That's a Nice Little Girl Is the Right Little Girl for Me" was the first syncopated number to become a hit that year, and "Come, Josephine, in My Flying Machine" was the second and bigger of the songs. It became the most familiar of all airplane songs and remains a classic, with cheerful lyrics by Alfred Bryan. With Bryan doing lyrics again in 1913, Fisher had another hit with "Peg o' My Heart," which drew inspiration from the play of the same name, starring Laurette Taylor. When it was revived by the Harmonicats in 1947, the disc sold over two million copies and continued the song's popularity (Vita Coustic 1).

It was around this time that Fisher started to compose songs with foreign cities or countries in their titles. Since many of them became hits, it seems his idea was sound. It started in 1913 with "I'm on My Way to Mandalay" and continued with "When It's Moonlight on the Alamo," "I Want to Go to Tokio," "Norway, the Land of the Midnight Sun," "Siam," "Ireland Must Be Heaven, for My Mother Came from There," "In the Land o' Yamo Yamo," "Lorraine, My Beautiful Alsace Lorraine," "When It's Night Time in Little Italy," and ending with "Fifty Million Frenchmen Can't Be Wrong."

Dolly Connolly helped make "There's a Broken Heart for Every Light on Broadway" (1915) famous, while SOPHIE TUCKER did the same for "You Can't Get Along with 'Em or Without 'Em" (1916). EDDIE CANTOR slayed 'em with "They Go Wild, Simply Wild, over Me" (1917). Fisher's biggest hit came in 1919, when he wrote the lyrics for and published Johnny Black's phenomenal tune "Dardanella." It was recorded first by Ben Selvin's Novelty Orchestra (Victor 18633) as an instrumental, selling more than six and a half million discs, but the song, with Fisher's lyrics, had a sheet music sale of more than two million. What made it so popular was not the melody but a highly original bass line. When JEROME KERN wrote "Ka-lu-a" for his show *Good Morning, Dearie*, using the identical recurring bass pattern, Fisher sued Kern and won, the judge ruling that Fisher's one measure of music was "essential and substantial" to his song.

In 1921, Fisher, in collaboration with Willie Raskin (1896–1942), wrote the lovely "I Found a Rose in the Devil's Garden," which PETE WENDLING made into a fine piano roll arrangement (QRS 1411). Another multimillion in sheet music sales came because of Max

Kortlander's brilliant piano roll arrangement of "Chicago" (1922) for the QRS company (QRS 2021) and PAUL WHITEMAN's scintillating version of the song for Victor records (Victor 18946). As the home of jazz during this decade, Chicago is perfectly evoked as "that toddlin' town." Fisher found himself with another hit when Bix Beiderbecke recorded "There Ain't No Sweet Man That's Worth the Salt of My Tears" (1927) in Tom Satterfield's arrangement for the Paul Whiteman Orchestra, with the Rhythm Boys as vocalists (Victor 21464). Sophie Tucker got another Fisher favorite in "Happy Days and Lonely Nights" (1928). It became so popular that two years later RUTH ETTING interpolated it into *Simple Simon.*

With the coming of talking pictures, Fred Fisher went to Hollywood in 1929. His first song hit there was "I Don't Want Your Kisses" from *So This Is College* (1929). His next one was "Blue Is the Night" used in *Their Own Desire* (1930). In 1931, Fisher wrote a pop song, "I'm All Dressed Up with a Broken Heart," which bandleader Ben Bernie played to success. And at the end of that decade, he wrote "Your Feet's Too Big," which FATS WALLER made his own (Bluebird 10500). It was so closely identified with Waller that it was included in a potpourri of his own songs for the hit revue *Ain't Misbehavin'* (1978).

# Mark Fisher

Songwriter, bandleader (b. Philadelphia, Pennsylvania, March 24, 1895; d. Long Lake, Illinois, January 2, 1948). Fisher is remembered today for two 1920s standards: 1924's "Oh, How I Miss You Tonight," written with JOE BURKE and lyricist BENNY DAVIS, and 1928's "When You're Smiling," composed with Larry Shay (1897–1988) and lyricist Joe Goodwin (1889–1943). Fisher had a million-selling hit with "Oh, How I Miss You" when he recorded it as vocalist and banjo player with TED FIO RITO's Oriole Terrace Orchestra in 1924 (Brunswick 2874); LOUIS ARMSTRONG had the first recording of "When You're Smiling" (Okeh 41298). Both became standards and were recorded by countless others; Perry Como helped revive both songs during the 1950s.

# Ella Fitzgerald

Popular singer (b. Newport News, Virginia, April 25, 1918; d. Beverly Hills, California, June 15, 1996). Fitzgerald was the most highly acclaimed jazz vocalist of her day. However, she began her career in pop music, singing with Chick Webb's orchestra. She scored her first hit with "A-Tisket, A-Tasket" (Decca 1840), which became the best-selling record of the decade. After Webb died in 1939, Fitzgerald took over the band until World War II made it impossible to keep it on the road. She started a solo career in 1942, playing clubs, theaters, and concerts, touring extensively through this country and Europe. Her second million-selling disc came in 1944, the double-sided hit "I'm Making Believe" and "Into Each Life Some Rain Must Fall" (Decca 23356), both recorded with the Ink Spots on harmony vocals. In 1946, she had a hit with "(I Love You) for Sentimental Reasons" (Decca 23670), with the Delta Rhythm Boys. Her last big pop hit came in 1949 with the Academy Award–winning song "Baby It's Cold Outside" (Decca 24644), from the film *Neptune's Daughter*.

In the 1950s, Fitzgerald's career was closely managed by recording executive/jazz promoter Norman Granz. Through his "Jazz at the Philharmonic" tours and the famed "Songbook" albums he released on Verve Records, he molded her into a major jazz star. Each Songbook focused on a key pop composer—including COLE PORTER, RICHARD RODGERS and LORENZ HART, GEORGE GERSHWIN, and HAROLD ARLEN—and helped keep their songs alive and make them a vital part of the jazz repertoire. Fitzgerald continued to be a popular touring and recording artist through the 1980s, until her career was finally slowed by diabetes. She died of complications of the disease in 1996.

# Fox-Trot

The standard and ubiquitous social dance, which led to the rise of jazz bands and dance orchestras. The dance is generally credited to vaudevillian Harry Fox, who first performed it as part of a roof-top revue at the New York Theatre in May 1914; it was then quickly picked up by the famous dance team of VERNON AND IRENE CASTLE. Set to a moderate-paced, syncopated 4/4 rhythm, the dance—with its combination of quick and slow steps—is easy to perform and has remained a ballroom staple for decades.

Describing the new recording of "Dumbell" by ZEZ CONFREY and his orchestra, the Victor Records bulletin of March 1923 commented, "The fox trot today is the greatest social dance of the entire world. It has gone far beyond the waltz, the polka, the tango. Where the old-time dancer 'knew' a dozen dances, the fox trotter only needs to know one. Everything that can be readily stepped off has been incorporated . . .—light kicks of the polka, the whirls of the waltz, the long curves of the tango, a lot of baby-steps anyone ought to pick up without trouble in two minutes, and a lot more from dances the present generation never heard of . . . instruments appear when least expected, and do the least expected things; but you are fox trotting all the time, without a falter, and wondering, probably, why it is you are dancing so well."

# Arthur Freed

Lyricist and film producer (b. Charleston, South Carolina, September 9, 1894; d. Los Angeles, Calif., April 12, 1973). Freed began his career as a music plugger in Chicago, where he met Minnie Marx, who invited him to join her four sons in their vaudeville act as a vocalist. He then teamed with Gus Edwards, and began writing lyrics with various composers. His first hit was 1923's "I Cried for You" with music by bandleaders Abe Lyman and Gus Arnheim, both of whom featured it with their bands. Judy Garland revived it in *Babes in Arms* (1939), and it became identified with her. In 1929, Freed moved to Hollywood, where his primary composing partner was Nacio Herb Brown, beginning that year with the score for *The Broadway Melody.* Their hits included the title song along with "You Were Meant for Me"; "Alone," written for the Marx Brothers' film *A Night at the Opera* (1935), and sung by Kitty Carlisle and Allan Jones; and "Good Morning," originally sung by Mickey Rooney and Judy Garland in *Babes in Arms* (1939) and then reprised in the nostalgic *Singin' in the Rain* (1952). The latter film was produced by Freed and was a veritable festival of Brown-Freed songs, including the title number, introduced in the film *Hollywood Revue of 1929* by Cliff Edwards (aka Ukulele Ike), who also had the #1 record (Columbia 1869-D). Freed became a producer at MGM in 1939, and headed the famous musicals unit that produced many classic films through the mid-1950s.

# Cliff Friend

Composer (b. Cincinnati, Ohio, October 1, 1893; d. Las Vegas, Nevada, June 27, 1974). Friend was active during the 1920s and 1930s, mostly working with lyricist Dave Franklin. Friend's father was a classical violinist, and Cliff was trained as a pianist at the Cincinnati Conservatory of Music. However, a chance meeting with singer Harry Richmond led to work in vaudeville, with the duo eventually reaching California in the late 1910s; there they teamed up with another would-be songwriter/performer, Buddy De Sylva. There, they were heard by Al Jolson, who urged them to come to New York, and began promoting their songs. Their first hit was "You Tell Her—I Stutter," with lyrics by Billy Rose, which was a hit in vaudeville and on disc for the Happiness Boys (Victor 19340). Friend worked with various lyricists through the 1920s, and then partnered with Dave Franklin. From the late 1920s through the 1940s, the duo wrote a number of hits for GUY LOMBARDO's orchestra, including 1934's "The Sweetest Music This Side of Heaven" (the band's theme song, co-composed with Carmen Lombardo), "When My Dream Boat Comes Home" (1936), 1937's "The Merry-Go-Round Broke Down" (which became the theme music for Warner Bros. *Looney Tunes* cartoons), and the #1 hit "The Anniversary Waltz" (1947; Decca 10267).

# Rudolf Friml

Composer (b. Prague, Czechoslovakia, December 7, 1879; d. Los Angeles, California, November 12, 1972). Friml studied at the Prague Conservatory under Antonin Dvořák and became an accompanist to violinist Jan Kubelik, who toured Europe and the United States. On his visit to America in 1906, Friml decided to stay. While he was pursuing a concert career, he was asked to work on an operetta for opera star Emma Trentini, who had just scored a huge success in VICTOR HERBERT's *Naughty Marietta*. Herbert was expected to write her next show, with a book by OTTO HARBACH, but he and Trentini had a falling-out, so he withdrew from the musical. Thus publisher Rudolph Schirmer obtained the commission for Friml.

*The Firefly* (December 2, 1912) was the musical that resulted, and it was Friml's first success. "Love Is Like a Firefly," "Sympathy," and "Giannina Mia" were the outstanding songs in the score. When it was turned into a film (1937) starring JEANETTE MACDONALD and Allan Jones, Friml reworked his "Chansonette" (of 1923) to make "The Donkey Serenade." It is always included in revivals of the stage show.

Friml composed steadily for the Broadway stage, but it wasn't until 1924 that he had his next success. He was best-known for old-fashioned, European-styled operetta. *Rose Marie* (September 2, 1924), set in the Canadian Rockies, signaled a brief return to more gracious times. Its score included five major songs: "Rose Marie," "Song of the Mounties," "The Door of My Dreams," "Totem Tom-Tom," and the million-selling "Indian Love Call," with lyrics by Otto Harbach and OSCAR HAMMERSTEIN II. This show, too, was turned into a film, starring Jeanette MacDonald and NELSON EDDY (1936).

*The Vagabond King* (September 21, 1925), with lyrics by Brian Hooker, starred Dennis King. The rich score included the stirring "Song of the Vagabonds," "Huguette Waltz," "Love Me Tonight," "Some Day," and "Only a Rose." The film version (1930), starring Dennis King and Jeanette MacDonald, has sustained the score's popularity through the years.

*The Three Musketeers* (March 13, 1928), with lyrics by P. G. WODEHOUSE and CLIFFORD GREY, was Friml's last important show. It starred Dennis King and Vivienne Segal, who shared "March of the Musketeers" and "Your Eyes," both with Wodehouse lyrics, and "My Sword and I," "Ma Belle," "All for One and One for All," and "The He for Me," with lyrics by Grey.

# Jane Froman

Deep-voiced popular singer of the 1930s–1950s, (b. Ellen Jane Froman, St. Louis, Missouri, November 10, 1911; d. Columbia, Missouri, April 22, 1980). Froman popularized several standards of the 1930s, beginning with her first appearance in the *Ziegfeld Follies of 1934*.

Her mother was a college music teacher in Columbia, Missouri, and Froman showed early skills as a singer. She began singing in local clubs while still a teen, and then attended college from 1922 to 1926. After graduate journalism study, Froman attended the Conservatory of Music in Cincinnati, Ohio, from 1928 to 1930, but did not graduate; she also did radio work in the area. In 1931, she moved to Chicago and was hired by NBC to perform on its local station. In 1933, Froman moved to New York for a spot on the Chesterfield show, which was hosted by BING CROSBY. This exposure led in 1934 to her Broadway debut in that year's edition of the *Ziegfeld Follies*. In this show, Froman introduced E. Y. HARBURG and VERNON DUKE's song "Suddenly" and Dana Seusse and EDWARD HEYMAN's "You Ought to Be in Pictures." That same year, she had a record hit with her cover of AL DUBIN and HARRY WARREN's "I Only Have Eyes for You." She had other hits through the 1930s, becoming closely associated with "With a Song in My Heart," written in 1929 by RICHARD RODGERS and LORENZ HART. (Froman revived it in 1952 in her biopic, named for the song, in which she sang the sound track while Susan Hayward portrayed her on screen.) In 1943, Froman was seriously injured in a plane crash en route to Europe to sing for World War II soldiers. She recovered, and continued performing through the 1950s, including three years (1952–1955) hosting her own television variety program. Froman retired to her hometown of Columbia, Missouri, in 1962.

# Gaiety Building

The Gaiety Building housed many Tin Pan Alley publishers during the late 1910s and throughout the 1920s. Located at 1547 Broadway, it was home to several black publishers, notably PACE AND HANDY and PERRY BRADFORD Music Company.

# Judy Garland

Famed singer and film actress (b. Frances Ethel Gumm, Grand Rapids, Michigan, June 10, 1922; d. London, England, January 22, 1969). Garland began her career as charismatic actress in movie musicals, did many radio guest shots, and then concerts and recordings. She made thirty-four films and starred in most of them. She auditioned successfully for MGM in 1935 and began appearing in films as a teenager, often paired with Mickey Rooney. She also began performing on radio that year, and although she never had her own program, she became a mainstay on radio over the next two decades. In November 1935, she auditioned for Decca Records, and signed a contract with the firm the next year.

Garland's vocal performances in films helped to relaunch several older songs and popularize new ones. In the film *Broadway Melody of 1938*, she revived the 1913 song "You Made Me Love You," sung to a photo of Clark Gable (Decca 1463). In 1939 she revived a 1923 song, "I Cried for You," in the film *Babes in Arms*. Also that year, she appeared in the film *The Wizard of Oz* and sang what became her theme, "Over the Rainbow," which won the Academy Award for Best Song (Decca 2672). The following year she sang a 1921 song, "I'm Nobody's Baby," in the film *Andy Hardy Meets Debutante* and recorded it for a #3 hit (Decca 3174). In 1942 she had another #3 hit, this time a revival of a 1917 song, "For Me and My Gal," in the film of the same name (Decca 18480). Although she recorded it in 1939, "Zing! Went the Strings of My Heart" wasn't released until 1943 (Decca 18543). "The Trolley Song" came from the 1944 film *Meet Me in St. Louis* and reached the #4 position (Decca 23361). "On the Atchison, Topeka, and the Santa Fe" came from *The Harvey Girls* and won the Academy Award for the Best Song of 1946. Her recording reached #10 (Decca 23436). Her last big hit, "The Man That Got Away" (Columbia 40270), came from the 1954 film *A Star Is Born*. It is her second most memorable song.

Garland became a television and concert artist in her last years, despite bouts of poor health. Most of her recording activity was done live, including 1961's *Judy at Carnegie Hall*, which reached #1 on the pop charts, and *Judy Garland at Home at the Palace: Opening Night*, recorded in 1967. She died from an accidental drug overdose while touring in 1969.

# Clarence Gaskill

Lyricist (b. Philadelphia, Pennsylvania, February 2, 1892; d. Fort Hill, New York, April 29, 1947). Gaskill was active primarily in the 1920s and early 1930s, working with various composers, and employed by Irving and Jack Mills. His best-known songs were 1924's "Doo-Wacka-Doo," a veritable anthem of the Flapper era, written with Will Donaldson and George Horther; and 1927's "I Can't Believe You're in Love With Me," written with JIMMY MCHUGH for the revue *Gay Paree*, and revived in 1954's dramatic film *The Caine Mutiny*. He also wrote 1931's "Minnie the Moocher" with CAB CALLOWAY and Irving Mills, which became Calloway's theme song. His last hit was 1932's "Prisoner of Love," which was revived in 1946 by the Ink Spots and Billy Eckstine, both scoring Top 10 hits, and a year later by Perry Como for a #1 hit.

# Percy Gaunt

Composer of 1890s musical comedies (b. Philadelphia, Pennsylvania, 1852; d. Palenville, New York, September 5, 1896). Gaunt is best remembered for his hit "The Bowery," written for the 1892 hit musical *A Trip to Chinatown*, presented by Charles Hoyt (1859–1900), who also wrote the lyrics. Not much is known about Gaunt's early years, although he was already working as musical director for the Barry and Fay touring troupe by the early 1880s. Gaunt joined Hoyt's touring company in 1883, writing his first score that year for Hoyt's *A Bunch of Keys*, which premiered in San Francisco. The duo's most successful production was *A Trip to Chinatown*, which opened in New York in November 1891, after having been on the road for nearly a year. It played for 657 performances, a record that wasn't broken for nearly thirty years. That show spawned road companies that toured for five years. During that time, songs came and went, but of the five original songs, "The Bowery" endured and eventually sold over a million copies of sheet music. Two other songs from the show, "Push Dem Clouds Away" and "Reuben and Cynthia," helped convince publisher T. B. HARMS that publishing songs from musicals was a profitable venture. In 1893, Gaunt had his other major song hit, "Love Me Little, Love Me Long," for which he wrote the lyrics. Gaunt left Hoyt in 1894 to write an operetta, but ill health dogged him, and he died before being able to complete this more "serious" work.

# George Gershwin

One of the greatest American composers of popular music (b. Jacob Gershvin, Brooklyn, New York, September 26, 1898; d. Los Angeles, California, July 11, 1937). After taking classical piano lessons, he was told by his friend Ben Bloom, who was working for JEROME H. REMICK, that the company had an opening for a demonstrator and song plugger. In May 1914, Gershwin applied for and obtained that job, which paid fifteen dollars a week. There was a conflict of interest, however, because Gershwin was much more interested in showing off his own compositions than in playing the firm's. When he finally submitted some of his own songs for consideration by Remick, he was told that he was hired as a demonstrator, not a composer.

Gershwin got his first break when SOPHIE TUCKER took his manuscript of "When You Want 'Em, You Can't Get 'Em, When You've Got 'Em, You Don't Want 'Em" to HARRY VON TILZER. Von Tilzer liked it, and on May 15, 1916, he became the first publisher to print a Gershwin song. Since lyricist Murray Roth had sold his share in the song to Gershwin for $15.00, Gershwin decided to gamble on a royalty. He got $5.00 in advance, and the song sold so few copies that this was the only money he would make on it.

Gershwin's piano playing was a cause of comment around the Remick offices. He was using advanced harmonies and striking rhythms in his playing, not just "pounding it out" like his colleagues. Other pluggers who heard Gershwin when they were working the music stores agreed that he had "something else." In late 1915, Gershwin started making piano rolls for the Standard Music Roll Company, manufacturers of Perfection Rolls. He turned them out with regularity, and they appeared not only under his own name but also credited to James Baker, Bert Wynn, or Fred Murtha, all "house names" of fictitious Perfection artists. Felix Arndt, composer of "Nola," was instrumental in getting him into the Aeolian Company in 1916. Aeolian was a large outfit with several labels, and Gershwin would make over one hundred rolls for it.

After Gershwin left Remick in March 1917, the firm immediately accepted a rag he wrote with Will Donaldson (1891–1954) and published "Rialto Ripples" in June. In late September, Gershwin became rehearsal pianist for *Miss 1917*, an extravaganza with music by VICTOR HERBERT and Gershwin's idol, JEROME KERN (with lyrics by P. G. WODEHOUSE). Gershwin not only met the eminent composers, but also got a chance to play some of his

George Gershwin (left) with his idol, Jerome Kern, in the 1920s.

songs for the chorus and stars. After the show closed, one of the young stars, Vivienne Segal, took "You-oo Just You," with words by IRVING CAESAR, to sing in vaudeville. It, too, was published by Remick but this time the sale was handled much differently. Seated behind his desk was the formidable Fred Belcher, general manager of the largest publishing house in the Alley. The young and inexperienced Irving Caesar sang while Gershwin played their song for the great man. They had been hoping to get $25.00 apiece for their effort. After the demonstration, Belcher said, "Well, boys, how about two hundred and fifty dollars?" Caesar and Gershwin looked at each other, speechless. Seeing them hesitate, Belcher then said, "Tell ya what, boys, I'll pay you five hundred dollars instead."

Early in 1918, Gershwin was hired by MAX DREYFUS at T. B. HARMS to write songs for $35.00 a week, plus a $50.00 advance and three cents a copy royalty on each song accepted. From this time on, Harms was Gershwin's publisher. The first occasion Dreyfus had to place a Gershwin song was in NORA BAYES's show *Ladies First* (October 24, 1918), where she sang "Some Wonderful Sort of Someone." The lyrics were by sometime Kern lyricist Schuyler Greene (1880–1927), and the published song was issued when the show was in tryouts on the road and still titled *Look Who's Here*. The next interpolation came in February 1919, when *Good Morning, Judge* opened with two Gershwin-Caesar songs. "I Was So Young (You Were So Beautiful)" became a hit.

The first complete Broadway score by Gershwin was for *La, La, Lucille*, which opened on May 26, 1919. It contained seven published songs, none distinguished, but at least Gershwin had a score to his credit. The show ran a respectable 104 performances and produced "Nobody but You," which was added after the opening. The post-Broadway tour was mounted by the son of the show's producer, Alex Aarons, who, with Vinton Freedley, would produce six Gershwin musicals, five of them hits.

Later in 1919, Gershwin was asked to write a couple of numbers for the opening of the Capitol Theatre, a new movie palace on Broadway. This event was to be celebrated by a revue called *Demi-Tasse* (October 24, 1919). One Gershwin entry was "Swanee," with lyrics by Irving Caesar. It was used in the show as a production number, with dance master Ned Wayburn choreographing the song for sixty chorus girls wearing electric lights on their slippers. Despite this impressive setting, the demand for the sheet music sold in the lobby was next to nothing. It wasn't until Irving Caesar took the song to his friend, AL JOLSON, and asked him to sing it, that the song became a hit. Jolson put it into *Sinbad*, his current show at the Winter Garden, and made a recording of it for Columbia (A-2884). With a full-page head shot of Jolson on the cover, "Swanee" sold over a million copies of sheet music and two million copies of his disc. It became the biggest-selling song Gershwin would have in his life.

George White (1890–1968), the dancer-director-turned-impresario, created his *Scandals* to rival Ziegfeld's *Follies*. From the second *Scandals*, the edition of 1920, Gershwin had six songs published. Of them, "Scandal Walk" achieved mild success. It was introduced in the show by dimple-kneed Ann Pennington, usually a star of the *Follies*.

"Waiting for the Sun to Come Out" was George's first collaboration with his brother IRA. Ira wrote it under the combined names of one of his brothers and one of his sisters, "Arthur Francis." It was interpolated into *The Sweetheart Shop* (August 31, 1920) and later published with a show cover. Previously, Ira had written lyrics to George's music for "The Real American Folk Song (Is a Rag)" (1918) for *Ladies First*, but this wasn't published until 1959, after ELLA FITZGERALD had included it in an album of Gershwin songs, with a special ragtime piano accompaniment by Lou Busch, better known as Joe "Fingers" Carr.

"The Yankee Doodle Blues," with lyrics by Irving Caesar and B. G. De Sylva, was interpolated into *Spice of 1922*. It didn't sell much sheet music until Al Jolson started plugging it and jazz bands recorded it. The best versions came from The Virginians and Ladd's Black Aces. The Black Aces' record on Gennett competed with that of Jazzbo's Carolina Serenaders (a second pseudonym for the same band, the Original Memphis Five) on Cameo. Isham Jones's orchestra also did a nice version (Brunswick 2286).

*George White's Scandals of 1922* provided one big Gershwin hit and a monumental flop that led to the strangest commission of all. The hit was "I'll Build a Stairway to Paradise," which Winnie Lightner sang to success, backed by an impressive production featuring George White himself with the rest of the dancing cast. The resounding flop really had no business in a revue. It was a one-act opera called *Blue Monday*, which Gershwin composed to a libretto by De Sylva. It was a twenty-five minute ballet that, after opening night, White decided was too gloomy, so he shelved it. But it impressed Paul Whiteman, whose orchestra was playing the show. Whiteman filed away the fact that Gershwin was trying to incorporate jazz and blues elements into a more "serious," setting and commissioned him to write "Rhapsody in Blue" for the Whiteman concert at Aeolian Hall a year and a half later.

For the Charles Dillingham revue *Nifties of 1923*, Gershwin saw his and Irving Caesar's "Nashville Nightingale" interpolated. Waring's Pennsylvanians recorded it (Victor 19492), as did Phil Ohman and Victor Arden, the two-piano team who would shortly become the mainstays of the orchestras for several Gershwin shows (Brunswick 2512).

It was "Rhapsody in Blue" that established Gershwin's reputation as a composer. One critic called it "the foremost serious effort by an American composer," and another described it as "one of the most significant works in twentieth century music." The two Whiteman recordings, with the composer at the piano, sold incredibly well, the acoustic performance in 1924 being put on Victor's classical blue label (Victor 55225). The electric recording was done in 1927 (Victor 35822). "Rhapsody" has since been performed extensively in concert halls both here and abroad, and it has been used as the basis of several ballets. It was sold to Universal Studios for a record price for use in *King of Jazz* (1930), in which pianist Roy Bargy is featured with the Whiteman orchestra. Although it was originally scored for jazz band and piano, and next written out for two pianos, it has since been transcribed for every conceivable combination of instruments and even for unaccompanied chorus.

The last *Scandals* with a Gershwin score was the sixth edition, in 1924. It boasted eight published songs, one of which became a smash hit, thanks to Paul Whiteman's recording. As with Gershwin's other *Scandals* hit of two years before, it fell to Winnie Lightner to introduce "Somebody Loves Me." The lyric was by De Sylva and Ballard MacDonald. The song was recorded by Marion Harris (Brunswick 2735), and it has remained timeless.

The first of Gershwin's complete Broadway scores since *Lucille* was *Lady, Be Good!* (December 1, 1924). Of seven songs published, four were hits and another was an impressive syncopated dance number. The show starred Fred and Adele Astaire and featured the duo-piano team of Victor Arden and Phil Ohman in the orchestra. This double-piano innovation was repeated by the Gershwins in four of their other shows (*Tip-Toes*, *Oh, Kay!*, *Funny Face*, and *Treasure Girl*). "Oh, Lady, Be Good" became popular as sung by Walter Catlett in the show. Artie Shaw revived it in 1939, in a swing arrangement that gave dancers a perennial favorite (Bluebird 10430). "Fascinating Rhythm" provided the Astaires with a great song-and-dance number and gave Arden and Ohman a chance to make a nice recording with Carl Fenton's orchestra (Brunswick 2790). "Little Jazz Bird" gave Cliff Edwards a solo in the show. "The Half of It, Dearie, Blues" was interestingly structured, but the best of all, "The Man I Love," was dropped from the show during the Philadelphia tryouts, when audiences failed to respond to Adele Astaire's performance. The song was tried in three later shows, only to be dropped from each of them. Finally, the song was so well known through vaudeville and nightclub performances that the brothers stopped trying to put it into a show. It had become a standard despite production flops.

*Tip-Toes* (December 28, 1925) was produced by Alex Aarons and Vinton Freedley, the team that had produced the Gershwin brothers' previous show, and the book was written by Guy Bolton and Fred Thompson, the team who had written *Lady, Be Good.* "Looking for a Boy" was introduced in the show by Queenie Smith, who had last starred in the Kern-Wodehouse show *Sitting Pretty* (1924). The Knickerbockers (Columbia 549-D) and ROGER WOLFE KAHN's orchestra (Victor 19939) made lovely recordings of it. "Sweet and Low-Down" and "That Certain Feeling" are the two other songs from *Tip-Toes* that have remained standards.

It is generally agreed that the score for *Oh, Kay!* (November 8, 1926) is the brothers' best, and the book, by P. G. Wodehouse and Guy Bolton, was the funniest written during the 1920s. Aarons and Freedley gave this material their usual attractive production, which starred Gertrude Lawrence, Oscar Shaw, and Victor Moore. It was perfect casting. The title song is one of the Gershwins' gems, and so, in their ways, are "Fidgety Feet," "Clap Yo' Hands," and "Do-Do-Do." The last two numbers were often to be found back-to-back on the same double-sided disc, paired by the various artists who recorded them. Gershwin himself recorded them as piano solos (Columbia 809-D), while Ohman and Arden recorded the pair with their orchestra (Brunswick 3377), as did Fred Rich's orchestra (Columbia 802-D), and the Missouri Jazz Band (Banner 1888). Curiously, Victor split a recorded pairing, with Roger Wolfe Kahn's orchestra doing "Clap Yo' Hands" on one side and George Olsen and His Music's "Do-Do-Do" on the other side (Victor 20327).

Gertrude Lawrence, who became a star in *Oh, Kay!*, introduced its most-played number, "Someone to Watch over Me." She recorded the song twice—once accompanied by Tom Waring at the piano (Victor 20331) and again in London a year later, accompanied by His Majesty's Theatre Orchestra, led by Arthur Wood (English Columbia 4618). As late as the mid-1980s, pop singer Linda Ronstadt, backed by Nelson Riddle's orchestra had a hit recording of the song (Asylum). George Gershwin also made a piano solo of it and coupled it with "Maybe" (Columbia 812-D). "Maybe" is a lovely ballad that, in the show, contrasted nicely with "Heaven on Earth," a show-stopper featured by comedian Victor Moore. When *Oh, Kay!* was revived off-Broadway in 1960, an original cast album was made (Fox 4003), with Wodehouse's lyrics for "The '20s Are Here to Stay," "The Pophams," and "You'll Still Be There."

With a book by George S. Kaufman, the first version of *Strike Up the Band* (1927) never made it to Broadway. It included "The Man I Love" and the title song, which was used with a rewritten book in 1930.

The next Aarons-Freedley production with the Gershwins was *Funny Face* (November 22, 1927), which was called *Smarty* during its tryouts. The producers opened a new theater called the Alvin (the first syllable of each producer's given name) with this show, which starred Fred and Adele Astaire, Victor Moore, and Allen Kearns. "The Babbitt and the Bromide" was Ira's attempt to write a Wodehousian comic number, and it succeeded. "High Hat," "He Loves and She Loves," "How Long Has This Been Going On?," "Let's Kiss and Make Up,"

"My One and Only" (originally published as "What Am I Gonna Do?"), and " 'S Wonderful" were the hit songs from the show. *Funny Face* was the basis of a later Broadway production, *My One and Only* (May 1, 1983), proving again the durability of the Gershwins' songs.

Florenz Ziegfeld Jr., aimed to produce an elaborate show for Marilyn Miller, and he chose *Rosalie* (January 10, 1928), with music by SIGMUND ROMBERG and George Gershwin. Romberg used lyricist P. G. Wodehouse. Gershwin used his brother Ira and, for two numbers, Wodehouse. The two collaborations with Wodehouse, "Oh, Gee! Oh, Joy!" and "Say So!" were the only hits in the show.

*Show Girl* (July 2, 1929) was a flop that starred Ruby Keeler, Al Jolson's nineteen-year-old wife, and the comic team of Clayton, Jackson, and Durante. The only song that attained any status was "Liza," which was to be sung by NICK LUCAS and danced by Ruby Keeler. On opening night, however, Al Jolson, who was in the audience, leaped onto the stage and sang it to his wife while she came down a huge staircase. He was to sing it again on *The Jolson Story*'s sound track.

When the revised version of *Strike Up the Band* (January 14, 1930) came to Broadway, it had a new book by Morrie Ryskind, and it included "I've Got a Crush on You," which FRANK SINATRA would revive in 1948 (Columbia 38151). The show also introduced the cute "Mademoiselle in New Rochelle," "Soon," and the title song, which would be sung in the 1940 movie of the same name by JUDY GARLAND and Mickey Rooney.

The last of the great Aarons-Freedley-Gershwin shows was *Girl Crazy* (October 14, 1930), starring ETHEL MERMAN, GINGER ROGERS, Allen Kearns, Willie Howard, and William Kent. Merman became a star when she introduced "Sam and Delilah" and "I Got Rhythm." Gershwin liked this last song so much that he used it as the basis for a concert work, "Variations on 'I Got Rhythm' " (1934). It has been a favorite of jazz pianists, too. Ginger Rogers introduced two beautiful ballads, "But Not for Me" and "Embraceable You." Fred Astaire helped to choreograph this last number, and he taught the routines to Rogers. Two films called *Girl Crazy* were made, though only the second used the show's story line. For the 1932 version, which starred Bert Wheeler and Robert Woolsey, the Gershwins wrote "You've Got What Gets Me." After the release of the 1943 Judy Garland–Mickey Rooney film, "Treat Me Rough!" was finally published. The Foursome, a male quartet, introduced "Bidin' My Time" in the 1930 show.

With the help of George S. Kaufman and Morrie Ryskind, the Gershwins embarked on a short series of politically conscious shows, starting with *Of Thee I Sing* (December 26, 1931). 1932 was an election year, so it was logical to build a musical around the presidency. The stars were William Gaxton, Lois Moran, and Victor Moore. It was the first musical to win a Pulitzer Prize (for drama), and the award went to Kaufman, Ryskind, and Ira Gershwin. It seemed that George's musical contribution didn't count with the committee. The score included "The Illegitimate Daughter," "Love Is Sweeping the Country," "Who Cares?," and the title song. The original production had the longest Broadway run of all the Gershwin shows, and had the further distinction of having its libretto published by Knopf, the first hardcover presentation ever for a book of a musical. Not until the show was revived in 1952 was "Wintergreen for President" published.

Gershwin's last work for the stage was, many feel, his finest. *Porgy and Bess* (October 10, 1935) starred Todd Duncan, Anne Brown, John W. Bubbles, and Warren Coleman. The songs, most of which are classics, include "Bess, You Is My Woman (Now)," "My Man's Gone Now," "A Woman Is a Sometime Thing," "I Got Plenty o' Nuttin'," "It Ain't Necessarily So," and, with a lyric by librettist DuBose Heyward, perhaps George's most majestic song, the one with which Abbie Mitchell opened the show, "Summertime." Anne Brown sang "Summertime" in *Rhapsody in Blue* (1945), the biographical Gershwin film.

Even before the movies could talk, theme songs were written to promote them. IRVING BERLIN wrote several, and Gershwin wrote one. It was called "The Sunshine Trail" (1923), for the film of the same name, starring Douglas MacLean and produced by Thomas H. Ince. Gershwin's debut in a film for which he wrote the entire score did not come until 1931, with the Janet Gaynor–Charles Farrell starrer, *Delicious.* None of the songs were especially memorable, although "Blah, Blah, Blah" has continued to have a life in cabarets. Ira spoofs the Moon-June-Croon-Spoon lyrics typical of the 1920s and 1930s, possibly thinking specifically about the J. FRED COOTS–Lou Davis song, "I'm Croonin' a Tune about June" (1929).

When the Gershwin brothers returned to Hollywood in 1936, it was to work for RKO on two pictures, both with Fred Astaire, the star of *Lady, Be Good!* and *Funny Face*. The first film was with Astaire's dancing-singing partner, Ginger Rogers, who had made her Broadway debut in *Girl Crazy*. In *Shall We Dance* (1937), the brothers returned to their lighthearted, pre-1930s, less socially significant themes with "Slap That Bass," "Walking the Dog" (which was published many years later as "Promenade"), the great comic number "Let's Call the Whole Thing Off," and one of George's most endearing and enduring ballads, "They Can't Take That Away from Me."

*A Damsel in Distress* (1937) was the next film to have a complete score by the Gershwins, with Fred Astaire once again in the leading role (but for the first time in four years without Ginger Rogers). Joan Fontaine, a dramatic actress, was given the assignment of the heroine in the story, basically taken from P. G. Wodehouse's 1919 novel of the same name (he also contributed to its screenplay). George Burns and Gracie Allen were a delight in this film and surprised audiences with their dancing abilities, sharing equally with Astaire in a tap routine, then doing an extended dance through an amusement park, winding up in front of trick mirrors. Allen sang the comic "Stiff Upper Lip," while Astaire sang "A Foggy Day (In London Town)." The film's hit song was the amusing "Nice Work If You Can Get It."

After *Damsel*, the brothers went to work for Samuel Goldwyn on the score for *The Goldwyn Follies* (1938). Five songs for the film had been completed before George suddenly became incapacitated by headaches. Two ballads became hits, "Love Walked In" and "(Our) Love Is Here to Stay," the last song George wrote. It was more or less thrown away in this film, but when it was used in Gene Kelly's *An American in Paris* (1951), it became the standard it should have been all along.

George Gershwin died of a brain tumor at the age of thirty-eight. However, his music has lived on in concert, on film and stage, and in nightclubs. Two "new" Broadway shows were created using Gershwin material, 1983's *My One and Only* and 1992's *Crazy for You.*

## American Published Individual Songs by George Gershwin

"Across the Sea" (1922), *George White's Scandals* (show)
"All the Livelong Day" (1964), *Kiss Me, Stupid* (film)
"Aren't You Kind of Glad We Did?" (1946), *The Shocking Miss Pilgrim* (film)
"Argentina" (1922), *George White's Scandals* (show)
"At Half Past Seven" (1923), *Nifties* (show)
"Babbitt and the Bromide" (1927), *Funny Face* (show)
"Back Bay Polka" (1946), *The Shocking Miss Pilgrim* (film)
"Beautiful Gypsy" (1927), *Rosalie* (show)
"Because, Because" (1931), *Of Thee I Sing* (show)
"Beginner's Luck" (1937), *Shall We Dance* (film)

"Bess, You Is My Woman" (1935), *Porgy and Bess* (show)
"Best of Everything" (1919), *La, La, Lucille* (show)
"Bidin' My Time" (1930), *Girl Crazy* (show)
"Blah-Blah-Blah" (1931), *Delicious* (film)
"Blue, Blue, Blue" (1933), *Let 'Em Eat Cake* (show)
"Blue Monday" (1976)
"Boy Wanted" (1921), *A Dangerous Maid* (show)
"Boy! What Love Has Done To Me!" (1930), *Girl Crazy* (show)
"But Not for Me" (1930), *Girl Crazy* (show)
"By and By" (1922), *Hayseed* (show)
"By Strauss" (1936), *The Show Is On* (show)
"Changing My Tune" (1946), *The Shocking Miss Pilgrim* (film)
"Cinderelatives" (1922), *George White's Scandals* (show)
"Clap Yo' Hands" (1926), *Oh, Kay!* (show)
"Come to the Moon" (1919), *Capitol Revue* (show)
"Cossack Love Song" (1925), *Song of the Flame* (show)
"Could You Use Me?" (1930), *Girl Crazy* (show)
"Dance Alone with You" (1927), *Funny Face* (show)
"Dancing Shoes" (1921), *A Dangerous Maid* (show)
"Dawn of a New Day" (1939)
"Dear Little Girl" (1958), *Star* (film)
"Delishious" (1931), *Delicious* (film)
"Dixie Rose" (1921)
"Do, Do, Do" (1926), *Oh, Kay!* (show)
"Do It Again" (1922), *The French Doll* (show)
"Do What You Do!" (1929), *Show Girl* (show)
"Drifting Along with the Tide" (1921), *George White's Scandals* (show)
"Embraceable You" (1930), *Girl Crazy* (show)
"Everybody Knows I Love Somebody" (1927), *Rosalie* (show)
"Fascinating Rhythm" (1924), *Lady, Be Good!* (show)
"Feeling I'm Falling" (1928), *Treasure Girl* (show)
"Feeling Sentimental" (1929), *Show Girl* (show)
"Fidgety Feet" (1926), *Oh, Kay!* (show)
"Foggy Day" (1937), *A Damsel in Distress* (film)
"For You, for Me, for Evermore" (1946), *The Shocking Miss Pilgrim* (film)
"From Now On" (1919), *La, La, Lucille* (show)
"Funny Face" (1927), *Funny Face* (show)
"Got a Rainbow" (1928), *Treasure Girl* (show)
"Half of It Dearie Blues" (1924), *Lady, Be Good* (show)
"Hang On to Me" (1924), *Lady, Be Good* (show)
"Hangin' Around with You" (1929), *Strike Up the Band* (show)
"Harlem River Chanty" (1968), *Tip-Toes* (show)
"Harlem Serenade" (1929), *Show Girl* (show)
"Has Anyone Seen My Joe?" (1968)
"He Loves and She Loves" (1927), *Funny Face* (show)
"Heaven on Earth" (1926), *Oh, Kay!* (show)
"Hey! Hey! Let 'Er Go!" (1924), *Sweet Little Devil* (show)
"High Hat" (1927), *Funny Face* (show)
"Hi-Ho!" (1967)
"How Long Has This Been Going On?" (1927), *Funny Face* (show)
"How've You Been" (1923), *George White's Scandals* (show)
"I Can't Be Bothered Now" (1937), *A Damsel in Distress* (film)
"I Don't Think I'll Fall in Love Today" (1928), *Treasure Girl* (show)
"I Found a Four Leaf Clover" (1922), *George White's Scandals* (show)
"I Got Plenty o' Nuttin'" (1935), *Porgy and Bess* (show)
"I Got Rhythm" (1930), *Girl Crazy* (show)
"I Loves You, Porgy" (1935), *Porgy and Bess* (show)
"I Mean to Say" (1929), *Strike Up the Band* (show)
"I Must Be Home by Twelve o'Clock" (1929), *Show Girl* (show)
"I Need a Garden" (1924), *George White's Scandals* (show)
"I Want to Be a War Bride" (1930), *Strike Up the Band* (show)
"I Was Doing All Right" (1938), *The Goldwyn Follies* (film)
"I Was So Young" (1919), *Good Morning, Judge* (show)
"I Won't Say I Will" (1923), *Little Miss Bluebeard* (show)
"Idle Dreams" (1920), *George White's Scandals* (show)
"I'll Build a Stairway to Paradise" (1922), *George White's Scandals* (show)
"Illegitimate Daughter" (1932), *Of Thee I Sing* (show)
"I'm a Poached Egg" (1964), *Kiss Me, Stupid* (film)
"In the Mandarin's Orchid Garden" (1930)
"Innocent Ingenue Baby" (1922), *Our Nell* (show)
"Isn't It a Pity?" (1932), *Pardon My English* (show)
"It Ain't Necessarily So" (1935), *Porgy and Bess* (show)
"It's a Great Little World" (1926), *Tip-Toes* (show)
"I've Got a Crush on You" (1930), *Strike Up the Band* (show)

"I've Got to Be There" (1933), *Pardon My English* (show)
"Jijibo" (1923), *Sweet Little Devil* (show)
"Jolly Tar and the Milk Maid" (1937), *A Damsel in Distress* (film)
"Just Another Rhumba" (1959)
"Just to Know You Are Mine" (1921), *A Dangerous Maid* (show)
"Katinkitschka" (1931), *Delicious* (film)
"Kickin' the Clouds Away" (1925), *My Fair Lady* (show)
"King of Swing" (1936)
"Kongo Kate" (1924), *George White's Scandals* (show)
"K-Ra-Zy for You" (1928), *Treasure Girl* (show)
"Let 'Em Eat Cake" (1933), *Let 'Em Eat Cake* (show)
"Let's Be Lonesome Together" (1923), *George White's Scandals* (show)
"Let's Call the Whole Thing Off" (1937), *Shall We Dance* (film)
"Let's Kiss and Make Up" (1927), *Funny Face* (show)
"Life of a Rose" (1923), *George White's Scandals* (show)
"Limehouse Nights" (1920), *Morris Gest Midnight Whirl* (show)
"Little Jazz Bird" (1924), *Lady, Be Good* (show)
"Liza" (1929), *Show Girl* (show)
"Lo-La-Lo" (1923), *George White' s Scandals* (show)
"Looking for a Boy" (1925), *Tip-Toes* (show)
"Lorelei" (1932), *Pardon My English* (show)
"Love Is Here to Stay" (1938), *The Goldwyn Follies* (film)
"Love Is Sweeping the Country" (1931), *Of Thee I Sing* (show)
"Love of a Wife" (1919), *La, La, Lucille* (show)
"Love Walked In" (1938), *The Goldwyn Follies* (film)
"Lu Lu" (1920), *Broadway Brevities of 1920* (show)
"Luckiest Man in the World" (1933), *Pardon My English* (show)
"Mademoiselle in New Rochelle" (1930), *Strike Up the Band* (show)
"Mah-Jongg" (1923), *A Perfect Lady* (show)
"Making of a Girl" (1916), *The Passing Show of 1916* (show)
"Man I Love" (1924), *Lady, Be Good* (show)
"Maybe" (1926), *Oh, Kay!* (show)
"Midnight Bells" (1925), *Song of the Flame* (show)
"Military Dancing Drill" (1927), *Strike Up the Band* (show)
"Mine" (1933), *Let 'Em Eat Cake* (show)
"Mischa, Yascha, Toscha, Sascha" (1932)
"My Cousin in Milwaukee" (1932), *Pardon My English* (show)
"My Fair Lady" (1925), *My Fair Lady* (show)
"My Lady" (1920), *George White's Scandals* (show)
"My Log-Cabin Home" (1921), *The Perfect Fool* (show)
"My Man's Gone Now" (1935), *Porgy and Bess* (show)
"My One and Only" (1927), *Funny Face* (show)
"Nashville Nightingale" (1923), *Nifties* (show)
"Nice Baby" (1925), *Tip-Toes* (show)
"Nice Work If You Can Get It" (1937), *A Damsel in Distress* (film)
"Night Time in Araby" (1924), *George White's Scandals* (show)
"Nightie-Night" (1925), *Tip-Toes* (show)
"No One Else but That Girl of Mine" (1921)
"Nobody but You" (1919), *La, La, Lucille* (show)
"Of Thee I Sing" (1931), *Of Thee I Sing* (show)
"Oh, Bess, Oh, Where's My Bess?" (1935), *Porgy and Bess* (show)
"Oh, Gee! Oh, Joy!" (1928), *Rosalie* (show)
"Oh, Kay!" (1926), *Oh, Kay!* (show)
"Oh, Lady, Be Good" (1924), *Lady, Be Good* (show)
"Oh, So Nice" (1928), *Treasure Girl* (show)
"Oh, What She Hangs Out" (1922), *George White's Scandals* (show)
"On and On and On" (1933), *Let 'Em Eat Cake* (show)
"On My Mind the Whole Night Long" (1920), *George White's Scandals* (show)
"One, Two, Three" (1946), *The Shocking Miss Pilgrim* (film)
"Oo, How I Love to Be Loved by You" (1920), *Ed Wynn's Carnival* (show)
"Pepita" (1923), *A Perfect Lady* (show)
"Poppyland" (1920), *Morris Gest Midnight Whirl* (show)
"Promenade" (1960)
"Real American Folk Song Is a Rag" (1959)
"Rhapsody in Blue" (1924)
"Rialto Ripples Rag" (1917)
"Rosalie" (1927), *Rosalie* (show)
"Rose of Madrid" (1923), *George White's Scandals* (show)
"'S Wonderful" (1927), *Funny Face* (show)
"Sam and Delilah" (1930), *Girl Crazy* (show)
"Say So!" (1928), *Rosalie* (show)
"Scandal Walk" (1920), *George White's Scandals* (show)
"Seventeen and Twenty-one" (1927), *Strike Up the Band* (show)
"Shall We Dance" (1937), *Shall We Dance* (film)
"She's Just a Baby" (1921), *George White's Scandals* (show)

"Show Me the Town" (1926), *Oh, Kay!* (show)
"Signal" (1925), *Song of the Flame* (show)
"Simple Life" (1921), *A Dangerous Maid* (show)
"Slap That Bass" (1937), *Shall We Dance* (film)
"Snow Flakes" (1920), *Broadway Brevities of 1920* (show)
"So Am I" (1925), *Lady, Be Good* (show)
"So Are You!" (1929), *Show Girl* (show)
"So What?" (1932), *Pardon My English* (show)
"Some Rain Must Fall" (1921), *A Dangerous Maid* (show)
"Some Wonderful Sort of Someone" (1918), *Look Who's Here* (show)
"Somebody from Somewhere" (1931), *Delicious* (film)
"Somebody Loves Me" (1924), *George White's Scandals* (show)
"Somehow It Seldom Comes True" (1919), *La, La, Lucille* (show)
"Someone" (1922), *For Goodness' Sake* (show)
"Someone Believes in You" (1923), *Sweet Little Devil* (show)
"Someone to Watch over Me" (1926), *Oh, Kay!* (show)
"Something About Love" (1919), *The Lady in Red* (show)
"Song of the Flame" (1925), *Song of the Flame* (show)
"Song of Long Ago" (1920), *George White's Scandals* (show)
"Soon" (1929), *Strike Up the Band* (show)
"Sophia" (1964), *Kiss Me, Stupid* (film)
"South Sea Isles" (1921), *George White's Scandals* (show)
"Spanish Love" (1920), *Broadway Brevities of 1920* (show)
"Stiff Upper Lip" (1937), *A Damsel in Distress* (film)
"Strike Up the Band" (1927), *Strike Up the Band* (show)
"Strike Up the Band for U.C.L.A." (1936)
"Summertime" (1935), *Porgy and Bess* (show)
"Sunshine Trail" (1923), *The Sunshine Trail* (film)
"Swanee" (1919), *Capitol Theatre Revue* (show)
"Swanee Rose" (1921)
"Sweet and Low-Down" (1925), *Tip-Toes* (show)
"Tee-Oodle-Um-Bum-Bo" (1919), *La, La, Lucille* (show)
"Tell Me More!" (1925), *Tell Me More* (show)
"That American Boy of Mine" (1923), *The Dancing Girl* (show)
"That Certain Feeling" (1925), *Tip-Toes* (show)
"That Lost Barber Shop Chord" (1926), *Americana* (show)
"There Is Nothing Too Good for You" (1923), *George White's Scandals* (show)
"There's a Boat Dat's Leaving Soon for New York" (1935), *Porgy and Bess* (show)
"There's More to the Kiss Than the Sound" (1919), *La, La, Lucille* (show)
"There's More to the Kiss Than the X-X-X" (1919), *Good Morning, Judge* (show)
"These Charming People" (1925), *Tip-Toes* (show)
"They All Laughed" (1937), *Shall We Dance* (film)
"They Can't Take That Away from Me" (1937), *Shall We Dance* (film)
"Things Are Looking Up" (1937), *A Damsel in Distress* (film)
"Three Times a Day" (1925), *My Fair Lady* (show)
"Throw 'Er in High" (1923), *George White's Scandals* (show)
"Till Then" (1933)
"Tomale (I'm Hot for You)" (1921)
"Tra-La-La" (1922), *For Goodness' Sake* (show)
"Treat Me Rough" (1944), *Girl Crazy* (film)
"Tum On and Tiss Me" (1920), *George White's Scandals* (show)
"Tune In to Station J.O.Y." (1924), *George White's Scandals* (show)
"Two Waltzes in C" (1971)
"Under a One-Man Top" (1923), *A Perfect Lady* (show)
"Union Square" (1933), *Let 'Em Eat Cake* (show)
"Virginia" (1923), *Sweet Little Devil* (show)
"Vodka" (1925), *Song of the Flame* (show)
"Waiting for the Sun to Come Out" (1920), *The Sweetheart Shop* (show)
"Walking Home with Angeline" (1922), *Our Nell* (show)
"We're Pals" (1920), *Dere Mable* (show)
"What Are We Here For?" (1928), *Treasure Girl* (show)
"When Do We Dance?" (1925), *Tip-Toes* (show)
"When You Want 'Em, You Can't Get 'Em" (1916)
"Where East Meets West" (1921), *George White's Scandals* (show)
"Where Is She?" (1923), *George White's Scandals* (show)
"Where Is the Man of My Dreams?" (1922), *George White's Scandals* (show)
"Where You Go, I Go" (1933), *Pardon My English* (show)
"Where's the Boy? Here's the Girl!" (1928), *Treasure Girl* (show)
"Who Cares?" (1931), *Of Thee I Sing* (show)

"Why Do I Love You?" (1925), *Tell Me More* (show)
"Wintergreen for President" (1932), *Of Thee I Sing* (show revival, 1952)
"Woman Is a Sometime Thing" (1935), *Porgy and Bess* (show)
"World Is Mine" (1927), *Funny Face* (show)
"Yan-kee" (1920)
"Yankee Doodle Blues" (1922), *Spice of 1922* (show)
"Yankee Doodle Rhythm" (1927), *Strike Up the Band* (show)
"Year After Year" (1924), *George White's Scandals* (show)
"You and I" (1923), *George White's Scandals* (show)
"You Are You" (1925), *Song of the Flame* (show)
"You-oo Just You" (1918)
"You've Got What Gets Me" (1932), *Girl Crazy* (film)

# Ira Gershwin

Lyricist (b. Israel Gershvin, New York City, December 6, 1896; d. Beverly Hills, California, August 19, 1983). In addition to writing for Broadway and Hollywood with brother George, Ira wrote with Jerome Kern, Vincent Youmans, Harold Arlen, Vernon Duke, Arthur Schwartz, Kurt Weill, Richard Whiting, and Burton Lane. His first great hit was "Oh, Me, Oh, My, Oh, You" from the 1921 Broadway musical *Two Little Girls in Blue*. It got a fine recording by Paul Whiteman's orchestra (Victor 18778). From the 1924 show *Lady, Be Good* came "Oh, Lady Be Good," and with it another hit recording by Whiteman (Victor 19551). Its flip side was "Fascinating Rhythm," from the same show. "The Man I Love" was written for this show but was dropped before the opening. However, The Troubadours made a splendid recording (Victor 21233). Ira wrote exclusively with George from 1925 until George's death in 1938.

Ira started to work with others as early as 1934, when he helped Harold Arlen and E. Y. Harburg write "Let's Take a Walk Around the Block" for the Broadway musical *Life Begins at 8:40*. His first major work after George's death was the 1941 Broadway show *Lady in the Dark*, with music by Kurt Weill. The show made a star of Danny Kaye, who performed the show-stopping comic patter song, "Tchaikowsky (and Other Russians)." Several less successful Broadway productions followed, and then Ira turned his attention again to movies. In the 1944 movie *Cover Girl*, he had a hit with "Long Ago (and Far Away)," with a #2 recording by Helen Forrest and Dick Haymes (Decca 23317). "The Man That Got Away" was from the film *A Star Is Born* in 1954, but when Frank Sinatra sang it, it was called "The Gal That Got Away" (Capitol 2864). Ira retired after the release of this film. There are several biographies of George Gershwin, but the best book on both brothers is *The Gershwins*, by Robert Kimball and Alfred Simon (1973).

# L. Wolfe Gilbert

Lyricist and composer (b. Louis Wolfe Gilbert, Odessa, Russia, August 31, 1886; d. Los Angeles, California, July 12, 1970). Gilbert came to the United States as a young boy, and initially worked as an actor and singer on the vaudeville circuit. By the early 1910s, he was writing lyrics as well as writing for *The New York Clipper*, a newspaper aimed at the theatrical community. In 1911, in the paper he attacked a song written by LEWIS MUIR, who shortly afterward confronted Gilbert; the duo began writing together, producing their first hit, "Waiting for the Robert E. Lee." They worked together through 1914 producing many hits, including most notably 1913's "Hitchy Koo," popularized by AL JOLSON. In 1921, he produced both lyrics and music for the classic "Down Yonder"; he even published it himself. It was interpolated by the Brown Brothers, a saxophone sextet, in *Tip Top* after that show's Broadway opening. It was spectacularly revived by pianist Del Wood (Tennessee 775) in 1951; Joe "Fingers" Carr also sold over a million copies with his version (Capitol 1777). It has since become a favorite of country musicians as well as ragtime-style pianists. "Lucky Lindy," composed by Abel Baer (1893–1976), came in 1927; it was the first song to celebrate Charles Lindbergh's landing in Paris, and is the best remembered of all the songs celebrating his achievement. 1930 saw the jazz classic "The Peanut Vendor," composed by Moises Simons, with lyrics by Marion Sunshine and Gilbert. It was memorably recorded by Cuban bandleader Don Azpiazu (Victor 22483). In 1935, Gilbert moved to Hollywood to write for EDDIE CANTOR's popular radio show. From 1941 to 1944, Gilbert served as head of ASCAP. In 1931, he had a hit with "Marta," composed by Simons. It was introduced and used as a radio theme by Arthur Tracy, "The Street Singer" (Brunswick 6216). He was more or less inactive after world war II.

# Lottie Gilson

Vaudeville singer (b. Pennsylvania 1871; d. New York City, June 10, 1912; full dates unknown). Gilson, nicknamed "The Little Magnet" because of her drawing power at the box office, introduced and plugged more songs to hit classification than any other vaudeville star in the 1890s. She was the first to have a singer planted in the audience to sing the second chorus along with her. Then she got the rest of the audience to join in. She made the Joe Stern–Ed Marks 1896 "Mother Was a Lady" an even bigger hit than she did their first song, "The Little Lost Child." Two years earlier, in 1894, she made famous Charles Lawlor and James Blake's "The Sidewalks of New York" ("East Side, West Side"). She took a John Bratton–Walter Ford song, "The Sunshine of Paradise Alley" (1895), and made such a success of it that she was identified with it thereafter. This was unusual, since singing publisher Julius Witmark had introduced it for his firm and should have had an edge on the competition. The same year that Maggie Cline turned the tearjerker "Mother Was a Lady" into a smash hit, Gilson did the same for the Stanley Carter–Harry Braisted comic song, "You're Not the Only Pebble on the Beach." Throughout the 1890s, she was the favorite at Tony Pastor's and other leading vaudeville houses in New York. When she was on tour, she met and encouraged Harry Von Tilzer to come to New York to try his luck placing his songs. Gilson remained a stage favorite for over twenty years.

# Arthur Godfrey

Singer, ukulele player, and radio and television personality (b. New York City, August 31, 1903; d. New York City, March 16, 1983).

Pleasant-voiced Godfrey was a fixture on radio and television for several decades. He learned to play the ukulele while serving in the Navy in the early 1920s. He joined the Coast Guard in 1927, and began to perform as part of an entertainment unit. After leaving the Coast Guard in 1930, Godfrey worked as a radio announcer until the mid-1930s, and then focused on performing on radio. He was hired by CBS Radio in 1945 to host the *Talent Scouts* program; it quickly became the top-rated radio program and was transferred to TV three years later, remaining on the air for a decade. He also hosted a variety-format program (*Arthur Godfrey and His Friends*) from 1949 to 1959. His TV "family" consisted of announcer Tony Marvin and singers Frank Parker, Marion Marlowe, the McGuire Sisters, Janette Davis, the Mariners, Lu Ann Simms, and Julius LaRosa. His pleasant baritone gave him several hit recordings, starting with the 1947 hit, "Too Fat Polka" (Columbia 37921). In 1950, with the Mariners, he had "Candy and Cake" (Columbia 38721). His big hit in 1951, with the Chordettes, was "Dance Me Loose" (Columbia 39632). Godfrey retired from radio and TV in the 1960s but did commercials into the 1970s.

# E. Ray Goetz

Lyricist, composer, and playwright (b. Buffalo, New York, June 12, 1886; d. Greenwich, Connecticut, June 12, 1954). Goetz was active as a composer and lyricist on Broadway from 1907 through 1930. He is best remembered for his contributions to two hits, both from 1916: "For Me and My Gal," with lyrics cowritten with EDGAR LESLIE and music by GEORGE W. MEYER, and revived in the 1942 movie musical of the same name; and the Hawaiian-flavored novelty "Yaaka Hula Hickey Dula," with lyrics cowritten with JOE YOUNG and music by PETE WENDLING. AL JOLSON popularized the latter song in his show *Robinson Crusoe, Jr.* (1916), and also made a best-selling recording of it (Columbia A-1956). Goetz contributed words and music to a number of Broadway revues, including the 1907 edition of *Ziegfeld's Follies, Hitchy-Koo of 1917*, and the 1922 version of *George White's Scandals*. He also contributed to the musical plays of others, most notably COLE PORTER's 1928 show *Paris*, and produced the works of others. Goetz's sister, Dorothy, was IRVING BERLIN's first wife, and Berlin and Goetz remained friends following her tragic death; the two collaborated on "Alexander's Bag-pipe Band," an obvious followup to Berlin's big earlier hit, in 1912. Goetz's songwriting activity ended in 1930.

# Jean Goldkette

Bandleader (b. Valenciennes, France, March 18, 1899; d. Santa Barbara, California, March 24, 1962). A child prodigy pianist, Goldkette settled in the United States when he was just twelve years old. He moved to Chicago, where he worked as a pianist/leader for dance band syndicator Edgar Benson. Using the knowledge he acquired from Benson, Goldkette formed his big dance band, which started recording for Victor in 1924, when he bought and ran Detroit's Greystone Ballroom. His recording band made only twenty sides, between October 12, 1926, and September 15, 1927, but it was arguably the finest dance band of the 1920s. With minor changes through the recording year (the addition of Billy Murray as vocalist on "I'm Looking over a Four Leaf Clover," Danny Polo's replacing Don Murray on clarinet,

Itzy Riskin's replacing Paul Mertz on piano), the band's personnel consisted of Bix Beiderbecke, cornet; Fuzzy Farrar and Ray Lodwig, trumpets; Bill Rank and Spiegle Wilcox, trombones; Don Murray, clarinet, alto sax, and baritone sax; Doc Ryker, alto sax; Frank Trumbauer, C melody sax; Joe Venuti, violin; Paul Mertz, piano; Howdy Quicksell, banjo; Eddie Lang, guitar; Steve Brown, string bass; Chauncey Morehouse, drums; and Bill Challis as arranger. The entire jazz core of the Goldkette band defected to join PAUL WHITEMAN in 1927. Goldkette continued to manage regional bands and dancehalls through the 1950s. He then returned to concertizing on the piano until shortly before his death.

# Benny Goodman

Bandleader and clarinetist (b. Benjamin David Goodman, Chicago, Illinois, May 30, 1909; d. New York City, June 13, 1986). Goodman was known as "The King of Swing." The name wasn't mere press agentry. Unlike PAUL WHITEMAN's "King of Jazz" tag, the masterful clarinetist deserved his title. Goodman's band, like most of the big bands, changed its personnel regularly as sidemen grew to star stature and others made their reputations. But when asked, "Which was your favorite big band?" and "Which did you enjoy playing in the most?" many players over the years gave the same answer: "Benny Goodman had the most exciting band of all, and we had a ball playing in it. But, my God, what a taskmaster!" Perhaps Goodman was not the most exacting of leaders (GLENN MILLER comes to mind), but he did expect precision playing, which called for regular rehearsals. For men scarcely out of their teens, this kind of discipline was too much like work. But the talented musicians and the skilled arrangers, led by pioneer FLETCHER HENDERSON, made its members regard the Goodman orchestra with utmost affection.

Goodman's parents emigrated from Russia to Chicago, where his father found work as a tailor. From his early teens, Goodman took clarinet lessons at Hull-House, a local settlement house for children of immigrants. He started his professional career at age thirteen. He came to New York City with the Ben Pollack band and began to record extensively as a sideman. His beautiful, full tone was easily identifiable, even though his name was not often found on early record labels. He also did pit band work for Broadway musicals, and was even busier doing freelance work in radio bands. In the summer of 1932, he organized his first band, which accompanied singer RUSS COLUMBO. He formed another band in the summer of 1934 to play at BILLY ROSE's Music Hall. This second band also made some fine recordings, and began to get some recognition when, from December 1934 to May 1935, they appeared on the weekly three-hour NBC radio program *Let's Dance*. They shared the program with XAVIER CUGAT's Latin music and Kel Murray's sweet dance music.

After six months on the program, the Goodman band toured the country to dismal response until they hit the Palomar Ballroom in Los Angeles, where their hot swing was a huge success. They went on to play at Chicago's Congress Hotel for eight months, during which time they were heard nightly on radio. The band's first hit recording featured Fletcher Henderson arrangements of the two kinds of tunes the band would perform throughout this decade: the medium bounce hot instrumental, and the slow, dreamy ballad. The disc that put them on the map carried JELLY ROLL MORTON's "King Porter Stomp" and VINCENT YOUMANS's "Sometimes I'm Happy" (Victor 25090). The band's theme, "Let's Dance," a 1935 song by Gregory Stone, Fanny May Baldridge, and Joe Bonime, wasn't recorded until 1939 (Columbia 35301). Its closing theme was "Good-Bye" (1935), by bandleader Gordon Jenkins (Victor 25215).

Henderson's arrangements often broke the fourteen-piece band into sections and had them competing with one another (e.g., the brass section accompanying Goodman's clarinet solo, or alternating accompaniment between the brass and reed sections). They also used the riffs as underlying motifs throughout the pieces. The "riff" was a rhythmic phrase of two measures which was repeated in the background. Riffs underlay the basis for many jazz-inspired songs, such as "Sing, Sing, Sing," "One o'Clock Jump," and "String of Pearls." Other arrangers who contributed over the years to the Goodman band's repertoire were Edgar Sampson, Jimmy Mundy, and Horace Henderson.

Just as Paul Whiteman wanted to make (what he considered) jazz respectable for the educated middle and upper classes in the 1920s, so Benny Goodman wanted to do the same for (what he was calling) jazz in the 1930s. On January 16, 1938, Goodman and his band

Benny Goodman pictured on the sheet music for his closing theme song, "Good-Bye," by composer Gordon Jenkins.

rented Carnegie Hall to present the first jazz concert ever held in that bastion of classical music. It was a complete success, as recordings made during the concert attest. These were finally issued in 1950, as a set of two LPs that became an all-time best-seller (Columbia OSL-160, *Carnegie Hall Jazz Concert*). The musicians on that historic evening included Harry James, Ziggy Elman, and Gordon Griffin, trumpets; Red Ballard and Vernon Brown, trombones; Benny Goodman, clarinet; Hymie Schertzer and George Koenig, alto saxes; Arthur Rollini and Babe Russin, tenor saxes; Jess Stacy, piano; Allen Reuss, guitar; Harry Goodman, string bass; Gene Krupa, drums; and Martha Tilton, vocalist.

The band's hot numbers included "Stompin' at the Savoy" (Victor 25247), "House Hop" (Victor 25350), "Riffin' at the Ritz" (Victor 25445), "Rosetta" (Victor 25510), "Sing, Sing, Sing" (Victor 36205), "Don't Be That Way" (Victor 25792), "Lullaby in Rhythm" (Victor 25827), "And the Angels Sing" (Victor 26170), "Jumpin' at the Woodside" (Columbia 35210), "Stealin' Apples"/"Opus Local 802" (Columbia 35362), "Benny Rides Again" (Columbia 55001), "Solo Flight" (Columbia 36684), "Air Mail Special" (Columbia 36254), "Clarinet a la King" (Okeh 6544), "Jersey Bounce"/"String of Pearls" (Okeh 6592), and "Six Flats Unfurnished" (Columbia 36652). Besides his big band, Goodman also featured, at various times, his trio, quartet, quintet, sextet, and septet. They all contributed to his success.

Goodman and the band appeared in several films, with prominent roles in *Hollywood Hotel* (1938), *The Powers Girl* (1943), *The Gang's All Here* (1943), and *Sweet and Lowdown* (1944). They made a soundtrack for Disney's *Make Mine Music* (1946). Goodman's life was given the Hollywood treatment, with Steve Allen in the title role of *The Benny Goodman Story* (1955).

# Gotham-Attucks Music Company

Publishers. Black songwriters, while relatively few in number, were on the scene in Tin Pan Alley from the beginning. Major firms such as JOSEPH W. STERN and Company, HOWLEY, HAVILAND, AND COMPANY, and M. WITMARK AND SONS published talented black composers and lyricists. The tearjerkers of GUSSIE DAVIS sold in the millions, as did the COON SONGS of the prolific Chris Smith, Ernest Hogan, Irving Jones, Willis Accooe, and Shepard Edmonds, and the show music of Tom Lemonier, COLE AND JOHNSON BROTHERS, Alex Rogers, James Vaughn, James Tim Brymn, Bert Williams, and Cecil Mack.

The first black-owned and operated Tin Pan Alley firm was Attucks Music Publishing Company, started in 1903 by Shepard N. Edmonds (1876–1957). He sold it to Richard C. McPherson (1883–1944) and WILL MARION COOK two years later. They, in the meantime, had started Gotham Music Company, and with this merger in mid-1905, the new firm became known as Gotham-Attucks Music Company. They quickly signed WILLIAMS AND WALKER to an exclusive contract and published songs from their shows, *Abyssinia* and *Bandanna Land.* A lyricist, McPherson wrote such hits as "He's a Cousin of Mine," "Good Morning, Carrie," "That's Why They Call Me Shine," and "You're in the Right Church but the Wrong Pew." Gotham-Attucks lasted until 1911, when McPherson decided that running a publishing company was not worth the effort. He continued to write lyrics throughout the 1920s and 1930s. Probably his most famous lyric was written to JAMES P. JOHNSON's music for "The CHARLESTON."

# Bud Green

Lyricist (b. Austria, November 19, 1897; d. Yonkers, New York, January 2, 1981). Green was most active in the 1920s and 1930s, working with a number of collaborators. Among his best-known songs was 1924's "Alabamy Bound," with lyrics by B. G. DE SYLVA and music by RAY HENDERSON, which sold over a million copies of sheet music. AL JOLSON introduced it, but it was more often associated with EDDIE CANTOR, who interpolated it into *Kid Boots.* In 1925, Green wrote "I Love My Baby (My Baby Loves Me)" with HARRY WARREN; Waring's Pennsylvanians made it a hit (Victor 19905). Two years later, Warren and Green scored again with "Away Down South in Heaven." Green partnered with composer SAM STEPT for two hits, 1928's "That's My Weakness Now," followed a year later by "Do Something," both written for Helen Kane. Among Green's later hits was 1937's "Once in a While," with music by Michael Edwards. It was introduced by TOMMY DORSEY and his orchestra, with a vocal by Jack Leonard (Victor 25686). 1938 saw the jazz hit "The Flat Foot Floogee," which became a theme number for the duo of Slim (Gaillard), who wrote the music, and Slam (Stewart); the duo also took colyricist credits. Green's last big hit was "Sentimental Journey," written with Les Brown and Ben Homer in 1944, which was a major hit for Brown's band featuring a young DORIS DAY (Columbia 36769). The song has become a standard in the American pop repertoire.

# Johnny Green

Composer and arranger (b. New York City, October 10, 1908; d. Beverly Hills, California, May 15, 1989). Green was a composer best remembered for his pop song hits of the 1930s and his later work on film sound tracks (when he went by the name John W. Green).

A musical prodigy, Green began playing piano at the age of five, and had taught himself the rudiments of orchestration by his early teens. He attended Harvard University, where he led a dance band during school breaks and on weekends; he worked one summer for GUY LOMBARDO. His first song, "Coquette," was written with GUS KAHN and Lombardo's brother, Carmen. On graduating college, Green worked on Wall Street, but continued to study music on the side, eventually giving up his day job in 1928. Green had several hits in the early 1930s, primarily with lyricist EDWARD HEYMAN. Their best-remembered number is 1930's "Body and Soul" (written with Robert Sour and Frank Eyton), introduced by Libby Holman, which has become a jazz classic. Other hits for Heyman and Green included "I Cover the Waterfront" (1933) and "I Wanna Be Loved" (1934; with additional lyrics by BILLY ROSE). Green augmented his income by leading a dance band and also serving as a musical director for several Broadway shows through the 1930s. In 1942, he moved to Hollywood, where he worked as a composer and arranger. He won two Oscars for music arrangement, first for 1948's *Easter Parade* and then for 1951's *An American in Paris* (he would win two more Oscars in the 1960s for his work on *West Side Story* and *Oliver!*). Green became general director for music at MGM in the 1950s, and served as a guest conductor for the Los Angeles Philharmonic during the 1960s and 1970s.

# Clifford Grey

Lyricist and playwright (b. Percival Davis, Birmingham, England, January 5, 1887; d. Ipswich, England, September 25, 1941). Initially performing under his birth name in various companies playing Britain's coastal resorts, Davis took the stage name Clifford Grey in 1907. He had his first major success providing lyrics to Nat Ayer's "If You Were the Only Girl in the World" in 1916. He began writing librettos for musicals in London, and came to New York in 1920 when JEROME KERN asked him to collaborate with himself, Guy Bolton, and P. G. WODEHOUSE on their new production, *Sally*. Grey remained in the United States and worked on shows with a number of composers, most successfully with VINCENT YOUMANS on the popular 1927 musical *Hit the Deck!*, which featured the big hit "Hallelujah," written with LEO ROBIN. In 1928, Grey provided lyrics for several numbers for *The Three Musketeers*, RUDOLF FRIML's last musical production. When talking pictures were introduced, Grey went to Hollywood and contributed screenplays to fourteen films, including adaptations of his earlier stage successes along with original musical comedies. His biggest latter-day hit was "Got a Date with an Angel," written in 1931 with Oscar Levant and JOHNNY GREEN. Hal Kemp and his orchestra, with vocalist Skinnay Ennis, made the best-selling recording (Brunswick 7319) in 1934. Grey returned to England in 1932, continuing to work in theater and film. He died following a performance to entertain soldiers in an encampment in Ipswich, a victim of an asthma attack. Grey also had a career as an Olympic athlete, winning gold medals as a member of the U.S. bobsled team in 1928 and 1932 (despite the fact that he wasn't a U.S. citizen).

# Ferde Grofé

See *Paul Whiteman*

# Mose Edwin Gumble

Famous song plugger (b. 1876; d. 1947; full dates unknown). Gumble had a long career as a song plugger, promoting several major hits of the 1910s and 1920s, as well as helping build the careers of several songwriters. Gumble was from the Midwest, originally managing Maurice Shapiro's Chicago music store. In late 1904, JEROME REMICK purchased Shapiro's business, and brought Gumble to New York to run his professional department. Just before leaving the Midwest, Gumble wed Clara Ella Black, who would become well known as a vaudeville chanteuse and recording star performing under the name Clarice Vance (b. Louisville, Kentucky, March 14, 1871; d. Napa, California, August 24, 1961); the couple divorced in 1914. In his position at Remick, Gumble hired several young musicians to work as song pluggers, including GEORGE GERSHWIN in 1914 and VINCENT YOUMANS five years later. Gumble was the key behind making several songs into major hits. In 1910, he took Jean Schwartz's and William Jerome's song "Chinatown, My Chinatown," and made it into a multimillion-seller; he worked similar magic seven years later when he took a song written and self-published by a Midwest composer, Lee S. Roberts, called "Smiles," and made it into a three-million-selling hit. In October 1928, Gumble left Remick to join with composer WALTER DONALDSON and Walter Douglas to form a new firm to publish the score of Donaldson's Broadway musical,

Mose Gumble in the 1920s.

*Whoopee*. The firm was bought by Warner Bros. in the early 1930s, and Gumble continued to work as a plugger for Warner's music holdings. He was killed in a train crash in 1947 while traveling for Warners on business.

# H

## Oscar Hammerstein II

Lyricist (b. New York City, July 12, 1895; d. Doylestown, Pennsylvania, August 12, 1960). Hammerstein came from a distinguished theatrical family. His grandfather, Oscar I, was a world-famous opera impresario, whose Manhattan Opera Company was bought by the Metropolitan Opera Association. He also built the Victoria Theatre and produced vaudeville shows. The Victoria was managed by William Hammerstein, Oscar's father. His uncle, Arthur, was a successful producer of Broadway plays and musicals.

Hammerstein started writing books and lyrics while attending Columbia College, working on the varsity show. His first musical comedy, *Always You* (January 5, 1920), was produced on Broadway by his uncle Arthur. With OTTO HARBACH, Hammerstein shared the book and lyric writing for VINCENT YOUMANS's *Wildflower* (1923). Hammerstein made musical history with JEROME KERN when they wrote *Show Boat* (1927) and *Music in the Air* (1932). They won an Academy Award for "The Last Time I Saw Paris" (1940), which was interpolated into the film *Lady, Be Good!* (1941). Hammerstein also wrote book and lyrics for three of the greatest American operettas: RUDOLF FRIML's *Rose Marie* (1924) and SIGMUND ROMBERG's *The Desert Song* (1926) and *The New Moon* (1928).

However, Hammerstein is best remembered for his partnership with RICHARD RODGERS and their contributions to musical theater in the 1940s. Rodgers sought a new partner after LORENZ HART turned down the offer to transform Lynn Riggs's play *Green Grow the Lilacs* (1931) into a musical for the Theatre Guild. Hart didn't think it would work. Rodgers, who had known Hammerstein since his own school days at Columbia, invited him to lunch to discuss the project. Hammerstein confided to Rodgers that he had thought of the same project when he was working with Kern, but that Kern, too, had turned it down. Rodgers remembered of that first meeting: "Oscar and I hit it off from the day we began discussing the show."

Rodgers's new partnership was a complete contrast to his old one. Whereas Rodgers and Hart lived totally separate lives, and Hart wrote to Rodgers's music, Rodgers and Hammerstein became great friends, shared similar values, and lived similar lives. And Hammerstein created the lyrics first. As he worked with his words, Hammerstein would make up his own dummy tunes. His wife, Dorothy, once described them as "so terrible that they want to make you cry."

The result of Rodgers and Hammerstein's shared passion for *Green Grow the Lilacs* was *Oklahoma!* (March 31, 1943), which refined the musical comedy form when Hammerstein's lyrics, like the dialogue, for the first time advanced the plot. The only exception to their working method in their first score was "People Will Say We're in Love." Rodgers composed the music immediately after they had discussed the kind of song it was to be, without waiting for Hammerstein's lyric. While the show was trying out in New Haven, it was titled *Away We Go!* The musical play had no stars, no chorus girls, no big laughs, and no popular dance routines. The word-of-mouth to Broadway from New Haven was "no girls, no gags, no

Oscar Hammerstein II (standing) with Richard Rodgers in a studio portrait, c. 1950s.

chance." After its March 31 opening, the slogan could have been changed to "no girls, no gags, no tickets." It ran for 2,248 performances. The marvelous score included "All 'Er Nothin'," "I Cain't Say No," "Kansas City," "Many a New Day," "Oh, What a Beautiful Mornin'," "Oklahoma!," "Pore Jud," and "The Surrey with the Fringe on Top." This show was the first to issue a full original-cast recording, a Decca album that sold over a million copies, starting the now standard practice of offering the complete score of a show on a disc featuring the original Broadway cast. The Broadway cast toured for a year, and a second national company toured for another ten years. To handle *Oklahoma!*'s songs, Rodgers and Hammerstein established their own publishing company, Williamson Music, Inc., named after both their fathers. The film, starring Shirley Jones and Gordon MacRae, was released in 1955.

*State Fair* (1945) was offered to the team because producer Darryl F. Zanuck wanted a film that contained the same kind of homespun feeling that *Oklahoma!* engendered. "It's a Grand Night for Singing" was a classic example of a song never coming near the *Hit Parade* yet becoming a standard. "It Might as Well Be Spring" took Hammerstein an agonizing week to work out, but it took Rodgers less than an hour to compose. It also won them the Academy Award for Best Song, and became one of the team's all-time hits. Dick Haymes had the hit recording (Decca 18706). This one did get on *Your Hit Parade*—and stayed on for seventeen weeks! *State Fair* was the team's only original film score, although Hollywood made successful film versions of their Broadway musicals. *State Fair* was remade in 1962, starring Pat Boone and Ann-Margret, with five new songs having words and music by Rodgers alone. Unfortunately, no hits were among them.

*Carousel* (April 19, 1945) was based on the Theatre Guild's 1921 production of Ferenc Molnar's *Liliom*. "If I Loved You," the hit of the show, was introduced by Jan Clayton and John Raitt, while "You'll Never Walk Alone" provided a lasting inspirational number. "June Is Bustin' Out All Over" and "A Real Nice Clambake" lend a gaiety to the score, along with the "Carousel Waltz." The dramatic "Soliloquy" proved to be the longest pop song ever published, at fifteen pages.

*Allegro* (October 10, 1947) was an experiment that failed, although hits were made of "A Fellow Needs a Girl," and "The Gentleman Is a Dope." The last had a successful recording by Jo Stafford (Capitol 15007).

*South Pacific* (April 7, 1949) ran for 1,925 performances and won the 1950 Pulitzer Prize for drama. It was based on James Michener's 1948 book *Tales of the South Pacific* (which had won a Pulitzer Prize for fiction). Opera star Ezio Pinza negotiated a contract that called for him to sing the equivalent of two operatic performances a week. Therefore, his singing role consisted of only "This Nearly Was Mine" and "Some Enchanted Evening." The latter's recording sold extremely well (Columbia 4559), and the original cast album sold over a million copies. Two million total copies of sheet music were sold of "Bali Ha'i," "A Cockeyed Optimist," "Dites-Moi," "Happy Talk," "Honey Bun," "I'm Gonna Wash That Man Right Outta My Hair," "There Is Nothin' like a Dame," "A Wonderful Guy," and "Younger Than Springtime." In addition to earning $9 million on Broadway, *South Pacific*'s film version (1958) was one of the highest money earners in Hollywood history up to that time.

The speed with which Rodgers composed must have dismayed Hammerstein, who labored over his lyrics. Once during dinner, while finishing coffee, Hammerstein gave his partner the lyrics he had carefully worked out for "Bali Ha'i." While conversation went on, Rodgers created the melody in five minutes. Later, when Rodgers was sick in bed, Hammerstein sent over his words to "Happy Talk" by messenger. Twenty minutes later, he called Rodgers, asking if the lyrics had arrived. Rodgers told him, "I've already written the melody."

*The King and I* (March 29, 1951) starred Gertrude Lawrence and Yul Brynner, and ran 1,246 performances. It was based on a movie—the first time Broadway had used a film as the framework for a show—*Anna and the King of Siam* (1946). Lawrence saw the film and went to Rodgers and Hammerstein to ask if they could make a musical out of it for her. For the first time, Rodgers approached the story through music, in contrast to his approach to *Oklahoma!*, where he and Hammerstein concentrated first on dialogue and lyrics. "Hello, Young Lovers" leads the score, the most popular number of several that have become standards. Others are "Getting to Know You," "I Whistle a Happy Tune," "Shall We Dance?," "We Kiss in a Shadow," and the instrumental "March of the Siamese Children." The film starred Yul Brynner and Deborah Kerr (1956).

*Me and Juliet* (May 28, 1953) was a letdown after the team's two previous shows. It contained only one popular song, "No Other Love." Perry Como had the best-selling recording (RCA Victor 20-5317). The melody came from the tango section of "Beneath the Southern Cross" from *Victory at Sea* (1952–1953), a television documentary for which Rodgers composed background music for twenty-five hours of film.

*Flower Drum Song* (December 1, 1958) gave the team another chance to work in the "Broadway-Oriental" vein. The hit of the show was "I Enjoy Being a Girl." Also in the score were "Grant Avenue," "Don't Marry Me," and "Fan Tan Fanny," which was given a super treatment by Joe "Fingers" Carr (Capitol F-4163). The film version starred Nancy Kwan (1961).

*The Sound of Music* (November 16, 1959) was the last of the team's shows and, with 1,433 performances on Broadway, one of their biggest hits. The main song in this show was "My Favorite Things," introduced by Mary Martin and Patricia Neway. In the film version (1965), the song was sung by Julie Andrews and a children's chorus. "Climb Ev'ry Mountain," "Do-Re-Mi," "Edelweiss," "Sixteen Going on Seventeen," and the title song sold over ten million copies on both the Broadway cast album and the movie sound track. *The Sound of Music* is still the biggest-grossing musical film of all time.

# Lou Handman

Composer (b. New York City, September 10, 1894; d. Flushing, New York, December 9, 1956). Like the archetypal composers of the 1920s, Handman started out as a piano accompanist for singers in vaudeville, then worked as a demonstrator for publishing firms. His first big hit was "Blue (and Broken Hearted)" (1922), with lyrics by Grant Clarke and EDGAR

Leslie. The Virginians, a "jazz" band within the Paul Whiteman Orchestra, made the hit instrumental (Victor 18933), while Marion Harris started her association with Handman songs by making it a hit (Brunswick 2310). Zez Confrey made an outstanding arrangement (QRS 2020) on piano rolls.

"My Sweetie Went Away" (1923) found its best plug in the Cotton Pickers' version (Brunswick 2461). This was Brunswick's name for the Original Memphis Five. Also, Joe Raymond and his orchestra recorded it (Victor 19110). "Lovey Came Back" (1923), with words by veterans Sam Lewis and Joe Young, sounded good to Marion Harris, who had previously scored with "Blue," and Ray Miller and his orchestra performed it often. The Original Memphis Five (under their real name) liked it, too, and plugged it (Banner 1292). "I Can't Get the One I Want" (1924) was a favorite with dance bands. Paul Whiteman, Vincent Lopez, Paul Specht, Ray Miller, and Lanin's Arcadians all recorded it.

"I'm Gonna Charleston Back to Charleston" (1925) was not only a cute play on words, but a gem of a dance number as well. The California Ramblers, as well as Lou Gold's orchestra, featured it. "Are You Lonesome Tonight?" (1927) was the musical question Handman asked, and Vaughan DeLeath answered with a hit recording (Edison 52044). Elvis Presley revived it with his hit recording in 1960 (RCA Victor 47–7810).

Although Handman composed throughout the 1930s, only "Puddin' Head Jones" (1933) was successful, as featured by the up-and-coming Ozzie Nelson Orchestra (Vocalion 2582).

# W. C. Handy

Composer, lyricist, publisher, trumpeter, and bandleader (b. William Christopher Handy, Florence, Alabama, November 16, 1873; d. New York City, March 29, 1958). As Scott Joplin and his "Maple Leaf Rag" were to ragtime, so W. C. Handy and his "St. Louis Blues" were to blues. He composed and published the most significant blues for twenty years (1912–1932), and through various media, promoted the blues as part of popular music and jazz.

As a youth, Handy played cornet in bands and formed his own band. He became a schoolteacher, toured with Mahara's Minstrels as lead cornet and bandmaster, and played Chicago's World's Fair in 1893. He led a local band in Memphis, Tennessee, where he started composing and met future collaborator and publishing partner Harry Herbert Pace (1884–1943). His first blues was "Memphis Blues," which he published in 1912. With Pace, he formed the Pace and Handy Music Company and issued "Jogo Blues" in 1913. He took the trio section and used it as the trio for his next composition, "St. Louis Blues," the following year. Though this incredible tune was being exposed locally, it took several years for it to take off nationally. Prince's Band was the first to record it (Columbia A-5772) in 1916, and

W. C. Handy in the 1940s.

Handy's "Saint Louis Blues" in its first edition.

Marion Harris had the first hit record as a song (Columbia A-2944) in 1920, but it wasn't until the ORIGINAL DIXIELAND JAZZ BAND recorded it the following year that it became a permanent part of the repertoire (Victor 18772).

"Yellow Dog Blues" started out life in 1914 as "Yellow Dog Rag," but it wasn't until Joseph C. Smith's orchestra recorded it in 1920 that it became a standard (Victor 18618). It took Handy's Memphis Blues Band until January 1922 to record both numbers (Paramount 20098). "Joe Turner Blues" and "Hesitating Blues" were published in 1915, and Prince's Band recorded both numbers the following year (Columbia A-5854, Columbia A-5772, respectively). The trouble with the Prince recordings were that they were issued on twelve-inch 78 rpm discs, making them more expensive to purchase and an awkward size to store (most pop recordings were on ten-inch discs). "Ole Miss Rag" came out in 1916, and Handy's Orchestra of Memphis launched it on disc when they came to New York City in September 1917 specifically to record for Columbia Records. It was issued with the flip side containing his "Hooking Cow Blues (Columbia A-2420). "Beale Street" also was published that year, and was immediately recorded by Earl Fuller's Jazz Band (Victor 18369). The following year saw the patriotic "The Kaiser's Got the Blues." 1921 was a banner year with "Aunt Hagar's Children Blues" coming out on disc by the Original Memphis Five (Pathe 020900), ISHAM JONES's orchestra (Brunswick 2358), and the Virginians (Victor 19021). The same year Noble Sissle and his Sizzling Syncopators recorded "Loveless Love" (Pathe 20493). When it was published again in 1925, the name was changed to "Careless Love," and Bessie Smith made a classic recording (Columbia 14083-D).

Handy wrote his autobiography, *Father of the Blues*, in 1941. The same year Henry "Hot Lips" Levine and the Dixieland Jazz Group recorded an album of Handy's tunes with vocalist Lena Horne (Victor p-82). In 1954, LOUIS ARMSTRONG recorded an album called *Plays W.C. Handy* (Columbia CL-591). In 1958, the year of his death, Hollywood made his biopic, *St. Louis Blues*, starring Nat "King" Cole.

# James F. Hanley

Composer (b. Rensselaer, Indiana, February 17, 1892; d. Douglaston, New York, February 8, 1942). He attended Chicago Musical College and had his first hit with a World War I number, "The Ragtime Volunteers Are Off to War" (1917), with lyrics by Ballard Macdonald. It was featured by EMMA CARUS. Later that same year, the team created "(Back Home Again in) Indiana," first recorded by the ORIGINAL DIXIELAND JAZZ BAND (Columbia A-2297). Joe Goodwin joined the team to help produce "Breeze, Blow My Baby Back to Me" (1919).

FANNY BRICE sang the Hanley-Macdonald "Rose of Washington Square" (1920) in the *Ziegfeld Midnight Frolic*, and it became a smash hit. Hanley followed it the next year, with

Grant Clarke writing the words, with "Second Hand Rose," which Fanny Brice sang in the *Ziegfeld Follies of 1921*. The Virginians made a hit recording of the Hanley-Goodwin collaboration "Gee! But I Hate to Go Home Alone" (1922) (Victor 18965). With B. G. De Sylva, Hanley wrote "Just a Cottage Small" (1925) for John McCormack, who sang it to success (Victor 1113). For *Honeymoon Lane* (September 20, 1926), Hanley collaborated with Eddie Dowling on the score, the big hit of which was "The Little White House (at the End of Honeymoon Lane)." And with Gene Buck, Hanley produced "No Foolin' " for *Ziegfeld's American Revue of 1926* (June 24, 1926). Sam Lanin's Troubadours made a nifty version on disc (Banner 1753). Hanley's last hit came with "Zing! Went the Strings of My Heart," written for Hal LeRoy and Eunice Healey in *Thumbs Up!* (December 27, 1934). Judy Garland sang it in *Listen, Darling* (1938).

# Otto Harbach

Lyricist (b. Otto Abels Harbach, Salt Lake City, Utah, August 18, 1873; d. New York City, January 24, 1963). Harbach began his career as a college professor of English (1895–1901), newspaper writer (1902–1903), advertising agency writer (1903–1910), then full-time lyric writer and librettist for Broadway musicals. His first big hit was "Cuddle Up a Little Closer" from the show *The Three Twins* (1908), which had music by Karl Hoschna. Hoschna and Harbach also collaborated on "Every Little Movement," which came from their 1910 musical *Madame Sherry*, and it was sung on disc by Harry MacDonough and Lucy Isabelle Marsh (Victor 5784).

Hoschna died in 1911, so Harbach sought new collaborators. "Sympathy," from the operetta *The Firefly* (1912), with music by Rudolf Friml, had a hit recording by contralto Helen Clark and tenor Walter van Brunt (Victor 17270). For the 1920 musical, *Mary*, Harbach wrote what was to become George Burns and Gracie Allen's radio and television theme, "The Love Nest." Joseph C. Smith's orchestra had the hit recording (Victor 18678). In 1924, Harbach had two winners in *Rose Marie*, also in collaboration with Friml: the title song, which Irish tenor John McCormack recorded (Victor 1067), and "Indian Love Call," which Paul Whiteman's orchestra made into an instrumental hit (Victor 19517). When the film of this show was made in 1936, Jeanette MacDonald and Nelson Eddy made another million-seller of "Indian Love Call" (Victor 4323).

Jerome Kern's 1925 musical *Sunny* sported two hits. "Who?" was recorded by George Olsen and His Music (the show's pit band), whose disc sold over a million copies (Victor 19840). Tommy Dorsey and his orchestra revived "Who?" in 1937 in a sensational arrangement (Victor 25693). "Sunny" was the flip side of George Olsen's disc. Two more hits came from the 1926 show *The Desert Song*: "One Alone" and "The Riff Song," both recorded by Nat Shilkret and the Victor Orchestra (Victor 20373). In 1931, from the show *The Cat and the Fiddle*, Harbach again had two hits, both recorded by Leo Reisman and his orchestra: "The Night Was Made for Love" and "She Didn't Say 'Yes' " (Victor 22839). Yet again, he had two hits from the 1933 musical *Roberta*: "Smoke Gets in Your Eyes" (a #1 hit by Paul Whiteman, with Bunny Berigan on trumpet [Victor 24455]), and "Yesterdays," recorded by Leo Reisman (Brunswick 6701). Harbach was president of ASCAP from 1950 to 1953.

# E. Y. "Yip" Harburg

Lyricist (b. Edgar Y. Harburg, New York City, April 8, 1896; d. Beverly Hills, California, March 5, 1981). Born to immigrant parents, Harburg earned the Yiddish nickname "Yipsel" (meaning squirrel), which was subsequently shortened to "Yip." He attended high school with IRA GERSHWIN, and the two worked together on the school newspaper. After he graduated, Harburg worked as a journalist in South America in the late 1910s, and then established an electrical supply business in New York City during the 1920s. However, the stock market crash ended his business, and he turned to his first love: lyric writing.

Harburg began writing lyrics in 1929. His primary collaborators were HAROLD ARLEN and Jay Gorney. For the show *Americana* in 1932, he and Gorney wrote the great Depression song, "Brother, Can You Spare a Dime," with which both BING CROSBY (Brunswick 6414) and RUDY VALLEE (Columbia 2725-D) had #1 hits. Also in 1932, he wrote "April in Paris," which appeared in VERNON DUKE's *Walk a Little Faster*. From *Crazy Quilt of 1933* came "It's Only a Paper Moon," given a hit recording by CLIFF EDWARDS (Vocalion 2587). It was revived in 1945 by ELLA FITZGERALD (Decca 23425). From *Ziegfeld Follies of 1934* came "What Is There to Say?" Emil Coleman and his orchestra had the hit (Columbia 2859-D).

There were two hits from the 1934 show *Life Begins at 8:40*. "You're a Builder Upper" had a hit recording by Leo Reisman's orchestra, with vocal by the song's composer, Harold Arlen (Brunswick 6941). "Fun to Be Fooled" was recorded by Henry King and his orchestra (Columbia 2941-D).The Arlen-Harburg duo then moved to Hollywood, contributing to various pictures. They provided songs for the satirical Broadway musical *Hooray for What!* in 1937, and then produced the score for what is arguably the best movie musical ever: 1939's *The Wizard of Oz*. "Over the Rainbow" and "We're Off to See the Wizard" are among the many classics from the film. "Happiness Is a Thing Called Joe" was written for the 1943 movie version of *Cabin in the Sky*. The beautiful "Evelina," from the 1944 musical *Bloomer Girl*, got a lovely recording by Bing Crosby (Decca 18635).

1947 was a special year, for that was when Harburg collaborated with BURTON LANE on the classic Broadway musical *Finian's Rainbow*, with its cornucopia of standards: "That

E. Y. "Yip" Harburg in the 1970s.

Great Come-and-Get-It Day," "When I'm Not Near the Girl I Love," "If This Isn't Love," "Look to the Rainbow," "Old Devil Moon," and "How Are Things in Glocca Morra," which got a hit recording by Buddy Clark (Columbia 37223). In 1961 Harburg wrote "The Happiest Girl in the World" for the musical of the same name. In 1962, he reunited with Arlen to provide songs for the Disney animated feature *Gay Purr-ee*. His career came to a close with the unsuccessful *Darling of the Day*, in 1968. He died in an automobile accident in March 1981.

# Leigh Harline

Composer (b. Salt Lake City, Utah, March 26, 1907; d. Hollywood, California, December 10, 1969). Harline was a film composer best remembered for his songs for the Disney animated film *Pinocchio*. Harline began his career scoring Disney shorts, notably 1934's "Silly Symphony" *The Grasshopper and the Ants*, which introduced the hit song "The World Owes Me a Living" (1934), with lyrics by Larry Morey (1905–1971). His best-loved score was for *Pinocchio* (1940), written with Ned Washington. The top songs were "Give a Little Whistle,"

"Hi-Diddle-Dee-Dee," "Jiminy Cricket," and the first of the two Academy Award–Winning Disney songs, "When You Wish upon a Star," which was used as the theme song for the Disney television show of the 1950s. CLIFF EDWARDS (aka Ukulele Ike) sang the song on the sound track and made the first hit recording. Harline left Disney shortly after completing this score, and subsequently worked for various studios. His most famous pure sound track was written for 1954's *Broken Lance*.

# T. B. Harms Company/Harms, Inc.

An old-line music publisher founded in 1875, Harms was a rather sleepy firm run by brothers Tom and Alex Harms until 1892, when they published the song hit "Daisy Bell" by William Jerome and Harry Dacre—better-known today as "A Bicycle Built for Two." That same year,

The Music Publishers Association of 1906. Seated at right, T. B. Harms; above him, F. B. Haviland; second from left, standing, E. T. Paull.

T. B. Harms building in 1910, after the firm moved uptown, at the corner of Broadway and 42nd Street.

the firm published the score for the landmark Broadway show *A Trip to Chinatown*, producing hits with "The Bowery" and "Push Them Clouds Away." In 1901, the firm really took off when MAX DREYFUS joined the ranks as an arranger. Dreyfus quickly acquired 25 percent of the firm, and in 1904 took over the entire operation. He had a keen ear for talent, and signed up promising young songwriters including JEROME KERN, VINCENT YOUMANS, and GEORGE and IRA GERSHWIN.

In 1917, Kern purchased one-quarter of the T. B. Harms firm. A separate firm, Harms, Inc., was formed by Dreyfus to hold non-Kern copyrights. Dreyfus entered into a separate partnership with the London based CHAPPELL AND COMPANY in 1920; Louis Dreyfus took over Chappell U.K. and Max continued to run both Chappell and Harms, Inc. Harms, Inc., was sold to Warner Bros. Pictures in 1929; Warners combined it with the JEROME REMICK and WITMARK catalogs it had purchased previously. The Dreyfuses continued to run Chappell. Rights to the Harms back catalog are now held by WARNER-CHAPPELL MUSIC.

T. B. HARMS (1875–1929)

| | |
|---|---|
| 1875–1891 | 819 Broadway |
| 1892–1904 | 18 East 22nd Street |
| 1904–1906 | 126 West 44th Street |
| 1907–1911 | 1431–1433 Broadway (Theatrical Exchange Building) |
| 1912–1933 | 62 West 45th Street |
| 1933–1935 | 1619 Broadway (owned by Warner Bros.) |

# Charles K. Harris

Songwriter, and publisher (b. Poughkeepsie, New York, May 1, 1867; d. New York City, December 22, 1930). His parents moved soon after his birth to Milwaukee, Wisconsin, where Harris spent his youth and the first decade of his professional years. He had his first number, "When the Sun Has Set," published by the Witmarks. He got his royalty statement six months later, along with a postal order for eighty-four cents in payment. He wrote to Isidore Witmark that it was the smallest return he had ever received for any song, and that he was going to frame the note with the caption: "The smallest royalty statement on record." Witmark wrote back to Harris: "Would say I am also framing your song and hanging it in a conspicuous place in my office, where all in the profession can see it. Underneath, I am writing this: 'The only song we ever published that did not sell.' " This incident made Harris start publishing his own songs.

Harris's dual career as songwriter and publisher was maintained by the extraordinary sales of one song, "After the Ball." Like many of the tearjerkers of its time, the song took its story from a true incident. Harris's youngest sister, Ada, had a girlfriend who lived in Chicago. She invited Ada to visit her and attend a ball given by a social club early in 1892. Charles was asked to chaperone Ada, taking her to Chicago from their home in Milwaukee. The evening of the ball was a momentous one for him for two reasons: he met his future wife there, and he witnessed a scene that he would alter and describe in a song. In the group was a charming couple, engaged to be married. Suddenly, Harris heard that the engagement had been broken that very evening. As they were leaving the party, Harris noticed the young man escorting not his fiancée but another young lady. The young man felt that if he caused his sweetheart a pang of jealousy, she would be willing to forget their quarrel. She, on the other hand, saw only that he was easily consoled. Tears came to her eyes, though she tried to hide them behind a smile and a careless toss of the head. On seeing this little drama, the words "Many a heart is aching after the ball" came into Harris's mind and stayed there.

The next day, as he was resting after the journey, he saw the estranged couple of the previous night whose pride had kept them apart. For his song, he set the scene with a little girl's climbing on her uncle's knee, asking, "Why are you single, why live alone?" The uncle recalls the time when he saw his sweetheart at a ball in the arms of another. She tried to explain, but he wouldn't believe her, thinking her faithless until years later, when he discovered that it was her brother who had been embracing her. When he had written three verses and a chorus, Harris sent for his arranger, Joseph Clauder, who took the song down on manuscript paper.

Harris's next thought was to get a star to include it in his repertoire. Playing at the Bijou Theatre in Milwaukee was the touring company of Charles Hoyt's *A Trip to Chinatown.*

Publisher-songwriter Charles K. Harris in 1926.

In the cast was the famous James Aldrich Libbey, billed as "the peerless baritone." Harris knew the company manager and, after hearing Libbey on opening night, asked the manager to arrange an appointment with the singer. The following morning, Libbey walked into Harris's office and was given the manuscript. Libbey liked the title of the song and proceeded to sing it straight through. He asked for an orchestration, and said he would put it into the show the following Wednesday. From the first time he sang it, audience response was overwhelming. He agreed to sing it for as long as the tour lasted. As the company moved from city to city, orders for the song poured into the Harris office. His first order was from the Oliver Ditson Company of Boston, for seventy-five thousand copies. Another order for one hundred thousand copies came soon after, and within a few months, Harris had sold two million copies, making "After the Ball" the first of the Alley's multimillion-selling hits. It would eventually sell over five million copies. The second edition featured a photograph of the "peerless baritone," who sang it for the rest of his professional life.

In addition to Libbey's plugging, John Philip Sousa included "After the Ball" in his daily program at the Chicago World's Fair in 1893, exposing it to crowds from all over the United States. This gigantic plug produced continuing sales.

With the money earned on "After the Ball," Harris continued to publish his own songs. He finally established a New York office in 1897, when he soon became a full-fledged publisher by taking on other songwriters' numbers. He hired vaudeville artist Meyer Cohen to run his business there, while he concentrated on composing and writing his sentimental ballads-with-a-story in Milwaukee. Harris never learned to read or write music, depending on Joseph Clauder to arrange and write out his piano and vocal parts for publication. Customers devoured his melancholy songs.

"After the Ball," Harris's most famous publication.

The bulk of his success continued to be with the publication of his own work. Harris moved to New York permanently in 1903, set at 31 West Thirty-first Street. Another of his weepers was the Spanish-American War favorite "Break the News to Mother." He also wrote and published the song that started AL JOLSON's career, "For Old Times' Sake," and the great sob-story telephone song, "Hello Central, Give Me Heaven." "Nobody Knows, Nobody Cares" and "Mid the Green Fields of Virginia" are the only other Harris songs that had sales of hit proportions. He continued to publish until his death.

# Lorenz Hart

Sharp-witted lyricist and librettist (b. Lorenz Milton Hart, New York City, May 2, 1895; d. New York City, November 22, 1943). Hart wrote mainly with RICHARD RODGERS from 1919 until his death. His hallmark was fashioning stylish and smart lyrics for Broadway and Hollywood.

Hart showed an early knack for writing witty lyrics and poems. As a teenager, he met nascent composer Richard Rodgers, and the two formed an immediate partnership. Hart's first hit came in 1925 with the *Garrick Gaieties* revue, which featured his "Manhattan," recorded by The Knickerbockers (Columbia 422-D). The same year "Here in My Arms" came from the musical *Dearest Enemy*, with Leo Reisman having the hit recording (Columbia 573-D). In 1926, Hart had *The Girl Friend*, with its title song jazzily played by George Olsen and His Music (Victor 20029), and "The Blue Room," sung by The Revelers (Victor 20082). The *Garrick Gaieties of 1926* produced "Mountain Greenery," recorded by ROGER WOLFE KAHN's orchestra (Victor 20071).

The next year Hart had two hits from *A Connecticut Yankee*, "Thou Swell" and "My Heart Stood Still," done on a single disc by Ben Selvin and his orchestra (Columbia 1187-D). *Present Arms* came to Broadway in 1928, and its hit song was "You Took Advantage of Me," with a hit recording by PAUL WHITEMAN (Victor 21398). *Spring Is Here* was the 1929 show that had "With a Song in My Heart," which got a hit disc by Leo Reisman and his orchestra (Victor 21923). JANE FROMAN had her hit when she revived it in her biopic of the same name in 1952 (Capitol 2044). Starting the new decade in 1930, *Simple Simon* appeared on Broadway with "Ten Cents a Dance" which RUTH ETTING made famous (Columbia 2146-D).

Hollywood beckoned in 1932, and from the film *Love Me Tonight* came three winners: "Isn't It Romantic?," with the hit recording by Harold Stern (Columbia 2718-D); "Mimi," by Maurice Chevalier, who introduced it in the movie (Victor 24063); and "Lover," by Paul Whiteman's orchestra (Victor 24283). "Blue Moon" was the only hit written by Hart that didn't come from a Broadway score or a movie. Published in 1934, it had hit recordings by Glen Gray and the Casa Loma Orchestra (Decca 312), BENNY GOODMAN (Columbia 3003-

D), and Ray Noble (Victor 24849). Mel Torme revived it in 1949 (Capitol 15428), as did Billy Eckstine (MGM 10311). Hart was back on Broadway in 1936 with *On Your Toes,* from which "There's a Small Hotel" gave Hal Kemp, leader of a popular sweet band, a #1 hit (Brunswick 7634). 1937 saw *Babes in Arms*, from which two standards emerged: "The Lady Is a Tramp," by Tommy Dorsey (Victor 25673), and "My Funny Valentine," a great favorite in nightclubs. *The Boys from Syracuse* was a nifty musical based on Shakespeare's *Comedy of Errors*. It gave "This Can't Be Love" to Horace Heidt for a hit (Brunswick 8257), as well as Benny Goodman (Victor 26099). "Falling in Love with Love" got a Frances Langford recording (Decca 2247). Benny Goodman had the hit recording of "I Didn't Know What Time It Was" (Columbia 35230), from *Too Many Girls,* in 1939. In 1941 *Pal Joey* contained "Bewitched," made by Leo Reisman's orchestra, featuring Anita Boyer as vocalist (Victor 27344). In 1950, it was revived by Chicago pianist-bandleader Bill Snyder in a million-selling hit (Tower 1473). Hart's last song was written for the Broadway revival of *A Connecticut Yankee* in 1943: "To Keep My Love Alive."

Increasingly unreliable due to alcoholism, Hart declined Rodgers's invitation to provide lyrics for a new show to be based on the play *Green Grow the Lilacs*. Rodgers instead partnered with Oscar Hammerstein II, and the result was *Oklahoma!*, a play that changed the musical theater. Hart died in November 1943. Five years later, Hollywood released a biopic about Rogers and Hart, *Words and Music*, starring Tom Drake and Mickey Rooney.

# Fletcher Henderson

African-American bandleader and arranger (b. Fletcher Hamilton [some sources give James Fletcher] Henderson, Jr., Cuthbert, Georgia, December 18, 1897; d. New York City, December 29, 1952).

Henderson's mother was a classical pianist, and his younger brother, Horace (1904–1988), would also become a pianist and bandleader. Henderson attended Atlanta University from 1916 to 1920, then moved to New York. He found a job as a pianist-demonstrator for the firm of Pace and Handy, and then was hired by the black-owned record label, Black Swan, to be its recording manager. He arranged for Ethel Waters's first recordings for this firm in the autumn of 1921, and they were immediately successful.

In 1924, at New York's Club Alabam, Henderson created a dance band with outstanding jazzmen that became most influential in the 1920s. He made many recordings, early with Louis Armstrong and Don Redman, and later with Chu Berry, Coleman Hawkins, and Benny Carter. The band lasted until 1934, when its members left en masse, and then Henderson formed a new group that played together until 1939. Meanwhile, to augment his income, Henderson began selling his distinctive arrangements to Benny Goodman, among other band leaders. He captured the essence of the Goodman band so that you didn't need to hear

Benny Goodman to recognize whose band it was in such arrangements as JELLY ROLL MORTON's "King Porter Stomp," backed by VINCENT YOUMANS's "Sometimes I'm Happy" (Victor 25090); "Christopher Columbus" (Victor 25279); "Star Dust" (Victor 25320); "I Want to Be Happy" (Victor 25510); and "Sugar Foot Stomp" (Victor 25678). Throughout the 1930s his arrangements drove the swing era. Henderson again led his own band from the 1940s through December 1950, when he suffered a stroke. He died two years later.

# Ray Henderson

Composer (b. Raymond Brost, Buffalo, New York, December 1, 1896; d. Greenwich, Connecticut, December 31, 1970). Born to musical parents, Henderson began playing at an early age, including a stint as church organist. After training at the Chicago Conservatory of Music, Henderson came to the Alley in 1918 to take a job as song plugger with LEO FEIST. Shortly after, he joined the FRED FISHER Company, where he was promoted from staff pianist to arranger. He next went to SHAPIRO, BERNSTEIN, AND COMPANY, where Louis Bernstein took an interest in him and got him jobs accompanying vaudevillian Elizabeth Brice, comedian Lew Brice, and several dance teams. These jobs gave him insight into the specific musical needs of performers in the two-a-day crucible of vaudeville. His first published song was "Humming" (1920), issued by T. B. HARMS, with lyrics by Lou Breau. Bernstein introduced Henderson to lyricist LEW BROWN, who became a collaborator and partner in the most famous songwriting trio of the 1920s. His first song with Brown was "Georgette" (1922), which was included in the revue *Greenwich Village Follies of 1922*; it was played by TED LEWIS, whose band also made a successful recording (Columbia A-3662).

His next song with Brown was "Annabelle" (1923), which didn't set the world on fire, but later that year, with MORT DIXON and BILLY ROSE, Henderson composed "That Old Gang of Mine," which did create sparks. This same team wrote "Follow the Swallow," which was placed in the *Greenwich Village Follies of 1924* and enjoyed a fine arrangement on George Olsen's recording (Victor 19428). They also came up with "I Wonder Who's Dancing with You Tonight," "Lucky Kentucky," and "You're in Love with Every One" (this last without Billy Rose).

The big year for Henderson was 1925, when, with assorted collaborators, he turned out six hits in a row. "Alabamy Bound," with lyrics by B. G. DESYLVA and BUD GREEN, sold over a million copies of sheet music. AL JOLSON introduced it, but it was more often associated with EDDIE CANTOR, who interpolated it into *Kid Boots*. " 'Bam, 'Bam, 'Bammy Shore," with lyrics by Mort Dixon, was made into a hit by ROGER WOLFE KAHN's recording (Victor 19808), and "If I Had a Girl Like You" (with help from Billy Rose) became a success largely because of Bennie Krueger's disc (Brunswick 2936). The Henderson-Dixon-Rose team then wrote "Too Many Parties and Too Many Pals." "Don't Bring Lulu" had Rose and Lew Brown as lyric writers and was helped to hit status by performances of The Avon Comedy Four in vaudeville, and on records by Jan Garber's orchestra (Victor 19661).

The two other Henderson hits in that fabulous year of 1925 had lyrics by SAM LEWIS and JOE YOUNG. "Five Foot Two, Eyes of Blue" didn't sell a million copies in its own time but has remained a favorite through the years. It caught the flapper era musically as John Held, Jr.'s, illustrations did visually. Strangely enough, it became a song for women singers, as Jane Gray (Harmony 114) and Esther Walker (Brunswick 3008) recorded it, each with piano accompaniment by RUBE BLOOM. "I'm Sitting on Top of the World" embodies the optimistic outlook of the times and was given beautiful arrangements on disc by ISHAM JONES's orchestra (Brunswick 3022) and Roger Wolfe Kahn's (Victor 19845). Canadian pianist Vera Guilaroff made an exquisite piano solo (Gennett 5750).

"Bye Bye Blackbird" (1926) had lyrics by Mort Dixon and Billy Rose, and for years it was the last song that Henderson would write with anyone other than his new partners, Lew Brown and Buddy De Sylva. This song was heavily plugged by Eddie Cantor, Georgie Price, and the Duncan Sisters.

After the partnership broke up, Buddy De Sylva remained in Hollywood as a film producer. Henderson and Brown stayed together for another three years. During that time, they wrote the score for *George White Scandals of 1931*. The biggest hit of that show was "Life Is Just a Bowl of Cherries," which was introduced and recorded by RUDY VALLEE (Victor 22783). Other hits from that revue were "This Is the Missus," "My Song," "That's Why Darkies Were Born," and "The Thrill Is Gone." Years later, this last became a favorite with TONY MARTIN. For the Shirley Temple film *Curly Top* (1935), Henderson, with lyricists TED KOEHLER and IRVING CAESAR, wrote "Animal Crackers in My Soup."

Although Henderson continued to work with Brown through the 1940s, the duo failed to achieve the success that they had enjoyed previously. Henderson was made a director of ASCAP in 1942, remaining in that position for nine years. His last major success was the wartime revue *Ziegfeld Follies of 1943*, starring Milton Berle, to which he contributed some songs with lyrics by JACK YELLEN. In 1956, the biopic *The Best Things in Life Are Free* celebrated the DeSylva-Brown-Henderson partnership. Henderson died of a heart attack in 1970.

See also *DeSylva, Brown, and Henderson*

# Victor Herbert

Composer (b. Dublin, Ireland, February 1, 1859; d. New York City, May 24, 1924), shortly after completing a tune and sending it to his arranger for scoring. Herbert was educated in Germany and studied cello at Stuttgart Conservatory. He married Theresa Forster, principal soprano of the Stuttgart Opera, and they came to New York in the summer of 1886 for her engagement at the Metropolitan Opera House. A few years later, Herbert became the leader of the 22nd Army Regimental Band. It was during this tenure that he began to write music for the theater. His first success was *The Wizard of the Nile* (November 4, 1895). The most popular song in the operetta was "Starlight, Star Bright." It was from this show that the phrase "Am I a Wiz?" entered the language and became a fad question of the day.

Herbert led a dual life, both writing for the musical stage and composing classical works. He also helped establish the careers of three sopranos. The first was Alice Neilsen, who was introduced to the public in his 1897 production *The Serenade*. As a follow-up to that success, Herbert created *The Fortune Teller* (September 26, 1898) for her. In it she played two roles and had a hit song in each part, "Always Do as People Say You Should" and "Romany Life." "Gypsy Love Song" (also known as "Slumber On, My Little Gypsy Sweetheart"), the biggest hit of the show, and one of the greatest of all time, was sung to her. From this show forward, Victor Herbert was published by M. WITMARK AND SONS.

After three years of devoting his time exclusively to conducting the famed Pittsburgh Symphony Orchestra, Herbert returned to Broadway with *Babes in Toyland* (October 13, 1903), an extravaganza that included three of his most endearing numbers, "Toyland," "March of the Toys," and "I Can't Do the Sum."

The second of Herbert's soprano "discoveries" wasn't so much a discovery as the remaking of a career. Fritzi Scheff was singing with the Metropolitan Opera Company when Herbert wanted her for a role in an operetta he had composed. It was a failure, but he made up for it when he wrote *Mlle. Modiste* (December 25, 1905) for her and gave her the immortal "Kiss Me Again." When she first heard the song, she did not want to sing it, feeling it was too low for her voice. His lyricist and producer agreed with her, but Herbert was adamant. Her success with this song kept it forever associated with her. One of Herbert's best comic numbers also came from this show, "I Want What I Want When I Want It."

The following year, Herbert wrote *The Red Mill* (September 24, 1906) for comedians Dave Montgomery and Fred Stone. Among the fine songs in this score are "In Old New York," "The Isle of Our Dreams," the haunting "Moonbeams," and the rousing "Every Day Is Ladies' Day with Me." The show ran 274 performances, more than any other Herbert show, and has frequently been revived. While the book is dated, the music never fails to captivate audiences.

Oscar Hammerstein—grandfather of the lyricist who worked with RICHARD RODGERS—started his career in the 1880s by building and managing vaudeville theaters and opera houses. He eventually built ten of them in New York City alone, starting with the Harlem Opera House. His first Manhattan Opera House was taken over by vaudeville producers Koster and Bial, who renamed it after themselves. In 1906, Hammerstein decided to build a second Manhattan Opera House, on Thirty-fourth Street between Eighth and Ninth avenues, and create an opera troupe to compete with the staid Metropolitan. He produced premiere performances of *The Tales of Hoffman*, *Pélleas et Mélisande*, *Thaïs*, and Strauss's *Elektra*, and he introduced American audiences to Nellie Melba, Mary Garden, Luisa Tetrazzini, and John McCormack. In 1910, Oscar Hammerstein sold his Manhattan Opera Company to the Metropolitan Opera for a million dollars. One condition of the sale was that he was to refrain from producing operas for ten years, so he turned to the Broadway stage. His first Broadway show was Herbert's *Naughty Marietta* (November 7, 1910), which starred the third opera singer important to Herbert, Emma Trentini. Possibly because he was working with so many

Victor Herbert, Irving Berlin, and John Philip Sousa, in 1924.

people from opera—including members of the chorus, the orchestra, and the orchestra's conductor—Herbert's score was his most ambitious yet. "Ah, Sweet Mystery of Life" has remained a classic, as have "Italian Street Song," "I'm Falling in Love with Someone," "Tramp, Tramp, Tramp," and " 'Neath the Southern Moon." A remarkable score.

Herbert wrote his last great show for a young actress, Christie MacDonald. *Sweethearts* (September 8, 1913) had such a uniformly fine score that a critic noted, "The abundant melodic flow is invariably marked by distinction, individuality, and a quality of superlative charm." Among the riches are the title song, "Pretty as a Picture," "The Angelus," "Wooden Shoes," and "Game of Love." Victor Herbert's last work was a tune composed for the Tiller Girls to dance in the *Ziegfeld Follies*.

# Edward Heyman

Lyricist (b. New York City, March 14, 1907; d. Los Angeles, California, March 30, 1981). Heyman was an important writer during the 1930s, collaborating with most of the Alley's leading tunesmiths.

Heyman attended the University of Michigan, and then returned to New York to work in the theater. His first song, "I'll Be Reminded of You," written with composer Ken Smith, came from the 1929 film *The Vagabond Lover*. The next year, his first big hit, "Body and Soul," was written for the Broadway show *Three's a Crowd*; Heyman's coauthors were JOHNNY GREEN, Robert Sour, and Frank Eyton. PAUL WHITEMAN's orchestra, with vocal by Jack Fulton, had the #1 recording (Columbia 2297-D). Vocalists Libby Holman, RUTH ETTING, Annette Hanshaw, and HELEN MORGAN also had top recordings. LOUIS ARMSTRONG revived it in 1932 (Okeh 41468), as did BENNY GOODMAN in 1935 (Victor 25115). It has been part of the standard repertoire in both pop music and jazz. Art Tatum, Coleman Hawkins, and Ziggy Elman have had hits with it, as have baritone Billy Eckstine in 1949 and Anita Baker in 1994. In a *Billboard* disc jockey poll, the song was voted the #3 favorite of all time.

Many of Heyman's big hits in the 1930s were written with composer Green. In 1931, they wrote the beautiful "Out of Nowhere," which BING CROSBY turned into a #1 hit (Brunswick 6090). "My Silent Love," written with composer Dana Suesse, came out in 1932 with a hit recording by ISHAM JONES and his orchestra, with vocal by Billy Scott (Brunswick 6308). Heyman's 1933 hits include "I Cover the Waterfront," composed by Johnny Green, and "This is Romance" composed by VERNON DUKE. GUY LOMBARDO and his orchestra featured his novelty "Two Buck Tim from Timbuctoo."

With BILLY ROSE, Heyman wrote "I Wanna Be Loved" in 1934, but had to wait until 1950, when the ANDREWS SISTERS made it a #1 hit (Decca 27007). 1934 also saw Heyman and Seusse's "You Oughta Be in Pictures" become a big hit, thanks to JANE FROMAN, who featured it in that year's edition of the *Ziegfeld Follies*. With RAY HENDERSON, Heyman wrote "When I Grow Up" for the 1935 Shirley Temple movie *Curly Top*. "For Sentimental Reasons" was given a boost in 1936 by MILDRED BAILEY (Vocalion 3367). TOMMY DORSEY and his Clambake Seven recorded the 1937 hit "Alibi Baby" (Victor 25577). In 1938, Mildred Bailey, with Red Norvo's orchestra, had a hit with "Have You Forgotten So Soon?" (Vocalion 4432). GLENN MILLER and his orchestra, with vocal by Ray Eberle, had a hit with Heyman's 1939 song "Melancholy Lullaby" (Bluebird 10423).

Heyman spent most of his time writing songs for the movies during the 1940s. They include such films as *So Proudly We Hail*, *Delightfully Dangerous*, *Love Letters*, *The Searching Wind*, *Northwest Outpost*, *The Kissing Bandit*, *On an Island with You*, and, in 1952, *One Minute to Zero*. His last hit came in 1955 when he wrote the TV theme "Blue Star" for *Medic*. Felicia Sanders had the hit recording (Columbia 40508). Heyman spent the rest of his career producing shows for an English-speaking theater troup in Mexico City.

# Bob Hilliard

Lyricist of the 1940s–1950s (b. New York City, January 21, 1918; d. Hollywood, California, February 1, 1971). Hilliard's first success was 1946's "The Coffee Song," with music by Dick Miles, a hit for FRANK SINATRA, followed by 1947's "The Big Brass Band from Brazil," with music by Carl Sigman, a hit on record for the ANDREWS SISTERS and Danny Kaye, among others. "Dear Hearts and Gentle People" (1949) has music by SAMMY FAIN. It was an enormously popular song, thanks to DINAH SHORE (Columbia 38605) and BING CROSBY (Decca 24798). In 1950, "Dearie" with music by Dave Mann (1916–2002), was a best-selling record by two great Broadway stars, Ray Bolger and ETHEL MERMAN (Decca 24873). Next, Hilliard worked with Broadway composer JULE STYNE on two musicals, the revue *Michael Todd's Peep Show*, which ran during the 1950–1951 season, and *Hazel Flagg* (1953). The latter produced major hits, among them "How Do You Speak to an Angel?," "Ev'ry Street's a Boulevard (In Old New York)," and "Money Burns a Hole in My Pocket," which were all used in the film version (retitled *Living It Up* [1954]), starring DEAN MARTIN and Jerry Lewis. He also collaborated on film scores, notably for Disney's *Alice in Wonderland* (1952), with Sammy Fain, most notable for "I'm Late." The popularity of teen pop in the later 1950s and early 1960s led to a decline in Hilliard's success, although he continued to work until his death.

# Hits

The first major publisher of popular music was M. WITMARK AND SONS, founded in 1886. It wasn't until 1892, when CHARLES K. HARRIS published his "After the Ball," that the Alley had a million-selling hit. Tin Pan Alley reached its peak in the 1920s, and sheet music was the mainstay of the music business until the end of World War II. The Alley set out to create hit songs and used whatever media were available for plugging to get hits—first vaudeville, then recordings, piano rolls, radio, talking pictures, television, and now MTV. As a by-product, it created the standard, a popular song that outlasts its original fame and enters the permanent repertoire of our memory.

See also *Charts*

# Hit Songs

## The 1890s

"The Bowery" (1892) came from Charles Hoyt's record-breaking show *A Trip to Chinatown*. The music was composed by PERCY GAUNT, with lyrics by Hoyt.

"Daisy Bell" (1892) was written by Englishman Harry Dacre (1860–1922). It was composed, so the story goes, when Dacre came through U.S. Customs for the first time. He had brought along his bicycle, and was unhappily surprised to find that he had to pay duty on it. A friend who came to pick him up, songwriter Billy Jerome, laughingly told him he was lucky the bicycle was not built for two, or the duty would have been twice as much. The song has always been known as "A Bicycle Built for Two."

"The Sidewalks of New York" (1894) is also better known by the beginning of its chorus ("East side, West side, all around the town"). It was composed by Charles B. Lawlor (1852–1925) and written by James W. Blake (1862–1935). Supposedly Lawlor, humming the melody, walked into the hat shop where Blake was working, and asked him to write some lyrics about New York. Blake agreed then and there, writing the words down as he waited on customers. When the song was finished, Lawlor took it to Pat Howley, who bought it outright. It was a great hit for HOWLEY, HAVILAND, AND COMPANY. Lawlor played and sang it wherever he was appearing, and LOTTIE GILSON plugged it nightly at the London Theatre on the Bowery, turning it into a hit.

"The Band Played On" was another song perhaps better known by the start of its chorus ("Casey would waltz with a strawberry blonde"). Both words and music were written by John F. Palmer, whose sister called his attention to a hurdy-gurdy melody that was playing outside their house. Palmer took it to publisher Charles B. Ward (1865–1917), who purchased it and gave himself credit as the composer. It was first published in the *New York Sunday World* on June 30, 1895, and when the sheet music came out, it was dedicated to that newspaper, which, by publishing it first, gave it a wonderful send-off.

"She Is More to Be Pitied Than Censured" ("The Beautiful Sensational Pathetic Song") was written by publisher William B. Gray in 1898. He issued it with this note on the cover: "The theme of this song is indeed a delicate one to handle, and is offered in sympathy, and not defense, for the unfortunate erring creatures, the life of one of whom suggested its construction." It became the epitome of the tearjerker. Today it has come down to us as a parody of itself. The Gay Nineties? Think again.

## The Turn of the Century

"Bill Bailey, Won't You Please Come Home?" (1902) was composed by HUGHIE CANNON. The song remained a standard for years, popularized by LOUIS ARMSTRONG, ELLA FITZGERALD, and Bobby Darin, to name just a few.

"Sweet Adeline" was composed by Harry Armstrong (1879–1951), with words by Richard H. Gerard (1876–1948). The melody was composed by Armstrong in 1896, but it wasn't until Gerard thought of a title, "You're the Flower of My Heart, Sweet Rosalie," that the song started to take shape. However, publisher after publisher rejected it, until the team saw a billboard advertising the farewell tour of opera singer Adelina Patti. The name was changed—not to Adelina, but to Adeline, to rhyme with "pine." M. WITMARK AND SONS published it in late 1903, when the Quaker City Quartette wanted a new number from the firm. The Quartette's lead singer, Harry Ernest, was featured on the cover of the first edition.

"Ida! Sweet As Apple Cider" (1903) was written by Eddie Leonard (1875–1941), a minstrel originally with Primrose and West. During his last performance, before he was asked to leave the troupe, he defied the manager by singing this song. It received such acclaim that Leonard was rehired immediately, and afterward "Ida" became his theme song. Eddie Cantor also used it as a theme on radio and television in tribute to his wife, who gave him five daughters.

"The Preacher and the Bear" (1904) was written by George Fairman and sold to Joe Arzonia, a partner of Philadelphia music publisher Arthur Longbrake. Arthur Collins had the first hit (Victor 4431). It was a fine comic number, revived in 1947 by bandleader-singer-comedian Phil Harris (RCA Victor 20-2143).

"Come Take a Trip in My Airship" was written by the same team who wrote "In the Good Old Summer Time," the minstrel-turned-vaudevillian George "Honey Boy" Evans (1870–1915) and Ren Shields (1868–1913). This was the first of the aviation songs, published by Charles K. Harris in 1904. Billy Murray had the hit in 1905 (Victor 2986).

"The Best I Get Is Much Obliged to You" (1907) was one of the funniest coon songs written in this period. Both words and music were created by Benjamin Hapgood Burt (1882–1950), who was originally an acting member of the Weber and Fields Company. Very much in the "Nobody" vein of Bert Williams, the point of the story here is that no one ever said, "Sylvester, you keep the change." The song was introduced by Louise Dresser in the hit musical *The Girl Behind the Counter* (February 4, 1907), which contributed greatly to its success.

"My Pony Boy" (1909) was an interpolation by Charlie O'Donnell and Bobby Heath (1889–1952) into the show *Miss Innocence* (November 30, 1908). Ada Jones had the hit (Victor 16356), and it remains a favorite children's song.

"Casey Jones" (1909) is the #1 favorite of railroad buffs. It was published in Los Angeles. The writers were two vaudevillians, Eddie Newton (composer) and T. Lawrence Seibert (lyricist), about whom nothing is known. The song inspired the townspeople of Jackson, Tennessee, to place a monument on the grave of the real "Casey," John Luther Jones. He had gotten his nickname from his hometown of Cayce, Kansas. The American Quartet sold a reported two million copies (Victor 16483).

"Heaven Will Protect the Working Girl" was composed by A. Baldwin Sloane (1872–1925) and written by Edgar Smith (1857–1938) for the show *Tillie's Nightmare* (May 5, 1910), starring Marie Dressler. It was a comic song parodying the tearjerkers of the 1890s, many of which Charles K. Harris made famous. Harris must have had a sense of humor, for he published it. Sloane also had a minor hit written with Clarence Brewster, "When You Ain't Got No Money (Well, You Needn't Come 'Round)" (1898), which May Irwin plugged.

"Meet Me Tonight in Dreamland" was the biggest hit of 1909, with music by Leo Friedman (1869–1927), who also published it, and lyrics by Beth Slater Whitson (1879–1930), who was utterly unknown. This perennial favorite featured Asher B. Samuels, equally unknown, on the cover of the first edition. Within three months of its publication, Will Rossiter of Chicago bought the song outright, with Reine Davies (who featured it in her vaudeville act in Chicago) on his cover, and immediately sold over two million copies. It is estimated that the song has sold around five million in all. Henry Burr had the original hit recording (Columbia A-905).

"Let Me Call You Sweetheart" (1910), again by Friedman and Slater, was an even bigger hit. As before, Friedman first issued this song himself, with a photo of Mae Curtis on the cover. Because the team didn't share in the royalties of their previous hit with Will Rossiter, Will's brother Harold, who had worked for him, opened his own publishing company, bought the song from Friedman, and gave him a royalty. It eventually sold over six million copies, making it one of the all-time best-sellers. The Peerless Quartet had the hit (Columbia A-1057). It is interesting to note that in 1904, CHRIS SMITH and Arthur J. Lamb wrote "Let Me Call You Sweetheart Once Again," which didn't set any records.

"Down by the Old Mill Stream" (1910) was the other multimillion-selling tune of that year, written and published by Tell Taylor (1876–1937). Tenor Harry MacDonough had the hit (Victor 17000).

This period saw the Alley flourishing, having introduced the intoxicating sounds of RAGTIME to the scene. Because of the tremendous influx of foreigners to America's shores during the last half of the nineteenth century, the Alleyites took advantage of this new audience by making fun of them as they tried to fit into a new way of life. ETHNIC SONGS proliferated, but hardly any survived this era. Of them, some of the coon songs managed to become memorable when the melody was particularly catchy and the lyrics more than usually funny. Vaudeville was still the most potent plug available to the Alley, and its top stars helped to turn songs into best-selling sheet music hits.

## The 1910s

"Oceana Roll" (1911) was composed by Lucien Denni (1886–1947) and written by Roger Lewis (1885–1948). It was a great rag song, revived in 1951 by Teresa Brewer (London 1083).

"Oh, You Beautiful Doll" (1911) was composed by Nat D. Ayer (1887–1952), with lyrics by Seymour Brown (1885–1947). Earlier that year, the team wrote the comic "If You Talk in Your Sleep, Don't Mention My Name." Ayer left the Alley to take his snappy syncopation to England, where he remained until the end of his life, composing mostly for the theater.

"Be My Little Baby Bumble Bee" (1912) was composed by Henry I. Marshall and Stanley Murphy, the same team who, two years later, wrote another million-seller, "I Want to Linger."

"Melancholy" was composed by Ernie Burnett (1884–1959), with words by George A. Norton (1880–1923), in 1912. Ragtime composer Theron C. Bennett, who published W. C. HANDY's "Memphis Blues" in the same year, first played and sang "Melancholy" at his own nightclub, The Dutch Mill, in Denver, Colorado. In late 1914, the title was changed to "My Melancholy Baby." That same year, Burnett published his famous piano piece "Steamboat Rag."

"Sailing Down the Chesapeake Bay" (1913) was the work of famous ragtime composer George Botsford (1874–1949) and lyricist Jean C. Havez (1874–1925). It is among the favorite rag songs of the era, continuing in favor among Dixieland bands today.

"The Trail of the Lonesome Pine" (1913) was the work of HARRY CARROLL and Ballard MacDonald. "By the Beautiful Sea" (1914) was the second of three million-selling successes in this decade by Carroll, this one with lyrics by Harold R. Atteridge (1886–1938). It is one of the few great and lasting songs about summertime.

"I Ain't Got Nobody" (1914) is a great ballad that both SOPHIE TUCKER and Bert Williams helped to make famous. However, its authorship is in dispute.

*(See Spencer Williams for a discussion of this controversy.)*

"Poor Butterfly" (1916) was the hit of the New York Hippodrome's production THE BIG SHOW. It was the only hit by the prolific hack composer Raymond Hubbell (1879–1954) and lyric-writing producer John L. Golden (1874–1955). The song was performed so often that it prompted Arthur Green and WILLIAM JEROME to write "If I Catch the Guy Who Wrote Poor Butterfly" (1917).

"After You've Gone" (1918) was composed by TURNER LAYTON and Henry Creamer. It was plugged by Sophie Tucker and became an important number in Broadway Music's catalog. The melody of the chorus starts like "Peg o' My Heart."

"I'm Always Chasing Rainbows" (1918) was the third of Harry Carroll's hits during this decade, even though he took his chorus from Chopin's Fantasie Impromptu in C# minor. The original lyrics were by JOSEPH MCCARTHY. It was first featured by dancer Harry Fox in the show *Oh, Look!*, but its fame increased when the show went on the road with the Dolly Sisters. It again became a hit when it was revived in the movie *The Dolly Sisters* (1945).

"Ja-Da" (1918) was written and composed by Bob Carleton (1896–1956). Its combination of catchy melody and nonsense lyric makes it a number that is sporadically revived.

"K-K-K-Katy" (1918) was written and composed by Geoffrey O'Hara (1882–1967), and it remains a favorite. During both world wars, it was sung as "K-K-K-K.P." In 1919, an answer was given in the song "Thtop Your Thuttering, Jimmy."

"Somebody Stole My Gal" (1918), written and composed by Leo Wood (1882–1929), had a strange history. It was first published by Meyer Cohen Music Company and introduced by Florence Milett. The song flopped. It was purchased by Denton and Haskins in 1922 and reissued, this time recorded by Ted Weems and his orchestra for a million-selling hit (Victor 19212). It was recorded again by Bix Beiderbecke and His Gang in 1927 (Okeh 41030). Johnny Ray revived it in 1953 (Columbia 39961). It has become a jazz band favorite.

"Beautiful Ohio" (1918) was composed by Robert A. King (1862–1932), using his pseudonym "Mary Earl," with lyrics by Ballard MacDonald. It was by far the biggest-selling song of 1918, topping five million copies, and the largest-selling song sheet published by SHAPIRO, BERNSTEIN, AND COMPANY. It has a chromatic theme similar to the middle section of Rimsky-Korsakoff's "Song of India." The beauty of the song has kept it in the permanent repertoire.

"Alice Blue Gown" was composed by HARRY TIERNEY, with lyrics by Joseph McCarthy, for *Irene* (November 1, 1919), the longest-running musical up to that time (a record held for twenty-eight years), with 675 performances. This waltz was introduced in the show by star Edith Day (Victor 45173).

"I'm Forever Blowing Bubbles" was written by "Jaan Kenbrovin" and "John William Kellette," pseudonyms for James Kendis (1883–1946), James Brockman (1886–1967) and Nat Vincent (1889–1979). It was introduced in *The Passing Show of 1918*, but was made famous by June Caprice. Henry Burr and Albert Campbell had the hit recording (Columbia A-2701).

"In Soudan" was composed by Nat Osborne (1878–1954), with words by Ballard MacDonald. It was in the "Tin Pan Alley Oriental" style of the day, coming at the height of "Dardanella's" popularity. ZEZ CONFREY, making piano rolls for QRS, was given many such songs, and he could usually come up with a brilliant arrangement, at once fresh and unstereotypical. He worked wonders with this one (QRS 786).

"Oh" was the inspiration of Byron Gay (1886–1945) and bandleader ARNOLD JOHNSON. Its catchy melody made it suitable for TED LEWIS's Jazz Band (Columbia A-2844). Pee Wee

Hunt and his dixieland band sold over a million copies with a recording of it in 1953 (Capitol 2442).

"Rose Room" was composed by San Francisco bandleader Art Hickman (1886–1930) as his instrumental theme in 1917. He published it and plugged it himself at the St. Francis Hotel, where his band performed in the Rose Room. His recording (Columbia A-2858) did so well that Sherman, Clay and Company took it over and published it as a song with words by Harry Williams (1879–1922).

"The World Is Waiting for the Sunrise" was written by two Canadians, Ernest Seitz and Eugene Lockhart (1891–1957). The Benson Orchestra's arrangement by ROY BARGY (Victor 18980) caused a sensation. So did Frank Banta's piano solo in 1928 (Victor 21821). The Firehouse Five Plus Two's revival in 1950 (Good Time Jazz L-12010) made it fresh all over again.

## The 1920s

### 1920

"Avalon" was "composed" by Vincent Rose (1880–1944), a California pianist and bandleader, who was trained as a classical musician. The main melodic theme of the chorus was stolen from the tenor aria "E Lucevan le Stelle," in Puccini's *Tosca* (1900). J. Bodewalt Lampe made the popular arrangement for JEROME H. REMICK AND COMPANY, which reportedly settled out of court with a $25,000 payment to Puccini.

"Jelly Bean" was the work of Jimmy Dupre, Sam Rosen, and Joe Verges, New Orleans songwriters who published the song through their Universal Music Publishing. It was revived in 1949 by "Chuck Thomas" and His Dixieland Band (Capitol 1011), in reality Woody Herman, who also sang it, with piano backing by Lou Busch.

"San" was pianist Lindsay McPhail's (1895–1965) only major song. Subtitled "Oriental Fox-Trot," it competed successfully with RICHARD WHITING's "Japanese Sandman." PAUL WHITEMAN had the hit version (Victor 19381), although the Benson Orchestra, The Georgia Melodians, Mike Markel's orchestra, and Ben Selvin didn't do badly with it. It was revived by Abe Lyman's Sharps and Flats in 1928 (Brunswick 3964), and again by Pee Wee Hunt in 1953, to sell more than a million discs (Capitol 2442).

"Whispering" was composed by John Schonberger (1892–1983) and Vincent Rose, with lyrics by Richard Coburn (1886–1952). It was a hit due solely to Paul Whiteman's recording (Victor 18690), which sold over two million copies. A deserving classic, it is still being performed.

### 1921

"Down Yonder" was the work of L. WOLFE GILBERT. It was interpolated by the Brown Brothers, a saxophone sextet, in *Tip Top* after that show's Broadway opening. It was spectacularly revived by pianist Del Wood (Tennessee 775) in 1951. Joe "Fingers" Carr also sold over a million copies with his version (Capitol 1777).

"Strut Miss Lizzie" was written by TURNER LAYTON and Henry Creamer. It was introduced by Van and Schenck in the *Ziegfeld Follies of 1921*.

"Sweet Lady" was composed by Frank Crumit (1889–1943) and Dave Zoob, with lyrics by Howard Johnson, for Julia Sanderson in *Tangerine*. It became a hit with Carl Fenton's orchestra (Brunswick 2143) and PAUL WHITEMAN's orchestra (Victor 18803). EUBIE BLAKE recorded it as a piano solo with a vocal chorus by Irving Kaufman (Emerson 10450), and this version sold tremendously.

"Three o'Clock in the Morning" was written by Julian Robledo and Dorothy Terriss, a pseudonym of Theodora Morse. Its middle strain echoes the famous Westminster chime of London's Big Ben. It was first heard in *Greenwich Village Follies of 1921*, and Paul Whiteman's recording sold over two million copies (Victor 18940).

### 1922

"Angel Child" was composed by Abner Silver (1899–1966), with lyrics by BENNY DAVIS. It was introduced by George Price in *Spice of 1922*. The Benson Orchestra (Victor 18870) had the big recording.

"Bees Knees" was composed by TED LEWIS and Ray Lopez (1889–1970), with words by Leo Wood (1882–1929). Lewis's band made the first recording of this great syncopated fox-trot (Columbia A-3730), but the Boston Syncopators (another pseudonym of the ORIGINAL MEMPHIS FIVE) made an outstanding version (Grey Gull 1138).

"China Boy" was the work of Phil Boutelje (1895–1979) and Dick Winfree. ARNOLD JOHNSON's orchestra made a hit recording (Brunswick 2355), and it was revived in 1952 by Pete Daily and His Dixieland Band (Capitol 2041).

"He May Be Your Man but He Comes to See Me Sometimes" was written by blues pianist Lemuel Fowler, who sold it to two publishers, PERRY BRADFORD in New York and Ted Browne in Chicago. When the Bradford edition sold extremely well, Browne stepped in and sued him. The best-selling instrumental version was by the Original Memphis Five (Pathe 202855).

"Hot Lips" was written by Henry Lange (1895–1985), HENRY BUSSE, and Lou Davis (1881–1961), when the first two were with PAUL WHITEMAN's orchestra. It became a popular feature for trumpeter Busse, and Whiteman's recording of it (Victor 18920) sold over a million copies. When Busse had his own orchestra in the 1930s, he used it as a theme song.

"Runnin' Wild" was composed by Arthur Harrington Gibbs (1895–1956), with lyrics by Joe Grey (1879–1956) and Leo Wood. It was such a hit that a show was named after it in 1923. The Southland Six made a fine recording (Vocalion 14476).

"Way Down Yonder in New Orleans" was written and introduced by TURNER LAYTON and Henry Creamer in *Spice of 1922*. It has been revived in practically every decade since, starting with the Frankie Trumbauer recording featuring Bix Beiderbecke in 1927 (Okeh 40843).

"Who'll Take My Place When I'm Gone" was composed by Billy Fazioli (1898–1924), with lyrics by Raymond Klages (1888–1947). Fazioli was the pianist-arranger with Ray Miller's orchestra (Columbia A-3695), but it was Bennie Krueger and his orchestra that had the finest recording (Brunswick 2303).

### 1923

"Blue Hoosier Blues" was composed by Abel Baer (1893–1976) and CLIFF FRIEND and written by Jack Meskill. Vincent Lopez and his Hotel Pennsylvania Orchestra (Okeh 4869) made the hit recording in a heavily competitive field.

"I Cried for You" was composed by two bandleaders, ABE LYMAN and GUS ARNHEIM, and written by Arthur Freed. It was assured of success with two bandleaders as composers, each plugging it in nightclubs and on radio and recordings, but when the lyricist became an executive producer for MGM, its continued success was certain. JUDY GARLAND sang it in *Babes in Arms* (1939), and it became identified with her from that time on.

"I Love You," by HARRY ARCHER and Harlan Thompson (1890–1966), was their only hit from *Little Jessie James*.

"Struttin' Jim" was written by Bob Carlton and Cliff Dixon. Its big recording was done by the ORIGINAL MEMPHIS FIVE (Perfect 14155).

"Yes! We Have No Bananas" was credited to Frank Silver (1896–1960) and Irving Conn (1898–1961), and supposedly was taken from the street cry of a Greek fruit peddler. However, it is known that the entire staff of SHAPIRO, BERNSTEIN had a hand in it. Sigmund Spaeth, in *A History of Popular Music in America*, traced the musical pedigree of this tune, ". . . the song had a most distinguished background, for its chorus melody was borrowed, consciously or unconsciously, from Handel's 'Hallelujah Chorus,' the finish of 'My Bonnie,' 'I Dreamt That I Dwelt in Marble Halls' (the middle strain), and 'Aunt Dinah's Quilting Party' (by way of Cole Porter's 'An Old Fashioned Garden'). It makes an amusing trick to sing the original words wherever possible, creating this extraordinary text: 'Hallelujah, Bananas! Oh, bring back my Bonnie to me. I dreamt that I dwelt in marble halls—the kind that you seldom see. I was seeing Nellie home, to an old-fashioned garden; but, Hallelujah, Bananas! Oh, bring back my Bonnie to me!' " The Pennsylvanian Syncopators made a fine recording (Emerson 10623), and SPIKE JONES and his City Slickers revived it in 1950 (Victor 20-3912).

**1924**

"Doo Wacka Doo" was written by CLARENCE GASKILL, Will Donaldson (1891–1954), and George Horther. PAUL WHITEMAN successfully featured it (Victor 19462), and Marion McKay's orchestra created a hit recording (Gennett 5615).

"Doodle-Doo-Doo" was composed by pianist Mel Stitzel (1902–1952), with lyrics by bandleader ART KASSEL. Naturally, when Kassel had a band, it was used as his theme song, but Jack Linx and his orchestra also made an exciting disc (Okeh 40188).

"I'm All Broken Up over You" was composed by Joe Murphy and Carl Hoeffle, with lyrics by JOE BURKE and Lou Herscher. Ted Weems and his orchestra did a magnificent arrangement (Victor 19286), featuring Dewey Bergman's novelty piano chorus and Walter Livingston on bass clarinet and alto saxophone.

"It Ain't Gonna Rain No Mo' " was taken by Wendell Hall (1896–1969) from an old Southern folk song and made into a hit by Carl Fenton's orchestra (Brunswick 2568).

"Me and the Boy Friend" was composed by JAMES MONACO, with words by Sidney Clare. Margaret Young made a hit recording of it (Brunswick 2736), as did Ray Miller and his orchestra (Brunswick 2753).

"There'll Be Some Changes Made" was composed by W. Benton Overstreet, with lyrics by Billy Higgins. Marion Harris helped make it a hit (Brunswick 2651), and Benny Goodman revived it in 1939 (Columbia 35210).

"Those Panama Mamas" was composed by publisher Irving Bibo (1889–1962), with words by Howard Johnson. EDDIE CANTOR helped make it a hit (Columbia 256-D), as did Belle Baker (Victor 19609). The Cotton Pickers (yet another nom-de-disc for the Original Memphis Five!) made a splendid version (Brunswick 2879), as did the Varsity Eight (Lincoln 2289).

### 1925

"Angry" was composed by Dudley Mecum (1896–1978), Henry and Merritt Brunies, and Jules Cassard. They recorded it as Merritt Brunies and His Friars Inn Orchestra in Chicago in November 1924 (Autograph 610). George Brunies (Merritt's brother) recorded it with the New Orleans Rhythm Kings in July 1923 (Gennett 5219), in Richmond, Indiana. The Arcadian Serenaders recorded it in St. Louis, Missouri, in October 1925 (Okeh 40517). Ray Miller and his orchestra recorded it, with Muggsy Spanier on cornet and Jules Cassard on string bass, in Chicago in January 1929 (Brunswick 4224). Bob Crosby's Bob Cats revived it in November 1939 (Decca 2839) on a best-selling disc.

"Cheatin' on Me" was composed by LEW POLLACK and written by JACK YELLEN. Eddie Frazier and his orchestra made a sensational recording (Sunset 1100), as did Warner's Seven Aces (Columbia 305-D). Sophie Tucker introduced it in vaudeville.

"Show Me the Way to Go Home" was by "Irving King," a pseudonym for the English songwriter-publishers Reg Connelly and Jimmy Campbell. They adapted it from an old Canadian folk song. Perry's Hot Dogs made a superb recording (Banner 1615).

### 1926

"Charmaine" was originally published in 1926 by Belwin as a theme song for the silent film *What Price Glory?* It was written by ERNO RAPEE and LEW POLLACK.

"Coney Island Washboard" was composed by Wade Hampton Durand (1887–1964) and Jerry Adams, with words by Ned Nestor and Claude Shugart. It became a favorite of jazz bands during the dixieland revival of the 1940s and has become a standard. The big recording came from Bob Scobey's Frisco Band (Good Time Jazz 49).

"Heart of My Heart" was written by Ben Ryan (1892–1968) and was also known as "The Gang That Sang 'Heart of My Heart.'" It was a big hit in the early 1950s, with recordings by Don Cornell, Alan Dale and Johnny Desmond (Coral 61076), and The Four Aces (Decca 28927).

"Hello, Bluebird" was composed by CLIFF FRIEND. It was featured by Harry Reser's Clicquot Club Eskimos (Columbia 795-D). It was revived on a best-selling record in 1952 by Teresa Brewer (Coral 60873).

"High, High, High Up in the Hills" was composed by MAURICE ABRAHAMS, with words by SAM LEWIS and JOE YOUNG. Abrahams wrote it for his wife, Belle Baker, who introduced it. Nat Shilkret and his orchestra made a splendid recording (Victor 20436).

"Hugs and Kisses" was composed by LOU ALTER, with lyrics by Raymond Klages, for *Earl Carroll's Vanities—Fifth Edition.* Art Landry and his orchestra had the hit recording (Victor 20285).

"I Never See Maggie Alone" was composed by Englishman Everett Lynton, with lyrics by Harry Tilsley. Irving Aaronson and his Commanders made the hit recording (Victor 20473).

"Moonlight on the Ganges" was composed by Englishman Sherman Myers, with lyrics by Chester Wallace. PAUL WHITEMAN and his orchestra had the best-selling record (Victor 20139).

### 1927

"Bye-Bye, Pretty Baby" was composed by pianist Jack Gardner (1903–1957) and bandleader George "Spike" Hamilton (1901–1957). Jan Garber and his orchestra had a marvelous version

(Victor 20833), and composer-singer-pianist Fred Rose accompanied himself for a touching rendition (Brunswick 3616).

"Diane" was written by Erno Rapee and Lew Pollack, as the theme song for the Janet Gaynor-Charles Farrell film *Seventh Heaven.* Published by Sherman, Clay, it became an outstanding hit with Nat Shilkret's arrangement (Victor 21000).

"Did You Mean It?" was written by bandleader Abe Lyman and comedians Phil Baker (1896–1963) and Sid Silvers (1907–1976). Baker and Silvers were a duo in vaudeville. This song was written for Marion Harris, who sang it in the revue *A Night in Spain*, also featuring the comedians (Victor 21116).

"(I Scream, You Scream, We All Scream for) Ice Cream" was composed by Robert King, with lyrics, most appropriately, by Howard Johnson (1887–1941; not the ice cream chain owner) and Billy Moll (1905–1968). The Six Jumping Jacks made a cute recording (Brunswick 3782), as did Fred Waring's Pennsylvanians (Victor 21099).

"I'm Gonna Meet My Sweetie Now" was composed by Jesse Greer (1896–1970), with lyrics by Benny Davis. Jean Goldkette and his orchestra made a fabulous recording (Victor 20675), as did vocalist Jane Green (Victor 20509).

"The Kinkajou" was composed by Harry Tierney, with words by Joseph McCarthy, for *Rio Rita* (1927). The song's title is the name of a bandit in the show. Most recordings featured this song backed by the show's title song. One of the best performances was by The Knickerbockers (Columbia 893-D). The song was copyrighted in 1926, and the show opened on Broadway on February 2, 1927.

"Lucky Lindy," composed by Abel Baer (1893–1976), with lyrics by L. Wolfe Gilbert, was the first song to celebrate Charles Lindbergh's landing in Paris. It was the best of nearly 100 other Lindy songs.

"Me and My Shadow" was composed by Dave Dreyer, with lyrics by Billy Rose. It was heavily plugged by Al Jolson, who sang it on radio, and it was introduced in *Harry Delmar's Revels* by Frank Fay. It later became the theme song of Segar Ellis and his orchestra. Ted Lewis used it as a feature in his performances. "Whispering" Jack Smith had the hit recording (Victor 20626).

"(Who's Wonderful, Who's Marvelous?) Miss Annabelle Lee" was composed by Lew Pollack, with words by Sidney Clare. It was introduced by Harry Richman. The Knickerbockers made a lovely dance arrangement (Columbia 1088-D) and Jane Gray, probably accompanied by Rube Bloom, made a nice version of it (Diva 2464-G).

"My Sunday Girl" was composed by Sam H. Stept, with words by Herman Ruby and Bud Cooper. It was given a superb recorded performance, with a fabulous novelty piano break by Frankie Carle, by Edwin J. McEnelly's orchestra (Victor 20589). On the Clicquot Club Eskimos' recording (Columbia 921-D), Harry Reser's banjo gets a good workout.

"Who's That Pretty Baby?" was written by Bobby Heath (1889–1952) and Alex Marr. Jack Crawford and his orchestra had a splendid recording (Victor 20847).

### 1928

"Oh, Baby" was written by Owen Murphy (1893–1965) for the show *Rain or Shine.* Jay C. Flippen plugged it.

"Sweet Sue" was composed by Victor Young, with lyrics by Will J. Harris (1900–1967). It was identified with the young actress Sue Carol. Charley Straight and his orchestra made a fine recording (Brunswick 3900), as did Pauline Alpert, as a piano solo, in 1946 (Sonora 1041).

" 'Tain't So, Honey, 'Tain't So" was written by Willard Robison (1894–1968) and popularized by PAUL WHITEMAN and his orchestra (Columbia 1444-D).

"That's My Weakness Now" was composed by SAM H. STEPT, with lyrics by BUD GREEN, for Helen Kane. Sam Lanin and his orchestra made a hit recording (Perfect 14999).

"When Sweet Susie Goes Steppin' By" was written by bandleader Whitey Kaufman, Fred Kelly, and publisher Irving Bibo. Nat Shilkret's orchestra made a fine recording (Victor 21515).

"When You're Smiling," composed by Larry Shay (1897–1988) and MARK FISHER, with lyrics by Joe Goodwin (1889–1943), was made famous by Seger Ellis (Columbia 1494-D). LOUIS ARMSTRONG made the first recording (Okeh 41298), and it has remained in the standard repertoire ever since.

### 1929

"Can't We Be Friends?" was composed by KAY SWIFT with lyrics by her husband, James P. Warburg (1896–1969), writing under the pseudonym "Paul James." It was introduced by Libby Holman in *The Little Show*.

"Do Something" was another song by the team of SAM STEPT and BUD GREEN. They wrote it for Helen Kane to perform in the film *Nothing but the Truth* (Victor 21917). It was revived in the 1980s by the contemporary vaudevillian Ian Whitcomb, in his act with piano accompanist Dick Zimmerman.

## The 1930s

### 1930

"Body and Soul" was composed by John W. Green (1908–1989), with lyrics by EDWARD HEYMAN, Robert Sour, and Frank Eyton. It first appeared in the revue *Three's a Crowd* (1930), sung by Libby Holman and danced to by Clifton Webb and Tamara Geva. PAUL WHITEMAN and his orchestra made the first hit recording (Columbia 2297-D), followed by tenor saxophonist Coleman Hawkins's 1939 version (Bluebird 10523), which has become a jazz classic.

"Bye Bye Blues" was written by Fred Hamm and Dave Bennett. It was recorded by Hamm in 1925 (Victor 19662) but was not published until 1930. Bert Lown and pianist Chauncey Gray somehow got their names on the sheet music after they recorded it in July 1930 (Columbia 2258-D). It became the theme song of Bert Lown and his Hotel Biltmore Orchestra.

"Fine and Dandy" was composed by KAY SWIFT and written by her husband, James P. Warburg (as Paul James), for the revue *Fine and Dandy*. It was introduced by Joe Cook and Alice Boulden.

"Goofus" was composed by bandleader Wayne King (1901–1985) and his violinist William Harold, and written by GUS KAHN. It was made into a novelty hit by King and his orchestra (Victor 22600). Phil Harris's recording in 1950 sold another million copies (Victor 20-3968).

"The Peanut Vendor" was composed by Moises Simons, with English lyrics by Marion Sunshine and L. WOLFE GILBERT. It was recorded by Cuban bandleader Don Azpiazu (Victor 22483), and was revived in the film *A Star Is Born* (1954).

"Please Don't Talk About Me When I'm Gone" was composed by Sam H. Stept, with lyrics by Sidney Clare. It was popularized in vaudeville by Bee Palmer, on radio by Kate Smith, and on record by Gene Austin (Victor 22635).

## 1931

"All of Me" was composed by Gerald Marks and written by Seymour Simons (1896–1949).

"As Time Goes By" was written by Herman Hupfeld for Frances Williams and Oscar Shaw in *Everybody's Welcome* (1931). Rudy Vallee's recording made the song a moderate success (Victor 22773). It was revived in the movie *Casablanca* (1942), as a musical theme throughout the film and also sung by Dooley Wilson. The song became so popular that Victor had to rerelease the Vallee recording because there was a recording ban by the musicians' union at the time. The rerelease became a #1 hit.

"Dream a Little Dream of Me" was composed by W. Schwandt and F. Andree, with lyrics by Gus Kahn. It was popularized by Kate Smith on radio and by Wayne King and his orchestra (Victor 22643). It ws revived in 1968 for a #12 pop hit by "Mama" Cass Elliott (Dunhill 4145).

"Got a Date with an Angel" was another English song hit, composed by Jack Waller and Joe Tunbridge and written by Clifford Grey and Sonnie Miller. Hal Kemp and his orchestra, with vocalist Skinnay Ennis, made the best-selling recording (Brunswick 7319) in 1934.

"Just Friends" was composed by John Klenner (1899–1955), with words by Sam M. Lewis. Russ Columbo had the hit (Victor 22909). It has become a jazz standard, with popular recordings by Chet Baker, Sarah Vaughan, and many others.

"Little Girl" was composed by guitarist Francis "Muff" Henry (1905–1953), with lyrics by Madeline Hyde (b. 1907). Henry was the guitarist with Guy Lombardo and his Royal Canadians, who introduced and popularized it. Joe Venuti's Blue Four, with Harold Arlen as vocalist, had a hit (Columbia 2488-D). The song was used as the theme for Fanny Brice's popular radio program *Baby Snooks*.

"Marta" was composed by Moises Simons and written by L. Wolfe Gilbert. It was introduced and used as a radio theme by Arthur Tracy, "The Street Singer" (Brunswick 6216).

"Out of Nowhere" was composed by Johnny Green and written by Edward Heyman. It was featured by Guy Lombardo, but the best-selling disc was made by Bing Crosby (Brunswick 6090). It was revived by Helen Forrest in the film *You Came Along* (1945).

"Penthouse Serenade" was composed and written by Will Jason (1910–1970) and Val Burton (1899–1981). It was recorded by the Arden-Ohman orchestra (Victor 22910). It has been a favorite of jazz pianists.

"That's My Desire" was composed by Helmy Kresa, with lyrics by Carroll Loveday (1898–1955). It was introduced on radio by Lanny Ross. It made the pop charts when, in 1947, singer Frankie Laine, who had been using the song in his nightclub act, was signed by Mercury Records to record it. His version sold over a million and a half copies, established Laine as a major pop singer, and made Mercury an important company (Mercury 5007).

"When It's Sleepy Time Down South" was written by Clarence Muse (1889–1979), Otis Rene (1898–1970), and Leon Rene (1902–1982). It was featured and used as a theme by Louis Armstrong and his orchestra (Okeh 41504).

### 1932

"In a Shanty in Old Shanty Town" was written by Little Jack Little (1900–1956), John Sims, and JOE YOUNG. It was introduced and featured by pianist Little Jack Little, and revived in 1940 by Johnny Long on a best-selling recording (Decca 23622). In the 1950s, the song was performed as a honky-tonk piano feature.

"My Silent Love" was composed by DANA SUESSE, with lyrics by EDWARD HEYMAN. It was adapted from Suesse's instrumental "Jazz Nocturne." ISHAM JONES and his orchestra had a hit disc (Brunswick 6308).

"Willow Weep for Me" was composed and written by Ann Ronell, with a dedication to GEORGE GERSHWIN. It was introduced by Irene Taylor and the PAUL WHITEMAN Orchestra, who also recorded it (Victor 24187).

### 1933

"Everything I Have Is Yours" was composed by BURTON LANE, with lyrics by HAROLD ADAMSON. It was introduced by Joan Crawford and Art Jarrett in the film *Dancing Lady*. Billy Eckstine had a hit recording in 1949 (MGM 10259), and it was sung by Monica Lewis in the film of the same name (1952).

"I Cover the Waterfront" was composed by JOHNNY GREEN and written by EDWARD HEYMAN to be used in the film of the same name starring Claudette Colbert and Ben Lyon. However, the movie was completed before the song was written, so it wasn't included on the sound track. After Ben Bernie and his orchestra plugged it on his radio show, the sound track was rescored to include the song.

### 1934

"I Wanna Be Loved" was composed by JOHNNY GREEN, with lyrics by EDWARD HEYMAN and BILLY ROSE. It was introduced in Rose's Casino de Paree in New York. It was revived in 1950 on a best-selling record by the ANDREWS SISTERS (Decca 27007).

"Moonglow" was composed by bandleaders WILL HUDSON and EDDIE DE LANGE, with lyrics by Irving Mills. It was introduced by the Hudson-De Lange Orchestra. It was revived in the nonmusical film *Picnic* (1955), and Morris Stoloff and his orchestra had the best-selling recording in a medley with the "Theme from Picnic" (Decca 29888).

"What a Diff'rence a Day Made" was a popular Spanish song composed by Maria Grever, with English lyrics by STANLEY ADAMS. The Dorsey Brothers Orchestra had the hit (Decca 283). It was revived by a best-selling recording of Dinah Washington's in 1959 (Mercury 71435).

"Winter Wonderland" was composed by Felix Bernard, with lyrics by Dick Smith. It was made popular by GUY LOMBARDO and his Royal Canadians (Decca 294). A perennial Christmas favorite, it was revived on a best-selling disc by the ANDREWS SISTERS in 1950 (Decca 23722).

"You Oughta Be in Pictures" was composed by DANA SUESSE, with lyrics by EDWARD HEYMAN. It was introduced in *Ziegfeld Follies of 1934* by JANE FROMAN. It was revived by DORIS DAY in the film *Starlift* (1951).

### 1935

"The Music Goes 'Round and 'Round" was composed by Ed Farley and Michael Riley, with lyrics by Red Hodgson. The composers were co-bandleaders and introduced this novelty song with newly formed Decca Records. It was Decca's first huge hit (Decca 578). It was revived by Danny Kaye in the film *The Five Pennies* (1959).

"Rosetta" was written by Earl Hines and Henri Woode in 1928, but was not published until 1935. It was first recorded by Earl Hines and his orchestra in 1933 (Brunswick 6541). Teddy Wilson made two superb piano solo recordings: one in 1935 (Brunswick 7563) and another in 1941 (Columbia 36632). Hines made his solo version in 1939 (Bluebird 10555).

"These Foolish Things Remind Me of You" was composed by Jack Strachey and Harry Link, with lyrics by Holt Marvell. It was introduced by Madge Elliott and Cyril Ritchard in the show *Spread It Around*, and was interpolated in the Olsen and Johnson film *Ghost Catchers* (1944).

### 1936

"Can't We Talk It Over" was composed by VICTOR YOUNG, with lyrics by NED WASHINGTON. It was made famous by BING CROSBY on radio, and on recordings by Bing with the MILLS BROTHERS (Brunswick 6240) and by Ben Bernie and his orchestra (Brunswick 6250).

"In the Chapel in the Moonlight" has words and music by Billy Hill (1899–1940). Shep Fields and his orchestra made the #1 recording (Bluebird 6640). It was revived with a million-selling record in 1954 by Kitty Kallen (Decca 29130), and again in 1967 by DEAN MARTIN (Reprise 0601).

"It's a Sin to Tell a Lie" had words and music by Billy Mayhew (1889–1951). It was introduced by KATE SMITH on radio and by Fats Waller with the #1 hit (Victor 25342). It was revived in 1955 with a best-selling record by Something Smith and the Redheads (Epic 9093).

"Pennies from Heaven" was composed by ARTHUR JOHNSTON, with lyrics by JOHNNY BURKE, for Bing Crosby in the film of the same title. The Crosby recording helped make it a standard (Deccca 947). The song was used in the nonmusical films *From Here to Eternity* (1953) and *Picnic* (1955). It was further revived in a film of the same name in 1981.

"San Francisco" was composed by Bronislau Kaper (1902–1983), with lyrics by GUS KAHN, for the film of the same name. It was sung by JEANETTE MACDONALD and others under the credits and was a recurring theme throughout. With such exposure, the song became a hit. The film has been frequently revived, and is popular with fans of MacDonald and costar Clark Gable. TOMMY DORSEY and his orchestra had the hit recording with a vocal by Edythe Wright (Victor 25352).

### 1937

"The Merry-Go-Round Broke Down" was written by CLIFF FRIEND and Dave Franklin. It was recorded in #1 selling editions by Shep Fields (Bluebird 7015) and by Russ Morgan and his orchestra (Brunswick 7888). It is still a favorite with vocal groups.

"Once in a While" was composed by Michael Edwards (1893–1962), with words by BUD GREEN. Edwards is a perfect example of the one-hit composer. But what a hit! It was introduced by TOMMY DORSEY and his orchestra, with a vocal by Jack Leonard (Victor 25686).

### 1938

"I Hadn't Anyone Till You" had words and music by RAY NOBLE, who introduced it and made the hit recording, with a vocal by TONY MARTIN (Brunswick 8079). Mel Torme revived it in the late 1940s (Capitol 880). It was also featured in the film *In a Lonely Place* (1950).

"Sunrise Serenade" was composed by bandleader-pianist Frankie Carle (1903–2001), with lyrics by JACK LAWRENCE. It was introduced and recorded by Glen Gray and his Casa Loma Orchestra, who had the #1 recording, featuring the composer at the piano (Decca 2321). GLENN MILLER and his orchestra also had a hit (Bluebird 10214). Carle used it as his band's theme (Columbia 37269).

### 1939

"If I Didn't Care" has words and music by JACK LAWRENCE. It was closely identified with The Ink Spots, a vocal quartet, whose recording was their most famous (Decca 2286).

"The Lady's in Love with You" has music by BURTON LANE and words by FRANK LOESSER. It was written for the Shirley Ross-Bob Hope film *Some Like It Hot.* GLENN MILLER and his orchestra made a memorable recording (Bluebird 10229).

"South of the Border, Down Mexico Way" had words and music by Jimmy Kennedy and Michael Carr. It was written for cowboy star GENE AUTRY for the film *South of the Border.* Autry's recording sold over three million copies in two years (Vocalion 5122).

## The 1940s

### 1940

"Blueberry Hill" was composed by Vincent Rose, with lyrics by Al Lewis and Larry Stock. GLENN MILLER and his orchestra (with vocal by Ray Eberle) made the first hit recording (Bluebird 10768). GENE AUTRY sang it in his film *The Singing Hills* (1941), and when it was revived in 1957 by Fats Domino, it sold over a million discs (Imperial 5407).

"Dance with a Dolly (with a Hole in Her Stocking)" was composed by pianist Terry Shand (1904–1977), with lyrics by Jimmy Eaton and Mickey Leader. It was made popular by Russ Morgan and his orchestra (Decca 18625).

"How High the Moon" was composed by Morgan Lewis (1906–1968), with lyrics by Nancy Hamilton (1908–1985), for the revue *Two for the Show* (1940), where it was sung by Frances Comstock and Alfred Drake. It was initially popularized by BENNY GOODMAN and his orchestra, with a vocal by Helen Forrest (Columbia 35391). In the early 1950s, Les Paul and Mary Ford's recording sold over a million copies (Capitol 1451).

"Johnson Rag" was originally composed by Guy Hall and Henry Kleinkauf as a piano instrumental in 1917. The composers, bandleaders from Wilkes-Barre, Pennsylvania, published it themselves. They also issued a song version that same year, "That Lovin' Johnson Rag." In 1940, Miller Music Corp. decided that it needed new lyrics, and asked JACK LAWRENCE to write them. He did, and Russ Morgan and his orchestra helped make it a hit (Decca 25442).

### 1941

"Elmer's Tune" was composed by Elmer Albrecht, with lyrics by Sammy Gallop. It was introduced by Dick Jurgens and his orchestra, and made famous by GLENN MILLER and his orchestra (Bluebird 11274). The version by BENNY GOODMAN and his orchestra (with a vocal by Peggy Lee, in her recording debut with Goodman) was also popular (Columbia 36359).

"How About You?" was composed by BURTON LANE, with lyrics by Ralph Freed, for Mickey Rooney and JUDY GARLAND, who introduced it in their film *Babes on Broadway.* Tommy Dorsey had a successful recording (Victor 27749). It was used in the non-musical film *Don't Bother to Knock* (1952).

"I Don't Want to Set the World on Fire" was composed by BENNIE BENJAMIN and Eddie Durham (1906–1987), and written by Eddie Seiler (1911–1952) and Sol Marcus (1912–1976). It was introduced by Harlan Leonard and His Rockets and was popularized by the Ink Spots (Decca 3987).

"Moonlight Cocktail" was composed by Luckey Roberts (1887–1968), with lyrics by Kim Gannon (1900–1974). The melody of the chorus was taken from Roberts's instrumental piano rag "Ripples of the Nile" (played by the composer on Circle Records 1028). GLENN MILLER and his orchestra had a million-seller with "Moonlight Cocktail" (Bluebird 11401).

"Racing with the Moon" was composed by Johnny Watson, with lyrics by Vaughn Monroe (1911–1973) and Pauline Pope. Monroe made it his theme song and sold over two million copies of his recording (Bluebird 11070).

### 1942

"Paper Doll" (actually written in 1915 but unpublished until 1930) had words and music by Johnny Black (September 30, 1891–June 9, 1936), who had composed "Dardanella." The MILLS BROTHERS turned it into a hit with their recording, which sold over a million copies (Decca 18318). Arthur Miller used it as a key element in his play *A View from the Bridge.*

"Who Wouldn't Love You?" was composed by Carl Fischer (1912–1954) with lyrics by Bill Carey (b. 1916). It was made famous by Kay Kyser and his orchestra, with a vocal by Harry Babbitt (Columbia 36526).

### 1943

"Holiday for Strings" was composed by David Rose (1910–1990), with lyrics added by Sammy Gallop (1915–1971). Rose's own orchestral version made it a hit (Victor 27853). He was musical director for comedian Red Skelton, who used it as his theme on both radio and television. Rose also composed "Our Waltz" and "Dance of the Spanish Onion." In 1962, he composed the instrumental novelty "The Stripper."

"Mairzy Doats" was composed by Jerry Livingston (1909–1987) and AL HOFFMAN, with lyrics by Milton Drake (b. 1916). The song was inspired when Drake's four-year-old daughter came home from kindergarten saying: "Cowzy tweet and sowzy tweet and liddle sharksy doisters." The Merry Macs had the hit record (Decca 18588), and the sheet music sold at the rate of thirty thousand copies a day for over a month.

### 1944

"Sentimental Journey" was written by Ben Homer (1917–1975), bandleader Les Brown (1912–2001), and BUD GREEN. It became Brown's theme song after his successful record with vocalist DORIS DAY (Columbia 36769). The song was featured in the film of the same name (1946). Television personality Dave Garroway used it as his theme.

"The Trolley Song" was composed by Ralph Blane (1914–1995), with lyrics by Hugh Martin (b. 1914), for JUDY GARLAND in the film *Meet Me in St. Louis.* Garland further popularized it with her hit recording (Decca 23361). The Pied Pipers also enjoyed a best-selling record (Capitol 168).

"Twilight Time" was written by Buck Ram (1907–1991), and The Three Suns (Morty Nevins, Al Nevins, and Artie Dunn). The group made the hit recording (Hit 7092). Ram also wrote "The Great Pretender" for The Platters in 1955, and that group revived "Twilight Time" in 1958 million-selling recording (Mercury 71289).

### 1945

"Cruising Down the River (on a Sunday Afternoon)" was written by two British women: music by Nell Tollerton, lyrics by Eily Beadell. Blue Barron and his orchestra made a million-selling record (MGM 10346), as did Russ Morgan and his orchestra (Decca 24568), both in 1949. The song was used in the film of the same name (1953), starring Dick Haymes and Audrey Totter.

"Day by Day" was composed by Axel Stordahl and Paul Weston, with words by Sammy Cahn. Jo Stafford made the hit recording (Capitol 227).

"Till the End of Time" was adapted by Ted Mossman from Chopin's Polonaise in A Flat Major and given words by Buddy Kaye. It sold over a million and a half copies of sheet music, and Perry Como's recording was a million-seller (RCA Victor 20-1709). It was also the title of a movie (1946), which featured its theme.

### 1946

"Do You Know What It Means to Miss New Orleans?" was composed by Lou Alter, with lyrics by Eddie De Lange. It was introduced in the film *New Orleans* by Billie Holiday and Louis Armstrong. It has become a standard with jazz bands and is often heard in clubs in New Orleans.

"(Oh Why, Oh Why, Did I Ever Leave) Wyoming" was a novelty hit with words and music by comedian Morey Amsterdam (1914–1996).

### 1947

"(Dance) Ballerina (Dance)" was composed by Carl Sigman, with words by Bob Russell (1914–1970). Vaughn Monroe made the hit recording (RCA Victor 20-2433), which sold over a million copies. It was successfully revived in 1957 by Nat "King" Cole (Capitol 3619).

"Near You" was composed by pianist-bandleader Francis Craig (1900–1966) with words by Kermit Goell (1915–1997). Craig had the hit recording (Bullet 1001), but the song got added exposure when Milton Berle chose it as the closing theme of his *Texaco Star Theatre* television program.

"Smoke Dreams" was written by Lloyd Shaffer (1901–1999), John Klenner, and Ted Steele (1917–1985) to be the theme song of radio's *Chesterfield Supper Club*, starring Perry Como, Jo Stafford, and The Starlighters.

"Tenderly" was composed by pianist Walter Gross (1909–1967), with lyrics by Jack Lawrence. It was popularized by Clark Dennis (Capitol 15307), and it was revived in 1952 in a hit recording by Rosemary Clooney (Columbia 39648). It was revived again in 1961 by Bert Kaempfert and his orchestra (Decca 31236).

## 1948

"Enjoy Yourself" was composed by CARL SIGMAN, with lyrics by Herb Magidson. When GUY LOMBARDO and his Royal Canadians recorded it in 1950, it became one of the biggest hits of that year (Decca 24839).

"Far Away Places" was composed by ALEX KRAMER, with words by ex-singer Joan Whitney (1914–1990). Two hit recordings made this a standard, one by BING CROSBY (Decca 24532), and the other by Perry Como (RCA Victor 20-3316).

"Mañana" was written by the husband-and-wife team of guitarist Dave Barbour (1912–1965) and singer Peggy Lee (1920–2002). Peggy Lee's recording sold over a million copies (Capitol 15022).

"Red Roses for a Blue Lady" was written by the team of Sid Tepper (b. 1918) and Roy Bennett (b. 1918). It was first popularized by Vaughn Monroe, (RCA Victor 20-3319), and was revived in 1965 by Bert Kaempfert and his orchestra (Decca 31722).

## 1949

"The Hot Canary" was composed by violinist Paul Nero (1917–1958), with lyrics added by Ray Gilbert (1912–1976). It was a showcase for violin virtuoso Florian Zabach, who made it a million-selling hit (Decca 27509).

"I Don't Care if the Sun Don't Shine" has words and music by Mack David (1912–1993). It was sung to success by Patti Page (Mercury 5396).

"I've Got a Lovely Bunch of Coconuts" has words and music by Fred Heatherton. Danny Kaye had a hit recording (Decca 24784), and there was a million-selling disc by Freddy Martin and his orchestra, with a vocal by Merv Griffin (RCA Victor 20-3554).

"The Old Piano Roll Blues" was composed and written by Cy Coben (b. 1919). Sammy Kaye and his orchestra, with vocals by Lisa Kirk and EDDIE CANTOR, made this a hit (RCA Victor 20-3751).

"Rudolph, the Red-Nosed Reindeer" has words and music by Johnny Marks (1909–1985). It was popularized by GENE AUTRY in a recording that has sold over six million discs (Columbia 38610). According to *Variety*, this is the second best-selling recorded Christmas song of all time (the first being "White Christmas"). There have been ninety different arrangements made, total recordings have sold over forty-five million copies, and the sheet music has sold in excess of seven million copies.

"The Third Man Theme" was composed by Anton Karas for the film *The Third Man*. It was recorded on zither by the composer, and became a two-million-selling disc (London 536).

The hardship on Tin Pan Alley caused by World War II, with critical shortages of paper and shellac, dominated the first half of this decade. Patriotic songs helped to win the war, as did such popular singers as FRANK SINATRA, who toured armed services bases, boosting the morale of G.I.s. GLENN MILLER, who led the most popular band of the time, enlisted in the Army and lost his life during the war. It was also a time for the Disney full-length cartoon films and their songs to help the civilians cope. Latin American music infiltrated dance, popular music, and films. RICHARD RODGERS and OSCAR HAMMERSTEIN II created the most popular musicals in Broadway history up to that time, and ALAN JAY LERNER and FREDERICK LOEWE were beginning their careers. Tin Pan Alley recovered from the war years and, unmindful of changing public tastes in pop music developed by and during the war, continued to supply all forms of entertainment with their songs.

## The 1950s

### 1950

"Be My Love" was composed by Nicholas Brodszky with lyrics by SAMMY CAHN. It was written for Mario Lanza's film *Toast of New Orleans*. Lanza's recording sold over a million copies (RCA Victor 20-1561).

"Dearie" had words and music by BOB HILLIARD and Dave Mann (1916–2002). It was an exercise in nostalgia, with a best-selling record by two great Broadway stars, Ray Bolger and ETHEL MERMAN (Decca 24873).

"Frosty the Snowman" was composed by Jack Rollins (1906–1973), with lyrics by Steve Nelson (b. 1907). It was a Christmas hit for GENE AUTRY (Columbia 38907), who had recorded "Rudolph" the previous year. An animated television version of the story is shown every Christmas, keeping this song a standard. The same writers produced "Peter Cottontail," an Easter classic, and "Smokey the Bear," the official song of the U.S. Forestry Service.

"Goodnight, Irene," was adapted by folklorist John Lomax from folksinger Leadbelly's song of the same name. It became popular in a recording by The Weavers, which was on the charts in the #1 position for thirteen weeks. It sold more than two million discs (Decca 27077). The Weavers (Pete Seeger, Lee Hayes, Fred Hellerman, and Ronnie Gilbert) gave annual concerts at Carnegie Hall. Other million-seller hits by them included "Tzena, Tzena, Tzena" (Decca 27053), "On Top of Old Smokey" (Deccca 27515), "So Long (It's Been Good to Know Yuh)" (Decca 27376), and "Kisses Sweeter Than Wine" (Decca 27670).

"(If I Knew You Were Comin') I'd've Baked a Cake" was written by Al Trace, BOB MERRILL, and AL HOFFMAN. Publisher Ben Barton's daughter, Eileen, had the hit recording (National 9103).

"Let's Do It Again" was written by Englishmen Desmond O'Connor and Ray Hartley, and was given a rousing treatment by Margaret Whiting, backed by (then-husband) Joe "Fingers" Carr (Capitol 1132).

"A Marshmallow World" was composed by Peter De Rose, with lyrics by CARL SIGMAN. It was De Rose's last song hit, made famous by radio-TV personality ARTHUR GODFREY.

"Music! Music! Music!" had words and music by Mel Glazer, but credit was given to Stephan Weiss and Bernie Baum. It became Teresa Brewer's first million-selling recording (London 604). Her perky, syncopated singing blended perfectly with the Jack Pleis Dixieland Band backing her. This rag song coincided with the first revival of ragtime, sparked by the piano recordings of Joe "Fingers" Carr on Capitol Records.

"My Heart Cries for You" was composed by bandleader Percy Faith (1908–1976), with lyrics by CARL SIGMAN. Faith adapted the melody from a French tune credited to Marie Antoinette! DINAH SHORE, as well as Guy Mitchell, had a hit recording (Columbia 39067).

### 1951

"Cry" had words and music by Churchill Kohlman (b. 1906). Although it was first recorded by Ruth Casey, it wasn't until Johnny Ray recorded it that this song (by a night watchman in a Pittsburgh dry cleaning plant) sold four million copies (Okeh 6840).

"I Get Ideas" was written by Sanders (d. 1942) (a rare example of the one-name composer), with lyrics by Dorcas Cochran. The melody was adapted from an Argentine tango, "Adios Muchachos," and transformed by TONY MARTIN into a best-selling recording (RCA Victor 20-4141).

"My Truly, Truly Fair" had words and music by BOB MERRILL. Guy Mitchell had the hit recording (Columbia 39415).

"Slow Poke" was written by Chilton Price and revised by Pee Wee King and Redd Stewart, who recorded the million-selling #1 disc (RCA Victor 47-0489).

## 1952

"How Much Is That Doggie in the Window" had words and music by BOB MERRILL. Patti Page made it a three-million seller (Mercury 70070).

"Lullaby of Birdland" composed by English jazz pianist George Shearing (b. 1919), with lyrics by B. Y. Forster, was named for a New York City jazz club. Shearing's own recording was a best-seller (MGM 11354).

"Say It with Your Heart" was composed by Norman Kaye (b. 1922), with lyrics by Steve Nelson. Bob Carroll made this a hit with a best-selling recording (Derby 814).

"Till I Waltz Again with You" had words and music by Sidney Prosen. Teresa Brewer made it a million seller (Coral 60873). Incidentally, the song is not a waltz.

## 1953

"I Need You Now" was written by Jimmie Crane (1910–1996) and Al Jacobs (1903–1985). Eddie Fisher had the million-selling disc (RCA Victor 47-5830).

"The Moon Is Blue" was composed by Herschel Burke Gilbert (b. 1918), with lyrics by Sylvia Fine, for the film of the same name. The best-selling record was by the Sauter-Finegan Orchestra, with a vocal by Sally Sweetland (RCA Victor 47-5359).

"Rags to Riches" was composed by RICHARD ADLER, with lyrics by Jerry Ross, as an independent number. It was their first big hit, and it led to their monumental Broadway shows *Pajama Game* (1954) and *Damn Yankees* (1955). Tony Bennett sold over two million copies of his recording (Columbia 40048).

## 1954

"Fly Me to the Moon" was written by Bart Howard (b. 1915). It was introduced by Felicia Sanders. Comedienne Kaye Ballard had a hit recording, and it was revived in 1962 by Joe Harnell.

"If I Give My Heart to You" was written as a bossa nova (Kapp 497) by Jimmie Crane, Al Jacobs, and Jimmy Brewster. Television songster Denise Lor introduced it and made the first recording (Major 27). The best-selling disc was by DORIS DAY (Columbia 40300).

"Miss America" had words and music by Bernie Wayne (1921–1993). It was for years the official song of the annual Miss America Pageant in Atlantic City, New Jersey, sung by emcee Bert Parks.

"Mister Sandman" had words and music by Pat Ballard (1899–1960). The Chordettes had the million-selling disc (Cadence 1247). It held the #1 spot on *Your Hit Parade* for eight weeks.

"No More" was composed by Leo De John, with lyrics by Julie and Dux De John. It isn't surprising that the De John Sisters had the hit recording (Epic 9085).

"Young at Heart" was composed by Johnny Richards, with lyrics by Carolyn Leigh (1926–1983). Frank Sinatra made a disc that sold a million copies (Capitol 2703). The song's title was given to a film starring Sinatra and Doris Day (also in 1954).

### 1955

"Dream Along with Me (I'm on My Way to a Star)" had words and music by Carl Sigman. It became familiar through weekly exposure as Perry Como's television theme.

"Hey, Mr. Banjo" was composed by Freddy Morgan (1910–1970), with lyrics by Norman Malkin. Morgan was the banjoist for Spike Jones and his City Slickers from 1947 to 1958. He formed the Sunnysiders to record his best-selling tune (Kapp 113).

"Wake the Town and Tell the People" was composed by Jerry Livingston, with lyrics by Sammy Gallop. Les Baxter and his orchestra made the best-selling recording (Capitol 3120).

"Zambezi" was composed by Nico Carstens and Anton De Waal, with lyrics by Bob Hilliard. The best-selling version was made by Lou Busch and his orchestra (Capitol 3272).

# Al Hoffman

Composer and lyricist (b. Minsk, Russia, September 25, 1902; d. New York City, July 21, 1960). Hoffman's family settled in Seattle, Washington when he was six years old; as a teen, he formed his own band there. In 1928, he moved to New York, and began composing in the early 1930s. His early hits included "I Don't Mind Walking in the Rain" (music by John Klenner), "Fit as a Fiddle" (with Al Goodhart and Arthur Freed), and "Little Man, You Had a Busy Day" (with Maurice Sigler and Mabel Wayne). Working with Goodhart and Sigler, Hoffman wrote prolifically for British stage productions and films during the later 1930s and early 1940s. In 1941, "The Story of a Starry Night" (with a melody by Hoffman and Jerry Livingston based on Tchaikovsky's Symphony No. 6 and lyrics by Mann Curtis), was a major hit for Glenn Miller. The composers followed this with a huge success, 1943's "Mairzy Doats," with lyrics by Milton Drake (b. 1916). The Merry Macs had the hit record (Decca 18588), and the sheet music sold at the rate of thirty thousand copies a day for over a month. For Disney's animated film *Cinderella* (1950), Hoffman, again composing with Livingston, but now working with lyricist Mack David, contributed "Bibbidi, Bobbidi, Boo," "The Work Song," "So This is Love," and "A Dream Is a Wish Your Heart Makes." The last was sung on the sound track by Ilene Woods. 1950 brought the major hit "(If I Knew

You Were Comin') I'd've Baked a Cake," written with Al Trace and Bob Merrill. Publisher Ben Barton's daughter, Eileen, had the hit recording (National 9103). Other novelties followed, including "Papa Loves Mambo" and "Hot Diggety." Hoffman continued to compose until his death, scoring minor pop hits.

# Billie Holiday

Great jazz vocalist (b. Elinore Harris Holliday, Baltimore, Maryland, April 7, 1915; d. New York City, July 17, 1959). Known as "Lady Day," she became an incomparable jazz singer accompanied by the best jazz musicians of her day. She teamed with Teddy Wilson's orchestra to record from 1935 to 1939. Their biggest hit came in 1937 with "Carelessly" (Brunswick 7867), a #1 pop record. During the 1930s, Holiday also recorded with Benny Goodman, Artie Shaw, and Count Basie. Her most famous recording came in 1939 with "Strange Fruit," a controversial song depicting a lynching in the South. It was released by the small jazz label Commodore Records (Commodore 526). It was banned from radio, but is considered a pop classic. She recorded her most famous composition, "God Bless the Child" in 1941 (Okeh 6270), backed by Roy Eldridge on trumpet and Eddie Heywood on piano. Holiday also recorded innumerable covers of Tin Pan Alley hits, always in her distinct, smoky-voiced style.

Holiday played in clubs, mostly in New York and Chicago, through the 1940s. In 1947, she appeared in the film *New Orleans* (also featuring Louis Armstrong, Arturo de Cordova, and Dorothy Patrick). A drug-related arrest led to a brief stay in jail and the loss of her cabaret card in the late 1940s; without the card, she could not perform in New York. She continued to record and perform until her death in 1959, but the quality of her later recordings suffered from her increasing drug and alcohol use.

# Joe Howard

Composer and singer (b. New York City, February 12, 1867; d. Chicago, Illinois, May 19, 1961). Howard ran away from home when he was eight years old and made his way to St. Louis, where he eked out a living selling newspapers and singing in saloons. He soon entered vaudeville, and next found a job with a traveling stock company. When he was seventeen, he met Ida Emerson and formed a song-and-dance act with her. She would be the second of his nine wives. They traveled throughout the Midwest, coming to Chicago as the stars of their own vaudeville show. They finally reached New York, where they appeared at Tony Pastor's Music Hall. In 1899, T. B. HARMS published their marvelous syncopated "ragtime" telephone song "Hello, Ma Baby," which sold over a million copies within a few months and has remained a standard since. In 1904, Howard wrote a follow-up called "Goodbye, My Lady Love," which was featured by Ida. The melody is derived from his earlier hit and William H. Myddleton's "Down South." Howard continued to perform it in vaudeville, where it was a big hit. He wrote the music for, and starred in, musical productions in Chicago from 1905 to 1915, and had his show songs published by CHARLES K. HARRIS. His biggest hit and the song most closely identified with him was "I Wonder Who's Kissing Her Now," with lyrics by Will M. Hough and Frank R. Adams, from their 1909 production *The Prince of Tonight*. It wasn't until the motion picture was made of Howard's life (using that song title as the title of the film) that Harold Orlob sued to establish that he wrote the melody. Orlob was working for Howard in Chicago, hired to supply music for the shows, with Howard claiming copyright and ownership of the material. When Orlob won his suit, he didn't want money, only recognition that he was sole composer of that song. Orlob is a classic example of one spending a lifetime in show business but being essentially a one-song composer. Howard continued to perform in clubs and on radio and television until his retirement, and did benefit shows thereafter.

# Howley, Haviland and Company (1893–1904)

One of the most successful of the Tin Pan Alley publishers. Patrick Howley (1870–1918), manager of Willis Woodward and Company, decided that there could be more to publishing than the sentimental ballads his firm bought. In 1893, he joined with Frederick Benjamin Haviland (1868–1932), New York sales manager for the Boston-based Oliver Ditson Company, which at that time was a classical and parlor-music publisher and sheet music wholesaler. They wanted to test the waters before quitting their jobs, so Howley and Haviland started the firm of George T. Worth, a name they made up to protect their identities. However, their respective employers caught on to their enterprise and forced them to quit their jobs. Thus, Howley, Haviland, and Company was born.

Howley, Haviland had great success with two of the Alley's most popular song styles: the sentimental ballad or tearjerker, and the COON SONG. They exploited these styles vigorously throughout the 1890s, becoming one of the most influential and envied firms of the time. Much of their success with coon songs could be attributed to illustrators Bert Cobb (1869–

Publisher F. B. Haviland pictured in 1908 after striking out on his own.

1936) and Edgar Keller (1867–1932), who designed their covers. Their artwork was, in large part, responsible for the sales that these songs enjoyed, so M. WITMARK AND SONS started using Cobb and Keller, too.

In 1900, new partner PAUL DRESSER was taken into the firm, which would remain active through 1904. Then, Haviland formed his own firm, with continuing success through his death in 1932. Dresser and Howley went on their own, but soon split. Dresser continued until his death in 1906, and Howley survived one more year; neither could achieve success without Haviland. In 1936, Jerry Vogel inherited the Haviland catalog.

HOWLEY, HAVILAND, AND COMPANY

| | |
|---|---|
| 1893 | 4 East 20th Street (as George T. Worth Company) |
| 1894–1898 | 4 East 20th Street (as Howley, Haviland, and Company). |
| 1898–1900 | 1260–1266 Broadway (at 32nd Street) |
| 1900–1903 | 1260–1266 Broadway (as Howley, Haviland, and Dresser) |
| 1903 | 1434–1440 Broadway |
| 1904 | 1440 Broadway (as Howley, Dresser Company) |
| 1905–1907 | 41 West 28th Street (as P. J. Howley Music Company) |
| 1905–1906 | 51 West 28th Street (as Paul Dresser Publishing Company) |

F. B. HAVILAND PUBLISHING COMPANY (1904–1932)

| | |
|---|---|
| 1904–1913 | 125 West 37th Street |
| 1914–1916 | Broadway and 47th Street (Strand Theatre Building) |
| 1916–1920 | 128 West 48th Street |
| 1920–1933 | 114 West 44th Street |

# Will Hudson

Bandleader and composer (b. Barstow, California, March 8, 1908; d. South Carolina, July 27, 1981). Hudson is best remembered for composing the standard "Moonglow." His family moved from California to Detroit, Michigan, when he was a teenager, and it was there that he founded his first band. By the mid-1930s, he was well established, having composed and arranged for a number of popular bandleaders in working for the music publisher Irving Mills (who often took "cocomposer" credit on Hudson's tunes). He teamed up with vocalist EDDIE DE LANGE in 1936, and the two worked together for two years before parting on less than amicable terms. De Lange provided lyrics for Hudson's biggest hit, 1934's "Moonglow," as well as "Deep in a Dream" and "Remember When." "Moonglow" was a hit for BENNY GOODMAN and ARTIE SHAW, and was revived for the film *Picnic* in 1955, giving it a second life. Hudson also composed some popular jazz-flavored instrumentals, most notably the 1936 hit "Organ Grinder's Swing," based on the traditional children's nursery rhyme "I like coffee, I like tea." ELLA FITZGERALD with Chick Webb's orchestra had the hit recording on Decca. Hudson was part of GLENN MILLER's Air Force band, serving as its head arranger from 1943 to 1945. After the war, he attended Juilliard and began writing in classical styles, leaving behind his work in popular music.

# Herman Hupfeld

Composer (b. Montclair, New Jersey, February 1, 1894; d. Montclair, June 8, 1951). Hupfeld was a Broadway and film composer of the 1930s and 1940s, most famous for a single song, "As Times Goes By." As a youngster he studied violin in Germany and then returned home to complete his education. After serving in World War I, he began performing as a pianist-singer, and writing songs for revues. His first minor hit came in 1930 with "Sing Something Simple," introduced in the *Second Little Show* by singer Ruth Tester. The next year, for the *Third Little Show*, he wrote the novelty "When Yuba Plays the Rumba on the Tuba," and his biggest hit, "As Time Goes By," introduced in the 1932 show *Everybody's Welcome*, by singer Frances Williams. At the time, RUDY VALLEE's recording made the song a moderate success (Victor 22773), but it really took off after it was revived in the movie *Casablanca* (1942), as a musical theme sung by Dooley Wilson. The song became so popular that Victor had to rerelease the Vallee recording because there was a recording ban by the musicians' union at the time. The rerelease became a #1 hit. 1932 also saw Hupfeld's last pop hit, "Let's Put Out the Lights and Go to Sleep," composed with Frederick Loewe, sung in *George White's Music Hall Varieties*. Hupfeld continued to compose and perform through the World War II years, and placed his last songs on Broadway in *Dance Me a Song* (1950), a flop that featured up-and-coming dancer Bob Fosse.

# I

## May Irwin

Singer and songwriter (b. Whitby, Canada, June 27, 1862; d. New York City, October 22, 1938). Irwin started in vaudeville with her sister Flora in 1875 and worked her way up to playing Tony Pastor's. She began to write her own songs in 1893, with "Mamie! Come Kiss Your Honey Boy." Her biggest success came in 1896, when she introduced Charles Trevathan's "The Bully Song." This song established her as the foremost coon shouter of the day. WEBER AND FIELDS booked her for their Music Hall, where she developed into a fine comedienne. She then took Ben Harney's "Mister Johnson, Turn Me Loose" into the show *Courted into Court* (December 29, 1896), and also began her collaboration with GEORGE M. COHAN, "Hot Tamale Alley," which scored a hit. In 1899, she introduced GUS EDWARDS and Will D. Cobb's COON SONG "I Couldn't Stand to See My Baby Lose." She became the first actress to appear on film when she reenacted her scandalous "kiss scene" from *The Widow Jones* in 1896. She was beloved by the industry and appeared in benefits long after she retired. She was one of the few performers to invest in real estate, and she spent her retirement in great comfort.

# J

## Jazz in the Tin Pan Alley Era

Jazz, a hybrid of RAGTIME and the BLUES, first found its way to the general public when the Victor Talking Machine Company issued the work of the ORIGINAL DIXIELAND JAZZ BAND (ODJB) early in 1917. LEO FEIST was the publisher of the ODJB compositions, but while the recordings sold well—as in rock and roll forty years later—the sheet music didn't. The major jazz performer was pioneer trumpeter/vocalist LOUIS ARMSTRONG, who first appeared with KING OLIVER'S CREOLE JAZZ BAND in 1923 on disc and in 1926 on sheet music. It was Armstrong who made singing pop songs in a jazzy manner the thing to do, adding to the jazz repertory.

"Jazz" doesn't refer so much to what is played as to how it is played. The ODJB started with five instruments (cornet, trombone, clarinet, piano, and drums). THE ORIGINAL MEMPHIS FIVE also used those same instruments, as did the Original Indiana Five. Yet these three bands don't sound much alike. The major difference is the way in which those five instruments were played. Intonation, the way in which brass and reed instruments are blown (and touch for the piano, that is, how the keys are struck), make them sound different. Jazz piano stylist JELLY ROLL MORTON cannot be mistaken for any other pianist, for his touch and his harmonic choices are immediately recognizable; he makes the piano sound like an entire dixieland band. He is easily distinguishable from EUBIE BLAKE, JAMES P. JOHNSON, and Willie "The Lion" Smith, each of whom also had an original and distinctive style. As Blake once said, "It's not that I play better than anybody else, it's the tricks I know."

Discs are the best way to familiarize oneself with jazzmen and jazz bands of the 1920s. Jazz in sheet music form, especially the tunes created for bands, didn't sell well, and was a discouragement to publishers. Indeed, the great jazz bands—King Oliver's Creole Jazz Band ("Sugar Foot Stomp"), Louis Armstrong's Hot Five ("Heebie Jeebies"), Jimmy Wade's Moulin Rouge Syncopators ("Mobile Blues"), The Original Memphis Five ("Shufflin' Mose"), and The Wolverines featuring Bix Beiderbecke ("Driftwood")—appeared only once or twice each on sheet music covers. Jazzmen such as Jack Teagarden, Muggsy Spanier, Red Nichols, Eubie Blake, and FLETCHER HENDERSON appeared on only a few more. The New Orleans Rhythm Kings were not pictured on their famous tune "Tin Roof Blues," but appear only on an edition of Jelly Roll Morton's "Wolverine Blues." Morton himself appeared only on the cover of Folio No.1 of his famous *Blues and Stomps for Piano*. His outstanding band, The Red Hot Peppers, never appeared on a sheet music cover.

These were the most important, most creative, and best-selling recording jazz bands and soloists of their time, but that popularity did not translate into sheet music sales. In fact, many of the published jazz tunes that became classics on records sold so poorly and had such limited press runs that they are almost never found today. The reverse, of course, was true of the pop singers who recorded. Their pictures on covers triggered widespread sales of sheet music.

The big bands of the 1930s did much to popularize Tin Pan Alley's songs. This was the height of the popularity of swing music, and it was not unusual for major bands to score Top 10 hits. BENNY GOODMAN and GLENN MILLER were perhaps the most successful, and they relied on the Alley to provide them with material. The bands also featured singers to put over the popular songs, and orchestras led by TOMMY DORSEY and ARTIE SHAW fought for the best available talent. Singers like FRANK SINATRA and DORIS DAY began their careers in front of bands. However, the coming of World War II led to a decimation in the ranks of the bands as members were drafted and the cost of gasoline made it difficult to continue touring. After the war, band singers broke away and became stars on their own, while the bands struggled to survive. Smaller combos were more economically feasible and soon took the place of the large bands, and jazz fell off the charts. However, jazz musicians continued to draw on the pop song repertoire for the basis of their improvisations. Even the revolutionary bebop musicians used the chord progressions of familiar pop numbers as the basis for their "new" compositions. And hits of the 1920s, 1930s, and 1940s continued to be reintroduced as jazz "standards" by performers as diverse as ELLA FITZGERALD, Sara Vaughan, Chet Baker, Miles Davis, and countless others.

# William Jerome

Turn-of-the-twentieth-century lyricist and music publisher (b. Cornwall-on-the-Hudson, New York, September 30, 1865 d. Newburgh, New York, June 25, 1932). Jerome was a vaudeville singer and dancer in his youth, working with various companies including Avory's

Hibernicon (beginning in 1882), followed by a stint with Barlow Wilson's Minstrels, and then came to New York to work, first at Tony Pastor's Fourteenth Street Theatre as a parody singer (in the late 1880s) and then with E. F. Albee's company at the Union Square Theatre from the early 1890s. Around this time, he wed the vaudeville singer Maude Nugent, who gained considerable fame for her 1896 song "Sweet Rosie O'Grady." In 1901, Jerome formed a successful partnership with composer JEAN SCHWARTZ that would last about a decade. Schwartz and Jerome started with the COON SONG "When Mr. Shakespeare Comes to Town," and followed it with "Rip Van Winkle Was a Lucky Man," which Nugent made famous. Schwartz and Jerome next had a tremendous success with 1903's "Bedelia (The Irish Coon Song Serenade)," which sold over three million copies. Blanche Ring sang it in *The Jersey Lily*, and she was constantly identified with the song. Next, the duo hit pay dirt big-time in 1910 with the publication of their all-time favorite, "Chinatown, My Chinatown." In 1915, Jerome worked with a new partner, composer WALTER DONALDSON, on the minor hit "Just Try to Picture Me Back Home in Tennessee," and in 1912 Jerome partnered with JAMES MONACO for the song "Row, Row, Row," featured in that year's edition of Ziegfeld's *Follies*. Around this time, Jerome founded his own music publishing business. He scored a huge success in 1917 when GEORGE M. COHAN gave him "Over There" to publish, perhaps the most popular song of the World War I era. Jerome was active in the founding of ASCAP and served as a director of the organization for many years. In his later years, Jerome retired to his hometown. In the spring of 1932, he was struck by a careless motorist, and never fully recovered from the accident. ("It was a Rolls Royce that hit me," Jerome told a local reporter. "Think of my feelings if a Ford had fixed me up this way.") Jerome died shortly thereafter.

# Jitterbug

The dance that started in Harlem's Savoy Ballroom, the blocklong building on Lenox Avenue, between 140th and 141st streets, and was first known as the Lindy, a dance that started in the late 1920s (named in honor of flying ace Charles Lindbergh). For swinging hepcats, the jitterbug was "real gone." Many rugs were cut by "killer-dillers" and "gates" in this dancing decade. This dance, which captivated bobbysoxers in the Depression years, literally swept people off their feet. By the mid-1930s, when swing was taking the country by storm, such fast, exhibition-style dancing was called the jitterbug. At the Savoy they danced to the music of Chick Webb and his orchestra. Johnny Hodges composed "Jitterbug's Lullaby" (1938), HAROLD ARLEN wrote "The Jitterbug" for *The Wizard of Oz* (1939), RUBE BLOOM wrote "Jitterbug Jamboree" (1939), and FATS WALLER composed "The Jitterbug Waltz" (1942).

# Jobbers

Sheet music wholesalers, otherwise known as jobbers, were very much a part of the publishing and plugging business. The major jobbers were Col. A. H. Goetting in Springfield, Massachusetts (who also owned Coupon Music Company in Boston and Enterprise Music Supply Company in New York); Plaza Music and Crown Music in New York City; Oliver Ditson in Boston; F. J. A. Forster and McKinley in Chicago; and Sherman, Clay in San Francisco. They did more than fill orders. They acted as selling agents for the smaller publishers, and they also undertook to plug certain numbers on their own. When Jack Robbins worked for the Enterprise Music Supply Company, he noticed a tune languishing on its shelves. He thought it could be a hit, so he pushed it. The tune was "Smiles," published by its composer, Lee S. Roberts, in Chicago. Robbins was so successful that JEROME H. REMICK bought the song from him, and MOSE GUMBLE, Remick's professional manager, turned it into a three-million seller. Plugging independently was such a natural for these go-getters that jobbers like Maurice Richmond (who worked for Goetting), Jack Robbins (who later worked for Richmond), JERRY VOGEL (who worked for Plaza), and Henry Waterson (who worked for Crown) eventually became full-time music publishers themselves.

# Arnold Johnson

Bandleader, pianist, and composer (b. Chicago, Illinois, March 23, 1893; d. St. Petersburg Florida, July 15, 1975). Johnson was a pop-jazz bandleader active from the late 1920s through the 1940s, who composed several popular hits, including "Oh" and "Does Your Heart Beat for Me?" Johnson began his career in Chicago, where he worked as a pianist in local restaurants and clubs, and also studied at the Chicago Music College. His first band job was with saxophonist Rudy Wiedoft. In 1919, he moved to New York, and scored his first and most enduring hit with "Oh," with lyrics by Byron Gay (1886–1945). It was initially a major hit for TED LEWIS's jazz band (Columbia A-2844), and it was very successfully revived in 1953 by Pee Wee Hunt, in a recording that sold over a million copies (Capitol 2442). Johnson remained in New York through about the mid-1920s, when he briefly retired to try to cash in on the Florida real estate boom. Returning to New York, Johnson made a major splash by providing the music for the 1928 editions of *George White Scandals* and the *Greenwich Village Follies,* and *Earl Carroll's Sketch Book* in 1929. During the intermission, new band vocalist (and future songwriter) HAROLD ARLEN sang a medley of his songs, accompanied by the Johnson band, helping to introduce the young songwriter to New York audiences. In the early 1930s, Johnson disbanded his orchestra and began working as a musical director for radio. He again led a band to entertain the troops during World War II, then returned to radio work until his retirement.

# Charles Leslie Johnson

Composer, publisher, and arranger (b. Kansas City, Kansas, December 3, 1876; d. Kansas City, Missouri, December 28, 1950). Johnson started taking piano lessons at the age of six, and ten years later studied theory and harmony. He had a fine ear and taught himself to play violin, banjo, guitar, and mandolin. In the twin cities, he organized string orchestras and played in theaters, hotels, restaurants, and dance halls. During the day, he demonstrated songs and pianos for the J. W. Jenkins Sons' Music Company, which published "Scandalous Thompson," his first rag, in 1899. Shortly after, he entered into partnership in the Central Music Publishing Company, which issued his Indian song "Iola." (Interestingly, both this song and CHARLES N. DANIELS's earlier "Hiawatha" were named for towns in Kansas, not Indians. The lyrics to both songs were added after they had become successful as instrumental numbers.) "Iola" didn't become a big hit until Daniels bought it for JEROME H. REMICK AND COMPANY and exploited it nationally. Coincidentally, Charles Johnson was working for Daniels's old firm, Carl Hoffman Music Company, at the time of the song's purchase in 1906.

Johnson was working over a new rag when Hoffman's bookkeeper asked him what the name of it was. The bookkeeper was carrying a container of dill pickles to accompany his dinner. Johnson noticed them and said, "I'll call it 'Dill Pickles Rag.' " After Daniels bought "Dill Pickles Rag" for Remick in 1907 (it had been published by Hoffman the year before) and turned it into a million-selling hit, Johnson started his own publishing company, which lasted until Harold Rossiter of Chicago purchased the firm in August 1910, with the stipulation that Johnson not reenter the publishing business again for one year (shades of Remick and Shapiro!).

Charles Johnson was one of the most prolific of the Alley composers and, like HARRY VON TILZER, wrote all of the types of songs and instrumentals then popular. He was published not only by his own firm but also by Remick, Vandersloot, Sam Fox, F. J. A. Forster, and WILL ROSSITER. Johnson was so prolific that he had to resort to pseudonyms, especially when he published his own songs, so it would appear that he had more than one composer on his staff. Among his pseudonyms was "Raymond Birch," who was credited with the RAGTIME hits "Powder Rag" and "Blue Goose Rag." Among Johnson's thirty-two rags, "Porcupine Rag" of 1909 and "Crazy Bone Rag" of 1913 became million-selling successes. "Cum-Bac" of 1911 was among his most clever. His 1916 "Teasing the Cat" enjoyed a huge popularity, thanks to the Van Eps Trio's recording (Victor 18226). Johnson's high sense of fun was reflected in his popular and well-constructed rags. His lyrical talent was evident in his biggest moneymaking song, the 1919 "Sweet and Low." Unlike other successful Tin Pan Alley composers, he elected to stay in his hometown.

# James P. Johnson

African-American composer and pianist (b. New Brunswick, New Jersey, February 1, 1894; d. New York City, November 17, 1955). He was called the "Father of Stride Piano" and composed the most famous stride rag, "Carolina Shout," which was used as a cutting contest piece. He recorded it twice, first in 1921 (Okeh 4495) and again in 1944 (Decca 24885).

Johnson also had a career as a Broadway songwriter. Notably, he composed the song that defined the Roaring Twenties, "The CHARLESTON." He never recorded his most famous tune, but ISHAM JONES and his orchestra, featuring Roy Bargy at the piano (Brunswick 2970), and the Tennessee Tooters, featuring RUBE BLOOM at the piano (Vocalion 15086), made up for it. That rhythm was insinuated into every fast fox-trot from 1925 to 1927. Johnson also wrote "Old-Fashioned Love" for the musical *Runnin' Wild* in 1923. Frank Crumit recorded it (Columbia A-3997). RUTH ETTING recorded his 1926 pop song "If I Could Be with You" (Columbia 2300-D), and in 1944, Johnson revived it himself (Decca 24883). His pupil, FATS WALLER, recorded his 1930 tune "A Porter's Love Song to a Chambermaid" (Victor 24648).

In the 1930s and 1940s, Johnson continued to compose, moving into longer concert works along with his piano pieces. He also worked in various New York clubs and recorded for several labels. A stroke left him an invalid and ended his career in 1951.

# Arthur Johnston

See *Sam Coslow*
and *Johnny Burke*

# Al Jolson

Singer and actor (b. Asa Yoelson, St. Petersburg, Russia, March 26, 1886; d. San Francisco, California, October 25, 1950). Jolson's father, Moses (Moishe), was a cantor, and came to the United States in April 1894, bringing his family afterward and settling in Washington, D.C; his mother died soon after. Asa and his older brother Hirsch sang on street corners for tips beginning when Asa was ten years old. They soon took the "stage names" of Al and Harry.

Jolson started his career as a singer in minstrel shows, winding up with the great Lew Dockstader's troupe from 1908 to 1909. He had entered vaudeville at the turn of the twentieth century, and first appeared on a sheet music cover for CHARLES K. HARRIS's "For Old Times' Sake" (1900), as part of the team of Joelson and Moore. His first performance on Broadway was at the Schuberts' newly opened Winter Garden Theatre, between Fiftieth and Fifty-first streets. It was in the revue *La Belle Paree* (March 20, 1911) that he sang JEROME KERN's "Paris Is a Paradise for Coons." With his next show, the same year, *Vera Violetta* (November 20), he headlined at the Winter Garden, a tradition that lasted for the next fifteen years. Any song he sang became a hit, so pluggers beat a path to his door. His door was wide open, and he was the first star to insist upon being "cut in" on the writing credit of a song. He became the king of the cut-inners, with coauthorship credit on many copyrights and a share of royalties on many of the biggest hits of his era. It is known that he never wrote anything in his life, yet he shared "authorship" of some of the greatest songs in the Alley. He made more hits than any other performer of his time.

Jolson made his first recordings in December 1911, scoring his first major recorded hit with GEORGE M. COHAN's "That Haunting Melody," which came from *Vera Violetta*, and was issued on disc in the spring of 1912. Also that spring, Jolson appeared on Broadway in *The Whirl of Society*, portraying an African-American servant. In 1913, he premiered in *The Honeymoon Express*, in which he interpolated the song "You Made Me Love You," by JAMES V. MONACO and JOSEPH MCCARTHY, which became a disc hit for the singer that October.

Jolson would continue to appear in Broadway revues and shows for the following years, enjoying long runs followed by nationwide tours. His biggest record hit during this period was "Where Did Robinson Crusoe Go with Friday on Saturday Night?" (Columbia A-1976), from the show *Robinson Crusoe Jr.* (1916). His major hit show was *Sinbad*, which premiered in early 1918, and was presented on Broadway and on the road for the next three years. The big hit from it was "Rock-a-Bye Your Baby with a Dixie Melody." In January 1920, he recorded GEORGE GERSHWIN and IRVING CAESAR's "Swanee," which he also interpolated into *Sinbad*; the record became a huge hit, launching Gershwin's songwriting career (Columbia A-2884).

Al Jolson (right) with Irving Berlin on the links, c. 1920.

Jolson's next Broadway show was *Bombo*, opening in the fall of 1921. Hits from the show include "April Showers" and the interpolated "Toot Toot Tootsie! (Goo'bye)" (January 1923) and "California, Here I Come" (May 1924). His next show, *Big Boy* (January 1925) produced no record hits, but Jolson did score with the nonshow "When the Red, Red Robin Comes Bob-Bob-Bobbin' Along" in the fall of 1926. Jolson secured a historic role for himself in the entertainment industry when he starred in the first talking (more correctly, "singing") film, *The Jazz Singer* (1927). "Mother, I Still Have You" was written especially for this Warner Bros. picture by Louis Silver, Grant Clarke, and (oh, yes) Al Jolson. His performing trademarks were his blackface and his white gloves. The makeup came early in his career as a vaudevillian; a veteran headliner advised him to wear it to hide his nervousness.

*The Singing Fool* (1928), Jolson's next feature, was a bigger sensation than his first, and introduced the major hits "Sonny Boy" and "There's a Rainbow Round My Shoulder." However, Jolson's career then began to wane, and his following pictures did not do as well. He returned to Broadway in 1931, and a year later launched his first radio show. The 1930s saw him working primarily in radio, with bit parts in films. During World War II, he entertained the troops.

Immediately after the war, Jolson's career enjoyed a new life. He recorded an album of songs for Decca Records that was a major hit in 1946. Then, Jolson was the only subject ever to perform in his own screen auto-biography, not once but twice, when he recorded all of the songs for Larry Parks on the sound tracks of *The Jolson Story* (1946) and *Jolson Sings Again* (1949). Both sound track albums were great commercial successes. Jolson also returned to radio, but a heart attack in the fall of 1950 ended his life and career.

# Isham Jones

Composer, bandleader, and saxophonist (b. Coalton, Ohio, January 31, 1894; d. Hollywood, California, October 19, 1956). Jones started his musical training early and became proficient on the tenor saxophone. The first composition for which he wrote both words and music, "At That Dixie Jubilee," was published by him when he was living in Saginaw, Michigan, in 1915. From there he moved to Chicago, where he organized a band that played at the Green Mill. In 1920, he opened the Rainbow Gardens and started recording for the new Brunswick Records, which was headquartered in Chicago. The band quickly established a national reputation through its recordings and, in 1922, added Louis Panico as lead trumpeter. Al Eldridge was pianist and shared the arranging chores with Jones. Eldridge wrote a beautiful number, "Think of Me" (1923), which the band recorded (Brunswick 2374) and on which he is featured. The band then moved for six years to the College Inn at the Hotel Sherman, where they became the preeminent dance band in Chicago. In 1924, Roy Bargy (1894–1974), composer and pianist for the Benson Orchestra, joined Jones to become his chief arranger and pianist after Eldridge died. Bargy was featured on their recording of "Charleston" (Brunswick 2970).

Jones's band altered its style at the beginning of the 1930s. He was the first to change the tempo of "Star Dust" from a snappy fox-trot to a dreamy ballad, and his recording of it sent the song on its way to becoming one of the most recorded of all time (Brunswick 4586). The band reached its peak popularity during the years 1932–1934. Jones broke up the band in 1936, with Woody Herman, his clarinetist, hiring most of the players and reforming them into another band and making it a cooperative venture.

Jones's songwriting career was a typical 1920s success story, with his 1930s efforts not meeting much success. In 1922, he and JAMES P. JOHNSON composed "Ivy," with words by Bert Williams's lyricist, Alex Rogers. It was a middling success, recorded by Jones's band (Brunswick 2365). Also in 1922, Jones teamed with the prolific GUS KAHN, who was to be his collaborator for several years. They wrote "Broken-Hearted Melody" and "On the Alamo." By 1923, when they wrote the hardy perennial "Swinging Down the Lane," Jones was so famous that LEO FEIST put his photograph on the cover of the sheet music.

The number of million-sellers that the team created in 1924 is truly amazing. Jones' wife gave him a baby grand piano for his birthday that year, and *within an hour*, so the story goes, he composed "I'll See You in My Dreams," "The One I Love Belongs to Somebody Else," "Spain," and "It Had to Be You." Such a burst of creativity remains unparalleled, since each song is now a part of the standard repertoire. With such major hits, other good Jones songs have been overlooked. One such was his 1924 ballad "Never Again," which his band recorded (Brunswick 2577) and to which Ruth Mack gave a sumptuous arrangement on a piano roll (Vocalstyle 12994). Another was "Why Couldn't It Be Poor Little Me?" (1924), which Jones recorded with Ray Miller's orchestra (Brunswick 2788). But jazz fans will always prefer the version cornetist Muggsy Spanier (1906–1967) made with The Stomp Six (Autograph 626), which included Guy Carey, trombone; Volly de Faut, clarinet; Mel Stitzel, piano; Joe Gish, tuba; and Ben Pollack, drums.

In 1931 Jones and Charles Newman (1901–1978) wrote "You're Just a Dream Come True," which became the band's new theme song (Brunswick 6015). Jones continued to lead his band through the mid-1930s, and to compose until the decade's end, when he retired from the music business.

# Richard M. Jones

Blues pianist and songwriter (b. Richard Mariney Jones, Donaldsonville, Louisiana, June 13, 1892; d. Chicago, Illinois, December 8, 1945). As a teen, Jones played primarily wind instruments in New Orleans, working with the Eureka Brass Band around 1902, then switched to piano. He worked out of New Orleans as a pianist and bandleader until coming to Chicago in 1918, where he played with a number of different bands and also worked as a talent scout for Okeh Records, which was active in recording early jazz and dance bands, during the mid-1920s. He wrote a number of BLUES standards: 1915's "Lonesome Nobody Cares," a hit for SOPHIE TUCKER; 1923's "All Night Blues," which Callie Vassar recorded (Gennett 5172); and his best-remembered song, 1937's "Trouble in Mind." He worked in a Chicago defense plant during World War II, while continuing to perform at night, and made his last recordings in 1944.

# Spike Jones

Bandleader extraordinaire and performer on cowbells, pistol, and car horns (b. Lindley Armstrong Jones, Long Beach, California, December 14, 1911; d. Los Angeles, California, May 1, 1964). Jones began playing drums as a teenager, working in the Los Angeles area. He did a good deal of session work, and then formed his own band. Jones's City Slickers lampooned current and past songs on radio and television, in concerts and movies, and on recordings, three of which sold more than one million copies each. The first, the 1942 "Der Fuehrer's Face," featured vocals by Carl Grayson and Willie Spicer (Bluebird 11586). His 1945 version of "Cocktails for Two" again featured the singing of Grayson (Victor 20-1628). The 1948 offering "All I Want for Christmas (Is My Two Front Teeth)" featured the singing of trumpeter George Rock (RCA Victor 20-3177) and became an annual best-seller in each succeeding Christmas season.

# Scott Joplin

Composer and "father of ragtime piano" (b. Bowie County, Texas, November 24, 1868; d. New York City, April 1, 1917). He was one of six children of a musical family and was given piano lessons as a child. He made his way as an itinerant pianist throughout the Mississippi Valley, appearing in 1885 at the Silver Dollar Saloon in St. Louis. After performing near the Chicago World's Fair of 1893, he came to the small town of Sedalia, Missouri, where he joined the Queen City Concert Band as second cornetist. Joplin played piano in the Williams Brothers' saloon, whose social club on the second floor was named the Maple Leaf Club. During this time, he enrolled in the George R. Smith College in Sedalia and studied music theory, harmony, and composition. In 1897, he composed his greatest and most influential piece, "Maple Leaf Rag." It wasn't until 1899, however, that John Stark and Son, of Sedalia, published it. It became the first rag to be popular nationally, eventually selling a million copies of sheet music and establishing RAGTIME as a genre. His "Maple Leaf Rag" was the most imitated rag of all time and set the musical structure of rags from that time forward. It is no wonder, then, that Stark proclaimed in his advertising that Joplin was "King of Ragtime writers." Joplin's use of several sixteen-measure musical themes of complex syncopation with an even, steady duple rhythm was a most revolutionary musical idea at the turn of the twentieth century. Popular music would never be the same again. The essential gaiety of the beat fit the national mood; the toe-tapping qualities of this new music filled the air with excitement. This syncopated piano music eclipsed the nonpianistic CAKEWALK's popularity soon after the slightly syncopated COON SONG made its debut. The piano rag was more sophisticated musically and technically harder to play than any popular music had been up to this time. Still, the infectious lilt of its syncopated melodies charmed and delighted listeners, and sheet music sales soared. Joplin moved from Sedalia to St. Louis, following his publisher, John Stark, there in 1900.

Joplin's next works were in a different vein, combining the traditions of Afro-American folk tunes with nineteenth-century European romanticism. His imaginative use of black mid-

Scott Joplin pictured on a sheet music cover of one of his compositions.

western folk materials led Alfred Ernst of the St. Louis Choral Symphony Society to call Joplin, in a 1901 article in the *St. Louis Post-Dispatch*, "an extraordinary genius as a composer of ragtime music." That same year saw the publication of "Peacherine Rag" and "The Easy Winners." His "Elite Syncopations" and "The Entertainer" of 1902 proved equally exciting, this last rag being revived in 1973 as background and theme music for the award-winning motion picture *The Sting*. A recording of the rag that year sold over a million copies and topped the charts as the #1 record for several weeks, seventy-one years after its initial publication (MCA 40174)!

For the 1904 St. Louis World's Fair, Joplin composed "The Cascades," which became well-known. Following his publisher to New York in June 1907, Joplin set up an office at 128 West Twenty-ninth Street in which to compose and arrange ragtime. He made his first New York sale to JOSEPH W. STERN and Company, which published his "Search Light Rag" and "Gladiolus Rag" that year. His masterpiece in the exceptional year of 1908 was "Fig Leaf Rag," and it was fitting that his mentor, John Stark, issued it. His "Maple Leaf" variation, "Sugar Cane," was published by the new Seminary Music Company of New York in 1908, as was his brilliant "Pine Apple Rag," later that year. This last tune was such a successful seller that two years later words were added to make a charming "rag song." Joplin was the first to create a syncopated tango instrumental, and his "Solace" of 1909 remains hauntingly beautiful. His thirty-eight rags constitute a major achievement in the history of popular music.

# Gus Kahn

Lyricist (b. Gustave Kahn, Coblenz, Germany, November 6, 1886; d. Beverly Hills, California, October 8, 1941). Kahn worked with such top Alleyites as EGBERT VAN ALSTYNE, WALTER DONALDSON, ISHAM JONES, RICHARD WHITING, TED FIO RITO, VINCENT YOUMANS, GEORGE and IRA GERSHWIN, HARRY AKST, SIGMUND ROMBERG, and ARTHUR JOHNSTON.

Kahn's family immigrated to Chicago from Germany around 1891. His first published song was written with composer (and his future wife) Grace LeBoy, 1908's "I Wish I Had A Girl." His first hit came seven years later with "Memories," with music by Van Alstyne, which was sung by concert tenor John Barnes Wells (Victor 17968). "Pretty Baby," from the next year, with music by Van Alstyne and Tony Jackson, was recorded by Billy Murray (Victor 18102). The 1921 "Ain't We Got Fun?" (written with Richard Whiting and Ray Egan) was a #1 hit for Van and Schenck (Columbia A-3412), as was his 1922 "Carolina in the Morning" (music by Walter Donaldson; Columbia A-3712). That same year, AL JOLSON sang "Toot Toot Tootsie" (written with Ernie Erdman and Dan Russo) in the show *Bombo* and made a hit recording (Columbia A-3705). 1924 was a very good year, with "Charley, My Boy" sung by EDDIE CANTOR (Columbia 182-D; music by Ted Fio Rito); "I'll See You in My Dreams," recorded by the composer leading the Ray Miller orchestra (Brunswick

2788); "Nobody's Sweetheart" (written with Elmer Schoebel and Billy Meyers), with Isham Jones and his orchestra (Brunswick 2578); and "The One I Love," with music by Isham Jones, performed by Al Jolson (Brunswick 2567).

1925 started with "Alone at Last," with the COON-SANDERS orchestra (Victor 19728), followed by "I Never Knew" (with music by Fio Rito) by GENE AUSTIN (Victor 19864). Two big hits came with "baby" numbers written with composer Walter Donaldson: "Yes, Sir, That's My Baby," again by Gene Austin, a #1 hit (Victor 19656), and "I Wonder Where My Baby Is Tonight," by Henry Burr and Billy Murray (Victor 19864). They were followed by another Kahn-Donaldson hit, "That Certain Party," recorded by Dan Russo and Ted Fio Rito's Oriole Orchestra (Victor 19917). 1927 brought PAUL WHITEMAN's version of "Chloe" (Victor 35921), which SPIKE JONES revived in 1945 with vocal by Red Ingle (Victor 20-1654). 1928 was a great year, with "Love Me or Leave Me" by RUTH ETTING (Columbia 1680-D) and "Makin' Whoopee," introduced and recorded by Eddie Cantor (Victor 21831), both written for the show *Whoopee!*, in which Cantor and Etting appeared. Kahn wrote the songs, and frequent collaborator Donaldson contributed the music.

The 1930s continued to be kind to Kahn. 1931 saw "Dream a Little Dream of Me," recorded by Wayne King for a #1 hit (Victor 22643). In 1933, Kahn moved to Hollywood, collaborating with Vincent Youmans on the FRED ASTAIRE-GINGER ROGERS vehicle *Flying Down to Rio*. Kahn continued to write prolifically for film musicals through the 1930s. In 1934 Grace Moore introduced and recorded the #1 hit "One Night of Love," from the movie of the same name (Brunswick 6994). His last hit came in 1941, from the film *Ziegfeld Girl*, and Kay Kyser's orchestra, with vocal by Harry Babbitt, recorded "You Stepped Out of a Dream" (Columbia 35946), with music by NACIO HERB BROWN. Kahn died in the autumn of 1941, and a decade later his life story was told in the biopic *I'll See You in My Dreams*, starring Danny Thomas as Kahn and DORIS DAY as his wife, Grace LeBoy.

# Roger Wolfe Kahn

Bandleader (b. Morristown, New Jersey, October 19, 1907; d. New York City, July 12, 1962). Kahn came from a well-to-do background, and his band catered to New York's upper crust. He had a marvelous dance band from the mid-1920s up to World War II. During that time, he was also an aviation consultant and test pilot. He cocomposed "Crazy Rhythm" and "Imagination" for the 1928 musical *Here's Howe*, and recorded both (Victor 21368). He also recorded his 1927 compositions "All by My Ownsome" (Victor 20808) and "Following You Around" (Victor 20573). His hit recordings include the 1925 "Hot-Hot-Hottentot" (Victor 19616) and "A Cup of Coffee, a Sandwich, and You" (Victor 19935), 1926's "Mountain Greenery" (Victor 20071); and 1928's "She's a Great, Great Girl," with a neat Jack Teagarden solo (Victor 21326). In 1927, "Russian Lullaby" was a #1 hit (Victor 20602), and in 1928, so was "Let a Smile Be Your Umbrella" (Victor 21233). The Depression cut back on Kahn's work, and in 1932 he made his last recording. He focused on his other career as a test pilot thereafter.

# Bert Kalmar

See *Harry Ruby*

# Art Kassell

Bandleader and composer (b. Chicago, Illinois, January 18, 1896; d. Los Angeles, California, February 3, 1965). Kassell was a bandleader active primarily in Chicago in the 1920s, working the local hotels. He is best remembered for two hits, "Sobbin' Blues" (1922), written with drummer Vic Berton and initially recorded by the Benson Orchestra (Victor 19130) and Albert E. Short's Tivoli Syncopators (Vocalion 14600), and "Doodle Doo Doo" (1924), with lyrics by Mel Stitzel, which became his band's theme song and was a hit for EDDIE CANTOR. BENNY GOODMAN briefly played clarinet with the band in the early 1920s, as did other young Chicago jazzmen, including Jimmy McPartland and Bud Freeman. Kassell's band was typical of the dance-oriented groups of the era.

# Benjamin F. Keith

Producer, owner of a vaudeville theater chain, and head of largest vaudeville talent agency (b. 1846; d. 1914 [dates unknown]). When he opened his first vaudeville palace in 1893, he became known as the "father of vaudeville." Like Tony Pastor before him, he opened his theater to women and children. He was so successful that he created a chain of theaters on the East Coast, in partnership with E. F. Albee (and thus the chain became known as the Keith-Albee theaters). The jewel among his theaters was the Palace Theatre in New York City. Here, as in lowercase palaces around the country, a star singer introduced new songs, and with her personality (most of the leading vaudeville singers in the 1890s were women) imbued songs with unique personal qualities to "put them over." As Tony Pastor once wrote, "The ultimate success of these songs depends very largely on the person who sings them." If the chemistry were right between the singer and the song, the audience bought the sheet music.

# Jerome Kern

Composer (b. New York City, January 27, 1885; d. New York City, November 11, 1945). Musical theater in the United States wended its way from the burlesques of WEBER AND FIELDS, the VICTOR HERBERT shows set in some far-off European country, the brashness of the GEORGE M. COHAN musicals, and the resplendent revues of the extravagant Ziegfeld. What was wanted next was a musical show with a strong story line as its base, with songs adding either to the plot or to the characters' personalities to move the show along (but keeping plenty of dancing girls in pretty costumes to gladden the hearts of the audience).

Kern, working with librettist Guy Bolton (1884–1979) and lyricist P. G. WODEHOUSE, would permanently change the face of America's musical theater during this time in the Alley's history. The new team created a new type of musical comedy, on a smaller scale than the overblown imported operettas that dominated the Broadway scene. The Princess Theatre, located on Thirty-ninth Street between Sixth Avenue and Broadway, the home of these productions, had only 299 seats. The shows produced there dealt exclusively with contemporary American subjects in intimate productions. Frank Sadler orchestrated most of these scores in a light and lighthearted manner, using an orchestra of eleven instruments, far fewer than the standard Broadway pit orchestra of the time. Above all, the songs were integrated with the plot and could advance the action because the size of the theater and orchestra allowed the lyrics to be heard clearly. Bolton's stories were amusing and artfully clever. Wodehouse was the first important literate lyricist of the American musical stage. If IRVING BERLIN set the standard for pop tunes during the Alley's golden age, then Jerome Kern did the same for show tunes and theater, and film songs of his time.

Jerry, as he was called, saw his first musical show when he was ten years old. It was Victor Herbert's *The Wizard of the Nile* (November 4, 1895). Legend has it that when he came home, he sat down at the piano and played the score from memory. This show surely gave him the incentive to compose for the theater. After high school, he studied at the New York College of Music, and to earn extra money and learn the business, he worked after school at JOSEPH W. STERN's jobbing plant as a bookkeeper, since the main publishing house didn't have a vacancy at the time. In September 1902, Stern's subsidiary, the Lyceum Publishing Company, issued Kern's first number, a reverie titled "At the Casino." Like many other famous composers' first works, this one didn't create much of a stir. So Kern went to Europe for a year's further study. Upon his return in 1904, he attracted the attention of T. B. HARMS's publishing head, MAX DREYFUS, who was at that time producing imported British and European operettas. One result of Kern's new association with that firm was that he was asked to interpolate his own numbers when these shows were presented on Broadway, to "Americanize" them. His first such interpolation was "Wine, Wine!" in *An English Daisy* (January 18, 1904). In *Mr. Wix of Wickham* (September 19, 1904), Kern had four numbers, "Angling by the Babbling Brook" being the most memorable. It wasn't until a year later that he had his first real hit in "How'd You Like to Spoon with Me?" Georgia Caine sang it in *The Earl and the Girl* (November 4, 1905). It was so successful that it was also used the following year in *The Rich Mr. Hoggenheimer* (October 22, 1906).

During a short stay in London, Kern was asked by American producer Charles Frohman to freshen up Frohman's latest production there, *The Beauty of Bath* (1906). The starring actor-manager Seymour Hicks added Pelham Grenville Wodehouse to the show as lyricist and verse writer for the princely sum of £2 a week. For this production, Hicks particularly wanted a show-stopping comic song with several additional choruses for encores. Wodehouse's first meeting with Kern took place at the Aldwych Theatre, where Kern, in his shirtsleeves, was playing poker with several of the actors. "When I finally managed to free him from the card table and was able to talk to him," Wodehouse recalled, "I became impressed. Here, I thought, was a young man supremely confident of himself—the kind of person who inspires people to seek him out when a job must be done." Between them, the composer and the lyricist came up with a song called "Mr. Chamberlain," about the prime minister and his then-topical protective tariff policy. When the show opened at the Aldwych on March 19, 1906, the number proved to be everything that Hicks had hoped for, not only stopping the show but also taking London by storm. Had there been pop charts in London in those days, this song would have been at the top. The pleasant Kern-Wodehouse association wasn't to resume for another ten years, when it would produce revolutionary results. For the next six years, Kern would interpolate songs in thirty-five musicals, in both New York and London, with no major hits.

His first chance to do a complete score for Broadway came when he was called to work on *The Red Petticoat* (November 13, 1912). The best thing about this flop show was a song Kern slipped in called "The Ragtime Restaurant." His second complete score was *Oh, I Say!* (October 30, 1913), from which the nicely syncopated number "Katy-did" foretold his happiest efforts in *Leave It to Jane*. The following year he enjoyed his second big hit, "You're Here and I'm Here," originally in *The Laughing Husband* (February 2, 1914) and then put into the post-Broadway tour of *The Marriage Market* (New York opening, September 22, 1913), where Donald Brian sang it to further popularity. IRENE and VERNON CASTLE added it to the touring version of *The Sunshine Girl* (New York opening, February 3, 1913) and turned it into a fox-trot showcase. LEO FEIST purchased it from Harms and fully exploited it, placing it in six different Broadway shows. Most show songs appeared only once, in the show for which originally written. Feist's professional manager worked overtime to get this number featured in those productions. The nearest a pop song came to this record was in 1925, when SHAPIRO, BERNSTEIN's man interpolated "If You Knew Susie" into five Broadway musicals.

*The Girl from Utah* (August 24, 1914) sported seven interpolated numbers by Kern. One of them, "They Didn't Believe Me," became the first of his songs to sell two million copies of sheet music. It has remained a classic. Four more shows found music interpolated by Kern before managers F. Ray Comstock and Elisabeth (Bessie) Marbury took over the Princess Theatre and turned the productions there into small, two-set shows with small casts and orchestras. When Kern was approached to help create such a show, he informed Marbury that he and Guy Bolton had just completed exactly the thing. Comstock and Marbury produced *Nobody Home* (April 20, 1915), and it was at the opening night that Kern ran into his friend "Plum" Wodehouse in the lobby. Wodehouse was there to see the show as a reviewer for *Vanity Fair*, a magazine "Devoted to Society and the Arts." At a party at his home later in the evening, Kern invited his former partner to join him again in creating shows. Wodehouse accepted, and was duly introduced to Guy Bolton. A classic three-way friendship and collaboration was set to begin.

In addition to writing occasional lyrics for shows, Wodehouse was fast becoming a world-famous humorist, writing extremely funny short stories and novels appearing in the *Saturday Evening Post*, *Collier's*, and *Cosmopolitan*. The second Princess show, written by Kern and Bolton, was titled *Very Good Eddie* (December 23, 1915) and contained the hit song "Babes in the Wood."

*Have a Heart* (January 11, 1917) was billed as "The Up-to-the-Minute Musical Comedy" and was the first to be written by what a *New York Times* drama critic called "the trio of musical fame: Bolton and Wodehouse and Kern." Bolton and Wodehouse fashioned a funny story around which melodious songs were written, most notably "And I Am All Alone" and "You Said Something." The funniest number was sung by comedian Billy B. Van, whose interpretation of "Napoleon" secured Wodehouse's reputation as a humorous lyricist. His renown as the first great theater lyricist was confirmed later when lyricist Howard Dietz wrote in a letter to Wodehouse, quoted in my biography of the lyricist, "Over the years I have held [Wodehouse] as the model of light verse in the song form." And RICHARD RODGERS wrote in a letter to me, "Before Larry Hart, only P. G. Wodehouse had made any assault on the intelligence of the song-listening public." In partial answer to what made the trio's Princess shows so influential throughout the 1920s, Kern wrote: "It is my opinion that the musical numbers should carry the action of the play, and should be representative of the personalities of the characters who sing them."

The trio didn't have time to rest, for Comstock and Marbury wanted a replacement for *Eddie* at the Princess. They complied with *Oh, Boy!* which opened on February 20, 1917, and ran for a record 475 performances. In addition to "Ain't It a Grand and Glorious Feeling?," "Nesting Time in Flatbush," and "You Never Knew About Me," it had Kern's favorite of all his songs, "Till the Clouds Roll By," the title MGM used for his screen biography.

The team next adapted George Ade's play *The College Widow* and turned it into *Leave It to Jane* (August 28, 1917). The score is Kern's happiest, filled with charming and gay melodies, matched superbly by master lyricist Wodehouse. In addition to the title song, "The Crickets Are Calling," "Just You Watch My Step," "The Sun Shines Brighter," "Wait Till Tomorrow," and "The Siren's Song" highlighted the show. The big comic numbers were "Sir Galahad" and "Cleopatterer."

*The Riviera Girl* (September 24, 1917) featured one Kern interpolation with Wodehouse lyrics, inspired by the place on Long Island where Wodehouse was then living, "The Bungalow in Quogue" (rhymes with Patchogue).

On November 5, 1917, a revue called *Miss 1917* was presented by Charles Dillingham and Florenz Ziegfeld, with half the numbers written by Kern and Wodehouse, the other half written by Victor Herbert and Wodehouse. The one song to last was Kern's "The Land Where the Good Songs Go."

The last Princess show written by the trio was *Oh Lady! Lady!!* (February 1, 1918). This show ran 219 performances and, prior to its Broadway opening, contained "Bill," one of the all-time classic theater songs, later to become part of *Show Boat*. "Before I Met You," "When the Ships Come Home," and "You Found Me and I Found You" were part of this important score. Of this show Dorothy Parker wrote: "Well, Bolton and Wodehouse and Kern have done it again. Every time these three gather together, the Princess Theatre is sold out for months in advance. . . . I like the way they go about musical comedy. I like the way the action slides casually into the songs. I like the deft rhyming of the song that is always sung in the last act by two comedians and a comedienne."

GEORGE GERSHWIN, VINCENT YOUMANS, RICHARD RODGERS, IRA GERSHWIN, and LORENZ HART were all captivated by what they saw and heard at the Princess. They admitted by word and deed that the shows written by this "trio of musical fame" inspired them, and they tried to imitate the Princess shows in form and spirit. Kern's work had a profound effect on theater music for years to come.

*The Night Boat* (February 2, 1920) contained "Left All Alone Again Blues" and the sprightly "Whose Baby Are You?," both written with new lyricist Anne Caldwell. In time, she would become the most successful woman writer in Broadway musical history.

Kern's *Sally* (December 21, 1920) contained a blockbuster book by Guy Bolton, and outstanding songs such as "The Church 'Round the Corner," with lyrics by Wodehouse and Clifford Grey, and "Look for the Silver Lining" and "Whip-Poor-Will," both with lyrics by B. G. DESYLVA. An interpolated Wodehouse lyric was another historical funny, "You Can't Keep a Good Girl Down (Joan of Arc)." The show ran a fantastic 570 performances.

In *Good Morning, Dearie* (November 1, 1921) Kern's "Ka-lu-a" gave him his biggest hit since "Look for the Silver Lining." The lyrics were by Anne Caldwell, but what was memorable about the song was its insistent bass line. It was so memorable, in fact, that FRED FISHER successfully sued Kern for using it, claiming Kern had lifted it from "Dardanella" (1919), which Fisher had written and published. Although it was not uncommon to sue over stolen tunes, here was a unique instance in which a bass line was considered as important as a melody.

*Sitting Pretty* (April 8, 1924) united the trio one more time. The score was a good one and featured "Bongo on the Congo." That song made a deep impression on Ira Gershwin, who wrote during a later period of self-doubt: "I was still not completely satisfied with my contribution. I was bothered by there being no lyric I considered comic . . . Up to then I'd often wondered if I could do a comedy trio like the ones P. G. Wodehouse came up with—'Bongo on the Congo' from *Sitting Pretty*, for instance." Also in that score was "When It's Apple Blossom Time in Sing-Sing," which parodied the 1912 hit "When It's Apple Blossom Time in Normandie." Wodehouse may have recalled his and Kern's earlier parody from *Oh, Boy!*, "(When It's) Nesting Time in Flatbush."

*Sunny* (September 22, 1925) was written with OTTO HARBACH and OSCAR HAMMERSTEIN II. The score contained over twenty songs, but only "Who?" had a life after the show. It sold over a million copies of sheet music and, when revived in a 1937 recording by TOMMY DORSEY and his orchestra, sold over a million records. The reason for the success of Hammerstein's lyric was his choice of the word "who" to sustain the opening note for five beats. It was a word that had enough interest to be repeated and held five times during the chorus.

*Show Boat* (December 27, 1927), with Oscar Hammerstein's book based on Edna Ferber's novel, created the modern form of the musical play, distinct from operetta and the musical comedies of the time. It was the first musical to deal with adult themes in an intelligent fashion, as it followed the lives of two couples from the 1880s through the 1920s. The score was Kern's greatest endeavor, and Hammerstein's lyrics fitted the music perfectly. The songs include the classics "Ol' Man River," "Can't Help Lovin' Dat Man," "Make Believe," "Why Do I Love You," "You Are Love," and "Bill." This last song had been written by P. G. Wodehouse for Vivienne Segal to sing in *Oh, Lady! Lady!!* (February 1, 1918), but was dropped during out-of-town tryouts when it was found to be unsuitable for her voice. Since it was a situation song, it had to be featured where it would be pertinent to the plot. Nine years later, it found a home in *Show Boat*, and HELEN MORGAN immortalized it. The show was a complete success, the third longest-running Broadway show of the 1920s, completing 572 performances and then touring for an entire year. Its London production (1928) ran for 350 performances, with Paul Robeson singing "Ol' Man River." *Show Boat* has been revived by major companies many times over the years, most notably on Broadway in 1946, for a run of 418 performances. (It was for this revival that Kern wrote his last song, "Nobody Else but Me.") A 1971 revival in London's West End ran for 910 performances! It has had three film versions made of it (in 1929, 1936, and 1951). The show has become one of the few popular entertainments for all time.

*Sweet Adeline* (September 3, 1929) contained only one hit, "Why Was I Born?" The show was a nostalgic look at the Gay Nineties. The Wall Street crash put a premature end to the production, since most of the theatergoing public had lost much of its disposable income. *The Cat and the Fiddle* (October 15, 1931), called "A Musical Love Story," included the ballad "The Night Was Made for Love" and the coquettish "She Didn't Say Yes," both with lyrics by Otto Harbach. *Music in the Air* (November 8, 1932), with lyrics by Oscar Hammerstein, was another of Kern's musical plays with a European setting. The two hits from this show were "I've Told Ev'ry Little Star" and "The Song Is You."

*Roberta* (November 18, 1933) was a reversion to the more typical musical show. The lyrics were by Otto Harbach, and the story was about a fashion designer. There were the classics "Yesterdays," "The Touch of Your Hand," and the ever-popular "Smoke Gets in Your Eyes." But when Kern first presented this last song, with its dramatic sweep of melodic line, nobody (especially the actress Tamara, for whom it was written) cared much for it, because Kern had written it in a quick march tempo. When he saw the cast's reaction during rehearsal, he recast it, putting it in a more romantic mood to suit the glamorous Tamara, who stopped the show with it nightly. (Incidentally, *Roberta* was Bob Hope's first Broadway musical.)

Kern's film work up to 1935 consisted of his adapting *Show Boat*, *Sally*, *Sunny*, *The Cat and the Fiddle*, *Sweet Adeline*, *Music in the Air*, and *Roberta* for the screen. With *Roberta* (1935), the screen version was superior to the show, using most of the original Broadway score (rare in Kern's previously filmed shows). It included two new songs that became hits:

"Lovely to Look At" and "I Won't Dance," featuring one of FRED ASTAIRE's phenomenal tap routines.

Kern devoted the last part of his career to composing ten original scores for films. *I Dream Too Much* (1935) was his first original film score, but it wasn't an auspicious beginning. The only song to attain a modicum of popularity was the lilting "Jockey on the Carousel."

*Swing Time* (1936), on the other hand, with lyrics by DOROTHY FIELDS, contained an absolutely superb score. In fact, it was to be regarded as the best that Kern would write for Hollywood. The film starred FRED ASTAIRE and GINGER ROGERS and followed their greatest movie, *Top Hat*, with IRVING BERLIN's richest Hollywood score. Kern's music was especially well integrated with the plot and made the movie a stand-out. This new Kern-Fields collaboration brought "A Fine Romance," "Never Gonna Dance," and Kern's first Academy Award winner, "The Way You Look Tonight."

With three original film scores in a row producing very little that was memorable (*High, Wide and Handsome* [1937], *When You're in Love* [1937], and *The Joy of Living* [1938]), Kern decided to do another Broadway show with OSCAR HAMMERSTEIN II. They called it *Very Warm for May* (May 17, 1939). It was to be Kern's last for Broadway, and it wasn't successful. However, one of his best songs and one of the all-time classic melodies, "All the Things You Are," came from this show (which was made into a film called *Broadway Rhythm* in 1943). This great song is the most frequent answer given by fellow composers to the two questions, "What song do you wish you had written?" and "Which song do you most admire?"

*Lady Be Good* (1941) was a Hollywood version of the Gershwin brothers' 1924 Broadway show. Into it was interpolated a Kern song he composed out of affection for his friend Oscar Hammerstein, who had written a set of lyrics soon after the Nazis captured Paris in June 1940. They had no thought of using "The Last Time I Saw Paris" in any show or film (KATE SMITH had introduced it on the radio), but it fit in this film, with Ann Sothern's poignant rendition. For it, Kern won his second Oscar (after some controversy, since the song hadn't been written expressly for the film). Kern also felt he should not have won, going so far as to say that HAROLD ARLEN's "Blues in the Night" should have, and that the Academy should change its rules so that only songs composed expressly for films could be eligible. The Academy did this, but only after Kern had accepted his award.

*Cover Girl* (1944) starred Rita Hayworth and Gene Kelly, and paired Kern with lyricist Ira Gershwin for the only time in their careers. The film's best song and another classic, "Long Ago and Far Away," started out with the title "Midnight Music." Gershwin was a slow worker, and his procrastination infuriated Kern. So when Kern became impatient for a lyric for this tune, instead of venting his spleen, he merely sent Gershwin a dummy lyric beginning, "Watching little Alice pee . . . " This, wrote Kern biographer Gerald Bordman, made Gershwin ashamed of his slothfulness, and he immediately wrote the classic that was to become his largest royalty producer, including all of the songs written with his brother George.

*Can't Help Singing* (1944) paired Kern with E. Y. HARBURG, who was usually Harold Arlen's collaborator. It gave Deanna Durbin the best song she would ever sing in a film, "More and More," which made the *Hit Parade* for fifteen weeks, the last of the Kern songs to become a hit in his lifetime. *Centennial Summer* (1946) was the last film for which Kern wrote an original score. Two hits emerged: "In Love in Vain," with lyrics by LEO ROBIN, and "All Through the Day," written with Oscar Hammerstein. Although both made the *Hit Parade* (thirteen and twenty weeks, respectively), they did so after Kern's death.

*Till the Clouds Roll By,* MGM'S tribute to Kern, was a spectacular "biography," including fourteen stars and featuring nearly one hundred of his songs, most as background music only. This lavish musical was written by long-time librettist Guy Bolton, who invented an interesting "life" for his old collaborator, one more in the series of Hollywood biographies that bore no relation to their subjects' actual lives.

## American Published Songs by Jerome D. Kern

"Abe Lincoln Had Just One Country" (1941), *Hayfoot Strawfoot* (show)
"Aida McCluskie" (1908), *Fluffy Ruffles* (show)
"Ain't It a Grand and Glorious Feeling?" (1917), *Oh, Boy* (show)
"Ain't It Funny What a Difference Just a Few Drinks Make?" (1916), *Ziegfeld Follies* (show)
"Alice in Wonderland" (1915), *The Girl from Utah* (show)
"All Full of Talk" (1916), *Little Miss Springtime* (show)
"All I Want Is You" (1906), *My Lady's Maid* (show)
"All in Fun" (1939), *Very Warm For May* (show)
"All Lanes Must Reach a Turning" (1924), *Dear Sir* (show)
"All the Things You Are" (1939), *Very Warm for May* (show)
"All the Things You Are" (1940), *Very Warm for May* (show)
"All the World Is Swaying" (1918), *Head over Heels* (show)
"All Through the Day" (1946), *Centennial Summer* (film)
"All You Need Is a Girl" (1924), *Sitting Pretty* (show)
"Allegheny Al" (1937), *High, Wide and Handsome* (film)
"Alone at Last" (1913), *Oh, I Say* (show)
"And I Am All Alone" (1916), *Have a Heart* (show)
"And Love Was Born" (1932), *Music in the Air* (show)
"And Russia Is Her Name" (1943)
"Angling by a Babbling Brook" (1904), *Mr. Wix of Wickham* (show)
"Another Little Girl" (1915), *Nobody Home* (show)
"Any Moment Now" (1944), *Can't Help Singing* (film)
"Any Old Night Is a Wonderful Night" (1915), *Nobody Home* (show)
"Anything May Happen Any Day" (1930), *Ripples* (show)
"April Fooled Me" (1959)
"Armful of Trouble" (1933), *Gowns by Roberta* (show)
"At That San Francisco Fair" (1915), *Nobody Home* (show)
"At the Casino" (1902)
"Babes in the Wood" (1915), *Very Good Eddie* (show)
"Babes in the Wood Fox Trot" (1916), *Very Good Eddie* (show)
"Baby Vampire" (1917), *Love o' Mike* (show)
"Back in My Shell" (1940), *One Night in the Tropics* (film)
"Bagpipe Serenade" (1905), *The Rich Mr. Hoggenheimer* (show)
"Ballooning" (1907), *Fascinating Flora* (show)
"Be a Little Sunbeam" (1917), *Oh, Boy* (show)
"Before I Met You" (1918), *Oh, Lady! Lady!!* (show)
"Big Show" (1918), *Head over Heels* (show)
"Big Spring Drive" (1918), *Rock-a-Bye Baby* (show)
"Bill" (1918), *Oh, Lady! Lady!!* (show)
"Bill" (1927), *Show Boat* (show)
"Bill's a Liar" (1907), *White Chrysanthemum* (show)
"Blue, Blue" (1906), *The Rich Mr. Hoggenheimer* (show)
"Blue Bulgarian Band" (1910), *King of Cadonia* (show)
"Blue Danube Blues" (1921), *Good Morning, Dearie* (show)
"Bob White" (1920), *The Night Boat* (show)
"Bohemia" (1912), *The Girl from Montmartre* (show)
"Bojangles of Harlem" (1936), *Swing Time* (film)
"Bongo on the Congo" (1924), *Sitting Pretty* (show)
"Bought and Paid For" (1914), *The Laughing Husband* (show)
"Bread and Butter" (1926), *Criss-Cross* (show)
"Bring 'Em Back" (1921), *Hitchy Koo of 1920* (show)
"Buggy Riding" (1920), *Hitchy Koo of 1920* (show)
"Bull Frog Patrol" (1919), *She's a Good Fellow* (show)
"Bungalow in Quogue" (1917), *The Riviera Girl* (show)

"Business of Our Own" (1919), *Zip, Goes a Million* (show)
"By the Blue Lagoon" (1909), *The Girl and the Wizard* (show)
"By the Country Stile" (1913), *The Marriage Market* (show)
"Bygone Days" (1912), *The Polish Wedding* (show)
"Californ-i-ay" (1945), *Can't Help Singing* (film)
"Call Me Flo" (1912), *A Winsome Widow* (show)
"Can I Forget You" (1937), *High, Wide and Handsome* (film)
"Can't Help Lovin' Dat Man" (1927), *Show Boat* (show)
"Can't Help Singing" (1945), *Can't Help Singing* (film)
"Catamarang" (1909), *King of Cadonia* (show)
"Chaplin Walk" (1915), *Nobody Home* (show)
"Cheer Up! Girls" (1907), *The Dairymaids* (show)
"Chick! Chick! Chick!" (1920), *The Night Boat* (show)
"Chorus Girl" (1905)
"Church 'Round the Corner" (1920), *Sally* (show)
"Cinderella Girl" (1926), *Criss-Cross* (show)
"Cinderella Sue" (1946), *Centennial Summer* (film)
"Cleopatterer" (1917), *Leave It to Jane* (show)
"Come Along, Pretty Girl" (1909), *King of Cadonia* (show)
"Come Around on Our Veranda" (1907), *The Orchid* (show)
"Come On Over Here" (1912), *The Woman Haters* (show)
"Come On Over Here" (1913), *The Doll Girl* (show)
"Come, Tiny Goldfish, to Me" (1910), *Our Miss Gibbs* (show)
"Coo-oo-Coo-oo" (1909), *King of Cadonia* (show)
"Cover Girl" (1944), *Cover Girl* (film)
"Crickets Are Calling" (1917), *Leave It to Jane* (show)
"Cupid, the Winner" (1920), *Hitchy Koo of 1920* (show)
"Daisy" (1917), *Have a Heart* (show)
"Day Dreaming" (1941)
"De Goblin's Glide" (1911), *La Belle Paree* (show)
"Dear Old Prison Days" (1918), *Oh, Lady! Lady!!* (show)
"Dearly Beloved" (1942), *You Were Never Lovelier* (film)
"Didn't You Believe?" (1921), *Good Morning, Dearie* (show)
"Ding Dong, It's Kissing Time" (1920), *Hitchy Koo of 1920* (show)
"Dining Out" (1908), *Fluffy Ruffles* (show)
"Don't Ask Me Not to Sing" (1931), *The Cat and the Fiddle* (show)
"Don't Ever Leave Me" (1929), *Sweet Adeline* (show)
"Don't Tempt Me" (1917), *Love o' Mike* (show)
"Don't Turn My Picture to the Wall" (1912), *The Girl from Montmartre* (show)
"Don't You Want a Paper, Dearie?" (1906), *The Rich Mr. Hoggenheimer* (show)
"Don't You Want to Take Me?" (1920), *The Night Boat* (show)
"Down on the Banks of the Subway" (1919), *The Rose of China* (show)
"Downcast Eye" (1904), *English Daisy* (show)
"Dream a Dream" (1925), *Sunny* (show)
"Drift With Me" (1916), *Love o' Mike* (show)
"D'ye Love Me?" (1925), *Sunny* (show)
"Each Pearl a Thought" (1913), *Oh, I Say* (show)
"Eastern Moon" (1907), *The Morals of Marcus* (show)
"Easy Pickin's" (1921), *Good Morning, Dearie* (show)
"Edinboro Wiggle" (1911), *La Belle Paree* (show)
"Eight Little Girls" (1910), *Our Miss Gibbs* (show)
"Enchanted Train" (1924), *Sitting Pretty* (show)
"Eulalie" (1909), *Kitty Grey* (show)
"Evening Hymn" (1905)
"Every Day" (1917), *Oh, Boy* (show)
"Every Day in Every Way" (1922), *The Bunch and Judy* (show)
"Every Girl I Meet" (1909), *King of Cadonia* (show)
"Every Girl in All America" (1918), *Toot-Toot* (show)
"Everybody Calls Me Little Red Riding Hood" (1923), *The Stepping Stones* (show)
"Ev'ry Little While" (1932)
"Fan Me with a Movement Slow" (1911), *The Kiss Waltz* (show)
"Fine Romance" (1936), *Swing Time* (film)
"First Rose of Summer" (1919), *She's a Good Fellow* (show)
"Folks Who Live on the Hill" (1937), *High, Wide and Handsome* (film)
"Follow Me 'Round" (1911), *The Siren* (show)
"Forever and a Day" (1941
"Forget-Me-Not" (1919), *Zip, Goes a Million* (show)
"Frantzi" (1909), *The Girl and the Wizard* (show)
"Frieda" (1908), *The Girls of Gottenberg* (show)
"From Saturday to Monday" (1904), *Mr. Wix of Wickham* (show)
"Funny Little Something" (1918), *Head over Heels* (show)
"Funny Old House" (1945)
"Gay Lothario" (1908), *A Waltz Dream* (show)

"Ginger Town" (1919), *She's a Good Fellow* (show)
"Girlie" (1918), *Toot-Toot* (show)
"Girls in the Sea" (1920), *Hitchy Koo of 1920* (show)
"Give a Little Thought to Me" (1919), *Zip, Goes a Million* (show)
"Gloria's Romance" (1916), *Gloria's Romance* (film)
"Go, Little Boat" (1917), *Miss 1917* (show)
"Good Morning, Dearie" (1921), *Good Morning Dearie* (show)
"Good Night Boat" (1920), *The Night Boat* (show)
"Greenwich Village" (1918), *Oh, Lady! Lady!!* (show)
"Gypsy Caravan" (1924), *Dear Sir* (show)
"Happy Wedding Day" (1919), *She's a Good Fellow* (show)
"Have a Heart" (1916), *Ziegfeld Follies of 1916* (show)
"Have a Heart" (1916), *Have a Heart* (show)
"Have You Forgotten Me? Blues" (1922), *The Bunch and Judy* (show)
"Hay-Ride" (1907), *The Dairymaids* (show)
"He Is the Type" (1925), *The City Chap* (show)
"He Must Be Nice to Mother" (1912), *The Polish Wedding* (show)
"He'll Be There" (1904
"Head over Heels" (1918), *Head over Heels* (show)
"Head over Heels Fox-Trot" (1919), *Head over Heels* (show)
"Heart for Sale" (1920), *The Night Boat* (show)
"Heaven in My Arms" (1939), *Very Warm for May* (show)
"Heavenly Party" (1938), *Joy for Living* (film)
"Here Am I" (1929), *Sweet Adeline* (film)
"High, Wide and Handsome" (1937), *High, Wide and Handsome* (film)
"Hippopotamus" (1910), *King of Cadonia* (show)
"Home Sweet Home" (1919), *A New Girl* (show)
"Honeymoon Inn" (1916), *Have a Heart* (show)
"Honeymoon Land" (1917), *Toot-Toot* (show)
"Honeymoon Lane" (1913), *Sunshine Girl* (show)
"Hoop-La-La, Papa" (1912), *The Girl from Montmartre* (show)
"Hot Dog!" (1922), *The Bunch and Judy* (show)
"How Do You Do, Katinka?" (1922), *The Bunch and Judy* (show)
"How'd You Like to Spoon with Me?" (1905), *The Earl and the Girl* (show)
"Howdy! How D'You Do?" (1909), *The Golden Widow* (show)
"I Am So Eager" (1932), *Music in the Air* (show)
"I Believed All They Said" (1918), *Rock-a-Bye Baby* (show)
"I Can't Forget Your Eyes" (1913), *Oh, I Say!* (show)
"I Can't Say You're the Only One" (1908), *The Girls of Gottenberg* (show)
"I Don't Want You to Be a Sister to Me" (1910), *Our Miss Gibbs* (show)
"I Dream Too Much" (1935), *I Dream Too Much* (film)
"I Got Love" (1935), *I Dream Too Much* (film)
"I Have the Room Above" (1936), *Show Boat* (film)
"I Just Couldn't Do Without You" (1907), *The White Chrysanthemum* (show)
"I Know and She Knows" (1913), *Oh, I Say* (show)
"I Love the Lassies" (1920), *The Night Boat* (show)
"I Might Fall Back on You" (1928), *Show Boat* (film)
"I Never Thought" (1918), *Rock-a-Bye Baby* (show)
"I Saw the Roses and Remembered You" (1923), *The Stepping Stones* (show)
"I Still Suits Me" (1936), *Show Boat* (film)
"I Want My Little Gob" (1919), *She's a Good Fellow* (show)
"I Want to Be There" (1924), *Dear Sir* (show)
"I Want to Sing in Opera" (1910), *The Siren* (show)
"I Was Alone" (1930), *Sunny* (film)
"I Was Lonely" (1918), *Head over Heels* (show)
"I Watch the Love Parade" (1931), *The Cat and the Fiddle* (show)
"I Will Knit a Suit O' Dreams" (1917), *Toot-Toot* (show)
"I Wonder" (1912), *Look Who's Here!* (show)
"I Wonder Why" (1916), *Love o' Mike* (show)
"I Won't Dance" (1935), *Roberta* (film)
"I'd Like a Lighthouse" (1920), *The Night Boat* (show)
"I'd Like to Have a Million in the Bank" (1915), *Very Good Eddie* (show)
"I'd Like to Meet Your Father" (1907), *The Dairy Maids* (show)
"I'd Love to Dance Through Life with You" (1915), *A Modern Eve* (show)
"I'd Much Rather Stay at Home" (1908), *A Waltz Dream* (show)
"If" (1918), *Toot-Toot* (show)
"If I Find the Girl" (1915), *Very Good Eddie* (show)
"If the Girl Wants You" (1909), *Kitty Grey* (show)
"If Mr. Ragtime Ever Gets into That War" (1916)
"If We Were on Our Honeymoon" (1913), *The Doll Girl* (show)
"If You Only Care Enough" (1918), *Toot-Toot* (show)
"If You Think It's Love, You're Right" (1924), *Dear Sir* (show)

"If You Would Only Love Me" (1912), *Mind the Paint Girl* (show)
"I'll Be Hard to Handle" (1933), *Roberta* (show)
"I'll Be Waiting 'Neath Your Window" (1912), *The Girl from Montmartre* (show)
"I'm a Crazy Daffydil" (1911), *Ziegfeld Follies of 1911* (show)
"I'm Alone" (1932), *Music in the Air* (show)
"I'm Going to Find a Girl" (1917), *Leave It to Jane* (show)
"I'm Looking for an Irish Husband" (1913), *The Marriage Market* (show)
"I'm Old-Fashioned" (1942), *You Were Never Lovelier* (film)
"I'm So Busy" (1916), *Have a Heart* (show)
"I'm the Echo" (1935), *I Dream Too Much* (film)
"I'm the Human Brush" (1911), *La Belle Paree* (show)
"I'm the Old Man in the Moon" (1917), *Miss 1917* (show)
"I'm Well Known" (1907), *The Orchid* (show)
"In a Shady Bungalow" (1903)
"In Araby with You" (1926), *Criss-Cross* (show)
"In Arcady" (1915), *Nobody Home* (show)
"In Egern on the Tegern See" (1932), *Music in the Air* (show)
"In Love in Vain" (1946), *Centennial Summer* (film)
"In Love with Love" (1923), *The Stepping Stones* (show)
"In Other Words, Seventeen" (1939), *Very Warm for May* (show)
"In the Heart of the Dark" (1939), *Very Warm for May* (show)
"In the Valley of Montbijou" (1911), *The Siren* (show)
"Introduce Me" (1959)
"Isn't It Great to Be Married" (1915), *Very Good Eddie* (show)
"It Can't Be Done" (1916), *Love o' Mike* (show)
"It Wasn't My Fault" (1916), *Love o' Mike* (show)
"It's a Great Big Land" (1917), *Leave It to Jane* (show)
"It's a Hard, Hard World" (1918), *Oh Lady! Lady!!* (show)
"It's Delightful" (1971)
"I've a Little Favor" (1907), *The Rich Mr. Hoggenheimer* (show)
"I've a Million Reasons Why I Love You" (1907), *The Dairy Maids* (show)
"I've Been Waiting for You All the Time" (1919), *She's a Good Fellow* (show)
"I've Got Money in the Bank" (1913), *The Marriage Market* (show)
"I've Got to Dance" (1915), *Very Good Eddie* (show)
"I've Just Been Waiting for You" (1915), *A Modern Eve* (show)
"I've Taken Such a Fancy to You" (1912), *The Girl from Montmartre* (show)
"I've Told Ev'ry Little Star" (1932), *Music in the Air* (show)
"Jockey on the Carousel" (1935), *I Dream Too Much* (film)
"Journey's End" (1922), *The City Chap* (show)
"Jubilo" (1919), *She's a Good Fellow* (show)
"Just a Little Line" (1919), *She's a Good Fellow* (show)
"Just Because You're You" (1917), *Ziegfeld Follies of 1917* (show)
"Just Good Friends" (1909), *Kitty Grey* (show)
"Just Let Me Look at You" (1938), *Joy of Living* (film)
"Just You Watch My Step" (1917), *Leave It to Jane* (show)
"Ka-Lu-A" (1921), *Good Morning, Dearie* (show)
"Katy-Did" (1913), *Oh, I Say!* (show)
"Katy Was a Business Girl" (1907), *Fascinating Flora* (show)
"Keep Your Rabbits, Rabbi" (1920)
"Kettle Song" (1918), *Rock-a-Bye Baby* (show)
"Kiss a Four Leaf Clover" (1926), *Criss-Cross* (show)
"Land of 'Let's Pretend' " (1914), *The Girl from Utah* (show)
"Land Where the Good Songs Go" (1917), *Miss 1917* (show)
"Language of Love" (1919), *Zip, Goes a Million* (show)
"Last Time I Saw Paris" (1940), *Lady Be Good* (film)
"Leave It to Jane" (1917), *Leave It to Jane* (show)
"Left All Alone Again Blues" (1920), *The Night Boat* (show)
"Lena, Lena" (1910), *King of Cadonia* (show)
"Let Us Build a Little Nest" (1912), *A Polish Wedding* (show)
"Let Us Build a Little Nest" (1918), *Head over Heels* (show)
"Let's Go" (1918), *Toot-Toot* (show)
"Letter Song" (1919), *She's a Good Fellow* (show)
"Life upon the Wicked Stage" (1928), *Show Boat* (film)
"Lifelong Love Affair" (1971)
"Little Back Yard Band" (1919), *Zip, Goes a Million* (show)
"Little Billie" (1916), *Gloria's Romance* (film)
"Little Bit of Silk" (1913), *The Marriage Market* (show)
"Little Bungalow in Quogue" (1917), *The Riviera Girl* (show)
"Little Church Around the Corner" (1907), *Fascinating Flora* (show)
"Little Eva" (1907), *The Dairy Maids* (show)
"Little Golden Maid" (1912), *The Red Petticoat* (show)
"Little Love" (1915), *Miss Information* (show)
"Little Thing Like a Kiss" (1913), *The Doll Girl* (show)

"Little Tune, Go Away" (1918), *Rock-a-Bye Baby* (show)
"Lonely Feet" (1934), *Sweet Adeline* (film)
"Lonesome Walls" (1939), *Mamba's Daughters* (show)
"Long Ago and Far Away" (1944), *Cover Girl* (film)
"Look for the Silver Lining" (1920), *Sally* (show)
"Look in Her Eyes" (1913), *Lieber Augustin* (show)
"Look Me Over, Dearie" (1911), *La Belle Paree* (show)
"Lorelei" (1921), *Sally* (show)
"Love and the Moon" (1922), *Rose Briar* (show)
"Love Is Like a Rubber Band" (1911), *The Kiss Waltz* (show)
"Love Is Like a Violin" (1914), *The Laughing Husband* (show)
"Lovely to Look At" (1935), *Roberta* (film)
"Love's Charming Art" (1911), *The Kiss Waltz* (show)
"Lullaby" (1918), *Rock-a-Bye Baby* (show)
"Magic Melody" (1915), *Nobody Home* (show)
"Make Believe" (1927), *Show Boat* (show)
"Make Way for Tomorrow" (1944), *Cover Girl* (film)
"Man Around the House" (1919), *Zip, Goes a Million* (show)
"Manicure Girl" (1910), *The Henpecks* (show)
"Mary McGee" (1907), *The Dairy Maids* (show)
"McGuire Esquire" (1904)
"Meet Her with a Taximeter" (1908), *Fluffy Ruffles* (show)
"Meet Me at Twilight" (1906), *The Little Cherub* (show)
"Mind the Paint" (1912), *Mind the Paint Girl* (show)
"Mr. and Mrs. Rorer" (1924), *Sitting Pretty* (show)
"Mitzi's Lullaby" (1918), *Head over Heels* (show)
"Molly o'Hallerhan" (1905), *The Catch of the Season* (show)
"Moments of the Dance" (1918), *Head over Heels* (show)
"Moon of Love" (1920), *Hitchy Koo of 1920* (show)
"Moon Song" (1918), *Oh, Lady! Lady!!* (show)
"More and More" (1944), *Can't Help Singing* (film)
"Morning Glory" (1922), *The Bunch and Judy* (show)
"Mother and Father" (1910), *King of Cadonia* (show)
"Mrs. Cockatoo" (1908), *Fluffy Ruffles* (show)
"My Boy" (1918), *Rock-a-Bye Baby* (show)
"My Castle in the Air" (1916), *Miss Springtime* (show)
"My Celia" (1904), *The Silver Slipper* (show)
"My Heart I Cannot Give to You" (1911), *The Siren* (show)
"My Hungarian Irish Girl" (1906), *The Rich Mr. Hoggenheimer* (show)
"My Lady of the Nile" (1916), *Ziegfeld Follies of 1916* (show)
"My Lady's Dress" (1921), *Good Morning, Dearie* (show)
"My Otaheitee Lady" (1912), *The Amazons* (show)
"My Peaches and Cream" (1912), *Look Who's Here* (show)
"My Southern Belle" (1905), *The Earl and the Girl* (show)
"Napoleon" (1916), *Have a Heart* (show)
"Nesting Time" (1917), *Oh, Boy* (show)
"Never Gonna Dance" (1936), *Swing Time* (film)
"Never Marry a Girl with Cold, Cold Feet" (1907), *The Dairy Maids* (show)
"New Love Is Old" (1931), *The Cat and the Fiddle* (show)
"Niagara Falls" (1921), Good Morning Dearie (show)
"Nice to Be Near" (1959)
"Night Was Made for Love" (1931), *The Cat and the Fiddle* (show)
"No One Knows" (1925), *The City Chap* (show)
"No Question in My Heart" (1968)
"Nobody Else but Me" (1946), *Show Boat* (show)
"Nodding Roses" (1916), *Very Good Eddie* (show)
"Not Here! Not Here!" (1909), *The Dollar Princess* (show)
"Not Yet" (1918), *Oh Lady! Lady!!* (show)
"Not You" (1918), *Rock-a-Bye Baby* (show)
"Nothing at All" (1908), *The Girls of Gottenberg* (show)
"Now That We Are One" (1968)
"Nursery Fanfare" (1918), *Rock-a-Bye Baby* (show)
"Oh, Lady! Lady!!" (1918), *Oh Lady! Lady!!* (show)
"Oh, Mr. Chamberlain" (1905), *The Catch of the Season* (show)
"Oh, Promise Me You'll Write to Him Today" (1918), *The Canary* (show)
"Oh, You Beautiful Person" (1919), *She's a Good Fellow* (show)
"Oh, You Beautiful Spring" (1912), *The Red Petticoat* (show)
"Ol' Man River" (1927), *Show Boat* (show)
"Old Bill Baker" (1916), *Very Good Eddie* (show)
"Old Boy Neutral" (1916), *Very Good Eddie* (show)
"Old-Fashioned Wife" (1917), *Oh, Boy* (show)
"Old Town" (1920), *Hitchy Koo of 1920* (show)
"On a Desert Island with You" (1924), *Sitting Pretty* (show)
"On the Beam" (1942), *You Were Never Lovelier* (film)
"On the Sands of Wa-ki-ki" (1915), *Miss Information* (show)

"On the Shore at Le Lei Wi" (1916), *Very Good Eddie* (show)
"On with the Dance" (1920), *Sally* (show)
"Once in a Blue Moon" (1923), *The Stepping Stones* (show)
"Once There Were Two of Us" (1968)
"One Moment Alone" (1931), *The Cat and the Fiddle* (show)
"One More Dance" (1932), *Music in the Air* (show)
"One-Two-Three" (1918), *Rock-a-Bye Baby* (show)
"Ooo, Ooo, Lena" (1912), *The Girl from Montmartre* (show)
"Our Little Nest" (1918), *Oh, Lady! Lady!!* (show)
"Our Lovely Rose" (1923), *The Stepping Stones* (show)
"Our Song" (1937), *When You're in Love* (film)
"Out of the Blue" (1929), *Sweet Adeline* (show)
"Package of Seeds" (1917), *Oh, Boy* (show)
"Pal Like You" (1917), *Oh, Boy* (show)
"Pale Venetian Moon" (1922), *The Bunch and Judy* (show)
"Paris Is a Paradise for Coons" (1911), *La Belle Paree* (show)
"Peach Girl" (1922), *The Bunch and Judy* (show)
"Peach of a Life" (1917), *Leave It to Jane* (show)
"Peaches" (1917), *Miss 1917* (show)
"Pick Yourself Up" (1936), *Swing Time* (film)
"Picture I Want to See" (1917), *Miss 1917* (show)
"Pie" (1923), *The Stepping Stones* (show)
"Plain Rustic Ride" (1906), *The Little Cherub* (show)
"Poker Love" (1906), *The Rich Mr. Hoggenheimer* (show)
"Polly Believed in Preparedness" (1916), *Have a Heart* (show)
"Poor Pierrot" (1931), *The Cat and the Fiddle* (show)
"Poor Prune" (1917), *Leave It to Jane* (show)
"Put Me to the Test" (1944), *Cover Girl* (film)
"Raggedy Ann" (1923), *The Stepping Stones* (show)
"Ragtime Restaurant" (1912), *The Red Petticoat* (show)
"Raining" (1905), *The Catch of the Season* (show)
"Recipe" (1906), *The Rich Mr. Hoggenheimer* (show)
"Reckless" (1935), *Reckless* (film)
"Remind Me" (1940), *One Night in the Tropics* (film)
"Right Now" (1907), *Fascinating Flora* (show)
"Rip Van Winkle and His Little Men" (1920), *The Night Boat* (show)
"Road That Lies Before" (1916), *Have a Heart* (show)
"Road That Lies Before" (1917), *Have a Heart* (show)
"Rolled into One" (1917), *Oh, Boy* (show)
"Rose-Marie" (1921), *Good Morning, Dearie* (show)
"Sally" (1921), *Sally* (show)
"Same Sort of Girl" (1914), *The Girl from Utah* (show)
"Saturday Till Monday" (1904), *Mr. Wix of Wickham* (show)
"Saturday Night" (1916), *Miss Springtime* (show)
"Schnitza Komisski" (1921), *Sally* (show)
"Shadow of the Moon" (1924), *Sitting Pretty* (show)
"She Didn't Say Yes" (1931), *The Cat and the Fiddle* (show)
"Shine Out, All You Little Stars" (1910), *The Gay Hussars* (show)
"Shorty George" (1942), *You Were Never Lovelier* (film)
"Shufflin' Sam" (1924), *Sitting Pretty* (show)
"Simple Little Tune" (1917), *Love o' Mike* (show)
"Since the Days of Grandmama" (1912), *The Red Petticoat* (show)
"Sing Song Girl" (1921), *Good Morning, Dearie* (show)
"Sing Trovatore" (1911), *La Belle Paree* (show)
"Sir Galahad" (1917), *Leave It to Jane* (show)
"Siren's Song" (1917), *Leave It to Jane* (show)
"Sitting Pretty" (1924), *Sitting Pretty* (show)
"Smoke Gets in Your Eyes" (1933), *Roberta* (show)
"Society" (1915), *Cousin Lucy* (show)
"Some Little Girl" (1918), *Oh Lady! Lady!!* (show)
"Some One" (1916), *Miss Springtime* (show)
"Some Party" (1919), *She's a Good Fellow* (show)
"Some Sort of Somebody" (1915), *Miss Information* (show)
"Something Had to Happen" (1933), *Roberta* (show)
"Song Is You" (1932), *Music in the Air* (show)
"Ssh—! You'll Waken Mister Doyle" (1913), *When Claudia Smiles* (show)
"Star of Hitchy Koo" (1920), *Hitchy Koo of 1920* (show)
"Stepping Stones" (1923), *The Stepping Stones* (show)
"Subway Express" (1907), *Fascinating Flora* (show)
"Sun About to Rise" (1929), *Sweet Adeline* (show)
"Sun Shines Brighter" (1917), *Leave It to Jane* (show)
"Sun Starts to Shine Again" (1918), *Oh, Lady! Lady!!* (show)
"Sunny" (1925), *Sunny* (show)
"Sunshine" (1925), *Sunny* (show)
"Sure Thing" (1944), *Cover Girl* (film)
"Susan" (1904), *Mr. Wix of Wickham* (show)
"Susie" (1926), *Criss-Cross* (show)
"Suzette and Her Pet" (1909), *The Girl and the Wizard* (show)

"Sweetest Girl, Silly Boy, I Love You" (1908), *Fluffy Ruffles* (show)
"Sweetest Sight That I Have Seen" (1945)
"Sweetest Things in Life" (1924), *Peter Pan* (show)
"Sweetie" (1920), *Hitchy Koo of 1920* (show)
"Swing Your Sweetheart" (1945), *Can't Help Singing* (film)
"Sympathetic Someone" (1925), *The City Chap* (show)
"Ta Ta, Little Girl" (1911), *The Kiss Waltz* (show)
"Take a Chance, Little Girl" (1918), *The Canary* (show)
"Take a Step with Me" (1914), *The Laughing Husband* (show)
"Take Care" (1908), *Fluffy Ruffles* (show)
"Take Me on the Merry-Go-Round" (1905), *Catch of the Season* (show)
"Teacher, Teacher" (1919), *She's a Good Fellow* (show)
"Teepee" (1918), *Toot-Toot* (show)
"Telephone Girls" (1919), *Zip, Goes a Million* (show)
"Tell Me All Your Troubles, Cutie" (1917), *Miss 1917* (show)
"That Little Something" (1927), *Lucky* (show)
"That Lucky Fellow" (1939), *Very Warm for May* (show)
"That Peculiar Tune" (1916)
"That's All Right for McGilligan" (1911), *La Belle Paree* (show)
"There Is a Happy Land" (1911), *Little Miss Fix-It* (show)
"There It Is Again" (1917), *Leave It to Jane* (show)
"There's a Hill Beyond a Hill" (1932), *Music in the Air* (show)
"There's a Resting Place for Every Girl" (1911), *The Kiss Waltz* (show)
"There's No Better Use for Time Than Kissing" (1918), *Rock-a-Bye Baby* (show)
"There's Something Rather Odd About Augustus" (1908), *Fluffy Ruffles* (show)
"They All Look Alike" (1916), *Have a Heart* (show)
"They Didn't Believe Me" (1914), *The Girl from Utah* (show)
"Things I Want" (1937), *High, Wide and Handsome* (film)
"Thirteen Collar" (1915), *Very Good Eddie* (show)
"Those Come Hither Eyes" (1915), *Cousin Lucy* (show)
"Till the Clouds Roll By" (1917), *Oh, Boy* (show)
"Toddle" (1921), *Good Morning, Dearie* (show)
"Too Many Faces" (1971)
"Touch of Your Hand" (1933), *Roberta* (show)
"Try to Forget" (1931), *The Cat and the Fiddle* (show)
"Tulip Time in Sing-Sing" (1924), *Sitting Pretty* (show)
"Tulips" (1905), *The Catch of the Season* (show)
"Turkey Trot" (1911), *Little Miss Fix-It* (show)
"'Twas Not So Long Ago" (1929), *Sweet Adeline* (show)
"Two Heads Are Better Than One" (1915), *Cousin Lucy* (show)
"Two Hearts Are Better Than One" (1946), *Centennial Summer* (film)
"Two Little Bluebirds" (1925), *Sunny* (show)
"Under the Linden Tree" (1907), *The Little Cherub* (show)
"Up with the Lark" (1946), *Centennial Summer* (film)
"Vienna" (1908), *A Waltz Dream* (show)
"Waiting Around the Corner" (1918), *Oh Lady! Lady!!* (show)
"Waiting for You" (1904), *Mr. Wix of Wickham* (show)
"Walking Home with Josie" (1925), *The City Chap* (show)
"Waltz in Swing Time" (1936), *Swing Time* (film)
"Way Down Town" (1921), *Good Morning, Dearie* (show)
"Way You Look Tonight" (1936), *Swing Time* (film)
"We Belong Together" (1932), *Music in the Air* (show)
"We Were So Young" (1934), *Sweet Adeline* (film)
"Wedding Bells Are Calling Me" (1915), *Very Good Eddie* (show)
"Wedding in the Spring" (1942), *You Were Never Lovelier* (film)
"Weeping Willow Tree" (1924), *Dear Sir* (show)
"We'll See" (1916), *Love O' Mike* (show)
"We'll Take Care of You All" (1915), *The Girl from Utah* (show)
"We're Crooks" (1917), *Miss 1917* (show)
"We're Going to Be Pals" (1917), *Oh, Boy* (show)
"What I'm Longing to Say" (1917), *Leave It to Jane* (show)
"What's Good About Good-Night?" (1938), *Joy of Living* (film)
"Wheatless Day" (1918), *Oh Lady! Lady!!* (show)
"When a New Star" (1943), *Hayfoot, Strawfoot* (show)
"When I Discover My Man" (1920), *The Charm School* (show)
"When I Fell in Love with You" (1925), *The City Chap* (show)
"When the Bo-Tree Blossoms Again" (1927), *Lucky* (show)
"When the Lights Are Low" (1916), *Ziegfeld Follies of 1916* (show)
"When the Ships Come Home" (1918), *Oh, Lady! Lady!!* (show)
"When the Spring Is in the Air" (1932), *Music in the Air* (show)

"When Three Is Company" (1913), *The Doll Girl* (show)
"When You Wake Up Dancing" (1918), *Toot-Toot* (show)
"When You're in Love, You'll Know" (1916), *Go to It* (show)
"Where's the Boy for Me?" (1915)
"Where's the Girl for Me?" (1915), *The Lady in Red* (show)
"Whip-Poor-Will" (1919), *Zip, Goes a Million* (show)
"Whip-Poor-Will" (1920), *Sally* (show)
"Whistle When You're Lonely" (1910), *The Echo* (show)
"Whistling Boy" (1937), *When You're in Love* (film)
"Who?" (1925), *Sunny* (show)
"Who Cares?" (1916), *Love o' Mike* (show)
"Whose Baby Are You?" (1920), *The Night Boat* (show)
"Why?" (1917), *Leave It to Jane* (show)
"Why Do I Love You?" (1927), *Show Boat* (show)
"Why Don't They Dance the Polka Anymore?" (1914), *The Girl from Utah* (show)
"Why Was I Born?" (1929), *Sweet Adeline* (show)
"Wifie of Your Own" (1913), *Oh, I Say* (show)
"Wild Rose" (1920), *Sally* (show)
"Will It All End in Smoke?" (1913), *The Doll Girl* (show)
"Will You Marry Me Tomorrow, Maria?" (1937), *High, Wide and Handsome* (film)
"Windmill Under the Stars" (1942)
"Wine, Wine!" (1904), *English Daisy* (show)
"Without the Girl—Inside" (1907), *The Gay White Way* (show)
"Wonderful Dad" (1923), *The Stepping Stones* (show)
"Won't You Have a Little Feather?" (1907), *Peter Pan* (show)
"Won't You Kiss Me Once Before I Go?" (1905), *The Catch of the Season* (show)
"Won't You Let Me Carry Your Parcel?" (1908), *Fluffy Ruffles* (show)
"Words Are Not Needed" (1917), *Oh, Boy* (show)
"Worries" (1924), *Sitting Pretty* (show)
"Year from Today" (1924), *Sitting Pretty* (show)
"Yesterdays" (1933), *Roberta* (show)
"You and Your Kiss" (1940), *One Night in the Tropics* (film)
"You Are Love" (1928), *Show Boat* (show)
"You Can't Keep a Good Girl Down" (1920), *Sally* (show)
"You Couldn't Be Cuter" (1938), *Joy of Living* (film)
"You Found Me, and I Found You" (1918), *Oh, Lady! Lady!!* (show)
"You Know and I Know" (1915), *Nobody Home* (show)
"You Must Come Over" (1921), *Ziegfeld Follies of 1921* (show)
"You Never Can Tell" (1914), *The Girl from Utah* (show)
"You Never Knew About Me" (1917), *Oh, Boy* (show)
"You Never Spoke a Word" (1917)
"You Said Something" (1916), *Have a Heart* (show)
"You Tell 'Em" (1919), *Zip, Goes a Million* (show)
"You Were Never Lovelier" (1942), *You Were Never Lovelier* (film)
"You Will, Won't You?" (1926), *Criss-Cross* (show)
"Your Dream" (1940), *One Night in the Tropics* (film)
"You're Devastating" (1933), *Roberta* (show)
"You're Here and I'm Here" (1914), *The Laughing Husband* (show)
"You're the Only Girl He Loves" (1912), *The Polish Wedding* (show)

# King Oliver's Creole Jazz Band

Joe "King" Oliver (b. near Abend, Louisiana, May 11, 1885; d. Savannah, Georgia, April 8, 1938) assembled the first of the great black jazz bands in Chicago. He came from New Orleans, where he had played in Kid Ory's band. He left New Orleans permanently in 1918 and became popular with the Chicago public. He assembled his Creole Jazz Band in mid-1922 for a job at Lincoln Gardens on the South Side. He brought LOUIS ARMSTRONG to Chicago, and the band made its first recordings for Gennett Records in sessions from April 6 to October 5, 1923. The band consisted of King Oliver and Louis Armstrong, cornets; Honore Dutrey, trombone; Johnny Dodds, clarinet; Lil Hardin, piano; Bill Johnson, banjo; and Warren "Baby" Dodds, drums.

The Creole Jazz Band was the most popular band on the South Side at that time, and its two cornets playing at the same time created tremendous excitement. The amazing gift that Armstrong had of improvising a second cornet part to King Oliver's lead has never been duplicated. They ad-libbed duets!

As with the ORIGINAL DIXIELAND JAZZ BAND, the Creole Jazz Band's importance to the history of jazz lies in its contribution to jazz composition. The tunes were mostly composed by King Oliver, some with the help of Armstrong, others with Lil Hardin (later the second Mrs. Armstrong). Oliver's compositions included "Canal Street Blues," "Chimes Blues," "Dippermouth Blues," "Snake Rag," "Alligator Hop," "Zulu's Ball," and such later tunes as "Snag It," "West End Blues," and "Doctor Jazz." When MELROSE BROTHERS finally published "Dippermouth Blues" in 1926, its name was changed to "Sugar Foot Stomp." It was the first time the band's photo appeared on a sheet music cover.

# Ted Koehler

Lyricist (b. Washington, D.C., July 14, 1894; d. Santa Monica, California, January 17, 1973). Koehler began his career as a theater pianist, then produced floor shows in night clubs. He began his full-time songwriting career in the late 1920s. His first major collaborator was HAROLD ARLEN. He also wrote with RUBE BLOOM, SAMMY FAIN, HARRY BARRIS, RAY HENDERSON, and JIMMY MCHUGH. His first hit came in 1923 with "When Lights Are Low," which the Benson Orchestra of Chicago made famous (Victor 19198). His permanent songwriting career got off to a great start in 1930 with "Get Happy," when Nat Shilkret and the Victor Orchestra recorded it (Victor 22444). 1931 saw "Between the Devil and the Deep Blue Sea" and "Kickin' the Gong Around," from the revue *Rhyth-Mania*, as introduced in the show and on disc by CAB CALLOWAY and his orchestra (Brunswick 6209), as well as "Wrap Your Troubles in Dreams" which BING CROSBY helped promote to a standard (Victor 22701). 1932 brought "I Gotta Right to Sing the Blues," from *Earl Carroll's Vanities*, and "I've Got the World on a String," from the *Cotton Club Parade of 1932*, both hit recordings by Cab Calloway and his orchestra (Brunswick 6460 and 6424).

1933 saw Koehler's greatest hits: "Stormy Weather," from the *Cotton Club Parade*, as recorded by Leo Reisman and his orchestra, with vocal by Harold Arlen (Victor 24262), followed by ETHEL WATERS's definitive version and #1 hit (Brunswick 6564); "Stay on the Right Side of the Road" had Bing Crosby to sell it (Brunswick 6533); "Let's Fall in Love," the title song of the film starring Ann Sothern, was given a #1 recording by Eddy Duchin and his orchestra (Victor 24510). "Animal Crackers in My Soup," written for the 1935 Shirley Temple film *Curly Top*, was recorded by Don Bestor and his orchestra (Brunswick 7495). Koehler's last hit came in 1939, from the World's Fair edition of the *Cotton Club Parade*, when Hal Kemp and his orchestra, with vocal by Bob Allen, made a hit of "Don't Worry 'Bout Me" (Victor 26188). FRANK SINATRA revived it in 1954 (Capitol 2787). Koehler continued to write for the movies throughout the 1940s, then retired.

# Alex Kramer

Composer (b. Montreal, Canada, May 30, 1903; d. Fairfield, Connecticut, February 10, 1998). Kramer is best remembered for his collaborations with his wife, Joan Whitney (b. Pittsburgh, Pennsylvania, June 26, 1914; d. Westport, Connecticut, July 12, 1990), on a string of hits in the 1940s and 1950s. Kramer was trained at McGill Conservatory, and also worked on local radio as a pianist. He moved to the United States in the late 1930s, and soon after met Whitney, who was already establishing herself as a club singer. With Hy Zaret, the couple scored their first hits in 1941 with "My Sister and I," a #1 hit with fourteen weeks on the charts, and "It All Comes Back to Me Now," popularized by bandleaders Gene Krupa and Hal Kemp. Their first major hit came four years later with "Candy" (1944), written with lyricist Mack David, a #1 record for JOHNNY MERCER and Jo Stafford (Capitol 183); the same recording was used in the 1991 film *Bugsy*. In 1947, the couple wrote "Faraway Places," which was a hit for both BING CROSBY (Decca 24532) and Perry Como (RCA Victor 20-3316). They also formed their own publishing company that year. Further hits include recordings by Louis Jordan ("Ain't Nobody Here But Us Chickens," a 1946 #1 R and B hit), "Love Somebody" (a 1948 #1 hit for DORIS DAY, singing with bandleader Buddy Clark [Columbia 38174]), and "No Other Arms, No Other Lips" (written with Hy Zaret; revived by the Chordettes in 1959 for a Top 40 hit [Cadence 1361]).

# Helmy Kresa

Piano arranger (b. Meissen, Germany, November 7, 1904; d. Southampton, New York, August 19, 1991). His only hit was the 1931 "That's My Desire," which finally broke in 1947, thanks to Frankie Laine (Mercury 5007). Helmy Kresa is recognized as the premier

Helmy Kresa in the 1920s.

piano arranger and orchestrator, not only for Irving Berlin but for a list of songwriters who insisted that Kresa arrange their numbers on a freelance basis. The list of songwriters who used his services is a virtual "Who's Who" of Alley and Hollywood songwriters.

Kresa always worked out his arrangements in the key of C. Upon completion of an arrangement, he would then determine the actual key in which the song should be published, based upon the melodic range of the chorus (most girl singers with bands had ranges of an octave plus two notes). Although he worked quickly (most of his piano parts were completed in under an hour and a half), he caught the essential harmonies and voiced them in the most pleasing manner, making the songs fun to perform.

His favorite orchestration was the one he did for "God Bless America." Over the years, he made arrangements of Berlin's classic for every conceivable combination of instruments and vocal groups. Beginning with "Blue Skies" (1926), Kresa worked on every Berlin song for publication.

# L

## Burton Lane

Composer (b. Burton Levy, New York City, February 2, 1912; d. New York City, January 5, 1997). Lane studied piano as a child, then played various string instruments in his school's orchestra and also began composing. After finishing high school, he was hired by JEROME H. REMICK as a song plugger; there he met GEORGE GERSHWIN, who encouraged him to compose.

In 1929, Lane contributed songs to the Broadway revue *Three's a Crowd* (with lyricist HOWARD DIETZ), and then partnered with HAROLD ADAMSON to contribute songs to *Earl Carroll's Vanities of 1931*. Soon after, Lane traveled to Hollywood, where he wrote for a number of musicals. Again partnering with Adamson, Lane had a hit in 1933 with "Everything I Have Is Yours," written for Joan Crawford and Art Jarrett in the film *Dancing Lady*. It was revived by Billy Eckstine with a hit recording in 1949 (MGM 10259), and again by Monica Lewis in the film of the same name (1952). In 1939, Lane collaborated with lyricist FRANK LOESSER for "The Lady's in Love with You," for the Shirley Ross-Bob Hope film *Some Like It Hot*. GLENN MILLER and his orchestra made a memorable recording (Bluebird 10229). In 1941, Lane wrote "How About You?," with lyrics by Ralph Freed, for Mickey Rooney and JUDY GARLAND, who introduced it in their film *Babes on Broadway*. TOMMY DORSEY had a successful recording (Victor 27749), and the song was later used in the nonmusical film *Don't Bother to Knock* (1952). In 1951, Lane collaborated with ALAN JAY LERNER on the score for MGM's *Royal Wedding*, which brought forth the longest title of a pop song from the films,

"How Could You Believe Me When I Said I Love You, When You Know I've Been a Liar All My Life?"

After World War II, Lane returned to Broadway, partnering with E. Y. "Yip" Harburg, notably on 1947's *Finian's Rainbow*. The play produced several standards, including "How Are Things in Glocca Morra," which got a hit recording by Buddy Clark (Columbia 37223). After that success, however, Lane did not return to Broadway for eighteen years, when he collaborated again with Lerner in 1965 on the Broadway show *On a Clear Day You Can See Forever*, which produced the title song. The show was made into a 1970 film starring Barbra Streisand, who also sang the title song; it has since become a standard in her repertoire. Lane and Lerner paired again in 1968 for the musical *Carmelina*, a flop.

# Latin-American Dances

In the late 1930s, while the jitterbug and the fox-trot were still very popular, dancers began learning the rumba and samba, and many Latin songs were given English lyrics. "Green Eyes" (1929, 1941), by Nilo Menendez (d. September 25, 1987), with words by E. Rivera and E. Woods, sold over a million discs in the version by Jimmy Dorsey and his orchestra, with vocals by Helen O'Connell and Bob Eberly (Deccca 3698). "Frenesi" (1939), composed by Alberto Dominguez and written by Ray Charles and S. K. Russell, was popularized by Artie Shaw and his expanded orchestra in 1940, on a recording which sold over three million copies (Victor 26542). The early war years saw the rise of singer Carmen Miranda. Even Walt Disney got into the act with his animated feature *Saludos Amigos* (1942), which included "Brazil" and "Tico-Tico."

"Besame Mucho" (1941, 1943) was composed by Consuelo Velazquez with English lyrics by Sunny Skylar, and it was made famous by Jimmy Dorsey and his orchestra (Decca 18574). "Miami Beach Rumba" (1946) was composed by Irving Fields, with lyrics by Albert Gamse.

# Jack Lawrence

Lyrcist and composer (b. Brooklyn, New York, April 7, 1912). Lawrence is best remembered for a series of pop hits from the late 1930s through the 1950s. His first published song came in 1933 with "Play, Fiddle, Play" written with Arthur Altman, a composer Lawrence had met in grade school. In 1938, Lawrence provided lyrics for bandleader-pianist Frankie Carle's "Sunrise Serenade," which was used as Carle's band's theme (Columbia 37269). A year later, the Ink Spots had their first major hit with Lawrence's "If I Didn't Care" (Decca 2286), which remained on the *Hit Parade* for seven weeks. Also in 1939, Lawrence composed "All or Nothing at All," again working with Altman; FRANK SINATRA recorded it with Harry James's band shortly after, and when he became a teen idol on his own in 1943, Columbia reissued it as Sinatra's first "solo" record (Columbia 35587). Lawrence's 1940 composition "Yes, My Darling Daughter" was the first song sung by the new star DINAH SHORE when she debuted on EDDIE CANTOR's radio program. (She also recorded it on Bluebird 10920.)

During the war years, Lawrence headed a band to entertain soldiers at the Manhattan Beach Training Center in Brooklyn. His attorney, Lee Eastman, asked him to write a song for his five-year-old daughter, Linda, who was jealous of her sister Laura (who could point to the DAVID RAKSIN hit of the same title). The song went unrecorded until 1946, when it was a major hit for both Charlie Spivak's orchestra and Buddy Clark singing with RAY NOBLE's band. Linda Eastman would later become the well-known wife of Paul McCartney. In 1946, he wrote a lyric to pianist Walter Gross's instrumental that became the song "Tenderly." First recorded by Sarah Vaughan, it became a big hit when Rosemary Clooney revived it in 1955. Lawrence's 1948 song "Beyond the Sea" was revived twelve years later by teen popster Bobby Darin for a #6 pop hit (Atco 6158); it was Lawrence's last appearance on the pop charts.

# Turner Layton

African-American composer (b. John Turner Layton, Jr., Washington, D.C., July 2, 1894; d. London, England, February 6, 1978). Layton's father taught voice in Washington's public schools, holding the position of director of music for the district's "colored schools" beginning in 1895. His father also composed hymns and was active as director of the Metropolitan AME Church choir for forty years. Layton initially studied dentistry at Howard University, but left school to seek a career as a musician in New York. There, he met singer/lyricist Henry Creamer (b. Richmond, Virginia, June 21, 1879; d. New York City, October 14, 1930), and the two formed a partnership that began in 1917 and lasted until 1922. They wrote sixty-five songs together, with one of their biggest hits being "After You're Gone," which was introduced in early 1918 in the Broadway show *So Long, Letty*. However, it didn't become a hit until a decade later, following Besie Smith's 1927 recording, leading to covers by SOPHIE TUCKER (also 1927), PAUL WHITEMAN (1930), LOUIS ARMSTRONG (1932), and BENNY GOODMAN (1935). The duo continued to work together until 1922, with their second major hit being that year's "Way Down Yonder in New Orleans," introduced by the team in the musical revue *Spice of 1922*. Again it took a while for the tune to become successful, but it was finally launched in 1927 by Frankie Trumbauer's band recording, featuring cornetist Bix Beiderbecke (Okeh 40843). Fred Astaire and Ginger Rogers danced to it on film in 1939, Betty Hutton sang it in a film in 1952, Frankie Laine and Jo Stafford had a hit in 1953 (Columbia 40116), and Freddie Cannon made a million-selling recording of it in 1960 (Swan 4043).

Layton broke off with Creamer and formed a new partnership with Clarence "Tandy" Johnstone. In early 1924, the duo debuted as a performing act in Paris, and they soon became a sensation. They settled in London, where they spent the next decade, until Johnstone was named as a corespondent in a divorce case involving a white, classical musician. The scandal ended their partnership, and Johnstone returned to New York. Layton had a career into the early 1940s, but by the mid-1950s, he was out of the music business and running a pub.

# Lead Sheet

The notation of a melody line alone, sometimes with indication for harmony. Before a publisher commissioned an arranger to make a fully written-out score, he asked for a lead sheet, in case the songwriter forgot what he'd just written.

# Leeds Music Corp.

Music publishing company established in 1939 by Lou Levy (b. New York City, December 3, 1910; d. New York City, November 1, 1995). This was the first publishing company to exploit many different kinds of songs and the first to make many types commercially acceptable. Leeds continued to make hits into 1963, when it published "I Want to Hold Your Hand," before the Beatles were known in the United States.

Levy's motto was "Behind every great song is a greater song publisher." He was the era's most aggressive and, interestingly, best-liked publisher. He expressed his working philosophy this way: "If your competition is putting out blue dresses, you put out red ones." Levy acted upon that philosophy by publishing boogie-woogie when the other firms were publishing ballads. When they picked up on boogie, he put out polkas. When they took up polkas, Levy went to calypso. His folios of the works of Pete Johnson and Albert Ammons, for example, contained numbers that previously had been available only on their recordings.

Levy got more record performances for his songs than any other publisher of his time. Recordings generated a substantial income, thanks to the "mechanical royalty" clause in performance contracts, giving royalties to publishers as the owners of the songs' copyrights. Beginning in the mid-1920s, recording companies used microphones to catch sound, and records were clearer than those made by the old acoustic method of recording directly into a horn. The range of sound became wider, and more instruments could be heard fully than ever before. After World War II, when shellac became readily available, recordings started to bring more profits to the Alley than the sales of sheet music. Sheets remained a significant part of the business for another decade, but Levy was the first publisher to take advantage of record sales to fund the exploitation of unrecorded songs in his catalog.

As a young man, Levy was a champion dancer at Roseland in New York City, winning many contests to the music of Jimmy Lunceford's band. Later he became the manager of the ANDREWS SISTERS, eventually marrying Maxine. It was at a talent show in Harlem that he first heard "Bei Mir Bist du Schon," sung in Yiddish. Levy was convinced that the number could succeed if it had English lyrics. He persuaded his roommates, SAMMY CAHN and SAUL CHAPLIN, to write them, and he got the Andrews Sisters to record the song. It became a hit. Levy started Leeds Music to give the Sisters a repertoire. He looked for the offbeat song or style, and often found it. His energy as a plugger was legendary among his colleagues. His hired pluggers managed to get Leeds songs onto the *Sunday Enquirer*'s "Music Sheet List," the *Accurate Report*, and the *Peatman Report*, which listed every plug on radio in the New York metropolitan area. *Peatman* also graded the kinds of plugs, whether played on a local station or on the network, in a medley or alone.

Levy's first hit song was "Undecided." It was followed by "I'll Remember April," "All or Nothing at All," "He's My Guy," "For Sentimental Reasons," "The Gypsy," and "Now Is the Hour." When he took over the publication of "Heartaches," he made it a hit all over again. He loved novelties, and began issuing them with "She Had to Go and Lose It at the Astor." It was quickly followed by "Dry Bones," "He Plays the Horses," and "Open the Door, Richard!" His boogie hits included: "Beat Me, Daddy, Eight to the Bar," "Rhumboogie," "Boogie-Woogie Bugle Boy," and such hip numbers as "Well, All Right" and " 'Tain't What You Do." He had big hits with "Galway Bay" and "The Foggy, Foggy Dew." Along with such novelties as "Woody Woodpecker" and "The Old Piano Roll Blues," Levy popularized radio pianist-comedian Alec Templeton's satiric compositions: "Bach Goes to Town," "Mozart Matriculates," and "Undertaker's Toccata."

Considering the many song types that Levy exploited, it is startling to learn that his biggest-seller in sheet music was Stuart Hamblen's (1908–1989) religious song of 1950, "It Is No Secret." The same year, Levy also had success with Meredith Willson's "May the Good Lord Bless and Keep You."

It is not often that the personal taste of a publisher dictates a business decision, but when Levy purchased the J. W. Jenkins' Sons company, he did so because Jenkins owned his favorite blues number, RICHARD M. JONES's "Trouble in Mind" (1937), as well as the Phil Baxter (1896–1972) novelty "Piccolo Pete" (1929).

After acquiring Jenkins, CLARENCE WILLIAMS Music, and OLMAN Music, Levy created the Duchess and Pickwick music companies. He sold all of his companies to MCA, in 1969.

# Alan Jay Lerner

Lyricist and librettist (b. New York City, August 31, 1918; d. New York City, June 14, 1986). After graduating from Harvard University in 1940, Lerner came to New York and got a job at the Lord and Thomas advertising agency writing radio scripts, among them the amusing *Chamber Music Society of Lower Basin Street*, which featured Henry "Hot Lips" Levine and his Barefooted Philharmonic and Paul Lavalle and his Woodwindy Ten. Vocalists at different times on the program were DINAH SHORE, Linda Keene and Lena Horne. While working in radio, Lerner met FREDERICK LOEWE at the Lambs' Club in 1942. Thus began one of Broadway's most creative and successful partnerships.

Besides his work with Loewe, Lerner collaborated with KURT WEILL on the Broadway show *Love Life* (1948), which produced "Here I'll Stay" and "Green-up Time." Lerner's screenplay for *An American in Paris* (1951) won him an Academy Award. The same year he collaborated with BURTON LANE on the score for MGM's *Royal Wedding*, which brought forth the longest title of a pop song from the films, "How Could You Believe Me When I Said I Love You, When You Know I've Been a Liar All My Life?" They collaborated again in 1965 for the Broadway show *On a Clear Day You Can See Forever*, which produced the title song. It was Lerner's last major Broadway success.

Lerner and Loewe reunited briefly in 1973 to write songs for a new production of *Gigi* and the film *The Little Prince* (1974). Lerner teamed with Andre Previn in 1969 for the musical *Coco*, which succeeded thanks to a star performance by Katharine Hepburn, and then the ill-fated *1600 Pennsylvania Avenue*, with music by LEONARD BERNSTEIN, which opened and quickly closed in 1976. Lerner's last production, *Dance a Little Closer* (1983), written to showcase the talents of his last wife, actress Liz Robertson, closed after a single performance. He died of lung cancer in 1986, leaving several projects uncompleted.

# Edgar Leslie

Prolific lyricist of the 1920s and 1930s (b. Stamford, Connecticut, December 31, 1885; d. New York City, January 22, 1976). Leslie was raised in New York City, and at a young age began writing lyrics for vaudeville singers. He had his first published songs in 1909, including "Saide Salome," written with new composer IRVING BERLIN. Two years later, he partnered with composer LEWIS MUIR on three RAGTIME songs, "The Matrimony Rag" and the snappy "When Ragtime Rosie Ragged the Rosary," both hits on the vaudeville stage, and "Dancing

Dan, the Ragtime Battling Man." In 1915, singer EVA TANGUY scored a hit with the patriotic "America, I Love You," which Leslie wrote with composer Archie Gottlier. In 1917, Leslie cowrote the lyric for the enormously popular "For Me and My Gal" with E. RAY GOETZ to a melody by GEORGE W. MEYER. In 1919, Leslie partnered with lyricist Bert Kalmar and composer PETE WENDLING, producing four major hits: the two-million-selling "All the Quakers Are Shoulder Shakers Down in Quaker Town" and "Take Your Girlie to the Movies," and the million-selling "Oh! What a Pal Was Mary" and "Take Me to the Land of Jazz." In 1927, HARRY WARREN had his first hit, "Rose of the Rio Grande" (1922), which was cocomposed by Whiteman reed virtuoso Ross Gorman, with lyrics by Leslie. Naturally, Gorman's band, The Virginians, was the first to record it (Victor 19001). Warren and Leslie would pair up again, notably in 1931, providing "By the River Sainte Marie" to GUY LOMBARDO for a #1 hit in 1931 (Columbia 2401-D).

After moving to England in 1927, Leslie scored a big hit with "Among My Souvenirs," written with composer Horatio Nicholls (the publishing name of music executive Lawrence Wright) in 1928; the song would be a major hit again in 1959 for Connie Francis (MGM 12824). Leslie was back in the United States by the early 1930s; in 1931, along with BILLY ROSE and George W. Meyer, he formed the Songwriters Protective Association, the predecessor of the Songwriters Guild of America. Leslie made his last partnership with composer JOE BURKE. They enjoyed seven major hits during the 1930s, including four huge successes in 1935 alone, notably "Moon over Miami," a hit for TED FIO RITO and his orchestra. They scored again in 1936 with "Midnight Blue," an interpolation into *The New Ziegfeld Follies of 1936*, and "Robins and Roses," which BING CROSBY made famous (Decca 791). "It Looks Like Rain in Cherry Blossom Lane" (1937) was a big hit for Guy Lombardo (Victor 25572).

Leslie remained active in writing lyrics through the early 1940s, then turned his attention to managing his back catalog of songs.

# Lou Levy

See *Leeds Music Corp.*

---

# Sam M. Lewis

---

Lyricist (b. New York City, October 25, 1885; d. New York City, November 22, 1959). Lewis started his career singing in cafés, writing material for himself and later for VAN AND SCHENCK and Lew Dockstader. Although he started writing lyrics in 1912, it wasn't until he teamed with fellow lyricist JOE YOUNG that he began having hits. He worked with Young from 1916 to 1930. In the 1930s, he worked with GEORGE W. MEYER, WALTER DONALDSON, FRED AHLERT, RAY HENDERSON, HARRY WARREN, J. FRED COOTS, and others. In 1916, he cowrote "Where Did Robinson Crusoe Go with Friday on Saturday Night?," used in the musical *Robinson Crusoe, Jr.*, which AL JOLSON promoted into a hit (Columbia A-1976). In 1918, Jolson interpolated "Rock-a-Bye Your Baby with a Dixie Melody" into his show *Sinbad* (Columbia A-2560). The following year NORA BAYES made a hit of "How Ya Gonna Keep 'Em Down on the Farm" (Columbia A-2687). 1921 saw two hits, "Cry Baby Blues," with a super piano roll by JAMES P. JOHNSON (QRS 1673), and "Tuck Me to Sleep in My Old 'Tucky Home," with the Benson Orchestra of Chicago's instrumental (Victor 18820).

1925 was Lewis's biggest year. "Dinah" was featured in the *New Plantation Revue* by ETHEL WATERS, who had a hit disc (Columbia 487-D). BING CROSBY and THE MILLS BROTHERS revived "Dinah" in 1932 for a #1 hit (Brunswick 6240), as did FATS WALLER in 1936 (Victor 25471). "Five Foot Two, Eyes of Blue" was given a great instrumental treatment by Ernie Golden and his orchestra (Brunswick 2999), and Jane Gray sang it, accompanied by RUBE BLOOM (Harmony 114-H). "I'm Sitting on Top of the World" had three great instrumental arrangements: by ROGER WOLFE KAHN (Victor 19845), ISHAM JONES (Brunswick 3022); and The Ambassadors (Vocalion 15156). His 1926 hit was "In a Little Spanish Town." PAUL WHITEMAN's recording, with vocal by Jack Fulton, made a #1 hit (Victor 20266). 1927 saw "There's a Cradle in Caroline," recorded by Frankie Trumbauer's orchestra, featuring the cornet of Bix Beiderbecke (Okeh 40879). 1929 saw "I Kiss Your Hand, Madame" in a hit recording by Leo Reisman and his orchestra, with vocal by Ranny Weeks (Victor 21920). It was revived in 1948 by SPIKE JONES and His City Slickers (Victor 20-2949).

Lewis's career wound down in the 1930s, although he continued to have hits through the middle of the decade. His 1931 hit was "Just Friends" as sung by RUSS COLUMBO (Victor 22909). His 1934 hit was "For All We Know," which Hal Kemp and his orchestra recorded successfully (Brunswick 6947). His last big song, in 1935, was "I Believe in Miracles," which the Dorsey Brothers Orchestra made into a #3 charted hit (Decca 335), while Fats Waller's version reached #10 (Victor 24853).

# Ted Lewis

Bandleader, clarinet player, and composer (b. Theodore Leopold Friedman, Circleville, Ohio, June 6, 1892; d. New York City, August 25, 1971). Novelty-jazz bandleader Lewis originally performed as a clarinet soloist on the vaudeville circuit. He first played with Earl Fuller's Famous Jazz Band in 1917, and then formed his own band two years later. He was active in New York during the 1920s, appearing on radio and records, and in a number of Broadway revues, including several editions of the popular *Greenwich Village Follies* and *Ziegfeld Midnight Frolics*, in the early through mid-1920s. Lewis's band employed many top-notch jazzmen from time to time, including JIMMY DORSEY, George Brunies, and BENNY GOODMAN. His compositions included 1922's "Bees Knees," written with Ray Lopez (1889–1970), with words by Leo Wood (1882–1929), and Lewis's band made the first recording of this great syncopated fox-trot (Columbia A-3730). Among Lewis's other pop hits were 1920's "When My Baby Smiles at Me" (Columbia A-2908; revived as the theme song for a 1948 film of the same name, starring Dan Dailey and Betty Grable, and covered by BING CROSBY in 1956), 1925's "While We Danced 'Til Dawn," and his signature piece, "Is Everybody Happy Now?" written for the *Artists and Models* revue and recorded by the band for Columbia in 1927. His recordings also did much to make hits of songs by other composers, notably his popular version of IRVING CAESAR's "Just a Gigolo" (1930, Columbia 2378-D). In his heyday, Lewis was said to be Columbia's best-selling act. He continued to perform into the 1960s, largely as nostalgia.

# Sid Lippman

Composer (b. Minneapolis, Minnesota, March 1, 1914; d. North Bergen, New Jersey, March 11, 2003). He came to New York City with a scholarship to Juilliard and became a staff arranger at IRVING BERLIN, Inc. While there, he met Hal Dickenson, leader of The Modernaires, GLENN MILLER's vocal group. Dickenson needed a melody for some lyrics, and Lippman supplied it. "These Things You Left Me" (1940) became his first hit. Eddie Sauter made a superb arrangement for BENNY GOODMAN and his orchestra, with a vocal by Helen Forrest, for a best-selling recording (Columbia 35910). Another popular version was the one by Charlie Barnet and his orchestra, with a vocal by Bob Carroll (Bluebird 11004).

Lippman's main collaborator was lyricist Sylvia Dee (b. Josephine Proffitt Faison, Little Rock, Arkansas, October 22, 1914; d. New York City, June 12, 1967). Their first hit was "I'm Thrilled" (1941), which received a great Bill Finegan arrangement for Glenn Miller's orchestra (Bluebird 11287). The new team of Lippman and Dee stayed together for sixteen years. "Chickery Chick" (1945) was the team's successor to "Mairzy Doats." With nonsense syllables taken from an old folk song, it became immediately popular with children. Sammy Kaye and his orchestra (Victor 20-1726) and Gene Krupa and his orchestra, with vocalist Anita O'Day, (Columbia 36877), had two of several hit recordings.

"My Sugar Is So Refined" (1946) came about at a lunch one day when Dee looked at the wrapper on a sugar cube, which read "refined sugar." She remarked to Lippman, "Isn't that a cute idea?" JOHNNY MERCER thought so, too, and he had the hit recording (Capitol 268). *Barefoot Boy with Cheek* (April 3, 1947) was the team's only Broadway show. The hit song was "After Graduation Day."

" 'A' You're Adorable" (1948) had lyrics by Lippman's first collaborators, Buddy Kaye and Fred Wise. (The song was written several years before its publication.) The three would begin each work session by exchanging jokes. One was told about a man recommending a friend for a job by listing his qualifications alphabetically: A, he's amiable; B, he's benevolent; and so on. From this came the idea for the song. It was a hit for Jo Stafford and Gordon MacRae (Capitol 15393), and for Perry Como with the Fontane Sisters (RCA Victor 20-3381).

"Too Young" (1951) was Lippman and Dee's biggest song. It was introduced by Johnny Desmond, then recorded by Nat "King" Cole (Capitol 1449), whose disc sold over a million copies. "Too Young" was on the *Hit Parade* longer than any other song (twenty-seven weeks, in the #1 spot for twelve)! It is a great all-time standard. On her own, Dee wrote "The End of the World" with composer Arthur Kent, which was a major hit for Skeeter Davis in 1963 (RCA 8098).

# Livingston and Evans

(Jay Livingston, b. Jacob Harold Levison, McDonald, Pennsylvania, March 28, 1915; d. Los Angeles, California, October 17, 2001; Ray Evans, b. Raymond Bernard Evans, Salamanca, New York, February 4, 1915). Livingston studied piano and came to New York City in 1937 as a pianist and vocal arranger. He and his college roommate, Evans, who played saxophone, clarinet, and piano, went to Hollywood in 1944 to write for Paramount Pictures. Their first big hit was the title song for the film *To Each His Own* (1946). The best-selling recording, by Eddy Howard, sold over two million copies (Majestic 7188). The Ink Spots had a #1 hit recording (Decca 23615). The song also became a million-seller in sheet music and had a total record sale of three million. In 1961, it was revived by the Platters (Mercury 71697).

*The Paleface* (1948) starred Bob Hope and Jane Russell. They sang that year's Academy Award winner, "Buttons and Bows." Dinah Shore's record sold over a million copies (Columbia 38284). *Captain Carey, U.S.A.* (1950) gave the team their second Oscar, for "Mona Lisa." Nat "King" Cole's version sold over three million (Capitol 1010). *The Man Who Knew Too Much* (1956) provided them with their third Oscar. "Whatever Will Be, Will Be (Que Sera, Sera)" was introduced in the Alfred Hitchcock thriller by DORIS DAY. Her recording sold over a million copies (Columbia 40704). It was the first time a song was used in a Hitchcock film.

Jay Livingston (left) and Ray Evans in the 1960s.

*Tammy and the Bachelor* (1957) sported "Tammy," sung in the film by Debbie Reynolds. Her recording sold over a million copies (Coral 61851), which was not bad, considering the fact that over one hundred other artists also recorded the song, for a total sale of over ten million records. *Oh, Captain* (February 4, 1958) was the Broadway version of the Alec Guinness film *Captain's Pardise* (1953). "You're So Right for Me" was the hit of Livingston and Evans's charming score. Livingston and Evans were less active in the 1960s, primarily creating lyrics for film theme songs. They did write the classic *Mr. Ed* theme song, which Livingston sang for the famous TV talking horse. However, by 1970 the team had pretty much retired.

# Jerry Livingston

Composer (b. Jerome Levinson, Denver, Colorado, March 25, 1909; d. Beverly Hills, California, July 1, 1987). Livingston's father, Sam Levinson, traveled from Denver to New York at the age of nineteen, where he enjoyed a brief singing career. Returning to Denver, he established a family. Livingston began playing piano in local bands as a teenager. Around 1932, he settled in New York after playing a road job in Ohio, and began composing songs. By the late 1930s, he was heading his own band, and changed his name from the Jewish-sounding Levinson to the less ethnic Livingston. He also met singer Ruth Brent (b. Ruth Schwartz), who would become his wife. Walt Disney heard Livingston's novelty hit "Chi-Babba Chi-Babba (My Bambino Go to Sleep)," written with composer AL HOFFMAN and with lyrics by Mack David, and hired them to score his cartoon feature *Cinderella* (1950). The score included "Bibbidi, Bobbidi, Boo," "The Work Song," and "A Dream Is a Wish Your Heart Makes." Livingston's best-remembered song is "Mairzy Doats," also written with Al Hoffman, and with lyricist Milton Drake (b. 1916). The Merry Macs had the hit record (Decca 18588), and the sheet music sold at the rate of thirty thousand copies a day for over a month. Livingston continued to work in Hollywood through the early 1970s, composing TV themes such as "This Is It!," the opening number for *The Bugs Bunny Show* and finger-snapping themes for *77 Sunset Strip* and *Hawaiian Eye*, as well as scoring films such as *Cat Ballou.*

# Frank Loesser

Composer and lyricist (b. Frank Henry Loesser, New York City, June 29, 1910; d. New York City, July 28, 1969).

Loesser came from a musical family; his father taught piano, and his half brother was also a pianist and teacher. He briefly attended college and then worked in a variety of jobs through the 1920s, pursuing an interest in music on the side. He published his first song in 1931 but it wasn't until three years later that he had his first hit with "I Wish I Were Twins" (with colyricist EDDIE DE LANGE and music by JOSEPH MEYER); FATS WALLER had the hit on disc. Then, Loesser formed a partnership with Irving Actman, doing nightclub work, which led to a contract with Universal Pictures in 1937.

Loesser and Actman went to Hollywood, and soon Loesser was working with a variety of composers to produce a number of hits, including 1938's "Two Sleepy People," "Small Fry" (popularized by BING CROSBY) and "Heart and Soul," first popularized by Larry Clinton and his orchestra (all with music by HOAGY CARMICHAEL). The next year, he scored with "The Lady's in Love with You" (1939; music by BURTON LANE). "(I've Got Spurs That) Jingle, Jangle, Jingle" (1942; music by Joseph J. Lilley) came from the film *The Forest Rangers*. The hit recording came from Kay Kyser and his orchestra (Columbia 36604), which sold over a million copies. Loesser wrote the most popular World War II song, "Praise the Lord and Pass the Ammunition," the first song for which he wrote both lyrics and music; Kyser again had the hit recording. For the film *Christmas Holiday* (1944), Loesser wrote both words

Frank Loesser, c. the 1940s.

and music to "Spring Will Be a Little Late This Year." 1948 brought a top-ranking pop song, "On a Slow Boat to China," again with a Kay Kyser recording, with a vocal by Harry Babbitt and Gloria Wood (Columbia 38301), a million-seller.

Thereafter, Loesser would write both words and music, as he did for his first Broadway musical, *Where's Charley?* (October 11, 1948). The show was based on Brandon Thomas's 1892 farce, *Charley's Aunt*. It starred the remarkable dancer-comedian Ray Bolger, who made "Once in Love with Amy" his own (Decca 40065). In the show, Bolger pretended to forget the lyrics and had the audience sing along with him. It had been a long time since a star had planted a "stooge" in the theater to sing the chorus along with him, and the gimmick remained a high point of the show. "My Darling, My Darling" was the show's other hit, with DORIS DAY's recording selling over a million copies (Columbia 38353). For several weeks, this song alternated with "On a Slow Boat to China" at the top position on *Your Hit Parade*. It was for the *Where's Charley?* songs that Loesser established his own publishing business, Frank Music Corporation. *Neptune's Daughter* (1949) had "Baby, It's Cold Outside" in its score, sung first in the film by Esther Williams and Ricardo Montalban. When it was reprised as a comedy number, Red Skelton and Betty Garrett sang it. It won the Academy Award for Best Song.

*Guys and Dolls* (November 24, 1950) was based on short stories by Damon Runyon. It was a smashing success, running 1,200 performances. Loesser proved that he could write excellent comedy songs: "Fugue for Tinhorns (I've Got the Horse Right Here)," "Adelaide's Lament," "A Bushel and a Peck," "Luck, Be a Lady," "The Oldest Established," "Sit Down, You're Rockin' the Boat," "Take Back Your Mink," and "Guys and Dolls." That he could also turn out impressive ballads was illustrated by "I'll Know," "I've Never Been in Love

Before," "More I Cannot Wish You," and "If I Were a Bell." When the film version was made (1955), Loesser added the beautiful "A Woman in Love." *Hans Christian Andersen* (1952) starred Danny Kaye and had one of the finest original film scores of the 1950s. It contained such gems as "I'm Hans Christian Andersen," "Anywhere I Wander," "The Inch Worm," "No Two People," "Thumbelina," and "Wonderful Copenhagen."

*The Most Happy Fella* (May 3, 1956) was an unusual musical, nearly operatic in its scope, based on Sidney Howard's Pulitzer Prize-winning play *They Knew What They Wanted* (1924). "Big D" celebrated Dallas, Texas, and "The Most Happy Fella" and "Happy to Make Your Acquaintance" provided warmhearted moments. "Standing on the Corner" was the big hit of the show, with The Four Lads making a million-selling recording (Columbia 40674). A human dynamo, always in a whirl of excitement and activity, Loesser often worked a sixteen-hour day. It was, therefore, a surprise to friends when he told them the day after *The Most Happy Fella* opened that he was going to Las Vegas for a "long, long holiday—and this time I mean it. I'll be back in three days."

*How to Succeed in Business Without Really Trying* (October 14, 1961) was Loesser's longest-running show. It saw 1,417 performances in New York and won the Pulitzer Prize for drama. It starred Robert Morse and Rudy Vallee, who reprised their roles in the film version (1967). The song hits were "Brotherhood of Man," "Grand Old Ivy," and the narcissistic "I Believe in You." Loesser never could repeat his earlier success on Broadway after this, and died of lung cancer in 1969.

# Frederick Loewe

Composer (b. Vienna, Austria, June 10, 1904; d. Palm Springs, California, February 14, 1988). Loewe composed the European hit "Katrina" when he was fifteen, and by the time he was nineteen, he had graduated from the Stern Conservatory in Berlin, where he had studied piano and composition. He wrote a shimmy, "Kathrin," with words by R. H. Winter, in 1923. Loewe came to the United States the following year, gave a recital in Town Hall, and began a succession of jobs in and out of music. With scriptwriter Earle Crooker, he composed his first American pop song, "A Waltz Was Born in Vienna," which found success in the show *Salute to Spring*, produced in stock by the Municipal Opera of St. Louis in 1937. But it wasn't until he met radio scriptwriter ALAN JAY LERNER that either of them had a solid career in musical theater.

*Brigadoon* (March 13, 1947) was the first successful offering of the team. (*What's Up* in 1943 and *The Day Before Spring* in 1945 were flops, and produced no memorable songs.) Lerner created the book for the show. The score had delightful songs: "Come to Me, Bend to Me," "Down on MacConnachy Square," "From This Day On," "I'll Go Home with Bonnie Jean," "There But for You Go I," and the two hits "The Heather on the Hill" and

"Almost Like Being in Love," the latter sung in the show by David Brooks and Marion Bell. In the film version (1954), it was sung by Gene Kelly. It was the first hit song by the team and received much airplay. Sheet music sales were more than half a million copies. For a show song, this was a remarkable feat.

*Paint Your Wagon* (November 12, 1951) contained three numbers that survived the show to become standards: "I Talk to the Trees," "Wand'rin' Star," and "They Call the Wind Maria." This last became popular through the efforts of Robert Goulet, who revived it a decade later on television and in nightclubs. (It was the song he used to audition for the role of Lancelot in *Camelot.*) The film version (1969) retained all three songs.

*My Fair Lady* (March 15, 1956) was based on George Bernard Shaw's play *Pygmalion* (1912). It broke *Oklahoma*'s long-run record with 2,717 performances and became one of Broadway's most successful musical comedies. It earned the largest sum any musical had earned until that time, over $100 million from touring companies, foreign productions (the London run broke all records there, with 2,281 performances), film rights, recordings, and sheet music. The original cast recording, released by Columbia Records, sold over five million copies. There were more than twenty cast albums made in more than ten languages. Chappell and Company, which published the sheet music, reported that the show was the biggest thing it had seen since entering the business, pointing out that its London branch had been in business for three hundred years! The show starred Rex Harrison, Julie Andrews, and Stanley Holloway. The songs ranged from Cockney comedy songs ("Wouldn't It Be Loverly?," "Get Me to the Church on Time," and "With a Little Bit of Luck") to patter songs ("Why Can't a Woman Be More like a Man?," "I'm an Ordinary Man," "A Hymn to Him," and the

Frederick Loewe (left) and Alan Jay Lerner, c. 1960.

glorious "The Rain in Spain") to the hits of the show: "On the Street Where You Live," "I Could Have Danced All Night," and "I've Grown Accustomed to Her Face." The film version (1964) kept the male stars of the show. Audrey Hepburn (her singing done by Marni Nixon) replaced Julie Andrews, and the film was a critical and popular hit.

Lerner and Loewe's first original film score, *Gigi* (1958), accented period charm, as had *My Fair Lady*, and starred Leslie Caron, Maurice Chevalier, Louis Jourdan, and Hermione Gingold. The score was an especially rich one, yielding many standards, including "I Remember It Well," "I'm Glad I'm Not Young Anymore," "The Night They Invented Champagne," "Thank Heaven for Little Girls," and the title song, which won the Oscar for Best Song.

*Camelot* (December 3, 1960) starred Richard Burton, Julie Andrews, Roddy McDowall, and Robert Goulet. It produced the title song, "How to Handle a Woman," "The Lusty Month of May," "What Do the Simple Folk Do?," and the big hit, "If Ever I Would Leave You," which was sung in the show by Robert Goulet. Although the show ran for 873 performances and had a huge advance sale ($3 million), it was considered a disappointment by some of the team's devotees. The only thing wrong with the show was that it followed *My Fair Lady*, an "unfollowable" show. The film version (1967), which starred Richard Harris and Vanessa Redgrave, was a success.

The team broke up after *Camelot* but reunited briefly to write an original score for a film, *The Little Prince* (1974). Sad to say, there were no hit songs.

# Guy Lombardo

Bandleader (b. London, Ontario, Canada, June 19, 1902; d. Houston, Texas, November 5, 1977). Because of his brother Carmen's lead alto saxophone with its wide vibrato, his brother Lebert's lead trumpet, and their eminently danceable tempos, Guy Lombardo and his Royal Canadians were the most successful dance band of all time. It was said to play "the sweetest music this side of heaven."

Carmen (1903–1971) was key to the band's success. He wrote many of their arrangements, took vocal solos, led the vocal trio, and composed several hits, including: "Coquette" (1928), written with JOHNNY GREEN (Green's first published song), lyrics by GUS KAHN (Columbia 1345-D); "Sweethearts on Parade" (1928), lyrics by Charles Newman (Columbia 1628-D); "Boo Hoo" (1937), composed with John Jacob Loeb (1910–1970), with lyrics by EDWARD HEYMAN (Victor 25522); "Seems Like Old Times" (1946), again with Loeb, used by ARTHUR GODFREY as his radio and television theme (Decca 18738); "Powder Your Face with Sunshine" (1948), lyrics by Stanley Rochinski; and "Get Out Those Old Records" (1950), written with John Jacob Loeb (Decca 27336).

The band's personnel changed little through the years. It basically consisted of Guy Lombardo, leader; Lebert Lombardo, trumpet; Jim Dillon, trombone; Carmen Lombardo and Larry Owens, clarinets and alto saxes; Fred Higman, tenor sax; Victor Lombardo, baritone

Guy Lombardo featured on the cover of the song "Quicker Than You Can Say—Jack Robinson," published by Remick.

sax; Fred Kreitzer, piano; Francis Henry, banjo; Bernard Davis, tuba; and George Gowans, drums.

The band came to New York City in 1929 and had its own radio shows, besides being regularly featured on the Burns and Allen program. The Lombardo band appeared in several movies, notably *Many Happy Returns* (1934), *Stage Door Canteen* (1943), and *No Leave, No Love* (1946).

This band was the best plug a song could have during the 1930s. They made extensive recordings and created more hit songs than any other band. They had unusually long residences at New York's Hotel Roosevelt Grill, and they broadcast New Year's Eve celebrations for over forty years on radio and television. LOUIS ARMSTRONG was perhaps the band's biggest fan.

# Nick Lucas

Popular singer-guitarist of the 1920s (b. Newark, New Jersey, August 22, 1897; d. Colorado Springs, Colorado, July 28, 1982). Lucas began his career as a banjoist working local clubs before joining the popular dance band of TED FIO RITO in the early 1920s; there he established himself as a vocalist billed as "The Singing Troubador." He was signed to the Brunswick label in 1925, and had several big recorded hits during the 1920s, notably JOE BURKE and AL DUBIN's "Tip Toe Through the Tulips with Me." Other hits included "Ukulele Lady" and "Bye, Bye, Blackbird" (Brunswick E18878). His popularity was so great that the Gibson Company made a special "Nick Lucas" model guitar. He appeared on Broadway in the 1929 revue *Showgirl*, and then moved to Hollywood, where he performed in film shorts and clubs. Tiny Tim's revival of "Tip Toe" in the 1960s brought some new interest in Lucas's career, and Lucas sang the classic song on the sound track for the 1974 film *The Great Gatsby*.

# Abe Lyman

Composer and bandleader (b. Chicago, Illinois, August 4, 1897; d. Beverly Hills, California, October 23, 1957). Lyman started out as a drummer in silent movie houses, then moved to Los Angeles in 1919. He formed a band there and played at the Cocoanut Grove restaurant for four years in the early 1920s. While playing at Grauman's Chinese Restaurant in the early 1930s, he and the band appeared in several movie musicals. His band also played on many radio programs, notably *Waltz Time*, which ran from 1934 to 1948, when Lyman left the music business for the restaurant business.

In 1923 Lyman cocomposed "I Cried for You," which The Collegians recorded (Victor 19093). In 1926, he had two hits, "Mary Lou," by the Lyman orchestra (Brunswick 3135) and in a splendid recording by Frances Sper, accompanied by PETE WENDLING (Cameo 1064), and "What Can I Say After I Say I'm Sorry?" Jane Gray, accompanied by RUBE BLOOM, had a hit recording (Harmony 114-H). His 1927 hit "Did You Mean It?" came from the musical *A Night in Spain*. It was introduced in the show and got a splendid recording by Marion Harris (Victor 21116). Lyman's recording career spanned the years 1923–1946. His more famous records include the 1925 "All Alone" (Brunswick 2742), the 1929 "Sweethearts on Parade" (Brunswick 4117), the 1931 "Just One More Chance" (Brunswick 6125), the 1937 hit "Little Old Lady" (Decca 1120), the 1939 "Good Morning," from the film version of *Babes in Arms* (Bluebird 10424), and his last hit, in 1945, "Rum and Coca-Cola" (Columbia 36775).

# M

## Jeanette MacDonald

Popular soprano and film star (b. Philadelphia, Pennsylvania, June 18, 1901; d. Houston, Texas, January 14, 1965). MacDonald took singing and dancing lessons as a child and understudied the lead in a Broadway musical as a teenager. She had her first starring role on Broadway in 1927 and continued there until late 1929, when she went to Hollywood. There she made eight films with baritone NELSON EDDY, which made stars of them both. She and Eddy had a million-seller, "Indian Love Call" and "Ah, Sweet Mystery of Life" (both on Victor 4323). Their other hit recording was "Will You Remember?" and "Farewell to Dreams" (Victor 4329). She introduced "Beyond the Blue Horizon" in the film *Monte Carlo* (Victor 22514); "One Hour with You," from the film of the same name, in 1932 (Victor 24013); "Isn't It Romantic?," from the 1932 film *Love Me Tonight* (Victor 24067); and "Try to Forget," from the movie version of *The Cat and the Fiddle* (Victor 24754). After her 1949 film *The Sun Comes Up*, MacDonald retired.

# Cecil Mack

African-American lyricist and publisher (b. Norfolk, Virginia, November 6, 1883; d. New York City, August 1, 1944). As a songwriter, he mainly worked with Chris Smith, James P. Johnson, Eubie Blake, and Albert Von Tilzer. Mack's career spanned from the turn of the twentieth century to his death. He created the music publishing firm Gotham-Attucks to help African-American songwriters get their songs published. He also organized the Cecil Mack Choir for work in Broadway musicals.

Mack's first success as a lyricist came in 1901 with "Good Morning, Carrie," which the famed team of Williams and Walker turned into a hit (Victor 997). In 1906, he had another hit with "He's a Cousin of Mine," which Bert Williams made a #1 success (Columbia 3536). Arthur Collins and Byron Harlan made a hit with the 1908 song "Down Among the Sugar Cane" (Victor 5670). Also in 1908, Mack had a great comic song, "You're in the Right Church but the Wrong Pew," for Bert Williams to sing in the Broadway musical *Bandanna Land.* In 1923, he wrote lyrics for James P. Johnson's "The Charleston," for *Running Wild,* whose pit band, under Arthur Gibbs, made a splendid recording (Victor 19165). From the same show came "Old-Fashioned Love," which Noble Sissle and Eubie Blake recorded (Victor 19253). In 1924, Mack turned his 1910 song, "That's Why They Call Me Shine," into the hotsy "Shine," and bands like Herb Wiedoeft's (Brunswick 2542), The Virginians (Victor 19334), and the Original Memphis Five (Perfect 14275) recorded it. It was revived in a 1942 version by Henry "Hot Lips" Levine (Victor 27831). Mack's last hit came in 1925, with "The Camel Walk," recorded by the New Orleans Jazz Band (Banner 1618).

# Edward B. Marks

Music publisher (b. 1865; d. 1945 [full dates unknown]). Marks was a pioneer in the field. He was a young notions salesman who liked to write lyrics. He went to see Frank Harding, whose father had started a music publishing business in 1860 at 229 The Bowery, which

Frank had taken over at the same location in 1879. Harding put Marks in touch with William Loraine, a part-time hack composer and full-time lush. Harding published the result of their collaboration ("December and May") in 1893. Marks offered to take samples of Harding's song catalog on the road with him. Harding accepted, since he had no branch office and wanted his music available in places other than New York City. After Marks got the royalty statement for his one song, he decided it would be more profitable to publish his songs himself.

He teamed with another salesman, JOSEPH W. STERN, who wrote melodies. They opened a small office in 1894 under Stern's name, and issued their first collaboration, "The Little Lost Child," that same year. With the help of music hall singers Della Fox and LOTTIE GILSON, the song became a hit and established Joseph W. Stern and Company as a major player in Tin Pan Alley.

Marks created the song slide, which was used in theaters to illustrate lyrics through a series of photographs and illustrations. The slide songs were introduced into nickelodeons—so that audiences could sing between pictures—and vaudeville. The illustrated song slide became a valuable tool in the plugging of popular songs.

In December 1920, Joseph W. Stern retired and his firm became the Edward B. Marks Music Corporation, retaining its old address at 102–104 West Thirty-eighth Street until February 1922, when Marks purchased a building at 223–225 West Forty-sixth Street, adjacent to the JEROME H. REMICK Building. Marks went on to have hits through the 1930s and 1940s, including 1930's "The Peanut Vendor" and BILLIE HOLIDAY's classic 1939 hit "Strange Fruit."

Edward Marks pictured at the turn of the twentieth century, when he was working with Joseph W. Stern.

In 1980, music businessman Freddy Bienstock purchased the firm in partnership with the Rodgers and Hammerstein estates. He has maintained the imprint as part of his CARLIN MUSIC publishing company.

# Gerald Marks

Composer (b. Saginaw, Michigan, October 13, 1900; d. New York City, January 27, 1997). Marks was a songwriter best remembered for his 1931 hit "All of Me," written with lyrics by Seymour Simons. It was introduced in vaudeville and on radio by Belle Baker, and LOUIS ARMSTRONG had the first hit recording (Okeh 41552), followed by MILDRED BAILEY in 1932 (Victor 22879). From 1948 on, FRANK SINATRA was associated with this song for the rest of his career (Columbia 38163). The song and its title were featured in a 1984 film. It is one of the best-known songs of all time. The song's success led to Marks's becoming a member of ASCAP, and he remained active in the organization for decades, serving on its board of directors from 1970 to 1981.

In 1936, Marks, working with lyricist IRVING CAESAR, supplied AL JOLSON with the hit "Is It True What They Say About Dixie?" A year later, the duo wrote a collection of songs aimed at children, issued as a folio under the title *Sing a Song of Safety*. Marks toured as a enertainer for the troops during World War II. He wrote one of the first patriotic numbers during the war years in 1940, "Ev'ry One's a Fighting Son of That Old Gang of Mine," also with lyricist Caesar. After the war, Marks primarily worked as a music business executive.

# Dean Martin

Singer and actor (b. Steubenville, Ohio, June 17, 1917; d. Los Angeles, California, December 25, 1995). He started working with Jerry Lewis as a comedy-singing act in nightclubs in 1946. The duo appeared on Ed Sullivan's TV show in 1948 and costarred on the *Colgate Comedy Hour* two years later. Martin and Lewis made sixteen movies (1949–1956) before breaking up their partnership. As a single, Martin acted in many films and had his own television show from 1965 to 1974. He was noted for a relaxed style of singing. He made many recordings from 1948 to 1967 and had three million-selling hits: "That's Amore," from his 1953 film *The Caddy* (Capitol 2589), "Memories Are Made of This" (Capitol 3295) in 1955, and "Everybody Loves Somebody," which became his television theme in 1965 (Reprise 0281).

# Tony Martin

Singer and actor popular from the 1930s to the 1950s (b. Alvin Morris, Oakland, California, December 25, 1912). Despite his Anglicized stage name, Martin was born to Russian Jewish immigrant parents. He began playing saxophone as a teenager, and soon formed his own band to play in the San Francisco area. He graduated to singing with various local bands, including a group led by Tom Guran that featured a young Woody Herman. Herman and Martin traveled together to play at the 1933 Chicago World's Fair, and remained there to do club work. In 1934, Martin moved to Hollywood, and landed a big part in *Follow the Fleet* (1936), which led to a contract with 20th Century Fox in 1936; he also made his radio debut on the Burns and Allen show. In 1937, he married Hollywood star Alice Faye (they would later divorce, and Martin married actress-dancer Cyd Charisse in the early 1950s; the duo formed a nightclub act in later years). Martin appeared in films until 1957 and on radio into the 1950s. He also sang with GLENN MILLER's Air Force band during World War II.

Martin made many recordings from 1938 to 1956. His two million-sellers were "To Each His Own" in 1946 (Mercury 3022) and "I Get Ideas" in 1951 (RCA Victor 20-4141). He was a frequent guest on TV in the 1950s and 1960s, and played nightclubs into the 1970s. He made several well-received appearances at the London Palladium, beginning in 1948 and continuing through the mid-1990s.

# Joseph McCarthy

Lyricist (b. Somerville, Massachusetts, September 27, 1885; d. New York City, December 18, 1943). McCarthy was a cabaret singer in New York when he began writing lyrics in the early 1910s. His first major his was 1913's "You Made Me Love You," with music by JIMMY

Monaco; the pair scored again in 1916 with "What Do You Want to Make Those Eyes at Me For?," revived in 1945 by Betty Grable in the film *Incendiary Blonde*, a biopic of nightclub chanteuse Texas Guinan. Working with Harry Carroll in 1918 for the show *Oh, Look*, McCarthy provided the lyrics for the million-selling hit "I'm Always Chasing Rainbows." In 1919, McCarthy teamed with composer Harry Tierney to write the hit "Alice Blue Gown" as part of the musical show *Irene* (made into a film in 1940, and revived on Broadway in 1973), as well as writing for the *Ziegfeld Follies*. They continued to work together through 1928, scoring *Kid Boots* for Ziegfeld in 1923 and then the very successful 1927 show *Rio Rita*, which produced numerous hits, including the title number and "The Kinkajou." They had one further collaboration, *Cross My Heart* (1928), but unlike *Rita* it closed quickly. During the 1930s, McCarthy worked primarily with composer James Hanley. He died in the early 1940s.

# Jimmy McHugh

Composer (b. James Francis McHugh, Boston, Massachusetts, July 10, 1895; d. Beverly Hills, California, May 23, 1969). McHugh had a college degree in music, and worked as a rehearsal pianist at the Boston Opera House. He became a song plugger for the Boston office of Waterson, Berlin and Snyder, joining the more than twenty others who bicycled around town playing and singing the firm's songs. He came to New York City in 1921 and joined the new Mills Music as a staff pianist. His "Stop Your Kiddin' " (1922), a joint effort with Ferde Grofe, was plugged extensively on disc by the Original Memphis Five (Vocalion 14461, Pathe 020855). McHugh's first hit, written with singer Gene Austin, was "When My Sugar Walks Down the Street" (1924). "The Lonesomest Girl in Town" (1925) had lyrics by Al Dubin. "Everything Is Hotsy Totsy Now" (1925) was done with Irving Mills. "I Can't Believe That You're in Love with Me" (1926) was written with Clarence Gaskill.

*Blackbirds of 1928* (May 9, 1928) was the first Broadway show for McHugh and lyricist Dorothy Fields, a partnership that produced a number of classic songs. It contained "Digga Digga Do," "Doin' the New Low-Down" (for Bill Robinson's great tap dance), "I Must Have That Man," and the frequently revived "I Can't Give You Anything but Love." (It has been said that McHugh bought the last song from Fats Waller and Andy Razaf, and that Fields had no knowledge of this. Her name went on the song because she and McHugh were contractual partners for the show. When Andy Razaf was inducted into the Songwriter's Hall of Fame, Don Redman's wife asked which of his songs was his favorite. Razaf, in a wheelchair, motioned her closer and sang softly in her ear, "I can't give you anything but love, baby . . .") The song originally appeared in a flop revue, *Harry Delmar's Revels* (November 28, 1927), but it was placed in *Blackbirds* with great success.

*The International Revue* (February 25, 1930) was the next show the McHugh-Fields team wrote, and two hits emerged from the score. "Exactly Like You" and "On the Sunny

Side of the Street" were both given to HARRY RICHMAN (Brunswick 4747). Over the years, "On the Sunny Side of the Street" has been used in seven films and has been a favorite of such jazz performers as LOUIS ARMSTRONG, Connee Boswell, BENNY GOODMAN, Peggy Lee, Louis Prima, and Fats Waller. *Every Night at Eight* (1935) was the first film to have a complete score by McHugh and Fields. "I Feel a Song Coming On" and "I'm in the Mood for Love" were the hits. *King of Burlesque* (1935) sported McHugh tunes and TED KOEHLER lyrics. Alice Faye sang "I'm Shooting High," and FATS WALLER made the most of the cute "I've Got My Fingers Crossed."

*Streets of Paris* (June 19, 1939) was a Broadway revue for which McHugh and Al Dubin wrote the score. It featured Carmen Miranda, who scored big with "South American Way" (Decca 23130). When she went to Hollywood the next year, she sang it in her film debut, *Down Argentine Way*. *Hers to Hold* (1943) contained a Deanna Durbin wartime hit, "Say a Pray'r for the Boys Over There." Also in that year, McHugh and HAROLD ADAMSON wrote one of the better World War II songs, "Comin' In on a Wing and a Prayer."

*A Date with Judy* (1948) contained one of McHugh's happiest songs, "It's a Most Unusual Day," sung by Jane Powell. Margaret Whiting recorded it (Capitol 57-724) and helped make it a standard. McHugh's last hit came with 1955's "Too Young to Go Steady" (with music by Adamson), which was successfully recorded by Nat "King" Cole and Patti Page. The song was part of the score for a projected Broadway show for the duo, but it closed before reaching New York. From 1952, McHugh led a nightclub act known as Jimmy McHugh's Song Stars of Tomorrow; he also served as vice president of ASCAP during the later 1950s and 1960s.

# Melrose Brothers Music Company

The Melrose firm solidified Chicago's position as the preeminent jazz city during the 1920s. The Melrose brothers, Walter and Lester, along with Marty Bloom, owned a music shop in Chicago before adding a music publishing business to it early in 1923. They issued song sheets and published orchestrations for dance and jazz bands. Their songs added immeasurably to the jazz and dance band repertoire. Most of the Melrose publications would become standard fare for dixieland jazz bands. Their first three successes were all-time favorites: "Wolverine Blues" by JELLY ROLL MORTON, recorded by The Benson Orchestra of Chicago (Victor 19140), Albert E. Short and his Tivoli Syncopators (Vocalion 14554), Gene Rodemich and his orchestra from St. Louis, recording in Chicago (Brunswick 2455), and the New Orleans Rhythm Kings (Gennett 5102), whose photo is on the cover of the sheet music; "Tin Roof Blues," composed and recorded by the New Orleans Rhythm Kings (Gennett 5105); and

"Sobbin' Blues," written by future bandleader ART KASSELL and drummer Vic Berton, initially recorded by the Benson Orchestra (Victor 19130) and Albert E. Short's Tivoli Syncopators (Vocalion 14600). Melrose also issued "All Night Blues," by Chicago blues pianist RICHARD M. JONES, which Callie Vassar recorded (Gennett 5172).

The following year, 1924, Melrose issued such classics as Charlie Davis's "Copenhagen," which had been recorded instrumentally by jazz and dance bands but got its first recording as a song in the early 1950s, by Teresa Brewer (London 604); "Someday Sweetheart," which SOPHIE TUCKER belted to fame; "Tia Juana," composed and recorded by St. Louis band leader Gene Rodemich and his trombonist Larry Conley (Brunswick 2680), although the classic recording was by Jelly Roll Morton (Gennett 5632); and "Mobile Blues," by Fred Rose and Al Short, recorded by Jimmy Wade and his Moulin Rouge Orchestra (Paramount 20295).

The Melrose Brothers came back strong in 1925 with Charlie Davis' "Jimtown Blues," a favorite of Jimmy Wade's Moulin Rouge Syncopators; "Whoop 'Em Up Blues," introduced by the Benson Orchestra; and the now standard "Spanish Shawl," pianist Elmer Schoebel's clever tune that Boston-based Edwin J. McEnelly's orchestra recorded, with a superb piano solo by newcomer Frankie Carle (Victor 19851). "Sugar Babe" was Boyd Senter's tune, which he plugged nightly with his Senterpedes.

"Sugar Foot Stomp" (1926), the KING OLIVER classic—which he recorded with his Creole Jazz Band, featuring LOUIS ARMSTRONG—was better known to jazz fans as "Dippermouth Blues" (Gennett 5132). "Hangin' Around" (1926) was a collaboration between pianist Jack Gardner and bandleader Fred Hamm, both of Chicago.

Two jazz classics were first published by Melrose in 1927: King Oliver's "Doctor Jazz," which Jelly Roll Morton's Red Hot Peppers catapulted to fame (Victor 20415), and "Willie the Weeper," recorded initially by three big Chicago jazz bands—King Oliver's (Vocalion 1112), Louis Armstrong's (Okeh 8482), and Doc Cook's (Columbia 1070-D). Gospel composer Thomas A. Dorsey's solid blues "It's Tight Like That" was issued by the company in 1928.

The Melrose Brothers' folios of Jelly Roll Morton's compositions and Louis Armstrong's "50 Hot Choruses" were landmarks in jazz publishing. The numbers that the Melrose Brothers issued, as well as the bands and soloists they helped to record, gave Chicago pride of place in the jazz world during the 1920s.

# Johnny Mercer

Lyricist and composer (b. John Herndon, Savannah, Georgia, November 18, 1909; d. Los Angeles, California, July 25, 1976). Mercer's major collaborators were HAROLD ARLEN, HOAGY CARMICHAEL, JEROME KERN, ARTHUR SCHWARTZ, HARRY WARREN, JIMMY

McHugh, Johnny Green, Jimmy Van Heusen, Richard Whiting, Walter Donaldson, Rube Bloom, and Vernon Duke. Mercer once said, "There are certain writers who have a great feeling for *tunes*, no matter where they come from. I think I'm one of them." He was so prolific that he wrote with practically everybody: performers (Fred Astaire, Bobby Darin, Erroll Garner, Marian McPartland, Trummy Young, Blossom Dearie), bandleaders (Woody Herman, Artie Shaw, Duke Ellington, Benny Carter, Lionel Hampton), and composer-arrangers (Gordon Jenkins, Elmer Bernstein, Ralph Burns, Neil Hefti, Paul Weston, David Raksin, Dick Hyman, Bobby Troup, Henry Mancini, Alex North, Michel Legrand, and Andre Previn). He took an idea and a title sent to him by Sadie Vimmerstedt, an Ohio housewife who worked at a cosmetics counter in Youngstown. Mercer wrote the words and music based on her title, "I Wanna Be Around," and he shared the royalties with her. Tony Bennett made a hit recording (Columbia 42634). Vimmerstedt wrote Mercer letters telling him of the changes the song had made in her life. She was getting to be famous. People came into the store asking for her autograph. She was interviewed on Cleveland radio, then in Cincinnati. But when she was asked to go to New York City, she wrote him complaining that, despite her rounds of interviews and traveling, she still had to work at the department store. "I'm tired, Mr. Mercer," she said, "I've got to get out of show business!"

Mercer first came to New York with a local Savannah dramatic company in 1927. They went home, and he stayed. His first published song, "Out of Breath and Scared to Death of You," was composed by Everett Miller for *Garrick Gaieties of 1930* (June 4, 1930). His first real hit was "Lazybones" (1933), with music by Hoagy Carmichael, who was to be a recurring collaborator. "P.S. I Love You," (1934) has a melody by Gordon Jenkins and was revived by The Hilltoppers in 1953 (Dot 15085) (not to be confused with the Beatles hit with the same title in the 1960s).

"I'm an Old Cowhand" (1936) was the first hit with words and music by Mercer. It was written for a Bing Crosby film, *Rhythm on the Range*, and Crosby's recording gave it hit status (Decca 871). Roy Rogers revived it in *King of the Cowboys* (1943). With Matty Malneck, Mercer wrote "Goody Goody" (1936), which Benny Goodman turned into a hit with vocalist Helen Ward (Victor 25245).

"Hooray for Hollywood," music by Richard Whiting, was sung in the film *Hollywood Hotel* (1937). This team scored again with "Too Marvelous for Words," in *Ready, Willing and Able* (1937). Harry Warren joined Mercer in 1938 for "Jeepers Creepers," in *Going Places*, and "You Must Have Been a Beautiful Baby," in *Hard to Get*.

Pianist Rube Bloom joined Mercer for "Day In—Day Out" (1939) and "Fools Rush In" (1940), the latter popularized by Tony Martin (Decca 3119). Glenn Miller and his orchestra also made a best-selling recording (Bluebird 10728). Ricky Nelson revived it successfully in 1963 (Decca 31533).

"And the Angels Sing" (1939) gave Mercer the opportunity to provide lyrics to trumpeter Ziggy Elman's feature with the Benny Goodman Orchestra (Victor 26170). The same year, Jimmy Van Heusen wrote a tune for "I Thought About You," one of Mercer's most evocative lyrics.

Although they had written only one song together, nine years earlier, Mercer joined Harold Arlen in 1941 to write the film score for *Blues in the Night*. Many fans consider the work they did together to be the most important for each of them. They were both hip-deep in jazz and blues, both were affecting singers, and both were willing to experiment with the standard structure of the popular song. "Blues in the Night," for example, has no verse-chorus

Johnny Mercer, c. the 1940s.

organization, but is made of three themes: an A section of twelve measures, a B section of twelve measures, a C section of sixteen measures, and a return to an extended A section of sixteen measures.

"The Waiter and the Porter and the Upstairs Maid" was another song Mercer wrote himself. It was interpolated into the film *Birth of the Blues* (1941). It is made in the typical Mercer off-the-cuff manner, with a riff-based melody and a clever rhyming scheme.

1942 was a banner year for Mercer, giving him six hits with collaborators and one by himself. His own was a novelty called "Strip Polka," which had best-selling recordings by the Andrews Sisters (Decca 18470), Kay Kyser and his orchestra (Columbia 36635), and Mercer himself (Capitol 103). His film score with Kern, *You Were Never Lovelier*, produced two standards, "Dearly Beloved" and "I'm Old-Fashioned." His film score with Arlen, *Star Spangled Rhythm*, produced the jazzy "Hit the Road to Dreamland" and another convention-breaker, "That Old Black Magic." With Carmichael, he wrote the pensive "Skylark," and with film director Victor Schertzinger (1890–1941), he wrote "Tangerine" for *The Fleet's In*. This song, with its subtle alliteration and internal rhymes, was sung in the film by Helen O'Connell with the Jimmy Dorsey Orchestra (Decca 4123).

As if he weren't busy enough writing words, composing tunes, hosting his own network radio program, and recording other people's songs, Mercer, with lyricist B. G. De Sylva and record store owner Glenn Wallichs, formed Capitol records in 1942, with Mercet as its president. With a roster of artists that included Nat "King" Cole, Stan Kenton, Jo Stafford, the Pied Pipers, Ella Mae Morse, Margaret Whiting, and Mercer himself, the company was successful from the start. Mercer the vocalist's biggest record hits came from songs by other writers: "Candy" (1944), by ALEX KRAMER, Joan Whitney, and Mack David (Capitol 183), and "My Sugar Is So Refined" (1946), by Sid Lippman and Sylvia Dee (Capitol 268). He made over one hundred recordings in his career, including duets with Bing Crosby, Nat "King" Cole, JUDY GARLAND, Jo Stafford, Margaret Whiting, and Martha Tilton.

"G. I. Jive" (1943), by Mercer alone, combined military jargon with hipster slang. His own recording (Capitol 141) with Paul Weston's orchestra was a big seller. The same year, he and Arlen collaborated on the film score for *The Sky's the Limit*. "My Shining Hour" and "One for My Baby" were both sung by Fred Astaire and turned into hits by him.

*Here Come the Waves* (1944) produced the swing sermon "Ac-cent-tchu-ate the Positive," with music by Harold Arlen. "Dream" (1945) was composed and written by Mercer, who used it as the closing theme of his radio program, *Johnny Mercer's Music Shop*. Probably his most beautiful melody, "Dream" was first recorded successfully by the Pied Pipers (Capitol 185), and was later revived by the Voices of Walter Schumann in a magnificent arrangement (Capitol 1505).

*The Harvey Girls* (1946) gave Mercer the first of his four Oscars for "On the Atchison, Topeka and the Santa Fe," with music by Harry Warren. The same year Mercer wrote the lyrics to David Raksin's beautiful film theme "Laura." The lyrics were written after the film's release. Woody Herman and his orchestra had the best-selling recording (Columbia 36785).

*St. Louis Woman* (March 30, 1946) has a score by Arlen and Mercer, which fans of both think magnificent. It included the classic "Come Rain or Come Shine." "Autumn Leaves" (1950) has a melody by Frenchman Joseph Kosma, and "When the World Was Young" (1950) has a melody by M. Philippe-Gerard. Both got English lyrics by Mercer. "In the Cool, Cool, Cool of the Evening" was Mercer's second Oscar winner, with music by Hoagy Carmichael, from the film *Here Comes the Groom* (1951).

*Top Banana* (November 1, 1951) was the first Broadway musical about the remarkable new medium, television, and the only musical with a complete score, both words and music, by Mercer. The title song, "O. K. for T. V.," and "San Souci" were the show's highlights, along with star Phil Silvers. Mercer's first all-words-and-music film score was *Daddy Long Legs* (1955), in which Fred Astaire introduced the sizzling "Something's Gotta Give."

*Li'l Abner* (November 15, 1956) was Mercer's most commercially successful Broadway score. The swinging Gene de Paul (1919–1988) music combined with Mercer's Dogpatchese lyrics to provide hits with "If I Had My Druthers," "Jubilation T. Cornpone," and the rhyming extravaganza "The Country's in the Very Best of Hands."

"Satin Doll" (1958) joined Billy Strayhorn and Duke Ellington's melody with Mercer's lyrics. In "Bilbao Song" (1961) Mercer gave English lyrics to KURT WEILL's music, which scored a tremendous hit as recorded by Bobby Darin.

Mercer's third and fourth Oscars were for songs with music by Henry Mancini (1924–1994), for the nonmusical films *Breakfast at Tiffany's* ("Moon River") (1961) and the title song from *Days of Wine and Roses* (1962). Mercer spent the balance of the 1960s contributing lyrics to movie themes. In 1970, he collaborated with Mancini for the score of the musical film *Darling Lily*, starring Julie Andrews. His last work was *The Good Companions*, a 1974 stage musical presented in London, with music by Andre Previn. Two years later, he died following surgery to remove a tumor from his brain.

Besides his prolific work as a lyricist, Mercer was very active in the music industry. In addition to being a cofounder of Capitol Records, he served as president of ASCAP (1941–

1942) and the Academy of Television Arts and Sciences (1956–1957). Mercer was a cofounder and the first president of the Songwriters Hall of Fame.

# Ethel Merman

Distinctive singer and actress (b. Ethel Agnes Zimmermann, Astoria, New York, January 16, 1909; d. New York City, February 15, 1984). Merman's father was a bookkeeper by day and a pianist by night. Encouraged to sing, she began performing as a young child, entertaining at local military training facilities during World War II. She quickly moved into working in New York nightclubs and vaudeville houses. Her big break came in the Broadway musical *Girl Crazy* (1930). Her career on Broadway lasted from 1930 to 1959. Her best roles were in *Anything Goes* (1934), *Annie Get Your Gun* (1946), *Call Me Madam* (1950, and *Gypsy* (1959). She started her recording career in 1931, and by 1932 she had a hit, "Eadie Was a Lady," from the Broadway musical *Take a Chance* (Brunswick 6456). In 1934 another starring role provided her with back-to-back hits when she recorded "You're the Top" and "I Get a Kick Out of You" from *Anything Goes* (Brunswick 7342). In 1946 she created her most memorable character in *Annie Get Your Gun*, and her charted hit was "They Say It's Wonderful" (Decca 23586). From the 1950 musical *Call Me Madam*, she and Dick Haymes recorded IRVING BERLIN's great DOUBLE SONG "You're Just In Love" (Decca 27317). The same year she and Ray Bolger recorded "If I Knew You Were Comin' I'd've Baked a Cake" (Decca 24944). In 1953 she and Mary Martin starred on television on the *Ford 50th Anniversary Show*, after which she made many guest appearances through the 1970s.

# Bob Merrill

Lyricist (b. H. Robert Merrill Levan, Atlantic City, New Jersey, May 17, 1921; d. Los Angeles, California, February 17, 1998). Merrill served in World War II, and then settled in Hollywood, working as a dialogue coach and bit-part actor. Invited by singer/comedienne

Dorothy Shay to write some songs for an upcoming recording session, Merrill began to supply lyrics for popular songs. His first major hit was "If I Knew You Were Comin' I'd've Baked a Cake," written in 1950 with music by AL HOFFMAN and Clem Watts. Other notable hits included Patti Page's classic "(How Much Is That) Doggie in the Window?" He began writing for Broadway in the mid-1950s, scoring his first major success with *Carnival* in 1961, which featured several hits, including "Love Makes the World Go Round." His greatest success came in 1964 with *Funny Girl*, written for Barbra Streisand with composer JULIE STYNE. Further Broadway attempts ended in failure, and Merrill has since pursued a career as a screenwriter and teacher.

# George W. Meyer

Composer (b. Boston, Massachusetts, January 1, 1884; d. New York City, August 28, 1959). Meyer was a songwriter-plugger when FRED MILLS published his first hit song, "Lonesome," in 1909. He wrote the snappy "Brass Band Ephraham Jones" in 1911 with lyricist Joe Goodwin (1889–1943).

Meyer was a publisher for two years, starting in 1912 with the publication of "Variety Rag" by HARRY TIERNEY. He followed it up the same year with "That Entertaining Rag" by Arthur Wellesley and Abe Olman's fabulous "Red Onion Rag." The next year, Meyer published Harry Jentes and PETE WENDLING's "Soup and Fish Rag," and in 1914, he issued vaudeville team Lyons and Yosco's "Mardi Gras Rag."

AL JOLSON introduced one of Meyer's great comic hits, "Where Did Robinson Crusoe Go with Friday on Saturday Night?" (1916), with lyrics by SAM M. LEWIS and JOE YOUNG (Columbia A-1976). The next year Meyer's collaborators were EDGAR LESLIE and E. RAY GOETZ, for a two-million-selling hit, "For Me and My Gal." (The title is inscribed on the tombstone of Meyer's wife.) "Everything Is Peaches Down in Georgia" (1918) was a collaboration with Milton Ager on the music and Grant Clarke as lyricist. The American Quartet had the hit (Victor 18497).

Reactivating his collaboration with Lewis and Young, Meyer created his greatest triumph, "Tuck Me to Sleep in My Old 'Tucky Home" (1921), which country singer Vernon Dalhart helped make into a multimillion-selling hit (Victor 18807). In 1923, Meyer collaborated with lyricist GUS KAHN on one of his most beautiful melodies, "Sittin' in a Corner." The following year, Meyer wrote the score of his only Broadway show, a black revue first called *Plantation Follies*, then *Dixie to Broadway* (October 29, 1924). It contained two of his finest numbers, "I'm a Little Blackbird Looking for a Bluebird" and "Mandy, Make Up Your Mind," a tune jazz bands still enjoy. "Someone Is Losin' Susan" (1926) was given a bouncy treatment by Pete Wendling (Cameo 1021). In 1929, with Al Bryan, Meyer wrote "My Song of the Nile" for Richard Barthelmess's film *Drag*.

Gus Van made a hit of Meyer's 1932 "I'm Sure of Everything but You," which Pete Wendling helped compose to Charles O'Flynn's lyrics. Meyer and Wendling had another hit two years later, with lyrics by Sam Lewis, in "I Believe in Miracles." Meyer's last hit was "There Are Such Things," composed with Abel Baer, with lyrics by STANLEY ADAMS, in 1942.

# Joseph Meyer

Composer (b. Modesto, California, March 12, 1894; d. New York City, June 22, 1987). Meyer was a classically trained violinist who studied in Paris in the first decade of the twentieth century, returning to the United States in 1908. He served in World War I and then briefly worked in a nonmusical job before taking up songwriting in the early 1920s. Meyer entered the Alley in 1922 with an enormous hit, "My Honey's Lovin' Arms," with lyrics by Herman Ruby (1891–1959). It was a favorite of dance bands and jazz combos, with ISHAM JONES (Brunswick 2301), Ray Miller (Brunswick 3828), The Virginians (Victor 18881), and Jazzbo's Carolina Serenaders (another pseudonym of the ORIGINAL MEMPHIS FIVE) (Cameo 218) making solid arrangements on records.

"California, Here I Come" (1924) was an inspiration of B. G. DE SYLVA. Its message echoed the composer's life, since he had come from California to New York, and had written the song in New York. It would be some six years before he followed his own advice. After being cut in on the writing credit, AL JOLSON sang it in *Big Boy*. The song was a natural for Jolson, and he helped make it a million-seller (Brunswick 2569). He also sang it in three films: *Rose of Washington Square* (1939), *The Jolson Story* (1946), and *Jolson Sings Again* (1949). It was the theme song of the California Ramblers.

"A Cup of Coffee, a Sandwich and You" (1925) was placed in *Charlot's Revue of 1926*, sung by the stars, Gertrude Lawrence and Jack Buchanan. BILLY ROSE and AL DUBIN wrote the lyrics. "Sugar Plum" (1925), with lyrics by B. G. De Sylva, was interpolated into *Gay Paree* and made famous by George Olsen and His Music (Victor 19859). "If You Knew Susie" (1925) was originally written for Al Jolson, but for once, he failed to deliver the expected hit, and it was EDDIE CANTOR who used it for the rest of his career. The song was placed in five different Broadway shows, and practically every male performer in vaudeville sang it. The sheet music sold well over a million copies. "Clap Hands! Here Comes Charley!" (1925) had lyrics by Billy Rose and Ballard MacDonald. Johnny Marvin helped to popularize it (Okeh 40558), and the Goofus Five made an instrumental hit recording (Okeh 40500). Meyer's "Crazy Rhythm" (1928) had lyrics by IRVING CAESAR. ROGER WOLFE KAHN cocomposed it and recorded it (Victor 21368), after having introduced it in *Here's Howe*.

Meyer continued to compose during the 1930s, including film work as well as writing for revues such as the *Ziefeld Follies of 1934* and *New Faces of 1936* (featuring the hit "It's High Time I Got the Low Down on You"). He wrote the music for lyricist EDDIE DE LANGE's first hit, "I Wish I Were Twins" (colyricist was FRANK LOESSER). He continued to compose for films through the mid-1940s.

# Glenn Miller

Bandleader (b. Clarinda, Iowa, March 1, 1904; d. English Channel, December 18, 1944). Miller joined Ben Pollack's band in Chicago in 1926 and came to New York City with them. He became a studio musician and arranger. He was a fine trombonist but not an outstanding soloist. He played in pit bands on Broadway that were led by Red Nichols, BENNY GOODMAN, and JIMMY and TOMMY DORSEY. He organized RAY NOBLE's first American band in 1935 and formed his own band in 1937. His second band, organized in 1938, clicked the next year when he played during the summer at Glen Island Casino in New Rochelle, New York, and made radio broadcasts. For this band, he created his famous "reed" sound, with clarinetist Wilbur Schwartz playing over the sax section.

Miller's recordings of the summer of 1939 took the music world by storm. He recorded a double-sided hit, with his theme song "Moonlight Serenade" and "Sunrise Serenade" on the same disc (Bluebird 10214). Arranger Bill Finegan made a swinging version of "Little Brown Jug" (Bluebird 10286), which was one of the band's most important tunes. Still later that summer, the band recorded Joe Garland's "In the Mood," in an arrangement by Miller himself (Bluebird 10416). His other big hits included Erskine Hawkins's "Tuxedo Junction" (Bluebird 10612); Jerry Gray's "Pennsylvania 6-5000" (Bluebird 10754), which was based on a riff from Larry Clinton's "Dipsy Doodle" (Victor 25693, Tommy Dorsey and his Orchestra); HARRY WARREN's "Chattanooga Choo Choo" (Bluebird 11230), featuring the vocal quartet The Modernaires; and Jerry Gray's "A String of Pearls" (Bluebird 11382).

The personnel for "In the Mood," recorded on August 1, 1939, were Clyde Hurley, Lee Knowles, and R. McMickle, trumpets; Glenn Miller, Al Mastren, and Paul Tanner, trombones; Wilbur Schwartz, clarinet; Hal McIntyre, alto sax; Tex Beneke, Al Klink, and Harold Tennyson, tenor saxes; Chummy MacGregor, piano; Richard Fisher, guitar; Rowland Bundock, string bass; and Moe Purtill, drums.

The band starred in two films, *Sun Valley Serenade* (1941) and *Orchestra Wives* (1942). The band broke up in September 1942, when Miller enlisted in the Army Air Force as a captain. He led a band in the service that performed, beginning in the spring of 1943, on radio and on Army bases and at bond rallies. In London with the band in June 1944, Miller

Glenn Miller gets "In the Mood," published by Shapiro, Bernstein.

boarded a plane to fly to Paris, which had just been liberated. The plane was lost over the English Channel, but the band continued to perform in various guises for years to come. The biopic *The Glenn Miller Story* (1954) featured Jimmy Stewart in the title role.

# Frederick Allen Mills

Publisher and composer (b. Philadelphia, Pennsylvania, February 1, 1869; d. Hawthorne, California, December 5, 1948). Mills wrote under the name of Kerry Mills. He composed CAKEWALKS as "Kerry" (and published them as "F. A.") through the 1890s, concentrating almost exclusively on this new, slightly syncopated dance craze. Popularized by the San Francisco team of WILLIAMS AND WALKER on the New York stage, and by Genaro and Bailey in vaudeville, Kerry Mills turned out a string of instrumental cakewalks that sold in vast quantities. His 1897 hit, "At a Georgia Campmeeting," is the granddaddy of cakewalks. At the end of 1899, advance orders for his "Impecunious Davis" totaled 265,000 copies. It eventually sold nearly 750,000. The cakewalk was almost an industry by itself; hundreds of other cakewalks were also published during the years 1895–1904. (Strangely, the cakewalk enjoyed a

Composer/publisher Kerry Mills, c. the 1910s.

short revival in 1915.) The firm of F. A. Mills pioneered this dance form, and maintained its high quality almost single-handedly. The cakewalk would be supplanted in the next decade by instrumental RAGTIME. Mills went bankrupt in 1915 and then made a brief comeback as a publisher from 1918 to 1920 before folding for good. He was not able to keep up with more modern song styles.

F. A. Mills (1895–1915)

| | |
|---|---|
| 1895–1899 | 45 West 29th Street |
| 1899–1906 | 48 West 29th Street |
| 1907–1908 | 32 West 29th Street |
| 1909–1914 | 122 West 36th Street |
| 1914–1915 | 207 West 48th Street |

# The Mills Brothers

Influential and popular black vocal-harmony group of the 1930s, 1940s, and 1950s. The four brothers (Herbert, b. April 2, 1912; d. April 12, 1989; Harry, b. August 9, 1913; d. June 28, 1982; Donald, b. April 29, 1915; d. November 13, 1999; John Jr., b. February 11,

1911; d. January 24, 1936), were all born in Piqua, Ohio. Their father was a concert singer-turned-barber who encouraged his young sons to harmonize. They were performing in vaudeville by the mid-1920s, and quickly gained fame for their vocal impressions of musical instruments. This led to a contract in 1930 with Brunswick Records, and their first hit, "Tiger Rag" (Brunswick 6197) came a year later. The group continued to make film appearances through the 1930s, and also enjoyed a string of hit records, both on their own and with BING CROSBY (notably on the 1932 million-seller "Dinah" backed by "Can't We Talk It Over" [Brunswick 6240]) with LOUIS ARMSTRONG, THE BOSWELL SISTERS, ELLA FITZGERALD, and others. When John, Jr., died in 1936, their father replaced him (John Sr., b. 1882; d. December 8, 1967) as bass vocalist in the group.

The Mills Brothers reached the peak of their popularity in the early 1940s. Their biggest hit came with the million-selling "Paper Doll" (Decca 18318; 1942), which was followed by another million-seller, "You Always Hurt the One You Love" (Decca 18599). They had further hits through the decade, and then scored big in 1952 with their version of "The Glow-Worm" (Decca 28384), a 1909 operetta song that was given new life with new lyrics by JOHNNY MERCER. John, Sr., finally retired in 1956, and the brothers soldiered on as a trio. The group continued to record through the late 1960s, having their last hit in 1968 with "Cab Driver" (Dot 17041), and performed until Harry's death in 1982. From the later 1980s until his death, Donald performed with his son, John Mills III; the younger Millses continue the family singing tradition, touring today.

# Mills Music, Inc.

The most productive publishing house of the 1920s. The emergence of Jack Mills (1891–1979) in July 1919, at 152 West Forty-fifth Street, was due to his days as a song plugger in the Alley. Most recently, he had been professional manager of McCarthy and Fisher Company. That experience spurred him to start his own firm. He established the genre of piano novelty RAGTIME with his purchase of ZEZ CONFREY's masterpiece, "Kitten on the Keys," in July 1921. This, along with nearly one hundred other pieces in this idiom that he eventually issued, gave him preeminence as a publisher of novelty rags. He also published many great blues and jazz numbers, such as "Down Hearted Blues," "I Just Want a Daddy I Can Call My Own," "Graveyard Dream Blues," "Farewell Blues," and "The Great White Way Blues."

In August 1928, the firm changed its name to Mills Music, Inc. The following year, in celebration of its tenth anniversary, Mills bought the catalogs of GUS EDWARDS Music, Stark and Cowan, Harold Dixon, McCarthy and Fisher, and FRED FISHER Music. In November 1931, Mills obtained the catalog of Waterson, Berlin and Snyder Company (minus the Berlin songs, which were already owned and published by IRVING BERLIN himself). From 1923 to 1932, the firm was located in the Mills Building, at 148–150 West Forty-sixth Street. Jack's brother Irving managed DUKE ELLINGTON (among other jazz performers) and the Mills firm published many of Ellington's compositions.

After World War II, the firm focused on classical music instructional publishing under the name of Belwin-Mills, Inc. Its back catalog is now part of WARNER/CHAPPELL MUSIC.

# James V. Monaco

Composer (b. Fornia, Italy, January 13, 1885; d. Beverly Hills, California, October 16, 1945). Monaco's family came to the United States when he was six years old, and settled in Albany, New York. He taught himself piano and began performing locally; his family then moved to Chicago in the first decade of the twentieth century, where he also worked local clubs. In 1910, Monaco moved to New York City, continuing his work as an itinerant pianist. He had his first publication in 1911 with "Oh, Mr. Dream Man," for which he wrote both words and music. His first big hit came in the *Ziegfeld Follies of 1912* when Lillian Lorraine sang "Row, Row, Row." It became such a hit that Ada Jones, Arthur Collins, and Byron Harlan and the American Quartet each had a hit recording. Through the years, it has been revived in several movies, and remains a standard.

AL JOLSON turned "You Made Me Love You" (with lyrics by JOSEPH MCCARTHY) into a major hit in 1913 (Columbia A-1374). Harry James revived it with a #5 hit in 1941 (Columbia 36296). McCarthy remained Monaco's primary lyricist through most of the 1910s. Al Jolson scored again in 1916 with "You're a Dog Gone Dangerous Girl" from his Broadway show, *Robinson Crusoe, Jr.* (Columbia A-2041). That same year, Ada Jones and Billy Murray had a hit with Monaco's "What Do You Want to Make Those Eyes at Me For?" (Victor 18224).

Monaco next had hits in 1920 with Bert Williams's recording of "Ten Little Bottles" (written with lyricist Ballard MacDonald), followed by "Caresses" (words and music by Monaco), a hit record for PAUL WHITEMAN. 1921 saw the hit "Dirty Hands, Dirty Face," sung by Al Jolson in the stage show *Bombo* (with lyrics by EDGAR LESLIE and Grant Clarke; typically Jolson also took a cut as "lyricist"). Jolson revived it in the film *The Jazz Singer*, and recorded it in March 1928, for a revival hit. 1924 saw Jane Green make a hit with "Me and the Boy

Friend" (Victor 19502). Mike Markel and his orchestra made a hit with the 1927 "Red Lips, Kiss My Blues Away" (Okeh 40805).

In 1930, Monaco moved to Hollywood to write for the movies; he scored an astounding twelve films that year, working primarily with lyricist CLIFF FRIEND. He had a few hits, but really hit it big when he signed with Paramount in 1936 to be staff composer for BING CROSBY's films, working with JOHNNY BURKE as his lyricist. Monaco's first big movie hit came from the his second Crosby score, 1938's *Sing, You Sinners*, which launched Crosby's #1 hit recording of "I've Got a Pocketful of Dreams" (Decca 1933). 1940 saw JIMMY DORSEY and his orchestra, with vocals by Helen O'Connell, scoring a #4 hit with "Six Lessons from Madame La Zonga" (Decca 3152). The same year, Monaco wrote the scores for the films *If I Had My Way*, *Rhythm on the River* (featuring the big hit "Only Forever," recorded by both TOMMY DORSEY and Eddie Duchin, and norminated as Best Song for the Oscars), and *Road to Singapore*. His major film scores include *Stage Door Canteen* (1943), *Pin-Up Girl* (1944), *Irish Eyes Are Smiling* (1944), *Sweet and Lowdown* (1944), and *The Dolly Sisters* (1945), from which he had his last hit, "I Can't Begin to Tell You," which Bing Crosby turned into a million-selling #1 hit (Decca 23457). Harry James and his orchestra, with Betty Grable as vocalist, had the #5 hit (Columbia 36867). Just as the record was breaking in the charts, Monaco died suddenly of a heart attack.

# Helen Morgan

Popular "torch singer" of the 1920s and 1930s (b. Helen Riggins, Danville, Ohio, August 2, 1890; d. Chicago, Illinois, October 8, 1941). Morgan got her start singing in Chicago nightclubs, and then came to New York to appear in *George White's Scandals* in 1925. Florenz Ziegfeld spotted her the next year in another revue, *Americana*, and signed her for the lead in Jerome Kern/Oscar Hammerstein's landmark, *Showboat* (1927). Her singing of the love ballads "Bill" and "Can't Help Lovin Dat Man" in that show made them huge hits, and made her a star. Her recording of "Bill" was a major seller in 1928 (Victor 21238). Morgan appeared in the 1929 and 1936 film adaptations of the show. Morgan's other major hit was GEORGE and IRA GERSHWIN's "The Man I Love."

During Prohibition, Morgan opened a series of speakeasies, and she became a heavy drinker. This led to health complications and her death in 1941. Her tragic death was a natural inspiration for a Hollywood biopic, and it came in 1957 with *The Helen Morgan Story*, in which the tragic singer was portrayed by Ann Blyth.

# Edwin H. Morris

Music publisher (b. Pittsburgh, Pennsylvania, December 18, 1906; d. Ventura, California, April 1, 1996). Morris began his career in music at age twenty-one, when he was hired by Warner Bros. Studios to build a music catalog for them. At Warners, he purchased several leading New York firms, including WITMARK, REMICK, and HARMS. In 1930, he was named to ASCAP's board of directors, and remained there for over three decades. In 1941, he struck out on his own, forming Edwin H. Morris Music, signing many of the leading Hollywood film composers, including IRA GERSHWIN, HAROLD ARLEN, JOHNNY MERCER, SAMMY CAHN, and JIMMY VAN HEUSEN. During the 1960s and 1970s, the firm turned its attention to Broadway, publishing the music for hits like *Hello, Dolly!* and *Mame* (Jerry Herman), *Bye Bye Birdie* and *Applause* (Charles Strouse and Lee Adams), and the all-time smash, *A Chorus Line* (Marvin Hamlisch and Ed Kleban). In 1976, the firm was purchased by MPL COMMUNICATIONS, INC.

# Theodore F. Morse

Composer (b. Washington, D.C., April 13, 1873; d. New York City, May 25, 1924). Morse came to New York City at the age of fourteen and worked for the Oliver Ditson Company as a junior clerk. He joined HOWLEY, HAVILAND AND COMPANY as a staff composer and plugger, left to become manager of F. A. MILLS, then left Mills to open his own firm, Morse Music Company in 1900. He sold his catalog two years later to Howley, Haviland and Dresser, and became manager of the professional department at American Music Company. American published his two-step "Happy Hooligan," based on the comic strip by Frederick Opper, then syndicated by the Hearst newspapers. In December 1903, Morse and F. B.

Haviland left American Music to form F. B. Haviland Publishing Company. It was incorporated in April 1904, with Haviland, Morse, and Richard Nugent as partners. At the new firm, Morse and lyricist Edward Madden (1878–1952) began their decadelong writing collaboration with "Blue Bell," which achieved a notable sale. Another succcess that year from the team was a COON SONG, "I've Got a Feelin' for You (Way Down in My Heart)." As an interpolation in a 1907 show, *Playing the Ponies*, they contributed "I'd Rather Be a Lobster Than a Wise Guy." The following year saw the team's greatest hit, "Down in Jungle Town." The next year, Morse left Haviland to start Theodore Morse Music Company, with Al Cook as his general manager. Morse's marriage to lyricist Theodora (Dolly) Terriss gave him a new professional collaborator. Their big hits came one after another, beginning in 1911 with the sensational rag song, "Another Rag." In 1912, they followed it with "When Uncle Joe Plays a Rag on His Old Banjo," which was featured in vaudeville by The Three Pickert Sisters and FRED and Adele ASTAIRE. The Pickerts also sang the married team's 1913 "Bobbin' Up and Down" to hit status. Morse teamed with lyricist Howard Johnson in 1915 for a FEIST hit, "M-O-T-H-E-R." Again for Feist, in 1917, Morse concocted his most famous song, from the music of Arthur Sullivan, when he and Dolly wrote "Hail! Hail! The Gang's All Here."

# Jelly Roll Morton

Composer and pianist (b. Ferdinand LaMott, New Orleans, Louisiana, October 20, 1890; d. Los Angeles, California, July 10, 1941). Morton created a way of arranging that encompassed other players' ideas and yet retained his own conceptions. Morton's piano style was distinctive and, once heard, was never forgotten or confused with anyone else's. He had definite ideas about his music and was the most articulate jazzman of his time. There was nothing haphazard or accidental in his performing, arranging, or composing; each musical device was well thought out and deliberately executed. As composer and performer, he created more diverse moods in his works than anyone else of his time. He also used unexpected rhythmic patterns to sustain audience interest. His use of sixths in the left hand provided uncommon voicings. What made his piano sound so distinctive, besides his touch, was his desire not to sound like a solo pianist, but to sound like an entire jazz band. His extraordinary left hand not only kept a steady rhythm like that of a tuba or string bass, but also incorporated the counterpoint of a trombone. His right hand alternated between the clear-cut melody line, as usually played by a trumpet, and the embellishments and flourishes of a clarinet. In performance, to complete the resemblance to a band, he would usually place a drumstick in his inner left shoe to beat against his bench or chair while playing.

Morton, playing and acting in a vaudeville comedy sketch, was the first jazzman to travel extensively around the country, from the time he was fourteen until he settled in Chicago in 1923, at the age of thirty-three. There he became an arranger and composer for the newly formed MELROSE BROTHERS MUSIC COMPANY. Although he had had one piece published earlier ("The 'Jelly Roll' Blues," issued by WILL ROSSITER in September 1915), his steady publishing, recording, and performing careers dated from his arrival in Chicago. Encouraged by the sales of "Wolverine Blues" (1923), Walter Melrose set up recording sessions with Gennett Records of Richmond, Indiana. This company eventually recorded every major dixieland jazz band (with the sole exception of the ORIGINAL DIXIELAND JAZZ BAND) and most of the important individual jazzmen of the 1920s.

Between July 1923 and June 1924, Morton recorded nineteen now-classic piano solos, sixteen of them his own compositions: all of these were eventually published by Melrose. The solo piano recordings were the start of his legend among his peers. His publications are important not only as vehicles for himself, but also as permanent parts of the jazz repertoire. The majority of his work was published by Melrose between 1923 and 1928.

"King Porter Stomp" was recorded more often by Morton and others than any of his other compositions. It was the first piano solo (Gennett 5289) he recorded at his first solo session on July 17, 1923, and it was among the last (General 4005) he recorded in his last solo session on December 14, 1939. This work started the swing era, when FLETCHER HENDERSON arranged it for BENNY GOODMAN's band in 1935 (Victor 25090). It has the distinction of being in the ragtimer's repertoire as well as those of dixieland bands and swing bands. Melrose published it in 1924.

"Milenberg Joys" led the eight Morton tunes published in 1925. Although it is a standard today and has been recorded by dance and jazz bands through the years, it is the only one not recorded by Morton himself. His famous rags "Kansas City Stomp" and "Grandpa's Spells," as well as his "Chicago Break Down," "Shreveport Stomp," "New Orleans Blues," "London Blues," and "Tom Cat Blues," were all issued in that year.

Morton published six compositions in 1926. His "Sweetheart o' Mine" was a reworking of his earlier "Frog-I-More Rag," the lead sheet of which was entered for copyright in 1918. "Stratford Hunch" was the last of his original piano solos to be issued. Melrose obtained a contract with the Victor Company for Morton to record with a seven-piece band of his choosing. It was to be an ideal band, for Morton was allowed to request his favorite musicians, those usually working for other leaders. In an unusual arrangement, Morton handpicked his band for recordings only and called his group the Red Hot Peppers. He did not have a performance band at this time. Even as the personnel of the Red Hot Peppers changed during its four years of recording, the group never failed to provide stimulating jazz. The remaining tunes published in the exciting year of 1926 came from the recordings of the Red Hot Peppers: "Black Bottom Stomp," "Sidewalk Blues," "Dead Man Blues," and "Cannon Ball Blues."

Two old solos and four new ones account for his 1927 output. "The Pearls," with its clever use of the rudimentary timekeeping of the left hand, and "Mr. Jelly Lord" were finally issued. "Billy Goat Stomp," "Jungle Blues," "Wild Man Blues," and "Hyena Stomp" were other Peppers tunes. In 1928, Melrose published his "Boogaboo" and "Georgia Swing," a reworking of an earlier Melrose tune, Santo Pecora's "She's Crying for Me."

Morton reminisced, played, and sang his life story to Alan Lomax for the Library of Congress during a six-week period in May and June 1938. His reminiscences stand as the greatest audio documentary of a jazzman ever recorded. He made a few final recordings during the 1940s while living in New York, but did not live to see the dixieland revival of the post-World War II period.

# Lewis F. Muir

Composer (b. Louis Meuer, New York City, May 30, 1883; d. New York City, December 3, 1915). Meuer went to St. Louis for the World's Fair in 1904, impressing audiences there with his fantastic piano playing. He had long, tapered fingers and a reach of nearly two octaves. He was known to play only in the key of F sharp. Back in New York, he published his first song with Shapiro Music Publisher. This was a rag song, with lyrics by E. RAY GOETZ, titled "Play That Fandango Rag." It was sung in the *Follies of 1909* by Lillian Lorraine.

The following year, Muir went to publisher J. Fred Helf, to whom he submitted another rag song for the next *Follies*. It was called "Play That Barber Shop Chord," with words by William Tracey. Bert Williams performed it in the show. He did such a good job that Ballard Macdonald became angry, because he had had the original idea and written the dummy lyric, but had abandoned the song. Macdonald sued Helf for leaving his name off the sheet music and was awarded damages of $37,500, which forced Helf into bankruptcy. But before Helf closed shop, he published Muir's piano solo "Chilly Billy Bee Rag." It stirred enough interest for the publisher to have Ed Moran write words to it. Helf issued the song as "When My Marie Sings Chilly-Billy-Bee." The last song Muir wrote for Helf was "Oh, You Bear Cat Rag," composed with Fred Watson, with lyrics by William Tracey (1893–1957).

From Helf, it was a jump to the house of F. A. MILLS for Muir. He was teamed with EDGAR LESLIE in 1911 to write a couple of rag songs, "The Matrimony Rag" and the snappy "When Ragtime Rosie Ragged the Rosary." Both songs attracted attention. The second was fast becoming a hit, vaudevillians thinking it a cute song, when a jealous columnist for the trade paper *New York Clipper*, L. WOLFE GILBERT, ingenuously mentioned in his column that it was a "crime" to make the rosary the subject of a ragtime song. He also attacked Mills for publishing it and perpetrating such a sacrilege. A few days later, Gilbert ran into Muir, who was hopping mad. Who was Gilbert to criticize his song, anyway? What had Gilbert written? When Gilbert mentioned the few he had published, Muir shot back that he hadn't heard of them, and that if Gilbert thought himself a writer, why didn't he prove it by writing a song with him? That evening, the two of them got together at Muir's house and created a summertime love song called "Do You Feel It in the Air?" and a chorus for a Dixie song.

The next morning they took their songs to Fred Mills. He listened politely to their ballad and announced that it stank. Gilbert then sang the Dixie song they titled "Waiting for the Robert E. Lee." Mills said he didn't believe in Dixie songs anymore, that they were passé, but offered Gilbert a batch of professional copies of his songs to let Gilbert see the kind of music his firm published. Gilbert left the office steaming and, after he had walked a few blocks, realized that he hadn't taken the professional copies. He knew that his wife would like to play them, so back he went. As he entered the door, Mills asked him to step inside and sing his Dixie song again, since he couldn't get the tune out of his mind. AL

JOLSON introduced it a few weeks later in his show at the Winter Garden Theatre. Soon after, SOPHIE TUCKER plugged it on her tour, and newcomer Ruth Roye performed it at the Palace. The song sold over two million copies and established the team of Muir and Gilbert. For two years, they turned out hit after hit, but none of them sold as many copies or lasted as long as their first collaboration, which is still performed by singers and bands when they want to evoke steamboat days.

Before the song became a hit, Muir wrote another good rag song with Edgar Leslie, "Dancing Dan, the Ragtime Battling Man." With publisher-composer MAURICE ABRAHAMS, husband of singer Belle Baker, Muir wrote "Ragtime Cowboy Joe," with lyrics by newcomer Grant Clarke (1891–1931). It was a smashing success.

In the meantime, Muir and Gilbert turned out a string of hits in 1912, great rag songs like "Ragging the Baby to Sleep," "Take Me to That Swanee Shore," "Here Comes My Daddy Now," and a song that Al Jolson made famous, "Hitchy Koo." The following year the team followed up with "Little Rag Baby Doll" and a COON SONG, "Mammy Jinny's Jubilee." That same year saw Muir's second and final piano rag, "Heavy on the Catsup," published. The last year of their collaboration, 1914, saw "Buy a Bale of Cotton for Me," "Camp meeting Band," and "Mootching Along." Muir died the following December.

# Billy Murray

Singer (b. Philadelphia, Pennsylvania, May 25, 1877; d. Jones Beach, New York, August 17, 1954.) Murray was the first singer to make his reputation on recordings rather than live performance. He started his recording career as a tenor, singing for the Edison Record Company at the beginning of the twentieth century, and made his last recording during World War II. By the 1910s, he was a star and had recorded most of the hits of his era. His recordings were big plugs for the songs that he chose and were a great boost for the Alley. He specialized in comic, novelty, and topical songs, and sang duets with Bob Roberts, Len Spencer, Ada Jones, Gladys Rice, Henry Burr, and Aileen Stanley. He was also a member of the Haydn Quartet, the American Quartet, and the Heidelberg Quintet. His first hits came in 1904 with "Bedelia" (Edison 8550, a cylinder), "Navajo" (Columbia 1655), and "Meet Me in St. Louis, Louis" (Victor 2850). In January 1905, he recorded the first song to honor the Wright Brothers' historic flight from Kitty Hawk, "Come Take a Trip in My Air-Ship" (Victor 2986). He became a champion of GEORGE M. COHAN's works, establishing many of them as hits, starting in 1905 with "Yankee Doodle Boy" (Columbia 3051), "Give My Regards to Broadway" (Columbia 3165), and "The Grand Old Rag" (Victor 4634), which became the biggest seller Victor had during this decade. "In My Merry Oldsmobile" was inspired by the first transcontinental auto race (Victor 4467). "Take Me Out to the Ball Game" remains the most celebrated song of our national pastime, and Murray's 1908 recording established it as a #1 hit (Victor 5570).

Murray started recording Irving Berlin songs in 1910, with "Sweet Italian Love" (Edison 10427). In 1916, he recorded Berlin's own favorite, "I Love a Piano" (Victor 17945). That same year, he recorded Berlin's first double song, "Simple Melody," with Elsie Baker (the real name of "Edna Brown") (Victor 18051), and Tony Jackson's "Pretty Baby," from *The Passing Show of 1916* (Victor 18102). In 1920, he recorded Berlin's great Prohibition song "I'll See You in C-U-B-A" (Victor 18652). His final hit came in 1927 a duet with Aileen Stanley, "Bridget O'Flynn (Where've Ya Been?)" (Victor 20240).

# Music Box Revues

See *Irving Berlin*

# N

## Ray Noble

Composer, bandleader, and radio actor (b. Brighton, England, December 17, 1903; d. Santa Barbara, California, April 3, 1979). Noble's extensive musical training showed in his dance bands with jazzy overtones. His father was an amateur songwriter and musician, and Noble was trained as a chorister as a boy, then attended university, and eventually studied at London's Royal Academy of Music.

In 1926, Noble broke into popular music when he submitted a dance band arrangement to a popular music magazine *Melody Maker*, as part of a contest; he won, which led to work with several British dance bands. He was musical director of HMV Records in England from 1929 to 1934. He recorded there under the name New Mayfair Orchestra, and his 1931 composition "Good Night, Sweetheart" (HMV 5984) became a favorite for bands to end their dances. Noble was the first British bandleader to achieve success on records in the United States. His 1933 "Love Is the Sweetest Thing" made the #1 chart hit with his band's recording (Victor 24333). In 1934 he came out with "The Very Thought of You" (Victor 24657), which Vaughn Monroe revived ten years later (Victor 20-1605). Also in 1934, he came to the United States to form an American band, calling on a young Glenn Miller to help him build it. His beautiful 1938 "I Hadn't Anyone Till You" (Brunswick 8079) was featured in a 1950 film, *In a Lonely Place.* 1938 also saw his instrumental "Cherokee" become the theme of Charlie Barnet and his orchestra (Bluebird 10373). Noble's American bands were respected by musicians for their great players, as well as their arrangements featuring unusual harmonies mixed with jazz rhythms.

Noble appeared as an actor on the *Burns and Allen,* radio show in the late 1930s and became a sporadic regular on the Edgar Bergen-Charlie McCarthy show from 1941 to the early 1950s. Noble and his band were featured in such films as *The Big Broadcast of 1936* (1935), *A Damsel in Distress* (1937), *Here We Go Again!* (1942), and *Out of This World* (1945). He retired in 1955.

# Abe Olman

Composer (b. Cincinnati, Ohio, December 20, 1888; d. Rancho Mirage, California, January 4, 1984). After working for Chicago publishers, Olman came to New York City as manager of the short-lived GEORGE W. MEYER Music Company in 1912. (This firm was backed by GUS EDWARDS, who, for contractual reasons, couldn't operate it under his own name.) In 1914, Olman formed his own company in Chicago, the LaSalle Music Publishing Company, to publish his latest song, "Down among the Sheltering Palms," with lyrics by James Brockman. Olman plugged it so well locally that LEO FEIST, who had a branch office in Chicago, heard about the song's success and purchased it. Feist gave it to AL JOLSON to sing in a stage production, and that boost turned the song into a three-million copy seller.

Olman's next big hit was published in 1917 by Forster, with lyrics by Ed Rose (1875–1935). "Oh, Johnny! Oh!" was introduced by NORA BAYES, and it sold well over a million copies. It was revived by the ANDREWS SISTERS in 1939 and sold over a million again (Decca 2840). Olman's last major success was his 1920 hit, originally entitled "O-HI-O," with lyrics by JACK YELLEN. It initially sold over three million copies because EDDIE CANTOR introduced it; it was next taken up by Lou Holtz, TED LEWIS, Al Jolson, and VAN AND SCHENCK in vaudeville and on stage. Unlike today's recording artists, who won't, as a rule, record another singer's hit, all of these top 1920s performers sang the song, and their fans bought the sheet music in great numbers. Because the pop music scene of today seems to require only one version of a song, the impact of several stars making a hit with the same song is not something we are familiar with. It is our loss, since each artist has something unique to bring to a song. "O-HI-O" was revived by the Andrews Sisters in 1940, under the title "Down by the Ohio," and it sold another million copies (Decca 3065).

Olman's lifelong success in the Alley came as a publisher, not only with his own firm but also as general manager of The Big Three from 1935 on. He retired to act as consultant to his nephew, Howard Richmond of The Richmond Organization. One of their projects was the formation of the National Academy of Popular Music and its Songwriters Hall of Fame. The Academy came into being in 1969, with Johnny Mercer as its first president. Olman gave special attention to the archives of the Academy, which now includes over 50,000 pieces of sheet music, 800 piano rolls, and 3,000 record albums, numerous playbills, and photographs. Contributions continue to swell this collection, and the collection makes available to those interested in popular music original artifacts for study and enjoyment. This organization is dedicated to the preservation of popular music, and it appears to be the only one of its kind in the world. The archives are currently housed at Long Island University's C. W. Post Campus in Brookville, New York.

# George Olsen

Bandleader (b. Portland, Oregon, March 18, 1893; d. Paramus, New Jersey, March 18, 1971). Olsen started his career by forming a band at the University of Michigan, then headed to the West Coast and later New York, where he worked for Florenz Ziegfeld. Olsen led the pit bands for Ziegfeld's Broadway musicals *Kid Boots* (1924), *Ziegfeld Follies of 1924*, *Sunny* (1925), *Good News* (1927), and *Whoopee* (1928). His wife, Ethel Schutta, was his female vocalist, and Fran Frey was his male singer.

The Olsen band's years of greatest popularity were 1925–1935. His first hit came in 1924 with "He's the Hottest Man in Town" (Victor 19375). "Who?," his only million-seller, came from the 1925 musical *Sunny* (Victor 19840). He had the #1 Irving Berlin hit "Always" in 1926 (Victor 19955). That same year he had a #3 hit with George Gershwin's "Someone to Watch over Me," from *Oh, Kay!* (Victor 20392), and a #2 hit, "Blue Skies," from *Betsy* (Victor 20455). "At Sundown" was his first hit in 1927 (Victor 20476), followed by "The Best Things in Life Are Free" (Victor 20872), "Varsity Drag," and " 'Good News," from the hit musical of the same name (Victor 20875). "My Heart Stood Still," from the 1928 *A Connecticut Yankee* (Victor 21034), and "Doin' the Raccoon" (Victor 21701) were big hits for him. Also in 1928, he recorded "A Precious Little Thing Called Love," which topped the charts (Victor 21832). It came from an early talkie, *The Shopworn Angel.* "Say It Isn't So" was Olsen's big hit in 1932 (Victor 24124), and his last #1 hit, "The Last Round-Up" (Columbia 2791-D), came the following year from the musical revue, *Ziegfeld Follies of 1934.* Upon the death of Orville Knapp, Olsen took over his band. They played on radio and entertained troops during World War II and in the early 1950s. Then, Olsen left the band business and bought a restaurant that featured tapes of his old records.

# Original Dixieland Jazz Band (ODJB)

An extremely popular recording and performing ensemble of the late teens, the ODJB helped make several Tin Pan Alley compositions into enormous record and sheet music successes.

1917—Jazz was in the air! As early as 1911, bands were playing in cabarets and for dancing in New Orleans. These were called "ragtime bands," as opposed to marching bands, because they tried to imitate piano rags on their various instruments.

Several members of Jack Laine's Reliance Band went to Chicago in March 1916 to play at Schiller's Café. With some personnel changes, this band joined Johnny Fogarty's Dancing Review at McVicker's, a famous vaudeville house, in August. Fogarty was known to Chicago audiences for his classy society dancing act. His interest in the fox-trot was evident from his group's photograph on the sheet music of the fox-trot arrangement of Shelton Brooks's "Walkin' the Dog." Johnny Fogarty signed the "Jass" (as it was then called) Band to appear with his act, and *Billboard* reported them to be a sensation. In early November 1916, the band members were chosen to come to New York to make the first jazz recordings in late January 1917.

The Original Dixieland Jazz Band (ODJB) consisted of New Orleans natives: Nick LaRocca (1889–1961), cornet; Eddie Edwards (1891–1963), trombone; Larry Shields (1893–1953), clarinet; Henry Ragas (1891–1919), piano; and Tony Sbarbaro (1897–1969), drums. The band's impact was immediately felt in the Alley. Chicago-based Henry I. Marshall (1883–1958) and Gus Kahn wrote the first tune about the group, "That Funny Jass Band from Dixieland," which was the first song to use the word for the new musical form in the title. It was published in November 1916 by Jerome H. Remick. Another pair of Chicagoans, Eddie Gray and Jerry Joyce, followed quickly with "When I Hear That 'Jaz' Band Play," issued in late 1916 by Frank K. Root and Company of Chicago. Bert Williams, an early admirer of the band, is featured on the cover of this number. The band's popularity did not

The Original Dixieland Jazz Band pictured on the cover of "Barnyard Blues," published by Leo Feist.

go unnoticed by the show business crowd. AL JOLSON raved about them upon his return to New York from Chicago, and he sent agent Max Hart to Chicago to hear them. Hart immediately signed them to open at the new Reisenweber's Restaurant, which was to launch its new Paradise Ballroom in mid-January. After the band's first week there, they were asked to open the new 400 Club Room at the end of the month. With Reisenweber's skillful promotion highlighting the jazz band's music for dancing, patrons flocked to the 400 Club.

Columbia Records stole a march (nay, a one-step) on its rival, the Victor Talking Machine Company, when it signed the ODJB, as it was now known, to a contract. They were to make two sides on January 30, 1917. When the band arrived at the Columbia studio, they were handed two brand-new songs to learn and record that afternoon; SHELTON BROOKS's "Darktown Strutters' Ball" and JAMES F. HANLEY's and Ballard MacDonald's "(Back Home Again in) Indiana." Since the others couldn't read music, Henry Ragas and Larry Shields had to play these songs over and over until all the members knew them and could work out their improvisations. The Columbia engineer was not sympathetic to the band, and neither was the artists and repertoire director. They decided after the session to shelve the two recordings. It was only after ODJB had a hit disc for Victor that Columbia released its recordings, in September 1917 (Columbia A-2297).

With all of Reisenweber's ballyhoo, Victor executives decided they should be the first to record this new type of band, unaware that the band had already recorded for Columbia. They scheduled a recording session for the band on February 26, 1917. Taking infinitely more pains than the Columbia engineer, Charles Souey made hundreds of test recordings to obtain the best placement of the five instruments, and Eddie King, head of Victor's artists and repertoire department, allowed them to record their own compositions. As a result, the Victor acoustic recordings stand up today. We can still enjoy the ODJB's work; the sound is clear, and their enthusiasm and vitality remain contagious. Their first number was "Livery Stable Blues" (published under the ODJB banner as "Barnyard Blues"), followed by the "Dixieland Jass Band One-Step" (later known as "The Original Dixieland One-Step"). Released on Victor 18255 on April 1, these two tunes comprised the first jazz record ever! The *Victor Bulletin* of March 17 announced their new discovery this way: "Spell it Jass, Jas, Jaz or Jazz—nothing can spell a Jass band . . . Anyway, a Jass band is the newest thing in the cabarets, adding greatly to the hilarity thereof."

The Victor record received nationwide distribution and created a monster, causing as much concern among guardians of the public morality as RAGTIME had twenty years earlier (and foreshadowing the rumpus rock and roll would cause almost forty years later). Everyone, from clergy to concerned parents to doctors, inveighed against this free expression. The ODJB's collective improvisations on their own compositions created an ensemble sound refreshing to the young, and the tunes, not quite as syncopated as piano rags, were far jauntier than the pop songs rendered by brass recording bands or by dance orchestras led by violinists. The initial ODJB recordings for Victor ended with their July 17, 1918, session, with a total of twelve issued sides.

LEO FEIST signed the ODJB to publish exclusively with his firm. He first issued several of their original compositions: "Tiger Rag," "Ostrich Walk," "Sensation," "At the Jazz Band Ball," "Barnyard Blues," "Skeleton Jangle," and "Look at 'Em Doing It." During the next year, as their Victor records kept coming, Feist issued "Bluin' the Blues," "Clarinet Marmalade," "Fidgety Feet," "Mournin' Blues," and "Lazy Daddy." He was surprised to discover, given the music's popularity, that sales were sluggish.

Feist labeled the ODJB originals as either "fox-trots" or "one-steps." This latter designation was new and used primarily to describe the band's faster numbers. (Other good one-steps included "Honky-Tonky" by Chris Smith, "Fluffy Ruffles" by George Hamilton Green, "Step with Pep" by Mel B. Kaufman, and "Limber Jack" by Don Richardson.) Younger members of the piano-playing public couldn't get enough of this good stuff. However, because the piano part in the sheet music arrangements could not convey, much less duplicate, the excitement and the spontaneity of jazz band performance, the Alley publishers abandoned the publication of jazz tunes because of poor sales. This decision foreshadowed the demise of the Alley in the 1950s. The sound of recorded rock and roll songs could not be duplicated from sheet music, because so much of the style depended on the recorded performance rather than on the content of the tunes. Tin Pan Alley could no longer compete with record companies for dominance of the popular music scene.

# Original Memphis Five

The exciting, vibrant sounds of the Original Memphis Five are still joyous to hear. They were unlike any other small jazz band of the 1920s. They are rarely mentioned in jazz history books, yet they exerted the greatest influence of all jazz bands on the public. They did not play at the usual dance halls (or unusual ones, for that matter), nor did they make the obligatory tours that so exhaust musicians. They were a studio group, in existence only to make records, not perform live for the public. And make records they did—more than any other group of their time! Just how many they made is still a question, since they recorded for many record companies under a host of pseudonyms. In addition to their "official" name, they recorded as Bailey's Lucky Seven, The Cotton Pickers, Jazzbo's Carolina Serenaders, Ladd's Black Aces, Lanin's Southern Serenaders, McMurray's California Thumpers, New Orleans Blackbirds, and the Tennessee Ten.

Even their "official" name is misleading—they didn't come from Memphis, nor were they always five in number. The founding members, Frank Signorelli (piano) and Phil Napoleon (trumpet), were the original groupies of the ORIGINAL DIXIELAND JAZZ BAND. They and their friends Miff Mole (trombone), Jimmy Lytell (clarinet), and Jack Roth (drums) would follow the ODJB from job to job, even sitting in with their idols when one or several didn't show up for the evening. Frank Signorelli (1901–1975) was the luckiest of the admirers; he actually got to record with the ODJB.

The Original Memphis Five's prolificacy gave them unique standing in the record business. Their special sound (mainly emanating from Napoleon) and easy tempos made their music ideal for dancing. The distinctive sound of this group is at its purest when the two leaders play a chorus together. Phil Napoleon (1901–1991) invariably mutes his trumpet for an intimate feeling, allowing Signorelli's sensitive and rhythmical piano backing to provide the animation and impetus for the rest of the band. Jimmy Lytell's clarinet is directly inspired by the ODJB's Larry Shields, but has a fuller tone. The Five's drive and their ability to ad-lib made their music ideal for listening and fun to dance to. As a result, the Original Memphis Five made a profound impression on the record-buying public during the 1920's, one that is still not fully appreciated. This is probably the only jazz group to remain fairly anonymous despite a readily identifiable sound. Their collective record sales were phenomenal.

It is not surprising to find Jack Mills publishing the compositions of the Original Memphis Five (or, more properly, those by Napoleon and Signorelli), because the band plugged so many of Mills' hot numbers on records. The best of the published Napoleon-Signorelli tunes seem to come from 1923, although their recordings of them started in late 1922. "Memphis Glide" became the group's theme song (Perfect 14132). "Great White Way Blues" (Vocalion 14527) and "Shufflin' Mose" (Perfect 14150) were published by Mills and achieved some success in sheet music. "Snuggle Up a Bit" and "Teasin' Squeezin' Man o' Mine" (both on Pathe 036043) and "Just Hot," written with JIMMY MCHUGH (Brunswick 2507), were big record sellers. "Sioux City Sue" (1924) (Pathe 036072), written with WALTER DONALDSON, is not to be confused with the 1945 pop song of the same name. The first one didn't go anywhere. In 1924, Napoleon and Signorelli composed "The Meanest Blues" (Perfect 14323) and "Mama's Boy" (Pathe 036168). In the 1930s, Signorelli was the composer of such song hits "A Blues Serenade," "I'll Never Be the Same," and "Stairway to the Stars."

While their output was unusually large, the Original Memphis Five's repertoire was not correspondingly large, because they would record the same tune for a dozen different companies. But this apparent drawback affords us the opportunity to see just how creative they were. Each rendition was a separate and individual one, not the same stock arrangement take after take. The band still communicates its excitement and enthusiasm to listeners.

# P

## Pace and Handy Music Company

The second black-owned music publishing company. It was formed in Memphis, Tennessee, by W. C. HANDY and Harry Herbert Pace (1884–1943). Harry Pace supplied the money and business contacts, while Handy ran the firm and composed much of its music. They had written their first song together in 1907, "In the Cotton Fields of Dixie," published by George Jaberg of Cincinnati. The first number they published themselves was Handy's "Jogo Blues" in 1913. The idea to start publishing actually came the year before, when Handy formed Handy Music Company to issue his "Memphis Blues." Shortly after he published it, he sold his copyright to songwriter-publisher Theron Bennett for $50.00, after he was assured that the tune was too difficult for the average player. Bennett had words added by George A. Norton a year later, and transferred the publishing of it to the Joe Morris Music Company.

Pace and Handy had a banner year in 1914, with the publication of Handy's "The St. Louis Blues," which became the most famous BLUES ever written. For his trio, Handy reused the trio section of his "Jogo Blues." The song was slow in getting established because the blues concept was too new for wide public acceptance. It wasn't until Handy's company

Pace & Handy's front office, c. 1923.

moved to New York that the tune finally took off. Later in 1914, Handy published his "Yellow Dog Rag," changed in 1919 to "Yellow Dog Blues," when Joseph C. Smith's orchestra recorded it for the Victor Talking Machine Company, featuring the laughing trombone of Harry Raderman (Victor 18618).

Sales of the "rag" version, while not spectacular, were encouraging enough for Pace and Handy to continue the business venture. Being a local publisher in the South, with a small catalog, the firm didn't have national exposure but depended on Chicago jobbers for distribution. Their only advertising was done through ads and publicity in the black press, notably the *Chicago Defender*. In 1915, Pace and Handy issued Handy's "Joe Turner Blues" and a takeoff on Franz Schubert called "Shoeboot's Serenade." The following year saw the publication of Handy's "Ole Miss Blues" and William King Phillips's "The Florida Blues." The cumulative effect of sales enabled the firm to move in 1917 to Chicago, where increased exposure of its blues catalog increased its sheet music sales. The first tunes published in the new office were Charles Hillman's "Preparedness Blues" and Douglas Williams's "The Hooking Cow Blues," to which Handy added some "jazz and blues." That year Handy wrote and published his "Beale Street," the first edition of which was issued, appropriately enough, in Memphis. It proved a huge success.

Other publishers had noted the sales generated by Pace and Handy's catalog, and tried to emulate them. Early in 1915, Will Rossiter, published Jelly Roll Morton's "The 'Jelly Roll' Blues" as an instrumental number. Sheet music sales were sluggish, but the tune later became a favorite of jazz bands and pianists.

In September 1917, Handy was asked to bring his band to New York to record for Columbia Records. Early in 1918, Handy decided to settle his publishing partnership in New

York and make it a specialty house in Tin Pan Alley. Pace and Handy found offices in the Gaiety Building, at 1547 Broadway. Their New York business began with Eddie Green's (1901–1950) "A Good Man Is Hard to Find," which SOPHIE TUCKER turned into a smash hit. The firm quickly followed, in mid-1918, with Clarence A. Stout's "O Death, Where Is Thy Sting," to cash in on Bert Williams's hit recording of it (Columbia A-2652). Handy himself contributed to the war effort that year with "The Kaiser's Got the Blues."

Pace and Handy made a good deal of its money from mechanical royalties paid on its recorded songs. One of the firm's biggest hits was spurred by the ORIGINAL DIXIELAND JAZZ BAND's recording of "The St. Louis Blues" (Victor 18772). The money generated from this record enabled the firm to move, in August 1920, to 232 West Forty-sixth Street and again, in July 1921, to still more spacious quarters at 165 West Forty-seventh Street. Harry Pace had sold his interest in the firm to Handy in April 1921, when Pace opened the first black-owned and operated record company, Black Swan Records. Handy renamed the firm Handy Brothers Music Company.

# Mitchell Parish

Lyricist (b. Shreveport, Louisiana, July 10, 1900; d. New York City, March 31, 1993). For the most part, Parrish wrote without benefit of collaboration. Many of his hits resulted when he put words to a melody long after the melody had been composed. In some cases, the tune had been a hit before his lyrics appeared. In every case, the song became a greater hit, and often a standard, because of the addition of his words.

Parish began his career when publisher Joe Morris hired him to write special material for vaudeville singers—recitations, punch lines, extra verses, and alternate lyrics to songs. Parish's first published song was "Carolina Rolling Stone" (1921), with music by the husband-and-wife team of Eleanor Young and Harry Squires. It was published by Morris and was featured by Willie and Eugene Howard in vaudeville. Bailey's Lucky Seven made a fine recording (Gennett 4868).

His big chance came when he was hired as staff lyricist by Jack Mills. Mills was the first to give Parish already famous melodies to turn into songs. "Sweet Lorraine" (1928) was composed by Cliff Burwell and was helped to popularity by RUDY VALLEE on radio. (It was this song that started jazz pianist Nat "King" Cole's vocal career in 1937, when a drunk in a club insisted that he sing it. He agreed reluctantly because he had never sung in public, having achieved popularity as pianist in the King Cole Trio. The reception was so great that he henceforth included singing in his act.)

"Lazy Rhapsody" (1929) was composed by Harry Sosnik (1906–1996) and Howard Jackson. Over the years, it has become a standard in nightclubs. It was given special treatment in an album of the same name, arranged and performed by Lou Busch (Capitol T-1072).

When "Star Dust" (1929) was first given to Parish, he declined to write lyrics for it because he didn't like it as a swing tune. But he did so after he heard VICTOR YOUNG's ballad arrangement for the ISHAM JONES Orchestra (Brunswick 4586). "Mood Indigo" (1931) was ostensibly written by Irving Mills to music by DUKE ELLINGTON and Barney Bigard. It was actually Bigard's melody and Parish's lyric, but Ellington and Mills claimed credit. It is the only Parish song for which he is not named as lyricist on the sheet music.

"Sentimental Gentleman from Georgia" (1932) was composed by Frank Perkins (1908–1988). The BOSWELL SISTERS helped make this a standard (Brunswick 6395). "The Scat Song" (1932) was composed by Perkins with help from CAB CALLOWAY, who made it "his" song (Brunswick 6272). "One Morning in May" (1933) was composed by HOAGY CARMICHAEL, who also introduced it. "Sophisticated Lady" (1933) is probably Duke Ellington's most famous melody. Until Parish put lyrics to it, it was only a piece of special material for the Ellington band. Since then, it has become an evergreen.

"Hands Across the Table" (1934) was composed by Jean Delettre for Lucienne Boyer to sing in the revue, *CONTINENTAL VARIETIES*. "Sidewalks of Cuba" (1934) has a melody of Ben Oakland's (1907–1979). It was introduced in the twenty-fifth edition of the *Cotton Club Parade*. Woody Herman and his orchestra revived it in 1946 (Columbia 37197).

"Stars Fell on Alabama" (1934) has a marvelous melody by Frank Perkins. It has been identified with Ozzie Nelson and his orchestra, and with Woody Herman in the 1940s. Jack Teagarden also performed it memorably (Brunswick 6993).

"Stairway to the Stars" (1935, 1939) was taken from a theme in Matty Malneck (1904–1981) and Frank Signorelli's "Park Avenue Fantasy," first published in 1935. After Parish wrote the lyrics, it became a smash hit, featured in GLENN MILLER, Ozzie Nelson, and PAUL WHITEMAN renditions. "Organ Grinder Swing" (1936) and "Mr. Ghost Goes to Town" (1936) had melodies by swing bandleader WILL HUDSON.

"Don't Be That Way" (1938) was arranger Edgar Sampson's melody. It was recorded by Chick Webb and his orchestra as an instrumental in November 1934 (Decca 483). By the time Parish wrote the words, BENNY GOODMAN's name had been added as cocomposer. Goodman also helped make it a hit (Victor 25792). "Riverboat Shuffle" was published in 1925 as an instrumental by Hoagy Carmichael. In 1939, Parish made it famous again by putting words to it.

"Deep Purple" (1939) was another example of a famous instrumental becoming even more popular after Parish worked his miracles. Peter De Rose (1900–1953) wrote this beloved melody in 1934, but after the Parish lyrics, Larry Clinton's Orchestra with vocalist Bea Wain had a best-selling recording (Victor 26141). It has been recorded through the years, and in 1963 Nino Tempo and April Stevens revived it (Atco 6273). Their record received a Grammy.

"Moonlight Serenade" (1939) was composed by bandleader Glenn Miller, who made it his theme song. It has been a favorite through the years. "All My Love" (1950) was composed by Paul Durand from Ravel's "Bolero." Patti Page made a best-selling recording (Mercury 5455).

In 1950, Parish wrote lyrics to "The Syncopated Clock," "Serenata," and "Sleigh Ride," all composed by LEROY ANDERSON. He later added words to Anderson's "Blue Tango" (1952) and "Forgotten Dreams" (1962).

Mitchell Parish in his later years.

"Tzena" (1950) was an Israeli pop tune that Julian Grossman adapted, with words by Parish. Gordon Jenkins and the Weavers made the hit recording (Decca 27077). "Ruby" (1953) was composed by Heinz Roemheld for the nonmusical film *Ruby Gentry*. It was popularized by Les Baxter and his orchestra (Capitol 2457). "Volare" (1958) was composed by Domenico Modugno, who had the #1 million-seller (Decca 30677). "Ciao, Ciao, Bambina" (1959) was the last big hit Parish had, to the music of Domenico Modugno.

*Stardust* (February 19, 1987), a magnificent Broadway revue, brought together the best of Mitchell Parish's songs. It was a richly deserved tribute to one of the Alley's most creative lyricists.

# Maceo Pinkard

African-American composer (b. Bluefield, West Virginia, June 27, 1897; d. New York City, July 21, 1962). Pinkard started with a theatrical agency in Omaha, Nebraska, where he had his first song published. It was called "I'm Goin' Back Home" (1915). From this inauspicious beginning, he came to New York, where he collaborated with William Tracey on his first million-selling hit, "Mammy o' Mine" (1919). His next success was "I'm Always Stuttering" (1922), which was styled after Zez Confrey's "Stumbling." This similarity was not lost on Confrey, who was asked to arrange it for piano roll (QRS 2079). Confrey took full advantage of the resemblance by including "Stumbling" rhythms whenever possible.

In the mid-1920s Pinkard hit his stride. For five years, he knocked out hit after hit, starting with "Sweet Georgia Brown" (1925), with lyrics by Ken Casey (1899–1965). It was introduced by bandleader Ben Bernie, who, for plugging purposes, cut himself in on the song as cocomposer although he did no writing. The same year, with Roy Turk as his collaborator, Pinkard wrote "Sweet Man," a fox-trot that was given a royal treatment on piano roll by Zez Confrey (Ampico 206571).

The team of Pinkard and Turk hit it big again in 1926 with "Gimme a Little Kiss, Will Ya, Huh?" which was introduced by Guy Lombardo and given another big boost by Whispering Jack Smith, who cut himself in on the writing credits (Victor 19978). The same year, the team created the snappy fox-trot "I Wonder What's Become of Joe?," introduced by Harry Reser's Seven Little Polar Bears (Lincoln 2536).

Working with Billy Rose, Pinkard turned out "Here Comes the Show Boat" (1927), introduced by Ethel Waters in *Africana*, and later used in the first movie version of *Show Boat* (1929). It was also the theme for *Maxwell House Show Boat*, a radio variety program. The same year, with Sidney Mitchell, he composed "Sugar," popularized by Ann Howe.

In 1928, Pinkard teamed with Archie Gottler (1896–1959) and Charles Tobias (1898–1970) to produce two big hits, "Don't Be Like That," which became a Helen Kane favorite, and "Lila," which Waring's Pennsylvanians recorded on a big-selling disc (Victor 21333).

Pinkard alone wrote "I'll Be a Friend with Pleasure" (1930), which Bix Beiderbecke and his orchestra recorded successfully, the orchestra including such latter-day bandleaders as Benny Goodman, Jimmy Dorsey, and Gene Krupa (Victor 23008). For his last two hits in this Depression year, Pinkard returned to his first New York partner, William Tracey, to write "Okay, Baby," recorded by McKinney's Cotton Pickers (Victor 23000), and "Them There Eyes," which had several revivals, including a recording by Billie Holliday (Vocalion 5021). Throughout his songwriting career, Pinkard collaborated mostly with white lyricists.

# A. J. Piron

African-American composer, violinist, and bandleader (b. Armand John Piron, New Orleans, Louisiana, August 16, 1888, d. New Orleans, February 17, 1943). After an accident at age seven left him unable to walk for a few years, Piron began playing the violin, inspired by his father and two brothers, who were musicians. He began playing violin in local bands as a teenager, and in 1913 took over Freddie Keppard's Olympians as bandleader. He hired pianist Clarence Williams in 1914 and began composing songs; they formed their own publishing company to promote them a year later. Williams expanded the business to Chicago in 1917, and Piron briefly joined him there in early 1919, but decided he preferred bandleading and life in New Orleans. The duo broke up, and Piron formed his own publishing company back home. His biggest hit song was 1922's "I Wish I Could Shimmy Like My Sister Kate," a hit for the ORIGINAL MEMPHIS FIVE, as well as LOUIS ARMSTRONG and FATS WALLER, and still a dixieland standard.

# Plugging

As business picked up, publishers' promotional efforts became more sophisticated. They hired scores of men known as "pluggers" to perform songs in their catalogs. Pluggers, who reported to the firms' professional managers, were men of great personal charm and many contacts. They sold songs by demonstrating them in music stores (and in the music sections of department stores) during the daytime, and by making the rounds of theaters, beer halls, and vaudeville houses during the evening. The best pluggers concentrated on getting vaudeville headliners to sing their songs, sometimes singing along with them from the audience when the song was introduced. To get leading performers to sing the songs whenever they appeared was always the goal of the plugger. Favorite performers could put the songs over to the audiences, who would then buy the sheet so they could learn and perform the songs themselves.

As the Alley developed, plugging remained essentially the same, but the methods changed with technology. After the vaudeville era, when radio captured audiences, airtime became a precious commodity, and pluggers (now sometimes called "contact men") concentrated on orchestra leaders who had their own programs. It didn't matter to the plugger how famous or obscure the performer was. If he had airtime and could perform a song during that time, he became a target. While getting the song recorded was desirable, the main thrust of plugging before the Presley era was to sell sheet music.

# Politics

There have always been songs and instrumentals written for political figures (mostly presidential candidates, governors, and mayors). Some of these became popular enough to merit publication and recording. Perhaps the most famous of all was "The Memphis Blues," originally written by composer W. C. HANDY on commission from Memphis mayoralty candidate Edward Crump in 1909. The tune remained popular long after the election, leading Handy to self-publish it in 1912.

Politicians also were not above borrowing popular song hits for their own use. During the Depression, for the 1932 presidential election the Democrats adopted a pop song, "Happy Days Are Here Again," as their party's theme. Harry Truman had EUBIE BLAKE and Noble Sissle's "I'm Just Wild About Harry" thrust on him at the beginning of his presidency, and it dogged him until the end of his life.

# Lew Pollack

Composer, lyricist, and pianist (b. New York City, June 16, 1895; d. Hollywood, California, January 18, 1946). Pollack was most active in New York in the 1920s and then in Hollywood through the mid-1940s.

Pollack had songs in Broadway shows and revues in the early 1920s, including *The Whirl of New York* and *The Midnight Rounders of 1921*, both in 1921. He collaborated with composer ERNO RAPEE on two major hits of the 1920s, "Charmaine" (1926) and "Diane" (1927). "Charmaine" was originally published in 1926 by Belwin as a theme song for the silent film *What Price Glory?*, with composer credit going to Rapee and lyrics by "Louis Leazer." When it was published with a new copyright in 1927 by Sherman, Clay, the lyricist's name appeared as Lew Pollack. When the song was first performed, Pollack thought it lousy and didn't want his name associated with it. When it became a hit a year later, he reconsidered and thought his name should appear in its rightful place. "Diane" was written by Rapee and Pollack, as the theme song for the Janet Gaynor-Charles Farrell film, *Seventh Heaven*. Published by Sherman, Clay, it became an outstanding hit with Nat Shilkret's arrangement (Victor 21000). Also in 1927, Pollack wrote "(Who's Wonderful, Who's Marvelous?) Miss Annabelle Lee," with words by Sidney Clare. It was introduced by HARRY RICHMAN. The Knickerbockers made a lovely dance arrangement (Columbia 1088-D), and Jane Gray, probably accompanied by RUBE BLOOM, made a nice version of it (Diva 2464-G). Also during the 1920s, Pollack and lyricist JACK YELLEN wrote an enormous hit for SOPHIE TUCKER, "My Yiddishe Momme," which was released on a two-sided 78, one side in English, the other in Yiddish. Pollack's instrumental "That's A-Plenty" has become a dixieland jazzband standard.

After moving to Hollywood in the early 1930s, Pollack scored several films, including JUDY GARLAND's 1936 *Pigskin Parade*, with lyricist Sidney Mitchell, and 1944's *Lady, Let's Dance*, which garnered an Oscar nomination for best song for Pollack's "Silver Shadows and Golden Dreams," with lyrics by Charles Newman. He died in Hollywood two years later.

# Cole Porter

Composer and lyricist (b. Peru, Indiana, June 9, 1893; d. Santa Monica, California, October 15, 1964). Porter studied violin and piano as a child. He came from wealth and social position, yet he wanted to become part of the Alley. More precisely, he wanted to write musical comedies. His first hit, "Old-Fashioned Garden" (1919), was a simple, sentimental song from *Hitchy-Koo of 1919*, not the smart, sophisticated stuff he had been writing as an undergraduate at Yale. His next hit, "I'm in Love Again," was introduced by the Dolly Sisters in *Greenwich Village Follies of 1925*. Ben Bernie and his orchestra helped popularize it (Brunswick 3496).

*Paris* (October 8, 1928) was the first hit show that Porter enjoyed on Broadway, and the principal song of the show was "Let's Do It," introduced by stars Irene Bordoni and Arthur Margetson. With this catalog of the amatory habits of assorted animals, fish, and insects, Porter earned his place as a writer of sophisticated lyrics. When it was interpolated into the film *Can-Can* (1960), it was sung by FRANK SINATRA and Shirley MacLaine.

*Fifty Million Frenchmen* (November 27, 1929) sported two hits, "You've Got That Thing," which was sung by Jack Thompson and Betty Compton, and "You Do Something

A dapper Cole Porter, c. the 1930s.

to Me," introduced by stars William Gaxton and Genevieve Tobin. Irving Berlin liked this score so much that he took an ad in newspapers to say that this show had "one of the best collections of song numbers I have ever listened to. It's worth the price of admission to hear Cole Porter's lyrics."

*Wake Up and Dream* (December 30, 1929) first opened in London (March 27, 1929) with star Jessie Matthews. Frances Shelley introduced the hit song "What Is This Thing Called Love?," which was followed by Tilly Losch's dance to it. Porter was believed to have gotten the basic melody from listening to native music in Marrakesh, Morocco. It still suits American audiences, often in the repertoire of nightclub singers.

With his successes, Porter joined the small club of writers, such as George M. Cohan, Irving Berlin, and Walter Donaldson, who could supply both words and music for hit songs. He once described his method of working: "First I think of an idea for a song and then I fit it to a title. Then I go to work on a melody, spotting the title at certain moments in the melody. Then I write the lyric—the end first—that way, it has a strong finish. It's terribly important for a song to have a strong finish. I do the lyrics the way I'd do a crossword puzzle. I try to give myself a meter which will make the lyric as easy as possible to write, but without being banal . . . I try to pick my rhyme words from a long list with the same ending."

*The New Yorkers* (December 8, 1930) contained "Love for Sale," a song about the world's oldest profession, introduced by the provocative Kathryn Crawford. For years this classic was banned from radio play because of its suggestive lyrics. But there were plenty of customers for Fred Waring's Pennsylvanians' recording, vocal by the Three Waring Girls (Victor 22598).

*Gay Divorce* (November 29, 1932) featured the great "Night and Day," which was introduced by Fred Astaire and Claire Luce. When the film was made (renamed *The Gay Divorcee*) (1934), Astaire sang it again, in his first film pairing with Ginger Rogers. The song was responsible for keeping the show alive. Frank Sinatra made a best-selling recording of the song in the 1940s (Bluebird 11463). As with "What Is This Thing Called Love?," Porter was alleged to have gotten his inspiration for this song from listening to a native tune in Morocco.

"Miss Otis Regrets" (published in 1934) was one of many party songs Porter wrote during the 1920s. He wrote it for his friend Monty Woolley, who impersonated a butler and delivered the lyrics, to Porter's accompaniment, at Elsa Maxwell's soirees. Woolley sang it for posterity in the Porter screen biography, *Night and Day* (1946).

*Anything Goes* (November 21, 1934) was one of the two greatest scores Porter wrote. "Blow, Gabriel, Blow" and the title song were introduced by star Ethel Merman, who also sang them in the first film adaptation of the musical (1936). Mitzi Gaynor sang them in the second film version (1956). "You're the Top," another of Porter's famous catalog songs, had its genesis in the early 1920s when Porter and his friend Mrs. Mackintosh, would amuse themselves after dinner by trying to concoct a list of superlatives that would rhyme. It was introduced by Ethel Merman and leading man William Gaxton. The same couple introduced "I Get a Kick Out of You" early in the show. The unorthodox placing of a strong number so early in the show was shrewd in this case. Part of the impact of Merman's singing came from the way she split the word "terrifically." She wrote in her autobiography, "I paused in the song after the syllable 'rif.' It was just a way of phrasing, of breaking a word into syllables, and holding on to one syllable longer than I ordinarily would, but for some reason the pause killed the people." She sang it in the first film version with Bing Crosby, and Crosby sang it with Mitzi Gaynor in the second.

*Jubilee* (October 12, 1935) contained two Porter gems. "Just One of Those Things," written overnight during the show's tryout, and "Begin the Beguine." Porter's inspiration came from the rhythms of an exotic dance he saw at Kalabahi in the Dutch East Indies. "Begin the Beguine" would likely have remained an obscurity during the 1930s if bandleader ARTIE SHAW hadn't wanted to record it. He had just signed with RCA-Victor's Bluebird label, and the recording director wanted Shaw to do a swing version of Friml's "Indian love Call." Shaw agreed, on the condition that he could also record "Begin the Beguine," as arranged by Jerry Gray. The disc sold over two million copies and was the turning point in Shaw's career (Bluebird 7746).

*Born to Dance* (1936) was Porter's first full-score film. It starred Eleanor Powell and James Stewart. It was Stewart who introduced "Easy to Love," and in spite of his thin singing, the song became popular, even appearing on the *Hit Parade*. Frances Langford sang it in a reprise. "I've Got You Under My Skin" was sung by sultry Virginia Bruce. It was given special treatment on record by Hal Kemp and his orchestra (Brunswick 7745). In 1951, Stan Freberg made a devastating parody of it, but by that time it was secure as a classic (Capitol 1711).

*Red, Hot and Blue!* (October 29, 1936) returned Porter to Broadway. It wasn't much of a show, but it did contain two Porter standards. "Ridin' High" was introduced by Ethel Merman, and she and Bob Hope sang "It's De-Lovely." In the second film version of *Anything Goes* (1956), "It's De-Lovely" was sung by Donald O'Connor and Mitzi Gaynor.

*Rosalie* (1937) contained two Porter gems, and both gave him trouble. While the story was the same as the one for the Broadway show (1928), Porter was hired to write a brand new score, to replace the original songs by GEORGE GERSHWIN and SIGMUND ROMBERG. The title song gave Porter a headache. He composed five tunes before he hit upon one he liked. When he played it for Louis B. Mayer, head of MGM, Mayer told him it was too highbrow. He advised Porter to go home and "write a honky-tonk song" and forget that it was NELSON EDDY who was to sing it. Porter was peeved, and in exasperation, wrote the corniest song he could think of, using all of the Alley's melodic and lyric clichés for a love song. When it became a hit, Porter was insulted. Irving Berlin advised him to "never hate a song that's sold half a million copies." The other song that became a standard, "In the Still of the Night," was also to be sung by Eddy, but he didn't like its long, seventy-two-measure chorus and complained that it wasn't suitable for his voice. Porter went back to Mayer and insisted that it remain and that Eddy sing it. Porter won. Not only did Eddy sing it beautifully in the film, he used it in his concert repertoire for many years.

*Leave It to Me!* (November 9, 1938) also contained two Porter standards. "Get Out of Town" belonged to Tamara Geva, and "My Heart Belongs to Daddy" made a star of Mary Martin. Veteran SOPHIE TUCKER, whose only Broadway book show this was, advised Martin to sing it in an innocent, babylike voice. The effect was to elevate Martin to stardom (Decca 8282). She sang it again in the Porter film biography, *Night and Day* (1946). Marilyn Monroe sang it in the film *Let's Make Love* (1960).

*Dubarry Was a Lady* (December 6, 1939) contained one solid hit and another that would achieve success years later when interpolated into the film *High Society* (1956). The second was "Well, Did You Evah?" The solid hit was "Friendship," which was introduced by Ethel Merman and Bert Lahr.

During rehearsals for *Mexican Hayride* (January 28, 1944), Porter talked over a scene with producer Michael Todd. Todd asked him what was the most clichéd title in the world. Porter's reply was "I Love You." Todd then bet him that he could take those three words and use only three notes—one for each word—and make a simple tune that would become the hit of the show. Porter took the challenge. Bing Crosby made a best-selling recording of it (Decca 18597).

*Hollywood Canteen* (1944) used "Don't Fence Me In," a cowboy number sung by Roy Rogers in this wartime movie. It was originally written for an unproduced film (*Adios Argentina*, 1935). It has been said that Porter paid a real cowboy $150 for the title and lyrics. Roy Rogers liked it so much that he got Porter's permission to use the title for his own western movie (1945) and sing it again. KATE SMITH helped to make it a hit by plugging it on her radio program, and Bing Crosby and the ANDREWS SISTERS sold over a million copies of their recording (Decca 23364).

*Kiss Me, Kate* (December 30, 1948) is, by general consent, the best and most successful of the Porter shows. It ran 1,077 performances. Based on *The Taming of the Shrew* (1603), by William Shakespeare, the show juxtaposed the latest swing ("Too Darn Hot") with Shakespeare ("I've Come to Wive It Wealthily in Padua" and "Where Is the Life That Late I Led?"). The score also contains "Always True to You in My Fashion," "Another Op'nin', Another Show," "Brush Up Your Shakespeare," and "So in Love." This last, in the early 1950s, was revived on a best-selling record by Patti Page (Mercury 5230). Dick Wellstood made a splendid stride piano solo, turning it into the "So in Love Rag." When MGM made the film (1953), the studio added "From This Moment On," which had originally been part of the score of a flop Porter show, *Out of This World* (1950). In the film, it was sung by Ann Miller and Tommy Rall. It was also used for a ballet sequence.

*Can-Can* (May 7, 1953) was Porter's last hit Broadway show. "I Love Paris" was inspired by set designer Jo Mielziner's rendering of Parisian rooftops. It was introduced in the show by French star Lilo, making her American debut. In the film (1960), it was sung by Frank Sinatra and Maurice Chevalier. It received a million-selling version by Les Baxter and his orchestra (Capitol 2479).

*High Society* (1956) was a musical film based on Philip Barry's romantic comedy *The Philadelphia Story* (1940). It starred Bing Crosby, Frank Sinatra, and Grace Kelly, with a happy sequence involving LOUIS ARMSTRONG. The score provided "I Love You, Samantha" for Crosby, while Sinatra got "Mind If I Make Love to You" and "You're Sensational." The title song (a calypso) was sung by Armstrong. Sinatra and Celeste Holm sang "Who Wants to Be a Millionaire?," and Crosby and Armstrong joined forces for "Now You Has Jazz." Interpolating "Well, Did You Evah!," gave Crosby and Sinatra the longed-for duet, with Porter revising his original lyrics for the occasion. "True Love" became Porter's all-time biggest movie song. The sound track recording of Crosby and Kelly singing it sold over a million copies (Capitol 3507).

*Aladdin* (1958), Porter's last orginal score, was done as a television musical. He died in 1964.

## American Published Individual Songs of Cole Porter:

"Abracadabra" (1944), *Mexican Hayride* (show)
"Ace in the Hole," (1941), *Let's Face It* (show)
"After You (Who?)," (1932), *Gay Divorce* (show)
"Agua Sincopada" (1929), *Wake Up and Dream* (show)
"Allez-Vous En" (1953), *Can-Can* (show)
"All I've Got to Get Now Is My Man" (1940), *Panama Hattie* (show)
"All of You" (1955), *Silk Stockings* (show)
"All Through the Night" (1934), *Anything Goes* (show)
"Altogether Too Fond of You" (1918), *Buddies* (show)

"Always True to You in My Fashion" (1948), *Kiss Me, Kate* (show)
"American Punch" (1922), *Hitchy-Koo of 1922* (show)
"Another Op'nin', Another Show" (1948), *Kiss Me, Kate* (show)
"Another Sentimental Song" (1919), *Hitchy-Koo of 1919* (show)
"Anything Goes" (1934), *Anything Goes* (show)
"As On Through the Seasons We Sail" (1955), *Silk Stockings* (show)
"At Long Last Love" (1938), *You Never Know* (show)
"Band Started Swinging a Song" (1944), *Seven Lively Arts* (show)
"Bandit Band" (1922), *Hitchy-Koo of 1922* (show)
"Banjo" (1929), *Wake Up and Dream* (show)
"Be a Clown" (1948), *The Pirate* (film)
"Begin the Beguine" (1935), *Jubilee* (show)
"Between You and Me" (1940), *Broadway Melody of 1940* (film)
"Bianca" (1948), *Kiss Me, Kate* (show)
"Bingo Eli Yale" (1910)
"Blow, Gabriel, Blow" (1934), *Anything Goes* (show)
"Bobolink Waltz" (1902)
"Boogie Barcarolle" (1941), *You'll Never Get Rich* (film)
"Bridget" (1910)
"Bring Me Back My Butterfly" (1919), *Hitchy-Koo of 1919* (show)
"Brittany" (1924), *Greenwich Village Follies* (show)
"Brush Up Your Shakespeare" (1948), *Kiss Me, Kate* (show)
"Buddie-Beware" (1934), *Anything Goes* (show)
"Bull Dog" (1911)
"But in the Morning, No" (1939), *Dubarry Was a Lady* (show)
"Buy Her a Box at the Opera" (1916), *See America First* (show)
"By the Mississinewah" (1943), *Something for the Boys* (show)
"Ca, C'est L'Amour" (1957), *Les Girls* (film)
"Calypso" (1956), *High Society* (film)
"Can-Can" (1953), *Can-Can* (show)
"Carlotta" (1944), *Mexican Hayride* (show)
"C'est Magnifique" (1953), *Can-Can* (show)
"Cherry Pies Ought to Be You" (1950), *Out of This World* (show)
"Climb Up the Mountain" (1950), *Out of this World* (show)
"Close" (1937), *Rosalie* (film)
"Come Along with Me" (1953), *Can-Can* (show)
"Come On In" (1939), *Dubarry Was a Lady* (show)
"Could It Be You?" (1943), *Something for the Boys* (show)
"Count Your Blessings" (1944), *Mexican Hayride* (show)
"Do I Love You?" (1939), *Dubarry Was a Lady* (show)
"Don't Fence Me In" (1944), *Hollywood Canteen* (film)
"Don't Look at Me That Way" (1928), *Paris* (show)
"Down in the Depths" (1936), *Red, Hot and Blue* (show)
"Dream Dancing" (1941), *You'll Never Get Rich* (film)
"Easy to Love" (1936), *Born to Dance* (film)
"Esmeralda" (1915), *Hands Up* (show)
"Ever and Ever Yours" (1916), *See America First* (show)
"Ev'ry Day a Holiday" (1939), *Dubarry Was a Lady* (show)
"Ev'ry Time We Say Goodbye" (1944), *Seven Lively Arts* (show)
"Ev'rything I Love" (1941), *Let's Face It* (show)
"Far Away" (1938), *Leave It To Me* (show)
"Farewell, Amanda" (1949), *Adam's Rib* (film)
"Farming" (1941), *Let's Face It* (show)
"Fated to Be Mated" (1957), *Silk Stockings* (film)
"Find Me a Primitive Man" (1929), *Fifty Million Frenchmen* (show)
"For No Rhyme or Reason" (1938), *You Never Know* (show)
"Frahngee-Pahnee" (1944), *Seven Lively Arts* (show)
"Fresh as a Daisy" (1940), *Panama Hattie* (show)
"Friendship" (1939), *Dubarry Was a Lady* (show)
"From Alpha to Omega" (1938), *You Never Know* (show)
"From Now On" (1938), *Leave It to Me* (show)
"From This Moment On" (1950), *Out of This World* (show)
"Get Out of Town" (1938), *Leave It to Me* (show)
"Gigolo" (1929), *Wake Up and Dream* (show)
"Girls" (1944), *Mexican Hayride* (show)
"Give Him the Oo-La-La" (1939), *Dubarry Was a Lady* (show)
"Glide, Glider, Glide" (1943)
"Goodbye, Little Dream, Goodbye" (1936), *Red, Hot and Blue* (show)
"Good-Will Movement" (1944), *Mexican Hayride* (show)
"Great Indoors" (1930), *The New Yorkers* (show)
"Gypsy in Me" (1934), *Anything Goes* (show)
"Happy Heaven of Harlem" (1929), *Fifty Million Frenchmen* (show)
"Harbor Deep Down in My Heart" (1922), *Hitchy-Koo of 1922* (show)
"Hark to the Song of the Night" (1950), *Out of This World* (show)
"Hasta Luego" (1942), *Something to Shout About* (film)
"Heaven Hop" (1928), *Paris* (show)

"Hence It Don't Make Sense" (1944), *Seven Lively Arts* (show)
"Here Comes the Band Wagon" (1929), *The Battle of Paris* (film)
"He's a Right Guy" (1943), *Something for the Boys* (show)
"Hey, Babe, Hey!" (1936), *Born to Dance* (film)
"Hey, Good Lookin" (1943), *Something for the Boys* (show)
"Hot House Rose" (1927)
"How's Your Romance" (1932), *Gay Divorce* (show)
"I Adore You" (1958), *Aladdin* (TV show)
"I Always Knew" (1942), *Something to Shout About* (film)
"I Am Ashamed That Women Are So Simple" (1948), *Kiss Me, Kate* (show)
"I Am in Love" (1953), *Can-Can* (show)
"I Am Loved" (1950), *Out of This World* (show)
"I Concentrate on You" (1940), *Broadway Melody of 1940* (film)
"I Get a Kick Out of You" (1934), *Anything Goes* (show)
"I Happen to Be in Love" (1940), *Broadway Melody of 1940* (film)
"I Happen to Like New York" (1931), *The New Yorkers* (show)
"I Hate Men" (1948), *Kiss Me, Kate* (show)
"I Hate You, Darling" (1941), *Let's Face It* (show)
"I Introduced" (1919), *Hitchy-Koo of 1919* (show)
"I Love Paris" (1953), *Can-Can* (show)
"I Love You" (1944), *Mexican Hayride* (show)
"I Love You, Samantha" (1956), *High Society* (film)
"I Loved Him But He Didn't Love Me" (1929), *Wake Up and Dream* (show)
"I Never Realized" (1921)
"I Sing of Love" (1948), *Kiss Me, Kate* (show)
"I Want to Go Home" (1938), *Leave It to Me* (show)
"I Worship You" (1929), *Fifty Million Frenchmen* (show)
"If You Loved Me Truly" (1953), *Can-Can* (show)
"If You Smile at Me" (1946), *Around the World* (show)
"I'm Getting Myself Ready for You" (1930), *The New Yorkers* (show)
"I'm in Love" (1929), *Fifty Million Frenchmen* (show)
"I'm in Love Again" (1925)
"I'm in Love with a Soldier Boy" (1943), *Something for the Boys* (show)
"I'm Unlucky at Gambling" (1929), *Fifty Million Frenchmen* (show)
"In Hitchy's Garden" (1919), *Hitchy-Koo of 1919* (show)
"In the Still of the Night" (1937), *Rosalie* (film)
"Is It the Girl (Or Is It the Gown)?" (1944), *Seven Lively Arts* (show)
"It Might Have Been" (1942), *Something to Shout About* (film)
"It Must Be Fun to Be You" (1944), *Mexican Hayride* (show)
"It Was Written in the Stars" (1939), *Dubarry Was a Lady* (show)
"It's a Chemical Reaction, That's All" (1955), *Silk Stockings* (show)
"It's All Right with Me" (1953), *Can-Can* (show)
"It's De-Lovely" (1936), *Red, Hot and Blue* (show)
"I've a Shooting Box in Scotland" (1916), *See America First* (show)
"I've a Strange New Rhythm in My Heart" (1937), *Rosalie* (film)
"I've Come to Wive It Wealthily in Padua" (1948), *Kiss Me, Kate* (show)
"I've Got an Awful Lot to Learn" (1916), *See America First* (show)
"I've Got My Eyes on You" (1940), *Broadway Melody of 1940* (film)
"I've Got Somebody Waiting" (1919), *Hitchy-Koo of 1919* (show)
"I've Got You on My Mind" (1932), *Gay Divorce* (show)
"I've Got You Under My Skin" (1936), *Born to Dance* (film)
"I've Still Got My Health" (1940), *Panama Hattie* (show)
"Jerry, My Soldier Boy" (1941), *Let's Face It* (show)
"Josephine" (1955), *Silk Stockings* (show)
"Just One of Those Things" (1930), *The New Yorkers* (show)
"Just One of Those Things" (1935), *Jubilee* (show)
"Katie Went to Haiti" (1939), *Dubarry Was a Lady* (show)
"Kling-Kling Bird on the Divi-Divi Tree" (1935), *Jubilee* (show)
"Language of Flowers" (1916), *See America First* (show)
"Leader of a Big-Time Band" (1943), *Something for the Boys* (show)
"Les Girls" (1957), *Les Girls* (film)
"Let's Be Buddies" (1940), *Panama Hattie* (show)
"Let's Do It" (1928), *Paris* (show)
"Let's Fly Away" (1930), *The New Yorkers* (show)
"Let's Misbehave" (1928), *Paris* (show)
"Let's Not Talk About Love" (1941), *Let's Face It* (show)
"Let's Step Out" (1930), *Fifty Million Frenchmen* (show)
"Lima" (1916), *See America First* (show)
"Little One" (1956), *High Society* (film)

"Little Rumba Numba" (1941), *Let's Face It* (show)
"Little Skipper from Heaven Above" (1936), *Red, Hot and Blue* (show)
"Live and Let Live" (1953), *Can-Can* (show)
"Look What I Found" (1946), *Around the World* (show)
"Looking at You" (1929), *Wake Up and Dream* (show)
"Lotus-Bloom" (1942), *Something to Shout About* (film)
"Love for Sale" (1930), *The New Yorkers* (show)
"Love of My Life" (1948), *The Pirate* (film)
"Love Letter Words" (1922), *Hitchy-Koo of 1922* (show)
"Love Me, Love My Pekinese" (1936), *Born to Dance* (film)
"Mack the Black" (1948), *The Pirate* (film)
"Make Ev'ry Day a Holiday" (1924), *Greenwich Village Follies* (show)
"Make It Another Old-Fashioned, Please" (1940), *Panama Hattie* (show)
"Maria" (1938), *You Never Know* (show)
"Me and Marie" (1935), *Jubilee* (show)
"Mind If I Make Love to You?" (1956), *High Society* (film)
"Miss Otis Regrets" (1934)
"Mister and Missus Fitch" (1954)
"Montmartre" (1953), *Can-Can* (show)
"Most Gentlemen Don't Like Love" (1938), *Leave It to Me* (show)
"My Cozy Little Corner in the Ritz" (1919), *Hitchy-Koo of 1919* (show)
"My Heart Belongs to Daddy" (1938), *Leave It to Me* (show)
"My Long Ago Girl" (1924), *Greenwich Village Follies* (show)
"My Mother Would Love You" (1940), *Panama Hattie* (show)
"Never Give Anything Away" (1953), *Can-Can* (show)
"Night and Day" (1932), *Gay Divorce* (show)
"Nina" (1948), *The Pirate* (film)
"No Lover" (1950), *Out of This World* (show)
"Nobody's Chasing Me" (1950), *Out of This World* (show)
"Now You Has Jazz" (1956), *High Society* (film)
"Oh, Bright Fair Dream" (1916), *See America First* (show)
"Old-Fashioned Garden" (1919), *Hitchy-Koo of 1919* (show)
"Only Another Boy and Girl" (1944), *Seven Lively Arts* (show)
"Ours" (1936), *Red, Hot and Blue* (show)
"Ozarks Are Calling Me Home" (1936), *Red, Hot and Blue* (show)
"Paree, What Did You Do to Me?" (1929), *Fifty Million Frenchmen* (show)
"Paris Loves Lovers" (1955), *Silk Stockings* (show)
"Peter Piper" (1919), *Hitchy-Koo of 1919* (show)
"Picture of Me Without You" (1935), *Jubilee* (show)
"Pipe-Dreaming" (1946), *Around the World* (show)
"Pity Me, Please" (1916), *See America First* (show)
"Please Don't Make Me Be Good" (1929), *Fifty Million Frenchmen* (show)
"Please Don't Monkey with Broadway" (1940), *Broadway Melody of 1940* (film)
"Prithee, Come Crusading" (1916), *See America First* (show)
"Queen of Terre Haute" (1929), *Fifty Million Frenchmen* (show)
"Quelque Chose" (1928), *Paris* (show)
"Rap Tap on Wood" (1936), *Born to Dance* (film)
"Red, Hot and Blue" (1936), *Red, Hot and Blue* (show)
"Ridin' High" (1936), *Red, Hot and Blue* (show)
"Ritz Roll and Rock" (1957), *Silk Stockings* (film)
"Rolling Home (1936), *Born to Dance* (film)
"Rosalie" (1937), *Rosalie* (film)
"Rub Your Lamp" (1941), *Let's Face It* (show)
"Sailors of the Sky" (1943)
"Satin and Silk" (1955), *Silk Stockings* (show)
"See America First" (1916), *See America First* (show)
"See That You're Born in Texas" (1943), *Something for the Boys* (show)
"Shootin' the Works for Uncle Sam" (1941), *You'll Never Get Rich* (film)
"Should I Tell You I Love You?" (1946), *Around the World* (show)
"Siberia" (1955), *Silk Stockings* (show)
"Silk Stockings" (1955), *Silk Stockings* (show)
"Sing to Me, Guitar" (1944), *Mexican Hayride* (show)
"Since I Kissed My Baby Goodbye" (1941), *You'll Never Get Rich* (film)
"Slow Sinks the Sun" (1916), *See America First* (show)
"So in Love" (1948), *Kiss Me, Kate* (show)
"So Near and Yet So Far" (1941), *You'll Never Get Rich* (film)
"Something for the Boys" (1943), *Something for the Boys* (show)
"Something to Shout About" (1942), *Something to Shout About* (film)
"Something's Got to Be Done" (1916), *See America First* (show)
"Stereophonic Sound" (1955), *Silk Stockings* (show)
"Swingin' the Jinx Away" (1936), *Born to Dance* (film)
"Take Me Back to Manhattan" (1930), *The New Yorkers* (show)

"Taking the Steps to Russia" (1938), *Leave It To Me* (show)
"Thank You So Much, Missus Lowsborough Goodby" (1934)
"That Black and White Baby of Mine" (1919), *Hitchy-Koo of 1919* (show)
"There He Goes, Mister Phileas Fogg" (1946), *Around the World* (show)
"There Must Be Someone for Me" (1944), *Mexican Hayride* (show)
"There'll Always Be a Lady Fair" (1936), *Anything Goes* (film)
"They All Fall in Love" (1929), *The Battle of Paris* (film)
"Tom, Dick or Harry" (1948), *Kiss Me, Kate* (show)
"Tomorrow" (1938), *Leave It to Me* (show)
"Too Darn Hot" (1948), *Kiss Me, Kate* (show)
"True Love" (1956), *High Society* (film)
"Trust Your Destiny to Your Star" (1958), *Aladdin* (TV show)
"Two Big Eyes" (1915), *Miss Information* (show)
"Two Little Babes in the Wood" (1928), *Paris* (show)
"Use Your Imagination" (1950), *Out of This World* (show)
"Visit Panama" (1940), *Panama Hattie* (show)
"Vivienne" (1928), *Paris* (show)
"Wait for the Moon" (1924), *Greenwich Village Follies* (show)
"Wake Up and Dream" (1929), *Wake Up and Dream* (show)
"Waltz Down the Aisle" (1934), *Anything Goes* (show)
"Washington Square" (1920), *As You Were* (show)
"We Open in Venice" (1948), *Kiss Me, Kate* (show)
"Wedding Cake-Walk" (1941), *You'll Never Get Rich* (film)
"Well, Did You Evah?" (1939), *Dubarry Was a Lady* (show)
"Were Thine That Special Face" (1948), *Kiss Me, Kate* (show)
"Weren't We Fools?" (1927)
"What Is That Tune?" (1938), *You Never Know* (show)
"What Is This Thing Called Love?" (1929), *Wake Up and Dream* (show)
"What Shall I Do?" (1938), *You Never Know* (show)
"When I Had a Uniform On" (1919), *Hitchy-Koo of 1919* (show)
"When I Used to Lead the Ballet" (1916), *See America First* (show)
"When I Was a Little Cuckoo" (1944), *Seven Lively Arts* (show)
"When Love Beckoned" (1939), *Dubarry Was a Lady* (show)
"When Love Comes Your Way" (1935), *Jubilee* (show)
"When My Baby Goes to Town" (1943), *Something for the Boys* (show)
"When My Caravan Comes Home" (1922), *Hitchy-Koo of 1922* (show)
"Wherever They Fly the Flag of Old England" (1946), *Around the World* (show)
"Where Have You Been?" (1930), *The New Yorkers* (show)
"Where Is the Life That Late I Led?" (1948), *Kiss Me, Kate* (show)
"Where, Oh Where?" (1950), *Out of This World* (show)
"Which" (1928), *Paris* (show)
"Who Knows" (1937), *Rosalie* (film)
"Who Wants to Be a Millionaire?" (1956), *High Society* (film)
"Who Would Have Dreamed?" (1940), *Panama Hattie* (show)
"Why Am I So Gone (About That Gal)?" (1957), *Les Girls* (film)
"Why Can't You Behave?" (1948), *Kiss Me, Kate* (show)
"Why Should I Care" (1937), *Rosalie* (film)
"Why Shouldn't I?" (1935), *Jubilee* (show)
"Without Love" (1955), *Silk Stockings* (show)
"Wow-Ooh-Wolf" (1944), *Seven Lively Arts* (show)
"Wunderbar" (1948), *Kiss Me, Kate* (show)
"You Can Do No Wrong" (1948), *The Pirate* (film)
"You Do Something to Me" (1929), *Fifty Million Frenchmen* (show)
"You Don't Know Paree" (1929), *Fifty Million Frenchmen* (show)
"You Don't Remind Me" (1950), *Out of This World* (show)
"You Irritate Me So" (1941), *Let's Face It* (show)
"You Never Know" (1938), *You Never Know* (show)
"You'd Be So Nice to Come Home To" (1942), *Something to Shout About* (film)
"You're a Bad Influence on Me" (1936), *Red, Hot and Blue* (show)
"You're in Love" (1932), *Gay Divorce* (show)
"You're Just Too, Too" (1957), *Les Girls* (film)
"You're Sensational" (1956), *High Society* (film)
"You're the Top" (1934), *Anything Goes* (show)
"You've Got Something" (1936), *Red, Hot and Blue* (show)
"You've Got That Thing" (1929), *Fifty Million Frenchmen* (show)

# Product Songs

This category of pop song started early in the nineteenth century, when music publishers who owned music stores starting putting lithographs of their buildings on sheet music covers. This was followed by piano companies and other music stores selling song sheets advertising their show rooms and instruments. Clothing and fashion wear soon followed. Newspaper owners, drug companies, food and drink manufacturers, tobacco products, household aids, automobile manufacturers and auto suppliers, department stores, organizational lodges, hotels and resorts either published songs themselves or allowed the use of their brand names, logos, and likenesses on song sheets. These are not to be confused with popular songs that contained advertisements on the back cover or along the margins. The advertising sheet exists for the sole purpose of promoting or illustrating a product. Many product song sheets were designed as giveaways—to be mailed to valued customers by the store owner—and thus always have folds. One must pay attention also to the inside front cover and back cover, which often contain photos or drawings of the product.

# Pseudonyms

Most often writer pseudonyms were used by publishing firms who didn't want it known that they had only one or two songwriters on their staff. Harry Lincoln was the mainstay of Vandersloot Music (also as "Abe Losch" and "R. A. Fischler"), while CHARLES L. JOHNSON sometimes wrote under the names "Raymond Birch" and "Ethel Earnist." CHARLES N. DANIELS wrote hits under his own name as well as "Neil Moret," and J. RUSSEL ROBINSON used "Joe Hoover." Some songwriters used pseudonyms as a means of getting out of exclusive arrangements with publishers.

# Publishing a Popular Song

A great deal of time, labor, skill, and money was involved in the creation of the song in sheet music form. First, the professional composer and lyricist, who were on the publisher's staff, demonstrated their new song to the publisher. If he liked it, he asks for a lead sheet (the melody line of the song) and the lyric. He then issued the writers a contract on a royalty basis (the amount depended upon how recently the writers had a hit song). The songwriters got a weekly draw against the royalty, so if the song hit big, their royalty was deducted from their draw. Someone in the arranging department decided what key to put it in, to suit the ability of the average pianist.

The arranger then made the manuscript piano copy, which he sent to the music engraver, who engraved the music and lyrics on a metal plate. (Music printing was a lithograph process, unlike commercial printing.) After the plates were proofread and corrected, the publisher ordered the copyright copies. These were sent with the copyright form to the registrar of copyrights at the Library of Congress and to foreign countries so that the song was protected. Professional copies were ordered (printed on cheap newspaper stock) for the purpose of teaching the song to professional singers.

At the same time, the publisher ordered orchestrations, which were parts for twelve to sixteen instruments in the original key and in four other keys (two higher and two lower). Also, reworked special versions might be ordered, including extra choruses. These versions required the lyrics for various acts so that the song might be used by a man, a woman, two men, two women, or a man and a woman. These versions were never used on the commercial copy of the song, but the publisher needed them to interest performers. Big publishers often had a dozen or so piano rooms for demonstrating and teaching songs to performers.

In the 1890s and early 1900s, sets of seven or eight glass slides (containing lyrics along with illustrations or photos) were prepared for use by motion picture organists and professional pluggers at theaters. The orchestrations prepared for dance bands were different from the vocal orchestrations. A typical dance arrangement consisted of an introduction, a first chorus for the entire band, a second chorus featuring stop time and novelty breaks for the brass section, the verse in another key, then a third chorus for a trombone solo with violin obbligato, a fourth chorus for saxophone solo, finishing up with the first chorus for the entire band. These orchestrations were given free to bandleaders as part of the exploitation of the song.

If, after all this, the publisher felt that the public might go for the song, then, and only then, the publisher asked for commercial copies to sell to the public.

The publisher assigned a graphic artist to design the cover and make the cover plates, usually in two colors. Then the retail copies were printed and distributed to the dealers. Advertisements were taken in newspapers and magazines, and display material was prepared for in-store use. Player piano rolls and recordings were sought to promote the songs. Pluggers were sent to dime stores and music counters to push the song.

## Contracts and payment

The standard contract between composer/lyricist and publisher included provision by the publisher to copyright the song, pay the songwriters a royalty per sheet music copy (for the more successful, a royalty of three cents), plus half of all monies received by the publisher from the sale of printed pianoforte copies and orchestrations; mechanical reproduction for phonograph records, music rolls, and electrical transcriptions; for motion picture use in the United States and Canada, and from publishers authorized by the publisher to issue the song outside of the United States and Canada. Advance payment against royalties upon signing would range from $100 to $10,000, depending upon the status of the songwriters (e.g., how many hits they had recently). Before the turn of the twentieth century, and for many songwriters up until the end of World War I, lump-sum payments instead of royalty arrangements were the normal way of doing business.

In 1909, with the new Copyright Act, a further stream of income for publishers and songwriters came with the establishment of "mechanical rights." The manufacturers of player piano rolls wanted to release popular songs; the publishers naturally wanted a royalty payment for this use. The Copyright Act mandated that publishers give "mechanical rights" to the player piano roll manufacturers in return for a fixed royalty rate. This provision was later expanded to include sound recordings.

Both mechanical and print rights could generate substantial income for publishers. Songwriters realized that they were getting the short end of the stick, and many either entered into partnership arrangements with other publishers or became publishers on their own. IRVING BERLIN is perhaps the most famous example of a songwriter who became his own publisher; because he was so popular and prolific, he was able to supply his publishing firm with enough hits without signing other songwriters.

# R

## Radio

Radio was a tremendous force in promoting songs from the mid-1920s on. At first, songs were performed live at radio stations by singers and orchestras. Then, during the late 1930s, disc jockeys became the rage, with announcers playing records and interviewing performers. Many disc jockeys became quite knowledgeable about the music business, and they would spread news concerning the current favorites, the better ones getting the jump on their competitors by previewing upcoming discs. Pop songs were also heard during the evening hours, in variety shows, and comedians always had a singer or bandleader to feature songs midway through the program. Even after television became the main entertainment vehicle, radio continued to be influential by programming all-music stations with a Top 40 format.

The most famous of the radio programs promoting popular songs in the days before DJs was *Your Hit Parade.* It was created by the advertising agency Batton, Barton, Durstine & Osburn in 1935 for their client Lucky Strike cigarettes. It premiered on NBC that year on April 20. The show did not feature the original artists singing their hits; rather, it had a house cast of singers and a house band who each week performed the seven most popular songs in America. Unlike the later TV show, the radio show had different casts through its long life, including singers Buddy Clark, Georgia Gibbs, Lanny Ross, Bea Wain, Barry Wood, FRANK

SINATRA, Joan Edwards, Andy Russell and Eileen Wilson. Orchestra leaders included Lennie Hayton, Leo Reisman, AXEL STORDAHL, and Mark Warnow, who conducted for most of the 1940s. The TV show (which aired from July 10, 1950, to April 24, 1959) continued the popular format. However, with the growth of rock and roll, and a focus on the performer of the song, the show lost much of its following and was replaced by DJ-inspired fare such as Dick Clark's *American Bandstand.*

# Rag Song

The format of the popular song, whether tearjerker or COON SONG, was the same throughout its first decade: there was a verse (that nobody knew) and a chorus (that everybody knew). While the verse might be any length, the chorus was usually either sixteen or thirty-two measures long. During the RAGTIME age, the tearjerker gave way to the pleasant love song ("On a Sunday Afternoon," "In the Good Old Summertime," "Meet Me in St. Louis, Louis," "Wait Till the Sun Shines, Nellie," "By the Light of the Silvery Moon," "Let Me Call You Sweetheart"). Peppier songs used the word "rag" or "ragtime" in their titles and have come to be known as "rag songs." As a musical fact, however, they are constructed exactly like other popular songs: with a verse (that nobody knows) and a chorus (that everybody knows). Such titles during this time were "That———Rag" (fill in the blank with "African," "Beautiful," "College," "Devil," "Epidemic," "Fussy," "Gossiping," "Hypnotizing," "Indian," "Kleptomaniac," "London," "Moving Picture," "Nightmare," "Operatic," "Puzzlin'," "Raggedy," "Shakespearian," "Teasin'," "Universal," "Whistling," "X-Ray," "Yodeling," etc., etc.). Then there are "Ragging the Baby to Sleep," "The Ragtime Boardinghouse," and "Rag, Rag, Rag"—not forgetting the most famous rag song of all, "Alexander's Ragtime Band."

# Ragtime

Ragtime, the joyous syncopated piano music from the Midwest, had its first publication in 1897. It wasn't until 1899 that John Stark and Son published SCOTT JOPLIN's "Maple Leaf Rag," in Sedalia, Missouri. From there, Stark moved to St. Louis, where the rag eventually

Original sheet music for Scott Joplin's "Maple Leaf Rag" (1899), published by John Stark and son.

sold more than one million copies of sheet music, thus establishing ragtime as a solid genre of popular music nationally and, during its first decade, internationally. Joplin was its leading composer, and such was his brilliance, that seventy-two years after he published "The Entertainer," it became a hit all over again, on a recording selling more than two million copies, taken from the sound track of the film *The Sting* (Universal, 1973). Of the approximately two thousand rags issued in sheet music, most were published in small towns far from Tin Pan Alley. Of all popular music, it was ragtime that attracted women to compose in the pop idiom—not surprising, since they were the ones who took piano lessons.

# Ralph Rainger

Composer (b. Ralph Reichenthal, New York City, October 7, 1901; d. Beverly Hills, California, October 24, 1942). In 1923, before starting law school, Rainger, under his birth name, had his first rag published. He also recorded "Piano Puzzle" (Bell P-193). After graduating from law school, he got a job as rehearsal pianist and (later) pianist in the pit for a Broadway show, *Queen High* (1926). He joined with Edgar Fairchild to become a duo-piano team on Broadway and in vaudeville that rivaled Victor Arden and Phil Ohman. Rainger next accompanied the vaudeville team of Clifton Webb and Mary Hay. When Webb went into *The Little Show* (1929), Rainger went into the orchestra pit as pianist. During rehearsals it was proposed that a blues song was needed, so Rainger and lyricist Howard Dietz supplied "Moanin' Low." It was Rainger's first song and his first big hit. Libby Holman sang it with great success in the show, and she and Webb performed a sensuous dance to it. Rainger was a fine pianist and musician, as evidenced by his remarkable novelty rag "Pianogram" (1929), which Robbins Music published. It has rhythms not often found in music of its time.

Rainger was offered a job with Paramount Pictures at the end of 1930, when he was teamed with lyricist Leo Robin. The first film they worked on was *The Big Broadcast* (1932), in which Bing Crosby introduced "Please." He sang it first in a rehearsal scene, with Eddie Lang accompanying him on the guitar. Later, Crosby sang it with a full orchestra at the end of the film. It was the first of many standards this fine writing team would produce. Bing Crosby's recording was a best-seller (Brunswick 6394).

"Love in Bloom" (1934) was written for Bing Crosby to sing in *She Loves Me Not*. His recording (Brunswick 6936) helped make this a half-million sheet music seller. The song's greatest success came from Jack Benny's use of it as his radio and television theme, and as his practice piece when taking violin lessons from Professor LeBlanc.

"June in January" (1934) was introduced by Bing Crosby in *Here Is My Heart*. Its title came first, an unusual occurrence, since Rainger preferred to compose the tune first. "I Wished on the Moon" (1935) was written with Dorothy Parker for Bing Crosby to sing in *The Big Broadcast of 1936* (1935).

"Blue Hawaii" (1937) was a Bing Crosby feature in *Waikiki Wedding* (1937). It was also used as the title song for an Elvis Presley film (1961) and in Presley's *Paradise, Hawaiian Style* (1965). Presley's recording on the sound track was a best-seller (RCA Victor LPM-2426).

"Thanks for the Memory" (1937) was written for Bob Hope and Shirley Ross in *The Big Broadcast of 1938* (1937). It won the Academy Award for Best Song. The next movie that Hope made was named for the song (1938). Hope started his radio show later that year and used it as his theme. He maintained its use on his television shows, and it will be forever identified with him, as "Love In Bloom" is with Jack Benny.

Rainger and Robin continued to work through 1942, when Rainger was killed in a plane crash.

# David Raksin

Film composer (b. Philadelphia, Pennsylvania, August 4, 1912). Raksin is best remembered for the big hit theme song for the film *Laura* (1944). He studied piano and woodwinds with his father, who was a musician, and led his own pop bands as a teenager. He went to Hollywood in 1935 to work with Charlie Chaplin on the score for *Modern Times* (1936). He would go on to write over hundred film scores, but his sole hit was the theme song for *Laura*. After the film's release, the popular melody was given lyrics by JOHNNY MERCER, and it has become a standard. In 1956, Raksin joined the faculty of UCLA. He has also composed classical works.

# Erno Rapee

Composer (b. Budapest, Hungary, June 4, 1891; d. New York City, June 26, 1945). Rapee is best remembered for his mid-1920s hits written with LEW POLLACK. He was originally a conductor, first working at the Dresden Opera House and then leading concert tours through

South America in the early 1910s. He settled in New York in 1912, and began scoring silent films, publishing two very successful collections of "themes" for orchestras to play to accompany films during the mid-1920s. Rapee's best-remembered score was for 1926's *What Price Glory*? For that film, he contributed a melody that he had first written about a decade earlier; a year later, with lyrics by Pollack, it became the big hit song "Charmaine." GUY LOMBARDO had the original hit recording. The same year, the duo produced "Diane," and two years later "Angela Mia," both themes for films and both major hits. Rapee was music director at New York's Roxy Theater from 1926 to 1931, and then at the newly opened Radio City Music Hall from 1932 until his death; he also did work as a conductor for NBC radio.

# Andy Razaf

Talented African-American lyricist (b. Andreamenetania Paul Razafinkeriefo, Washington, D.C., December 16, 1895; d. North Hollywood, California, February 3, 1973). Razaf wrote with the best African-American composers: FATS WALLER, EUBIE BLAKE, and JAMES P. JOHNSON. Razaf's father, the nephew of the queen of Madagascar, died before his son's birth; Razaf's mother was the daughter of John Lewis Waller, an African-American who was the first ambassador to Madagascar. Razaf was born in Washington but raised in Harlem. By his teens, he was writing songs, and he sold his first song, "Baltimo," when he was seventeen years old. Sometime in the early 1920s, he partnered with pianist/organist Thomas "Fats" Waller; the two would write many of the greatest hits of the jazz era.

In 1928 he wrote "Louisiana," and PAUL WHITEMAN recorded it (Victor 21438). "Take Your Tomorrow" was given a splendid treatment by Edwin J. McEnelly's orchestra, with a hot piano break by Frankie Carle (Victor 21773). The same year, "My Handy Man" had both lyrics and music written by Razaf.

1929 was a banner year for Razaf. He had four hits, starting with "Ain't Misbehavin'," recorded as an instrumental by composer Waller (Victor 22108) and by Leo Reisman's orchestra, with vocal by Lew Conrad, sending it to the #2 spot on the charts (Victor 22047). That and "Black and Blue" were written for the 1920s' best revue, *Connie's Hot Chocolates*. "Honeysuckle Rose" was written for *Connie's Load of Coal*, but became a standard later in the 1930s. "My Fate Is in Your Hands" was recorded by the most popular male vocalist of the late 1920s, GENE AUSTIN, backed by composer Waller at the piano (Victor 22223).

1930 got off to a great start with "Memories of You" (music by Eubie Blake) from *Blackbirds of 1930* being recorded by LOUIS ARMSTRONG (Okeh 41463). The same year Razaf created "Blue, Turning Gray over You." Fats Waller made a fine recording (Victor 36206). In 1932 Louis Armstrong recorded "Keepin' out of Mischief Now" and set it on its way

(Okeh 41560). In 1936 Razaf wrote "Make Believe Ballroom" as the theme song for the first radio disc jockey, Martin Block, on New York's WNEW. The same year BENNY GOODMAN adopted "Stompin' at the Savoy" as his band's theme song (Victor 25247). The last hit written and composed by Razaf, "That's What I Like About the South," (1944), was taken by Phil Harris as his trademark; he sang a snatch of it on every Jack Benny radio show (Victor 20–2089).

Razaf suffered a stroke in the early 1950s and was confined to a wheelchair for the rest of his life.

# Record Industry

Flat discs began to be sold commercially in 1897. They were an invention of Emile Berliner, who also invented the gramophone on which to play them. Earlier, in 1877, Thomas Edison had invented a phonograph that played cylindrical records, but by 1908 the gramophone and its flat discs became the public's preferred machine and playback device. It wasn't until the 1920s that record sales enjoyed enough popularity to interest Tin Pan Alley. Record companies needed Tin Pan Alley's products, and Tin Pan Alley needed plugging provided by continual, permanent performances. Publishers also did not mind the two-cents-a-copy mechanical royalty due them from the record companies after the Copyright Law of 1909 was enacted.

There were two major labels during the 1920s, Victor and Columbia, both also manufacturers of gramophones; Edison was a distant third because of the inventor's insistence on using a different means of cutting his discs (and thereby limiting playback to his own equipment). Victor held the patent for disc manufacture for many years, insisting on a royalty payment if other labels wanted to use its technology. However, this was successfully challenged in the early 1920s by an independent label, showing that others had made flat discs using methods similar to Victor's prior to its patent application. Thereafter, many independents flourished, further promoting popular music. Some publishers also became record producers, such as Jack and Irving Mills, who established their own labels in the mid-1930s. However, most chose to leave recordmaking to the major producers.

The Depression and the growth of radio temporarily slowed record sales. The major labels were both absorbed into radio conglomerates (Victor into RCA and Columbia and several smaller labels into CBS). ASCAP resisted radio play of recordings, fearing this would put live musicians out of work; several battles were fought between the publishers and the radio/recording industry through the mid-1940s, when a compromise position was finally reached. After World War II, the recording industry replaced the Alley as the mainstay of the music business. With the coming of rock and roll, the transition was complete, and recorded performances became the most important aspect of popular music.

# Jerome H. Remick and Company

Publisher Jerome H. Remick (1869–1931), a Detroit businessman, bought the old-line Detroit firm of Whitney Warner Publishing Company, with offices at 10 Witherell Street, in 1902. It did not take him long to determine that most of the publishing action was in New York City. At the end of 1902, Remick purchased CHARLES N. DANIELS's Indian intermezzo, "Hiawatha," for the then unheard-of sum of $10,000 and installed Daniels in Detroit as his general manager. The following year, he bought out Louis Bernstein's half of SHAPIRO, BERNSTEIN AND COMPANY to become a partner with Maurice Shapiro in Shapiro, Remick and Company, also proprietors of the Whitney Warner Company, located at 45 West 28th Street in New York.

At the end of 1904, Jerome Remick bought out Maurice Shapiro with the stipulation that Shapiro not engage in music publishing in the United States for two years. The beginning of 1905 saw the establishment of Jerome H. Remick and Company. Remick retained Fred E. Belcher (1869–1919), of the Whitney Warner staff in Detroit, to look after his office in New York during the partnership with Shapiro. Upon establishing his own company, Remick kept Belcher in charge of the New York office, where his duties included overseeing the more than fifty retail stores Remick owned around the country. MOSES EDWIN GUMBLE, composer and plugger supreme, who had worked in 1902 as branch manager in Chicago for Shapiro, was brought to New York and put in charge of Remick's professional department, becoming the number two man in the office, after Belcher.

Remick kept his editorial headquarters in Detroit. Under the direction of composer Charles N. Daniels (usually writing under the pseudonym of Neil Moret), the firm prospered. It not only published over one hundred rags, but established an enormous catalog of every kind of popular song, with many hits. So large was his output that Remick was forced to buy a printing plant in 1907. His volume of published songs remained the largest of any Tin Pan Alley firm until the end of World War I. Like other major firms—LEO FEIST, M. WITMARK, JOSEPH W. STERN, and Shapiro—the Remick Company had a branch office in theater-filled Chicago, managed for years by Harry Werthan. When Daniels left Detroit in 1912 to move to the West Coast, the Remick editorial office moved to 131 West Forty-first Street in New York City under the guidance of Gumble. Fred Belcher became vice president and secretary of the Remick Company, supervising the empire from its new office. The firm took a twenty-year lease.

The first million-selling rag issued by Remick was CHARLES L. JOHNSON's "Dill Pickles Rag," which had first been published in 1906 by Carl Hoffman in Kansas City. Charles Daniels, who had previously worked for Hoffman, bought the copyright in 1907, launched an extensive plugging campaign, and made it a huge success. The company's next million-selling rag was George Botsford's "Black and White Rag," in 1908. And so they continued until the end of the war.

About two thousand rags were published, most of them originating from RAGTIME's regional, small-town roots. For all the influence that ragtime had on the popular music business, the form developed and took root far from New York City. While major publishers Stern, SNYDER, ROSSITER, Forster, Kremer, Vandersloot, Witmark, Mentel Bros., and Jenkins all issued more rags than the rest of the other publishers, and had their share of ragtime hits, the total output of these nine firms did not equal the combined number of rags published by Stark and Remick.

The Remick firm was purchased by Warner Brothers Pictures in 1929 and merged with their other music holdings. Its back catalog is now part of WARNER/CHAPPELL MUSIC, INC.

JEROME H. REMICK and COMPANY (1904–1928)

| | |
|---|---|
| 1905–1908 | 45 West 28th Street |
| 1908–1911 | 131 West 41st Street |
| 1912–1931 | 219–221 West 46th Street |
| 1931–1935 | 1657 Broadway (Hollywood Building, owned by Warner Bros.) |

# Harry Richman

Singer (b. Harry Reichman, Cincinnati, Ohio, August 10, 1895; d. Los Angeles, California, November 3, 1972). Richman had an important career in nightclubs and films, Broadway musicals, and radio. His persona as dapper man-about-town, with cane and top hat, gave him a theatrical flair. It helped him achieve top billing in vaudeville, playing the Palace Theatre and nightclubs.

Richman began performing as a twelve-year-old in a duo act in Chicago as "Remington and Reichman." At age eighteen, he took the Americanized name of Richman and moved to San Francisco. He then worked as a pianist for vaudevillians The Dolly Sisters and Mae West, among others. He first appeared on Broadway in 1922, but didn't have a major success until he was featured in *George White's Scandals of 1926*. His record hits also started in 1926 with "Muddy Water" (for which he claimed coauthorship credit). He followed it in 1927 with "Miss Annabelle Lee" which The Knickerbockers recorded with vocal by Irving Kaufman (Columbia 1088-D).

In 1930, Richman wrote and introduced his two hits, "Singing a Vagabond Song" and "There's Danger in Your Eyes, Cherie," from the film in which he starred, *Puttin' on the Ritz* (Brunswick 4678). He also made famous the IRVING BERLIN song whose title came from the title of that film (Brunswick 4677). After the mid-1940s, Richman played clubs and theaters for another decade, and then retired.

During his career heyday, Richman ran his own speakeasy, Club Richman, and drove around Broadway in a large Rolls Royce, announcing his presence by handing out gold $10.00 coins to passersby. He also was an amateur aviator, setting the world altitude record for an amphibious plane in 1935, and then, in partnership with another pilot, flying from the United States to England and back in a single-engine plane a year later.

# The Richmond Organization (TRO)

Founded by Howard Richmond (b. 1918) in 1949, this was probably the first firm to truly recognize the power of the deejay in promoting hit songs. While most publishers were happy to have one or two hits a year, Richmond had six in his first full year of publishing ("Hop Scotch Polka," "Music! Music! Music!," "Goodnight, Irene," "Molasses, Molasses," "Tzena, Tzena, Tzena," and "The Thing"). He accomplished this amazing feat alone, as a one-man operation! Before entering publishing (he was the son of jobber-publisher Maurice (Morris) Richmond and the nephew of publisher Jack Robbins), he was an assistant to a Broadway publicist. The publicist to whom he was apprenticed, started plugging his clients' recordings, and Richmond soon joined his cousin Buddy Robbins in a similar enterprise. By the time Richmond formed his own publishing companies (Cromwell, Hollis, and Essex), he knew over three hundred disc jockeys on a first-name basis. He spent a good part of his time on the phone with them, talking up the recordings of his songs, which he airmailed to them. He usually got his records airtime on their shows. His track record at this new kind of plugging was spectacular. His organization became international, and it is now run by his son, Larry Richmond (b. 1954). The firm's publishing imprints include Cheshire Music, Cromwell Music, Devon Music, Essex Music, Folkways Music Publishers, Hampshire House Publishing, Hollis Music, Ludlow Music, Melody Trails, Musical Comedy Productions, Total Music Services, Words and Music, and Worldwide Music Services. Composer/artists represented by the firm include Black Sabbath, The Who, Pink Floyd, Justin Hayward and the Moody Blues, Pete Seeger, Huddie Ledbetter, Woody Guthrie, and many more. The TRO catalog also contains a great range of popular standards such as "Fly Me to the Moon," "Dream a Little Dream," "Only You," "I Believe," "A Guy Is a Guy," "Band of Gold,"

"September Song," and "I'll Be Around." TRO's Muscadet Productions works with the master recordings of Joe Cocker, T Rex, Procol Harum, and others.

# Blanche Ring

Singer and actress (b. Boston, Massachusetts, April 24, 1877; d. Santa Monica, California, January 13, 1961). Ring first appeared in vaudeville in her hometown before coming to New York City, where she made her debut on Broadway in *The Defender* (July 3, 1902). She interpolated in the show George Evans and Ren Shields's "In the Good Old Summer Time," with which she was identified thereafter. She witnessed in the song's creation when she and the two songwriters were having dinner at Coney Island. Evans looked around and said there was "nothing like the good old summer time," and Shields picked up the phrase and wrote it down. When handed the lyrics, Evans hummed the tune on the spot.

Ring was a marvelous interpreter of the popular songs of her day. Toward the end of the decade, she had three stupendous hits in a row. The outstanding song success of 1908 was the John Flynn–Will Cobb "Yip-I-Addy-I-Ay," which she added to her permanent repertoire. In 1909, she was given her theme song by the English team of Scott, Weston, and Barnes, when they wrote "I've Got Rings on My Fingers." Ring was asked to join the cast of *The Midnight Sons* (May 22, 1909), in which she sang this interpolated number. The song was so closely identified with her that in order to satisfy her fans, she also had to interpolate it into her next show, *The Yankee Girl* (February 10, 1910), where it proved to be a hit again. The same year she performed another classic, the Fred Fisher–Alfred Bryan airplane song, "Come, Josephine, in My Flying Machine." She continued to be a favorite in vaudeville and on the stage until 1938. She also sang on radio.

# Robbins Music Corporation

A new company was formed on January 1, 1922, when Maurice Richmond, a major jobber and a minor publisher (who had bought the F. A. MILLS catalog in 1915), created a firm with his nephew and general manager, John J. Robbins (whose nickname was Jack; 1894–

1959), to form Richmond-Robbins, at 1658 Broadway. When Robbins became a partner with Harry Engel two years later (Robbins-Engel), the new firm stayed at the same address. From 1927 to 1935 (when Robbins sold out to MGM), the firm was known as Robbins Music Corporation, at 799 Seventh Avenue.

Robbins had under contract popular lyricist MITCHELL PARISH, and several of the key composers of the 1920s and 1930s, including JIMMY MCHUGH, NACIO HERB BROWN, Peter De Rose, DUKE ELLINGTON, SAMMY CAHN, JIMMY VAN HEUSEN, JOHNNY MERCER, and LOU ALTER.

In 1935, MGM formed the BIG THREE combine, including the holdings of LEO FEIST, Miller Music, and Robbins.

# Leo Robin

Lyricist (b. Pittsburgh, Pennsylvania, April 6, 1900; d. Los Angeles, California, December 29, 1984). Robin's major collaborator was RALPH RAINGER, but he also worked with JEROME KERN, VINCENT YOUMANS, RICHARD WHITING, HAROLD ARLEN, JULE STYNE, and HARRY WARREN.

Robin was educated at the University of Pittsburgh law school. His first big song came in 1926 with ALBERT VON TILZER, "My Cutey's Due at Two-to-Two Today," with the Clevelanders making it a novelty hit (Brunswick 3279). In 1927 he wrote "Hallelujah" for the Broadway musical *Hit the Deck*, which Nat Shilkret and the Victor Orchestra made famous (Victor 20599). "Louise," from the 1929 film *Innocents of Paris*, was written for and introduced by Maurice Chevalier, who also recorded it to standard status (Victor 21918). A year later, "Beyond the Blue Horizon" came from the movie *Monte Carlo*, which starred JEANETTE MACDONALD, who introduced it in the film and recorded it (Victor 22514).

He wrote throughout the 1930s for the movies (working for Paramount from 1932 to 1938 and for 20th Century-Fox from 1938 to 1942). In Robin's first assignment with Rainger, they turned out "Please" for the 1932 movie *The Big Broadcast*, which starred BING CROSBY, who introduced it (Brunswick 6394). They next wrote "One Hour with You" for the film of the same name. Jimmie Grier made it famous (Victor 22971).

For the 1934 film *She Loves Me Not*, starring Bing Crosby, Robin and Rainger wrote "Love in Bloom," with which Crosby had a #1 hit (Brunswick 6936). Crosby had another Robin hit with "Love Is Just Around the Corner," from the 1934 film *Here Is My Heart* (Decca 310). Shep Fields and his Rippling Rhythm had the hit recording of "Moonlight and Shadows," introduced in the 1937 film *Jungle Princess* (Bluebird 6803). Shep Fields also had the next Robin hit, "Thanks for the Memory," from *The Big Broadcast of 1938* (Bluebird

7318). Field's record was a #1 hit, the song won an Oscar for Best Song of 1937, and it became Bob Hope's theme for radio and television. Helen Forrest and Dick Haymes had the hit record of "In Love in Vain," which was written for the 1946 film *Centennial Summer* (Decca 23528). Robin's last big hit, "Diamonds Are a Girl's Best Friend," came from the 1949 Broadway musical *Gentlemen Prefer Blondes*, in Jo Stafford's recording (Capitol 824). Robin retired in the mid-1950s.

# Bill "Bojangles" Robinson

Dancer and singer (b. Richmond, Virginia, May 25, 1878; d. New York City, November 25, 1949). Robinson started tap dancing at age five. He appeared in the 1910s in vaudeville, in the act Cooper and Robinson. From 1928, he appeared as a single on Broadway in such shows as *Blackbirds of 1928*, where he introduced "Doin' the New Low Down" (Brunswick 4535); *Brown Buddies*; *Blackbirds of 1933*; and *Blackbirds of 1934*. He was in Hollywood from 1935 to 1938, gaining great fame in Shirley Temple films (*The Little Colonel*, *The Littlest Rebel*, *Rebecca of Sunnybrook Farm*, and *Just Around the Corner).* Robinson was known for humorous dance routines, such as his stairstep dance. In 1939, he starred in the Broadway musical *The Hot Mikado*. His last show, in 1945, was *Memphis Bound*.

# J. Russel Robinson

Composer and pianist (b. Indianapolis, Indiana, July 8, 1892; d. Palmdale, California, September 30, 1963). He and his brother John were known as the Famous Robinson Brothers as they toured regionally, with Russel at the piano and John playing drums. Russel had his first composition, "Sapho Rag," published in 1909 by John Stark. "That Eccentric Rag" was published in his hometown in 1912 by a local music store. After it was reissued by Mills

Music in 1923 as "Eccentric" (and with a recording by the New Orleans Rhythm Kings [Gennett 5009]), it became a favorite of jazz bands. It remains a standard in their repertoire. From 1917 to 1925, Robinson worked for the Imperial Player Rolls Company. Later, at QRS, he was advertised in their catalog as "the White Boy with the colored fingers." During the day he worked as a demonstrator for Leo Feist's Chicago branch. In 1919, Feist published a tune Robinson had written with Theodore Morse, called "Lullaby Blues in the Evening," which was the melodic parent of "Margie." The following year, the Original Dixieland Jazz Band's recording sold over a million copies (Victor 18717).

Robinson came to New York to join Pace and Handy as an arranger and as Handy's personal manager. He met minstrel singer Al Bernard (1888–1949), and they formed a vaudeville team, the Dixie Stars. They recorded for Columbia, Brunswick, Cameo, and Okeh. They were the white counterparts of Noble Sissle and Eubie Blake, Bernard singing while Robinson played piano (and occasionally joined in singing). They composed and made famous "Blue-Eyed Sally," "Let Me Be the First to Kiss You Good Morning," "Never Gettin' No Place Blues," and "Let My Home Be Your Home," among others.

Robinson briefly joined the Original Dixieland Jazz Band for their tour to London in 1919, then rejoined them on their return to the United States to make six successful sides with the band, including "Margie" and "Palesteena."

Robinson teamed with Roy Turk (1892–1934) to write "Aggravatin' Papa (Don't You Two-Time Me)" (1922) and "Beale Street Mama" (1923). Also in 1923 came "St. Louis Gal," featured by the St. Louis orchestra leader Gene Rodemich. In 1926, Robinson wrote the classic "Mary Lou," which was introduced by Abe Lyman and his orchestra (Brunswick 3135) and recorded by Pete Wendling, with a vocal by Frances Sper (Cameo 1064). Using the pseudonym "Joe Hoover," Robinson wrote another jazz favorite, "Rhythm King," which was first recorded by Bix Beiderbecke and His Gang (Okeh 41173). Robinson moved to California to freelance, and in 1936, wrote "Swing, Mister Charlie."

Robinson continued to publish through the early 1950s but was unable to adapt to new song styles and failed to produce further hits. He retired thereafter.

# Richard Rodgers

Composer (b. Hammels Station, New York, June 28, 1902; d. New York City, June 29, 1979). When he was six years old, he was taken to see *The Pied Piper*, a children's show composed and written by Manuel Klein and R. H. Burnside. The show was significant only because it sparked Rodgers's fascination with the theater. Soon after, he was taken to his first Broadway show, *Little Nemo*, based on the cartoon characters of Windsor McKay and featuring music by VICTOR HERBERT. Although the score has been mercifully forgotten, it so entranced the six-year-old Rodgers that he made up his mind to make theater his life's work. As the young JEROME KERN had been taken with Herbert's music, so was Rodgers. In a few years, it would be JEROME KERN's music, especially that from *Very Good Eddie*, that made an indelible impression on Rodgers. Rodgers has said that he went to see *Eddie* six times. Rodgers was in high school when the Princess Theatre shows were produced, and the experience of seeing them—and hearing Kern's music and P. G. WODEHOUSE's lyrics—was the biggest impetus to starting his career in musical theater.

Rodgers composed songs in summer camps and for assemblies in grade school and high school. His older brother Mortimer, who was then going to Columbia University, asked him to compose the music for a benefit show that his club was putting on. Rodgers's involvement in *One Minute, Please* (1917) was a turning point in his life. One member of the club, Philip Leavitt, saw the need for Rodgers to have a lyricist, and he knew of one who happened to need a composer. On a Sunday afternoon in 1918, Leavitt took Rodgers to meet LORENZ HART at his home, and the two discovered mutual likes, dislikes, and theories about the musical theater. They both admired the Princess shows, and although Hart was seven years older than Rodgers, they got along famously. As Rodgers later wrote in his autobiography, *Musical Stages*, "In one afternoon I acquired a career, a partner, a best friend—and a source of permanent irritation," referring to Hart's erratic work habits.

Within a few weeks of their first meeting, Rodgers and Hart turned out fifteen songs, one of which, "Any Old Place with You," was interpolated into *A Lonely Romeo* (June 10, 1919), sung by Eve Lynn and Alan Hale. It was the first of their songs to be published,

Richard Rodgers (left) and Lorenz Hart in the early 1930s.

issued by JEROME H. REMICK AND COMPANY. The show was produced by Lew Fields, formerly of WEBER AND FIELDS, and he liked the new team enough to encourage them. He signed them to do the score for his next show, *Poor Little Ritz Girl* (July 28, 1920), but had second thoughts during tryouts and hired SIGMUND ROMBERG to add eight numbers, reducing the team's contribution to eight. Of the published songs, "Love's Intense in Tents" was the only one to indicate the cleverness of the lyricist. The team met Lew Fields's son, Herbert, who wanted to write librettos for musicals, taking jobs acting, directing, and choreographing shows as a way of being in the theater until he got the chance to write. For the next five years, the three created musicals that no one wanted.

*Garrick Gaieties* (May 17, 1925) came about when junior members of the Theatre Guild wanted a smart revue to raise money to buy tapestries for the Guild's new theater on Fifty-second Street, then under construction. The revue would be a showcase for these talented newcomers. The cast included Sterling Holloway, Edith Meiser, Romney Brent, and June Cochrane. When the show opened at the Garrick Theatre (originally scheduled for two performances, but ran for 161), Rodgers and Hart made a name for themselves with two songs, "Sentimental Me (and Romantic You)" and "Manhattan." This second song was helped by PAUL WHITEMAN and his orchestra's recording (Victor 19769). Through the years, it has been featured in assorted movies, notably as a theme in Bob Hope's film biography of former New York mayor (and Tin Pan Alley lyricist) James J. Walker, *Beau James* (1957). It was the first in a long line of song classics the team would produce.

*The Girl Friend* (March 17, 1926) told the story of a six-day bicycle race. It was written by Herbert Fields and produced by his father, Lew. The show starred Eva Puck and her husband, Sammy White, who sang the show's two big hits, "The Blue Room" and "The Girl Friend." The title song, a CHARLESTON-inspired number with clever lyrics, hit the spot. It became an instant favorite, with marvelous recordings by Sam Lanin's Troubadours (Banner 1753) and George Olsen's Orchestra (Victor 20029). The two hit songs were recorded back-to-back by the famous piano duo Arden and Ohman (Brunswick 3197). When the second edition of the *Garrick Gaieties* (May 10, 1926) opened, it contained another Rodgers and Hart hit, "Mountain Greenery."

The team was invited by English producer Charles B. Cochran to create a revue for the London Pavilion. It was called *One Dam Thing After Another* (May 20, 1927). Shortly before taking up their duties, the team spent a few days in Paris. As the pair were taking a taxi ride with two young ladies, they barely escaped colliding with another car. One of the women remarked, "My heart stood still." Hart said that would make a good song title, and Rodgers jotted it down. During their first evening in London, Rodgers found his note, sat down and composed the song, and gave it to Hart, who had forgotten about the incident. He fashioned a lyric and it was put into the revue. Rodgers liked the song so much, he bought the rights from Cochran to include it in their next Broadway show.

*A Connecticut Yankee* (November 3, 1927), based on Mark Twain's novel, contained not only "My Heart Stood Still" but also the cheery "Thou Swell." "Thou Swell" was introduced in the show by stars William Gaxton and Constance Carpenter, and it was given a marvelous recording by Bix Beiderbecke and His Gang (Okeh 41030).

*Present Arms!* (April 26, 1928) was a curiosity, not only because it imitated the vague plot of VINCENT YOUMANS's *Hit the Deck* (also written by Herbert Fields) but also because it took that show's star, Charles King, as *its* star. While the Youmans plot involved the Navy, *Present Arms!* was about the Marines. The hit of the show, "You Took Advantage of Me," was not sung by the principals but by Joyce Barbour and Busby Berkeley, who, in addition to being dance director for the show, was its second male lead. Rodgers and Hart were surprised, although gratified, by the song's success, for they had hoped "Do I Hear You Saying (I Love You?)" would be the hit. Indeed, they had practically insured that it would be, by placing it in the first scene and again in the third scene. It was also played during intermission and as part of the finale. It was the last music the audience heard as it left the theater. Rodgers wrote, "But people forgot it as soon as they reached the sidewalk. Maybe the title was too long, maybe the music was too delicate, maybe, maybe, maybe."

*Spring Is Here* (March 11, 1929) was notable only for its hit song, "With a Song in My Heart." It appeared in the film adaptation of the musical (1930), sung by Alexander Gray and Bernice Claire. It became so identified with singer Jane Froman that her 1952 screen biography was given the song's title. She sang it for Susan Hayward on the sound track (Capitol 2044).

*Simple Simon* (February 18, 1930) began the 1930s with what should have been a scintillating score. It was a Ziegfeld production to star comedian Ed Wynn and torch singer RUTH ETTING. However, during the show's Boston tryout, Lee Morse became the female lead, and "Ten Cents a Dance" was hurriedly written (in less than an hour) for her. This taxi dancer's lament was next given to Etting, who had replaced Morse by the time the song went into rehearsal. It stole the show and became identified with Etting (Columbia 2146D). It was sung by DORIS DAY in the Etting film biography, *Love Me or Leave Me* (1955).

*America's Sweetheart* (February 10, 1931) was the last Broadway show the team would write for five years. They were going, like everyone else, to Hollywood. The show starred Ann Sothern, using her real name (Harriette Lake), and Jack Whiting, who sang the show's only hit, "I've Got Five Dollars." This became a popular Depression song. It was revived by Jane Russell and Scott Brady in the film *Gentlemen Marry Brunettes* (1955).

*Love Me Tonight* (1932) starred Maurice Chevalier and JEANETTE MACDONALD. The team sang three memorable songs in this film, one solo apiece and a duet. "Mimi" was for Chevalier. He used it during his entire career, reviving it in the film *A New Kind of Love* (1963). "Lover" was MacDonald's song, and Peggy Lee revived it in the film *The Jazz Singer* (1953). Her disc sold over a million copies (Decca 28215). "Isn't It Romantic" gave us one of Rodgers's lovliest tunes. However, though it was sung by both stars, they didn't sing it together. It was first sung by Chevalier to a customer in a shop, who sang it to a taxi driver, who then sang it to another, until it reached MacDonald, who finally reprised it. It was also featured in a film of the same name (1948). Although never in the hit class, the song has been a standard since its debut.

The team was invited by MGM to write the score for an update of MGM's early film musical *Hollywood Revue of 1929*, to be called *Hollywood Party* (1934). One of the songs they wrote, for Jean Harlow, was "Prayer," but when she dropped out of the film, they shelved the song. When asked to contribute a song to *Manhattan Melodrama* (1934, starring Clark Gable, Myrna Loy, and William Powell), Hart rewrote the lyric and called it "The Bad in Every Man." When Rodgers and Hart went to publisher Jack Robbins to discuss publishing the song, he told them that the tune was all right, but the lyrics were not commercial enough. Reportedly, Hart replied, "Commercial? I suppose it should be something corny like 'Blue Moon' "? Robbins quickly agreed that that was a good commercial title. Hart worked on it, and Robbins published it as an independent number. It was the largest-selling song Rodgers and Hart had had up to that time, and it was their only song that wasn't written for a show or film (at least not in its final form). It was featured by TED FIO RITO and sold more than a million copies of sheet music. When The Marcels recorded it in 1961, it was a #1 hit (Colpix 186). It is said that Hart hated "Blue Moon."

*Mississippi* (1935) gave BING CROSBY "It's Easy to Remember (And So Hard to Forget)" and "Soon." Both made the *Hit Parade* and can be heard today in many cabaret singers' repertoires.

*Jumbo* (November 16, 1935) brought the team back to Broadway for a BILLY ROSE production that starred Jimmy Durante, Big Rosie (an elephant), Gloria Grafton, and Paul Whiteman and his orchestra. The three hits of the show were "My Romance," "Little Girl Blue," and "The Most Beautiful Girl in the World," a lovely waltz introduced by Donald Novis and Gloria Grafton. When *Jumbo* was filmed in 1962, the third song was sung first by Stephen Boyd, then reprised by Jimmy Durante, twenty-seven years after he appeared in the stage show.

*On Your Toes* (April 11, 1936) brought together some of the theater's savviest talents: playwright George Abbott, choreographer George Balanchine, producer Dwight Deere Wiman, and designer Jo Mielziner. It made stars of Ray Bolger and Tamara Geva, who danced the ballet "Slaughter on Tenth Avenue." This extended number would have an independent life in the concert hall. The hit song was "There's a Small Hotel," originally written for *Jumbo* but cut during rehearsal. It was introduced by Doris Carson and Ray Bolger. It was later used in the film *Pal Joey* (1957), sung by FRANK SINATRA. The show was revived on Broadway in 1954 and again in 1982, directed both times by George Abbott. When the last revival took place, Abbott was ninety-five.

*Babes in Arms* (April 14, 1937) provided a score with four hits sung by an especially talented cast. "Where or When?" was introduced by Mitzi Green and Ray Heatherton. It was revived in 1960 in a best-selling record by Dion and The Belmonts (Laurie 3044). "The Lady Is a Tramp" was introduced by Mitzi Green in the show, sung by Judy Garland when it was adapted for a film (1939), and later used in the film version of *Pal Joey*, sung by Frank Sinatra. It was also played at a White House function when President Gerald Ford asked Queen Elizabeth for the first dance. "Johnny One Note" was introduced by Wynn Murray. "My Funny Valentine" was introduced by Mitzi Green, but after Judy Garland sang it in the film version, it became one of her specialties. It is a favorite of nightclub singers.

*I Married An Angel* (May 11, 1938) was originally conceived in 1933 as a movie project for JEANETTE MACDONALD, with a book by the team. It was finally produced on the stage in 1938, bringing together the stars of RUDOLF FRIML's *The Three Musketeers* (1928), Dennis King and Vivienne Segal. They got to sing "Spring Here." When the film was finally made in 1942, the song was sung by NELSON EDDY and Jeanette MacDonald, nine years after MacDonald was to star in the project written for her.

*The Boys from Syracuse* (November 23, 1938) had the finest score Rodgers and Hart wrote in the 1930s, fully integrated to the story line, which producer-director-librettist George Abbott adapted from Shakespeare's *Comedy of Errors*. The songs work beautifully within the context of this charming musical, and many of them have had lives independent from the show. "Falling in Love with Love," a lovely waltz, was sung by Muriel Angelus. "Oh, Diogenes!," "Sing for Your Supper," "What Can You Do with a Man?," "Dear Old Syracuse," "The Shortest Day of the Year," and the hauntingly beautiful "You Have Cast Your Shadow on the Sea," as sung by Marcy Westcott and Eddie Albert, have worn exceedingly well. "This Can't Be Love" was also introduced by Westcott and Albert, and was helped on its way when

BENNY GOODMAN and his orchestra recorded it (Victor 26099). When the film was made in 1940, the team added "Who Are You?" to the score. A marvelous off-Broadway production in 1963 demonstrated the show's lasting qualities.

*Too Many Girls* (October 18, 1939) included two of Hart's cleverest lyrics, "Give It Back to the Indians" and "I Like to Recognize the Tune." This last was a dig at the swing era's penchant for overarranging a melody. The hit song was "I Didn't Know What Time It Was," introduced by Marcy Westcott and Dick Kollmar, also used in the film of *Pal Joey*.

*Higher and Higher* (April 4, 1940) contained one hit, "It Never Entered My Mind," introduced in the show by Shirley Ross.

*Pal Joey* (December 25, 1940) was an offbeat musical based on short stories by John O'Hara, featuring an antihero and an aging prostitute. The nasty, self-centered "Joey" was played on Broadway by Gene Kelly, with Vivienne Segal as his paramour. "I Could Write a Book" was introduced by Kelly, and "Bewitched, Bothered and Bewildered" was delivered by Segal. The cute "Zip," done by a stripper played by Jean Casto, is a takeoff on the literary pretensions of Gypsy Rose Lee. The show had a successful revival on Broadway in 1952, with Vivienne Segal re-creating her original role for her final Broadway appearance.

*A Connecticut Yankee* (November 17, 1943) was the last show Rodgers worked on with Lorenz Hart. For this major Broadway revival, produced by Rodgers, the team created three new songs. "To Keep My Love Alive" is one of Hart's best comic lyrics and the last song he wrote. He died five days after the opening.

Rodgers and Hart's contributions to stage, films, and the Alley give them top ranking during the 1930s. They contributed enormously to the quality of popular music. While it was usually difficult for a show song to stand on its own as a hit or standard, Rodgers and Hart's enduring works are proven exceptions.

*(For the continuing career of Rodgers, see* HAMMERSTEIN, OSCAR II*).*

## American Published Individual Songs by Richard Rodgers:

"All at Once" (1937), *Babes in Arms* (show)
"All at Once You Love Her" (1955), *Pipe Dream* (show)
"All Dark People" (1937), *Babes in Arms* (show)
"All Dressed Up" (1939), *Too Many Girls* (show)
"All 'er Nothin'" (1943), *Oklahoma* (show)
"All I Owe Ioway" (1945), *State Fair* (film)
"All Points West" (1937)
"Amarillo" (1941), *They Met in Argentina* (film)
"Any Old Place with You" (1919), *A Lonely Romeo* (show)
"April Fool" (1925), *Garrick Gaieties* (show)
"Are You My Love" (1936), *Dancing Pirate* (film)
"As Once I Loved You" (1976), *Rex* (show)
"As Though You Were There" (1940)
"Asiatic Angles" (1919), *Up Stage and Down* (show)
"Auto Show Girl" (1917)
"Away from You" (1976), *Rex* (show)
"Babes in Arms" (1937), *Babes in Arms* (show)
"Baby's Awake Now" (1929), *Spring Is Here* (show)
"Baby's Best Friend" (1928), *She's My Baby* (show)
"Bali H'ai" (1949), *South Pacific* (show)
"Barnard! Barnard!" (1964)
"Be My Host" (1962), *No Strings* (show)
"Better Be Good to Me" (1928), *Chee-Chee* (show)
"Bewitched" (1940), *Pal Joey* (show)
"Big Black Giant" (1953), *Me and Juliet* (show)
"Blue Moon" (1934)
"Blue Ocean Blues" (1928), *Present Arms* (show)
"Blue Room" (1926), *The Girl Friend* (show)
"Bombardier Song" (1942)
"Boys and Girls Like You and Me" (1943), *Away We Go* (show)
"Breath of Springtime" (1920), *You'd Be Surprised* (show)
"Butterfly Love" (1919), *Up Stage and Down* (show)
"Bye and Bye" (1925), *Dearest Enemies* (show)
"Can't You Do a Friend a Favor?" (1943), *A Connecticut Yankee* (show)

"Careless Rhapsody" (1942), *By Jupiter* (show)
"Carousel Waltz" (1945), *Carousel* (show)
"Cheerio!" (1925), *Dearest Enemy* (show)
"Cinderella March" (1957), *Cinderella* (TV show)
"Cinderella Waltz" (1957), *Cinderella* (TV show)
"Circus on Parade" (1935), *Jumbo* (show)
"Climb Ev'ry Mountain" (1959), *Sound of Music* (show)
"Cock-eyed Optimist" (1949), *South Pacific* (show)
"Come and Tell Me" (1926), *Betsy* (show)
"Come Home" (1947), *Allegro* (show)
"Crazy Elbows" (1928), *Present Arms* (show)
"Cutting the Cane" (1941), *They Met in Argentina* (film)
"Dancing on the Ceiling" (1931)
"Dear Friend" (1944)
"Dear, Oh Dear!" (1928), *Chee-Chee* (show)
"Diavolo" (1935), *Jumbo* (show)
"Did You Ever Get Stung?" (1938), *I Married an Angel* (show)
"Dites-Moi" (1949), *South Pacific* (show)
"Do I Hear a Waltz?" (1965), *Do I Hear a Waltz?* (show)
"Do I Hear You Saying" (1928), *Present Arms* (show)
"Do I Love You?" (1957), *Cinderella* (TV show)
"Do It the Hard Way" (1940), *Pal Joey* (show)
"Do-Re-Mi" (1959), *Sound of Music* (show)
"Do You Love Me?" (1925), *Garrick Gaieties* (show)
"Don't Be Afraid of an Animal" (1967), *Androcles and the Lion* (TV show)
"Don't Marry Me" (1958), *Flower Drum Song* (show)
"Don't Tell Your Folks" (1930), *Simple Simon* (show)
"Down by the River" (1935), *Mississippi* (film)
"Down by the Sea" (1928), *Present Arms!* (show)
"Eager Beaver" (1962), *No Strings* (show)
"It's Easy to Remember" (1935), *Mississippi* (film)
"Edelweiss" (1959), *Sound of Music* (show)
"Ev'ry Day" (1979), *I Remember Mama* (show)
"Ev'ry Sunday Afternoon" (1940), *Higher and Higher* (show)
"Ev'rything I've Got" (1942), *By Jupiter* (show)
"Everybody's Got a Home But Me" (1955), *Pipe Dream* (show)
"Fair Is Fair" (1964)
"Falling in Love with Love" (1938), *Boys from Syracuse* (show)
"Farmer and the Cowman" (1943), *Oklahama!* (film)
"Father of the Man" (1972)
"Fellow Needs a Girl" (1947), *Allegro* (show)
"From Another World" (1940), *Higher and Higher* (show)
"Gentleman Is a Dope" (1947), *Allegro* (show)
"Getting to Know You" (1951), *King and I* (show)
"Girl Friend" (1926), *The Girl Friend* (show)
"Give Her a Kiss" (1932), *Phantom President* (film)
"Give It Back to the Indians" (1939), *Too Many Girls* (show)
"Glad to Be Unhappy" (1936), *On Your Toes* (show)
"Good Fellow Mine" (1926), *The Girl Friend* (show)
"Grant Avenue" (1957), *Flower Drum Song* (show)
"Guadalcanal March" (1952), *Victory at Sea* (TV series)
"Hallelujah, I'm a Bum" (1932), *Hallelujah, I'm a Bum* (film)
"Happy Christmas, Little Friend" (1952)
"Happy Hunting Horn" (1952), *Pal Joey* (show)
"Happy Talk" (1949), *South Pacific* (show)
"Have You Met Miss Jones?" (1937), *I'd Rather Be Right* (show)
"He Dances on My Ceiling" (1930), *Simple Simon* (show)
"He Was Too Good to Me" (1930), *Simple Simon* (show)
"Heart Is Quicker Than the Eye" (1936), *On Your Toes* (show)
"Hello, Young Lovers" (1951), *King and I* (show)
"Here in My Arms" (1925), *Dearest Enemy* (show)
"Here We Are Again" (1965), *Do I Hear a Waltz?* (show)
"Here's a Hand" (1942), *By Jupiter* (show)
"Here's a Kiss" (1925), *Dearest Enemy* (show)
"Hollywood Party" (1934), *Hollywood Party* (film)
"Honey Bun" (1949), *South Pacific* (show)
"How About It?" (1931), *America's Sweetheart* (show)
"How Can You Forget?" (1938), *Fools for Scandal* (film)
"How to Win Friends and Influence People" (1938), *I Married an Angel* (show)
"How Was I to Know?" (1927), *She's My Baby* (show)
"Hundred Million Miracles" (1958), *Flower Drum Song* (show)
"I Blush" (1927), *A Connecticut Yankee* (show)
"I Cain't Say No" (1943), *Oklahoma* (show)
"I Can Do Wonders with You" (1929), *Heads Up!* (show)
"I Could Write a Book" (1940), *Pal Joey* (show)
"I Didn't Know What Time It Was" (1939), *Too Many Girls* (show)
"I Do Not Know a Day I Did Not Love You" (1970), *Two by Two* (show)
"I Enjoy Being a Girl" (1958), *Flower Drum Song* (show)
"I Feel at Home with You" (1927), *A Connecticut Yankee* (show)
"I Have Confidence" (1965), *Sound of Music* (film)
"I Have Dreamed" (1951), *King and I* (show)

"I Haven't Got a Worry in the World" (1946), *Happy Birthday* (show)
"I Like to Recognize the Tune" (1939), *Too Many Girls* (show)
"I Love You More Than Yesterday" (1929), *Lady Fingers* (show)
"I Married an Angel" (1938), *I Married an Angel* (show)
"I Must Love You" (1928), *Chee-Chee* (show)
"I Still Believe in You" (1930), *Simple Simon* (show)
"I Want a Man" (1931), *America's Sweetheart* (show)
"I Whistle a Happy Tune" (1951), *King and I* (show)
"I Wish I Were in Love Again" (1937), *Babes in Arms* (show)
"I'd Like to Poison Ivy" (1924), *Melody Man* (show)
"I'd Rather Be Right (Don't Have to Know Much)" (1937), *I'd Rather Be Right* (show)
"I'd Rather Be Right (Than Influential)" (1937), *I'd Rather Be Right* (show)
"I'll Do It Again" (1932), *Hallelujah, I'm a Bum* (film)
"I'll Tell the Man in the Street" (1938), *I Married an Angel* (show)
"I'm a Fool, Little One" (1928), *Present Arms!* (show)
"I'm Gonna Wash That Man Right Out of My Hair" (1949), *South Pacific* (show)
"I'm Your Girl" (1953), *Me and Juliet* (show)
"I've Got Five Dollars" (1931), *America's Sweetheart* (show)
"If I Loved You" (1945), *Carousel* (show)
"If I Were You" (1926), *Betsy* (show)
"Impossible" (1957), *Cinderella* (TV show)
"In My Own Little Corner" (1957), *Cinderella* (TV show)
"Isn't It Kinda Fun?" (1945), *State Fair* (film)
"Isn't It Romantic?" (1932), *Love Me Tonight* (film)
"It Feels Good" (1953), *Me and Juliet* (show)
"It Is Not the End of the World" (1979), *I Remember Mama* (show)
"It Might as Well Be Spring" (1945), *State Fair* (film)
"It Must Be Heaven" (1929), *Heads Up!* (show)
"It Never Entered My Mind" (1940), *Higher and Higher* (show)
"It's a Grand Night for Singing" (1945), *State Fair* (film)
"It's Got to Be Love" (1936), *On Your Toes* (show)
"It's Me" (1953), *Me and Juliet* (show)
"It's the Little Things in Texas" (1962), *State Fair* (film)
"Johnny One Note" (1937), *Babes in Arms* (show)
"June Is Bustin' Out All Over" (1945), *Carousel* (show)
"Jupiter Forbid" (1942), *By Jupiter* (show)
"Kansas City" (1943), *Oklahoma!* (film)
"Keep It Gay" (1953), *Me and Juliet* (show)
"Keys to Heaven" (1926), *Garrick Gaieties* (show)
"Kiss for Cinderella" (1928), *Present Arms!* (show)
"La-La-La" (1962), *No Strings* (show)
"Lady Is a Tramp" (1937), *Babes in Arms* (show)
"Lady Must Live" (1931), *America's Sweetheart* (show)
"Lady Raffles, Behave" (1920), *Poor Little Ritz Girl* (show)
"Like Ordinary People Do" (1930), *Hot Heiress* (film)
"Little Birdie Told Me So" (1926), *Peggy-Ann* (show)
"Little Dolores" (1935)
"Little Girl Blue" (1935), *Jumbo* (show)
"Little House in Soho" (1926), *She's My Baby* (show)
"Little Souvenir" (1926), *Garrick Gaieties* (show)
"Loads of Love" (1962), *No Strings* (show)
"Loneliness of Evening" (1951)
"Lonely Goatherd" (1959), *Sound of Music* (show)
"Look No Further" (1962), *No Strings* (show)
"Love Is Not in Vain" (1919), *Up Stage and Down* (show)
"Love, Look Away" (1958), *Flower Drum Song* (show)
"Love Makes the World Go" (1962), *No Strings* (show)
"Love Me by Parcel Post" (1919), *Up Stage and Down* (show)
"Love Me Tonight" (1932), *Love Me Tonight* (film)
"Love Never Went to College" (1939), *Too Many Girls* (show)
"Love Will Call" (1920), *Poor Little Ritz Girl* (show)
"Love's Intense in Tents" (1920), *Poor Little Ritz Girl* (show)
"Lovely Night" (1967), *Cinderella* (TV show)
"Lover" (1933)
"Maine" (1962), *No Strings* (show)
"Man I Used to Be" (1955), *Pipe Dream* (show)
"Man Who Has Everything" (1962), *No Strings* (show)
"Manhattan" (1925), *Garrick Gaieties* (show)
"Many a New Day" (1943), *Oklahoma!* (show)
"Maria" (1959), *Sound of Music* (show)
"Marriage Type Love" (1953), *Me and Juliet* (show)
"Mary, Queen of Scots" (1920), *Poor Little Ritz Girl* (show)
"Maybe It's Me" (1926), *Fifth Avenue Follies* (show)
"Maybe It's Me" (1926), *Peggy-Ann* (show)
"Me for You!" (1929), *Heads Up!* (show)
"Mimi" (1932), *Love Me Tonight* (film)
"Mister Snow" (1945), *Carousel* (show)
"Money Isn't Everything" (1947), *Allegro* (show)

"Moon in My Window" (1965), *Do I Hear a Waltz?* (show)
"Moon of My Delight" (1928), *Chee-Chee* (show)
"Moonlight Mama" (1924), *Melody Man* (show)
"More Than Just a Friend" (1962), *State Fair* (film)
"Most Beautiful Girl in the World" (1935), *Jumbo* (show)
"Mountain Greenery" (1926), *Garrick Gaieties* (show)
"Muchacha" (1935)
"My Best Love" (1958), *Flower Drum Song* (show)
"My Favorite Things" (1959), *Sound of Music* (show)
"My Funny Valentine" (1937), *Babes in Arms* (show)
"My Girl Back Home" (1958), *South Pacific* (film)
"My Heart Stood Still" (1927), *A Connecticut Yankee* (show)
"My Lord and Master" (1951), *King and I* (show)
"My Man Is on the Make" (1929), *Heads Up!* (show)
"My Romance" (1935), *Jumbo* (show)
"Never Say "No" (1962), *State Fair* (film)
"Next Time It Happens" (1955), *Pipe Dream* (show)
"No More Waiting" (1967), *Androcles and the Lion* (TV show)
"No Other Love" (1953), *Me and Juliet* (show)
"No Strings" (1962), *No Strings* (show)
"Nobody Told Me" (1962), *No Strings* (show)
"Nobody's Heart Belongs to Me" (1942), *By Jupiter* (show)
"Nothing but You" (1940), *Higher and Higher* (show)
"Oh, Diogenes!" (1938), *Boys from Syracuse* (show)
"Oh, What a Beautiful Mornin" (1943), *Oklahoma* (show)
"Oklahoma!" (1943), *Oklahoma!* (show)
"Old-Fashioned Girl" (1925), *Garrick Gaieties* (show)
"Old Man" (1970), *Two by Two* (show)
"On a Desert Island with Thee!" (1927), *A Connecticut Yankee* (show)
"On with the Dance" (1925), *Garrick Gaieties* (show)
"On Your Toes" (1936), *On Your Toes* (show)
"Ordinary Couple" (1959), *The Sound of Music* (show)
"Our State Fair" (1962), *State Fair* (film)
"Out of My Dreams" (1943), *Oklahoma!* (show)
"Over and Over Again" (1935), *Jumbo* (show)
"People Will Say We're in Love" (1943), *Oklahoma!* (show)
"Perhaps" (1965), *Do I Hear a Waltz?* (show)
"Plant You Now, Dig You Later" (1940), *Pal Joey* (show)
"Pore Jud" (1943), *Oklahoma!* (film)
"Poor Apache" (1932), *Love Me Tonight* (film)
"Princess of the Willow Tree" (1920), *You'd Be Surprised* (show)
"P. T. Boat Song" (1943)
"Queen Elizabeth" (1926), *Garrick Gaieties* (show)
"Quiet Night" (1936), *On Your Toes* (show)
"Real Nice Clambake" (1945), *Carousel* (show)
"Regents March" (1971)
"Rhythm of the Day" (1933), *Dancing Lady* (film)
"Rich Man, Poor Man" (1929), *Spring Is Here* (show)
"Send for Me" (1930), *Simple Simon* (show)
"Sentimental Me" (1925), *Garrick Gaieties* (show)
"Shall We Dance?" (1951), *The King and I* (show)
"She Could Shake the Maracas" (1939), *Too Many Girls* (show)
"She Is Beautiful" (1958), *Flower Drum Song* (show)
"Ship Without a Sail" (1929), *Heads Up!* (show)
"Shortest Day of the Year" (1938), *Boys from Syracuse* (show)
"Simpatica" (1941), *They Met in Argentina* (film)
"Sing" (1926), *Betsy* (show)
"Sing for Your Supper" (1938), *Boys from Syracuse* (show)
"Singing a Love Song" (1928), *Chee-Chee* (show)
"Sixteen Going on Seventeen" (1959), *Sound of Music* (show)
"Sky City" (1929), *Heads Up!* (show)
"Sleepyhead" (1926), *Girl Friend* (show)
"Sleepyhead" (1926), *Garrick Gaieties* (show)
"So Far" (1941), *Allegro* (show)
"So Long, Farewell" (1959), *The Sound of Music* (film)
"Soliloquy" (1945), *Carousel* (show)
"Some Enchanted Evening" (1949), *South Pacific* (show)
"Someone Should Tell Them" (1927), *A Connecticut Yankee* (show)
"Someone Like You" (1965), *Do I Hear a Waltz?* (show)
"Something Doesn't Happen" (1970), *Two by Two* (show)
"Something Good" (1965), *The Sound of Music* (film)
"Something, Somewhere" (1970), *Two by Two* (show)
"Something Wonderful" (1951), *The King and I* (show)
"Soon" (1935), *Mississippi* (film)
"Sound of Music" (1959), *The Sound of Music* (show)
"Spring Is Here" (1938), *I Married an Angel* (show)
"Stay" (1965), *Do I Hear a Waltz?* (show)
"Stepsisters' Lament" (1957), *Cinderella* (TV show)

"Stonewall Moskowitz March" (1926), *Betsy* (show)
"Strangers" (1967), *Androcles and the Lion* (TV show)
"Sunday" (1958), *Flower Drum Song* (show)
"Surrey with the Fringe on Top" (1943), *Oklahoma!* (show)
"Suzy Is a Good Thing" (1955), *Pipe Dream* (show)
"Sweet Peter" (1925), *Dearest Enemy* (show)
"Sweet Sixty-five" (1937), *I'd Rather Be Right* (show)
"Sweet Thursday" (1955), *Pipe Dream* (show)
"Sweetenheart" (1930), *Simple Simon* (show)
"Sweetest Sounds" (1962), *No Strings* (show)
"Take and Take and Take" (1937), *I'd Rather Eat Cake* (show)
"Take Him" (1952), *Pal Joey* (show)
"Take the Moment" (1965), *Do I Hear a Waltz?* (show)
"Tartar Song" (1928), *Chee-Chee* (show)
"Ten Cents a Dance" (1930), *Simple Simon* (show)
"Ten Minutes Ago" (1957), *Cinderella* (TV show)
"Thank You So Much" (1965), *Do I Hear a Waltz?* (show)
"That's for Me" (1945), *State Fair* (film)
"That's Love" (1934), *Nana* (film)
"That's the Way It Happens" (1953), *Me and Juliet* (show)
"Theme from Victory at Sea" (1954), *Victory at Sea* (TV series)
"There Is Nothin' Like a Dame" (1949), *South Pacific* (show)
"There's a Boy in Harlem" (1938), *Fools for Scandal* (film)
"There's a Small Hotel" (1936), *On Your Toes* (show)
"There's Music in You" (1953), *Main Street to Broadway* (film)
"There's So Much More" (1931), *America's Sweetheart* (show)
"This Can't Be Love" (1938), *Boys from Syracuse* (show)
"This Funny World" (1926), *Betsy* (show)
"This Isn't Heaven" (1962), *State Fair* (film)
"This Nearly Was Mine" (1949), *South Pacific* (show)
"Thou Swell" (1927), *A Connecticut Yankee* (show)
"Time" (1979), *I Remember Mama* (show)
"To Keep My Love Alive" (1943), *A Connecticut Yankee* (show)
"Too Good for the Average Man" (1936), *On Your Toes* (show)
"Tree in the Park" (1926), *Peggy-Ann* (show)
"Twinkle in Your Eye" (1938), *I Married an Angel* (show)
"Twinkling Eyes" (1919), *Up Stage and Down* (show)
"Two by Two (by Two)" (1965), *Do I Hear a Waltz?* (show)
"Two by Two" (1970), *Two by Two* (show)
"Valiant Years" (1961), *Winston Churchill* (TV show)
"Velvet Paws" (1967), *Androcles and the Lion* (TV show)
"Very Special Day" (1953), *Me and Juliet* (show)
"Wait Till You See Her" (1942), *By Jupiter* (show)
"Way Out West" (1937), *Babes in Arms* (show)
"We Kiss in a Shadow" (1951), *The King and I* (show)
"We'll Be the Same" (1931), *America's Sweetheart* (show)
"We're on Our Way" (1944)
"What Do You Want with Money?" (1932), *Hallelujah, I'm a Bum* (film)
"What Is a Man?" (1952), *Pal Joey* (show)
"What's the Use of Talking" (1926), *Garrick Gaieties* (show)
"What's the Use of Wond'rin' " (1945), *Carousel* (show)
"When I Go on the Stage" (1928), *She's My Baby* (show)
"When the Children Are Asleep" (1945), *Carousel* (show)
"When We Are Married" (1920), *You'd Be Surprised* (show)
"When You're Dancing the Waltz" (1936), *Dancing Pirate* (film)
"Where or When?" (1937), *Babes in Arms* (show)
"Where's That Little Girl?" (1926), *Fifth Avenue Follies* (show)
"Where's That Rainbow?" (1926), *Peggy-Ann* (show)
"Whispers" (1917)
"Who Are You?" (1940), *Boys from Syracuse* (film)
"Whoopsie" (1927), *She's My Baby* (show)
"Why Can't I?" (1929), *Spring Is Here* (show)
"Why Do I?" (1926), *The Girl Friend* (show)
"Why Do You Suppose?" (1929), *Heads Up!* (show)
"Willing and Eager" (1962), *State Fair* (film)
"With a Song in My Heart" (1929), *Spring Is Here* (show)
"Wonderful Guy" (1949), *South Pacific* (show)
"You Always Love the Same Girl" (1943), *A Connecticut Yankee* (show)
"You Are Beautiful" (1958), *Flower Drum Song* (show)
"You Are Never Away" (1947), *Allegro* (show)
"You Are So Lovely and I'm So Lonely" (1935), *Something Gay* (show)
"You Are Too Beautiful" (1932), *Hallelujah, I'm a Bum* (film)
"You Can't Fool Your Dreams" (1920), *Poor Little Ritz Girl* (show)
"You Could Not Please Me More" (1979), *I Remember Mama* (show)
"You Don't Tell Me" (1962), *No Strings* (show)

"You Have Cast Your Shadow on the Sea" (1938), *Boys from Syracuse* (show)
"You Mustn't Kick It Around" (1940), *Pal Joey* (show)
"You Never Say Yes" (1929), *Spring Is Here* (show)
"You Took Advantage of Me" (1928), *Present Arms!* (show)
"You'll Never Walk Alone" (1945), *Carousel* (show)
"You're Nearer" (1940)
"You're the Cats" (1930), *Hot Heiress* (film)
"You're the Mother Type" (1926), *Betsy* (show)
"You're What I Need" (1927), *She's My Baby* (show)
"You've Got the Best of Me" (1941), *They Met in Argentina* (film)
"You've Got to Be Carefully Taught" (1949), *South Pacific* (film)
"Younger Than Springtime" (1949), *South Pacific* (show)
"Yours Sincerely" (1929), *Spring Is Here* (show)
"Zip" (1962), *Pal Joey* (film)

# Alex Rogers

See *Williams and Walker*

# Ginger Rogers

Singer and film actress (b. Independence, Missouri, July 16, 1911; d. Medford, Oregon, April 15, 1995). She won a Charleston dance contest in Chicago, and the prize was a vaudeville engagement with the Paul Ash band. She came to New York in 1929 and landed small roles on Broadway. She appeared in a slew of movies in the early 1930s, including her first with Fred Astaire, *Flying Down to Rio* (1933). They were a hit team in nine films. She later branched out as a serious actress and comedienne. She appeared in seventy-three films, the last in 1966. The year before, she had succeeded Carol Channing on Broadway in *Hello, Dolly!*

Ginger Rogers and Fred Astaire sang and danced to "Carioca" in *Flying Down to Rio*, "The Continental" in *The Gay Divorcee* (1934), "I Won't Dance" in *Roberta* (1935), "Cheek to Cheek" and "Top Hat, White Tie and Tails" in *Top Hat* (1935), "A Fine Romance" and "The Way You Look Tonight" in *Swing Time* (1936), and "They Can't Take That Away from Me" in *Shall We Dance?* (1937).

# Sigmund Romberg

Composer (b. Nagy Kaniza, Hungary, July 29, 1887; d. New York City, November 9, 1951). Romberg came to the United States in 1909 and got jobs playing piano in Hungarian restaurants in New York City. He later began conducting a small salon orchestra at Bustanoby's, a fashionable restaurant. After he instituted the playing of American trots and glides for social dancing, the place became a favorite rendezvous of the rich and famous. Romberg's first published compositions were "Some Smoke" and "Leg of Mutton," both issued by JOSEPH W. STERN and Company in 1913.

When Louis Hirsch resigned as staff composer of the Shubert organization, J. J. Shubert hired Romberg as his replacement. His first assignment: to write the score for the Shubert brothers' elaborate revue at the Winter Garden, *The Whirl of the World* (January 10, 1914). Unlike Friml's debut, Romberg's was inauspicious. While his trots had brought him some attention (and the notice of J. J. Shubert), his popular songwriting left a lot to be desired. It took him fifteen more Shubert musicals (in three years) before he struck it rich. As he kept learning his craft at the expense of his audiences, he became something of a hack, churning out uninspired tunes to suit various stars of Shubert shows.

*Maytime* (August 16, 1917), with lyrics by Rida Johnson Young, had one outstanding song, "Will You Remember (Sweetheart)?" It was spotted as a leitmotif throughout the story. When the movie was made (1937), JEAETTE MACDONALD and NELSON EDDY sang it to immortality.

For *Love Birds* (March 15, 1921), with lyrics by Ballard MacDonald, Romberg wrote a cheerful song called "I Love to Go Swimmin' with Wimmen," which has gone unnoticed except by Al Stricker, who has sung it with the St. Louis Ragtimers for thirty-five years. Their recording of it is one of their best (Paseo 102).

*Blossom Time* (September 29, 1921), with lyrics by Dorothy Donnelly, who was a playwright, lyricist, and actress. The play was based on the life and music of Franz Schubert. This was one of the most popular shows of all time, with various touring companies playing it for over thirty years. The score's best-known numbers include "Three Little Maids," "The Serenade," "My Springtime Thou Art," "Tell Me Daisy," and the major hit, "Song of Love," taken from the first movement of Schubert's Unfinished Symphony.

*The Student Prince* (December 2, 1924), again with lyrics by Dorothy Donnelly, proved to be Romberg's finest score. He had found his metier in the Viennese operetta tradition instead of the Alley's, and in the year of RUDOLF FRIML's success with *Rose Marie*, Romberg's *Prince* had a run of 608 performances. The score is filled with standards: "Students' Marching Song," "Serenade," "Just We Two," "Drinking Song," "Golden Days," and the favorite of them all, "Deep in My Heart, Dear." Rise Stevens and Nelson Eddy made the hit recording (Columbia 4510-M).

*The Desert Song* (November 30, 1926) took its theme from the headlines of the day. It was great romantic stuff, and, with the help of OTTO HARBACH and OSCAR HAMMERSTEIN II, Romberg fashioned a score rich in memorable songs. They include "The Riff Song," "It," "The Desert Song," and the hauntingly beautiful "One Alone."

According to Gerald Bordman, in his biography of Jerome Kern, at a bridge game Kern tried to give his partner, Sigmund Romberg, a clue as to how many trumps he was holding by humming "One Alone." When the scheme failed and the hand was lost, Kern got him aside and said, "You dumb Dutchman. What was I humming to you?" Romberg replied, "One of my songs." Kern: "What was the title?" Romberg: "Who knows from lyrics?"

*The New Moon* (September 19, 1928), with lyrics by Oscar Hammerstein II, was the last of the great operettas that Broadway produced in the flurry that spanned the seven years from *Blossom Time* to *The New Moon*. For this successful show (519 performances), Romberg created five hits: "Softly, as in a Morning Sunrise," "One Kiss," "Stout Hearted Men," "Wanting You," and the perennial "Lover, Come Back to Me."

Romberg followed many other popular composers to Hollywood in 1930. He continued to write for stage and screen, and beginning in 1934 hosted his own radio program sponsored by the Swift meat packing firm. *The Night Is Young* (1935) was an MGM film for which Oscar Hammerstein II wrote lyrics to Romberg's music. It contained "When I Grow Too Old to Dream," made famous by Nelson Eddy (Victor 4285). However, following films and shows were less successful, and in 1942 Romberg formed an orchestra to tour and record. In 1945, he returned triumphantly to Broadway with *Up in Central Park* (with lyrics by DOROTHY FIELDS), which included the hit "Close as Pages in a Book," which was recorded by BENNY GOODMAN. The show was filmed in 1948.

In 1951, Romberg had his last hit with "Zing Zing-Zoom Zoom," which he had originally written as a novelty for his 1950 Christmas greeting. Perry Como had the chart hit. After his death, *The Girl in the Pink Tights* was mounted on Broadway, which included the hit "Lost in Loveliness" (written with lyricist LEO ROBIN), recorded by Dolores Grey and Billy Eckstine.

# Billy Rose

Lyricist and Broadway producer (b. William Samuel Rosenberg, New York City, September 6, 1899; d. Jamaica, West Indies, February 10, 1966). Rose studied shorthand in high school and won a shorthand contest for speed. He became the secretary to financier Bernard Baruch. Rose entered show business in the early 1920s as a lyricist and idea man who had a knack for song titles.

Rose's best years were 1923–1936. His first song was "Barney Google," which Ernie Hare and Billy Jones recorded (Columbia A-3876). That same year saw two more hits: "That Old Gang of Mine," which had a top recording by Billy Murray and Ed Smalle (Victor 19095), and "You've Got to See Mama Ev'ry Night," which Bennie Krueger's orchestra played in a splendid arrangement (Brunswick 2390). "I Can't Get the One I Want" had three different lovely arrangements: by Vincent Lopez and his orchestra (Okeh 40152), by PAUL WHITEMAN and his orchestra (Victor 19381), and by Ray Miller and his orchestra (Brunswick 2643). Rose's great novelty song of 1924 was "Does the Spearmint Lose Its Flavor on the Bedpost Overnight?" The hit recording was by Ernest Hare and Billy Jones (Cameo 504). British skiffle star Lonnie Donegan revived it in 1961 for a #5 hit (Dot 15911). 1925 saw three Rose hits: "A Cup of Coffee, a Sandwich and You" from *Andre Charlot's Revue of 1925*, which was introduced by Gertrude Lawrence and Jack Buchanan in the show and recorded by them (Columbia 512-D); "Don't Bring Lulu," sung on a hit recording by Billy Murray (Victor 19628); and "Clap Hands! Here Comes Charlie," which Arthur Fields, accompanied on the piano by LEW POLLACK, made a hit (Harmony 80-H). In 1926, Rose had "Tonight You Belong to Me," which the Cavaliers recorded (Columbia 860-D) and which had a million-selling revival in 1956, when Patience and Prudence recorded it (Liberty 55022). In 1928 Rose had "Here Comes the Showboat," recorded by Vaughn DeLeath (Edison 52104), and "Back in Your Own Back Yard," recorded by RUTH ETTING (Columbia 1288-D). From the 1929 Broadway musical *Great Day!* came the title song and "Without a Song," both recorded by Paul Whiteman and his orchestra (Columbia 2098-D), and Ruth Etting had the haunting "More Than You Know" (Columbia 2038-D). GENE AUSTIN had the hit recording of "I've Got a Feeling I'm Falling (Victor 22033).

In 1931, for his Broadway musical *Crazy Quilt*, Rose wrote "I Found a Million Dollar Baby (in a Five-and-Ten-Cent Store)," which Fred Waring's Pennsylvanians made into a hit (Victor 22707). He put "It's Only a Paper Moon" into *Crazy Quilt of 1933*, but when it flopped, he placed it in the movie *Take a Chance*, where CLIFF EDWARDS made a hit (Vocalion 2587). His last hit came in 1936 from his show, *Casa Mañana*, "The Night Is Young and You're So Beautiful." Jan Garber and his orchestra had the big recording (Brunswick 7800).

Rose turned his attention after this primarily to producing, including such lavish spectacles as aquacades for the 1939 New York and 1940 San Francisco World's Fairs. He owned two nightclubs as well as two of Broadway's best theaters, the Ziegfeld and his own Billy Rose Theatre. Rose retired from the music and theatrical world in the 1950s.

# Fred Rose

Composer, singer, pianist, and publisher (b. Evansville, Indiana, August 24, 1897; d. Nashville, Tennessee, December 1, 1954). Rose started in Chicago, playing and singing in honky-tonks. He also made records for Brunswick and had his own radio show. Since Chicago was the hometown of 1920s jazz, Rose's earliest compositions show the city's influence more than the songs of most composers of his day. They are highly syncopated.

Rose's first hit was "Sweet Mama, Papa's Getting Mad" (1920), recorded by the ORIGINAL DIXIELAND JAZZ BAND (Victor 18722) and featured in vaudeville by SOPHIE TUCKER and her Kings of Syncopation. "Don't Bring Me Posies" (1921) was his next hit. He wrote several more songs, but it wasn't until the end of 1923 that he scored again, with "Mobile Blues," which he wrote in collaboration with bandleader Albert E. Short. Jimmy Wade's Moulin Rouge Syncopaters made the hit recording of it (Paramount 20295), quickly followed by Muggsy Spanier and his Bucktown Five (Gennett 5405).

"Red Hot Mamma" (1924) was a favorite of jazz bands, especially after the ORIGINAL MEMPHIS FIVE's version (Emerson 10782). Ray Miller's dance band came out with a recording of it (Brunswick 2681), and Sophie Tucker plugged it in vaudeville. As if to show his versatility, Rose produced the waltz-ballad "Honest and Truly" (1924), which sold over a million copies and began a brief association with PAUL WHITEMAN and publisher LEO FEIST. With Whiteman, in 1925, Rose wrote "Charlestonette" (Victor 19785) and "Flamin' Mamie," the latter recorded and plugged by the COON-SANDERS NIGHTHAWKS (Victor 19922). The last hit Rose produced for Feist, in 1925, was "Red Hot Henry Brown," which the Charleston Chasers made famous (Columbia 446-D). Back in Chicago, Rose wrote "'Deed I Do" (1926), which Ben Bernie popularized, and "Deep Henderson" (1926), which was plugged and recorded by the Coon-Sanders Nighthawks (Victor 20081).

In the 1930s, Rose settled in Nashville, where he composed a series of country hits; started the most successful country music publishing company, Acuff-Rose, in partnership with country star Roy Acuff; and was influential in creating the sound of country and western music in the 1940s. As a publisher, he is credited with the discovery of Hank Williams. His son, Wesley Rose, became a major force in country music when he took over the publishing company.

# Monroe H. Rosenfeld

Songwriter who named Tin Pan Alley (b. Richmond, Virginia, April 22, 1862; d. New York City, December 12, 1918). As a young man, he was a journalist in Cincinnati, Ohio, where he came to the attention of old-line publisher Frank Harding. Harding encouraged him to go to New York. Rosie, as he was known, was a most versatile man. He played piano at Herman's Wine Room, wrote articles for newspapers, and became a press agent, short story writer, arranger, composer, and lyricist. He also sold song ideas to other lyricists. He was so prolific that he not only used pseudonyms, but sometimes put novice writers' names on his own works to help them get started. He discovered the talented EMMA CARUS and had friendships with Helene Mora and Imogene Comer, who helped plug his songs-with-morals.

Although many Alleyites were fond of their drink, Rosenfeld was abstemious. His devastating vice was playing the horses. He was a chronic loser, and most of his earnings went to

Monroe H. Rosenfeld pictured on the cover of his "Goodbye, My Honey, I'm Gone."

the track and stayed there. He was often desperate to raise money for his addiction to betting, and sold many of his songs outright for a few dollars. He was also known to sell the same song to several publishers, as well as to steal other people's tunes and pass them off as his own. He was a persuasive salesman, and when he needed cash for the races and didn't have the time to write a song, he would sell a publisher an idea for a ballad and receive an advance. He would then go to one of his impoverished writer friends to produce the song for a small consideration, and he acted as contractor. The next day he would pick up the completed manuscript, take it to the office, convince the publisher that it was going to be a smash hit, and collect another advance on it. On the rare days when this ploy didn't work, he forged checks. Once, when the police were about to arrest him, he jumped out of a second-story window and permanently injured one of his legs. Thereafter, he had a limp and wore bell-bottom trousers to hide the deformity that resulted from his jump.

He started composing while in Cincinnati, and in 1882 he had John Church publish "She's Sweet as She Can Be." His other tearjerkers included "Good-by, My Boy, Good-by," "With All Her Faults I Love Her Still," and his big ballad hit of 1897, "Take Back Your Gold." One of his few comic songs was titled "Her Golden Hair Was Hanging Down Her Back." Bert Williams created a success when he sang Rosenfeld's COON SONG, also of 1897, "I Don't Care If Yo' Nebber Comes Back." Probably his last published song was his 1916 "On a Dreamy Summer's Night." Late in his career, he was named founding editor in chief of *The Tuneful Yankee*, published by Walter Jacobs, Inc., a magazine for the trade and would-be songwriters.

# Jerry Ross

See *Richard Adler*

# Will Rossiter

Publisher (b. Wells, Somerset, England, March 15, 1867; d. Oak Park, Illinois, June 10, 1954). Will Rossiter became a major publisher when he began operations in Chicago in 1890. He was the first to hawk his wares in retail stores. Satisfying his urge to perform, he personally demonstrated songs to his customers. This go-getter, styling himself as "The Chicago Publisher," was the first to advertise songs in trade journals and theatrical papers. He was also the first to issue inexpensive song folios. However, he dropped out of the song business at the end of the 1890s and didn't resume his publishing career until 1905, when he came back to stay. He helped start the careers of several notable Alleyites by giving advice to CHARLES K. HARRIS, and by publishing WILLIAM JEROME, FRED FISHER, EGBERT VAN ALSTYNE, and PERCY WENRICH, all of whom, besides being top-notch songwriters, entered the publishing field themselves.

# Harry Ruby

Composer (b. Harry Rubinstein, New York City, January 27, 1895; d. Woodland Hills, California, February 23, 1974). Ruby's musical life began when he got a job as a staff pianist for GUS EDWARDS in his publishing house. While in vaudeville as the pianist of the Messenger Boys Trio, he met dancer Bert Kalmar, who also had a publishing company with Harry Puck (1890–1964). Ruby persuaded Kalmar to give him a job as staff pianist with his firm. (Puck worked with his sister Eva, and Kalmar and Puck had written the 1913 success "Where Did You Get That Girl?") It wasn't until he worked for Waterson, Berlin and Snyder that Ruby came up with his first hit, "What'll We Do on a Saturday Night When the Town Goes Dry?" (1919), for which he wrote both words and music. His mind was still on Prohibition when, the following year, he teamed with Bert Kalmar to write "Where Do They Go When They Row, Row, Row?" That same year the team came up with "So Long, Oo-Long." "My Sunny Tennessee" (1921) was featured by EDDIE CANTOR in *The Midnight Rounders*. "I Gave You Up Just Before You Threw Me Down" (1922) was made into a hit by Arthur Fields (Banner 1158). In the same year, Kalmar and Ruby wrote for VAN AND SCHENCK "The Sheik of Avenue B," a take-off of Ted Snyder's "The Sheik (of Araby)." And the team wrote the lyrics to Ted Snyder's 1923 melody "Who's Sorry Now?"

They wrote the score for *The Ramblers* (September 20, 1926), which starred Clark and McCullough, who made a hit of "All Alone Monday." For the score of *The 5 O'Clock Girl* (October 10, 1927), they wrote "Thinking of You." This later became Kay Kyser's theme song (Brunswick 7449). In *Good Boy* (September 5, 1928), they had "I Wanna Be Loved by You," and Helen Kane with her boop-boop-a-doop made it a hit in that show (Victor 21864). For Groucho Marx in *Animal Crackers* (October 23, 1928), they wrote "Hooray for Captain Spaulding," which was not published as a single sheet until 1956, when it became Groucho's theme for his television program.

Kalmar and Ruby went to Hollywood and shored up Amos 'n' Andy's film debut in *Check and Double Check* (1930) by inserting their multimillion-selling "Three Little Words."

It was next popularized on radio by RUDY VALLEE. "Nevertheless" (1931) was made a hit by Jack Denny and his orchestra (Brunswick 6114). It was revived in a recording made in 1950 by the MILLS BROTHERS (Decca 27253). For the film *Wake Up and Dream* (1945) Ruby wrote lyrics to RUBE BLOOM's music for "Give Me the Simple Life."

In 1950, MGM made a film biography of Ruby and Kalmar, *Three Little Words*, with Red Skelton playing Harry Ruby and FRED ASTAIRE as Bert Kalmar. The score was, of course, an anthology of their hits. One song of Ruby's we'll never get to hear is the gag song he once asked Eddie Cantor to sing: "I'm Sorry I Made You Cry But Your Face Looks Cleaner Now." Ruby retired after the early 1950s, although he continued to appear from time to time on television and at special events.

Ruby's first love throughout his life was baseball. He probably wished he had written "Take Me Out to the Ball Game," and he actually played in an exhibition game in 1931 with the Washington Senators against the Baltimore Orioles. He once bragged to writer David Ewen, "I also played in a few major league exhibition games, and in four official games in the Coast League with the Hollywood Stars and Los Angeles Angels. All this, you will admit, is more than Mozart, Berlin, Gershwin, and Chopin can say." Max Wilk recounts the story of a lunchtime discussion at the MGM commissary between Joseph L. Mankiewicz and Ruby, wherein Mankiewicz put Ruby to the supreme test. "Let's assume you're driving along a mountain road, high up," he hypothesized. "You see a precipitous cliff with a sheer six-hundred-foot drop. Two men are hanging there, desperate. One of them is Joe DiMaggio, the other is your father. You have time to save only one of them. Which one do you save?"

"Are you kidding?" replied Ruby instantly. "My father never hit over .218 in his life!"

# Dan Russo

See *Ted Fio Rito*

# S

## Santly-Joy, Inc.

Joe Santly (1886–1962), longtime plugger and composer in the Alley, decided to open his own firm in 1929, with his brothers Lester (1894–1983) and Henry (1890–1934), as Santly Brothers. Shortly after moving into the BRILL BUILDING in 1935, they became partners with George Joy, and changed the name of the firm to Santly Bros.-Joy. Their biggest hit makers were songwriters FATS WALLER, JERRY LIVINGSTON, BOB MERRILL, and VICTOR YOUNG. In 1938, it became known as Santly-Joy-Select, and in 1943, it was permanently changed to Santly-Joy, Inc. The firm continued to publish sheet music through the early 1950s.

## Elmer Schoebel

Composer and pianist (b. East St. Louis, Illinois, September 8, 1896; d. St. Petersburg, Florida, December 15, 1970). Schoebel's first jobs were playing piano and organ in movie houses. He went to Chicago in 1919, and in 1922, he recorded with the Friars' Society Orchestra (which later changed its name to the New Orleans Rhythm Kings). He was an excellent pianist, and his work caught the jazz spirit, as exemplified by his first published compositions in 1923: "Blue Grass Blues," "The House of David Blues," "Bugle Call Rag," and "Railroad Man," all with lyrics by Billy Meyers. Schoebel's "Farewell Blues" (1923) became the Rhythm Kings' theme song and one of the standard tunes of the dixieland repertoire. Cornetist Paul Mares and clarinetist Leon Roppolo shared composer credit.

In 1924, Schoebel wrote a great jazz tune called "Prince of Wails," a punning title that referred to the prince (later King Edward VIII) who was a jazz fan. The Friars' Society Orchestra made a superb recording of it in 1929 (Brunswick 4652), which featured Schoebel's piano playing. That year he also wrote, with the ubiquitous GUS KAHN and Ernie Erdman, "Nobody's Sweetheart."

Schoebel joined ISHAM JONES's orchestra in 1925 and played with them briefly in New York, where he composed "Everybody Stomp." Back in Chicago, he played with Louis Panico's band and also with Art Kassell's. During the day, he arranged and transcribed tunes for the MELROSE BROTHERS MUSIC COMPANY, which published his "Spanish Shawl" (1925). Like all of the better Chicago composers, he wrote with Gus Kahn. Besides "Nobody's Sweetheart," they wrote "Ten Little Miles from Town" (1928).

Schoebel spent over a decade (beginning in the mid-1930s) in New York City, where he was chief musical arranger for the Warner Bros.-owned Music Publishers Holding Corporation. He returned to working as a club pianist in the 1940s and then retired from the music business.

# Arthur Schwartz

Composer (b. Brooklyn, New York, November 25, 1900; d. Kintnersville, Pennsylvania, September 3, 1984). Schwartz studied to be a lawyer, but eventually succumbed to the lure of the Broadway stage. It took him several years to convince HOWARD DIETZ that they should team up to write for revues, but after he did, the team created the best of them. Schwartz began his writing with *The Grand Street Follies of 1926* (June 15, 1926). He convinced Dietz to join him for *The Little Show* (April 30, 1929), *The Second Little Show* (September 2, 1930), and *Three's a Crowd* (October 15, 1930).

*The Band Wagon* (June 3, 1931) gave the team their first real hits. The revue's sketches were by America's master comic playwright, George S. Kaufman, and the director was Hassard Short (who had done the *Music Box Revues* and was responsible for the revolving stage, mirrors, and novel lighting effects in *The Band Wagon*). The cast included Fred and Adele Astaire (their final appearance together), Helen Broderick, Frank Morgan, and dancer Tilly Losch. "I Love Louisa" was staged as a production number set in Bavaria, dominated by a merry-go-round. It was the first time a Broadway musical used a turntable. When performed in the movie version (1953), the song was a comedy number for FRED ASTAIRE, with support from Oscar Levant. "New Sun in the Sky" was introduced by Fred Astaire as he smartened himself up in front of a mirror. "Dancing in the Dark," one of their most successful numbers, was introduced in the show by John Barker, then danced to by Tilly Losch. It was written during rehearsals when Schwartz felt they needed "a dark song, somewhat mystical, yet in slow, even rhythm." He had it by the following morning. ARTIE SHAW's recording in 1941 sold over a million discs (Victor 27335). The title was used for a movie musical (1949), in which the song was sung under the credits, was used as a recurring theme throughout, and was featured by Betsy Drake in a production number. In the movie version of *The Band Wagon*, "Dancing in the Dark" was an effective dance sequence for Fred Astaire and Cyd Charisse.

*Flying Colors* (September 15, 1932) had a cast consisting of Clifton Webb, Charles Butterworth, Tamara Geva, and Patsy Kelly. It also contained three Dietz-Schwartz hits. "Alone Together," their follow-up to "Dancing in the Dark," was introduced by Clifton Webb and Tamara Geva. "Louisiana Hayride" was sung by the two in a production number in the first act finale, featuring a night-ride effect. It also provided Webb with one of his famous dance specialties. In the movie version of *The Band Wagon*, it was sung by Nanette Fabray. "A Shine on Your Shoes" was introduced on stage by Vilma and Buddy Ebsen, Monette Moore, and Larry Adler. In *The Band Wagon* film, it was sung and danced to by Fred Astaire.

*Revenge with Music* (November 28, 1934) was the team's first book musical, based on the novel *The Three-Cornered Hat* by Pedro de Alarcon. The stars were Charles Winninger, Libby Holman, and Georges Metaxa. The score boasted two hits. "If There Is Someone Lovelier Than You" was introduced by Metaxa. It was originally written for a radio serial, *The Gibson Family* (1933). Of all his songs, this was Schwartz's favorite. "You and the Night and the Music" was introduced by Metaxa and Holman. Al Bowlly made a hit recording (Victor 24855), and the great ballad was revived in the late 1940s by Frank Parker (Mercury 1008).

"That's Entertainment" (1953) was the last hit song the team wrote together. It was for the movie version of *The Band Wagon* and was introduced by Fred Astaire, Nanette Fabray, and India Adams (singing for Cyd Charisse). The song became the theme and title of two major film anthologies, *That's Entertainment* (1974) and *That's Entertainment II* (1976), MGM's collections of the best numbers from its musical films of the previous five decades.

From the 1940s through the 1950s, Schwartz worked with a variety of lyricist-collaborators. Notably, he collaborated with DOROTHY FIELDS on the 1951 hit *A Tree Grows in Brooklyn*, followed in 1954 by *By the Beautiful Sea*. In the later 1960s, Schwartz moved to England, where he scored a musical version of *Nicholas Nickleby* and recorded an album of his own material. He then returned to the United States and retired.

# Jean Schwartz

Composer (b. Budapest, Hungary, November 4, 1878; d. Los Angeles, California, November 30, 1956). Schwartz's family came to the United States to live in New York City when he was thirteen. He studied the piano and got a job as a demonstrator in the music department of Siegel-Cooper's, which boasted New York's first department store sheet music counter. He then joined SHAPIRO, BERNSTEIN and Von Tilzer as staff pianist and plugger. His first published composition was the CAKEWALK hit, "Dusky Dudes," in 1899. He formed a song-writing team with WILLIAM JEROME in 1901 and enjoyed a respectable string of hits during the next decade. Schwartz and Jerome started with a COON SONG made popular by Harry Bulger called "When Mr. Shakespeare Comes to Town," and followed it with "Rip Van Winkle Was a Lucky Man," which Jerome's wife, Maude Nugent, made famous. Schwartz and Jerome's hit with the overwhelmingly popular "Bedelia (The Irish Coon Song Serenade)" was due almost entirely to MOSE GUMBLE's plugging the number for Maurice Shapiro. It sold over three million copies. BLANCHE RING sang it in *The Jersey Lily*, and she was constantly identified with the song.

Schwartz got back into the syncopated game in 1908 with a huge success in "The Whitewash Man." It was a superior RAG and helped reaffirm RAGTIME's popularity during this decade. He scored twice more with instrumentals in 1910, "Black Beauty Rag" and "The Pop Corn Man." This same year saw JEROME REMICK's publication of Schwartz and Jerome's all-time favorite, "Chinatown, My Chinatown," again plugged to multimillion status by Mose Gumble, now head of Remick's professional department.

Jean Schwartz had many songs interpolated into Broadway shows, but it wasn't until 1904 that he wrote his first complete Broadway score, for *Piff, Paff, Pouf*, which starred Eddie Foy. Schwartz and Jerome owned their own publishing house for a few years before World War I, when they went their separate ways. Schwartz wrote for Broadway shows throughout the 1920s. His biggest successes came during World War I with AL JOLSON introducing "Hello Central! Give Me No Man's Land" and "Rock-a-Bye Your Baby with a Dixie Melody" in *Sinbad* in 1918. (The lyrics for both songs were by veterans JOE YOUNG and SAM M. LEWIS.) In 1930, Schwartz wrote his last hit, "Au Revoir, Pleasant Dreams," which Ben Bernie used as his radio theme (Brunswick 4943).

# Shapiro, Bernstein and Company (1898–present)

One of the leading publishers of Tin Pan Alley. Maurice Shapiro (1873–1911) started his career at the Adelphi Publishing Company at 229 West Twentieth Street, on January 1, 1897. At the end of that year, the company's name was changed to Consolidated Music Publishers, and the firm moved to 10 Union Square. The next year, Shapiro changed the name to Universal Music Department Company and moved the business to 48 West Twenty-

Publisher and founder of Shapiro, Bernstein, Maurice Shapiro, in 1909.

ninth Street, but not for long. The following year it expanded and moved around the corner to the Alley, at 49 and 51 West Twenty-eighth Street, as William C. Dunn and Company.

When HARRY VON TILZER entered the firm, at the end of 1899, the name became Shapiro, Bernstein and Von Tilzer, and the firm moved two doors away to 45 West Twenty-eighth Street. In the meantime, Shapiro bought the catalogs of Orphean Music Company, Myll Bros., and Horwitz and Bowers.

At the beginning of 1902, Harry Von Tilzer left to form his own company. JEROME REMICK bought Louis Bernstein's share of the business on January 2, 1904, and became Shapiro's partner in Shapiro, Remick and Company. This firm lasted exactly one year—Remick bought the entire company and its catalog from Shapiro.

Returning from his enforced retirement at the end of 1906, Shapiro began again from scratch. He purchased the catalog of Cooper, Kendis and Paley and established a new office in the Maxine Elliot Theatre, at 1416 Broadway, on the corner of Thirty-ninth Street. He named his new company Shapiro Music Publisher and assembled a brand-new staff. Composer Edgar Selden became his general manager and served extremely well. Upon Shapiro's death in 1911, his brother-in-law, Louis Bernstein (who had in the meantime become a successful dealer in New York real estate), took over the business, keeping Selden as general manager. In 1913, Bernstein changed the name of the firm again to Shapiro, Bernstein and Company. Louis Bernstein (1879–1962) thus reentered the music publishing business and, matching Shapiro's drive and business acumen, maintained the firm as one of the leading publishers of Tin Pan Alley for the rest of his life. Unlike most other Tin Pan Alley firms, Shapiro, Bernstein has not been absorbed into a major music-publishing conglomerate.

Louis Bernstein in the 1920s.

Shapiro Music Publisher building in 1910, on the corner of Broadway and 39th Street.

SHAPIRO, BERNSTEIN AND COMPANY

| | |
|---|---|
| 1897 | 229 West 20th Street (as Adelphi Pub. Co.) |
| 1897 | 10 Union Square (as Consolidated Music Pub.) |
| 1898 | 48 West 29th Street (as Universal Music Department Co.) |
| 1898–1899 | 49 and 51 West 28th Street (as William C. Dunn and Company) |
| 1899 | 45 West 28th Street (as Orphean Music Company) |
| 1900–1901 | 45 West 28th Street (as Shapiro, Bernstein and Von Tilzer) |
| 1902–1903 | 45 West 28th Street (as Shapiro, Bernstein and Company) |
| 1904 | 45 West 28th Street (as Shapiro, Remick and Company) |
| 1906–1912 | Corner Broadway and 39th Street (Maxine Elliot Theatre) (as Shapiro Music Publisher) |
| 1913–1914 | Corner Broadway and 39th Street (as Shapiro, Bernstein and Company) |
| 1914–1918 | 224 West 47th Street (Strand Theatre Building) |
| 1918–1931 | Corner Broadway and 47th Street (Central Theatre Building) |
| 1931–1936 | Corner Broadway and 51st Street (Capitol Theatre Building) |
| 1936–1959 | 1270 Sixth Avenue (RKO Building) |
| 1959–1973 | 666 Fifth Avenue |
| 1973– | 10 East 53rd Street |

# Artie Shaw

Bandleader and clarinetist (b. Arthur Jacob Arshawsky, New York City, May 23, 1910). Artie Shaw was a virtuoso of the clarinet, with a gorgeous tone that was especially telling on show tunes and ballads. His solos were well thought out, and his arrangements were startlingly effective. He joined bandleader Irving Aaronson in California in 1929, and came with him on tour to New York City, where he remained.

Shaw became an elite freelancer in the recording studios and, especially, in radio bands. After leading various combos, he formed a swing band in the spring of 1937 called Artie Shaw and His New Music. It didn't do particularly well until Jerry Gray arranged COLE PORTER's flop song "Begin the Beguine" (Bluebird 7746) for a July 1938 recording, which firmly established the band and made the song a classic. Shaw's own radio show, many recordings, and prestigious dance hall engagements kept his band on top. At the time of the "Beguine" recording, the band's personnel consisted of Chuck Peterson, John Best, and Claude Bowen, trumpets; George Arus, Ted Vesley, and Harry Rogers, trombones; Artie Shaw, clarinet; Les Robinson and Hank Freeman, alto saxes; Tony Pastor and Ronnie Perry, tenor saxes; Les Burness, piano; Al Avola, guitar; Sid Weiss, string bass; and Cliff Leeman, drums.

Among Shaw's hits were "What Is This Thing Called Love?" (Bluebird 10001), "It Had to Be You" (Bluebird 10091), "Donkey Serenade" (Bluebird 10125), "Rose Room" (Bluebird 10148), "Out of Nowhere" (Bluebird 10320), "Oh, Lady Be Good" (Bluebird 10430), and "All the Things You Are" (Bluebird 10492). With a thirty-two-piece band that included a thirteen-piece string section, on March 3, 1940, Shaw recorded "Frenesi," the biggest-selling recording of the World War years II (Victor 26542). In the fall of 1940, Shaw created his band-within-the-band, the Gramercy Five, with Johnny Guarnieri playing harpsichord! The group scored a hit with "Moonglow" (Victor 27405). The Shaw band appeared in two movies, *Dancing Cod* (1939) and *Second Chorus* (1940). His bands had the highest musical standards and contained some of the country's finest musicians.

Shaw was almost as well-known for his wives as for his music. Among his eight were novelist Kathleen Winsor and actresses Lana Turner, Ava Gardner, Doris Dowling, and Evelyn Keyes. Shaw retired from performing in the mid–1950s, famously turning his back on the music industry. Although he has continued to give interviews from time to time, Shaw often expresses bitterness toward the commercialism that he saw in the jazz world.

# Sheet Music

## Pre-Tin Pan Alley Sheet Music Publishing

Before Tin Pan Alley publishers made music publishing into a major industry, most publishing was done locally by printers or stationers (dealers in printed goods and paper). So-called broadsides or one sheets were first imported to the United States from Britain, and these were followed by sheet music. (Song sheets continued to be published in the United States through the nineteenth century; these featured just the words to popular songs, without the musical accompaniments.) The first major printing centers for sheet music in the United States were New York, Boston, Baltimore, and Philadelphia; Benjamin Carr (b. London, England, September 12, 1768; d. Philadelphia, May 24, 1831), who operated out of Philadelphia, is generally cited as the first publisher who focused on music. The output of early publishers like Carr was primarily limited to patriotic music and songs.

During the Civil War era, major hits were published by music dealers such as Oliver Ditson out of Boston; Ditson, like other music publishers, published a wide range of material, from classical music to pop songs. Stationers continued to be active in music publishing. Many of Stephen Foster's songs were published by Firth, Pond and Company of New York; popular Civil War songwriter Henry Work's songs were published by Chicago stationer Root & Cady, among others.

Charles K. Harris's publication of "After the Ball" in 1892 is generally credited as the "birth of Tin Pan Alley" publishing, in which a publisher actively promoted a song through stage performance (plugging). Its nationwide sale of over 2 million copies revealed a huge market for popular music, and many publishing houses were created specifically to cater to it.

## Sizes of Sheet Music

There are four main sizes of sheets. Before 1918, sheets were generally 13½ by 10½, inches, and these are known to collectors as large sheets. In 1918, two major publishers issued "wartime" sheets, 10¼ by 7 inches, referred to as miniature sheets. From 1919 to the present day, sheets have been issued in what we know as the standard size, 12 by 9 inches. From 1961 to 1978, some sheets were published in a smaller 11 by 8½ inch format, in addition to the regular 12 by 9 inches also being published.

## Pricing and Sales of Sheets

Throughout pop history, there have been inconsistencies in the pricing and printing prices on sheet music. During the early nineteenth century, sheet music sold for as little as twenty-five cents and as much as seventy-five cents. When the price was printed on the cover, it usually appeared as a single number (e.g., 5, which stood for fifty cents). Naturally, sheets with colored lithographs and engravings cost more than those in plain black and white. The price of fifty cents remained fairly standard throughout the late nineteenth century and into the twentieth up to the Depression (1930), when the price dropped to twenty-five (or thirty or thirty-five) cents.

Since there were so many independent publishers, prices varied. As seen in the chronological price list, prices have always been erratic. For example, the ninety-five-cent price started at the beginning of 1970 and lasted, for the most part, until the end of 1971. However, a few publishers continued to charge that amount until September 1972. While the majority of publishers started charging $1.00 for sheets at the beginning of 1972, some had originated that price as early as June 1971. Most publishers were charging $1.00 by July 1973, but as early as March of that year, some publishers had gone to $1.25. The price list that follows, therefore, is merely a guide to prices originally charged by publishers in general, with a great deal of overlapping at both ends of the spectrum. However, you can be certain that if you have a sheet first issued in 1982 but carrying a printed price of $3.50, you have a reprint, even if the original plates were used for the music and lyrics and the original photograph or design was used on the cover. The change of price is the giveaway. For the most part, prices are printed on either the front or the back cover. Sometimes they are not, usually during periods when the price has been the same for a long time (e.g., 1981–1984, 1984–1989).

Since sheet music prices remained fairly constant until about 1945, we begin just after the war, when the price rose from thirty-five to forty cents:

| | |
|---|---|
| 40¢ | 1946–1950 |
| 50¢ | 1950–1959 |
| 60¢ | March 1959–1964 |
| 75¢ | 1964–1968 |
| 85¢ | 1968–1969 (up to April 1970) |
| 95¢ | 1970–1971 (up to September 1972) |
| 1.00 | 1972–July 1973 (but started as early as June 1971) |
| 1.25 | March 1973–July 1974 |
| 1.50 | March 1974–December 1978 |
| 1.75 | April 1978–March 1979 |
| 1.95 | May 1979–1981 |
| 2.50 | 1981–1984 |
| 2.95 | 1984–1989 |
| 3.50 | 1989–1993 (up to December) |
| 3.95 | April 1993–Present |

Turn-of-the-century Woolworth's store featuring a five cent sheet music sale.

The biggest sales of sheet music were in five-and-dime chain stores (Woolworths, McCrory's), where a sheet sold for ten cents. At a music store (which also sold musical instruments, phonographs, records, and piano rolls), the retail price was twenty-five cents during the 1920s, rising to forty cents after World War II. After World War II, jukeboxes were in demand at restaurants and diners, where records of pop music could be heard for a nickel a side. Publishers advertised in music magazines for the public to join their sheet music clubs. For $1.00, a membership bought all songs they issued during that year (what a bargain!).

## Price-Cutting

Around the turn of the twentieth century, department stores became an important outlet for the sales of sheet music. The two largest department stores in New York City, Siegel, Cooper and Company ("Meet me at the fountain"), at Eighteenth Street and Sixth Avenue, and R. H. Macy and Company, at Thirty-fourth Street and Broadway, started a famous feud by cutting prices on their items. Macy's began selling sheet music at six cents per copy and daring other stores to undersell it. Five major music publishers got together to stop this price-cutting. In August 1907, Leo Feist, M. Witmark and Sons, F. B. Haviland, F. A. Mills, and Charles K. Harris formed American Music Stores to establish their own music counters in the principal department stores and to act as jobbers to the department store business in general. They also wanted to stop the Joseph W. Stern Company from monopolizing department store music counters with its contracts to feature Stern music. American Music Stores managed to secure contracts to supply over fifty stores with their combined publications.

The price war between Macy and Siegel-Cooper was the publishers' main worry. It was Isidore Witmark's idea to shock the two stores into pricing sheet music at fifty cents. The music cartel did this by announcing a one-day sale—on October 12, 1907—of their most popular songs for one cent apiece at Rothenberg and Company, on West Fourteenth Street. This sale was to include Witmark's current hit, "Love Me and the World Is Mine," which was being wholesaled at the feuding stores for twenty-three cents a copy. In addition to holding the sale, the publishers employed people to go to Macy's and to Siegel-Cooper's, demanding that these stores sell their sheets at the same price as Rothenberg's, brandishing the "We will not be under-sold" ad which had appeared in newspapers the previous day. Rothenberg's put on extra staff, and the rehearsed crowd went to Macy's and Siegel-Cooper's. Macy's clerks, becoming increasingly irritated, were calling the floor manager to approve every sale.

One of Isidore Witmark's friends went to the household department and bought some tin pots and pans. He then went to the music department, where he ordered a list of song sheets, which the salesgirl wrapped up. He was prepared to pay a penny apiece for them. When told that the price was six cents a copy, he created a fuss and showed her the Rothenberg ad. After a long harangue, he walked away, dropping pieces of tinware as he went, making quite a racket. It took most of the floorwalkers to get him out, but everyone knew he was there.

As the day came to an end, a representative of Macy's called the office of American Music Stores. When informed that the united publishers would fight the department stores if it took twenty such sales, Macy's capitulated, and the price-cutting of sheet music came to an abrupt end.

## Piracy

During the nineteenth century, lyric sheets called "songsters" were very popular. These were usually printed on newsprint and sold for a penny or two. The printers of songsters paid no royalties to the original publishers. This rampant piracy was one of the inspirations for the founding of societies to protect composers, first in Europe, and then in the United States with ASCAP. During the twentieth century, fake books were the main form of piracy, with hundreds of tunes being published in one book. But here, only the melody of the chorus was printed, with harmonic symbols above the melody. These were made for professional musicians (usually pianists playing in bars) and were sold to them under the counter.

## Cover Art

Along with getting a star to use a song in the act or on the air, publishers discovered early in the history of Tin Pan Alley that the song's cover art played an important role in the selling of the popular music sheet. Fancy-lettered, engraved black-and-white covers were issued prior to the birth of Tin Pan Alley, and black-and-white lithographs of scenes illustrating the titles of songs were also common. It wasn't until "After the Ball," which featured the photograph of its popularizer, James Aldrich Libbey, prominently on the cover, that the appeal of catchy cover art was recognized as a key to success in selling sheet music.

From the beginning of Tin Pan Alley, it was noticed that an attractive cover sold more songs. Previously, publishers issued plain white covers printed in black ink. With the resurgence of popularity of color lithograph covers, during the 1890s, fancy artwork designs, drawings, illustrations, and the use of photography (scenes, places, celebrities) became standard practice. While famous illustrators and cartoonists were often used, a legion of lesser-known graphic artists also designed sheet music covers When photos of entertainers were added to enhance the promotional value, the photos sometimes partially obscured the original design. The typical procedure when commissioning an artist to design a cover was to have him come to the publisher's office to hear the song played and sung by the house pianist. Then the artist would submit a small sketch of his design for approval. If his design was accepted, the artist would complete a full-scale drawing including typography, ready for the printer.

From the mid-1890s on, publishers took great care with their covers. Occasionally, famous illustrators of books, magazines, and posters created sheet music artwork or allowed their previous work to be used as cover art. They included James Montgomery Flagg, Archie Gunn, Maxfield Parrish, Grace G. Drayton, Edward Windsor Kemble, Charles Dana Gibson, Henry Hutt, Raeburn Van Buren, Howard Chandler Christy, Rose O'Neill, Russell Patterson, John Held, Jr., Alberto Vargas, and Norman Rockwell. Famous cartoonists also illustrated cover sheets: Richard Outcault, Palmer Cox, Rudolph Dirks, Bud Fisher, Frederick Opper, Windsor McCay, George McManus, Rube Goldberg, George Herriman, Billy DeBeck, Frank King, Sidney Smith, Carl Ed, Milt Gross, Al Hirshfeld, Ham Fisher, Walt Disney, Edwina, Charles Schulz, Stan MacGovern, Hank Ketcham, and Al Capp. Several commercial artists made sheet music covers their lifework: Fred W. Starmer, Bert Cobb, Edgar Keller, John Frew, Edward Henry Pfeiffer, Andre De Takacs, and Albert Barbelle.

Edward Taylor Paull (1858–1924) was the first and only publisher to regularly use five-color lithography for his covers. He started publishing (mostly marches) in 1894 and continued issuing his highly collectible sheets until his death.

A publisher sometimes used a performer's photograph on the cover as an incentive for the performer to retain the song in his repertoire. A photograph also served as a reminder of the time the potential purchaser saw and heard the performer sing the song, and encouraged the customer to buy the sheet as a souvenir. Today, these covers often hold the only extant photographs of some of the places and people of bygone eras, giving the sheets added desirability, importance, and value.

The artwork of each era in Tin Pan Alley's history is distinctive. As many people collect sheet music today as collect postcards, posters, and other works of popular art.

## Orchestrations/Arrangements

Along with the standard piano-vocal versions of hit songs, Tin Pan Alley publishers also produced arrangements of pop songs for a variety of instruments. By the turn of the twentieth century, these included piano solo, mandolin, banjo with piano accompaniment, and arrangements for dance bands, theater orchestras, military bands, concert bands, and combos for movie houses. For dance bands, a standard or "stock" arrangement was issued. Bands made whatever adjustments were necessary for their members. Many regional bands relied on these stock arrangements because they could not afford their own arrangers. Eventually, other musicians and listeners tended to view these as second-tier outfits, because of their lack of creativity.

## Sheet Music Collecting

The world, it seems to me, is made up of two kinds of people: collectors and noncollectors. Collectors may be interested in the music itself, some more interested in the covers, some in the subject of the song, some in all three. There are three principal areas or categories of sheet music collecting today—popular songs, show tunes, and film music—and they are usually collected by decade. Then there are special categories: RAGTIME, BLUES, COON SONGS, transportation (further broken down into sub-groupings such as automobiles, railroads, airplanes, boats, roller skates); theatrical celebrities, and personalities such as Judy Garland, Marilyn Monroe, Shirley Temple, Jeanette MacDonald, Nelson Eddy, and Mae West (the most collected today).

Other categories are states, cities, radio, television, Prohibition, dances, women's rights, cartoons, advertising, historical events, national celebrities, sports (again, particularized as baseball, football, golf, boxing, Ping-Pong), politicians (especially presidents, governors, and mayors), singers, band leaders, million-selling songs, minstrel songs, major or favorite composers (IRVING BERLIN, JEROME KERN, GEORGE GERSHWIN, COLE PORTER), Oscar winners, patriotic songs (World War I had the most songs written about it), famous illustrators, people's names (Mary and Sue are the leaders here), songs about your occupation, and so on.

The most widely collected category, I have found, is that of local imprints. Most collectors, regardless of of their interest in other categories, seem to collect songs published in their locale and songs that mention their hometown in either the title or the lyrics. While Manhattanites would have a tough time trying to collect all of the songs published there, they will collect songs with New York, Manhattan, Harlem, or a similar area in the title.

The history of sheet music collecting as a deliberate activity started during the 1920s. True, people bound their music sheets during the nineteenth century (that is how much of it has come down to us in such fine condition), but as these volumes show, there was no method of gathering them as they were being bound—just random acquisition in no particular order. Many single sheets from the nineteenth century, therefore, are slightly trimmed and have holes in the spine where they were sewn together when bound. Neither trimming nor unbinding affects the price of these sheets.

Naturally, the pioneer collectors dealt only with the eighteenth and nineteenth centuries. They continued to collect up until the 1950s, when they either died or donated their collections to libraries. Modern collecting started in the late 1950s and early 1960s, with mostly twentieth-century items. With great interest in ragtime in the 1970s, that collectible became prominent, and is still a category that intrigues today's collectors.

Music collecting today is a developing and expanding field. While it is true that much American popular sheet music can be purchased for a couple of dollars at flea markets and garage sales (because it was mass-produced and lots of it still exists), it is also true that prices of specialty items have risen dramatically during the past few years.

Awareness and specialized interest have led to an increased demand for information on all aspects of the field. Societies have been organized to bring collectors together, and monthly publications devoted to buying, selling, and trading have sprung up—including articles about favorite categories.

People like to point out that the prices of some sheets are astronomically high. The famed Streeter auction of Americana in 1967 saw a first edition of the "Star Spangled Banner" go to a dealer for $23,000. SCOTT JOPLIN's masterpiece, "Maple Leaf Rag," went for $10,000 in 1979. A copy of Gershwin's famous "Swanee," in the original edition, recently went for $1,500. Irving Berlin's first published song, "Marie from Sunny Italy," also went for that amount at a recent auction, and any of the five songs from Rodgers and Hammerstein's *Away We Go* fetch between $500 and $1,000. You don't know *Away We Go*? I don't blame you, for that title lasted for only three weeks in New Haven and Boston in March 1943. When the show came to Broadway, it was titled *Oklahoma!*

Perhaps the most pressing question today among collectors is how to identify the first edition of a song. As in first-edition book collecting, when the publisher does not identify it as such, there are various means of detection: checking the copyright copy at the Library of Congress; checking advertisements for other songs on the inside front, inside back, and back covers, finding out who first performed it—perhaps his or her photo is on the first edition; and so on. There is no easy answer.

Unfortunately, there is no formula for establishing the current value of a rare or desirable music sheet. The value of a sheet greatly depends upon how much a collector is willing to pay for it. The sheet may not be particularly scarce, but if it is the last one needed to complete a category, a collector will pay a higher price than might ordinarily be expected. Sheets vary in availability from one geographic area to another.

Some of the following criteria used to determine value will be obvious to the collector and non-collector alike: the scarcity or rarity of the item, the condition, the importance historically and qualitatively of the composer and/or lyricist, the significance of the publisher, the number of collectors wanting the same item and its generally limited availability, the artistic design of the cover, the photographs of artists on the cover, the date of original publication, and the general familiarity of the song itself.

As in most collecting, there are vogues for certain categories. In the early 1950s, nineteenth-century imprints were in great demand. Today, ragtime is the hottest category, closely followed by show tunes of the major Broadway writers and movie tunes with photographs of favorite stars. Coon songs are now coming into prominence, with prices accelerating greatly every year. In the 1990s, they were selling for an average of $12.00 apiece. Today, the average seems to be between $50.00 and $100.00 each.

The tremendous nostalgia that has taken hold since the early 1970s has made what was formerly considered trash—not worth saving, ephemeral in nature, made to be used up immediately and thrown away—sought after by collectors, all of us wanting to recapture our youth or symbols of happier times. No wonder Bakelite bracelets and art deco telephones are so expensive. Even vintage clothing has a ready market today. Further, there has been a legitimizing of sheet music as a worthwhile collectible. Specialized auctions are held regularly, and a growing number of dealers are producing informative catalogs.

One of the main points to be made about collecting sheet music today is that much of it is relatively inexpensive and plentiful. One can have a lot of fun specializing in several categories with a small outlay of cash. While brand-new contemporary songs retail for $3.95 a copy, many older hits can be obtained at flea markets for as little as a dollar.

# Shimmy

In the early 1920s, the shimmy, introduced by Gilda Gray (1898–1959), was the craze in vaudeville and on Broadway. ETHEL WATERS started her career as a shimmy dancer before she began singing and acting. Joe Gold and Eugene West summed it up in their song "Everybody Shimmies Now" (1918), which had a photo of Mae West on the cover. The dance was still going strong four years later, as evidenced by Armand J. Piron's "I Wish I Could Shimmy Like My Sister Kate" (1922).

# Dinah Shore

Singer (b. Frances Rose Shore, Winchester, Tennessee, March 1, 1917; d. Los Angeles, California, February 24, 1994). She began her career in Nashville on radio. She came to New York in 1938, and by the following year, she was recording with XAVIER CUGAT and singing on station WNEW. In 1940, she joined radio's *Chamber Music Society of Lower Basin Street* and made a few records with leader Henry "Hot Lips" Levine and his Barefooted Philharmonic. Eddie Cantor signed her for his radio show, and by 1941, she had her own program. She hosted a top-rated television variety program from 1951 to 1962, and had a popular talk show on TV from 1970 to 1980.

Shore's first million-seller was the 1942 "Blues in the Night," from the film of the same name (Bluebird 11436). She had a #1 hit in 1944, from the movie *Follow the Boys*, "I'll Walk Alone" (RCA Victor 20-1586). She had another #1 hit in 1946 with "The Gypsy" (Columbia 36964). In 1947, she had yet another #1 hit with "The Anniversary Song," from the film *The Jolson Story* (Columbia 37234). Her last million-seller came in 1948 with the #1 hit "Buttons and Bows," the Academy Award winner from *The Paleface* (Columbia 38284). She and Buddy Clark also recorded the Academy Award winner of 1949, "Baby, It's Cold Outside," from *Neptune's Daughter* (Columbia 38463). Also in that year, Shore scored with "Dear Hearts and Gentle People" (Columbia 38605). Late in 1950, she had another hit with "My Heart Cries for You" (RCA Victor 20-3978). In 1951 she had a #3 hit with "Sweet Violets." Then came rock and roll, and the end of her recording career.

# Carl Sigman

Composer and lyricist (b. Brooklyn, New York, September 24, 1909; d. Manhasset, New York, September 26, 2000). Sigman had a career composing songs that stretched from the 1940s through the 1970s and contributed several standards to the pop repertoire. The son of a shoe-store owner, he studied law at his mother's insistence, and was admitted to the bar after graduating from New York University. He studied piano for nine years, and became a friend of lyricist Johnny Mercer. One of his first big hits was "Pennsylvania 6–5000," written in tribute to Glenn Miller's New York home-away-from-home, the Hotel Pennsylvania. It was a Top 10 hit for the band and became their signature tune. In 1942, Sigman was drafted into the army, and while serving, he wrote the 82nd Airborne Division's official song, "The All American Soldier." "(Dance) Ballerina (Dance)," with words by Bob Russell (1914–1970), was a major hit for Vaughn Monroe in 1947 (RCA Victor 20-2433), selling over a million copies. It was successfully revived in 1957 by Nat "King" Cole (Capitol 3619). In 1948, Sigman composed "Enjoy Yourself," with lyrics by Herb Magidson. When Guy Lombardo and his Royal Canadians recorded it in 1950, it became one of the biggest hits of that year (Decca 24839). Sigman composed both melody and lyrics for the 1955 hit "Dream Along with Me (I'm on My Way to a Star)," which became Perry Como's television theme. Later hits for the composer include "What Now, My Love" in 1966, and the theme from the film *Love Story*, "Where Do I Begin?," a tearjerking ballad, in 1970. Sigman also wrote themes for television (notably 1955's *The Adventures of Robin Hood*) and many films.

# Frank Sinatra

Singer and actor (b. Francis Albert Sinatra, Hoboken, New Jersey, December 12, 1915; d. Beverly Hills, California, May 14, 1998). Sinatra was hired as a vocalist by Harry James in mid-1939. Although he recorded "All or Nothing at All" with the Harry James Orchestra (Columbia 35587), it wasn't released until 1943, after he had left James. He joined TOMMY DORSEY and his orchestra in early 1940 and had his first hit, "Polka Dots and Moonbeams" (Victor 26539), with the Dorsey band. He also made the films *Las Vegas Nights* (1941) and *Ship Ahoy* (1942) with the band. He left Dorsey to go on his own in late 1942. In January 1943, he made a sensational appearance at the Paramount Theatre in New York City, where screaming, swooning bobby-soxers proved his popularity.

Sinatra sang on radio as a regular on *Your Hit Parade* (the first time in 1944, and again from 1947 to 1949). AXEL STORDAHL became his music director and conductor for radio and recordings. The great debate during the 1940s and 1950s was Who is the top male singer, BING CROSBY or Frank Sinatra?

L to r: Hank Sanicola, Frank Sinatra, Irving Berlin, and Ben Barton at the opening of Sinatra's music publishing company, Barton Music, in the Brill Building, 1943.

Sinatra starred in two 1944 films, *Higher and Higher* and *Step Lively*, but it was in *Anchors Aweigh* (1945) that he got to show his ability to handle comedy. His film career floundered in the early 1950s, but was spectacularly revived in *From Here to Eternity* (1953), which won him an Oscar for Best Supporting Actor. His million-selling hit record of 1954, "Young at Heart" (Capitol 2703), became the title of a film (1954) starring Sinatra and DORIS DAY. His musical movie career was revived with the great *Guys and Dolls* (1955), *High Society* (1956), *Pal Joey* (1957), and *Can-Can* (1960). His recording career picked up as his acting career was at its height, when he scored a hit with "Love and Marriage," from the television production of *Our Town*, which starred Sinatra. It was the first hit song to come from a television production (Capitol 3260). This recording was later used as the theme song for the TV show *Married with Children*. His next hit, "(Love Is) The Tender Trap," came from the movie of the same name, in which he starred (Capitol 3290). In 1957, he had the hit recording of Academy Award winner "All the Way," from a film he starred in, *The Joker Is Wild* (Capitol 3793). The following year he had another hit in "Witchcraft" (Capitol 3859). In 1959, he again had the hit recording of an Academy Award winner, "High Hopes," from a film in which he starred, *A Hole in the Head* (Capitol 4214). In 1966, he had a #1 hit and million-seller with "Strangers in the Night," from the film *A Man Could Get Killed* (Reprise 0470). "Something Stupid" was his last million-seller, recorded in 1967 with his daughter Nancy (Reprise 0561). In 1969, he recorded a song that he used until the end of his life, "My Way" (Reprise 0817). His last hit, in 1980, was the theme from the film, *New York, New York* (Reprise 49233). He was a headliner for more than fifty-six years, and many think he was the best singer of the twentieth century.

# Noble Sissle

See *Eubie Blake*

# Chris Smith

African-American composer (b. Charleston, South Carolina, October 12, 1879; d. New York City, October 4, 1949). He started in show business with a black medicine show. He began a twenty-year partnership with his childhood friend, Elmer Bowman (1879–1916), when they came to New York City with their vaudeville act. There Smith met the best black talents of the day, and wrote for and with them. He also met CECIL MACK, who became his main lyricist. Starting in 1901 with his first big hit, "Good Morning, Carrie," he contributed songs to the WILLIAMS AND WALKER Company's shows. While writing for the Black Patti Company, he and principal comedian Jolly John Larkins wrote a hit comic song in 1904 called "Shame on You." To place a song in *Marrying Mary* (August 27, 1906), Smith allowed the show's composer, Silvio Hein, credit on the song. Marie Cahill, the star of the show, made "He's a Cousin of Mine" famous and boosted her own career as well. Also in that year, Smith and Mack wrote "All In, Down and Out." The team scored heavily in 1908 with "Down Among the Sugar Cane" and "You're in the Right Church but the Wrong Pew," which Bert Williams made into a hit in *Bandanna Land.*

In 1909, Smith left Mack (and GOTHAM-ATTUCKS) and went to JEROME REMICK's, with Jim Burris as his lyricist. The new team gave Remick's "There's a Big Cry-Baby in the Moon" and a marvelous novelty comedy song called "Transmagnificanbamdamuality (or C-A-T Spells Cat)." That same year, they went to JOSEPH W. STERN's with their comic song "Come After Breakfast, Bring 'Long Your Lunch and Leave 'Fore Supper Time," which became a success in vaudeville. Smith helped Bert Williams write his first *Ziegfeld Follies* song, "Constantly," in 1910, as well as "If He Comes In, I'm Going Out."

Smith created the first of his syncopated instrumentals in 1911 with "Honky Tonky Monkey Rag." The following year he went to Haviland with four numbers: "Beans, Beans, Beans," "That Puzzlin' Rag," and the Fanny Brice rag song "That Snakey Rag" (all written with Elmer Bowman), and the ballad "After All That I've Been to You," with lyrics by Jack Drislane. In 1913, he wrote by himself "Fifteen Cents" and the lyric to Luckey Roberts's fabulous "Junk Man Rag," which was featured by Maurice and Florence Walton, dancing rivals of the Castles.

It was while he was at Stern's turning Roberts's rag into a song that Smith and Jim Burris created the most famous fox-trot song of the decade, "Ballin' the Jack." Burris's lyrics don't exactly explain the dance step, but nobody cared then and nobody cares now. It immediately caught on with dancers and singers in vaudeville. It was so popular that it was interpolated into *The Girl from Utah* (August 24, 1914), for the star Donald Brian's specialty dance. The song version became so popular that in a reversal from the usual—making an instrumental into a song—bandleader/composer JAMES REESE EUROPE helped Smith turn the song into an instrumental! The whole world, it seemed, was dance-crazy, and Chris Smith gave it reason to be, with the era's favorite tune.

In 1915, Smith wrote another fox-trot, "Keep It Up," which was merely a variation of "Ballin' the Jack." The following year, Smith had two hits in a row for Broadway Music Corporation: "Down in Honky Tonk Town," with words by Charles McCarron (1891–1919), and "Never Let the Same Bee Sting You Twice," with words by Cecil Mack. He also published his first BLUES that year, with San Francisco publisher Sherman, Clay and Company, appropriately called "San Francisco Blues."

Throughout the 1920s, Smith contributed numbers, including two syncopated gems, "I've Got My Habits On" (1921), which he wrote to JIMMY DURANTE's music, and his own "If You Sheik on Your Mamma, Your Mamma's Gonna Sheba on You" (1924). After 1928, Smith's name mysteriously disappeared from sheet music, although he did have one publication in 1930 and two songs later in that decade.

# Kate Smith

Singer (b. Greenville, Virginia, May 1, 1909; d. Raleigh, North Carolina, June 17, 1986). Smith performed in vaudeville as the "Songbird of the South." She came to New York City in 1926 and played the Palace Theatre and a Broadway musical, *Honeymoon Lane*. Ted Collins became her manager in 1931 and got her a fifteen-minute radio show several nights a week. Her theme song was one she co-wrote, "When the Moon Comes Over the Mountain" (Columbia 2516-D). She had many different radio programs, either fifteen minutes or thirty minutes in length. One show in the late 1930s featured a new comedy team, Abbott and Costello. Before making movies, Smith had a #1 hit with GUY LOMBARDO's orchestra, "River, Stay 'Way from My Door" (Columbia 2578-D). Her most famous radio broadcast took place on November 11, 1938, when she introduced IRVING BERLIN's "God Bless America." Her hit recording was revived throughout World War II (Victor 26198). In 1940, Smith had the hit record of "The Last Time I Saw Paris," which won the Academy Award for Best Song of 1941 (Columbia 35802). Her last Top 10 hit came in 1945. "Don't Fence Me In" was from the film *Hollywood Canteen* (Columbia 36759).

Smith had a popular afternoon television show in the early 1950s but briefly retired upon the death of her longtime manager in 1954. She returned to show business the following year, doing guest shots on television variety shows and had her own singing show. She continued on TV and in nightclubs into the 1970s. Her clear soprano voice cheered radio and television audiences throughout her career.

# Ted Snyder Company/Waterson, Berlin and Snyder (1908–1928)

Ted Snyder and Company was one of the major publishing companies of the Ragtime Era. Ted Snyder (1881–1965) came to New York in 1904 after having worked as a staff pianist and plugger for publishing firms in Chicago. He landed a job on the professional staff of F.

A. MILLS Company, and had some numbers published by Mills. He obtained financial backing from Boston jobber George Krey to start a firm with lyricist Ed Rose (1875–1935). In July 1908, with the backing of Henry Waterson of the Crown Music Company, Snyder created the Ted Snyder Company and became sole owner of the catalog of Rose and Snyder. In September, he published his own successful rag, "Wild Cherries." A few months after starting his own firm, singer Amy Butler, a friend of Waterson's, took Snyder down to Jimmy Kelly's saloon, where she had heard a waiter singing original risqué parodies of popular songs. She believed his talents as a lyricist would be useful to the firm. Snyder was not overly impressed but, with Butler's persuasion, he hired the waiter to write lyrics for a weekly draw of $25.00 against future royalties. It is fitting that when Ted Snyder and his new lyricist, IRVING BERLIN, wrote "Kiss Me, My Honey, Kiss Me," Amy Butler's picture appeared on the cover of the sheet music.

The new team clicked and wrote "Next to Your Mother, Who Do You Love?," "Sweet Italian Love" (which featured a photo of Irving Berlin on the cover), "My Wife's Gone to the Country (Hurrah! Hurrah!)" (with lyrics co-written by George Whiting, whose wife divorced him because of this song), and rag songs: "That Beautiful Rag," "That Mysterious Rag," and "Wild Cherries Rag." This last was a song version of Snyder's instrumental. It, too, became extremely popular. After Irving Berlin's gigantic hit "Alexander's Ragtime Band," he was made a partner in the firm. In 1912 the name was changed to Waterson, Berlin and Snyder. Berlin left the firm in 1919 to start his own company.

Ted Snyder's biggest hit was published in 1921. In an interview, he told how he wrote it: "I had the melody of the chorus of the 'Sheik' written and I couldn't get any kind of verse that suited me. I have always considered the verse very important, and insist on having a good verse, which will show off the chorus of my songs. I played this chorus around the office, but nobody paid any attention to it. In my effort to get a suitable verse, I finally went into the Oriental and at last completed the song under the title of 'My Rose of Araby' ".

"Mr. Waterson had just read the book of *The Sheik* and he said that a book that could sell over two million copies was worth writing a song about, and he wanted to call my song 'The Sheik.' However, I couldn't connect the Sheik of the story with my 'Rose of Araby,' as we had written it. Mr. Waterson showed the way and a few days after the song was written, the moving picture was announced. So it was an all-round fortunate combination of circumstances which helped to make the song a hit."

The following year, the same team—Snyder, Harry B. Smith, and Francis Wheeler—wrote another hit for the company, "Dancing Fool," which was recorded by the most famous dance bands of the day. In 1923 Snyder, Bert Kalmar, and HARRY RUBY teamed up to write one of the great standards, "Who's Sorry Now." Snyder wrote of it, "Well, everybody knows that song crazes go in cycles. All the publisher can do is try to feel what the public may want next. When I saw all those 'cry' songs and none of them making the headway I thought they should, it made me feel they had not hit on the right idea of that type of song. So I tried my hand and was lucky enough to get the right song. It was a number deliberately written to fit conditions which I felt were in the air. I thought the public wanted that kind of song."

Snyder left his company in the summer of 1927 to go to California. Waterson, Berlin and Snyder went bankrupt in 1929, and Jack Mills (of MILLS MUSIC) bought its catalog for $5,000 in 1931.

TED SNYDER COMPANY

1908–1911 112 West 38th Street (as Ted Snyder Co.)

1912–1914 112 West 38th Street (as Waterson, Berlin and Snyder)

1914–1928 224 West 47th Street (Strand Theatre Building)

# Song Folios

Song folios were used to market older songs. Publishers issued folios during the 1920s, usually for $1.00 each, which would include six or seven numbers. These folios were often built around song themes or were collections of a composer's work. Publishers would also issue what they called dance folios, ten or twelve tunes without words, suitable for various dance styles.

# Song Form

The popular song of Tin Pan Alley was constructed of two parts: the verse (which nobody knew) and the chorus (which everybody knew). In the beginning of popular song publishing, the verse was used to tell the story and to build interest in the song. There were as many as five or six stanzas in the verse. By the end of the Alley, the song was reduced to just the chorus, which featured the catchy melody.

# Southern Music Company

Southern Music began in 1928, and opened a New York office two years later. It specialized in publishing songs that were recorded first, rather than creating songs and then trying to get them recorded. This firm started in the Paramount Building, but became the first tenant in the Brill Building a year later. It was also the first major publisher to concentrate on county music, representing Jimmie Rodgers and the Carter Family.

Southern was founded by Ralph Peer (b. Ralph Sylvester Peer, Kansas City, Missouri, May 22, 1892; d. Hollywood, California, January 19, 1960). Peer was born to the music business; his father sold phonographs and had a link with the Columbia Company, for whom Peer worked in his native Kansas City from 1911 to 1919. He was hired by a rival firm, the General Phonograph Company, in 1920 to run their Okeh division. His first job was to oversee the recordings of blues singer Mamie Smith, recording her "Crazy Blues" in 1920, said to be the first blues recording by a black singer. In 1923, he was contacted by an Atlanta furniture dealer who wanted him to record a local fiddler named Fiddlin' John Carson. The resulting record—Carson's rendition of "The Little Old Log Cabin in the Lane" backed with "The Old Hen Cackled"—is generally credited as the first successful country music recording.

In 1925, Peer moved to Victor Records, which offered him a unique arrangement: instead of paying him a salary, they offered him the publishing rights to any of the material he recorded. Because there were no publishing rights to traditional songs or tunes, Peer began to encourage his artists to write their own material. In 1928, Victor and Peer founded Southern Music, which became a leading publisher of blues and country material.

In the summer of 1927, Peer made a field trip to Bristol, Tennessee, that would become legendary in recording circles. At this session he "discovered" both Jimmie Rodgers and the Carter Family, overseeing their first recordings. His music publishing arm would naturally become the outlet for both of these acts' prolific compositions. In 1930, Victor fired Peer because they felt he was unfairly profiting from his music publishing activities; from that point, he turned his attention full-time to the publishing business.

In 1932, foreseeing the change in musical tastes, Peer branched out in his publishing business to sign popular songsmiths like Hoagy Carmichael while he also explored the international market. He was central in the founding of Broadcast Music Inc. (or BMI) in 1940, which challenged the more conservative ASCAP (American Society of Composers, Authors, and Publishers) in its dominance of the music licensing field.

In the 1940s and 1950s, Peer left the day-to-day operations of his company increasingly to his son while he pursued a lifelong interest in horticulture, becoming a world-renowned authority on camellias.

# John Stark and Son

Publisher (b. Spencer County, Kentucky, 1841; d. St. Louis, Missouri, November 20, 1927). Owner of a music store in Sedalia, Missouri, John Stark liked Scott Joplin's "Maple Leaf Rag" enough to publish it in September 1899. The first edition quickly sold out. When Stark wanted to order another edition from the printing firm in St. Louis, he was told he would have to wait his turn, as it was busy with larger orders. This so infuriated Stark that he went to St. Louis and bought the printing company. He then moved his business and family there, and became a full-time publisher, mostly of rags. His enthusiasm for RAGTIME was so great that he devoted his life to plugging it. Certainly, his catalog became the most important, containing many of the best works in the genre. In August 1905, Stark moved his editorial office from St. Louis to New York City, where he remained at 127 East Twenty-third Street until moving back to St. Louis permanently in 1910. He continued to publish rags until 1922. His number of published rags was second only to that of the JEROME H. REMICK firm.

# Sam Stept

Composer active in the 1930s and 1940s (b. Samuel H. Stept, Odessa, Russia, September 18, 1897; d. Los Angeles, California, December 1, 1964). The Stept family settled in Pittsburgh, Pennsylvania, after emigrating to the United States in 1900. As a teenager, Stept worked first as a pianist for a local music publisher, then as an accompanist on the vaudeville circuit. By the early 1920s, he was leading his own dance band. His first hit came in 1928 with lyricist BUD GREEN on "That's My Weakness Now," written for singer Helen Kane, who sang it in the film *Applause*. Kane also scored a hit a year later with the duo's "Do Something." Stept and Green continued to work for musical films through the early 1930s. In 1931, Stept had a major hit with "Please Don't Talk About Me When I'm Gone," with lyrics by Sidney Clare. It was popularized in vaudeville by Bee Palmer, on radio by KATE SMITH, and on record by GENE AUSTIN (Victor 22635), and revived in 1961 by FRANK SINATRA. Other Stept collaborators for film work included Sidney Mitchell, NED WASHINGTON, and TED KOEHLER. Stept also produced scores for several Broadway shows and revues in the later 1930s, most notably the 1939 hit *Yokel Boy*, with lyrics by LEW BROWN and Charles Tobias, which three years later was made into a film with Eddie Foy, Jr., in the title role. Also in 1942, the Stept-Brown-Tobias partnership produced the major ANDREWS SISTERS hit, "Don't Sit Under the Apple Tree," featured in the film *Private Buckaroo*. Stept continued to write for films and stage through the early 1950s, and then retired from composing to turn his attention to managing his music publishing holdings.

# Joseph W. Stern

Publisher (b. New York City, January 11, 1870; d. Long Island, New York, March 31, 1934). He and his silent partner, EDWARD B. MARKS, became the major competitor of the Witmarks. As general music publishers, Stern and Marks were strong on dance music—waltzes, schottisches, two-steps—especially the sensation of the 1890s, the CAKEWALK. They were quick to hear the difference that the black songwriter made, and hired the most prolific teams—Bob Cole writing first with comedian Billy Johnson, then COLE AND JOHNSON BROTHERS (no relation to Billy), John Rosamond and James Weldon, and WILLIAMS and WALKER. One of his best-known hits was "Under the Bamboo Tree" from 1902. The Stern Company was the first New York publisher to latch on to piano RAGTIME, when it bought the rights to Tom Turpin's 1897 St. Louis publication, "Harlem Rag," in 1899. Their black house arranger,

Music publisher Joseph W. Stern.

Will Tyers (1876–1924), rewrote it, and their new version became nationally known. Other hit songwriters included Chris Smith with "Ballin' the Jack," a major hit in 1914–1915. Stern retired in 1920, and Marks continued to operate the firm under his own name.

JOSEPH W. STERN and COMPANY (1894–1920)

| | |
|---|---|
| 1894 | 304 East 14th Street |
| 1895–1898 | 45 East 20th Street |
| 1898–1906 | 34 East 21st Street (Mark Stern Building) |
| 1907–1920 | 102–104 West 38th Street |

# Axel Stordahl

Arranger and composer (b. New York City, August 8, 1913; d. Encino, California August 30, 1963). Stordahl was originally a trumpet player, joining TOMMY DORSEY's band in 1936 as an arranger. While with Dorsey, he showed his skills arranging accompaniments for slower numbers and ballads, making him a favorite of young singer FRANK SINATRA. When Sinatra left the band, Stordahl went with him as his music director, serving in that capacity through the late 1940s. In 1945, Stordahl composed his best-known hit, "Day by Day" with PAUL WESTON, with words by SAMMY CAHN; Jo Stafford made the hit recording (Capitol 227). Through the 1950s, he worked in studio bands for radio and films, and worked again with Sinatra on record.

# Billy Strayhorn

See *Duke Ellington*

# Jule Styne

Composer (b. London, England, December 31, 1905; d. New York City, September 20, 1994). Styne came to the United States with his family when he was eight years old, and received thorough training in piano technique at Chicago Musical College.

"Sunday" (1926) was the first tune Styne created, while working as pianist-arranger for ARNOLD JOHNSON and his orchestra in Chicago. It wasn't until he joined Bennie Krueger's orchestra that he took the song to Rocco Vocco, head of LEO FEIST's Chicago office. Vocco assigned lyricist Ned Miller (1899–1990) to it and published the result. It was an immediate sensation for JEAN GOLDKETTE and his orchestra, featuring Bix Beiderbecke (Victor 20273). The orchestras of ABE LYMAN (Brunswick 3286) and Sam Lanin (Perfect 14726) also made successful recordings. Later "Sunday" was used as the radio theme of *The Phil Harris–Alice Faye Show* on NBC.

Styne formed his own dance band to play in Chicago hotels and clubs. In 1938, he went to Hollywood to work as an arranger and vocal coach. His first big hit, with lyrics by FRANK LOESSER, was "I Don't Want to Walk Without You," from the film, *Sweater Girl* (1942). The #1 hit recording came from Harry James and his orchestra (Columbia 36478).

In Hollywood, Styne teamed with lyricist SAMMY CAHN, and their first hit was "I've Heard That Song Before," introduced by Bob Crosby and his orchestra in the film *Youth on Parade* (1942). Harry James and his orchestra (with vocal by Helen Forrest) recorded it in 1943 and sold over a million discs (Columbia 36668). *Follow the Boys* (1944) contained the only song of Styne and Cahn's to sell over a million copies of sheet music, "I'll Walk Alone," introduced in the film by DINAH SHORE, who also had a best-selling record (RCA Victor 20-1586). It was revived by Don Cornell in 1952 (Coral 60659).

"It's Been a Long, Long Time" (1945) was an independent song by the team, introduced on radio by bandleader Phil Brito. Harry James and his orchestra (with vocal by Kitty Kallen) made a #1 hit recording (Columbia 36838). "Let It Snow! Let It Snow! Let It Snow!" (1945) was another nonfilm hit for the team. Vaughn Monroe made the #1 disc (RCA Victor 20-1759).

*High Button Shoes* (October 9, 1947) was Styne's first Broadway musical. The score, with lyrics by Cahn, included two hit songs, "Papa, Won't You Dance with Me?" and "I Still Get Jealous," both sung by Nanette Fabray in the show. A film, *Romance on the High Seas* (1948), brought the team's next big song, "It's Magic," introduced by DORIS DAY and Jack Carson. Day's recording sold over a million copies (Columbia 38188).

*Gentlemen Prefer Blondes* (December 8, 1949), Styne's second Broadway show, had lyrics by LEO ROBIN. They came up with two standards, "A Little Girl from Little Rock" and "Diamonds Are a Girl's Best Friend." Both were introduced in the show by Carol Channing, who became a star as a result of these numbers. When the show was adapted for film in 1953, Marilyn Monroe and Jane Russell sang these two songs.

Styne's *Hazel Flagg* (February 11, 1953), a Broadway musical with lyrics by BOB HILLIARD, had several hits, among them "How Do You Speak to an Angel," "Ev'ry Street's a

Boulevard (in Old New York)," and "Money Burns a Hole in My Pocket," which were all used in the film version (retitled *Living It Up* [1954]), starring DEAN MARTIN and Jerry Lewis.

Styne and Cahn were sitting in their Hollywood office in 1954 when producer Sol C. Siegel came to ask them if they could write a song called "Three Coins in the Fountain." Cahn replied, "We could write a song called 'Eh,' if you want us to." When asked for details, Siegel told them that the studio had just finished a picture in Italy called *We Believe in Love*, and that Siegel wanted the title changed. He figured that if a title song went along with the change, other studio executives would okay it. Unfortunately, all of the film's prints were being used in editing, and the script copies were still in Italy. When the songwriters asked what the film was about, Siegel summarized, "It's about three American girls in Italy who throw coins in a fountain." Styne and Cahn worked it out in an hour, and soon had FRANK SINATRA's promise to sing it on the sound track (Capitol 2816). The Four Aces had the #1 million-selling hit (Decca 29123). The song also received an Academy Award.

*My Sister Eileen* (1955) reunited Styne with Leo Robin, and the hit of the film was "Give Me a Band and My Baby." The biggest recording was by Joe Carr and the Joy Riders (Capitol 3231).

*Bells Are Ringing* (November 29, 1956) had lyrics by BETTY COMDEN and ADOLPH GREEN. The score of this Broadway musical is excellent and contained two enormous hits. "Just in Time" was introduced by Judy Holliday and Sydney Chaplin in the show, and by Dean Martin in the film version (1960). "The Party's Over" was sung in both show and film by Judy Holliday.

*Gypsy* (May 21, 1959), based on the memoirs of Gypsy Rose Lee, was another hit musical for Styne, writing with new lyric partner, Stephen Sondheim (b. 1930). They had a hit with "Let Me Entertain You" and also scored heavily with "Everything's Coming Up Roses," which ETHEL MERMAN belted to success in the show. When the film version was made (1962), the latter was sung on the sound track by Lisa Kirk for Rosalind Russell. *Do Re Mi* (December 26, 1960) reunited Styne with Comden and Green for one hit, "Make Someone Happy," sung in the show by Nancy Dussault and John Reardon.

*Funny Girl* (March 26, 1964), with lyrics by BOB MERRILL, was Styne's last Broadway show with song successes. "Don't Rain on My Parade," "The Music That Makes Me Dance," and "People" were all introduced by Barbra Streisand, who also sang them in the film (1968). Her recording of "People" received a Grammy (Columbia 42965).

# Dana Suesse

Composer and pianist (b. Kansas City, Missouri, December 3, 1910; d. New York City, October 16, 1987). One of the few women composers to score hits, Suesse is best remembered for "You Oughta Be in Pictures." Trained as a classical pianist, she came to New York with her mother, who was an opera singer. PAUL WHITEMAN invited her to write two "jazz concertos" for his orchestra to perform at Carnegie Hall; the reviewer in *The New Yorker* dubbed her "The Girl Gershwin." Her first song hit was 1932's "Have You Forgotten," with lyrics by LEO ROBIN. That same year she partnered with EDWARD HEYMAN, who provided lyrics to one of the melodies she had previously written for Whiteman. The new song was called "My Silent Love" and was a hit for ISHAM JONES (Brunswick 6308). The Heymann–Suesse duo scored a major success in 1934 when Jane Froman sang their "You Oughta Be in Pictures" in that year's edition of the *Ziegfeld Follies*. A year later, the duo scored the film *Sweet Surrender*, an odd hodgepodge of a musical filmed in Astoria, New York, and mostly featuring radio personalities (singer Frank Parker was the male lead, partnered by Broadway singer Tamara as his love interest). Bandleader ABE LYMAN was also prominently featured. Other hits for Suesse included 1937's "The Night Is Young and You're So Beautiful" (with lyrics by BILLY ROSE and Irving Kahal) and "Yours for a Song" (with Rose and Ted Fetter), the latter of which was introduced in *Billy Rose's Aquacade*, a lavish revue presented at the 1939 New York World's Fair. In later years, Suesse returned to concertizing and composing classical works.

# Kay Swift

Composer, lyricist, and librettist (b. Kay Faulkner, New York City, April 19, 1897; d. New York City, January 28, 1993). Swift was a classically trained pianist who broke into Broadway big time in 1929 when her song "Can't We Be Friends" was introduced by singer Libby Holman in the revue *The Little Show*. The lyric was provided by her husband, wealthy banker James P. Warburg, under the name "Paul James." They collaborated on a complete score in 1930 for the musical *Fine and Dandy*, producing their biggest hit, "Can This Be Love?" She then began an affair with GEORGE GERSHWIN, which continued until the composer's death, and led to the dissolution of her marriage. Meanwhile, she continued to contribute to Broadway revues and shows, notably 1935's *Parade*, a socially conscious period piece, and the music for George Balanchine's 1935 ballet, *Alma Mater*. Swift wed rancher Faye Hubbard and retired to life on the ranch in the later 1930s, writing a book of memoirs that was made into the film *Never a Dull Moment* in 1950 with Fred MacMurray and Irene Dunne. This marriage, too, ended in divorce. In later life, Swift's landmark status as an early female popular music composer, and her association with Gershwin, led to renewed interest in her work.

# T

## Eva Tanguay

Singer (b. Marbleton, Canada, August 1, 1878; d. Hollywood, California, January 11, 1948). Tanguay had a fairly ordinary voice but tremendous enthusiasm and energy. She was vaudeville's highest-paid star, personifying the idea of her most famous song, the 1905 Harry Sutton–Jean Lenox "I Don't Care." She became known as the "I Don't Care Girl," brazenly proclaiming to managers, directors, fellow performers, and even audiences that she really didn't care what they thought of her. Her love affairs were well known, although she hardly ever gave interviews to the press. She gave everything to putting over a song.

When she was just seventeen, Tanguay first appeared on a sheet music cover: "Shinny on Your Own Side," an 1895 tune by Charles Graham, the composer-author of the classic tearjerker of 1891, "The Picture That Is Turned to the Wall" (which established M. WITMARK AND SONS as a major publisher). Tanguay got Blanche Merrill (1885–1966) to write special material that parodied her own proclivities. One such song, "Egotistical Eva," went over with a bang. In 1910, she had Merrill write her a RAG SONG modestly titled "The Tanguay Rag." It was published with a photo showing the famous Tanguay legs on its cover. She had her last two hits in 1915: the Archie Gottler–EDGAR LESLIE "America, I Love You" and the veteran team of MONROE H. ROSENFELD and Arthur Lange's "What Money Can't Buy."

Eva Tanguay in full costume to perform the "Tanguay Rag," published by Will Rossiter.

Tanguay was a human dynamo whose performances exhausted her. It could be said that she burned herself out.

# Television Musicals

One of the attractions of early television was a remarkable number of original book musicals created for the medium. Many of Broadway's most famous composers and lyricists wrote them: Cole Porter (*Aladdin*, 1958), Richard Rodgers and Oscar Hammerstein II (*Cinderella*, 1957), Arthur Schwartz and Howard Dietz (*A Bell for Adano*, 1956), Jule Styne and Bob Merrill (*The Dangerous Christmas of Red Riding Hood*, 1965), Hugh Martin (*Hans Brinker*, 1958), Stephen Sondheim (*Evening Primrose*, 1966), Burton Lane and Dorothy Fields (*Junior Miss*, 1957), and Jimmy Van Heusen and Sammy Cahn (*Our Town*, 1955). This last featured "Love and Marriage"—the first hit song to come from this new medium. Since the mid-1960s, however, few new musicals have been written specifically for television, although some classic Broadway musicals have been remade as television features.

# James Thornton

Composer, and performer (b. Liverpool, England, December 5, 1861; d. New York City, July 27, 1938). Thornton's family came to the United States when he was eight years old and settled in Boston. As a young man, Thornton went to New York City, where he started his career as a singing waiter. He became a drinking companion of John L. Sullivan, the first heavyweight champion of the world. For several years, he was a singing partner of Charles B. Lawlor, composer of "The Sidewalks of New York," touring in vaudeville with him. Thornton's first song hit came in 1892, inspired by his wife Bonnie's pleading with him to come home right after his performance, instead of staying out drinking in saloons. When he refused to promise this, she asked if she was still his sweetheart. He airily replied, "My sweetheart's the man in the moon." The next morning he remembered the phrase and used it as the title of his song.

In 1894, he came up with another sentimental ballad, "She May Have Seen Better Days." But it was in 1898 that he published his most famous song, again inspired by his wife. Asked if he still loved her, Thornton replied: "I love you like I did when you were sweet sixteen." Thornton sold "When You Were Sweet Sixteen" to two different publishers for $15.00 each. After the Witmarks turned it into a giant hit, JOSEPH W. STERN and Company sued them, because Stern could prove that it, too, had purchased the song for $15.00. They settled out of court when Witmark paid Stern $5,000.00. The song is still a favorite of barbershop quartets.

Thornton's last hit came in 1900, when he wrote "The Bridge of Sighs," inspired by the structure that connects the Criminal Court Building with the Tombs Prison in New York City. He continued as an artist in vaudeville and made his last appearance in Jerome Kern's musical, *Sweet Adeline*, in 1929. He died broke.

# Harry Tierney

Popular composer of the 1920s (b. Harry Austin Tierney, Perth Amboy, New Jersey, May 21, 1890; d. New York City, March 22, 1965). Originally a concert pianist, Tierney got his first job on Tin Pan Alley working as a demonstrator for JEROME REMICK in the early 1910s. During the mid-1910s, he placed songs in several Broadway shows, but really scored big when he partnered with lyricist JOSEPH MCCARTHY. The duo's first smash was the show *Irene*

(1919), which produced the hit "Alice Blue Gown," among others. Several more shows followed, their next major success coming with *Kid Boots* (1923), which produced the standard "Someone Loves You." Next came 1927's *Rio Rita*, a major sensation that ran for over 500 performances and introduced the hit title song and "The Kinkajou," which were usually paired on recordings. After one final show with McCarthy (the flop *Cross My Heart* in 1928), Tierney went to Hollywood. With lyricist BENNY DAVIS he scored the film *Dixiana*, which produced the hit title song, but his career pretty much faded after that. Further attempts to return to Broadway were unsuccessful.

# Charles Tobias

Lyricist and singer (b. New York City, August 15, 1898; d. New York City, July 7, 1970). Tobias had a long career, beginning as a vaudeville singer. In 1923, he founded his own publishing house. Working with his brothers Harry (b. New York City, September 11, 1895; d. St. Louis, Missouri, December 15, 1994) and Henry (b. Worcester, Massachusetts, April 23, 1905; d. Los Angeles, California, December 5, 1997), he wrote the lyrics to two hits, "On a Dew-Dew-Dewy Day" and "Miss You." During the 1930s, Tobias mostly wrote songs for Broadway shows and revues, and then turned his attention to film work through the early 1950s. He had a major hit during World War II with the ANDREW SISTERS' "Don't Sit Under the Apple Tree" (Decca 18312), with colyricist LEW BROWN and music by SAM STEPT. After a decade of inactivity, Tobias returned to the charts in 1962 when he provided Nat "King" Cole with the hits "Those Lazy, Hazy, Crazy Days of Summer" (music by Hans Carste) and "All Over the World" (music by Al Frisch). Older brother Harry was also a successful lyricist and was active in music publishing. Younger brother Henry had a long career, composing melodies to Charles's lyrics for several editions of *Earl Carroll's Vanities* during the 1930s and after the war working as a musical director for CBS.

# Triangle Music Publishing Company

When Joseph M. Davis (b. New York City, October 6, 1896; d. Louisville, Kentucky, September 3, 1978) established the Triangle Company in 1919, he created a firm to rival the black publishers (he himself was white), issuing mostly BLUES and popular songs written by blacks.

Some of his hits were "I Wanna Jazz Some More," "Papa Will Be Gone," "Whicker Bill Blues," "My Lovin' Mamie," "Daddy, Your Mama Is Lonesome for You," and "Dreaming Blues." During the 1930s, Davis dropped the Triangle imprint and replaced it with Joe Davis, Inc. Davis sold the firm in December 1939 and went into the record manufacturing business, becoming a major independent record salesman as well. He kept his business going until the early 1960s. Among his most famous songwriters were FATS WALLER, ANDY RAZAF, CHRIS SMITH, Alex Hill, Paul Denniker, SPENCER WILLIAMS, Carson J. Robison, J. C. Johnson, and Claude Hopkins.

# Sophie Tucker

Famed, big-voiced singer (b. Sonia Kalish-Abuza, Russia, January 13, 1884; d. New York City, February 9, 1966). She continued working as a headliner in clubs and on television until her death. She was billed late in her career as "The Last of the Red Hot Mamas." Earlier, however, she was called "The Mary Garden of Ragtime." She, like EMMA CARUS, was a large woman with a strong voice and a wide vibrato. Her energy was enormous, and she went to great lengths to put over a song.

Tucker's exact place of birth is unknown; her parents were on the move somewhere between Russia and Poland at the time. When she was three, the family moved to the United States, and eventually settled in Hartford, Connecticut, where her father opened a small restaurant/café. Tucker was already performing there as a preteen singer, and in 1906 moved to New York and began working the cafés and burlesque, and vaudeville houses. She sometimes performed as a "coon shouter," including the requisite blackface makeup. Tucker's first hit was "Dat Lovin' Rag" (1908), by Bernie Adler and Victor Smalley, which convinced her to build a career on this type of syncopated song with upbeat, somewhat brassy lyrics. She introduced HARRY VON TILZER's "The Cubanola Glide" (1909), and also appeared in a small role in *Ziegfeld's Follies* that year. The following year, on the advice of her maid, she introduced black writer SHELTON BROOKS's "Some of These Days." This was so often requested that she made it her theme song. She also boosted Brooks's "Darktown Strutters' Ball" (1917) after the ORIGINAL DIXIELAND JAZZ BAND made its introductory recording.

In 1921, Tucker hired as her accompanist the pianist/songwriter Ted Shapiro, who remained her musical director for the rest of her career. Throughout the 1920s, Tucker made hits, mostly projecting her signature personality of a sassy, strong-willed woman: "Aggravatin' Papa," "You've Got to See Mama Ev'ry Night," "Papa, Better Watch Your Step," "Old King Tut," "Red Hot Mama," "Mama Goes Where Papa Goes," "Nobody Knows What a Red-Head Mama Can Do," "I Ain't Got Nobody," "After You've Gone," "There'll Be Some

Sophie Tucker immortalized in "The Tucker Trot," published by Will Rossiter.

Changes Made," "He's a Good Man to Have Around," "Real Estate Papa, You Ain't Gonna Sub-Divide Me," and "I'm the Last of the Red Hot Mamas." The last she sang in her first film, *Honky Tonk* (1929). The sentimental "My Yiddishe Mama" was written specially for her by JACK YELLEN and LEW POLLACK in 1925, and she made it an enormous hit, recording it in both English and Yiddish on a single 78. Tucker continued to be an enormous star on the Broadway stage, while also appearing in vaudeville and nightclubs.

After moving to Hollywood in 1929, Tucker had a spotty film career through the mid-1940s. She often appeared as herself, performing a number or two, but did not have any starring vehicles. During the 1930s, she made several acclaimed appearances in London, and last appeared on Broadway in 1941's revue *High Kickers* by COLE PORTER. She continued to make nightclub and TV guest appearances through the early 1960s. Her autobiography, *Some of These Days* (1945), showed her to be a loyal, hardworking performer who loved her business and was always on the lookout for new songs.

# Roy Turk

See *Fred E. Ahlert*

# V

## Rudy Vallee

Singer (b. Herbert Pryor Vallee, Island Pond, Vermont, July 28, 1901; d. Los Angeles, California, July 3, 1986). After graduation from Yale, Vallee worked at the Heigh-Ho Club in New York City in 1928, leading the Connecticut Yankees, whose name he took from the RICHARD RODGERS–LORENZ HART show of the previous season. His pianist, Cliff Burwell, and lyricist MITCHELL PARISH wrote "Sweet Lorraine," which Vallee plugged to success. Vallee was famous in the pre-electric microphone days for using a megaphone while singing in front of his band. He was also an alto saxophonist who changed his first name in honor of the great alto sax virtuoso, Rudy Wiedoeft.

Vallee's rise to stardom was swift. His first movie, *The Vagabond Lover* (1929), featured his song "I'm Just a Vagabond Lover." In 1929, he began hosting his own NBC radio show, which made Alice Faye, Frances Langford, and Edgar Bergen into stars and revived the career of comedian Frank Fay. The show, sponsored by Fleishman's yeast, was an enormous success and ran for a decade. Vallee's theme song was "My Time Is Your Time." In addition to plugging the songs of others, Vallee wrote a few hits himself, notably "Deep Night" (1929) and "Betty Coed" (1930), and he helped make famous "Good Night, Sweetheart," "The Whiffenpoof Song," and the "Stein Song." He made a comeback as the star of Broadway's

Rudy Vallee pictured on the cover of "So Close to the Forest," published by T. B. Harms.

long-running musical *How to Succeed in Business Without Really Trying* (October 14, 1961), and he played the same role in the film version (1967). He continued to make club appearances until his death in the mid-1980s.

# Van and Schenck

Comedy singers (Gus Van, b. August Von Glahn, Brooklyn, New York, August 12, 1887; d. Miami Beach, Florida, March 12, 1968; Joe Schenck, b. Joseph Thuma Schenck, Brooklyn, New York, 1891; d. Detroit, Michigan, June 28, 1930). Van and Schenck were popular performers in vaudeville, in Broadway musicals, and on radio, and had many record hits from 1917 to 1928.

Both were born to immigrant parents. Van worked as a trolley motorman by day and an amateur singer in local bars at night. He was soon supporting himself as an entertainer, and in 1905 hired teenage pianist Joe Schenck to be his accompanist. After Schenck's voice changed, he began singing tenor harmonies to Van's lead, and the duo was born. They hit vaudeville around 1910, and two years later WILL ROSSITER published their first original composition, "Teach Me That Beautiful Love."

In 1916, Van and Schenck were booked by Florenz Ziegfeld to appear in his shows, making their first Ziegfeld appearance in *The Century Girl.* This led to their first recordings for the small Emerson label, but they soon were signed by Victor. The duo scored their first big hit with their 1917 disc "For Me and My Gal" (Victor 18258). From 1918 to 1928, the duo recorded for Victor's rival Columbia, scoring hits with "Mandy" (Columbia A-2780), 1921's "Ain't We Got Fun?"(Columbia A-3412), and 1923's "Carolina in the Morning" (Columbia A-3712).

Through the 1920s, the duo continued to compose songs, usually working with another composer, but most of these are forgotten today and they are best remembered for making hits of others' compositions. They also did dialect routines typical of the day, including Jewish, Italian, and rural-rube characterizations. Besides recordings, the duo performed on radio (beginning in 1923), and also made several "talkie" shorts through the 1920s and one feature film, 1930's *They Learned About Women.* Two songs were issued on disc from the film, the duo's last record release.

In the spring of 1930, Schenck died of a heart attack while the duo was touring. Van continued to perform as a single through the 1930s, appearing in film shorts and occasionally recording. He retired to Miami Beach, Florida, in 1949, still making local appearances after his retirement. He died in March 1968 after being struck by an automobile.

# Egbert Van Alstyne

Composer (b. Merango, Illinois, March 5, 1878; d. Chicago, Illinois, July 9, 1951). Van Alystne was a musical prodigy who played the organ for Sunday school when he was seven years old, and was given a scholarship to Chicago Musical College, the Juilliard of its day. It was run by Florenz Ziegfeld, Sr., whose son would create the famous revue series, the *Follies.* During the first decade of the twentieth century, it was unusual for composers of popular music to have any formal training in classical music, and Van Alstyne was exceptional in this regard. (Two other Tin Pan Alleyites, PERCY WENRICH and ZEZ CONFREY, would later study at the Chicago Musical College.)

Van Alstyne went into vaudeville with lyricist Harry H. Williams (1879–1922) and turned out a string of hits, starting in 1903 with the fine Indian song "Navajo," introduced by Marie Cahill (1870–1933) in her show *Nancy Brown.* Van Alstyne and Williams scored again the following year with a COON SONG, "Back, Back, Back to Baltimore." In 1905, the team had their greatest hit with "In the Shade of the Old Apple Tree," which sold several million copies of sheet music. The next year the team produced "Won't You Come Over to My House," and followed that up in 1907 with another Indian song, "San Antonio," and the comic "I'm Afraid to Come Home in the Dark," the latter sung to great acclaim by MAY IRWIN. The following year, joined by lyricist Benjamin Hapgood Burt (1882–1950), Van Alstyne composed a sequel, "I Used to Be Afraid to Go Home in the Dark, Now I'm Afraid to Go at All." In 1910, the team scored with "What's the Matter with Father?," and in 1911, with a RAG SONG harking back to their first hit, "Oh, That Navajo Rag."

Van Alstyne was involved with piano rags as early as 1900, when he wrote "Rag Time Chimes," published in Chicago by WILL ROSSITER. It featured, for the first time, the "chimes" effect that would become a cliché in other ragtime compositions. He had a hit for JEROME REMICK in 1909 with "Honey Rag," whose second strain is a beauty. And in 1912 he wrote "Jamaica Jinger (A Hot Rag)," which again demonstrated his creativity in syncopation. Van Alstyne composed the verse to the Tony Jackson tune "Pretty Baby," which, because of its interpolation into the *Passing Show of 1916*, became a million-seller. His last hit was the 1931 "Beautiful Love."

# Jimmy Van Heusen

Composer (b. Edward Chester Babcock, Syracuse, New York, January 26, 1913; d. Rancho Mirage, California, February 7, 1990). Van Heusen was a popular composer of the 1940s and 1950s who worked primarily with lyricists JOHNNY BURKE and SAMMY CAHN.

While still in high school, Van Heusen had a radio program on a local station which featured his songs. It was then that he changed his name, taking his surname from the famous shirt manufacturer. He spent four years as a staff pianist in Tin Pan Alley, working for SANTLY Brothers and JEROME REMICK, before he was asked to write his first Broadway show, *Swingin' the Dream* (November 29, 1939), based on Shakespeare's *A Midsummer Night's Dream*. From that score, "Darn That Dream," with lyrics by EDDIE DE LANGE, became popular. BENNY GOODMAN, who introduced it in the show, recorded an Eddie Sauter arrangement of it, with vocalist MILDRED BAILEY (Columbia 35331). The following year, Van Heusen teamed with lyricist Johnny Burke to write "Polka Dots and Moonbeams" (1940), which became FRANK SINATRA's first hit with the TOMMY DORSEY Orchestra (Victor 26539).

Van Heusen's teaming with Johnny Burke led him to Hollywood in 1940, when BING CROSBY asked them to write for the Road pictures. For *The Road to Zanzibar* (1941), the team wrote the lovely "It's Always You." Tommy Dorsey and his orchestra (with a vocal by

Jimmy Van Heusen in his Hollywood days, c. the 1930s.

Frank Sinatra) made a hit with their version (Victor 27345). The follow-up *The Road to Morocco* (1942) sported two hits by Van Heusen and Burke, "Constantly" and "Moonlight Becomes You." Crosby's solo flick *Dixie* (1943) contained "Sunday, Monday or Always" and "If You Please." The former was sung in the film by Crosby, who also had a million-selling #1 hit recording (Decca 18561).

The Burke-Van Heusen team wrote prolifically for other film stars besides Crosby. *Lady in the Dark* (1944) included Van Heusen's interpolation "Suddenly It's Spring" (1943), sung by Ginger Rogers. It was popularized by Eugenie Baird, who sang it on the hit recording by Glen Gray and his Casa Loma Orchestra (Decca 18596). *And the Angels Sing* (1944) introduced "It Could Happen to You," sung by Dorothy Lamour and Fred MacMurray. *Going My Way* (1944) contained the duo's "Swinging on a Star," which was written for Crosby (Decca 18597) and won the Oscar for Best Song. It was the first of four Oscars that Van Heusen would win in his career, more than any other composer has won so far. The same year, Van Heusen, with comedian Phil Silvers as lyricist, wrote "Nancy with the Laughing Face" for Frank Sinatra's newborn daughter (Columbia 36868). It was a good omen, for she grew up to become a singing star in the late 1960s.

Reunited with Burke, Van Heusen wrote the songs for *The Road to Utopia* (1946), which featured Dorothy Lamour singing "Personality," a song that JOHNNY MERCER recorded for a #1 best-seller (Capitol 230). *The Road to Rio* (1947) contained "But Beautiful," which was sung in the film by Bing Crosby. *Riding High* (1950) included "Sunshine Cake" for Crosby.

*The Tender Trap* (1955) starred Frank Sinatra and had a hit title song (Capitol 3290) to begin the long, profitable partnership of Van Heusen and lyricist Sammy Cahn. As a team, they would win three Oscars for their movie songs. Just as Van Heusen had won a previous Oscar with someone else, so had Cahn ("Three Coins in the Fountain," with JULE STYNE). This film also began the new team's enduring association with Frank Sinatra.

*Our Town* (1955) was a television musical adaptation of Thornton Wilder's play (1938), with songs by Styne and Cahn. It produced the medium's first original song hit, "Love and Marriage," which Frank Sinatra sang in the show and then recorded on a best-selling disc (Capitol 3260). It was the first popular song to receive an Emmy. It also received a prestigious Christopher Award for its lyric approach to the song's subject. *The Joker Is Wild* (1957) was the screen biography of nightclub comedian Joe E. Lewis, played by Frank Sinatra. The only original song in the film was "All the Way," which received the team's first Academy Award for Best Song. Sinatra's recording ensured its success (Capitol 3793). *Some Came Running* (1958) gave Sinatra "To Love and Be Loved."

*A Hole in the Head* (1959) was another Sinatra starrer, and the song "High Hopes," hurriedly composed and filmed on the last day of shooting, won Van Heusen and Cahn the second of their three shared Oscars. Again, Sinatra's recording was the best-seller (Capitol 4214). When Senator John F. Kennedy was running for president, he asked Cahn for a campaign song, so Cahn revised "High Hopes." After Kennedy's election, it was agreed that the song had made a significant contribution. The team wrote many title songs for films, from the mid-1950s through 1968, including *Pardners* (1956), *Indiscreet* (1958), *Holiday for Lovers* (1959), *The World of Suzie Wong* (1960), *A Pocketful of Miracles* (1961), *Come Blow Your Horn* (1963), *Under the Yum-Yum Tree* (1963), *Thoroughly Modern Millie* (1967), and *Star!* (1968).

*Papa's Delicate Condition* (1963) was originally intended to be a starring vehicle for Fred Astaire in 1955, when the team wrote "Call Me Irresponsible." The film was made seven years later, starring television comedian Jackie Gleason. As was the case with several other of the team's best songs, this one was a last-minute inclusion. It won their third Academy Award. The duo's last work was for two Broadway musicals in the mid-1960s, *Skyscraper* (1965) and *Walking Happy* (1966), and then Van Heusen retired.

# Jerry Vogel Music Company

Jerry Vogel (1897–1980), longtime manager of Plaza Music, a major jobber in New York City, opened his own firm in 1934, when GEORGE M. COHAN gave him all of the Cohan copyrights in order to keep them in print. Vogel inherited the F. B. Haviland Publishing Company two years later. His firm's specialty was acquiring copyright renewals of proven hits. Mainly a reprint house, Vogel's slogan was "Old Songs Are the Best Songs." The company continues to operate as an independent in New York City.

# Albert Von Tilzer

Composer (b. Albert Gumm, Indianapolis, Indiana, March 29, 1878; d. Los Angeles, California, October 1, 1956). After brother Harry von Tilzer was made a partner in Shapiro, Bernstein and Von Tilzer, Albert was hired to work in the firm's Chicago office. By 1904, he had come to New York, and in that year he founded his own publishing house with another brother, Jack. Called the York Music Company, it was located at 40 West Twenty-eighth Street. For it, he and Cecil Mack wrote York's first big hit, "Teasin'." When Albert joined vaudevillian Jack Norworth in 1907, they created the hit "Honey Boy" in honor of the old minstrel George Evans. Norworth plugged it in vaudeville, as well as their two 1908 hits: "Smarty" and the song that became the anthem of baseball, "Take Me Out to the Ball Game." (Albert was said to have seen his first baseball game twenty years after he wrote "Take Me Out to The Ball Game.")

In 1910, Von Tilzer teamed up with vaudevillian Junie McCree to produce an all-time favorite, "Put Your Arms Around Me, Honey." He gave up York Music at the beginning of 1913 and joined the new firm of yet another brother: Will Von Tilzer's Broadway Music Corporation, which opened in April at 145 West Forty-fifth Street. With Stanley Murphy and Charles McCarron, Albert wrote "Oh, How She Could Yacki Hacki Wicki Wacki Woo," with which Eddie Cantor made his debut in the *Ziegfeld Follies of 1917*. Charlotte Greenwood helped to popularize "Oh, by Jingo!" in 1919. The next year Albert's smash hit was "I'll Be with You in Apple Blossom Time," which he followed in 1921 with "Dapper Dan," which Eddie Cantor sang in blackface in *The Midnight Rounders*.

Broadway Music Corporation went out of business in 1922. Albert then went into vaudeville as a headliner on the Orpheum circuit. In 1930, he went to Hollywood to work in film music.

# Harry Von Tilzer

Composer and music publisher (b. Harry Gumm, Detroit, Michigan, July 8, 1872; d. New York City, January 10, 1946). While ragtime was rapidly changing the beat of the Alley, and before Irving Berlin started writing his own songs, Harry Von Tilzer, who was to give

Berlin his first job on the Alley, as a plugger, decided to go into business for himself. Amicably leaving Maurice Shapiro in 1902 to form Harry Von Tilzer Music Publishing Company, he remained on Twenty-eighth Street for the first five years of his firm's business life. So prolific and versatile was he as a composer, and so successful, that his firm started with million-selling hits as varied as the tearjerker "A Bird in a Gilded Cage"; the waltz song "On a Sunday Afternoon"; the COON SONG "What You Gonna Do When the Rent Comes' Round?"; the friendship songs "Down Where the Wurzburger Flows," "Under the Anheuser Bush," and "Wait Till the Sun Shines, Nellie"; the kid song "All Aboard for Blanket Bay"; the syncopated dance sensation "The Cubanola Glide"; and the love song "I Want a Girl Just Like the Girl That Married Dear Old Dad." Unlike CHARLES K. HARRIS and PAUL DRESSER, who stayed with sentimental ballads throughout their careers, Von Tilzer wrote in all genres of popular song with equal success. That he was a master plugger goes without saying; as he was reported to have composed and published more than 100 songs that sold more than half a million copies each, as well as a large number of multimillion-copy-selling songs.

In an unsigned article published in *Metropolitan Magazine* in 1902, Harry Von Tilzer wrote about his job as a plugger and of a stunt he created for a song he had just published:

> I'm a song promoter. I'm the man who makes the popular songs popular. I earn big money and I've grown into a necessity to the music publishing house that employs me.
>
> The company works one big town at a time. It sends on, by freight, a stack of the music of the song to be made popular. It is not put on sale until I give the word.
>
> I get to a town after the music has been placed in the hands of the leading music houses. I arrange with two or three theatres to aid me in introducing the song.
>
> Maybe I go to the swellest theatre in town Monday night and sit in a lower box, in my evening clothes, like an ordinary patron. During the daytime I will have fixed the orchestra and had the music run over. Between the first and second act, perhaps, I stand up in my box and begin singing.

Harry Von Tilzer, c. the 1920s.

The audience is startled. Ushers run through the aisles. A policeman comes in and walks toward the box. About the time the policeman is where he can be seen by all the audience, I step out on to the stage in front of the curtain and begin the chorus, with the orchestra playing and the audience, that is now onto the game, clapping so hard it almost blisters its hands.

I have, maybe, a good whistler in the gallery, whom I have taught during the day. He helps me when I begin teaching the gallery to whistle the chorus. He leads the gods and before I am done they, and the whole house, have caught the air.

I usually get the orchestra to play the chorus as the audience is going out. Everybody goes home humming or whistling it. But long before the home-going, probably, I have walked singing down the aisle of another theatre between the second and third act, having been led out by an usher and having then come back and stood in front of the orchestra and taught that theatre's audience to sing and whistle the song.

The best thing I ever did to popularize a song was done right here in little old New York, in a roof garden theatre. My wife knew a girl who was making a hit at the garden, so we had to go and see the girl in her act. I put the thing off for a night or two and planned a little surprise.

I met the girl, who did a singing part, and fixed the thing up with her. The orchestra and the manager, an old friend of mine, readily fell into line. I was engaged in promoting the popularity for "Please Let Me Sleep," about this time, and I saw a chance to do some noble work.

My wife wanted to sit away up in front so her friend would see her, but I insisted on taking chairs in the rear of the garden, near the elevator landing. The crowd was large. The night was hot and the bill was good.

"I don't know what makes me so drowsy," I said to my wife as her friend came on. "I guess they must have put knock-out drops in that last glass of lemonade."

I leaned back in my chair with one elbow on the table. As the girl sang I began to snore. I snored so loud that it disturbed those listening to the singing. They looked around in disgust. My wife gave me a kick under the table.

"Wake up, Harry," she said. "You are attracting attention." I snored harder than ever. A waiter came over and shook me by the arm. My wife became alarmed and stood up.

Most of the folks in our part of the garden thought I was drunk. One man started toward the manager's office to complain, just as a policeman was brought my way by a second waiter.

The entire audience turned our way. Some persons stood on chairs and others moved out into the aisles. Just as the policeman and the waiter raised me out of my chair, I stretched and yawned like a man dead for slumber and began singing:

"Please go 'way an' let me sleep. Ah would rather sleep than eat."

Out of one corner of my eye, I noticed a great light spread over my wife's face. I kept singing as I was being carried and led to the elevator. I sang going down and I sang coming up.

As the elevator reached the landing, the girl on the stage struck into the chorus along with the orchestra, and the audience tumbled.

I never saw an audience go so nearly crazy over anything in my life. Men laughed until the tears came and women became hysterical. My wife was the happiest woman in all the town. She admitted for the first time that I was a sure enough actor, which I had made up my mind she should do if I had to scare her half to death to bring about the conviction.

Von Tilzer, one of five sons, all of whom entered the music publishing business, two of them as successful songwriters, including brother ALBERT VON TILZER. During his early childhood his parents moved to Indianapolis, where he grew up. When he was fourteen, he ran away from home to join Cole Brothers Circus. He next worked for a traveling repertory company, acting, accompanying singers at the piano, and writing songs for the productions. It was at this time that he changed his name, taking his mother's maiden name of Tilzer and adding "Von" as a sign of distinction; his other siblings would follow his lead.

When he was performing with a burlesque show in Chicago, he met the popular vaudeville star LOTTIE GILSON, who took an interest in him. She urged him to devote himself seriously to songwriting and to go to New York to advance his career. He came to New York in 1892 with $1.65 in his pocket. He rented a furnished room, and got a job as a pianist and singer in a saloon at $15.00 a week. He kept writing songs, some of which Tony Pastor sang in his Music Hall. Several other entertainers bought some of these early works outright for $2.00 each.

Six years later, Von Tilzer was still living in a furnished room, sharing one on East Fifteenth Street with his lyricist, Andrew B. Sterling (1874–1955). At one point, they were three weeks behind on their rent. When a final bill was slipped under their door, they used the paper to write a chorus and then a verse of what turned out to be their first successful publication, "My Old New Hampshire Home." Lyricist Bartley Costello heard about their song and advised them to take it to printer-publisher William C. Dunn, who ran the Orphean Music Company. Dunn liked it and bought it for $15.00.

Shortly thereafter, Dunn sold out to Maurice Shapiro, and Shapiro's edition of the song sold over a million copies. Shapiro then looked up Von Tilzer and asked him to join his firm as a partner, giving him $4,000.00 in royalties. Through the first decade of the twentieth century, the Harry Von Tilzer Music Publishing Company dominated the industry mainly by publishing and plugging its owner's wide-ranging compositions.

Von Tilzer's first number for the new firm, in 1899, was an "oo-oo" song, "I'd Leave Ma Happy Home for You," which featured the vaudeville act of Mr. and Mrs. Joe Keaton on the cover, with their four-year-old son, Buster. Von Tilzer's own first million-seller was published in 1900, when he worked out a tune for a lyric written by Arthur J. Lamb. Before he wrote the melody, he insisted that Lamb change the lyric so that the heroine of the story was married to the rich old man, not living in sin with him. Later that evening, Von Tilzer went to a party which ended at a house of ill repute. He sat down at the piano in the parlor to compose music to the words. When he finished, he noticed that some of the girls were crying, and their reaction convinced him of the song's possibilities. Von Tilzer later spoke of "A Bird in a Gilded Cage" as "the key that opened the door of wealth and fame" for him. It sold more than two million copies and became a memorable song, typical of the tearjerker in the public mind.

Lamb and von Tilzer teamed up again in 1902 to create a sequel to their big hit, called "The Mansion of Aching Hearts." This song quickly became another million-seller, plugged by a newly hired boy singer, Izzy Baline, who in a few short years would become the most famous Alley songwriter, IRVING BERLIN. Acting as inspiration, Harry Von Tilzer showed the young Berlin how to be a successful publisher and composer. The productive year of 1902, when Von Tilzer started his own publishing company, saw a series of hit songs from his pen. With the always reliable Sterling, he turned out an enormously popular song, the waltz favorite "On a Sunday Afternoon." On the beach sunning himself, he thought of the line "they work hard on Monday, but one day that's fun day," and went back to Sterling to have him write the rest of the lyric. With Sterling as his lyricist, Von Tilzer also turned out a series of coon songs that were very popular and whose melodies continue to please. Their previous 1901 collaboration, "Down Where the Cotton Blossoms Grow," was featured in vaudeville by Helene Mora. (Did his songwriting brother, Albert, remember this song when he wrote "Down Where the Swanee River Flows," in 1916, for AL JOLSON?)

In 1903, the Sterling–Von Tilzer team turned out "Good-bye, Eliza Jane," followed the next year by "Alexander (Don't You Love Your Baby No More)," a title Irving Berlin was to remember seven years later for his all-time hit. Von Tilzer got inspiration for his 1905 coon song hit that topped even "Alexander" when he overheard a black couple talking on the platform of a railway station. The wife called her husband "Rufus Rastus Johnson Brown." The rhythmic name was an inspiration to Sterling, who fashioned a lyric with the title "What You Goin' to Do When the Rent Comes Round?"

Von Tilzer's 1911 hit, with Will Dillon, was called "All Alone." This, too, stuck in Irving Berlin's mind when he composed a song with the same name for his 1924 *Music Box Revue*. Another Von Tilzer title, the 1909 "I Love, I Love, I Love My Wife, but Oh, You Kid" was sung by Harry Armstrong and Billy Clark that same year. Also that year, the first parody was published, "I Love My Pipe but Oh, You Pippin!" which spawned other, similar titles. Herbert Ingraham titled his 1910 song "I Love My Husband, but Oh, You Henry!" That same year saw "I Love My Steady, but I'm Crazy for My Once-in-a-While," but it wasn't until 1917 that GEORGE W. MEYER came up with "I Love My Billy Sunday, but Oh, You Saturday Night."

Von Tilzer's last hit came in 1925, when, with Dolph Singer, he wrote and published "Just Around the Corner." TED LEWIS and his band helped to make it famous (Decca 3846). Although he maintained his office and issued songs after this, Von Tilzer went more or less into retirement.

HARRY VON TILZER MUSIC PUBLISHING COMPANY (1902–1946)

| | |
|---|---|
| 1902–1903 | 42 West 28th Street |
| 1903–1907 | 37 West 28th Street |
| 1908–1916 | 125 West 43rd Street |
| 1916–1920 | 222 West 46th Street |
| 1921–1923 | 1658 Broadway (Roseland Building) |
| 1924–1946 | 1587 Broadway |

# "Fats" Waller

Composer, singer, and pianist (b. Thomas Wright Waller, New York City, May 21, 1904; d. Kansas City, Kansas, December 15, 1943). At age ten, Waller was already playing organ at his father's church, and piano at local parties. In 1918, he got his first paying job as a theater organist, playing to accompany silent films. A year later, after winning a Harlem piano contest performing JAMES P. JOHNSON's "Carolina Shout," he became a protégé of the composer and the best-known exponent of stride, a black piano style of the 1920s.

He was a prolific songwriter who knocked 'em out for hamburger money. His first big hit was "Squeeze Me," with CLARENCE WILLIAMS, in 1925. His biggest year was 1929, with such standards emerging as "Ain't Misbehavin' " (Victor 22092), "Sweet Savannah Sue" (Victor 22108), "What Did I Do to Be So Black and Blue?," "Honeysuckle Rose" (Victor 24826), "I've Got a Feeling I'm Falling" (Victor 22092), and "My Fate Is in Your Hands" (Victor 38568). He continued in 1930 with "Blue Turning Grey over You" (Victor 36206), and in 1932 with "Keeping Out of Mischief Now." Most of these had lyrics by ANDY RAZAF. Waller also wrote scores for the musicals *Keep Shufflin'* (February 27, 1928; with James P. Johnson and Clarence Todd), *Hot Chocolates* (June 20, 1929; with lyrics by Razaf), and *Early to Bed* (June 17, 1943). LOUIS ARMSTRONG's appearance in *Hot Chocolates*, singing with the

Fats Waller, c. the 1930s.

pit band during intermission ("What Did I Do to Be So Black and Blue?"), was a sensation, making Armstrong into a major star and the song into a great hit.

In addition to composing, Waller made piano rolls, as well as over five hundred records, had his own weekly network radio program, performed in Europe and England, and was featured in such films as *Hooray for Love*, *King of Burlesque*, and the classic 1943 musical film *Stormy Weather*. After filming his sequences for it, Waller spent some time in Hollywood, but died on his return train trip of complications from pneumonia. Waller's songs have been favorites in the jazz and pop repertoire since their composition. A revue featuring his songs (and songs associated with him), *Ain't Misbehavin'* (May 9, 1978), had a run of 1,604 performances on Broadway.

# War Songs

The first war to be sung about after the Alley was formed in 1885 was the Spanish-American War (1898), which inspired "Our Country, May She Always Be Right." However, World War I had the most songs published about and during it. This is not surprising, considering this was Tin Pan Alley's period of greatest dominance. Some of the era's hits include "Over There" (1917), "Au Revoir, but Not Good-bye, Soldier Boy"(1917), "Bring Back My Daddy to Me" (1917), "Good-bye Broadway, Hello France" (1917), "Liberty Bell—It's Time to Ring Again" (1917), "We'll Knock the Heligo—Into Heligo—Out of Heligoland" (1917), "When the Boys Come Home" (1917), "I'm Gonna Pin a Medal on the Girl I Left Behind" (1918), "If He Can Fight like He Can Love, Good Night, Germany" (1918), "Oh! How I Hate to Get Up in the Morning" (1918), "The Rose of No-Man's Land" (1918), "America, Here's My Boy" (1917), "They Were All Out of Step but Jim" (1918), and "Till We Meet Again" (1918).

While the number of World War II songs was far fewer than those written for World War I, the quality was much better, and the public got behind the ones for World War II as a gesture of patriotism. World War II brought many changes (and subjects for lyrics). Our lives were inconvenienced by food (especially sugar) and gas rationing, a shellac shortage (limiting the number of records pressed), a paper shortage (limiting the amount of sheet music), and blackouts. Top songwriters contributed to the war effort, often donating their revenue to military and civilian agencies. IRVING BERLIN led off with "Arms for the Love of America" (1941), for the Army Ordnance Department; GEORGE M. COHAN wrote "For the Flag, for the Home, for the Family" (1942); RICHARD RODGERS and LORENZ HART wrote "The Bombardier Song" (1942) for the bomber crews of the U. S. Army Air Forces; HOAGY CARMICHAEL wrote "The Cranky Old Yank (In a Clanky Old Tank)" (1942); the new team of Rodgers and OSCAR HAMMERSTEIN II wrote "The P.T. Boat Song" (1943) for the motor torpedo boats of the Navy; COLE PORTER also paid tribute to the Navy with "Sailors of the Sky" (1943); VERNON DUKE and HOWARD DIETZ wrote "The Silver Shield" (1943) in honor of the U.S. Coast Guard; and Meredith Willson wrote "Fire Up!" (1943), a marching song for the Chemical Warfare Service.

GERALD MARKS and IRVING CAESAR got an early start with "Ev'ry One's a Fighting Son of That Old Gang of Mine" (1940). Willie Lee Duckworth wrote "Sound Off" (1940) as part of "The Cadence System of Teaching Close Order Drill." J. FRED COOTS wrote the hit "Goodbye, Mama (I'm Off to Yokohama)" (1941), and Ernie Burnett and Jack Meskill took another vantage point with "Since Kitten's Knittin' Mittens (for the Army)" (1941).

JOE HOWARD, using an official slogan of the Army, Navy and Marines, wrote his "Keep Mum, Chum" (1942), and SAM STEPT and TED KOEHLER wrote "I'm Mighty Proud of That Old Gang of Mine" (1942). "Don't Sit under the Apple Tree" was another great wartime song by Stept, with lyrics by LEW BROWN and Charles Tobias. The best-selling records were made by the ANDREWS SISTERS (Decca 18312), and GLENN MILLER and his orchestra (Bluebird 11474). "When the Lights Go On Again" was the work of BENNIE BENJAMIN, Eddie Seiler, and Sol Marcus, with a best-selling recording by Vaughn Monroe (Victor 27945). The same year, FRANK LOESSER wrote what became the most popular song of World War II, "Praise the Lord and Pass the Ammunition!!" Kay Kyser had the million-selling #1 hit (Columbia 36640). JOHNNY MERCER contributed "G. I. Jive"; KAY SWIFT wrote "Fighting on the Home Front Wins," dedicated to the American housewife; JIMMY MCHUGH and HAROLD ADAMSON wrote one of the best, "Comin' In on a Wing and a Prayer"; and JULE STYNE and SAMMY CAHN celebrated prematurely with "Vict'ry Polka," all in 1943.

# Warner/Chappell Music, Inc.

A major music-publishing conglomerate, formed in 1987 through the marriage of the holdings of Warner Bros. Music and the venerable Chappell music publishing firm. At the birth of the "talking picture" era, Warner Bros. began a massive investment in song copyrights as a means of securing material for its pictures as well as a publishing arm for the material produced by its house composers. Its first acquisition was of M. Witmark and Sons 1928, followed by T. B. Harms (manged by Max Dreyfus), and then, in 1929 Jerome Remick. Music Publishing Holding Corporation was the name given to the new entity, and it was run by a young Warner employee, Edwin H. Morris. Other acquisitions followed, notably Advanced Music Corporation (which held the catalog of Ager, Yellen, and Bornstein), and through its Harms holdings, Warner took over New World Music Corporation, which from 1948 held the rights to the complete catalogs of George and Ira Gershwin. In 1967, Warner Bros. Pictures merged with Seven Arts, and the music publishing firm was renamed Warner Bros-Seven Arts Music; in 1969, the Kinney corporation purchased the company, and at the same time the catalog of Tamerlane Music was brought into the company, now named Warner-Tamerlane Publishing Corp. The name was simplified to Warner Bros. Music until 1987, when the large Chappell Music holdings was acquired.

# Harry Warren

Composer (b. Salvatore Guaragna, Brooklyn, New York, December 24, 1893; d. Los Angeles, California, September 22, 1981). Warren's parents were Italian immigrants; his shoemaker father changed the family name to Warren when Harry was five years old. As a youngster, Harry sang in the church choir and played his father's accordion; as a young teen, he got some work as a drummer that led to a brief tour with a carnival band. Around 1910, he began playing the piano, working in local cafés, clubs, and movie houses, and also began working as a stagehand at the Liberty Theatre, a combination vaudeville and movie house in Brooklyn. He then went to the Vitagraph Studio in Flatbush, where he became a property man. In those fledgling movie days, he did whatever needed to be done: movie extra; assistant director; offstage mood music pianist for love scenes, cabaret sequences, and chases. The young Warren's love for the movies never left him.

While working as the house pianist at Healy's Café in Sheepshead Bay, he was heard by two songwriters, who recommended him for a job as rehearsal pianist and song plugger for Stark and Cowan. It was there that he had his first song published and had his first hit, "Rose of the Rio Grande" (1922). It was cocomposed by Paul Whiteman reed virtuoso Ross Gorman, with lyrics by Edgar Leslie. Naturally, Gorman's band, The Virginians, was the first to record it (Victor 19001). "Chuck Thomas" (alias of Woody Herman) and his Dixieland Band revived it in 1949 (Capitol 746).

Warren went to Shapiro, Bernstein and Company in 1925, where with Bud Green he wrote "I Love My Baby (My Baby Loves Me)." Waring's Pennsylvanians helped make it a hit (Victor 19905). Two years later, Warren and Green scored again with "Away Down South in Heaven." And with Henry Creamer, Warren wrote "Clementine (from New Orleans)," which Blossom Seeley introduced, and which Jean Goldkette and his orchestra, featuring Bix Beiderbecke, made into a classic recording (Victor 20994). "Nagasaki" (1928), with Mort Dixon, which Paul Mares's Friars Society Orchestra recorded (Okeh 41574), and Bill Robinson featured at the Cotton Club, was the perennial favorite of stride pianist Willie "The Lion" Smith, who played and sang it at almost every engagement he had.

*Sweet and Low* (November 17, 1930) was a revue for which Warren wrote two hits, "Cheerful Little Earful," with lyrics by Ira Gershwin and Billy Rose, and "Would You Like to Take a Walk?" with lyrics by Mort Dixon and Billy Rose.

"Cryin' for the Carolines" (1930), with words by Sam Lewis and Joe Young, was written for *Spring Is Here* and sung in the film by Lawrence Gray. It was popularized by Guy

Harry Warren, 1930.

LOMBARDO and his Royal Canadians (Columbia 2062-D). Lombardo also turned the Warren and Edgar Leslie song "By the River Sainte Marie" into a #1 hit in 1931 (Columbia 2401-D). The same year found Warren writing for the revue *The Laugh Parade* (November 2, 1931), starring Ed Wynn. Warren's big song, written with Mort Dixon and Joe Young, was "You're My Everything," which was introduced by Jeanne Aubert and Lawrence Gray.

Billy Rose was a great title man. He wrote serviceable lyrics, but his forte was creating song titles and selling the resulting songs for more money than anyone else could have gotten for them. In 1926, he wrote a lyric called "I Found a Million Dollar Baby" to music by FRED FISHER. It didn't go anywhere, but since Rose still liked the title, he gave it to Warren and Mort Dixon. They fashioned "I Found a Million Dollar Baby in a Five and Ten Cent Store" for the revue *Billy Rose's Crazy Quilt* (May 19, 1931), which featured Ted Healy, FANNY BRICE (Mrs. Billy Rose at the time), Phil Baker, and Lew Brice. BING CROSBY's recording gave it the necessary boost (Brunswick 6140). It was also used in two movies called *Million Dollar Baby* (1935 and 1941).

Warner Brothers offered Warren a chance to compose a complete score for an original movie musical, and to team with AL DUBIN as lyricist, in 1932. The film they wrote was *42nd Street* (1933), and it became the prototype of the backstage musical, establishing Busby Berkeley as the most creative choreographer and director of production numbers in the history of Hollywood. Harry Warren's music inspired many Berkeley extravaganzas. For this film, Warren and Dubin wrote "Shuffle Off to Buffalo," "42nd Street," and "You're Getting to Be a Habit with Me." All became standards, the last the most frequently performed.

*Gold Diggers of 1933* was the next Warren-Dubin film to boast a number of hits. "The Gold Digger's Song (We're in the Money)" became a hopeful anthem during the Depression. "Pettin' in the Park" was an answer to the anti-petting ordinances in some cities. "The Shadow Waltz" also became a hit. "I Only Have Eyes for You" (1934) came from *Dames*, and was first sung by Dick Powell. It received a much more felicitous rendering when it was revived in *Tea for Two* (1950) by Doris Day and Gordon MacRae.

"Lullaby of Broadway" came from *Dames*'s sequel, *Gold Diggers of 1935*, and it won the first of Warren's three Oscars for Best Song. A movie with the song's title was made in 1951 with Doris Day and Gene Nelson. It would seem natural that Hollywood moguls, who were making money hand over fist with movie musicals, would trust their songwriters' talents, but such was not the case. Jack Warner did not want "Lullaby of Broadway" in *Gold Diggers of 1935*. After Warren played it for AL JOLSON, Jolson went to Warner to demand that he be allowed to use it in his current film, then in production. When Berkeley heard about Jolson's designs on the song, he demanded that Warner put it back into *Diggers*, as originally planned. Warner relented, and the song became a perennial.

The Dubin-Warren team continued to score hits through the mid-1930s. "Lulu's Back in Town" (1935) came from the film *Broadway Gondolier*, and was sung by Dick Powell and the MILLS BROTHERS. It was made into a hit recording by FATS WALLER and His Rhythm (Victor 25063). "With Plenty of Money and You" (1936) came from *Gold Diggers of 1937*, introduced by Dick Powell. Doris Day revived it in the film *My Dream Is Yours* (1949). "September in the Rain" (1937) was sung by James Melton in *Melody for Two*, and was revived in 1949 by pianist George Shearing, whose first hit it was (MGM 30250).

"You Must Have Been a Beautiful Baby" (1938) was the beginning of a brief teaming with lyricist JOHNNY MERCER. It was written for the film *Hard to Get* and sung by Dick Powell to Olivia de Havilland. Bobby Darin revived it in a 1961 best-selling record (Atco

6206). "Jeepers Creepers" (1938) was another Warren-Mercer collaboration, written for Louis Armstrong in the film *Going Places*. Armstrong used it throughout the rest of his career (Decca 2267).

"Down Argentine Way" (1940), with lyrics by new collaborator Mack Gordon, was introduced by Don Ameche and Betty Grable in the film of the same name. "Chattanooga Choo-Choo" (1941), again with lyrics by Gordon, was played in the movie *Sun Valley Serenade* (1941) by Glenn Miller and his orchestra, featuring individual band members, and underscoring a spectacular tap routine by the Nicholas Brothers. Glenn Miller's band made a million-selling #1 disc (Bluebird 11230).

*Orchestra Wives* (1942) again featured Glenn Miller and his orchestra, taking acting parts as well as performing "At Last," "Serenade in Blue," and "I've Got a Gal in Kalamazoo." Pat Friday sang the songs that actress Lynn Bari lip-synched in the film. "I Had the Craziest Dream" (1942) was sung by Harry James's vocalist, Helen Forrest, in the film *Springtime in the Rockies*. It became a million-selling #1 hit (Columbia 36659). "You'll Never Know" (1943) was written by Warren and Gordon for Alice Faye in *Hello, Frisco, Hello*. It won Warren his second of three Oscars. It also proved to be his biggest seller in sheet music. Dick Haymes had the #1 hit (Decca 18556). "I Wish I Knew" and "The More I See You," both with lyrics by Mack Gordon, were written for *Billy Rose's Diamond Horseshoe* (1945).

"On the Atchison, Topeka and the Sante Fe" (1945), written with Johnny Mercer, was used in *The Harvey Girls* (1946), first as a production number and later sung by Judy Garland. It won Warren his third Oscar (and Mercer his first), and Johnny Mercer and the Pied Pipers had a best-selling disc (Capitol 195).

"That's Amore" (1953), with lyricist Jack Brooks (1912–1971), was written for Dean Martin in the film *The Caddy*. Martin also made a best-selling recording (Capitol 2589), which was used in the 1987 film *Moonstruck*. In 1956, Warren returned to Broadway for the first time in a quarter-century with *Shangri La*, but it lasted for only twenty-one performances. "An Affair to Remember" (1957), with words by Harold Adamson and Leo McCarey, Warren's last big hit, was used as the theme for the film of the same name. It was sung by Vic Damone under the titles and was further popularized by his recording (Columbia 40945).

Warren continued to write film themes on occasion through the late 1960s, but his hits came only from revivals of earlier songs. Several revues featuring Warren's songs were staged in the 1970s, and then in 1980 came David Merrick's very successful stage version of the film musical *42nd Street*, which ran for nearly 3500 performances; it was revived again in 2000. Warren was too ill to see his final Broadway success, and died after a long illness in the fall of 1981.

# Ned Washington

Lyricist (b. Scranton, Pennsylvania, August 15, 1901; d. Beverly Hills, California, December 20, 1976). Washington came to New York City in the mid-1920s, and began contributing lyrics to various revues and shows, then moved to Hollywood in 1935. His first hit came in

1936 with "Can't We Talk It Over?," to a melody by VICTOR YOUNG. It was made famous by BING CROSBY on radio, and on record by Bing with the MILLS BROTHERS (Brunswick 6240) and by Ben Bernie and his orchestra (Brunswick 6250). This was followed by "I'm Getting Sentimental over You," composed by George Bassman (1914–1997), which was adopted by TOMMY DORSEY as his theme song (Victor 25236). Washington's next major hit was "The Nearness of You," with music by HOAGY CARMICHAEL, which was written for Gladys Swarthout to sing in the film *Romance in the Dark* (1938). It wasn't published until 1940, and then as a pop song, with no mention of its film connection. Also in 1940, his song "When You Wish Upon A Star" written for the Disney animated feature *Pinocchio*, with music by LEIGH HARLINE, won the Oscar for Best Song. In 1946, he collaborated again with Victor Young on the classic "Stella By Starlight," which Young had written as an instrumental theme for the 1944 film *The Uninvited*. The song became a favorite improvisation piece for bebop musicians, including Thelonious Monk, Miles Davis, and Chet Baker.

The 1950s saw Washington turn his attention to movie theme songs, although his best-remembered numbers were two incidental songs written for Rita Hayworth's 1953 film, *Miss Sadie Thompson*: "The Heat Is On" and "Sadie Thompson's Song." From 1957 to 1976, Washington was director of ASCAP, which he had first joined in 1930.

# Ethel Waters

African-American singer and actress (b. Chester, Pennsylvania, October 31, 1896; d. Chatsworth, California, September 1, 1977). She began her career in 1917 as a SHIMMY dancer and a BLUES singer. Her recording career began in 1921, with the black-owned Black Swan recording company, owned by Harry Pace, former partner of the PACE AND HANDY MUSIC COMPANY. Her backup was provided by the first FLETCHER HENDERSON band, which later toured with her. Her first double-sided hit was "Oh Daddy" and "Down Home Blues" (Black Swan 2010). Her next double-sided hit was "There'll Be Some Changes Made" and "One Man Nan" (Black Swan 2021). Her next hit was "Dinah" in 1925, when she switched to Columbia Records. Waters introduced this song in her Broadway show *The New Plantation Revue* (Columbia 487-D). "Am I Blue?," her next big hit, came from a 1929 film, *On with the Show* (Columbia 1837-D). In August 1930, she recorded EUBIE BLAKE's now-standard "Memories of You" (Columbia 2288-D). Her most important song, "Stormy Weather," was introduced by her in *The Cotton Club Parade of 1933* (Brunswick 6564). She also introduced "Heat Wave" in IRVING BERLIN's revue *As Thousands Cheer* (Columbia 2826-D). Her two big hits from her 1940 Broadway show *Cabin in the Sky* were "Honey in the Honeycomb" (Liberty L-311) and "Taking a Chance on Love" (Liberty L-310). After a full career in vaudeville, on Broadway, in dramas and musicals, in films, and on television, Waters got religion and during the 1960s and 1970s often appeared with evangelist Billy Graham.

Ethel Waters (left) aims her megaphone at Eubie Blake, c. 1930.

# Berlin Waterson and Snyder

See *Ted Snyder Company* and *Irving Berlin*

# Mabel Wayne

Composer (b. Brooklyn, New York, July 16, 1904; d. New York City, June 19, 1978). Wayne studied music in New York and then abroad, touring as a concert pianist and classical vocalist as a teenager. She switched to pop music in the mid-1920s, having her first publication with

"Don't Wake Me Up (Let Me Dream)," written with L. Wolfe Gilbert and Abel Baer. But Wayne's first big hit came in 1926 when Paul Whiteman recorded "In a Little Spanish Town" (with lyrics by Sam Lewis and Joe Young) and made it a #1 hit (Victor 20266). She became the most successful woman pop songwriter before rock and roll. In 1927, she collaborated again with Gilbert on her best-remembered song, "Ramona," written to be played behind the silent film of the same name, starring Delores Del Rio. In 1928, Whiteman's recording of the song was a #1 hit (Victor 21214), as was Gene Austin's, but Austin's recording sold over a million copies (Victor 21334).

Paul Whiteman continued to be Wayne's lucky charm as she wrote songs for his first movie, *King of Jazz* in 1930. The hit song was "It Happened in Monterey" (with lyrics by Billy Rose), which Whiteman recorded (Columbia 2170-D). "Little Man, You've Had a Busy Day" (written with Maurice Sigler and Al Hoffman) was her 1934 hit, which had a #2 hit recording by Emil Coleman and his orchestra with vocals by Jerry Cooper and the Harmonians (Columbia 2930-D). Though she wrote into the 1950s, her last big hit was "Why Don't You Fall in Love with Me?" (lyrics by Al Lewis), written in 1937 and a #3 hit recording by Dinah Shore in 1943 (and covered the same year for Top 10 hits by Dick Jurgens and Johnny Young).

# Weber and Fields Music Hall

The forerunner of the Weber and Fields shows was the burlesque of Harrigan and Hart, who had their own theaters—first the Theatre Comique and later the Park Theatre—in the 1870s and 1880s, as well as the services of their own composer, Dave Braham. Their songs were Irish, and so were their audiences. New York then had the largest Irish population in the world.

By the time Weber and Fields got their own theater, in 1896, coon songs were coming into their own, and John Stromberg, genial composer for Weber and Fields, wrote them and other comic songs and ballads. Weber, Fields, and Stromberg published their own material until they sold their catalog to M. Witmark and Sons in 1900. (Italian songs came into vogue after 1905, and Yiddish songs about four years later. Ethnic songs came to an apex of sorts in 1920 with the publication of "The Argentines, the Portuguese and the Greeks.")

When Joe Weber (1867–1942) and Lew Fields (1867–1941) opened their Music Hall on September 5, 1896, the "Dutch" comedians assembled a company of the finest stars of the popular musical theater. The 665-seat house, located on the corner of Twenty-ninth Street and Broadway, was formerly known as the Imperial Music Hall. Never a success before, under Weber and Fields's management, the place sold out. The first half of their annual show

Weber and Fields pictured in business clothes from their hit show *Twirly Whirly*, published by Witmark.

consisted of variety acts, with such talents as singer LOTTIE GILSON. It was the second half, though, the burlesque, that made their hall famous. They held matinees on Tuesdays (instead of the usual Wednesdays) so that their troupe could see the latest dramas at Wednesday matinees in order to burlesque them. This scheduling also gave the casts who were burlesqued a chance to see how Weber and Fields did it. Some of their famous shows were *Quo Vass Iss*, *Fiddle-Dee-Dee*, *Hurly-Burly*, *Whirl-I-Gig*, *Pousse Cafe*, and *Twirly-Whirly*. They were the only burlesque troupe to tour the country year after year. Pete Dailey, their leading comedian, extemporized his lines, throwing the other stars and players into confusion but also keeping them on their toes. Sam Bernard was the German comedian in the company, and David Warfield started his career there as a Jewish comedian. Marie Dressler; William Collier; Collier's wife, Louise Allen; Henry Dixey; Lillian Russell; Fay Templeton; Louis Mann; Frankie Bailey; Bessie Clayton; Vesta Tilley; Cissie Loftus; DeWolf Hopper; Carter DeHaven; and the McCoy Sisters were other high-priced stars who appeared at the Music Hall until it closed in 1904, when Weber and Fields went their separate ways.

Fields sired an impressive family of theater luminaries; his daughter DOROTHY FIELDS and son Herbert both became noted lyricists and librettists for major Broadway shows and film, and son Joseph became a noted playwright.

# Paul Francis Webster

Lyricist (b. New York City, December 20, 1907; d. Beverly Hills, California, March 22, 1984). Although Webster started writing pop songs in the early 1930s, he didn't hit his stride until the early 1950s when he had many hits from his film songs. He won three Academy Awards for Best Song, and his career lasted until 1972.

Webster attended Columbia University and New York University, but dropped out to work as a seaman. On returning to New York, he began working as a dance instructor in the late 1920s, and to dabbled with lyric writing. Webster's first hit came in 1932 when Ted Black and his orchestra recorded the #3 hit "Masquerade" (music by John Jacob Loeb; Victor 24046). The following year PAUL WHITEMAN and his orchestra, with vocal by Jack Fulton, recorded "My Moonlight Madonna" (music by William Scotti; Victor 24364). "Got the Jitters" (also with music by Loeb) came from the 1934 *Casino de Paree Revue*, and was made famous by Ben Pollack and his orchestra, with vocal by Nappy Lamare (Columbia 2870-D).

Also in 1934, Webster and lyricist LEW POLLACK were hired to write for films; the duo scored with "Two Cigarettes in the Dark," from the film *Kill That Story*, when JOHNNY GREEN and his orchestra, with vocal by George Bouler, had the #2 hit record (Columbia 2943-D); BING CROSBY and Frank Parker also had Top 10 recordings.

Webster continued to score hits on occasion through the 1940s. "I Got It Bad and That Ain't Good" came from the 1941 show *Jump for Joy*, for which DUKE ELLINGTON composed the score. The show was produced with an all-black cast in Los Angeles, and was unusual for its time because it addressed topical issues; nonetheless, it was never brought to Broadway. Ellington's recording of this song hit featured vocalist Ivy Anderson and reached the #13 position (Victor 27531). "Doctor, Lawyer and Indian Chief," one of several collaborations with HOAGY CARMICHAEL, came from the 1945 film *The Stork Club*, starring Betty Hutton, who had the #1 hit (Capitol 220).

Webster's career really took off in the 1950s. It was fitting that Mario Lanza, the most popular operatic tenor since Enrico Caruso, played the lead in the 1951 film *The Great Caruso* and recorded "The Loveliest Night of the Year," which sold over a million copies (Victor 20-3300; composed with Irving Aaronson and Juventino Rosas). He won his first Academy Award for Best Song for "Secret Love," from the 1953 film, *Calamity Jane*, (music by SAMMY FAIN), which DORIS DAY introduced in the film. Her #1 recording sold over a million copies (Columbia 40108). She followed it up the following year in the film *Lucky Me*, when she sang Webster and Fain's "I Speak to the Stars" (Columbia 40210). His second Academy Award winner was for "Love Is a Many-Splendored Thing" (also with music by Fain), from the 1955 film of the same name. The Four Aces had the million-selling #1 hit (Decca 29625). The following year Pat Boone had the #5 million-seller "Friendly Persuasion" (music by Dmitri Tiomkin) from the film of the same name (Dot 15490). Boone followed it up with another Webster hit the same year with the title song from the movie *Anastasia* (Dot 15521), composed by Alfred Newman. Boone did it again in 1957 with another million-seller from the title song of the film *April Love*, in which he introduced it (Dot 15660); the music was again by Fain. Webster's 1958 hit "A Certain Smile" came from the film of the same name and had a hit recording by Johnny Mathis (Columbia 41193). That same year he wrote the TV themes for *Maverick* and *Sugarfoot*. His songs appeared in such films as *Raintree County, Boy on a Dolphin, Imitation of Life, The Guns of Navarone, Return to Peyton Place, Tender Is the Night, Mutiny on the Bounty, Who's Afraid of Virginia Woolf?, An American Dream*, and *The Stepmother*. Webster's last Academy Award-winning song was for the 1965 "The Shadow of Your Smile," with music by Johnny Mandel, from *The Sandpiper*.

# Kurt Weill

Popular and theatrical music composer (b. Kurt Julian Weill, Dessau, Germany, March 2, 1900; d. New York City, April 3, 1950). Weill began his career in Germany as musical director for a small opera company. He wrote a symphony in 1921 (it went unperformed at the time) and then wrote several short operas, mostly on social-political topics. He collaborated with playwright Bertolt Brecht in 1927 on *Mahagonny*, a satire of American capitalism. The duo then created the 1928 *The Threepenny Opera*, an adaptation of John Gay's eighteenth-century comic opera *The Beggar's Opera*, which had great success touring throughout Europe for five years. Weill married his star, Lotte Lenya, and they came to the United States in 1935.

Weill's first Broadway show, *Johnny Johnson* (1936), provided no hits, but his second show, the 1938 *Knickerbocker-Holiday*, sported "September Song" (lyrics by Maxwell Anderson), introduced by actor Walter Huston, whose recording made it a standard (Brunswick 8272). In 1941, Weill collaborated with IRA GERSHWIN on the show *Lady in the Dark*, but again had no major hits from it. In 1943, Weill wrote "Speak Low" for the show *One Touch of Venus*, a collaboration with lyricist/poet Ogden Nash, that GUY LOMBARDO turned into a hit (Decca 18573). *Street Scene* (1947) contained a hit song, "Moon-Faced, Starry Eyed" (with lyrics by poet Langston Hughes), which Murray Arnold sang with Freddy Martin and his orchestra (RCA Victor 20-2176).

However, Weill's pop fame comes from just one song: "Mack the Knife," based on the theme from *Three Penny Opera*. Brecht and Weill's masterwork did not appear in America until 1954, when it made its Off-Broadway debut, eventually running for a record 2,611 performances and making a hit of "Mack the Knife." The Dick Hyman Trio had a million-selling hit of the theme, "Moritat," which as a song became known as "Mack the Knife" (MGM 12149). Marc Blitzstein revised Brecht's lyrics, and in 1959 Bobby Darin had the #1 million-selling hit (Atco 6147); in 1956, LOUIS ARMSTRONG also recorded a memorable version (Columbia 40587), which he continued to perform through the rest of his career. In 1961, Andy Williams had a hit with "The Bilbao Song," with lyrics by JOHNNY MERCER (Cadence 1398). Weill was working on a score for a new Broadway project, based on Mark Twain's classic American novel *Huckleberry Finn*, at the time of his death.

# Pete Wendling

Composer (b. New York City, June 6, 1888; d. Maspeth, New York, April 8, 1974). Wendling was a self-taught pianist who learned to play from watching and listening to his idol, Mike Bernard, a RAGTIME champ who performed at Tony Pastor's Music Hall. When he was eighteen, Wendling won a national ragtime piano contest sponsored by *The Police Gazette*. He was proud of the gold medal he won, and even prouder when FREDERICK A. MILLS took him on as a staff pianist. He joined piano-roll producer Rhythmodik in 1914 to cut rolls for the firm, and in 1919 went with QRS, where he made a great many rolls until he left in 1925. Wendling then became a staff pianist at Waterson, Berlin and Snyder, where he met

Lewis F. Muir and became his vaudeville partner. They would eventually play the London Hippodrome.

Wendling's first rag was a collaboration with Harry Jentes titled "Soup and Fish Rag" (1913), published by George W. Meyer and Company. After some tips on songwriting from both Muir and Irving Berlin, Wendling sold over a million copies of his first published song, "Yaaka Hula Hickey Dula," with lyrics by Joe Young and E. Ray Goetz. Of course, it helped that Al Jolson used the song in his show, *Robinson Crusoe, Jr.* (1916) (Columbia A-1956). Jolson also provided Wendling with his million-selling World War I favorite, "Oh! How I Wish I Could Sleep Until My Daddy Comes Home," with lyrics by Muir and Young.

Wendling formed a new partnership in 1919 with Bert Kalmar and Edgar Leslie. They produced two million-sellers and two nearly as successful. The two near-million-sellers were "All the Quakers Are Shoulder Shakers Down in Quaker Town" and "Take Your Girlie to the Movies." The million-sellers were "Oh! What a Pal Was Mary" and "Take Me to the Land of Jazz."

In August 1926, Wendling made four sides at Cameo Records, including two of his own brand-new songs, "Usen't You Used to Be My Sweetie?" and "I Meet Her in the Moonlight (But She Keeps Me in the Dark)," the latter sung on the recording by Frances Sper (Cameo 1021). Although Wendling made more than a thousand piano rolls, these four recordings do more to show the kind of pianist he was, because they demonstrate a light, bouncy touch with a lilting swing unlike that of any other pianist. It is a real loss that he didn't record more songs.

Wendling scored again in 1927, with "There's Everything Nice about You," lyrics by Alfred Bryan. Two other songwriters, Al Bernard and Sam Stept, made a lovely recording of it (Cameo 1141). "Red Lips, Kiss My Blues Away" (1927), also with lyrics by Bryan, got a marvelous recording by Mike Markel's orchestra (Okeh 40805) and a superb arrangement on piano roll by Jack Ward (Welte 75273). Wendling and Jack Meskill wrote "There's Danger in Your Eyes, Cherie!" (1929) for Harry Richman to sing in his film *Puttin' on the Ritz* (Brunswick 4678).

Wendling continued to publish songs through the 1930s, and his last major hit came in 1942 with "On the Street of Regret," with John Klenner's lyrics (1899–1955), published by Loeb-Lissauer. Sammy Kaye had the hit (Victor 27750). Thereafter, Wendling's style of songs fell out of favor, and his last publications came in the early 1950s.

# Percy Wenrich

Composer (b. Joplin, Missouri, January 23, 1880; d. New York City, March 17, 1952). Wenrich attended Chicago Musical College and worked for McKinley Music Company, where he wrote melodies to verses that would-be lyricists submitted. He also composed songs, rags, intermezzi, waltzes, and whatever else was needed. Wenrich's initial success came in composing rags. His first major effort was "Peaches and Cream" (1905) for JEROME REMICK. His biggest rag hit was "The Smiler" (1907), which was published by the Chicago firm of Arnett-Delonais. It became so big that Fred Forster bought the copyright and plugged it nationally. His finest rag, "Persian Lamb Rag," was issued the following year by Walter Jacobs of Boston.

Wenrich came to New York City with his wife, vaudevillian Dolly Connolly, in 1908 and was hired as a staff writer for Jerome H. Remick and Company. With lyricist Alfred Byran, he wrote a hit Indian song called "Rainbow." The next year, he immediately turned out a two-million seller, "Put on Your Old Gray Bonnet," with lyrics by Stanley Murphy (1875–1919). In 1910, he turned out two rags, "Southern Symphony" and "Egyptian Rag," as well as another million-seller, "Silver Bell," with lyrics by Edward Madden. This team then wrote a magnificent RAG SONG for Dolly Connolly, "Red Rose Rag" (1911) (Columbia A-1028), which George Burns sang for decades, as well as the male quartet's dream, "Moonlight Bay" (1912), also made famous by Connolly (Columbia A-1128). Wenrich's ragtime output included the 1911 "Ragtime Chimes" and "Sunflower Rag." "Ragtime Chimes" proved so successful that Edward Madden added lyrics a year later.

In 1912, Wenrich and Homer Howard formed the Wenrich-Howard Company to publish songs. In 1913 they issued the instrumentals "Kentucky Days" and "Whipped Cream Rag," and the great rag song "Snow Deer," with lyrics by Jack Mahoney (1882–1945). However, Wenrich quickly gave up his publishing company to devote himself to composing and to performing with his wife in vaudeville. He joined LEO FEIST and, with Mahoney, scored heavily in 1914 with "When You Wore a Tulip and I Wore a Big Red Rose." Dolly Connolly toured vaudeville houses for several years, accompanied by her husband and featuring mostly his songs. A great plugger, she also recorded for Columbia Records, which greatly increased sales of the song sheets. Wenrich gave another big hit to Connolly when he and JOSEPH MCCARTHY wrote "Sweet Cider Time When You Were Mine" (1916).

When America entered World War I, Wenrich and lyricist Howard Johnson (1887–1941) asked the musical question "Where Do We Go from Here?" Wenrich's last hit was the marvelous syncopated fox-trot song "All Muddled Up" (1922), which ZEZ CONFREY and his orchestra recorded with great artistic and commercial success (Victor 18973).

# Paul Weston

Bandleader, arranger, and composer (b. Paul Wetstein, Springfield, Massachusetts, March 12, 1912; d. Hollywood, California, September 20, 1996). Weston is best remembered as one of the first creators of "mood music"—lush, symphonic recordings beloved in suburban households of the 1950s.

After graduating from Columbia University in the early 1930s, Weston began his career as a big band arranger, working first for RUDY VALLEE and then for TOMMY DORSEY. While with Dorsey, he met singer Jo Stafford, whom he would later wed. Bob Crosby brought him to Hollywood to arrange the music for the film *Holiday Inn* in 1942. There, Weston met Johnny Mercer, who hired him as an A&R director for his new label, Capitol Records. And in 1945, Weston composed "I Should Care" for the film *Thrill of a Romance*, with Sammy Cahn's lyric; it was a hit for Frank Sinatra (Columbia 36791). A year later, Stafford achieved a major hit with "Day by Day (Capitol 227), composed by Axel Stordahl and Weston, and also with Cahn's lyrics; this is perhaps Weston's most famous pop song. In 1950, Capitol initiated a contest inviting listeners to write lyrics to an existing melody by a Capitol artist; the result was "When April Comes Again," with lyrics by contest winner William Schaefer to Weston's tune. Six years later, it was popularized by Mel Torme's recording, and remained in the singer's repertoire for decades. One of Weston's most unusual projects was a series of albums with wife Stafford parodying a bad pop lounge act; released as albums by "Jonathan and Darlene Edwards," they have become cult classics, and their second album, *In Paris* (1960), won a Grammy. Weston spent the 1960s composing for television, and then retired, along with his wife, in the early 1970s.

# Paul Whiteman

Bandleader (b. Paul Samuel Whiteman, Denver, Colorado, March 28, 1890; d. Doylestown, Pennsylvania, December 29, 1967). Whiteman was a large man, and it seemed that the size of his original band (nine) increased in proportion to his waistline as his career flourished in the 1920s. (His band stopped at thirty-four, but his waistline didn't.) His first group, called the Ambassador Orchestra, made its first recording for Victor on August 9, 1920. Whiteman was leader and violinist; Henry Busse, trumpet; Buster Johnson, trombone; Gus Mueller, clarinet and alto sax; Hale Byers, soprano sax, alto sax, and flute; Ferde Grofe, piano and arranger; Mike Pingatore, banjo; Sammy Heiss, tuba; and Harold McDonald, drums. It took three sessions to get a record that could be released—"Japanese Sandman," backed with "Whispering" (Victor 18690). It sold well over a million copies and made both songs hits and standards.

Ross Gorman (1890–1953) replaced Gus Mueller and became the most influential reed player in dance orchestras. He played every reed instrument (the bass clarinet is a particularly nice touch on "Nobody Lied When They Said That I Cried over You" on Victor 18913) and was the creator of the three-octave clarinet run at the beginning of George Gershwin's "Rhapsody in Blue." He played the "Rhapsody" at its Aeolian Hall debut and on the two recordings the band made for Victor (the first acoustical, on Victor 55225; the second electrical, on Victor 35822).

The band's first arranger was Ferde Grofe (1892–1972), who composed the well-known "Grand Canyon Suite" ("On the Trail" was the most famous section, thanks to its use by

Iconic image of Paul Whiteman on a sheet music cover from the 1930 film *King of Jazz*, published by Leo Feist.

Philip Morris cigarettes as their theme for radio commercials). Grofe created memorable arrangements of pop songs in the "symphonic jazz" style that gave the band its distinctive sound. He orchestrated the first version of Gershwin's "Rhapsody in Blue" for a concert on February 12, 1924, as well as all of the other selections performed that evening. Grofe was also in charge of making the arrangements for the tunes The Virginians recorded. This was a subgroup of the Whiteman orchestra used by Victor to fill the company's loss of the Original Dixieland Jazz Band when it disbanded. Victor didn't want another real jazz band like the ODJB, but rather a group it could call a jazz band, one that played with less abandon. The only catch for jazz fans was that everything the Virginians recorded was scored, whereas real jazz bands improvised. That Grofe succeeded at all was due to his skill in writing what sounded like improvisations. The Virginians were led by Ross Gorman, who, in the year of the group's creation, cowrote the hit "Rose of the Rio Grande" (1922) and recorded it (Victor 19001) in Grofe's arrangement.

From the jazz fan's perspective, the most interesting band Whiteman had was the one that existed from November 1927 through September 1929, when it included Bix Beiderbecke on cornet, Tommy Dorsey on trombone, Jimmy Dorsey on clarinet and alto sax—Frank Trumbauer on C melody sax, and Bill Challis as arranger.

The Whiteman band performed in the pit for such Broadway musicals as *George White's Scandals of 1922* (August 28, 1922), *Lucky* (March 22, 1927), and *Jumbo* (November 16, 1935), in which Whiteman rode an elephant while conducting his orchestra! In 1930, the band made its first film, *King of Jazz*, a title bestowed upon Whiteman by his press agent after the historic concert at Aeolian Hall.

In 1930, The Rhythm Boys (Harry Barris, Al Rinker, and Bing Crosby) became the band's first vocal group; Mildred Bailey was its first female vocalist. Some of Whiteman's sidemen and vocalists during the 1930s included Ramona Davies, Johnny Mercer, Jack Teagarden, Bunny Berigan, Miff Mole, Frank Signorelli, Clark Dennis, Joan Edwards, and The Modernaires. Throughout the 1930s, Whiteman appeared on radio, with his own show and as a frequent guest on other programs. He appeared in the films *Thanks a Million* (1935), *Strike Up the Band* (1940), *Atlantic City* (1944), and *Rhapsody in Blue* (1945). Whiteman became involved with television early on, hosting a teenage dance show in the early 1950s.

# Richard A. Whiting

Composer (b. Peoria, Illinois, November 12, 1891; d. Beverly Hills, California, February 10, 1938). Whiting started writing songs while in high school, but didn't try to publish them until a friend persuaded him to travel to Detroit for an interview with Jerome H. Remick.

The publisher was so impressed that he bought three of Whiting's songs and offered him the recently vacated job of professional manager of the Detroit office. Since the salary was only $25.00 a week, Whiting supplemented his income by playing piano for six Hawaiians in a hotel band. He had to wear brown makeup to pretend he, too, was a "native."

His first song was "The Big Red Motor and the Little Blue Limousine" (1913), with lyricist Earle C. Jones, who had previously worked with former manager CHARLES N. DANIELS. His second number, a RAGTIME song, "I Wonder Where My Lovin' Man Has Gone," was written in collaboration with Charles L. Cooke (1891–1958), who had written a marvelous rag, "Blame It on the Blues" (1914), and was, a decade later, known as Doc Cook, leader of the Dreamland Orchestra in Chicago.

The following year, Whiting wrote "It's Tulip Time in Holland" and acquired a Steinway grand piano. He had longed for one, and approached Remick with the idea of signing over his rights to this song in return for a piano. Remick, a good businessman, accepted the deal. Whiting was ecstatic at first, then realized that he got the worst of the bargain as "Tulip Time"'s sales climbed to one and a half million copies. The song would have netted him over $50,000.00. Steinway nine-foot, Model D concert grands at this time, cost about $1,600.00.

In 1916 Whiting teamed with a Detroit bank clerk, Raymond Egan, who hung out at the Remick office during his lunch breaks. He and Whiting were to write many hits. Their first was "Mammy's Little Coal Black Rose," which Blossom Seeley helped sell. Shortly after, the team created another hit with "They Made It Twice as Nice as Paradise and They Called It Dixieland." The following year, AL JOLSON helped sell "Where the Black-Eyed Susans Grow."

Whiting's next hit was his biggest seller of all and one of World War I's greatest numbers. The lyricist was, again, Ray Egan. When Whiting submitted the song to Remick, the publisher said he liked the tune but didn't think the title, "Auf Wiedersehen," was salable—American soldiers were being killed by the German army. When asked what it meant in English, Whiting replied, "Till we meet again." Remick thought that a good title, and so did over five million Americans who bought the sheet music!

The Roaring Twenties really did roar for Whiting. His first two songs published in this decade were multimillion-sellers, both with lyrics by Ray Egan. "Japanese Sandman" was a catchy tune, repeating two notes in a singsong way. NORA BAYES delighted audiences with it, ZEZ CONFREY made a superb piano roll arrangement of it (QRS 1160), and PAUL WHITEMAN's orchestra sold over two million copies (Victor 18690).

After he wrote the melody for "Bimini Bay," Whiting showed it to two lyricists, Ray Egan and GUS KAHN. This trio proved successful—TED LEWIS plugged this song, and VAN AND SCHENCK plugged "Ain't We Got Fun" to sell well over a million copies each (Columbia A-3412). "Bimini Bay" was introduced by Arthur West in *Satires of 1920*.

"Sleepy Time Gal" (1925) was composed with pianist Ange Lorenzo, who followed it up with his own "Dreamy Dream Girl," which was not a hit. Ben Bernie made the hit recording of "Sleepy Time Gal" (Brunswick 2992), and Canadian pianist Vera Guilaroff made a wonderful novelty solo recording of it (Gennett 5750).

"Ukulele Lady" (1925) was a natural for guitarist NICK LUCAS to plug. It had lyrics by Gus Kahn, and Vaughn DeLeath sang it to success on radio. The following year Al Jolson turned Whiting's "Breezin' Along with the Breeze" into a hit, and Lou Breese made it his orchestra's theme song. "Horses" had lyrics by Byron Gay (1886–1945) and was made famous by GEORGE OLSEN and his orchestra (Victor 19977). "Honey" (1928) was introduced by

Rudy Vallee, who made it a hit (Victor 21869), while Gene Austin made "She's Funny That Way" successful (Victor 21779). The melody of "She's Funny That Way" was composed by Charles N. Daniels, and the lyrics were written by Whiting. Ruth Etting made the most of "Guilty," which Whiting, Harry Akst, and Gus Kahn wrote for her in 1931 (Columbia 2529-D).

By then, Whiting was heavily involved with the movies. He started early in the talkie game, when he signed with Paramount to compose for their films. They teamed him with a new lyricist, Leo Robin, to write the score for *Innocents of Paris* (1929), starring Maurice Chevalier in his American debut. The big hit was "Louise," which Chevalier kept in his repertoire for the rest of his career (Victor 21918). In *Dance of Life* (1929), Hal Skelly scored with "True Blue Lou."

Writing the score for *Monte Carlo* (1930), Whiting and Robin came up with a rouser for Jeanette MacDonald, "Beyond the Blue Horizon" (Victor 22514). It was a genuine hit with several revivals. For *Playboy of Paris* (1930), the team wrote Whiting's own favorite of his songs, "My Ideal." The song's best interpreter was his daughter, Margaret, whose first recording was of that song and who turned it into a gigantic hit, as well as a standard (Capitol 134). *One Hour with You* (1932) was the last film on Whiting and Robin's contract for Paramount. It was an undistinguished film, but "(I'd Love to Spend) One Hour with You" became a standard when Eddie Cantor made it his radio theme, then carried it over to his television show in the 1950s. The year 1932 also brought Whiting to Broadway, where he collaborated with Nacio Herb Brown and B. G. DeSylva on *Take a Chance* (November 26, 1932), starring Ethel Merman, Jack Haley, and Jack Whiting. The hit song was "You're

Richard Whiting, c. the 1930s.

an Old Smoothie," kept current by its use on radio and television by Old Gold cigarettes in their commercials.

When Whiting was asked to write for Shirley Temple in her first starring film, *Bright Eyes* (1934), he couldn't get an idea. His daughter, Margaret, licking a large lollipop, came in to see him, and he told her to get away with that sticky stuff. He then realized that the lollipop might be a subject, and wrote one of the most famous children's songs ever, "On the Good Ship Lollipop."

In 1937, Whiting went to Warner Brothers, where he was teamed with lyricist JOHNNY MERCER for what would be his last three films. The first, *Ready, Willing and Able* (1937), contained a great production number, "Too Marvelous for Words," which outlasted the film's success to become a standard. *Hollywood Hotel* (1937) was based on a popular radio show of the same name hosted by gossip columnist Louella Parsons. The song "Hooray for Hollywood," which was used as the opener, became the unofficial theme of the film industry. It was sung in the film by Johnny "Scat" Davis and Frances Langford, backed by BENNY GOODMAN's orchestra. It was later used by Jack Benny to close his radio show every Sunday evening. While working on a Dick Powell feature, *Cowboy from Brooklyn* (1938), Whiting suffered a heart attack. His last song was "Ride, Tenderfoot, Ride," written with Johnny Mercer.

Whiting's daughter, Margaret (b. Detroit, Michigan, July 22, 1924), became a major pop vocalist in the late 1940s and 1950s, recording primarily for Capitol Records. She remained active on the nightclub circuit in later decades.

# Williams and Walker

(Egbert Austin Williams, b. Antigua, British West Indies, November 12, 1874; d. New York City, March 4, 1922; George Walker, b. Lawrence, Kansas, 1873; d. Islip, New York, January 6, 1911). Williams's parents brought him to Riverside, California, where he attended high school. He made his way to San Francisco, where he started his career by singing to his own banjo accompaniment. It was there he met Walker, who came to California from Lawrence, Kansas, in a touring medicine show. They formed a vaudeville act and were appearing in Chicago when they were asked to perform for the Show Managers of America. Producer Tom Canary, of Canary and Lederer, caught their act and rushed backstage to sign them up for his new show, *The Gold Bug* (September 21, 1896), with a score by VICTOR HERBERT. They didn't have roles, but they performed their act in the middle of the show and became a hit. It was a short-lived triumph, however, for the show closed in a week. It did bring them to Broadway, though, and to the attention of other managers. They were quickly booked to play Koster and Bial's vaudeville house, on Twenty-third Street near Sixth Avenue, where they were kept on for an extended run. It was during this time that Williams and Walker performed and popularized their highly distinctive CAKEWALK.

For the next thirteen years, they were to popularize many songs, some written by themselves and some by others. Their photographs—a selling tool—appeared on a sheet music cover ("Enjoy Yourselves") as early as 1897. That same year McIntyre and Heath, a white minstrel duo, sang the Williams and Walker tune "I Don't Like No Cheap Man," and made it a hit. Their own 1899 hit was "The Medicine Man." In 1901, the team made "Good Morning, Carrie" their biggest song written by others: CHRIS SMITH, his vaudeville partner Elmer Bowman, and lyricist R. C. McPherson, who would be better known under the pseudonym "Cecil Mack." Their 1902 hit, "When It's All Goin' Out and Nothin' Comin' In," featured them on the sheet music cover. In 1905, Williams first sang "Nobody," the number that would be associated with him for the rest of his career. Alex Rogers (1876–1930) wrote the very funny lyrics, and the music was composed by Williams. He once wrote of his melodies, "Perhaps it would be more correct to say that I assembled them. For the tunes to popular songs are mostly made up of standard parts, like a motor car. As a machinist assembles a motor car . . . I assembled the tunes to 'Nobody,' 'Believe Me,' and one or two others." Alex Rogers became a valued member of the Williams and Walker Company, not only for his lyric contributions but also for his singing and acting. He wrote most of Bert Williams's best material and helped Jesse Shipp with the libretti for their three Broadway musicals. Later he served in the same capacities for composer Luckey Roberts.

Signing with producers Hurtig and Seamon, the Williams and Walker Company created its first vaudeville musical, *The Policy Players*, which opened at Koster and Bial's on April 3, 1900. It toured vaudeville houses, and its success encouraged the team to continue with their repertory company. Their next production was *Sons of Ham*, which toured for two years, starting in 1900, and finally opened at the Grand Opera House in New York City on March 3, 1902. It was the first Williams and Walker show from which songs were published using a standard show cover, this one featuring drawings of them.

George Walker was the first to marry. In 1899, he wed Aida Overton, a young soubrette with the company. A year later, Bert Williams married dancer Lottie Thompson, also a member of the troupe.

Their landmark production, *In Dahomey*, opened on February 18, 1903, at the New York Theatre. This was the first full-length book musical written and performed by blacks at a major Broadway theater. The Williams and Walker Company contained many of the most creative black talents in show business. The cast included Alex Rogers, Jesse Shipp, J. Leubrie Hill, Hattie McIntosh, George Catlin, and Abbie Mitchell, as well as the stars' wives. A wonderful song for George Walker was "Me an' da Minstrel Ban'," and Bert Williams scored with Alex Rogers's "I'm a Jonah Man." They enjoyed a seven-month stay with the show in London, where the team appeared before King Edward VII. They returned to tour with the show for the 1904–1905 season and added "I May Be Crazy but I Ain't No Fool" for Williams. The song's title became a popular catchphrase.

*Abyssinia*, their next production, opened at the Majestic Theatre on February 20, 1906. Their new producer, Melville Raymond, provided elaborate scenery, a large cast, and live camels on stage. No songs from the score became popular.

F. Ray Comstock produced *Bandanna Land*, the last show, in which the team appeared together, at the Majestic Theatre (February 3, 1908). It contained songs by Tom Lemonier, Cecil Mack and Chris Smith, WILL MARION COOK, and Alex Rogers, J. Leubrie Hill, and

Joe Jordan. "Bon Bon Buddy, the Chocolate Drop" became George Walker's theme song, and "You're in the Right Church but the Wrong Pew" became a hit for Bert Williams. This show introduced Williams's famous pantomime, "The Poker Game," which became his trademark. (It can be seen in a silent film short, "Natural Born Gambler," made in 1916.) George Walker became ill during the Chicago run of the tour and retired from the stage.

Comstock produced the last of the Williams and Walker Company's Broadway shows, *Mr. Lode of Koal* (November 1, 1909), again at the Majestic Theatre, at Fifty-eighth Street and Columbus Avenue. Although George Walker was missing, the critics agreed that Bert Williams carried the show by himself. The big number was Williams's "Believe Me." Shortly after the show closed, Bert Williams accepted an offer to appear in Florenz Ziegfeld's *Follies of 1910*.

For the *Follies*, Williams composed, with lyrics by Chris Smith and Jim Burris, a riotous song in the "Nobody" vein, called "Constantly," and it became another hit for him. For the *Ziegfeld Follies of 1911*, he created, with lyricist Grant Clarke, another hit in "Dat's Harmony." It was also in this *Follies* that he caused a minor sensation singing IRVING BERLIN's "Woodman, Woodman, Spare That Tree." For the *Ziegfeld Follies of 1912*, Williams came up with "My Landlady" and "You're on the Right Road but You're Going the Wrong Way." For the *Ziegfeld Follies of 1914*, he again performed his famous poker game and introduced it by singing "The Darktown Poker Club." For his final *Follies* in 1919, the one generally acknowledged as the best of them all, he sang "You Cannot Make Your Shimmy Shake on Tea," a protest against the coming of Prohibition. His last Broadway show was a revue, *Broadway Brevities of 1920*, which made popular "The Moon Shines on the Moonshine." It is fitting that his

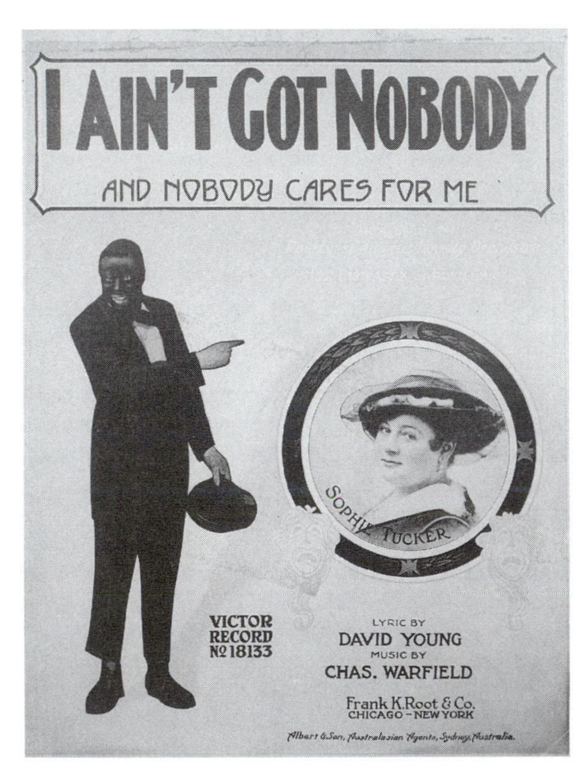


Bert Williams (left) points to Sophie Tucker on the cover of "I Ain't Got Nobody," which the two singers made into a hit.

last song in this show was written by Chris Smith, who went back to the beginning of Williams's career in New York, "I Want to Know Where Tosti Went (When He Said Goodbye)."

Despite his success, Bert Williams keenly felt prejudice when he appeared on stage in his own country. In his travels abroad, he met and performed for royalty and was accepted by them as a talented artist. At home he was always subjected to prejudice. He wrote an article for *American Magazine* (December 1917), in which he stated, "I have never been able to discover that there was anything disgraceful in being a colored man. But I have often found it inconvenient—in America." And, although he ended the article by saying, "I'm having a grand time," W. C. Fields, who worked with Williams in several *Follies*, once observed, "He was the funniest man I ever saw and the saddest man I ever knew."

# Clarence Williams

African-American composer and publisher (b. Plaquemine, Louisiana, October 8, 1893; d. Jamaica, New York, November 6, 1965). In 1915, Williams formed Williams and Piron Music Publishers with violinist-orchestra leader Armand John Piron (1888–1943) in New Orleans. It was the third black publishing firm, and the second of that decade. The company was formed to issue Williams's first song, "You Missed a Good Woman When You Picked All Over Me." The firm's partners published their first collaboration the following year, "Brown Skin, Who You For." It was recorded by the Victor Military Band (Victor 18203) and made money for them. The sale of his 1917 hit, "You're Some Pretty Doll," to SHAPIRO, BERNSTEIN the following year enabled Williams to move to Chicago, where he opened two music stores and reestablished the publishing company later in the year. In 1919, the firm published "Royal Garden Blues" and "I Ain't Gonna Give Nobody None o' This Jelly Roll," both with music by Williams and words by SPENCER WILLIAMS (no relation). When Clarence sold these songs to Shapiro, Bernstein, he was able to move to New York City late in 1921. He secured offices in the Gaiety Building and changed the name of his firm to Clarence Williams Music Publishing Company, having bought out Piron, who did not want to leave New Orleans. Piron subsequently started his own publishing firm there.

Williams started active publishing in New York in 1922, reaping five hits in his first year: "I Wish I Could Shimmy Like My Sister Kate," "Got to Cool My Doggies Now," "That Da-Da Strain," "My Pillow and Me," and "'Tain't Nobody's Biz-ness If I Do." The classic "Kate" was apparently based on a tune that Williams heard a young LOUIS ARMSTRONG perform (under the title "Keep Off Katie's Head") during the 1910s. Armstrong later asserted that Williams had stolen the song, but Williams claimed it was common around New Orleans:

"The tune is older than all of us. People always put different words to it. Some of them were too dirty to say in polite company. The way Louis did it didn't have anything to do with sister Kate."

In 1923, Williams's biggest hits were "Sugar Blues," which has had many revivals (notably by Clyde McCoy in the mid-1930s), and "Oh, Daddy, Blues," made famous by Bessie Smith. (Williams played piano on Smith's first session, and subsequently served as a scout/unofficial A&R man for Columbia and other labels for BLUES and jazz musicians; Williams also formed his own booking agency during the 1920s to promote his discoveries.)

Williams Music Publishing had a great year in 1924, when it issued "Cakewalking Babies from Home," "Mama's Gone, Goodbye," and "Everybody Loves My Baby." The next big year for hits was 1926, when Williams issued JAMES P. JOHNSON's "Carolina Shout," FATS WALLER's "Squeeze Me" and "How Could I Be Blue," and the Jack Palmer-Spencer Williams standard, "I've Found a New Baby." The firm published the King Oliver classic "West End Blues" in 1928, "Baby, Won't You Please Come Home" in 1930, and the famous New Orleans parade-stopper, "High Society," in 1933. Through the late 1930s, Williams published piano compositions by Johnson and Waller, among others, while continuing to issue songs.

In early 1943, Decca Records purchased Williams's back catalog of copyrights; according to some sources, Williams continued to hold a one-third interest in the publishing company and a half interest in his own songs. His last hits were 1946's "Ugly Chile" and "Sugar Blues" from a year later, both with lyrics by JOHNNY MERCER. Williams moved to Brooklyn, New York, in the early 1950s, and continued to make occasional appearances for a while. He was injured in an automobile accident in 1953, and he suffered from the complications from diabetes during his final decade.

# Spencer Williams

African-American composer and lyricist (b. New Orleans, Louisiana, October 14, 1889; d. Queens, New York, July 14, 1965). Williams, the son of a New Orleans prostitute, was raised by his aunt, a noted madam, after the death of his mother when he was eight years old. After a short stay in Birmingham, Alabama, with other relatives during his midteens, Williams moved to Chicago. A competent pianist, he worked as a Pullman porter while also playing the piano at a local amusement park, and tried to hawk his compositions to local publishers. He had his first success in 1912.

Spencer Williams's first hit was probably an adaptation of an existing song. "I Ain't Got Nobody" (1914) is a great ballad that both SOPHIE TUCKER and Bert Williams of WILLIAMS AND WALKER helped to make famous. It was first copyrighted as an unpublished composition in 1914 by Charles Warfield and David Young. A 1916 edition, published by Frank K. Root and Company of Chicago, gave credit to the same songwriters. However, in 1915, the song had been copyrighted as an unpublished composition credited to Dave Peyton and Spencer Williams, with the word "Much" at the end of the title. In February 1916, Craig and Company (whose manager was Roger Graham) published the song as being by Spencer Williams, music, and Roger Graham (1885–1938), lyrics. Later that year, Frank K. Root and Company bought the Craig edition, giving the firm two editions of the same song with two different sets of writers. (So who really wrote it? I vote for the unsophisticated team of Warfield and Young.) The Williams-Graham version is more syncopated and better constructed than the earlier song, and it is the one that has become the "standard."

In 1919, Williams partnered with the (unrelated) songwriter-music publisher CLARENCE WILLIAMS who both collaborated with Spencer and published their songs. First came "I Ain't Gonna Give Nobody None o' This Jelly Roll," a double-entendre-laced song; but it was "Royal Garden Blues" that would become the lasting hit. Although composed in 1919, it didn't have a hit recording until 1921, but then remained in the jazz and swing repertoires through the 1930s and beyond.

Spencer Williams followed Clarence to New York in 1921, although they were no longer partners. In the city he quickly met BLUES lyricist and publisher Perry Bradford and white publisher Joe Davis (owner of Triangle Music), who would become Williams's principal publisher. He also met pianist FATS WALLER, who cut Williams's "Got to Cool My Doggies Now," from the Schubert revue *The Passing Show of 1922*, as his first piano roll. The two collaborated on a few songs, with Williams writing lyrics and Waller providing the melodies.

Collaborating with white lyricist Jack Palmer in 1924, Williams wrote "Everybody Loves My Baby," which became a hit thanks to recordings by Alberta Hunter with the Red Onion Jazz Babies, LOUIS ARMSTRONG with the FLETCHER HENDERSON Orchestra, and Trixie Smith, who recorded it twice, with backing on one record by the ORIGINAL MEMPHIS FIVE and by the Henderson Orchestra on the other. The song was interpolated into two reviews, the *Ziegfeld Follies* (spring 1924) and *Earl Carroll's Vanities* (autumn 1924).

The song's success brought Williams to the attention of a wealthy socialite named Caroline Dudley Reagan, who hoped to assemble a show of jazz music and dance in Paris. She hired Williams to compose music for what would become a landmark show, *La Revue Negre*, which introduced a young dancer named Josephine Baker to the Paris stage. The show opened on October 2, 1925, and was an immediate sensation. Williams enjoyed life in Paris, and remained there for three years.

Williams returned to the U.S. in mid-1928, and had a major hit with the ballad "Susianna" a year later, with radio star Joe Davis plugging it heavily and Bing Crosby making the first recording. However, the stock market crash in October 1929 hit the music industry hard, particularly black songwriters, who were not able to find work in Hollywood. Williams had his last hit when BENNY GOODMAN and a recording band called the Charleston Chasers recorded "Basin Street Blues" in 1931 (it had been recorded by Louis Armstrong in 1928). A vocal part was added by trombonist Jack Teagarden, and GLENN MILLER did the arrangement. The song became closely associated with Teagarden through the rest of his career, and was a hit again when Bing Crosby recorded it as a duet with Connee Boswell for Decca in 1937.

Meanwhile, Williams returned to Paris in 1932, reuniting with Baker. Four years later, he wed a white English woman and settled in a London suburb. Williams started his own publishing company and continued to write on occasion. In 1954, he moved his family to Sweden, and three years later he made a final move back to the United States, to Queens, New York. In failing health, Williams spent his last years in seclusion.

# Williamson Music Inc.

See *Oscar Hammerstein II*

# M. Witmark and Sons

The first major full-line popular sheet music publisher of the 1890s, it developed the personal and professional creative and marketing skills that soon became standard throughout the industry. Like most new media enterprises, Tin Pan Alley was a young man's game. But the Witmarks, when they started, made it seem like a kid's game. Isidore (1869–1941), the eldest, was seventeen; Julius (1870–1929), the boy tenor, was sixteen; and baby Jay (1877–1950), the financial head, was all of nine when they started publishing music in 1886. "M." Witmark was their father, Marcus; his sole function in the firm was to sign legal papers, because his business-minded sons were all underage.

The Witmark brothers decided to enter the music publishing business after Willis Woodward not only neglected to pay Isidore a royalty on his first published number, "A Mother's a Mother After All," but also reneged on his promise to give Julius a percentage of sheet music sales for plugging Jennie Lindsay's "Always Take Mother's Advice," when she was on a bill with the Thatcher, Primrose, and West minstrel troupe.

The brothers entered the popular song field with gusto, taking an active lead in plugging their songs instead of waiting—as their competitors Willis Woodward, T. B. Harms, and Harding did—for singers to come to them. The Witmarks put composers and arrangers—with more than one piano, unusual at the time—on staff to demonstrate their songs.

Isidore Witmark, c. the 1920s.

The first building owned by a Tin Pan Alley firm. The Witmark Building, 144–146 W. 37th Street, c. 1905.

In the 1880s, as today, political rumors abounded—at first met with denials, and later with an admission of their truth. One day in 1886, Jay Witmark noticed in the newspaper that President Grover Cleveland was going to be married. This news sparked the Witmark brothers' daily business conference. They decided to publish a wedding march to mark the occasion, and Isidore was assigned the task of creating one. After a few hours, he had composed the piece, and the boys rushed to get it printed. During the next few days, it was reported that the announcement had been a hoax and that the president was not going to get married. It was too late to stop the presses, and the boys' publishing career nearly ended before it started. However, a few days after that, the president did announce his forthcoming marriage to Frances Folsom, and the Witmark brothers were ready with their first topical piece, "President Grover Cleveland's Wedding March." It could be said that they had stolen a march over all their competitors—an auspicious beginning to their business. It was the first attempt to capitalize on a national event in order to sell sheet music nationally. Although the tune did not become hit, its creation-on-demand was what publishers in the Alley became famous for, and its publication date marks the beginning of the Golden Age of Tin Pan Alley.

The Witmarks quickly found that topical songs alone could not sustain business. As the 1890s wore on, they branched out to become general publishers of popular music. They handled the show scores of VICTOR HERBERT, Chauncey Olcott, and the precocious GEORGE M. COHAN, which led also to the development of their fine Irish song catalog ("Mother Machree," "My Wild Irish Rose," "When Irish Eyes Are Smiling"). They competed early on with HOWLEY, HAVILAND in COON SONGS by hiring Ben Harney ("Mister Johnson, Turn Me Loose") and Sidney Perrin ("Mammy's Little Pumpkin-Colored Coons") to write exclusively for them.

In 1891, Tin Pan Alley became aware of a new development in the copyright laws, that, at first, sharply curtailed its revenues. And, as with President Cleveland's wedding, the Witmarks were the ones to leap upon this event and turn it into profit. Before 1891, copyright laws protected American writers from piracy only within the United States. And, much of what was published in America—royalty free—was the work of Englishmen. Also, tunes from the Continent—embellished with new lyrics by Americans—were published with no fee paid to the composer.

The International Copyright Law of 1891 changed the situation dramatically and, for the first time, afforded copyright protection to foreign compositions sold in America, as well as to American works published abroad. It became important for American publishers to secure international rights, especially for the English plays and musicals that had been published so freely and easily before. The Witmarks saw an opportunity to convince leading music publishers in London that they needed representation in the United States. They also saw the need to open an office in London to handle their own publications overseas.

Isidore was chosen to go to London to establish representation there. When he arrived, he was faced with a peculiar situation. British music publishers were generally leisurely in their dealings (and advanced in years), and they expected to deal with an American of similar attitude and deportment. Isidore, who was then twenty-three years old, resented their attitude. When he could no longer tolerate it, he said at one meeting, "See here! In my country, the type of man you have been expecting to meet in me is retired long ago or relegated to the position of bookkeeper!" He won them over and gained contracts with England's second largest publisher, Charles Sheard and Company, as well as one with specialist publisher Reynolds and Company. He also appointed an American actor, Charles Warren, who was living in London permanently, as personal representative of M. Witmark and Sons. Thus, the Witmarks became the first major U.S. music publisher with an overseas branch.

In 1893, when Julius Witmark was on the road singing his firm's songs with minstrel troupes, he went to Chicago, where the World's Fair was in progress. There he met an old friend, Sol Bloom, who was in charge of some exhibits. Before Julius left, he created a Chicago branch of Witmark's, putting Bloom in charge. It was a restless Bloom who, several years later, saw a viable business opportunity in acquiring music sections in department stores. He left the Witmarks to pursue it, and later turned publisher himself. After a few successful years, he got out of the music publishing business and sold his catalog to the Witmarks. He eventually went into other businesses, finally becoming a congressman representing New York State.

It was this same year, 1893, that saw the Witmarks move to Twenty-eighth Street from Union Square, becoming the first important firm to move to the still-unnamed "Alley." Their move uptown gave recognition to the shift in the location of the theatrical houses and to the new form of popular entertainment, vaudeville. It also acknowledged that the firm needed larger quarters as its business grew. The Witmarks took over the buildings at 49–51 West Twenty-eighth Street.

As they were settling down, a new kind of music began to attract the interest of the public. It came at first in high-spirited songs with syncopated accompaniment, and the Witmarks hired Max Hoffman in Chicago to write such "rag accompaniments" for their new coon songs. On the stage, a dance called the CAKEWALK appeared, with syncopated music written especially for it. Its final form was as an instrumental in 2/4 time for the piano, and it was called "Rag Time." It became the sensation of the mid-1890s and vied with the waltz as a favorite time signature.

In 1896, for every "Sweet Rosie O'Grady" that was published, there was a coon song: MAY IRWIN's "Bully Song," Bert Williams's "Oh, I Don't Know," Ernest Hogan's "All Coons Look Alike to Me," W. T. Jefferson's "My Coal Black Lady," Ben Harney's "Mister Johnson, Turn Me Loose," Barney Fagan's "My Gal Is a Highborn Lady," and Theodore Metz's "Hot Time in the Old Town."

Two years later, the Witmarks moved again, this time around the corner to 8 West Twenty-ninth Street, a five-story building that they completely occupied. Their business had grown to include not only a professional department, with its staff songwriters and pluggers, but also the Witmark Music Library of special arrangements of medleys, overtures, and popular operatic productions for rental, operatic selections, oratorios, masses, vocal parts for chorus, band scores, and orchestra scores; the minstrel department, which furnished not only music but also books, gags, scripts, costumes, accessories, makeup, and instruments; and a booming mail-order business outfitting complete minstrel shows for amateur productions. Their mail-order "Black and White Series" contained not only their semiclassical numbers, but also their most famous ballads, standard features and steady sellers through the years. These backlist items carried them through downturns in the economy that produced sluggish frontlist sales, and kept such composers as Ernest Ball and Caro Roma in print. To keep the music world informed of their various activities, the Witmarks began the first of the Alley house organs, *The Witmark Monthly*.

Over the years, Witmark had absorbed many other publishers, including Prophetic (which owned the rights to African-American composer GUSSIE L. DAVIS, among others), WEBER AND FIELDS, GUS EDWARDS, and Sol Bloom. In 1928, the Witmark firm was the first purchase made by Warner Brothers Pictures in its attempt to build a large catalog of popular music, and was quickly followed by JEROME REMICK and T. B. Harms in Warner Brothers's new publishing operation.

M. WITMARK and SONS (1886–1934)

| | |
|---|---|
| 1886–1887 | 402 West 40th Street |
| 1888 | 32 East 14th Street |
| 1889–1893 | 841 Broadway |
| 1893–1898 | 49–51 West 28th Street |
| 1898–1903 | 8 West 29th Street |
| 1903–1923 | 144–146 West 37th Street |
| 1923–1929 | 1650 Broadway (corner 51st Street) |
| 1929–1934 | 1657 Broadway (owned by Warner Bros.) |

# P. G. Wodehouse

Lyricist, author, playwright, foremost humorist of the twentieth century, creator of Jeeves and Bertie Wooster, wrote 33 musicals and 18 straight plays, 97 books and 285 short stories, (b. Guildford, England, October 15, 1881; d. Remsenburg, New York, February 14, 1975.) Working Guy Bolton, librettist, and JEROME KERN, composer, Wodehouse pioneered the development of American musical comedy. He worked with the greatest theatre composers of his time: Kern, GEORGE GERSHWIN, SIGMUND ROMBERG, RUDOLF FRIML, Emmerich Kalman, and COLE PORTER.

Wodehouse started writing lyrics for shows in the West End of London in 1904 and first came to Broadway with *Miss Springtime* (September 25, 1916) at the New Amsterdam Theatre. His big hit was "My Castle in the Air," introduced in the show by George MacFarlane, who also had the hit recording (Victor 45110). 1917 was a banner year for Wodehouse, who had five shows running simultaneously on Broadway and one which closed out of town. For *Have a Heart* (January 11, 1917), he wrote "And I Am All Alone," which Henry Burr recorded (Pathe 2014l); "Napoleon" was one of Wodehouse's great comic songs, introduced in the show by Billy B. Van, who also recorded it (Columbia A-2307); and "You Said Something," which Alice Green and Harry MacDonough successfully recorded (Victor 18260). His second show of the year, *Oh, Boy!*, was also his most successful (February 20, 1917), as it ran for 475 performances. "Nesting Time in Flatbush" was neatly recorded by Ada Jones and Billy Murray (Victor 18270), and "Rolled into One" was recorded by the star who introduced it in the show, Anna Wheaton (Columbia A-2238). Jerome Kern's own favorite of his songs was "Till the Clouds Roll By" (it was also the title of his screen biography). Anna Wheaton and James Harrod sang it on disc (Columbia A-2261). "You Never Knew About Me" and "An Old-Fashioned Wife" got splendid recordings by Edna Brown and Alice Green (Victor 18259).

*Leave It to Jane* (August 28, 1917) was Wodehouse's third musical of 1917 and the one with the best score. A medley of the rich score can be heard on recording by Joseph C. Smith and his orchestra (Victor 35660), and Jack Warner sang the title song (Emerson 7304). Emma Stephens sang "The Crickets Are Calling" (Pathe 20265), and Gladys Rice and Helen Clark sang "The Siren's Song" (Edison 80382). *The Riviera Girl* was the fourth show that year (September 24, 1917), with "Let's Build a Little Bungalow in Quogue" being introduced by Sam Hardy and Juliette Day in the show, and Billy Murray and Rachel Grant making a hit disc (Edison 80381). Alice Green recorded the other important song from the show, "Just a Voice to Call Me Dear" (Victor 18399). The fifth show Wodehouse had during this year was *Miss 1917* (November 5, 1917), produced by Charles Dillingham and Florenz Ziegfeld, Jr. Despite its lavishness of production and its having both Victor Herbert and Jerome Kern as composers, the show lasted only forty-eight performances and boasted only one hit song, Kern's "The Land Where the Good Songs Go," which Alice Green and Charles Harrison sang (Victor 18410).

1918 started off with another big hit as *Oh, Lady! Lady!!* came to the stage (February 1, 1918) and stayed for 219 performances. The title song was given a nice rendition by the Waldorf-Astoria Dance Orchestra (Victor 18477). A medley of songs was done by the Victor Light Opera Company (Victor 35672). *Oh, My Dear!* came at the end of the year (November 27, 1918) and had "City of Dreams" recorded by Joe Phillips (Okeh 1161). Wodehouse wrote the libretto for what is arguably the greatest musical comedy of the 1920s, the Gershwins' *Oh, Kay!* (November 8, 1926). He allowed his greatest song, "Bill," to be included in *Show Boat,* with HELEN MORGAN introducing and having the hit recording (Victor 21238) in 1928. *Rosalie* (January 10,1928) featured five songs by Wodehouse, but only "Say So" and "Oh Gee, Oh Joy" got recorded by Johnny Johnson's Statler Pennsylvanians (Victor 21224).

Wodehouse's last work for Broadway was the original libretto for Cole Porter's *Anything Goes* (November 21, 1934). When the show was transferred to London the following year, Wodehouse supplied additional lyrics to "Anything Goes" and "You're the Top."

Besides his work as a theatrical lyricist, Wodehouse is best remembered for authoring a series of comic novels featuring the young British fop Bertie Wooster and his ever trustworthy manservant Jeeves.

# Harry Woods

Composer (b. Harry MacGregor Woods, North Chelmsford, Massachusetts, November 4, 1896; d. Glendale, Arizona, January 14, 1970). Woods was born with no fingers on his left hand, yet he learned to play the piano and could manage enough of a two-note bass line that he could play professionally during his songwriting career.

Woods loved fishing and farming in his native New England. He began to dabble in songwriting in 1923, when he collaborated with Abner Silver (1899–1966) on "I'm Goin'

South," which AL JOLSON sang in *Bombo*. Lanin's Arcadians (Pathe 020992) and Bennie Krueger's Orchestra (Brunswick 2445) recorded "Long Lost Mamma (Daddy Misses You)" (1923), which enjoyed substantial sales. But songwriting was still a hobby for Woods, who remained on his farm on Cape Cod. However, when CLIFF EDWARDS interpolated Woods's "Paddlin' Madeline Home" (1925) in *Sunny*, Woods began to have second thoughts about songwriting (Pathe 025149).

The clincher that turned Harry Woods into a full-time songwriter was his 1926 song "When the Red, Red Robin Comes Bob, Bob, Bobbin' Along," which sold over a million copies. The same year, he had minor hits with "Poor Papa (He's Got Nothin' at All)," with lyrics by BILLY ROSE, which was recorded successfully by both Fred Rich (Harmony 119-H) and Irving Aaronson (Victor 20002). "Me, Too" had words by Al Sherman and Charlie Tobias. Tobias introduced it in vaudeville and got PAUL WHITEMAN to make a record of it (Victor 20197). "Side by Side" (1927) was a tremendous hit when Paul Whiteman recorded it (Victor 20627), and the Duncan Sisters sang it in vaudeville. Kay Starr revived it in 1953 for a #3 hit (Capitol 2334).

"Just Like a Butterfly That's Caught in the Rain" (1927) was the work of Woods and lyricist MORT DIXON. It was sung successfully by Blossom Seeley. This new team came up with a perennial that same year when they wrote "I'm Looking over a Four Leaf Clover." It is the theme song of the Mummers' Parade held in Philadelphia each year. "She's a Great, Great Girl" (1928) received a nice arrangement on ROGER WOLFE KAHN's Orchestra's recording (Victor 21326).

"A Little Kiss Each Morning (A Little Kiss Each Night)" (Victor 22193) and "Heigh Ho! Everybody, Heigh Ho!" (Victor 22029) were written for RUDY VALLEE and his Connecticut Yankees for their film debut in *Vagabond Lover (1929)*. "The Man from the South" (1930) was a collaboration with RUBE BLOOM which Ted Weems and his orchestra made into a #1 hit record (Victor 22238).

"When the Moon Comes over the Mountain" (1931) became KATE SMITH's radio theme and the title of her first film. "River, Stay 'Way from My Door" (1931), lyrics by Mort Dixon, was given a splendid piano roll arrangement by Lou Penn (Paramount 5876).

Before Woods went to England in 1932 to write for British-Gaumont films, he and Mort Dixon collaborated on "Pink Elephants," which GUY LOMBARDO plugged (Brunswick 6399). This was also the year of Woods's only collaboration with GUS KAHN. They wrote "A Little Street Where Old Friends Meet," which was played on radio and in clubs by Vincent Lopez. Later that year, he joined the English songwriting-publishing team of Reg Connelly and Jimmy Campbell to write "Try a Little Tenderness," which RUTH ETTING made popular in America (Melotone 12625) and Ray Noble and his orchestra made popular in England. Campbell, Connelly, and Woods also collaborated on "Just an Echo in the Valley," which BING CROSBY sang in the film *Going Hollywood* (1933). In 1935, Woods wrote the cute "I'll Never Say 'Never Again' Again."

A favorite story about Harry Woods typifies both the insouciance and the values of the Alleymen of his day. Woods's terrible temper and his love for strong drink were well known to his songwriter friends, as well as to bartenders and customers of the clubs where he played piano. Woods once got into a yelling match with an equally inebriated customer. When the row escalated to the physical, the bartender called the police. As the police arrived, they found Woods sitting astride the chest of his foe, clutching his throat with his right hand and pounding a dent in the unfortunate patron's forehead with the stump of his left hand. As the combatants were separated, a woman entering the bar recoiled from the bloody sight. "Who is that horrible man?" she asked. Woods's crony, sitting at the bar, replied proudly, "That's Harry Woods. He wrote 'Try a Little Tenderness.' "

In the early 1940s, Woods retired from songwriting. He eventually settled in Arizona, and died there following an automobile accident.

# Willis Woodward

Pioneer publisher (d. September 1908; full birth and death dates unknown). Woodward, who appeared on the scene at the beginning of the 1880s, had his office at 842 Broadway, the Star Theatre Building, at Thirteenth Street and Broadway. He was known as the King of Tearjerkers with hits like "White Wings," "The Song That Reached My Heart," and "Always Take Mother's Advice." Woodward published Isadore Witmark's first song. When Witmark's royalty statement came, he was so disgusted at his meager earnings that he and his brothers went into business for themselves. In 1888, PAUL DRESSER gave Woodward his "Convict and the Bird." Jacob Henry Ellis, young composer of marches and CAKEWALKS ("Remus Takes the Cake"), bought a partnership in the firm in September 1900. This firm moved to 48 West Twenty-eighth Street in February 1908. Ellis kept the company going for another four years.

# Allie Wrubel

Composer (b. Middletown, Connecticut, January 15, 1905; d. Twentynine Palms, California, December 13, 1973). Wrubel studied to be a doctor at Columbia University while also playing saxophone in various dance bands, including a one-year engagement with PAUL WHITEMAN. He had his first song published in 1931, and three years later began writing for films. Often partnering with lyricist MORT DIXON, Wrubel provided songs for a slew of 1930s features under contract to Warner Bros. Dixon and Wrubel's "I See Two Lovers" (1934) was the last big seller for pop crooner RUSS COLUMBO, who recorded it two days before his death; it was featured in the film *Sweet Music* (featuring Columbo's rival RUDY VALLEE in the lead). Wrubel's other well-known songs of the era include "Gone with the Wind" (with lyrics by Herb Magidson [1906–1986]) and "Music, Maestro, Please," popularized by TOMMY DORSEY.

Wrubel worked through the 1940s and into the early 1950s, most notably on Disney's 1946 combined animated and live-action film, *Song of the South*, which produced perhaps his best-known song today, "Zip-A-Dee-Doo -Dah," with lyrics by Ray Gilbert (1912–1976). It was sung in the film by James Baskett, and it had its hit recording by JOHNNY MERCER with the Pied Pipers (Capitol 323). Wrubel was less active in the 1950s, although he did produce a few more movie songs towards the end of the decade, and then retired. Ironically, Wrubel died of a heart attack in Twentynine Palms, California—the subject of his song "The Lady from Twentynine Palms."

# Y

## Jack Yellen

Lyricist (b. Razcki, Poland, July 6, 1892; d. Springfield, New York, April 17, 1991). Yellen's family came to the United States when he was five years old and settled in Buffalo, New York. Yellen worked as a reporter for a local newspaper and began dabbling in song lyrics. He moved to New York in the early 1910s, and then served in the Army during World War I. His first major hits were written with composer George L. Cobb, a fellow Buffalonian. They first scored with 1913's "All Aboard for Dixie Land," which was made into a hit by stage singer Elizabeth Murray. Two years later, she introduced another of their songs, "Listen to That Dixie Band," and then "Alabama Jubilee," which sold nearly a million copies. Their final Southern-themed hit was "Are You from Dixie?" (1915).

After the war, Yellen established a primary partnership with composer Milton Ager, and the duo produced many of the classic songs of the 1920s, including "Ain't She Sweet," "Crazy Words, Crazy Tune," and "Hard-Hearted Hannah, the Vamp of Savannah." They also formed a publishing company with their manager, Ben Bornstein, in August 1922. In 1925, working with composer Lew Pollack, Yellen wrote the classic "My Yiddishe Momme," inspired by the death of his own mother; it became a signature tune for Sophie Tucker. Ager and Yellen went to Hollywood in 1928, and continued to produce hits, including "The

Last of the Red Hot Mommas," written for Tucker's screen debut in the film *Honky Tonk*, and 1929's "Happy Days Are Here Again," which became closely associated with Franklin D. Roosevelt's presidency. Yellen and Ager broke up in 1930.

Yellen continued to write lyrics for films through the 1930s, then returned to Broadway in the early 1940s. Among his later hits was 1939's "Are You Having Any Fun?," written for Ella Logan to sing in *George White's Scandals of 1939*. She also made the hit record (Columbia 35251). After World War II, he retired from the songwriting business. A founding member of ASCAP, he served on its board from 1951 to 1969.

# Vincent Youmans

Composer (b. Vincent Miller (Millie) Youmans, New York City, September 27, 1898; d. Denver, Colorado, April 5, 1946). Youmans worked with IRA GERSHWIN as lyricist on the first Broadway show for each of them. Just as GEORGE GERSHWIN, who was only one day older than Youmans, was the first to experiment with BLUES and jazz ideas in Broadway music, so Youmans took the temper of the times and expressed himself just as individually. There is no mistaking much of Youmans's or Gershwin's music as coming from any time but the 1920s.

Just as George Gershwin began his recording career for Aeolian, so did Youmans, and also in 1916. Felix Arndt, as he had done for Gershwin a few months earlier, hired Youmans to orchestrate songs for piano rolls and taught him to make rich arrangements. Youmans enlisted in the U.S. Navy during World War I and was at the Great Lakes Training Station, where he was to prepare musical shows for the sailors and act as rehearsal pianist. The bandmaster there was none other than John Philip Sousa, who liked one tune Youmans had written, programmed it in his concerts frequently, and gave it to other Navy bands to play. Nine years later, with words added, it became "Hallelujah," the runaway hit of *Hit the Deck* (1927).

Upon returning to civilian life in 1919, Youmans got a job with MOSE GUMBLE at JEROME REMICK's, where Gershwin had worked just a few years before. Youmans was given the same duties: demonstrating songs to performers and plugging them in stores. He was soon given a chance to work for VICTOR HERBERT on *Oui, Madam* (1920), which closed out of town. Youmans, in an interview later in his life, said, "There are no treatises or instruction books on how to write an opera or musical comedy. Working with a man like Victor Herbert was the luckiest thing that happened to me. No money could have bought the training I received in less than a year."

Youmans published his first song in January 1920, when Remick's issued "The Country Cousin," with lyrics by Alfred Bryan (1871–1958). It was inspired by a silent movie of the

Vincent Youmans, c. the 1920s.

same name, starring Elaine Hammerstein, whose photo appears on the cover. Like most first songs by top composers, this one didn't create a ripple in the Alley's pond.

By the fall of 1920, Youmans was ready to write for the theater, so he took his wares to MAX DREYFUS of T. B. HARMS, who, as he had done for Gershwin, hired Youmans to compose. It was at Harms that he met lyricist IRVING CAESAR and the Gershwin brothers. George took an immediate liking to Youmans. When they learned of the proximity of their birthdays, Youmans called George "Old Man," and George responded by calling Youmans "Junior."

When young Alex Aarons, who had produced the road tour of Gershwin's *La, La Lucille*, began his next show, *Two Little Girls in Blue* (May 3, 1921), George urged Aarons to hire Youmans to write the score. Youmans, in turn, asked Ira to write the lyrics. One of the first songs they worked on turned out to be the hit of the show. Ira recalled that when he wrote "Oh, Me! Oh, My! (Oh, You!)," it was merely a dummy lyric to translate the rhythm into sounds. Later on, he thought, he would find a real lyric subject and change it. But Youmans expressed delight with the original inspiration. Ira later said, "That was fine with me because I couldn't think of anything else." (Another set of dummy lyrics would provide Youmans with his greatest hit a few years later.) One of the reasons "Oh, Me! Oh, My!" became such a smash was PAUL WHITEMAN's Victor recording of Ferde Grofe's orchestration, which caught the public's attention with its snappy syncopation (Victor 18778).

*Wildflower* (February 7, 1923) was Youmans's second Broadway score and his longest-running show, with 477 performances. The two hit songs, "Bambalina" and "Wildflower," firmly established him. His next two shows, *Mary Jane McKane* (December 25, 1923) and *Lollipop* (January 21, 1924), were moderately successful but didn't contain any outstanding songs. Youmans had a penchant for revising and reusing songs in subsequent shows. One of his greatest hits, "Sometimes I'm Happy" (with lyrics by Irving Caesar), was placed first in *A Night Out* (1925), which closed during its pre-Broadway tour in Philadelphia, and later put into *Hit the Deck* (1927), where it became a classic. The song was originally known as "Come on and Pet Me," with lyrics by OSCAR HAMMERSTEIN II and William Cary Duncan, from *Mary Jane McKane*. Also from that show was "My Boy and I," the melody of which later turned up in *No, No, Nanette* (1925) as the title song, with a lyric by OTTO HARBACH.

*No, No, Nanette* (September 16, 1925) had a strange history. It was first performed in a Detroit tryout on April 23, 1924, but ran into horrendous book problems. Before the show moved to Chicago (where it was a smash hit), the book was overhauled, cast members were replaced, and five new songs were written. Lyricist Irving Caesar remembered working a long day with Youmans on one of the new songs and trying to get a brief nap before they were to attend a party. He had just fallen asleep on the couch when Youmans woke him, wanting to play a new tune he had just worked out. Couldn't it wait until tomorrow? No. Caesar was dragged to the piano to hear it. Youmans wanted a lyric. Couldn't it wait? No, again. He wanted it now. While Youmans played it over, Caesar sleepily jotted down dummy lyrics to fit the rhythm, intending to replace it the next day with a permanent set. When Caesar was finished, Youmans thought the lyrics and title were great and insisted on keeping what Caesar had just written. The song, Youmans' greatest hit, was "Tea for Two." The other *Nanette* song to remain a favorite, "I Want to Be Happy," also has charming lyrics by Caesar. And, not to be outdone by his idol, JEROME KERN, who had flirted with the BLUES in an early 1920s show, Youmans wrote "'Where Has My Hubby Gone?' Blues" for this score. By the time *Nanette* opened on Broadway, it had had nearly a year's run in Chicago, two road companies and a London production (March 11, 1925), which ran for 665 performances. The Broadway production ran for 321 performances, and when *Nanette* was revived on Broadway on May 16, 1973, it ran for 861 performances.

*Oh, Please!* (December 17, 1926) was the next Youmans show. It starred Beatrice Lillie and it bombed. However, it contained one of his catchiest melodies, "I Know That You Know," which jazz pianists still like to perform. The initial recording by Ohman and Arden with their orchestra started it on its way (Brunswick 3410). An interesting sidelight is that both of Youmans's future wives were in the chorus of this show.

*Hit the Deck* (April 25, 1927), the first show produced by Youmans himself, had a Broadway run of 352 performances. The two major songs were the classic "Hallelujah!," with words by LEO ROBIN and CLIFFORD GREY, and "Sometimes I'm Happy," with lyrics by Caesar (used without Caesar's permission in this show). However, since it became a hit, Caesar benefited tremendously. *Great Day!* (October 17, 1929), with lyrics by BILLY ROSE and Edward Eliscu (1902–1998), contained three all-time standards: "Great Day!," "Without a Song," and a gorgeous ballad, "More Than You Know." The show was a flop, but these songs are evergreens.

*Smiles* (November 18, 1930) was a Ziegfeld bomb. Starring Marilyn Miller and FRED and Adele ASTAIRE, this lavish production should have been a success but lasted only sixty-three performances. However, with lyrics by HAROLD ADAMSON and Mack Gordon, Youmans turned out the enduring "Time on My Hands." *Through the Years* (January 28, 1932) was another flop for Youmans, with only a twenty-performance run. But, as had been the case with his other unsuccessful shows, two standards emerged: "Drums in My Heart" and "Through the

Years," both with lyrics by Edward Heyman. *Take a Chance* (November 26, 1932) was Youmans's last Broadway show, but he didn't write the entire score. His biggest contribution was "Rise 'n' Shine," sung by Ethel Merman.

Youmans's only original movie score was for RKO's *Flying Down to Rio* (1933), in which Fred Astaire and Ginger Rogers danced together for the first time. Their first dance was to Youmans's "Carioca," a samba with a maxixe tinge, with lyrics by Gus Kahn and Edward Eliscu. "Orchids in the Moonlight" was another hit from the score, a tango for Astaire and Dolores Del Rio. Clearly, Youmans was in the vanguard of Latin American music, which swept the country in the 1940s. "Flying Down to Rio" became a hit thanks to Astaire's performance (Columbia 2912-D).

In the early 1930s, Youmans contracted tuberculosis, which cut short his creative output. Another blow came in 1934 when his publishing firm went under, and he subsequently was forced into bankruptcy. In 1943, he made a grand comeback attempt, a classical dance show featuring choreography by Leonide Massine to European and Latin-American classical music, *The Vincent Youmans Ballet Revue*. It was a major disaster, drawing pans from the critics and losing over $4 million. Youmans subsequently retired to Colorado, where he died.

# Joe Young

Lyricist (b. New York City, July 4, 1889; d. New York City, April 21, 1939). Young's early career was spent as a singer and song plugger in the Alley. In 1916, he teamed with lyricist Sam M. Lewis, collaborating with him on many hits.

"You're My Everything" was written with Mort Dixon in 1931 for *The Laugh Parade*, and was recorded by the Arden-Ohman Orchestra, with vocal by Frank Luther (Victor 22818). The same year saw a collaboration with Sammy Fain, "Was That the Human Thing To Do?," with a hit recording by Bert Lown's orchestra and vocal by Elmer Feldkamp (Victor 22908). In 1932, Young wrote "In a Shanty In Old Shanty Town," which Ted Lewis and his band made into a #1 hit (Columbia 2652-D). His two standards from 1933 were "Two Tickets to Georgia" and "Annie Doesn't Live Here Anymore," which Guy Lombardo turned into a hit (Brunswick 6662). His biggest hit of the decade came in 1935, when he and Fred Ahlert wrote "I'm Gonna Sit Right Down and Write Myself a Letter," which gave Fats Waller a chance to spread out (Victor 25044) and the Boswell Sisters their last hit (Decca 671). It was revived in 1957 by Billy Williams in a million-selling #3 hit (Coral 61830). 1936 saw two more collaborations with Fred Ahlert, "The 'Goona Goo'," a #5 hit for Clyde McCoy and his orchestra (Decca 1109), and "There's Frost on the Moon," which gave Artie

Joe Young, c. the 1920s.

SHAW his first big hit, early in 1937 (Brunswick 7771). After this last hit, illness prevented Joe Young from writing more songs.

# Victor Young

Composer, bandleader, and violinist (b. Chicago, Illinois, August 8, 1900; d. Palm Springs, California, November 11, 1956). Young's father was an opera tenor who abandoned his children after the death of Young's mother. Young was sent to Warsaw, Poland, in 1910, to be raised by his grandparents. Trained as a violinist, he studied at the Warsaw Conservatory, and played with several European orchestras until the beginning of World War I. He returned to the United States, and after the war became a concert violinist and also worked in theater orchestras. Young left the classical world and settled in Chicago. He became the lead violinist and arranger for TED FIO RITO's popular dance band, and in 1931 formed his own band, which backed many of the day's popular singers (it's his band that's heard behind Judy Garland on her 1939 recording of "Over the Rainbow"). Beginning in the mid-1930s, Young was an orchestrator and composer for Paramount Studios in Hollywood, and was said to have worked on over 300 films by the time of his death in 1956.

As a songwriter, Young's first hit was the peppy 1928 song "Sweet Sue," with lyrics by Will Harris. Young often collaborated with Ned Washington, and they scored several major hits: 1936's "Can't We Talk It Over?" popularized by Bing Crosby; "A Hundred Years from Today" (cocomposed by Joe Young), for the 1935 film *Straight Is the Way*; the classic 1946 ballad, "Stella By Starlight" (based on a theme that Young wrote for the film *The Uninvited* two years earlier) and the theme song for the 1956 film *Around the World in 80 Days*, which was Young's last completed score. He died suddenly in November 1956, leaving incomplete a musical based on the life of Mark Twain that was finished by composer/orchestrator Ferde Grofe.

# Z

## Ziegfeld Follies

No other revue series made such an impression on the public and none yielded as many song hits, even though they were mostly interpolated into the shows. Before the *Follies*, which premiered on July 8, 1907, the Broadway revue had been merely vaudeville, extravaganza, and burlesque, dressed up with outrageous costumes and lavish sets. With the coming of Florenz Ziegfeld, Jr. (b. Chicago, Illinois, March 21, 1867; d. New York City, July 22, 1932) and his *Follies*, the revue added girls—not just a handful, but forty to fifty of them, all beauties. For all his meticulous attention to detail, the one element Ziegfeld ignored was the music for his shows. He imported stars, dressed (and undressed) his showgirls magnificently, and spent fortunes on scenery, but for the most part hired hacks to write the songs. Consequently, the talents of Tin Pan Alley weren't as vital to the *Follies* as might be supposed. Except for the two *Follies* shows written by IRVING BERLIN, all of the hit songs from other editions were interpolations, songs added to the shows and not composed by the original writers of those shows.

The first Ziegfeld song hit, from the *Follies of 1908* (June 15, 1908), was made by headliners NORA BAYES and Jack Norworth singing their own composition, "Shine On, Harvest Moon," as an interpolation. In the *Follies of 1910* (June 20, 1910), Bert Williams

Sheet music cover from the 1916 edition of Ziegfeld's *Follies*, published by T. B. Harms.

and Fanny Brice made their *Follies* debuts. Williams featured his own tune, "You're Gwine to Get Somethin' What You Don't Expect," and the Ford Dabney–Cecil Mack number "That Minor Strain." Fanny Brice scored with Joe Jordan's "Lovie Joe." Ford Dabney (1883–1958), a black writer, managed to place "The Pensacola Mooch" as the show's dance sensation. For the *Ziegfeld Follies of 1911* (June 26, 1911), Irving Berlin contributed the only standout, with Bert Williams interpreting his "Woodman, Woodman, Spare That Tree." The 1912 edition (October 21, 1912) contained an interpolated hit by James Monaco and William Jerome, with Elizabeth Brice singing their "Row, Row, Row."

By all accounts, *the Ziegfeld Follies of 1919* (June 16, 1919) was the most important in the series. Irving Berlin wrote its theme song, one that served this show and has served hundreds of beauty pageants and fashion shows ever since: "A Pretty Girl Is Like a Melody," which John Steel originally sang (Victor 18588). Berlin also created such diverse gems as "Mandy," sung by Van and Schenck (Columbia A-2780); "You Cannot Make Your Shimmy Shake on Tea," performed by Bert Williams; and the million-selling hit that Eddie Cantor sang, "You'd Be Surprised" (Emerson 10102). Alleyites Harry Tierney and Joseph McCarthy had an interpolated hit with "My Baby's Arms."

# Bibliography

*American Musician and Art Journal* (New York: 1906–1914).

American Society of Composers, Authors, and Publishers. *ASCAP Biographical Dictionary*. 3rd ed. New York: ASCAP, 1966.

American Society of Composers, Authors, and Publishers. *ASCAP Biographical Dictionary*. 4th ed. New York: Bowker, 1980.

Anderson, Jervis. *This Was Harlem, 1900–1950*. New York: Farrar, Straus and Giroux, 1982.

Appelbaum, Stanley, ed. *Show Songs from "The Black Crook" to "The Red Mill."* New York: Dover, 1974.

Atkinson, Brooks. *Broadway*. New York: Macmillan, 1970.

Baral, Robert. *Revue*. New York: Fleet, 1962.

Barrett, Mary Ellin. *Irving Berlin: A Daughter's Memoir*. New York: Simon and Schuster, 1994.

Bennett, Tony, with Will Friedwald. *The Good Life*. New York: Pocket Books, 1998.

Bloom, Ken. *American Song: The Complete Musical Theatre Companion*. 2nd ed., 2 vols. New York: Schirmer Books, 1996.

Bloom, Ken. *Hollywood Song: The Complete Film and Musical Companion*. New York: Facts on File, 1995.

Bloom, Ken. *Tin Pan Alley Song*. New York: Schirmer Books, 2001.

Bloom, Sol. *Autobiography*. New York: Putnam, 1948.

Bordman, Gerald. *American Musical Comedy: From* Adonis *to* Dreamgirls. New York: Oxford University Press, 1982.

Bordman, Gerald. *American Musical Revue: From* The Passing Show *to* Sugar Babies. New York: Oxford University Press, 1985.

Bordman, Gerald. *American Musical Theatre: A Chronicle*. 2nd ed. New York: Oxford University Press, 2001.

Bordman, Gerald. *American Operetta: From* H.M.S. Pinafore *to* Sweeney Todd. New York: Oxford University Press, 1981.

Bordman, Gerald. *Days to Be Happy, Years to Be Sad: The Life and Music of Vincent Youmans*. New York: Oxford University Press, 1982.

Bordman, Gerald. *Jerome Kern: His Life and Music*. New York: Oxford University Press, 1980.

Bordman, Gerald. *The Oxford Companion to American Theatre*. 2nd ed. New York: Oxford University Press, 1992.

Bradford, Perry. *Born with the Blues*. New York: Oak Publications, 1965.

Brunn, H. O. *The Story of the Original Dixieland Jazz Band*. Baton Rouge: Louisiana State University Press, 1960.

Burton, Jack. *The Blue Book of Broadway Musicals*. Watkins Glen, New York: Century House, 1952.

Burton, Jack. *The Blue Book of Hollywood Musicals*. Watkins Glen, New York: Century House, 1953.

Cahn, Sammy. *I Should Care*. New York: Arbor House, 1974.

Cantor, Eddie. *Take My Life*. New York: Garden City, Doubleday, 1957.

Castle, Irene. *Castles in the Air.* Garden City, New York: Doubleday, 1958.
Charosh, Paul, and Robert A. Fremont, eds. *Song Hits from the Turn of the Century.* New York: Dover, 1975.
Charters, Ann. *Nobody: The Story of Bert Williams.* New York: Macmillan, 1970.
Charters, Samuel, and Leonard Kunstadt. *Jazz: A History of the New York Scene.* Garden City, New York: Doubleday, 1962.
Chilton, John. *Who's Who of Jazz.* Philadelphia: Chilton, 1972.
Christensen, Axel, ed. *Christensen's Ragtime Review.* (Chicago, 1914–1916).
Churchill, Allen. *The Great White Way.* New York: Dutton, 1962.
Clooney, Rosemary, with Joan Bartel. *Girl Singer: An Autobiography.* New York: Random House, 1999.
Cohan, George M. *Twenty Years on Broadway.* New York: Harper Bros., 1924.
Coslow, Sam. *Cocktails for Two.* New Rochelle, New York: Arlington House, 1977.
DeLong, Thomas A. *Pops: Paul Whiteman, King of Jazz.* Piscataway, N.J.: New Century, 1983.
Dietz, Howard. *Dancing in the Dark.* New York: Quadrangle, 1974.
Duke, Vernon. *Passport to Paris.* Boston: Little, Brown, 1955.
Ewen, David. *Complete Book of the American Musical Theater.* New York: Henry Holt, 1958.
Ewen, David. *Popular American Composers.* New York: H. W. Wilson, 1962.
Ewen, David. *The Life and Death of Tin Pin Alley.* New York: Funk and Wagnalls, 1964.
Ewen, David. *American Popular Songs from the Revolutionary War to the Present.* New York: Random House, 1966.
Ewen, David. *Great Men of American Popular Song.* Rev. and enl. ed. Englewood Cliffs, N.J.: Prentice-Hall, 1972.
Farnsworth, Marjorie. *The Ziegfeld Follies.* New York: Putnam's, 1956.
Feather, Leonard, and Gary Gitler. *The Biographical Encyclopedia of Jazz.* New York: Oxford University Press, 1999.
Feist, Leonard. *An Introduction to Popular Music Publishing in America.* New York: National Music Publishers' Association, 1980.
Flinn, Denny Martin. *Musical! A Grand Tour.* New York: Schirmer Books, 1997.
Fordin, Hugh. *The Movies' Greatest Musicals.* New York: Ungar, 1984.
Fowler, Gene. *Schnozzola: The Story of Jimmy Durante.* New York: Viking Press, 1951.
Freedland, Michael. *Al Jolson.* New York: Stein & Day, 1972.
Freedland, Michael. *A Salute to Irving Berlin.* New ed. London: W. H. Allen, 1986.
Fremont, Robert A. *Favorite Songs of the Nineties.* New York: Dover, 1973.
Friedwald, Will. *Jazz Singing: America's Great Voices from Bessie Smith to Bebop and Beyond.* New York: Da Capo, 1996.
Friedwald, Will. *Sinatra! the Song Is You: A Singer's Art.* New York: Da Capo, 1997.
Furia, Philip. *Ira Gershwin: The Art of the Lyricist.* New York: Oxford University Press, 1996.
Furia, Philip. *Irving Berlin: A Life in Song.* New York: Schirmer Books, 1998.
Furia, Philip. *The Poets of Tin Pan Alley: A History of America's Great Lyricists.* New York: Oxford University Press, 1990.
Furia, Philip, ed. *American Song Lyricists, 1920–1960.* Detroit: Gale Group, 2002.
Gänzl, Kurt. *The Encyclopedia of the Musical Theatre.* 2nd ed. New York: Schirmer Books, 2001.
Gänzl, Kurt. *The Musical: A Concise History.* Boston: Northeastern University Press, 1997.
Gershwin, Ira. *Lyrics on Several Occasions.* New York: Knopf, 1959.
Gilbert, L. Wolfe. *Without Rhyme or Reason.* New York: Vantage, 1956.
Goldberg, Isaac. *Tin Pan Alley.* New York: John Day, 1930.
Gottlieb, Robert, and Robert Kimball, eds. *Reading Lyrics.* New York: Pantheon, 2000.
Gourse, Leslie. *Louis's Children: American Jazz Singers.* New York: Quill, 1984.
Green, Stanley. *Broadway Musicals, Show by Show.* 2nd ed. Milwaukee, Wis.: Hal Leonard Books, 1987.
Green, Stanley. *Encyclopaedia of the Musical Film.* New York: Oxford University Press, 1981.
Green, Stanley. *Encyclopaedia of the Musical Theatre.* New York: Dodd, Mead, 1976.

Green, Stanley. *Hollywood Musicals Year by Year*. Milwaukee, Wis: Hal Leonard Books, 1990.
Green, Stanley. *The Rodgers and Hammerstein*. Fact Book. Rodgers and Hammerstein, 1955.
Green, Stanley. *The World of Musical Comedy: The Story of the American Musical Stage as Told Through the Careers of Its Foremost Composers and Lyricists*. 4th ed. New York: Da Capo Press, 1984.
Hammerstein, Oscar II. *Lyrics*. New York: Simon and Schuster, 1949.
Hammond, John. *On Record*. New York: Ridge Press, 1977.
Handy, W. C. *Father of the Blues*. New York: Macmillan, 1941.
Harris, Charles K. *After the Ball*. New York: Frank-Maurice, 1926.
Hart, Dorothy. *Thou Swell, Thou Witty*. New York: Harper & Row, 1976.
Hart, Dorothy, and Robert Kimball, eds. *The Complete Lyrics of Lorenz Hart*. New York: Da Capo Press, 1995.
Hemming, Roy. *The Melody Lingers On: The Great Songwriters and Their Movie Musicals*. New York: Newmarket Press, 1986.
Huff, Mac, arr. *Irving Berlin, a Century of Song: Words and Music by Irving Berlin*. New York: Irving Berlin Music, 1988.
Isman, Felix. *Weber and Fields*. New York: Boni & Liveright, 1924.
Jablonski, Edward. *Alan Jay Lerner: A Biography*. New York: Henry Holt, 1996.
Jablonski, Edward. *Gershwin: With a New Critical Discography* (New York: Da Capo Press, 1998).
Jablonski, Edward. *Harold Arlen: Happy with the Blues*. New York: Da Capo Press, 1985.
Jablonski, Edward. *Irving Berlin: American Troubadour*. New York: Henry Holt, 1999.
Jackson, Richard, ed. *Popular Songs of 19th Century America*. New York: Dover, 1976.
Jasen, David A. *A Century of American Popular Music (1899–1999): 2000 Best-Loved and Remembered Songs*. New York: Routledge, 2002.
Jasen, David A. *P. G. Wodehouse: A Portriat of A Master*. New York: Schirmer, 2002.
Jasen, David A. *The Theatre of P. G. Wodehouse*. London: Batsford, 1979.
Jasen, David A., and Gene Jones. *That American Rag*. New York: Schirmer Books, 2000.
Jasen, David A., and Gene Jones. *Spreadin' Rhythm Around: Black Popular Songwriters, 1880–1930*. New York: Schirmer Books, 1998.
Jasen, David A., ed. *"Alexander's Ragtime Band" and Other Favorite Song Hits, 1901–1911*. New York: Dover, 1987.
Jasen, David A., ed. *Beale Street and Other Classic Blues: 38 Works, 1901–1921*. Mineola, New York: Dover, 1998.
Jasen, David A., ed. *For Me and My Gal and Other Favorite Song Hits, 1915–1917*. New York: Dover, 1994.
Jasen, David A., ed. *"A Pretty Girl Is like a Melody": and Other Favorite Song Hits, 1918–1919*. Mineola, New York: Dover, 1997.
Jasen, David A., ed. *35 Song Hits by Great Black Songwriters*. Mineola, New York: Dover, 1998.
Jasen, David A., and Gene Jones. *Black Bottom Stomp: Eight Masters of Ragtime and Early Jazz*. New York: Routledge, 2001.
Jay, Dave. *The Irving Berlin Songography*. New Rochelle, New York: Arlington House, 1969.
Johnson, James Weldon. *Along the Way*. New York: Viking, 1913.
Johnson, James Weldon. *Black Manhattan*. New York: Knopf, 1930.
Kahn, E. J., Jr. *The Merry Partners: The Age and Stage of Harrigan and Hart*. New York: Random House, 1955.
Kernfeld, Barry, ed. *The New Grove Dictionary of Jazz*. 2nd ed. London: Grove's Dictionaries, 2001.
Kimball, Robert, ed. *Cole*. New York, Holt, Rinehart & Winston, 1971.
Kimball, Robert, ed. *The Complete Lyrics of Cole Porter*. New York: Da Capo Press, 1992.
Kimball, Robert, ed. *The Complete Lyrics of Ira Gershwin*. New York: Da Capo Press, 1998.
Kimball, Robert, and William Bolcom. *Reminiscing with Noble Sissle and Eubie Blake*. New York: Cooper Square Press, 2000.
Kinkle, Roger D. *The Complete Encyclopedia of Popular Music and Jazz, 1900–50*. New Rochelle, New York: Arlington House, 1974.
Klamkin, Marian. *Old Sheet Music*. New York: Hawthorne, 1975.

Lange, Horst. *The Fabulous Fives.* Chigwell, U.K.: Storyville, 1978.
Larkin, Colin, ed. *The Encyclopedia of Popular Music.* 3rd ed. London: Muze, 1998.
Levy, Lester S. *Give Me Yesterday: American History in Song, 1890–1920.* Norman: University of Oklahoma Press, 1975.
Levy, Lester S. *Grace Notes in American History: Popular Sheet Music from 1820–1900.* Norman: University of Oklahoma Press, 1967.
Levy, Lester S. *Picture the Song.* Baltimore: John Hopkins University Press, 1976.
Lomax, Alan. *Mister Jelly Roll.* New York: Duell, Sloan, 1950.
Lopez, Vincent. *Lopez Speaking.* New York: Citadel, 1960.
Lord, Tom. *Clarence Williams.* Chigwell, U.K.: Storyville, 1976.
Marks, Edward B. *They All Sang: From Tony Pastor to Rudy Vallee.* New York: Viking, 1934.
Marmorstein, Gary. *Hollywood Rhapsody: The Story of Movie Music, 1900–75.* New York: Schirmer Books, 1997.
Marx, Samuel, and Jan Clayton. *Rodgers & Hart: Bewitched, Bothered and Bedeviled.* New York: Putnam's, 1976.
McCabe, John. *George M. Cohan: The Man Who Owned Broadway.* Garden City, New York: Doubleday, 1973.
McGuire, Patricia Dubin. *Lullaby of Broadway.* Secaucus, New Jersey: Citadel, 1983.
*Melody* (Boston, 1918–1934).
*Music Trade Review* (New York, 1899–1933).
Osgood, Henry O. *So This Is Jazz.* Boston: Little, Brown, 1926.
Petkov, Steven, and Leonard Mustazza, eds. *The Frank Sinatra Reader.* New York: Oxford University Press, 1995.
Rice, Edward Le Roy. *Monarchs of Minstrelsy.* New York: Kenny, 1911.
Rodgers, Richard. *Musical Stages.* New York: Random House, 1975.
Rose, Al. *Eubie Blake.* New York: Schirmer Books, 1979.
Rosenfeld, Monroe H., ed. *The Tuneful Yankee.* Boston: 1917.
Rust, Brian. *Jazz Records, 1887–1942.* 2 vols. New Rochelle, New York: Arlington House, 1978.
Rust, Brian. *The American Dance Band Discography, 1917–1942.* 2 vols. New Rochelle, New York: Arlington House, 1975.
Rust, Brian, and Allen G. Debus. *The Complete Entertainment Discography.* New Rochelle, New York: Arlington House, 1973.
Sampson, Henry T. *Blacks in Blackface.* Metuchen, N.J.: Scarecrow, 1980.
Shapiro, Nat. *Popular Music: An Annotated Index of American Popular Songs.* 5 vols. New York: Adrian Press, 1965–1969.
Shaw, Arnold. *The Rockin' '50s.* New York: Hawthorne, 1974.
Simon, George T. *The Big Bands.* 4th ed. New York: Schirmer Books, 1981.
Southern, Eileen. *Biographical Dictionary of Afro-American and African Musicians.* Westport, Conn.: Greenwood Press, 1982.
Southern, Eileen. *The Music of Black Americans: A History.* 3rd ed. New York: W. W. Norton, 1997.
Spaeth, Sigmund. *The Facts of Life in Popular Song.* New York: Whittlesey House, 1934.
Spaeth, Sigmund. *A History of Popular Music in America.* New York: Random House, 1948.
Stagg, Jerry. *The Brothers Schubert.* New York: Random House, 1968.
Sudhalter, Richard M. *Bix: Man & Legend.* New Rochelle, New York: Arlington House, 1974.
Sudhalter, Richard M. *Stardust Melody: The Life and Music of Hoagy Carmichael.* New York: Oxford University Press, 2002.
Suskin, Steven. *More Opening Nights on Broadway.* New York: Schirmer Books, 1997.
Suskin, Steven. *Opening Nights on Broadway.* New York: Schirmer Books, 1990.
Suskin, Steven. *Show Tunes.* 3rd ed. New York: Oxford University Press, 2000.
Taylor, Deems. *Some Enchanted Evenings.* New York: Harper, 1953.
Taylor, Theodore. *Jule: The Story of Composer Jule Styne.* New York: Random House, 1979.
Tucker, Sophie. *Some of These Days.* Garden City, New York: Doubleday, Doran, 1945.
Tyler, Don. *Hit Parade, 1920–1955.* New York: Morrow, 1985.

Walker, John, ed. *Halliwell's Film and Video Guide*. New York: Harper Collins, 2000.
Waller, Maurice, and Anthony Calabrese. *Fats Waller*. New York: Schirmer Books, 1977.
Waters, Ethel, and Charles Samuels. *His Eye Is on the Sparrow*. Garden City, New York: Doubleday, 1951.
Westin, Helen. *Introducing the Song Sheet*. Nashville, Tenn.: Thomas Nelson, 1976.
Whitcomb, Ian. *After the Ball: Pop Music from Rag to Rock*. New York: Simon and Schuster, 1973.
Whitcomb, Ian. *Irving Berlin and Ragtime America*. New York: Limelight Editions, 1988.
Whiteman, Paul, and Mary Margaret McBride. *Jazz*. New York: J. H. Sears, 1926.
Whiting, Margaret, and Will Holt. *It Might as Well Be Spring*. New York: William Morrow, 1987.
Wilder, Alec. *American Popular Song: The Great Innovators, 1900–1950*. New York: Oxford University Press, 1972.
Wilk, Max. *They're Playing Our Song*. New York: Atheneum, 1973.
Winer, Deborah Grace. *The Night and the Music: Rosemary Clooney, Barbara Cook, and Julie Wilson Inside the World of Cabaret*. New York: Schirmer Books, 1995.
Winer, Deborah Grace. *On the Sunny Side of the Street: The Life and Lyrics of Dorothy Fields*. New York: Schirmer Books, 1997.
Winkler, Max. *A Penny from Heaven*. New York: Appleton-Century-Crofts, 1951.
Witmark, Isidore. *From Ragtime to Swingtime*. New York: Lee Furman, 1939.
Wodehouse, P. G., and Guy Bolton. *Bring on the Girls!* New York: Simon and Schuster, 1953.
Woll, Allen. *Dictionary of the Black Theatre*. Westport, Conn.: Greenwood Press, 1983.
Woollcott, Alexander. *The Story of Irving Berlin*. New York: Putnam's, 1925.
Wright, Laurie. *Mr. Jelly Lord*. Chigwell, U.K.: Storyville, 1980.
Young, Jordan R. *Spike Jones and His City Slickers*. Beverly Hills, Calif.: Disharmony Books, 1984.

# General Index

Page numbers in **boldface** indicate a subject with its own entry.

# Index of Songs